INSIDERS' GUIDE® TO
CALIFORNIA'S WINE COUNTRY

Help Us Keep This Guide Up to Date

Every effort has been made by the author and editors to make this guide as accurate and useful as possible. However, many things can change after a guide is published—establishments close, phone numbers change, facilities come under new management, etc.

We would love to hear from you concerning your experiences with this guide and how you feel it could be improved and be kept up to date. While we may not be able to respond to all comments and suggestions, we'll take them to heart and we'll also make certain to share them with the author. Please send your comments and suggestions to the following address:

The Globe Pequot Press
Reader Response/Editorial Department
P.O. Box 480
Guilford, CT 06437

Or you may e-mail us at:

editorial@GlobePequot.com

Thanks for your input, and happy travels!

Insiders' Guide®
to California's
Wine Country

Including Napa, Sonoma, Mendocino, and
Lake Counties

SIXTH EDITION

Jean Saylor Doppenberg

Guilford, Connecticut
An imprint of The Globe Pequot Press

Copyright © 2002, 2003 by The Globe Pequot Press
Previous editions of this book were published by Falcon Publishing, Inc. in 1998, 1999, and 2000.

Front cover photo © Ed Gifford/Masterfile
Back cover photos by Todd Grosser and Jean Saylor Doppenberg
Maps by Geografx © The Globe Pequot Press

ISSN: 1539-9923
ISBN: 0-7627-2722-5

Manufactured in the United States of America
Sixth Edition/First Printing

Contents

Preface xii

Acknowledgments xiii

How to Use This Book 1

Area Overview 3

Getting Here, Getting Around 14

History 28

Golden Gateway 43

Flora, Fauna, and Climate 48

Hotels, Motels, and Inns 53

Bed-and-Breakfast Inns 72

Spas and Resorts 98

Camping 109

Restaurants 116

Nightlife 145

Wineries 154

Attractions 196

Festivals and Annual Events 218

Shopping 240

Arts and Culture 262

Parks and Recreation 277

Lake County 299

On the Water 307

Spectator Sports 316

Kidstuff 326

Day Trips 335

Real Estate 341

Retirement 354

Education and Child Care 366

Health Care 381

Media 388

Worship 396

Index 405

About the Author 425

Directory of Maps

California's Wine Country Overview vii

Napa County Wine Trails viii

Sonoma County Wine Trails ix

Mendocino County Wine Trails x

Lake County Wine Trails xi

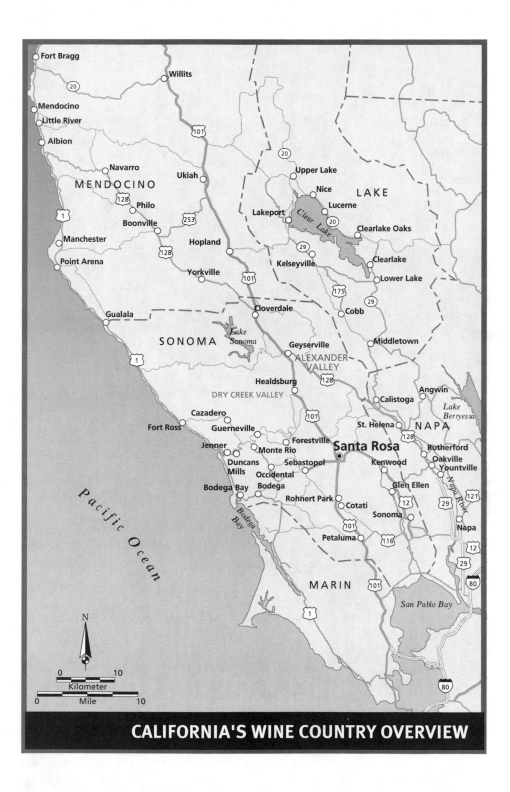

CALIFORNIA'S WINE COUNTRY OVERVIEW

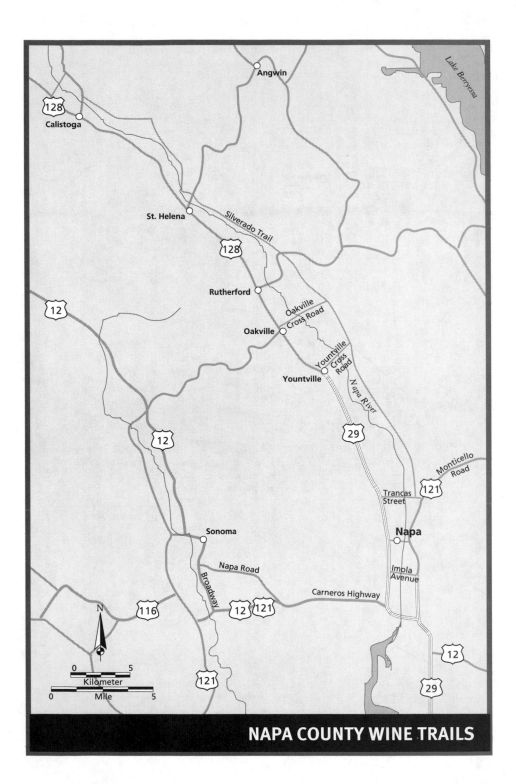

NAPA COUNTY WINE TRAILS

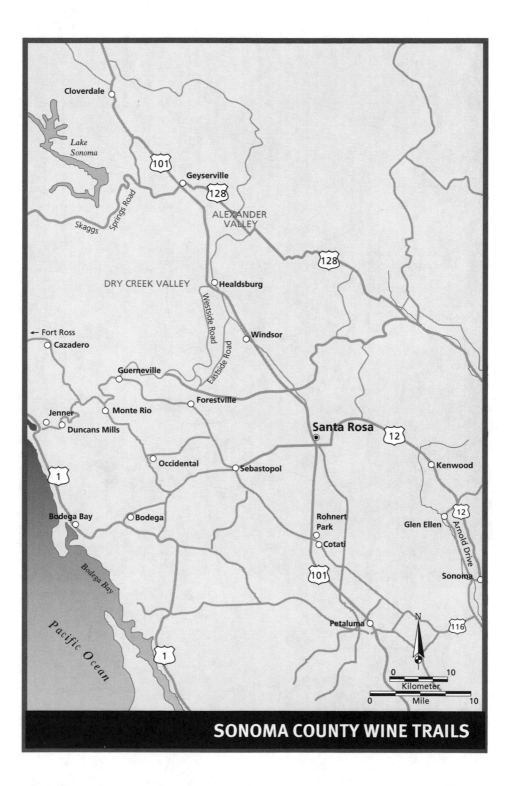

SONOMA COUNTY WINE TRAILS

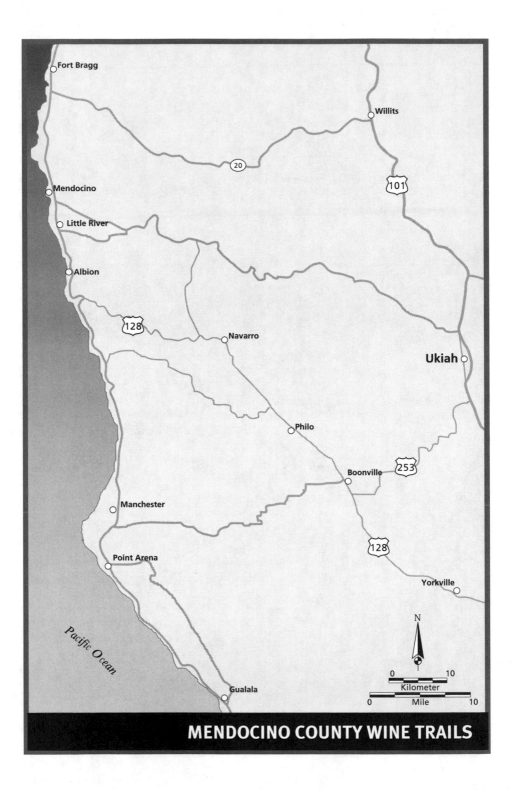

Fort Bragg

Willits

20

101

Mendocino

Little River

Albion

128

Navarro

Ukiah

Philo

Boonville

253

Manchester

128

Point Arena

Yorkville

Pacific Ocean

N

0 — 10
Kilometer
0 — Mile — 10

Gualala

MENDOCINO COUNTY WINE TRAILS

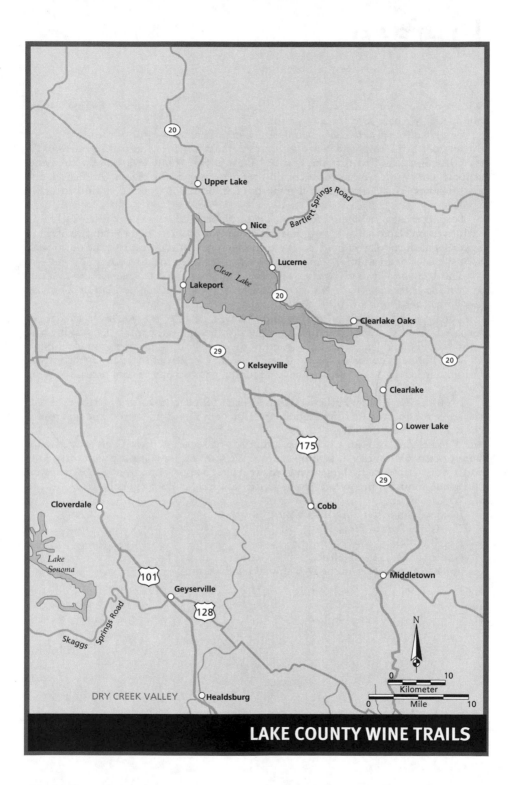

20

Upper Lake

Bartlett Springs Road

Nice

Lucerne

Clear Lake

Lakeport

20

Clearlake Oaks

29

20

Kelseyville

Clearlake

Lower Lake

175

29

Cloverdale

Cobb

Lake Sonoma

101

Geyserville

128

Middletown

Skaggs Springs Road

N

0   10
Kilometer
0   10
Mile

DRY CREEK VALLEY

Healdsburg

LAKE COUNTY WINE TRAILS

Preface

With so many "wine country" guides on the market, you may wonder what makes this one special. We have several reasons to brag:

First, *Insiders' Guide to California's Wine Country* offers what most of the other guides do not: in-depth listings and insights into restaurants, wineries, inns, and attractions fit for all budgets. Add to that the practical information about real estate, retirement, schools, and health care for those considering relocating to the region. (And check out the "Insiders' Tips," those helpful nuggets of information you won't find in other books.)

Second, those other guides focus mostly on Napa and Sonoma Counties, and some exclusively on Napa Valley. Many guides do a good job of scratching the surface of these regions, but the book you hold in your hands goes several steps beyond the norm with an inside look at an additional must-visit wine region: Mendocino County.

Third, *Insiders' Guide to California's Wine Country* gives a nod to Lake County, a lesser known locale for visitors to Northern California, yet a popular destination for those who love water sports and off-the-beaten-path wine tasting.

But we don't stop there. As you flip through these pages, you'll see that we've included detailed information on getaway destinations and attractions along the Sonoma and Mendocino coastlines—some of the most beautiful scenery you will find in all of California, if not on the planet. There's also an overview of the many attractions to be found in nearby San Francisco and ideas for day trips beyond the boundaries of Wine Country.

It's your choice, but we believe this guide—page for page—is superior to the others in the sheer volume of data offered about the Northern California region known around the world as "Wine Country."

Whether visiting Wine Country as a tourist or a settler, *Insiders' Guide to California's Wine Country* welcomes you with open arms. We want to know if the book worked for you. If you discover something we missed, we'd like to know about that, too. We update this guide annually, and we want to be as accurate and helpful as possible.

Write to us at:
Insiders' Guide to California's Wine Country
The Globe Pequot Press
P.O. Box 480
Guilford, CT 06437-0480
You can also visit us on the Web at www.insiders.com.

Acknowledgments

Only one author's name appears on the cover of this book, but pulling together so much information is not accomplished without the help and cooperation of scores of friends, acquaintances, and even total strangers. I have nearly as many people to thank for their assistance as there are grapes in Wine Country. It's impossible to name them all, but here are several that stand out, in no particular order:

My gratitude goes to Lisa Walter of the Sonoma Valley Harvest Wine Festival for her support of the book, and to Tom Fuller of the Napa Valley Wine Auction for his help. (Thanks to you both for a couple of memorable afternoons!) Clay Gregory, president of the board of directors of the Napa Valley Vintners Association and former general manager of Robert Mondavi Winery, and Nick Frey, executive director of the Sonoma County Grape Growers Association, were generous with their time and provided true insiders' insight and information. Catherine De Prima of the Sonoma County Film Commission, Susan Kashack of Sonoma State University, and photographer Derrick Story also contributed their expertise.

Fact-checker Tricia Jornada labored over the details of listings in several chapters, and for her help I am grateful. My sister, Jan Blanchard, lent many of her photos for use in the book, while my husband, Loren, displayed patience and understanding when piles of my writing and research were littering the house. Jan Cronan, my editor at Globe Pequot Press on the last two editions of this book, has been a rock. Thank you, Jan.

John and Gertrude Saylor, my parents, are responsible for my lifelong desire to visit new places. Thanks to their own love of travel, before my 10th birthday I had hiked the circumference of Devil's Tower, waded in the Gulf of Mexico, posed for pictures in front of Mt. Rushmore, gawked at Jayne Mansfield's hot pink mansion in Hollywood, and been kissed by a cockatoo in Miami. Covering Wine Country has been almost as exciting.

A common sight in Wine Country: hot air balloons floating over vineyards. PHOTO: NAPA VALLEY CONFERENCE AND VISITORS BUREAU

How to Use This Book

Napa County
Sonoma County
Mendocino County

Skimming through *Insiders' Guide to California's Wine Country* is a bit like channel surfing with your TV's remote control—you flip here and there, back and forth, looking for something to grab your attention. It might be a striking image or an interesting name that leaps out and demands closer investigation.

Go ahead and chapter surf to your heart's content, and land on any page that strikes your fancy, whether it's for a restaurant, winery, or lodging listing. That's okay. Data-heavy books such as this one are designed for thumbing through. But at some point you might want to find a particular "thing" by region, so it will help to understand the book's structure.

The table of contents breaks down the chapter topics, but if any questions remain, a quick peek at chapter introductions should answer them. Beyond that, we organized each chapter geographically, more or less, with Napa County listings first, followed by those of Sonoma County and Mendocino County. In general, the listings for hotels, attractions, wineries, and so forth appear in order in the book as you would encounter them while driving in each region, approximately south to north and east to west. (To make the Sonoma County listings more manageable—there are scads of them—we further divided the county into Northern, Southern, Sonoma Coast, and West County/Russian River subheadings.) Refer to the list below for the general order by town and city. (Lake County has its own chapter. Please see the table of contents.)

Note: We understand that many of our world-class eateries are known by name and not necessarily by their location. So we've organized our Restaurants chapter using the same geographical method explained above, then listed the restaurants alphabetically within their respective towns and regions.

Napa County

Napa, Yountville, Oakville, Rutherford, St. Helena, Angwin, Lake Berryessa, Calistoga

Sonoma County

Southern Sonoma
Sonoma, Glen Ellen, Kenwood, Petaluma, Cotati, Rohnert Park, Santa Rosa

Northern Sonoma
Windsor, Healdsburg, Geyserville, Cloverdale, Alexander Valley, Dry Creek Valley, Lake Sonoma, Westside Road

Sonoma Coast
Bodega, Bodega Bay, Jenner, Fort Ross

West County/Russian River
Sebastopol, Occidental, Forestville, Guerneville, Monte Rio, Cazadero, Duncans Mills

Mendocino County

U.S. 101
Hopland, Ukiah, Willits

Highway 128
Yorkville, Boonville, Philo, Navarro

Mendocino Coast
Gualala, Point Arena, Albion, Little River, Mendocino, Fort Bragg

Be aware that several chapters cover topics that venture beyond the Wine Country or otherwise defy a strict county-by-county organization. These include our Golden Gateway (San Francisco) and Day Trips chapters, which focus on more distant destinations. Likewise, the Spectator Sports chapter covers professional teams in and beyond Wine Country and is thus organized by sport. The Flora, Fauna, and Climate chapter and, to some extent, the Getting Here, Getting Around chapter, deal with phenomena that have no respect for county lines and thus have their own unique breakdowns. And the Festivals and Annual Events chapter logically follows a chronological order.

Finally, you'll note that some material teeters on the categorical fence that divides some chapters, so we have cross-referenced information wherever it made sense, briefly mentioning a related event, activity, or locale where appropriate and referring you to the chapter where it is described in more detail.

We hope the book answers all your questions and raises a few you might not have considered. If you find anything you believe to be inaccurate or misleading, we urge you to let us know.

Area Overview

Napa, Sonoma, and *Mendocino*—three words synonymous with beauty and the good life. Although I live here and gaze upon that beauty every day, I'm endlessly fascinated by its changing vistas. Trust me, visitors never go away disappointed by the scenery.

Although it is promoted as a nirvana for foodies and as "Eden to a wine grape," the Wine Country has much more to offer than its famous agricultural crops. I'm happy to report that it's composed of vibrant small cities, sleepy rural communities, a coastline blissfully free of commercialism, some of the tallest trees in the world, and an endless collection of colorful characters that call it home.

In this chapter, Wine Country is put under the microscope to reveal the various cities and towns you'll encounter as a visitor to the region.

Napa County

Of the Wine Country counties profiled in this book, Napa is by far the most dependent on wine and tourism and the region most associated with those two industries in the minds of visitors. Always rural in nature, Napa County has seen the rise and fall of wheat, cattle, and prunes as the dominant product. Today it is ultrapremium wine grapes—and the visitors who love them—that drive the economy.

In the last decade, Napa County's total population grew 12 percent (according to 2000 census figures), to 124,279, yet it remains the Bay Area's least populated county. Most of the residents are hardworking, average Joes and Jills, with the median household income in the city of Napa at $46,000. But we have a good share of celebrity residents, too, who earn a bit more. Property owners in Napa Valley and its environs include Francis Ford Coppola (see our Wineries chapter), Robin Williams, Robert Redford (who has been spotted bicycling through the valley), Woody Harrelson, Joe Montana, Boz Scaggs, Danielle Steele, David Wolper, and Mario Andretti. Other household names who have shopped for homes and property here but apparently haven't signed on the dotted line (yet) include Barbra Streisand and Eric Clapton.

Even if they don't commit to buying their very own villa or vineyard, celebs (A-list, B-list, and even C-list varieties) flock to the area for getaway jaunts the same as you, the probably-not-world-famous visitor. Because of this growing number of high-rollers and famous faces flitting about, filmmaker/wine baron/longtime resident Coppola recently quipped to the local press that he feared Napa Valley was turning into the East Hampton of the West Coast. Be that as it may, if you should stumble upon La Streisand noshing at the Model Bakery in St. Helena, please play it cool.

The southern gateway to Napa Valley is the city of Napa, which, at about 72,000 people, makes up more than half of the county's population. Napa has several gracious, older districts left over from the horse-and-buggy days—the lettered streets known as Old Town, the Fuller Park area south of downtown, and Alta Heights—connected by more down-to-earth neighborhoods. It is home to most of the budget- and family-oriented accommodations and eateries in the valley.

Yet downtown Napa is rapidly undergoing a major renovation that was triggered by the development and construction of Copia (see our Attractions chapter) and a $238 million flood control project along the Napa River that will take several years

3

to complete. Where once it was seen primarily as the commercial core of the valley proper, lacking an abundance of tourist-oriented amenities, the city of Napa is becoming a destination in itself. New hotels and B&Bs have opened, many new eateries are getting rave reviews, and the city center in general is being spiffed up and transformed. Some historic buildings are facing demolition in the flood control zone, yet others are getting multimillion-dollar makeovers. Plans for proposed hotels and other attractions are announced almost weekly, with several projects waiting for the green light so that groundbreaking can begin.

Though Napa owes much of its prosperity to the wine industry, government is the largest employer in the city. Napa is the seat of the county government, and the Napa Valley Unified School District and Napa State Hospital account for hundreds of jobs.

To the north of the city of Napa is Yountville, named after Napa Valley pioneer George Yount (see our History chapter). It is a small community (population 3,000) that self-proclaims more fine restaurants per capita than any city in America—and we don't doubt it. New subdivisions built in the late 1990s have increased the population slightly, but this is a town that caters almost exclusively, and with a lot of class, to visitors.

Oakville and Rutherford appear frequently in addresses throughout the book, but usually the reference is to nearby, countryside locales. The towns themselves are minuscule; hardly more than bulges around Highway 29. This is, however, a beautiful part of the valley—a midway sector where the mountains begin to encroach upon the valley floor. Every experienced picnicker in the region knows the Oakville Grocery Company, an unpretentious little pit stop along the highway famous for its gourmet delights. This is also the stretch of road where you will begin to come upon the showplace wineries—Robert Mondavi, Niebaum-Coppola, and so on.

When most visitors imagine the quintessential Wine Country village, they envision St. Helena—with its gingerbread cottages painted glistening white, canopied sidewalks of a thriving-yet-nostalgic downtown, pocket gardens with not a blade of grass out of place, and only three traffic lights! Though it has its peripheral subdivisions and apartment complexes, the overall look of St. Helena is defined by high-priced neatness (see our Real Estate chapter). Much of the housing is pre-World War II and nearly all has been immaculately maintained, and the residential streets in the heart of town are lushly lined with mature trees. The north end of town is dominated by the imposing structures of the Beringer and Charles Krug wineries and the Culinary Institute at Greystone (see our Education and Child Care chapter). About a quarter of the town's approximately 6,000 residents are 65 or older, making it a popular spot for retirees with comfortable bank accounts. Due east of St. Helena is Deer Park, a small community with about 1,800 souls.

The hilltop hamlet of Angwin, up Deer Park Road/Howell Mountain Road off the Silverado Trail, orbits around Pacific Union College. The town's population tops out at about 3,100, most of them college students—a full 61 percent of the inhabitants here are under age 30. The town is so heavily Seventh-day Adventist that it's said to be one of only two in the nation where the post office delivers mail on Sunday rather than Saturday.

To the east of Angwin, man-made Lake Berryessa figures prominently in our On the Water chapter. The settlements thereof tend to lie on the western and southern shores of the lake, especially along Berryessa-Knoxville Road. The eastern perimeter is virtually inaccessible to any vehicle. Unlike Clear Lake in Lake County, Berryessa is not encircled by hotels and restaurants. There are a few, but it is known more as a spot for vacation homes. As such, it empties out a bit in the winter.

Calistoga, the northernmost town of Napa Valley, is an iconoclastic slice of California, a burg that sees itself as "real" and unadulterated even as it supports itself almost entirely through tourist dollars, with the corner on the spa and mud bath market. As one local wag likes to describe it, "Calistoga is to pickup trucks what St.

The friendly facade of City Hall in Calistoga is just one of this small town's many charms. PHOTO: JEAN SAYLOR DOPPENBERG

Helena is to Range Rovers." The population hovers at around 5,200, with about 28 percent age 65 and older. Calistoga's easy-going mood can crack when the locals feel threatened by rampant development, however. PepsiCo tried to open some fast-food franchises in town a few years ago, but the citizenry hastily mobilized and ran the scoundrels out of town. That led to a bold prohibition of all new "formula" businesses. And just for the record, wine isn't the only refreshment bottled in Napa Valley: On the east side of Calistoga are two major suppliers of mineral water, Calistoga and Crystal Geyser, and some excellent beers are brewed and bottled at the Calistoga Inn.

Sonoma County

Encompassing nearly 1,600 square miles from the Pacific coast to the Mayacmas Mountains and San Pablo Bay, Sonoma County is the most populous of the four Wine Country counties. But most of the approximately 458,600 residents live in a relatively narrow corridor along U.S. 101 from Santa Rosa to Petaluma. The rest of the county—approximately 56 percent—is farmland. The farms consist of apple, peach, and plum orchards, livestock rangeland and dairy farms, and, of course, vineyards.

It's no surprise that grapes and wine are the most prized agricultural commodities, with an annual value of approximately $232 million—dairy comes in second at $95 million. Yet agricultural employment accounts for less than 4 percent of the total workforce. The services, retail trade, and manufacturing sectors by far employ the most people—approximately 62 percent. The state's Employment Development Department (EDD) expects these sectors to grow the fastest in Sonoma County over the next four to five years.

Santa Rosa is the county seat and the largest city, with a population of 147,600. In May 2002, *Forbes* magazine ranked the city number two in its list of the top 10 dynamic economic regions in the nation.

The largest employers include Agilent Technologies, a spin-off company of electronics giant Hewlett Packard; aerospace and medical supplier Optical Coating; high-tech medical equipment manufacturer Medtronic; and county and state government offices. As in Napa County and the rest of California, the Hispanic population is booming in Sonoma County (currently at 15 percent). Asian peoples are the second largest minority (4 percent), followed by Blacks and Native Americans (each at 1 percent).

Santa Rosa's downtown is split in two by U.S. 101—a planning decision that many have long since regretted. To the west of the highway are multiple antiques shops and historic Railroad Square, whose sturdy buildings were constructed of locally quarried stone. To the east, especially along Fourth Street, are restaurants, coffee houses, music stores, and similar hangouts. The Luther Burbank Home and Gardens (see our Attractions chapter) are also nearby.

Due south of Santa Rosa are the residential communities of Cotati, Rohnert Park, and Petaluma. The latter is the third-largest town in Wine Country, with more than 54,500 people and stately homes and Art Deco commercial palaces (such as the McNear Building).

On the southeastern edge of the county is the town of Sonoma. This small enclave of approximately 9,100 residents is largely defined by its historic sites, especially those along the town's eight-acre central plaza. There you'll find the Mission San Francisco de Solano, the Sonoma Barracks, the Swiss Hotel, and several nearby wineries within walking distance (see our Wineries, Hotels, Motels, and Inns, and Bed-and-Breakfast Inns chapters). The square is a National Historic Landmark and is a great spot to relax on a sunny afternoon. For a further description of the town of Sonoma, turn to our History chapter.

North of Sonoma are several tiny hamlets, including Glen Ellen and Kenwood. Tucked away from the traffic of Highway 12, Glen Ellen's Main Street is only two blocks long, so you might have to invent an excuse to spend the whole day here. One possibility is Jack London State Historic Park, just west of town (see our Attractions chapter). Kenwood is equally small, if not smaller, but no less charming. From the center of town (don't stand there; it's the middle of Highway 12), you can see the forested crests of two state parks, Annadel and Sugarloaf Ridge (see our Parks and Recreation chapter).

At the north end of the county is the town of Healdsburg, with a population of 10,700. Like Sonoma, the town has a delightful core centered around a classic town square. There you can find good food, good books, and a good dose of fine old relics and shopping options.

Just a short hop north on U.S. 101 from Healdsburg is Geyserville, named for an area northeast of the town where natural steam vents from the earth. These fumaroles, as they are called, are visible from many points in the county, particularly on cool mornings. (See our Lake County chapter for more information about the geothermal activity along the Sonoma County/Lake County border.)

Still farther north on U.S. 101 is Cloverdale, a small, pleasant town of 6,800 souls nestled at the far end of the peaceful Alexander Valley, one of the county's prime grape-growing regions. From this point north, the coast redwoods start to take over (see "The Big Trees" in our Day Trips chapter), though there are still lots of grape-growing fields to be found in Sonoma's northern neighbor, Mendocino County.

The Alexander Valley south of Cloverdale offers wine tasters a more relaxed alternative to the relative bustle of Napa and Sonoma Valleys. It may not have as many wineries, but it does have some good ones (see our Wineries chapter), and the traffic is comparatively light. In spring, when the winter rains have turned the hills a vivid green, the valley is especially charming—like a wee bit of the rolling Irish countryside.

Another smaller and similarly charming vale is the Dry Creek Valley, which lies west of Alexander Valley above Healdsburg. Here row upon row of vineyards line the rich valley floor and terraces climb up the gentle hillsides. At one time, Dry Creek Valley extended farther to the north, but much of it was submerged when Warm Springs Dam was built in 1982. The dam gave birth to Lake Sonoma, a recreational area profiled more thoroughly in our On the Water chapter.

Finally, let it be known that there is life in western Sonoma County, despite the scarcity of wineries. Bodega Bay is the gateway to the Pacific, and it is where Highway 1 kisses the coast and begins its circuitous trek northward. Much of the Alfred Hitchcock thriller *The Birds* was filmed in 1963 in both Bodega Bay and the slightly inland

The Potter School, made famous in Alfred Hitchcock's movie The Birds, *dominates a hillside in the small town of Bodega.* PHOTO: JEAN SAYLOR DOPPENBERG

enclave of Bodega. The movie featured Bodega's Potter School, a one-room schoolhouse built a century before Hitchcock's cameras rolled into town.

Bodega Bay is one of the largest fishing ports between San Francisco and Eureka, and in September and October, the locals like to celebrate what they call "secret summer," when temperatures are relatively mild and the morning fog quickly disperses. The hook-shaped peninsula that shields the harbor from the open sea is Bodega Head. You can drive out on the headland along Westshore Road, which offers brilliant views and access to beaches and cliffs. Also on Bodega Head is the Bodega Marine Lab, a University of California field station that is open to the public every Friday from 2:00 to 4:00 P.M.

The town of Jenner lies about 7 miles north of Bodega Bay, at the point where the Russian River meets the sea. Dozens of harbor seals congregate near the town, growing fat on steelhead and other fish that migrate upriver. North of Jenner the coastal settlements are few and far between. Once the easternmost outpost of Czarist Russia, Fort Ross is now a State Historic Park (see our History and Attractions chapters).

Russian geographers will also recognize the name Sebastopol. The Wine Country town with a population of 7,700 that shares this name with the Crimean city is located halfway between Santa Rosa and the coast. Sebastopol rose to prominence on the cores of a billion Gravenstein apples—the delectable fruit that got its start here. The community has honored the revered apple by naming Highway 116, which runs through the heart of town, the Gravenstein Highway, and every summer it hosts the Gravenstein Apple Fair (see our Festivals and Annual Events chapter).

West and north of Sebastopol is the town of Forestville, which serves as a way station for travelers headed to the Russian River and the Pacific coast. Nearby is the all-but-forgotten town of Occidental, perched at the top of a hill in the middle of redwood country. Many know Occidental as the place for sublime Italian dinners—at Negri's and the Union Hotel (see our Restaurants chapter). It's also delightfully romantic, but what would you expect of a village whose main thoroughfare goes by the name Bohemian Highway?

Where the Bohemian Highway meets the Russian River just north of Occidental is the tiny town of Monte Rio. Here you can catch a movie at the funky Rio Theater before heading upriver to Guerneville (pronounced GURN-ville). This former lumber capital–cum–summer resort is sometimes referred to as the Gay Riviera, because of the large gay population that lives and weekends here.

While Guerneville is the largest town in the Russian River resort area, Duncans Mills is one of the smallest. Located about 4 miles before Highway 116 joins Highway 1, the town looks much as it did when it was the western terminus of the Northwest Pacific Railroad. A museum recalls the glory days of the beloved choo-choo, and a host of art and antiques shops and restaurants provide plenty of distractions.

Mendocino County

Mendocino County is double the size of Sonoma County, covering nearly 3,500 square miles. The population, currently at 86,200, is widely dispersed, with only a quarter of the residents living in urban areas. Most people find employment in the service sector, specifically tourism. The county's economy has historically

The quaint village of Duncans Mills hangs out its welcome along Highway 12 in west Sonoma County.

PHOTO: JEAN SAYLOR DOPPENBERG

been centered in the lumber and fishing industries, and both still have a foothold here. In inland areas such as the Yokayo Valley, agriculture is paramount. And because of the large holdings of public land in Mendocino County, the state parks system has become another important employer.

Hopland is a town that came by its name honestly. Awash in a field of hops in the early 1900s, it was the perfect choice as a home base for Mendocino Brewing Company, when in 1982 it became California's first brewery since Prohibition. At the south end of Hopland is the Real Goods Solar Living Center (see our Attractions chapter), a 12-acre site created by Real Goods, retailer of alternative energy products and services. Real Goods' 5,000-square-foot building is made of rice-straw bales, and wind generators and solar panels provide all of its electrical needs.

With a population of 15,500, Ukiah is Mendocino's largest town. It is set in the Yokayo Valley between the Coast Range and Lake Mendocino. Lumber is the chief commodity here, as it has been for decades, but Ukiah also has become the financial, business, medical, and service center not only for Mendocino County, but also for portions of Sonoma, Lake, and Humboldt counties. The town is home to many descendants of the Pomo tribe, the first inhabitants of the area.

Willits, to the north, also was kick-started during the 19th-century lumber boom, and most of the larger companies in the area are involved in manufacturing wood products. Driving along U.S. 101 6 miles south of town, look for a boulder directly across the highway from White Deer Lodge—it was a reputed hideout of Black Bart, the stagecoach robber who roamed the area more than 100 years ago. You probably won't catch a glimpse of Bart, but you might see a white fallow deer on Ridgewood Summit. Herds of the deer, purchased from William Randolph Hearst's San Simeon Ranch, were released here in 1949.

Highway 128 courses through the Anderson Valley, linking the tiny towns of

Phone Numbers for Tourists

Napa County
Napa Valley Conference & Visitors
Bureau
1310 Napa Town Center, Napa
(707) 226–7459
www.napavalley.com

Napa Chamber of Commerce
1556 First Street, Napa
(707) 226–7455
www.napachamber.org

Yountville Chamber of Commerce
6516 Yount Street, Yountville
(707) 944–0904
www.yountville.com

St. Helena Chamber of Commerce
1010 Main Street, St. Helena
(707) 963–4456
www.sthelena.com

Calistoga Chamber of Commerce
1458 Lincoln Avenue, Calistoga
(707) 942–6333
www.calistogafun.com

Sonoma County
Hispanic Chamber of Commerce of
Sonoma County
2435 Professional Drive, Santa Rosa
(707) 526–7744

Sonoma Valley Visitors Bureau
453 First Street E., Sonoma
(707) 996–1090
www.sonomavalley.com

Sonoma Valley Chamber of Commerce
651 Broadway, Sonoma
(707) 996–1033
www.sonomachamber.com

Petaluma Chamber of Commerce
800 Baywood Drive, Petaluma
(707) 762–2785
www.petaluma.org

Petaluma Visitors Program
799 Baywood Drive, Petaluma
(707) 769–0429
www.petaluma.org/visitor

Cotati Chamber of Commerce
8109 La Plaza, Cotati
(707) 795–5508
www.cotati.org

Rohnert Park Chamber of Commerce
5000 Roberts Lake Road, Rohnert Park
(707) 584–1415
www.rpchamber.org

Santa Rosa Convention & Visitors Bureau
and California Welcome Center
9 Fourth Street, Santa Rosa
(707) 577–8674
www.visitsantarosa.com

Santa Rosa Chamber of Commerce
637 First Street, Santa Rosa
(707) 545–1414
www.santarosachamber.com

Sonoma County Tourism Program
520 Mendocino Avenue, Suite 210, Santa
Rosa
(707) 565–5383
www.sonomacounty.com

Mark West Area Chamber of Commerce
4795 Old Redwood Highway, Santa Rosa
(707) 578–7975
www.markwest.org

Windsor Chamber of Commerce
8499 Old Redwood Highway, Windsor
(707) 838–7285
www.windsorchamber.com

Healdsburg Chamber of Commerce
217 Healdsburg Avenue, Healdsburg
(707) 433–6935
www.healdsburg.org

Geyserville Chamber of Commerce
Information Center
21060 Geyserville Avenue, Geyserville
(707) 857–3745
www.geyservillecc.com

North Coast Wine and Visitors Center
105 North Cloverdale Boulevard,
Cloverdale
(707) 894–0818
www.cloverdale.net

Sonoma Coast Visitor Information/
Bodega Bay Area Chamber of Commerce
850 Highway 1, Bodega Bay
(707) 875–3422
www.bodegabay.com

Jenner Visitors' Center
10451 Highway 1, Jenner
(707) 865–9433

Sebastopol Chamber of Commerce
265 South Main Street, Sebastopol
(707) 823–3032
www.sebastopol.org

Monte Rio Chamber of Commerce
(707) 865–1533

Forestville Chamber of Commerce and
Visitors Center
6652 Front Street, Forestville
(707) 887–1111

Russian River Region Visitors Bureau and
Chamber of Commerce
16209 First Street, Guerneville
(707) 869–9000, (800) 253–8800
www.russianriver.com

Occidental Chamber of Commerce
(707) 874–3279
www.occidental.org

Mendocino County
Hopland Chamber of Commerce
(707) 744–1379

Ukiah Chamber of Commerce
200 South School Street, Ukiah
(707) 462–4705
www.ukiahchamber.com

Willits Chamber of Commerce
239 South Main Street, Willits
(707) 459–7910

Anderson Valley Chamber of Commerce
(707) 895–2379

Redwood Coast Chamber of Commerce
(707) 884–1080, (800) 778–5252
www.redwoodcoastchamber.com

Fort Bragg-Mendocino Coast Chamber of
Commerce
332 North Main Street, Fort Bragg
(707) 961–6300, (800) 726–2780
www.mendocinocoast.com

Yorkville, Boonville, Philo, and Navarro. The valley's northern latitude and salty breezes make it appropriate for growing cool-weather grapes such as Gewurztraminer and Riesling. Anderson Valley also brings forth a healthy supply of apples and sheep, and mushrooms are gathered in the soggy forests on either side of the valley.

Gualala, pronounced "Wah-LA-la," is the southern gateway to the Mendocino Coast. Along with Anchor Bay, 4 miles to the north, it forms what locals call the Banana Belt, a relatively warm and fog-free pocket of coastline. Gualala was a thriving lumber town until the supply of unprotected trees dwindled in the 1960s. Today the town is something of an arts community, with resident painters, sculptors, photographers, writers, and musicians (see our Arts and Culture chapter).

About 16 miles north of Gualala is Point Arena. With about 474 people, it's one of the smallest incorporated cities in the state. Once a lumber and fishing center, Point Arena now sticks mostly to the tourist trade. Surfers say the harbor is one of the best surfing spots in Northern California. Point Arena Lighthouse, rebuilt after the 1906 earthquake, is a favorite stop for visitors.

Moving up the coast, Albion (between Whitesboro Cove and the Albion River) and Little River (near the waterway of the same name) are further possibilities for weary Highway 1 drivers and white-knuckled passengers. Most people who stop there, other than those on their way to the Little River Inn (see our Spas and Resorts chapter), are heading for Mendocino, a village with about 1,000 residents that stood as a popular monument to social freedom even before the Sir Douglas Quintet sang about it in the late 1960s. It was little more than an economically depressed former lumber town when the Mendocino Art Center was founded in 1959, seeding an artists' colony that revitalized the community. The Art Center lives on, offering more than 200 classes, workshops, and seminars each year (see our Attractions and Arts and Culture chapters).

The village of Mendocino, a National Historic Preservation District, is a delightful mix of gingerbread architecture, steep gables, and white picket fences that seem straight out of an Edward Hopper painting of New England. Yet some people have been critical of Mendocino's "perfection"— one local called it "more of a movie set than a town." A few of the more outstand-

Insiders' Tip

The surge in demand for wine fueled an unprecedented expansion of vineyards in Sonoma County in the late 1990s. Approximately 3,500 to 4,000 acres of new vines were planted in the county each year between 1995 and 2000. The frenzied growth enraged local environmentalists, who complained that the new vineyards would increase soil erosion and transform the county into a "Grape Republic." In 1999, a county ordinance went into effect limiting vineyard expansion onto fragile hillside areas.

ing architectural structures include the Mendocino Hotel, the Ford House, and the Presbyterian Church of Mendocino, all on Main Street. The latter building is the oldest continuously operating Presbyterian church in California.

Almost as charming, and more diversified economically, is Fort Bragg, originally established as a military outpost in 1857 as a check on the nearby Mendocino Indian Reservation. With a population of 7,000, its beaches are prized for beachcombing, surf fishing, and picnicking. Noyo Harbor, on the south end of town, is a bustle of activity when fishing boats arrive to unload their hauls and clean up. It's one of the largest ports between San Francisco and Eureka, and it is preferred by the vast majority of local seals and sea lions. You can get a map for a walking tour of the town from the Fort Bragg Chamber of Commerce at 332 North Main Street.

Getting Here, Getting Around

By Automobile
By Air
By Bus/Train
Public Transportation
By Limousine
By Taxi

It's about 142 miles from Infineon Raceway at the southern tip of Sonoma County to the town of Piercy at the north end of Mendocino County. And that's as the crow flies somewhat diagonally across the map; it is considerably farther as the tourist weaves. So before you set out, understand that this three-county region covers one massive chunk of California real estate, and it may take more time than you might first think to get where you want to go.

As explained in How to Use This Book, major Wine Country thoroughfares run north-south, generally along the principal valleys. They are occasionally linked by roads and highways that run east-west, with the latter often traversing the hills and ranges that divide the region. We cover the major highways here, starting with the four primary routes. Unless otherwise stated, all roads mentioned are two-lane highways.

In addition to the route descriptions, we've provided information on public and private transportation, including airports, shuttle services, Amtrak and Greyhound, taxis, limousines, and public buses.

One last word of advice: Use your common sense when it comes to wine tasting and driving. If you plan to drive to a series of tasting rooms, please designate one person to drink in moderation (or literally only "taste"—as in swirl, sniff, sip, and spit) or, preferably, rent a limo and see the Wine Country safely and in style. Remember, the legal blood-alcohol threshold in California is .08 percent. That is lower than some visitors are accustomed to, and it is possible to be over this limit without feeling particularly buzzed. So play it safe. If you're not sure, you probably are drunk, at least by California Highway Patrol standards. Finally, even if you are white-eyed sober, others on the road might not be. As the public-service ads say, drive defensively.

By Automobile

The Main North-South Arteries

Highway 29

This is the main traffic corridor of Napa Valley, not to mention the perimeter route for half of Lake County's Clear Lake. The highway begins in Vallejo and, after passing through the city of Napa about 12 miles later, quickly becomes a ride in a wine-theme amusement park. It passes through some of the finest wine-grape country in America and connects the valley's towns: Napa, Yountville, Oakville, Rutherford, St. Helena, and Calistoga. Its shoulders are weighed down by chateaux, fortresses, Victorians, and renowned restaurants. Wine Country heavyweights such as Robert Mondavi and Domaine Chandon are here, and so are great historic wineries like Beringer and Charles Krug (see our Wineries chapter). Highway 29, the tourism artery of Napa Valley, is commonly referred to as "St. Helena Highway," and you will see it used frequently in addresses, as in this book. You will also see and hear the expression "upvalley" from time to time. This generally refers to St. Helena and points north.

Highway 29 is four lanes from Vallejo to Yountville; two thereafter. The road makes a sharp right when it gets to Calistoga and proceeds through the mostly vintage downtown. It leaves Calistoga and heads due north, climbing the flank of Mt. St. Helena and dropping into the flats of Lake County. The highway then takes a serpentine path up to Lower Lake, where it veers sharply and heads northwest, skirting the southern and western shores of Clear Lake. Highway 29 hits Kelseyville and Lakeport, then heads north and dies at the town of Upper Lake.

Highway 12

Highway 12 travels east-west for most of its length, but it garners acclaim for a relatively short north-south stretch that runs through the Sonoma Valley. Soon after joining with Highway 29 just below Napa, Highway 12 breaks west, hooking up with Highway 121 and skirting the Carneros Valley before crossing the Napa-Sonoma border. It then splits north to begin its renowned tour past wineries and hot springs and through classic Wine Country towns. It veers west after Kenwood, soon passing through the heart of bustling Santa Rosa and on to Sebastopol.

U.S. 101

U.S. 101, also known as the Redwood Highway, doesn't have the charm of Highways 29 or 12. As the major artery of Sonoma and Mendocino counties, it serves commuters, truckers, farmers, and all manner of passersby, who may travel it south to Hollywood or north to Oregon.

U.S. 101 enters Sonoma County about 5 miles south of Petaluma, and continues on to Rohnert Park, Santa Rosa, Healdsburg, Cloverdale, Ukiah, Willits, Laytonville, and other, smaller towns. The southern Wine Country stretch of U.S. 101—from Petaluma to Windsor—is rather developed and populated, and traffic tends to bog down close to rush hour, but snarls can occur any time of day. U.S. 101 is four lanes to the Marin border; north it alternates at intervals between two lanes and six.

Highway 1

Highway 1 is a destination unto itself. Though this Sonoma-Mendocino section of the highway may not be as celebrated as the

The Russian River Valley and most other areas of Wine Country guide visitors to local wineries by means of street signs. PHOTO: JEAN SAYLOR DOPPENBERG

Big Sur–Carmel section to the south, it does offer approximately 135 miles of breathtaking coastal landscape, jaw-dropping vistas of the craggy coastline and the ocean to the west, and stands of coastal live oak, pine, fir, or coast redwoods to the east.

The highway intersects about two dozen state parks, state beaches, state reserves, regional parks, and county parks on its ascent through the Wine Country (see our Parks and Recreation chapter). It also is the main artery for such towns as Jenner, Gualala, Point Arena, Albion, Mendocino, and Fort Bragg. If you've been there before, the names are enough to make you smell salt air and clam chowder.

Cypress trees tower over a lonely stretch of Highway 1. PHOTO: JOHN NAGIECKI

Snaking its way north through Marin County, Highway 1 cuts over to the ocean at Bodega Bay, about 8 miles after it enters Sonoma County. The highway leaves the sea again north of Rockport in the upper reaches of Mendocino County. You'll notice that between Bodega Bay and Fort Bragg in Mendocino County, the road is often designated as Coast Highway 1. And one note of realism: This is not 135 miles that you can drive in two hours. The route regularly curves up, down, and around the rocky coast—expect to stop often if you have passengers prone to car sickness. Doing the entire trip in one full day will leave little time for beachcombing and otter spotting.

Other Wine Country Roadways

Highway 121

This highway joins Sonoma with the Lake Berryessa highlands, via Napa. The route

is born at Sears Point, site of the famed Infineon Raceway (formerly known as Sears Point) at the southern tip of Sonoma County (see our Spectator Sports chapter). It heads north, then makes a sharp right to join Highway 12 on its way to Napa Valley.

Highway 121 travels through the Carneros grape-growing region, which has only a few wineries but some of the most coveted vineyards in the state. The road intersects Highway 29 and is lured north, but it quickly departs with three sharp turns—right, left, and right again—through the city of Napa. Highway 121 then assumes a winding northeasterly course into the hills before it enters Highway 128 not far from Lake Berryessa.

Highway 128

Highway 128, best known as the path through the Alexander Valley wine region, is a rambling roadway that periodically hitches northward rides to augment its own northwesterly journey. It enters Napa

County from the east, navigating the steep hills that hug Lake Berryessa. It sneaks around the southwest fingers of the lake, then follows Sage Creek west into Napa Valley. When it gets to Rutherford, Highway 128 joins Highway 29 on a northern jaunt through the vineyards. But when Highway 29 makes a right turn into Calistoga, Highway 128 continues northwest, into rustic Knights Valley and then lovely Alexander Valley with its first-rate wineries.

Highway 128 meets U.S. 101 just north of Geyserville and follows it to Cloverdale. It then breaks away again, heading northwest through Boonville and Philo on one of California's most unheralded scenic routes. Before it hits Highway 1 near Navarro Point, Highway 128 cuts into Navarro River Redwoods State Park, a skinny swath that basically straddles the highway.

Highway 20

If you want a detailed lesson in California geology, with a minor course in history, don't bother with a textbook. Just drive the length of Highway 20, which begins high in the Sierra Nevada Mountains, descends through gold country, and crosses the fertile Sacramento Valley on its search for the ocean. Highway 20 enters the Wine Country in eastern Lake County and bears generally west along the northern edge of Clear Lake through towns such as Clearlake Oaks and Lucerne. The highway passes north of Lake Mendocino just before it hits U.S. 101 at the town of Calpella. The two highways then merge on a northerly course. Highway 20 breaks away from U.S. 101 at Willits, where it embarks on a jittery, handsome west-by-northwest track to the coast. It meets Highway 1 just south of Fort Bragg.

Highway 116

Highway 116 is the paved shadow of the Russian River for a good part of its length. After connecting Sonoma and Petaluma in southern Sonoma County, it joins with U.S. 101 up to Cotati, then splits off and heads northwest through Sebastopol and Forestville. It's a perfectly nice highway during all of that, but Highway 116 really

shines just as it reaches Guerneville and follows the river to the coast. The water sparkles, the sunlight blinks through the trees, and the ocean feels just a few curves away.

Highway 253

Crooked Highway 253 connects Boonville and Ukiah in Mendocino County; in other words it connects U.S. 101 and seaward Highway 128. If, by contrast, you want to go from Boonville to the coast, take Mountain View Road.

Highway 175

Highway 175 is an alternative to Highway 20 as a connection between Sonoma and Lake Counties. It's also a pleasing drive, one of the roads less traveled in the Wine Country. Highway 175 leaves Middletown in Lake County and proceeds north past the town of Cobb and Boggs Mountain State Forest. It joins Highway 29 and goes almost to Lakeport before it breaks west. It then wiggles through the Mayacmas Mountains and ends up in Hopland at U.S. 101.

By Air

Three major airports "service" the Wine Country on its periphery—San Francisco,

Insiders' Tip

Highway 1 several miles north of Jenner follows a steep serpentine route—affectionately, but unofficially, called Dramamine Drive. The highway climbs high up the Coast Range, offering spectacular views of the ocean below.

Oakland, and Sacramento—each of them as inconveniently located as the next.

Among the big three airports profiled here, the Oakland and Sacramento airports are slightly more efficient if you are entering the Wine Country through Napa or the town of Sonoma. Figure on taking 75 to 90 minutes to drive from Oakland or Sacramento to Napa, and about the same from San Francisco to Santa Rosa. Of course, San Francisco offers a longer lineup of airlines. Six major rental car companies—Hertz, Avis, Budget, Dollar, National, and Alamo—serve all three airports.

Major Airports

San Francisco International Airport
San Francisco
(650) 876–2377
www.flysfo.com

With about 40 million passengers a year, San Francisco International Airport (SFO) is the fifth busiest airport in the United States and the world's ninth busiest. Located 14 miles south of downtown San Francisco, the airport is surrounded by more than 2,700 acres of undeveloped tidelands. The runways you see today were built on land reclaimed from San Francisco Bay.

Insiders' Tip

If you find yourself in slow moving traffic on U.S. 101 or any other multilane highway in California, don't be alarmed if you see a motorcycle passing cars in between the lanes of stalled or slow traffic. Such riding is legal in the state of California.

The airport has undergone a huge renovation and expansion at a cost of approximately $3 billion. This includes a 2.5-million-square-foot international terminal—priced at more than $900 million alone—that increased the number of gates from 10 to 24; two parking garages; a centralized rental car facility; a BART (Bay Area Rapid Transit) station; and an AirTrain system to move passengers between terminals. Construction will continue for some time, as the old international terminal is converted to domestic use.

Along with this renovation come some nice surprises, including Ebisu, a Japanese restaurant and sushi bar. And if you have time to kill—and what else are airports for?—there are rotating art exhibitions and a permanent collection administered by the San Francisco Art Commission. An Aviation Library and Archival Research Center were also added during the renovation.

Every major airline carrier, and virtually every smaller carrier with any sort of presence in the western United States, touches down at SFO. If you're in doubt about service from a specific airline, contact the airport or your travel agent. There are outlets for all the expected rental car companies at the airport.

Here are the contact numbers you will need: National, (650) 616–3000; Budget, (650) 877–0998; Dollar, (650) 244–4131; Hertz, (650) 624–6600; Avis, (650) 877–3156; and Alamo, (650) 347–9911.

Parking fees are $1.00 for 15 minutes, $28.00 for the first full day, and $35.00 for the second.

Oakland International Airport
Oakland
(510) 577–4000
www.flyoakland.com

The Oakland International Airport (OAK) is smaller and less ambitious than its neighbor to the west, and that is exactly what makes it more attractive to many Wine Country visitors. With only two terminals and a dozen airlines, it can be a painless experience.

South of downtown Oakland, take the Hegenberger Road exit from I-880 to reach OAK. Once inside there are 14 boarding gates at Terminal One and 8 at Terminal Two, where no gate is farther than 400 feet from the curb. Terminal Two is devoted entirely to Southwest Airlines, which bases 300 of its pilots and nearly 500 flight attendants in Oakland.

There are Laptop Lane services in both terminals, so if you absolutely, positively must conduct business coming or going, this is the place. Private mini-offices are equipped with Pentium II personal computers, laser printers, fax machines, and T-1 lines for Internet and e-mail access.

Several major and regional airlines service OAK. These include Alaska, American, America West, Continental, Delta, jetBlue, Southwest, and United. Seven major car rental companies operate at the airport. Local numbers are: Hertz, (510) 639–0200; Avis, (510) 577–6370; Budget, (510) 568–6150; Dollar, (510) 638–2750; National, (510) 639–2411; Thrifty, (510) 568–1279; and Enterprise, (510) 638–8600.

All the parking lots charge $1.00 for the first 20 minutes, but the rates vary for a day: It's $25.00 in the hourly lot, $15.00 long-term in the daily lot, and $12.00 in economy.

Sacramento International Airport
Sacramento
(916) 929–5411
www.airports.co.sacramento.ca.us

It used to be that politicians shuttling back and forth between their constituents and the State Capitol created most of the traffic at Sacramento International Airport (SMF), about 10 miles north of downtown Sacramento (and accessible from I-5). But this is now the 46th busiest airport in the nation, and a new terminal that opened in October 1998 effectively doubled the size of the facility.

Ten major air carriers serve the Sacramento airport—Alaska, America West, American, Continental, Delta, Frontier, Horizon, Northwest, Southwest, and United. Several of the usual rental car agencies can provide you with wheels at SMF. Local numbers are: Hertz, (916) 927–3882; Avis, (916) 922–5601; Budget, (916) 922–7317; National, (916) 568–2415; and Alamo, (916) 646–6020. Park-

ing (12,000 vehicle capacity) runs about $1.00 for the first hour, $2.00 per hour thereafter in the hourly lot, with a maximum of $24.00 a day. The daily lots charge $7.00 to $10.00 per day.

Charles M. Schulz–Sonoma County Airport
2200 Airport Boulevard, Santa Rosa
(707) 565–7240

This airport, one of Wine Country's best, was renamed in 2000 to honor the late Charles Schulz of "Peanuts" fame, who lived in Santa Rosa for several decades. A $3 million upgrade of this airport's runways and main taxiways was completed in 2001. Valley Air Express began service to Oakland in late 2002 on a nine-passenger Cessna; at press time, the airport was in negotiations to add a larger carrier.

Meanwhile, private planes are always welcome, and 20 hangars were built in late 2001 to accommodate them. There are no landing fees, though the overnight rate is $6.00 to $17.00, and the monthly rate can range from $36.00 to $109.00 (depending on wingspan).

The airport is about 7 miles north of downtown Santa Rosa, 2.2 miles west of U.S. 101 on Airport Boulevard. Hertz, (800) 654–3131 or (707) 528–0834, and Avis, (800) 331–1212 or (707) 571–0465, both offer rental car services at this airport. The daily rate for long-term parking is $5.00.

Smaller Wine Country Airports

The region includes at least a dozen smaller airports open to private planes. Here is an alphabetical listing of the most accessible, with numbers you can call for details. Unless otherwise stated, figure on no landing fees and an overnight charge of $4.00 or $5.00.

Angwin Airport
100 Angwin Avenue, Angwin
(707) 965–6219

The airport is off College Avenue, behind Pacific Union College. The overnight fee is $5.00 (single engine) or $7.00 (double).

Boonville Airport
Airport Road, Boonville
(707) 895–9918

The airport is northwest of town, off Ornbaun Road.

Cloverdale Municipal Airport
220 Airport Road, Cloverdale
(707) 894–1895

The airport is south of town, off Asti Road.

Healdsburg Municipal Airport
1580 Lytton Springs Road, Healdsburg
(707) 433–3319

The airport is north of town, accessible from U.S. 101 or Dry Creek Road.

Little River Airport
43001 Airport Road, Little River
(707) 937–5129

The airport is east of town, off Little River Airport Road. The overnight fee is $7 for a single-engine plane, $8 for a double-engine.

Napa County Airport
2030 Airport Road, Napa
(707) 253–4300
www.co.napa.ca.us

Perhaps the most elaborate of the small airports, Napa County offers Bridgeford Flying Service and Jonesy's Famous Steakhouse. Japan Air Lines maintains a multimillion-dollar pilot training facility on the grounds. The airport is 1 mile west of the intersection of Highways 12 and 29. There is no landing fee for private planes. The overnight fee is $5.00 for a single-engine plane, $8.00 for a double-engine, and $20.00 for a commercial plane.

Petaluma Municipal Airport
601 Sky Ranch Road, Petaluma
(707) 778–4404

The airport is on the east end of town, off East Washington Street.

Sonoma Sky Park
21870 Eighth Street East, Sonoma
(707) 996–2100

The airport is just south of Sonoma, near the community of Schellville.

Sonoma Valley Airport
23980 Arnold Drive, Sonoma
(707) 938–5382

This is another airport just south of Sonoma, near the junction of Highways 116 and 121.

Ukiah Municipal Airport
1411 South State Street, Ukiah
(707) 467–2817

The airport is on the south end of town, off South State.

Airport Shuttles

If you enter the Wine Country via San Francisco, Oakland, or Sonoma County Airport, you don't have to be stranded at the baggage carousel. The following carriers specialize in airport transportation.

Evans Airport Service
4075 Solano Avenue, Napa
(707) 255–1559, (800) 428–5612
www.evanstransportation.com

Evans Airport Service, long the prime mode of getting to SFO from Napa (or vice versa), now goes to OAK, too. Evans has 11 daily departures on weekdays, 9 Saturday, and 10 Sunday to San Francisco; and 8 on weekdays, 7 on weekends to Oakland. The buses are full-size and comfortable. The fare is $18 one-way

Insiders' Tip

To toodle around downtown Napa, take the trolley. There's a fixed route, with several stops in key locations for hopping on and off. The trolley operates from 11:00 A.M. to 10:00 P.M. on weekends, and 11:00 A.M. to 7:00 P.M. on weekdays.

from Evans' large, patrolled lot, but children younger than 13 ride for half price. The office is open from 5:00 A.M. to midnight, and you can leave a reservation with the answering service if no one is home. To get to Evans take Highway 29 to Trower Avenue and go west one mini-block to Solano Avenue, the frontage road. Turn right and look for the first building past the fire station. Parking is $2.00 per day.

Sonoma County Airport Express
4246 Petaluma Boulevard North, Petaluma
(707) 837–8700, (800) 327–2024
www.airportexpressinc.com

The Airport Express makes 23 daily runs from the Sonoma County Airport to San Francisco International Airport and 10 runs daily to Oakland International Airport. There are three intermediate pickup/drop-off points: 601 Mendocino Avenue in downtown Santa Rosa, the DoubleTree Hotel at 1 DoubleTree Drive in Rohnert Park, and at the company's office in Petaluma at 4246 Petaluma Boulevard North. The one-way cost to either airport is $24 for adults, $12 for kids ages 3 to 11, and $22 for seniors. Long-term parking at the Sonoma County Airport is $5.00 per day, parking is free (for 72 hours maximum) at the DoubleTree lot, and secured parking at the Petaluma site costs $4.00 per day.

Sonoma Airporter
500 West Napa Street, Sonoma
(707) 938–4246, (800) 611–4246

The Airporter makes six daily runs (five on Saturday) from Sonoma Valley to SFO, with a connection in San Rafael. The nine-passenger vans will pick you up practically anywhere in Sonoma, Boyes Hot Springs, Glen Ellen, Kenwood, or Oakmont, and deposit you at your terminal about one hour and 40 minutes later. The fare is $33.00 for adults, $23.00 for children 2 to 12 (free for infants with an adult chaperone), but it's $5.00 less if you pick up the bus at Sonoma City Hall.

By Bus/Train

Amtrak
1275 McKinstry Street, Napa
(800) 872–7245
www.transitinfo.org/Amtrak

The only viable railroad lines in the Wine Country are tourist-oriented puffers described in our Attractions chapter. There are no Amtrak stations, but the company has contracted Amador Stage Lines to run buses from Napa, Petaluma, Rohnert Park, Santa Rosa, Cloverdale, Ukiah, and Willits. These buses will drop you off at an Amtrak station, or deliver you from a station. The fee varies with destination but generally is quite reasonable. From Martinez the rail line can take you practically anywhere in the country. Call Amtrak for details.

Greyhound Bus Lines
435 Santa Rosa Avenue, Santa Rosa
(707) 545–6495, (800) 231–2222
www.transitinfo.org/Greyhound

Greyhound's only true Wine Country station is in Santa Rosa. Other towns—Napa, Petaluma, Sonoma, Willits, and Ukiah included—are "flagstop" stations. That means they have infrequent but regular pickups at specific corners and parking lots. Call for details.

Public Transportation

Public buses and vans might not be a viable option for a week of exploring and wine tasting, but they are handy for specific errands. And for those of you who live here or stay with friends for any significant time, they can be a blessing. The Wine Country has an extensive network of inter-city and intracity public vehicles, many of which are connected by a transfer system. Only basic information is provided below; please call for more details.

Vintage Railroad:
All Aboard the Napa Valley Wine Train

As soon as you set foot in Napa County, the ads are everywhere. Tourist brochures, billboards, and bus benches urge you to ride it with someone you love. Napa motels promote themselves as "minutes from" it. Leaflets lie in the living rooms of practically every bed-and-breakfast inn in the land.

And if you spend any significant time driving the length of the valley, you will eventually see it: a chain of exquisite railroad cars, painted "burgundy, champagne gold, and grapeleaf green," rumbling along at a luxuriously unhurried gait. It's the Napa Valley Wine Train, the uncontested champion of Napa tourist attractions.

Before the first Napa Valley Wine Train ever rolled down the line, crews laid some 16,000 tons of ballast rocks along the track bed. Six miles of new track at stations and terminals were installed and about 16,000 old railroad ties replaced, many of which dated to the '40s. All in all, the track renovation cost $1.7 million. Limited passenger service finally began September 16, 1989.

The train cars are beautiful, with Honduran mahogany paneling, brass bathroom fixtures, etched glass partitions, crystal chandeliers, and wool carpeting. Norman Roth, the San Francisco–based designer who oversaw the interior design, patterned the cars after early-20th-century classics such as the Venice-Simplon Orient Express and the Andalusian Express, and they aren't far off the mark. (In the summer of 1997 the Wine Train added a double-decked dome car, built for the Milwaukee Road Rail-

The Napa Valley Wine Train is popular among locals and visitors. PHOTO: TINA LUSTER-HOBAN

road Line in 1947.) With plush seats that swivel 360 degrees, you can point yourself at the window and watch the Wine Country pass by at a leisurely 15 to 20 miles per hour. It's a hypnotic sensation.

The Wine Train Depot is at 1275 McKinstry Street in Napa, near the corner of Soscol Avenue and First Street. Before you board, a Wine Train representative conducts a quickie seminar, explaining how the senses of taste, smell, and touch combine to help you enjoy that complimentary glass of wine you're holding.

Kelly Macdonald, a one-time sous-chef with Mustards Grill, came aboard the Wine Train in late 2001 as executive chef.

The food is complemented by some 40 still wines and a small selection of sparkling wines; some are big names, some small, but all are from Napa Valley.

All in all, you'll travel 36 miles from Napa to St. Helena, past 26 wineries and countless acres of vines. St. Helena is the midpoint, and there is no turnaround loop there. The two engines, connected back-to-back, are moved along parallel tracks to the back of the train, which then becomes the front. And then it's time for you to move, too.

Unless you are in the dome car, you will either start with an hors d'oeuvres course in the parlor and move to a dining car for lunch, or eat the first two courses in a dining car, then retire to the parlor for dessert.

For now, the luncheon train takes three hours and boards at 11:00 A.M. Monday through Friday, 12:10 P.M. on Saturday and Sunday. The dinner train is a three-hour cruise that boards at 6:00 P.M. Monday through Friday, 5:30 P.M. on Saturday and Sunday. The Champagne brunch train runs for two and a half hours and boards at 8:30 A.M. on Saturday and Sunday.

All-inclusive tariffs (for train fare and food) are $59.50 for the champagne brunch, $70.00 for lunch, and $79.00 for dinner. Lunch and dinner in the Vista Dome Car are about $20 higher. If that's too rich for your blood, you can ride in the deli car for $35, then purchase your lunch a la carte. Twice monthly, on a Thursday or a Friday, you can sign up for "Murder on the Wine Train Express," a full dinner and "real-life theatre," with characters in 1915 period dress. The cost for that is $105 per person.

The Wine Train accepts most credit cards. Smoking is not permitted anywhere on board.

Whenever you ride the Napa Valley Wine Train, and whichever package you choose, reservations are a must. You can call (707) 253–2111 or (800) 427–4124, or visit the Web site at www.winetrain.com.

Napa County

The VINE (Napa Valley Transit)
1151 Pearl Street, Napa
(707) 255–7631, (800) 696–6443,
(707) 226–9722 (TDD)
www.napavalleyVINE.net

The VINE is a multiline municipal bus service within Napa Valley. Five lines are within the city of Napa and its environs; a sixth runs all the way from Vallejo to Cal-istoga (this was formerly known as the Napa Valley Transit line, and locals might still refer to it as NVT). The basic fare in town is $1 for adults (more for the longer route), 75 cents for students, and 50 cents for seniors and the disabled. All the buses are accessible by wheelchairs and have bicycle racks. Seven-day-a-week service is offered, but weekend schedules are slightly more limited.

Sonoma County

Golden Gate Transit (Santa Rosa to San Francisco)
Pioneer Way and Industrial Drive
(707) 541–2000, (415) 257–4554 (TDD)
www.transitinfo.org/GGT

Golden Gate Transit (GGT) is a comprehensive network that connects San Francisco with that amorphous region known as the North Bay. Most of the routes end in Marin County, but several continue north into the Wine Country. There are service points in the Valley of the Moon, Petaluma, Cotati, Rohnert Park, Santa Rosa, and Sebastopol. The basic adult fare is $5.00 or $5.75 to San Francisco, depending on where you embark. There are discounts for kids, seniors, and the disabled. Once in the city you get transfer privileges for the Bay Area Rapid Transit system (BART) and the San Francisco Municipal Railway (Muni). Call for schedule information and locations of GGT's 11 park-and-ride lots in the Wine Country.

Healdsburg Municipal Transit
401 Grove Street, Healdsburg
(707) 431–3324
www.transitinfo.org/Healdsburg

This in-city bus has only one route, but it tries its damnedest to hit every corner in town, making almost 60 stops. The busier pickup points get hourly service between 8:30 A.M. and 4:30 P.M. The standard adult fare is $1.00, falling to 75 cents for students and 60 cents for seniors and the disabled.

Petaluma Transit
482 Kenilworth Drive, Petaluma
(707) 778–4460
www.transitinfo.org/Petaluma

Three routes serve downtown Petaluma and its surroundings. Buses generally run every hour between 6:30 A.M. and 6:00 P.M. with a condensed schedule on Saturday and no service on Sunday. Adults and students ride for 80 cents, seniors and the disabled for 40 cents, and children five or younger for free. Discounted monthly and multiride passes are available.

Santa Rosa CityBus
Second and B Streets, Santa Rosa
(707) 543–3333, (707) 543–3926 (TDD)
www.transitinfo.org/SantaRosa

This network offers 13 convenient routes within the Santa Rosa city limits plus free transfers to Golden Gate Transit or Sonoma County Transit. Most CityBuses operate from 6:00 A.M. to 8:00 P.M. Monday through Friday, 8:00 A.M. to 5:30 P.M. on Saturday, and 10:00 A.M. to 5:00 P.M. on Sunday. The fares are $1.00 for adults, 75 cents for students, 50 cents for seniors, and free for children five or younger. Monthly passes are available.

Sonoma County Transit (Petaluma to Cloverdale)
335 West Robles Avenue, Santa Rosa
(707) 576–7433, (800) 345–7433
www.transitinfo.org/SCT

Sonoma County Transit (SCT) serves an area bounded by Petaluma to the south, Sonoma to the east, Cloverdale to the north, and Occidental to the west, with most of the action in the vicinity of U.S. 101. Basic adult fares run from 95 cents to $2.35, depending on distance. Kids get a small discount, while seniors and the disabled get a larger one. SCT offers transfers to Santa Rosa CityBus, Golden Gate Transit, and the Sonoma County municipal transit systems that lie within a designated area. Most buses run from 5:00 A.M. to 10:30 P.M. during the work week and 7:00 A.M. to 7:00 P.M. on weekends.

Volunteer Wheels of Sonoma County
153 Stony Circle, Santa Rosa
(707) 573–3377, (800) 992–1006

Volunteer Wheels, a door-to-door service in Sonoma County, is part of the Americans with Disabilities Act program, administered locally as a nonprofit organization. As its name implies, all drivers work on a volunteer basis. The one-way fare is $2.00 within the Santa Rosa city limits and between $1.80 and $4.30 elsewhere in Sonoma County.

Mendocino County

Mendocino County Dial-a-Ride
241 Plant Road, Ukiah
(707) 462–3881 (Ukiah), (707) 459–9038
(Willits), (707) 964–1800 (Fort Bragg)
www.4mta.org
Though the phone numbers are different, these three lines are coordinated by the same office. Service is door-to-door, with customers sharing vans. The fare is $2.50–$3.00 within the respective city limits, and rates climb as you travel through concentric, mapped-out zones. The high end is about $15.00. Seniors and kids get discounts.

Mendocino Transit Authority (Santa Rosa to Fort Bragg)
241 Plant Road, Ukiah
(707) 462–1422, (800) 696–4682
www.4mta.org
MTA has four lines in Sonoma and Mendocino counties. Taken as a whole, they form a long rectangle with U.S. 101 (Santa Rosa to Willits) on the east, Highway 20 (Willits to Fort Bragg) on the north, coastal Highway 1 (Bodega Bay to Fort Bragg) on the west, and Bodega Highway (Santa Rosa to Bodega) on the south. One other route cuts across the rectangle from Ukiah to Albion, on Highway 253–Highway 128. The MTA buses run only once or twice a day, so don't miss the one you're after. Fares vary wildly according to distance. Call for specifics or check their Web site. Seniors and the disabled ride for half-price; children younger than six ride for free.

By Limousine

You see so many stretch limos in some parts of the Wine Country that you'll swear the Academy Awards are at the next intersection. And it makes sense when you think about it. If no one in your group volunteers for designated-driver duties, a limousine will escort you from tasting room to tasting room, freeing you up to daydream and act silly.

Many of the limo services provide drivers who are knowledgeable about the region and its vintages. But we must draw a distinction. Companies offering something that clearly goes beyond transportation—lunch at an exclusive winery or unscheduled informational tours—are included in our Attractions chapter, under the subheading "Tours." If transportation is the primary service, then the companies are listed here regardless of how far they go to help you plan your itinerary. Most limousine businesses prefer not to quote rates because the variables—type of car, size of party, distance, etc.—are multiple. If they do offer basic rates, we report them here.

Napa County

Antique Tours
Napa
(707) 226–9227
www.antiquetours.net
This company stands out for one simply luxurious reason: its small fleet of restored 1947 Packard convertible limos (and one 1948 hardtop). Little did you know that postwar Packards were equipped with AM/FM stereo cassette players, ice drawers, and air conditioning. The Packards accommodate up to seven passengers, and the charge is $70 per hour on weekdays, $90 on weekends; there is a four-hour minimum.

Executive Limousine
Napa
(707) 257–2949
www.napalimousine.com
Executive generally operates within a 50- to 70-mile radius around Napa, but show 'em the money and they'll go anywhere. They have a range of vehicles from short to long (10 passengers), and they usually charge by the hour; basic rates vary from $55 in a stretch job to $45 in a sedan.

Napa Valley Crown Limousine
Napa
(707) 257–0879, (800) 286–8228
www.napalimo.com
The proprietors of this service have plenty of experience in the tourist biz. Before getting behind the wheel they ran a bed-

and-breakfast inn and a tourist information office, and they still get many recommendations from wedding planners and tourist bureaus. They go anywhere (even to Mexico once!), and their winery knowledge is superior. Basic eight-passenger rentals are $65 an hour during the week, $75 an hour on weekends.

Royal Coach Limousine Service
Napa
(800) 995–7692
www.royalcoachlimousine.com
You have a choice of six- or eight-passenger cars and a range of itineraries. Ask for Matt if you want to customize something special.

Napa Winery Shuttle
(707) 694–4877
www.wineshuttle.com
Sip, swish, and spit all you wish, then leave the driving to these folks. Though not a traditional limo service, this shuttle service operates much like one but for lots less bucks. With regularly scheduled, door-to-door pickups and drop-offs at Napa Valley's major hotels (and stops at B&Bs by appointment), the cheerful drivers chauffeur you to a series of wineries, with pit stops at a couple of restaurants, too. Upon request, they can also personalize your journey and pack picnic lunches, and they will pick up and deliver your wine purchases, too. The service's fleet of white, 14-passenger, nonsmoking vans is top of the line, with plush interiors for extra comfort. The drivers, all longtime valley residents, provide interesting commentary and history as you glide worry-free from one place to the next. A full-day excursion with unlimited stops runs about $38 per person.

Sonoma County

California Wine Tours
22455 Broadway, Sonoma
(707) 939–7225, (800) 294–6386
www.californiawinetours.com
These operators deserve mention for their extensive wine knowledge and detailed

suggestions. They offer a standard, five-hour tasting tour for $49 per person. Customized tours begin at $55 per hour, with a four-hour minimum on weekends.

Pure Luxury
Sonoma County
(707) 775–2920, (800) 626–LIMO
www.pureluxury.com
Pure Luxury will take you anywhere in the Wine Country, for any reason: wine tours, weddings, airport transportation—you name it. Call to customize a tour.

Pacific Limousine
Rohnert Park
(707) 792–1500
www.pacificlimo.com
Pacific has been operating since 1990. They charge $45 per hour for a town car limo. The flat rate to either San Francisco International or Oakland International Airport is $135.

Just D-Vine Limousine Service
Santa Rosa
(707) 576–1725
www.winelimo.com
This owner-operated company (established 1985) prefers to stay within Sonoma and Napa counties. They offer a two-person, six-hour tour for $199.

Heaven on Wheels
Windsor
(707) 838–7778
Greg Baker, the company's owner/operator, checks out all wineries before suggesting them for tours. His basic package is four hours. Rates are customized, and the cars go anywhere in Northern California.

Odyssey Limousine
Windsor
(707) 836–0672, (800) 544–1929
This is another service that customizes by car and number of people. Odyssey has been gliding around Napa and Sonoma counties since 1988.

Mendocino County

Mendocino Wine Tours
Fort Bragg
(707) 964–8294
www.mendocinowinetours.com

Stephen Seago Sr. has run limo services for 12 years. "This is my life," he says, and he makes the most of it. Seago offers complete limousine and transportation services, covering all of the Mendocino and Lake County Wine Country—and occasionally venturing to Napa, Sonoma, Sea Ranch, or Bay Area airports. Choose either a seven-passenger luxury van ($50 an hour) or a Lincoln Town Car stretch limo that seats between seven and eight ($65 an hour).

By Taxi

Your chances of flagging down a taxi on the roads of the Wine Country are statistically smaller than your odds of being trampled by a cow. Here, "hailing a cab" means saluting a robust Cabernet Sauvignon. But there are plenty of companies to get you from curb to curb. The standard rate is $2.50–$2.80 baseline and $2.50 per mile thereafter.

In Napa County, you'll find Black Tie Taxi, (707) 259-1000 or (888) 544-8294; Napa Valley Cab, Napa, (707) 257-6444; Taxi Cabernet, St. Helena, (707) 963-2620 or (707) 942-2226; or Yellow Cab of Napa, (707) 226-3731 or (866) 226-3731.

In Sonoma County, there's A-1 Taxi of Petaluma, (707) 763-3393; A-C Taxi, Santa Rosa, (707) 526-4888; Bear Flag Taxi, Sonoma, (707) 996-6733; Bill's Taxi Service, Guerneville, (707) 869-2177; George's Taxi/Yellow Cab, Santa Rosa, (707) 546-3322 or (707) 544-4444.

Mendocino County's cab services are provided by Fort Bragg Door to Door, (707) 964-8294 or (888) 961-8294. In the Ukiah area, it's Hey Taxi, Inc. at (707) 461-1200.

History

Napa County
Sonoma County
Mendocino County

The flags of Spain, England, Imperial Russia, Mexico, and the Bear Flag Republic have all flown over Wine Country at one time or another, a testament to the ambition, struggle, victories, and bitter disappointments of numerous explorers and conquerors. But before all the hubbub started, the region was home to Miwok, Pomo, Mayacoma, Yukia, and other indigenous peoples. Early descriptions of their lives evoke visions of a kind of Eden, where food was abundant and the mild climate permitted a life without the burden of clothes.

The Gold Rush of 1849 is perhaps the most renowned and defining event of Northern California history. The accidental discovery of one tiny nugget in 1848 by James Marshall, a moody carpenter working a sawmill in the Sierra foothills, set off one of the most frenzied mass migrations in history.

California was then newly a part of the United States, having been acquired from the Republic of Mexico—a remote, sparsely populated region cut off from the United States by 1,800 miles of broiling desert and nearly impassable mountain ranges. As news of the California Eldorado spread, hordes of gold seekers stampeded West, while others sailed from the East Coast around South America's Cape Horn. Some came from as far off as Germany, England, Wales, Ireland, and China. By the summer of 1849, more than 100 vessels floated empty in San Francisco Bay, their passengers and crew having forsaken all for a chance in the mines.

Through all of this, the various settlers of the region had experimented with growing vines north of San Francisco. However, the area's potential was not fully recognized until a man by the name of Count Agoston Haraszthy arrived on the scene (see our Close-up in this chapter). Not long afterward, vineyards began to stretch in neat rows to the horizons. With time, numerous wineries sprang up and the region began to slowly gain international fame as the California Wine Country.

Napa County

For 10,000 years or more, the Pomos were the undisputed occupants of the lands of the upper Sonoma and Napa valleys, on up to Clear Lake and the surrounding lands. They lived an orderly life, with the men carrying on the outdoor work and often specializing in fishing or crafting arrowheads. Marriage was conducted in traditional fashion, and babies were the domain of the women—mothers, grandmothers, aunts, and cousins.

The Pomos lived peacefully and enjoyed a relatively easy existence compared to tribes in other regions of California. The climate was mild; the streams abounded with fish. The Pomos were the first to discover the value of the mineral and hot springs south of Clear Lake. They were also on friendly terms with the Nappa tribe to the south near the Napa River.

The first white settler in the Napa Valley was George Yount—frontiersman, hunter, trapper, and mountain man. He had left his wife and three children in Missouri in 1832 to drive mules with a pack train to Santa Fe. The job fizzled, but Yount saw no reason to return to Missouri. Instead, his restless feet took him to California's coast, where he trapped beaver for a while. He eventually made his way north in the summer of 1834 to the mission in Sonoma.

There he was welcomed with considerable enthusiasm by Padre Jose Quijas, who had been praying for someone to repair the mission buildings. It appeared that Yount was a resourceful man who could do almost anything.

In time Yount became acquainted with the Mexican commandant Vallejo, who, it turned out, also needed work done—a new roof for his hacienda. Soon Yount was turning out 1,000 shingles a day and training the mission workers to help. Yount's payment likely came via a 12,000-acre Napa Valley land grant he received, with Vallejo's help.

Upon Yount's arrival in Napa Valley, he hiked up an old Indian trail leading to the top of Mount St. Helena. From there he could look across the entire valley, and he was ready to settle down. In 1836 he set about building a Kentucky-style blockhouse for himself. He got on well with the Pomos and Nappas and taught them how to help. Then he erected a flour mill and sawmill, planted wheat and potatoes, and started a small vineyard. But like most God-fearing Missourians who made their way to Napa, he believed grapes were for eating, not for making wine. Yount's name would eventually live on into future generations—the town of Yountville was named in his honor.

Soon another settler appeared on the scene—Dr. Edward Bale, a young English surgeon. His marriage to a niece of General Vallejo made him a Mexican citizen, and as such he was given a land grant north of Yount's. Bale established a sawmill to cut timber, and a grist mill (still standing and known as Bale Mill) to grind the settlers' grain. The mills became centers of great activity and supplied work for new settlers, but the best was yet to come for Bale. When gold diggers poured into the state, flour became a premium product, and Bale's mill was a gold mine in its own right.

The near-wilderness aspect of the Napa Valley changed dramatically after gold was discovered in the Sierra foothills, 100 miles east of San Francisco, in 1848. The city by the bay, which boasted a population of less than 450, was virtually abandoned in the rush to the gold fields. And although Napa was 40 miles to the north—not exactly on the direct route to the foothills—large numbers of gold seekers did wander off course and find their way into the valley, on foot or on horseback. If anyone in town had a horse for sale, the sale was quickly made. Sometimes the horse was simply stolen.

Miners also found the valley a popular wintering place when rains drowned the mines. Some stayed in the area. In two years Napa's population tripled to 450. A census two years later showed a jump to 2,116 (including 252 women). In just one decade, wilderness had transformed to populace.

City on the River

The first town in the valley, founded in 1836, was Napa City—not that it amounted to much. But soon after the discovery of gold, prosperity set in. The chief places of business were saloons, and the method of payment was likely to be gold dust. In fact, the change brought about by gold was amazing.

The only route into town, the Napa River, soon opened the region to the world. The channel was deep, so before long steamboats were plying the river, transporting passengers to San Francisco and Sacramento for a $1.00 fare, lunch included. But the river's main value was for moving freight. The valley's fertile soil was producing such a profusion of fruits and vegetables that ships lined up daily at the Napa docks to load up for the San Francisco market.

In the outlying Berryessa Valley, some 30 miles inland, wheat grew so abundantly it became an international product. Ships from foreign ports arrived regularly at the Napa Embarcadero to load Napa County wheat. The river brought in industry that would last until the end of the century. Lined up along its shores were potteries, iron works, tile factories, and tanneries. The term "Napa leather" earned its own listing in Webster's dictionary as "a type of leather resembling the original glove leather made in Napa by tanning sheepskins with a soap and oil mixture."

Many residents prospered beyond their wildest dreams, and by the 1880s Napa had achieved fame for both its charm and vast wealth. That reputation brought in the bankers, who were by no means above ostentation in the building of their great Victorian mansions. Some of those homes still stand today as an architectural reminder of other times.

But it came to an abrupt end. Napa's river traffic was killed by a single structure—a bridge built across the Carquinez Straits between Martinez and Vallejo. That allowed trucks to come into Napa Valley for the first time.

Those Amazing Hot Springs

During the 1860s it became fashionable all over the country to "take the waters." Soaking in hot mineral baths or mineral-rich mud was touted to cure virtually every known ailment. The first entrepreneur to capitalize on these bubbling springs was Sam Brannan, who had become a millionaire selling shovels and picks to miners.

Some of that wealth was spent acquiring 1 square mile of land in the northern valley. It was Brannan's vision to build an extravagant resort spa that would become a holiday retreat for San Francisco's shamefully rich. He called the place Calistoga—a combination of his fondness for Saratoga Springs and the word California. On the grounds there soon appeared a lavish hotel, 25 gingerbread cottages, an observatory tower, large stables with many fine horses, a winery, and a distillery. Brannan imported great herds of merino sheep from England and silkworms and mulberry trees from China. The benefits of the hot springs, of course, were obvious and needed no further publicity.

But success soon slipped away from Sam Brannan. His flair for moneymaking deserted him in Calistoga, in San Francisco, and in the gold country in general. His beautiful Calistoga hotel burned. He was shot in the back by a disgruntled mill hand and harassed by his creditors. Sick and discouraged, he left Calistoga. Brannan never recovered the promise of his early youth, but he wrote a fantastic chapter in the history of Napa Valley. He died in Southern California in 1889, penniless and practically alone.

In time, another hot springs resort, Napa Soda Springs, was developed 5 miles east of Napa City and took the place of Calistoga in the fickle favor of San Franciscans accustomed to lavish living. Banked against a flower-carpeted hillside, it presented an unequaled view of Napa Valley and San Pablo Bay. A good deal of faith was put in the healing powers of "a course at the springs." According to the report of a Dr. Anderson, the waters were beneficial "in the treatment of chronic metritis and ovaritis, for Bright's disease, acid blood, and dyspepsia."

The Silver Commotion

In the winter of 1858, rumors started percolating that silver had been discovered in the mountains. In no time at all, every unemployed man had turned prospector. Most of those wielding a pick knew nothing of the characteristics of silver ledges, and outcrops of barren rock of any description were equally valuable to their ignorant eyes. The commotion continued for several weeks. A local assay office was even opened, run by an assayer who gave such discouraging reports that nobody believed him. So miners instead hauled their rocks to San Francisco, where reports came back "no silver at all" or "a trace." Fortune quickly turned to folly, and tons of shiny rocks were unloaded by the disenchanted miners to make paving material for the streets of Napa.

Of more serious import were the quicksilver mines that developed in the 1860s in the Mayacmas Mountains that separate the Napa and Sonoma valleys. Mining quicksilver, or mercury, was a hazardous process, and newspapers of the day were filled with accident stories. A typical one involved a foreman: "While inspecting a piece of ground there fell without warning a mass of rock weighing half a ton, rendering him insensible for nearly an hour." (Only an hour?)

In the 1870s, silver fever struck again. A vein of silver was discovered in the Calis-

The Father of California Viticulture

Although many early settlers had started vineyards north of San Francisco, the first individual to recognize the area's potential for growing fine wine grapes was Count Agoston Haraszthy.

A flamboyant man who may or may not have been a true aristocrat, Haraszthy fled political turmoil in his native Hungary to seek his fortunes in America. His first endeavor in the New World was founding Sauk City, Wisconsin, where he built homes, mills, and stores; planted hops; and started a vineyard. The town remains to this day.

Once weary of that project, he headed to California along the Santa Fe Trail. He arrived at the gold fields on horseback, an Argonaut in silken shirt, red sash, and velour hat, seeking whatever opportunities might exist. Haraszthy was working as an assayer at the San Francisco mint when General Vallejo heard of the man's interest in viticulture. Vallejo invited him to Sonoma in 1856, whereupon Haraszthy quickly recognized the potential of Sonoma's soil. Convinced that grapes could prosper without irrigation, he sailed for Europe and returned with 300 varieties of grape cuttings, the basis for his 6,000-acre vineyards.

The winery he built was of massive stones, with cellars dug into the hillsides. For himself, he built a grand Pompeian-style villa. His fame spread quickly, and vintners from other parts of California, as well as those newly arrived from Europe, came to him for advice and for cuttings. It created something of a "grape rush" in the Sonoma and Napa valleys.

But by 1868 the count was again restless and decided to turn his enthusiasm to raising sugar in Nicaragua. He left his two sons (who had married Vallejo daughters) to run the winery business. They never saw their father again, for he vanished mysteriously in the jungle. According to legend, he fell from a tree into a river and was devoured by crocodiles.

The villa he built in Sonoma was destroyed by the passage of time, but in the 1980s, townsfolk rebuilt a replica next to the first vineyards he planted. Both are there to see today.

This is a modern replica of Agoston Haraszthy's Sonoma home.
PHOTO: LOU ZAUNER

toga hills, and a new town sprang up around the diggings—Silverado City. The hillsides soon were pocked with mining claims, and the city prospered briefly. The vein was short-lived, but the town's hotel and mining office became famous, for it was here that Robert Louis Stevenson brought his bride on a honeymoon.

It was a strange entourage that straggled into the Napa Valley on a warm May day in 1880—gaunt, ailing Robert Louis Stevenson; his new bride, Fanny; her 12-year-old son; and a setter-spaniel named Chuchu. They had decided to honeymoon in Calistoga, hoping to cure the Scottish author's lung problems. They arrived at the Springs Hotel, where they lived a short time in a "cottage on the green," but after a couple of weeks they located cheaper quarters. They moved into the assayer's office and the bunkhouse of an abandoned silver mine as squatters, paying no rent.

With a secondhand cookstove and a few household effects pulled up the mountain by a new neighbor who was also a squatter, they settled down for the summer, living the free life of gypsies. Here Stevenson wrote in his journal the notes that became his first literary success, *The Silverado Squatters*.

The Emergence of Fine Wine

Although Yount and Bale were the first to raise grapes in Napa Valley, it seems doubtful either had the inclination to cultivate fine wines. That distinction came to several German immigrants who arrived in the 1870s: Jacob Schram (who barbered by day and planted vines by moonlight), Charles Krug (known as the father of Napa viniculture), Jacob and Frederick Beringer (Jacob was Krug's winemaker until he built his own winery), and Gottlieb Groezinger (his winery stands as Yountville's Vintage 1870).

The 1870s marked tremendous growth in the Napa Valley wine industry. Local viticulture clubs began organizing in 1875, with Charles Krug chosen president of the largest. (A note that will come

in handy: Generally speaking, we use "viticulture" when talking specifically about the science and practice of growing grapes, and "viniculture" to discuss the process of making wines.) About the same time, the Beringer brothers established their winery, complete with a cellar dug into a hillside by Chinese laborers and reinforced with stone—a feat of advanced architecture as well as masonry. Adding to the growth of the industry was an outbreak of phylloxera (a ravenous louse that eats the plant's roots) in French vineyards. Napa wineries continued to expand, with some 140 wineries producing almost five million gallons of wine.

Unfortunately, this led to overproduction. In the late 1880s growers were all feeling the pinch, and Charles Krug's vineyards and cellar went into receivership. More bad times loomed in the form of a general nationwide depression in 1890. But the blow that brought valley growers to their knees was the discovery that the dreaded, grapevine-ravaging phylloxera—for which there was no cure—had infected the vineyards of the entire area. By the turn of the century, almost every vineyard had been ruined.

Plantings of resistant varieties brought fresh hope. Viticulture looked to be getting back on track. But those bright hopes were dashed by a new cataclysm called Prohibition. For the Old World grape-growers, who considered wine the elixir of life, the law was inexplicable madness.

The plague of Prohibition lasted for 14 years, from 1920 to 1933. Some vintners survived it by making sacramental or pharmaceutical wines. But for others it would take years to build back their businesses. Still, one thing was clear: There would be no returning to wheat or cattle raising. Napa County was on its way to becoming America's premier wine region.

By 1966 wine was becoming fashionable, not only in California but across the nation. Between 1966 and 1972 wine consumption doubled. Visitors started pouring into the area to look, sample, and buy. By the mid-'70s, there were again more than 50 wineries in operation in Napa Valley, and a new promotional technique had been developed—wine tastings. To let the public see how great the product was, vintners opened their doors and uncorked their bottles for sampling. Many offered their cellars for touring.

In the 1980s viticulture became a sort of dream occupation—a creative endeavor that could be both financially rewarding and personally satisfying. New wineries popped up almost overnight, many operated by individuals drawn into the field because they savored living close to the soil. Wineries started gaining public acceptance by offering extra attractions—Shakespearean plays and readings in the caves and Mozart played on expansive green lawns. Wine Country golf courses and croquet courts drew international competition. Cooking classes featured famous chefs. It all drew attention to the work of the winemaker.

Sonoma County

In 1823, a zealous young Spanish priest, Father Jose Altimira, arrived in California and established the Mission San Francisco de Solano, northernmost in a chain of missions spaced a day's journey apart along California's coast. This mission was the only one to be dedicated after Mexico overthrew Spanish rule earlier that year. In fact, not everyone in the mission hierarchy thought it was a good idea. But Altimira was nothing if not enthusiastic, and he convinced his colleagues it would be a better climate than San Francisco for the Native American converts.

Compared to other, grander missions, Altimira's was unimpressive—a flimsy wooden structure that was swept twice by fire before achieving its present, fireproof adobe state. Within six years, Altimira claimed 1,000 converts (some may have been transfers). An adobe chapel had been added, as had a number of small shops where converts could learn weaving and agricultural skills.

But the mission was doomed from the start. A decree was passed down from the Mexican government that all church properties would be "secularized" (that is, confiscated). In 1834, a young lieutenant, the aforementioned Mariano Vallejo, was sent from Monterey to seize all mission property and dispose of grain fields and thousands of head of cattle, sheep, and horses. It was outright thievery carried out under the guise of eminent domain.

The converts—turned loose to fend for themselves—were likely to have been grateful. They didn't much like Altimira, a cold and impersonal man, and they didn't care for the Spanish or the Mexicans, who were sometimes oppressive. In any case, the Mexican government had another, more serious reason to send an emissary into the territory—to discourage foreign invaders. Trappers were arriving in ever-increasing poaching forays over the Sierra Nevada Mountains, and some were staying on as settlers. And on the north coast Russian settlers had arrived from Alaska.

Meanwhile, young Lieutenant Vallejo brought his beautiful, cultured wife, Francisca Benicia, to this rough, untamed land and set up house in the abandoned mission. In one of its 37 rooms, their first daughter was born. In time, Vallejo set about creating the town of Sonoma. Using a pocket compass, he laid out an eight-acre plaza around which the town would rise. The plaza would serve as a promenade area for the populace as well as a parade ground where young soldiers could drill and practice their horsemanship skills. At the same time, Vallejo was preoccupied with developing a 66,000-acre ranch in the grasslands of Petaluma Valley, some 10 miles away. Built as a defense against intruders, the structure's walls were 3 feet thick, braced by redwood beams. It became a second home for the growing Vallejo family, which eventually numbered 15 children.

Some 2,000 American Indians (most of them transfers from the mission ranks) answered roll call daily in the courtyard before going to work making saddles and boots. These products were marketed to settlers or shipped to coastal communities as far south as San Blas, Mexico. Though it all seemed like a sustainable arrangement, trouble was brewing behind the scenes. That trouble was the Bear Flag Republic.

The Bear Flag Rebellion

"About half past five in the morning of Sunday, June 14, a group of desperados surrounded the house of General Vallejo and arrested him," wrote his sister. "Vallejo, dressed in the uniform of a General, was the prisoner of this group of rough-looking men, some wearing on their heads caps made with the skins of coyotes or wolves . . . . Shoes were to be seen on the feet of 15 or 20 among the whole lot."

The issues surrounding this drama were complex. England, France, and the United States were each vying for the California territory, which Mexico was sure to relinquish (whether by force or purchase). General Vallejo argued in favor of American rule, while his rivals, Gen. Pio Pico of Los Angeles and Gen. Jose Castro of Monterey, strongly preferred the English or French to the Americans. Adding to this tense situation was the unexpected arrival in Monterey of Lt. John Charles Frémont of the U.S. Topographical Service, a surveyor purportedly on a mission to map a more direct route to the Pacific. Frémont rode in accompanied by a contingent of 62 armed U.S. cavalry.

Frémont did not hesitate in inciting the Mexican generals, going so far as to raise the Stars and Stripes over his camp. After some fierce posturing but no real fighting, Frémont moved north to Oregon. Following his departure, rumors began circulating that the Mexicans were about to evict all Americans from California. The story incited rage among local settlers, having been lured to California by the Mexican government's promise of land. They decided to take matters into their own hands.

Thirty-three renegade malcontents went to the Sonoma presidio to dispose of the Mexicans. Along the way they hastily fashioned a flag for the new republic, made of a woman's red flannel petticoat and a length of unbleached muslin. For their emblem they used berry juice to paint on it the picture of a bear (it looked more like a pig) and the words *California Republic*. The ever-cordial Vallejo brought up some wine for the group, and they spent some time in convivial conversation. But in the end, he was carried off to Sutter's Fort in Sacramento, where Vallejo's friend John Sutter reluctantly jailed him.

The California Republic lasted 26 days. On July 9, 1846, U.S. Navy Lt. Joseph Revere lowered the bear flag and replaced it with the American Stars and Stripes. Vallejo was released from jail August 6. He had been away no more than a month, but in that time his horses and cattle had been stolen, his fields stripped of grain.

The New State of California

The months that followed the rebellion brought mass confusion. Nobody knew who was in charge. A group of military volunteers known as Company C from New York City's Bowery arrived. But since there wasn't much for the soldiers to do (unless they wanted to stoop to manual labor), they improved their leisure by riding spirited horses, hunting waterfowl, and staging cruel bear-and-bull fights in a makeshift stadium behind their barracks.

The discovery of gold suddenly shifted everyone's attention. Settler and soldier alike left Sonoma to the womenfolk. The village sank into stagnation. Vallejo, on the other hand, wasn't too bad off. He had seen what was coming and had hedged his bets. While serving Mexico loyally (virtually without pay), he had also taken steps to ingratiate himself with the United

States. In time he actually became a California senator.

But Vallejo's plans of becoming a prominent American somehow went awry. Lawsuit after lawsuit went against him, and his land empire disappeared. He slipped deeper into debt. One by one his dreams vanished. He did manage to hold onto his Sonoma home, Lachryma Montis, and here his wife—once pampered—sold dried fruit and chili peppers for the San Francisco market. In old age, Vallejo became a symbol of the link between an idealized Mexican era and the Yankee-dominated present. In his unfailing dignity and hospitality, he seemed to personify all that was best about the past.

By the mid-1860s, Sonoma had become almost totally neglected. There were no trees, and the plaza had degenerated. A fire in 1866 destroyed much of what the early settlers had built. Some of the early pioneers responded by organizing a Pioneer Society of 340 members to revitalize the town. They planted trees, built fences, and cleaned up the plaza (appointing one member to be in charge of keeping livestock out of that area of town). Gradually the town took on a more respectable look, though the society itself fizzled out.

About 1888, many Italian immigrants came to quarry cobblestones for the streets of San Francisco. Among them was Samuele Sebastiani, who quickly recognized the possibilities for growing wine grapes. In no time at all he was supplying the demand of the growing Italian community for wine, and making a name for his winery. Today, the strong Italian influence remains in and around Sonoma, where Italian restaurants line the streets around the plaza.

One of Vallejo's mandates when he took over as commandant was to ensure that lands north of San Francisco were settled. At the time, this northern frontier was a lonesome wilderness, and Vallejo had some trouble convincing any of his fellow Californians to apply for grants. But he had plenty of relatives, so most of them fell heir to large tracts. In 1837, he convinced his widowed mother to leave her San Diego adobe and travel 700 miles to an area near Santa Rosa Creek. She packed up her nine children and seven-trunk wardrobe and built the Cabrillo adobe, the first bona fide home in the Santa Rosa Valley. In time it became the nucleus of a settlement.

Santa Rosa

In 1854, the town of Santa Rosa was little more than a trading post. A few small businesses and houses had sprung up along the creek, and the town had a representative in the state senate. That man was William Bennett, another former Missourian, and his ambition was to snatch the county seat away from Sonoma. To help voters make up their minds on the issue, he hosted a big Fourth of July barbecue attended by, according to one historian, "the lame, the halt and blind if they could influence a vote." Not surprisingly the vote went in favor of Santa Rosa. At daybreak a group of Santa Rosans, fearing Sonoma wouldn't release the county records, hired a wagon and raced to Sonoma, grabbed the records, and raced back to Santa Rosa.

Reporting the hijacking, the *Sonoma Bulletin* editor wrote, "We are only sorry they did not take the adobe courthouse too . . . its removal would have embellished our plaza." Within three years, according to the newly launched *Sonoma Democrat*, Santa Rosa had grown to 100 buildings. After the arrival of the railroad in 1870, the town's population exploded to 6,000.

About this time a shy, trim New Englander named Luther Burbank opened a nursery in the town and began experimenting on flowers, fruits, and vegetables. His uncanny talent for interpreting the results of his experiments earned him the lasting title of "plant wizard" (see our Attractions chapter).

A wizard of a different sort next appeared in town—spiritualist-sage Thomas Harris, a man of magnetic personality and piercing eyes "like revolving lights." In the outlying area called Fountain Grove, Harris established the esoteric Brotherhood of New Life, a colony of communal living that separated its members from their spouses (and their cash) to await their celestial mates in another world. Harris claimed these other worlds were revealed to him during his conversations with the angels. It was left to a woman reporter to provide the impetus to drive Harris from the gates of his Eden. She joined the group long enough to write a lurid exposé that sent the preacher packing.

The infamous 1906 earthquake that leveled San Francisco also struck Santa Rosa—nearby Petaluma, Santa Rosa's then rival, escaped virtually unscathed. The courthouse collapsed, and downtown buildings suffered devastating damage. Nearly 100 people died in the rubble, but the city's spirit survived. While some residents did head for other parts, many townsfolk simply rolled up their sleeves and began to rebuild. Only one minor case of looting was reported during the period. County Supervisor Tom McNamara made off with a portion of the statue of Minerva that had stood on top of the courthouse. Despite the county's requests, McNamara never returned it.

Petaluma

Before the advent of the railroads in the mid-1880s, rivers were the principal means of shipping goods inland. In the Petaluma River, steamboats—introduced to California during the Gold Rush—operated regularly during the 1850s, hauling wool, butter, cream, eggs, and live chicks down the twisting tidal river to San Francisco Bay. By the 1890s, Petaluma was the third-busiest waterway in the state.

But it was neither the river nor steamboats that gave Petaluma its enduring fame. In the 1880s, it became known as the "Egg Basket of the World" when the first practical chicken incubator was invented there and marketed on a mass scale. Immigrants from Europe thronged to Petaluma to set up hundreds of hatcheries and thousands of chicken-feed mills. As many as 600 million eggs per year were shipped to worldwide points. But chicken-related prosperity declined in the 1930s due to high feed costs. Leghorn hens were replaced by Holstein cows. Today the Petaluma countryside is mostly dairy land.

Insiders' Tip

Take a brief walking tour of Petaluma's historic Victorian homes beginning on Fifth Street at A Street, and continuing on Liberty Street, switching over to Sixth Street, up D Street, and then down Fifth Street.

Jack London in Glen Ellen

Glen Ellen, 9 miles north of Sonoma, lies in an area forested with oak, madrone, redwood, and buckeye trees. Author Jack London came to this countryside in 1903 at the invitation of friends who owned the Wake Robin Lodge. There, at age 30, he met their vivacious niece, Charmian. Instantly attracted to one another, the couple spent their days riding horseback and having sprightly conversations. They were perfectly matched, adventurous individuals, and London stayed on to marry Charmian.

At first they lived at her family's lodge, but London fell in love with the land locally known as "the valley of the moon." He started accumulating property until he had a 1,500-acre tract, and here the Londons lived in a simple white house. He called the place Beauty Ranch, and it was there he wrote most of his prodigious output of books. London's success as an author had initially been spurred by the appearance of a Yukon story in *Atlantic Monthly* magazine and confirmed by publication of *The Call of the Wild* when he was 22.

Within eight years, he was America's highest paid author. In his short lifetime, he wrote 54 books, 1,300 articles, and 188 short stories, some translated into 30 languages. His house overflowed with guests—scientists, actresses, writers, and socialites. And exuberance marked just about everything London did. He took up scientific farming and designed a pigpen that gave each pig family an apartment. Later, he took a long sea voyage with Charmian on a ship he designed himself.

But London's most wondrous dream was Wolf House, his 26-room mansion, an imposing affair of redwood and huge stone blocks, with arched windows opening onto forested slopes and offering views of the entire valley. London wrote, "It will last one-thousand years, God willing." But one midnight in August 1913, billows of black smoke filled the sky as a raging fire burned out of control. The author watched silently from a nearby hill

The cottage in which Jack London lived—and ultimately died—is part of a state park in Sonoma County. PHOTO: JEAN SAYLOR DOPPENBERG

as his dream crumbled to the earth. London never quite recovered from the calamity. Three years later he died at age 40. The official cause was uremic poisoning, but rumors persisted it was suicide. The magnificent ruins of Wolf House, as well as all of Beauty Ranch, live on as a California state park.

Northern Sonoma County

The Pomo tribe lived for centuries in what is now northern Sonoma County. In 1841, Mexico granted a portion of their domain to a New England sea captain, Henry Fitch (nobody consulted the Pomos, of course), who had eloped with General Vallejo's sister. But Fitch, having received such an excellent dowry, saw no reason to live out his life in such a lonely land. He hired Cyrus Alexander to manage a ranch there with immense herds of cattle. The names of both men live on as landmarks—Fitch Mountain looms over the town of Healdsburg and to the east lies Alexander Valley, Cyrus's payment for work on the ranch.

Healdsburg itself bears the name of Harmon Heald, a disenchanted '49er who arrived on the scene in 1852 and claimed land for a town site. He surveyed the town and sold lots for $15 apiece around a central plaza. By the end of the decade, Healdsburg had a population of 500.

Russian River and Western Sonoma County

Called Slavyanka (Slavic girl) by Russian settlers during their tenure in California, the Russian River flows from the hilly regions above Hopland, past Cloverdale, Healdsburg, Guerneville, Duncans Mills, and finally Jenner, where it meets the Pacific. The Russians explored the length of the river basin—a territory that the Spanish had largely ignored—initially to scout out a suitable settlement site and thereafter to occasionally chase down otter. They saw the area for what it was, a rich river valley dense with towering virgin redwood stands, bounded by fertile plains, and awash with fish. But the Russians abandoned their foothold in California before ever establishing a settlement upriver, leaving the region behind for others to exploit.

When the first American loggers arrived in the Russian River valley, they could hardly believe what they saw. The trees were enormous, some measuring as wide as 23 feet in diameter and 300 feet in height. The first sawmill opened in the valley in 1861, with others springing up soon thereafter. Stumptown, renamed Guerneville in 1870 after lumberman George Guerne, was the region's logging epicenter.

The trees offered the woodsmen a rich bounty for a time. However, around the turn of the century many had been harvested, and the mills began to close. In an effort to shore up profits, the Northwest Pacific Railroad—which had been servicing the mills—began to promote the Russian River area as a tourist destination. Urban vacationers from San Francisco and other parts were soon hopping aboard trains in droves to escape to the region—with the railroad cars rolling right onto a ferryboat for the ride across the Golden Gate. Hotels and resorts sprang up, as did bevies of summer cottages. In the 1930s, revelers boogied all night at the Rio Nido Inn to the sounds of Benny Goodman's clarinet and Ozzie Nelson's band.

Not far from the Russian River, the town of Sebastopol got its start when Joaquin Carillo, another Vallejo relative, received the standard family land grant (this one of 13,000 acres). After American settlers overran his lands, he turned his house into a hotel.

Another popular local name also harks back to a Russian source. Settlers at Fort Ross introduced the Gravenstein apple to the county in the mid-19th century. In 1883, Nathaniel Griffin demonstrated that "Gravs" could be grown commercially, and he was dubbed "Grandfather of the Gravenstein." The apple became popular in the county because of its exceptional flavor and early ripening. The fruit was so well liked that locals inaugurated an annual celebration—the Gravenstein Apple Festival—in 1910 in its honor. The festival continues to be held today.

The Russian Orthodox community occasionally holds services at the historic Fort Ross chapel on the Sonoma County Coast. PHOTO: JOHN NAGIECKI

Other western Sonoma towns include Valley Ford, Bloomfield, Forestville, and Occidental. The latter was first settled by Bill Howard, who had survived a shipwreck off New York, malaria in Africa, and a revolution in Brazil. He and a sawmill operator lured a railroad into the territory and after that success built the whole town of Occidental in four months. Italian woodcutters from Tuscany worked the forests, and a few opened restaurants where a traditional Italian feast could be had for two bits. Today, Occidental is still the place to go for Italian dinners; it is also a hub for artists and environmental activists. If you're feeling deficient in either of these subjects, consider a short course or workshop at the Occidental Arts and Ecology Center. Located on 80 gorgeous acres off Coleman Valley Road, the center can help you take that first step toward a new career as a blacksmith or beekeeper or learn all about landscape painting or restoration forestry.

The Sonoma Coast

For almost 60 miles along the jagged coastline, Sonoma County's Highway 1 (called Coast Highway 1 in many locales) snakes through rangeland and small towns that lie between the Coast Range and the Pacific. Centuries ago Miwok and Pomo tribes fished these coastal waters. Later, Russians and the Aleut hunters they brought down from Alaska harvested otter here—to near extinction—in nimble kayaks called baidarkas. The hunters skillfully negotiated their small craft through the surf and swells of the rugged coastline, occasionally seeking refuge in one of the few protected coves hidden among the bluffs. Bodega Bay, near Sonoma County's southern border, was one of the few places where larger ships could safely drop anchor. It thus wasn't long before the bay became a shipping center, dispatching lumber and agricultural products to San Francisco and beyond.

Bodega Bay became famous as the site where Alfred Hitchcock filmed his classic thriller, *The Birds*. A wall-size photo at Bay View Restaurant at the popular Inn at the Tides (see our Hotels, Motels, and Inns chapters) commemorates Hitchcock's work.

Mendocino County

Rumors of gold brought the first adventuring white pioneers to Mendocino County in the 1840s. The rumors were false, but the land itself was pleasant—a good place to settle down and raise sheep, plant fruit trees, and grow hops. Sam Orr, a Kentuckian, arrived in 1857 with his wife, along with a quantity of grape cuttings to start a vineyard. Soon another American wandered in, a prospector from the gold country named Seward. He bought some of Orr's cuttings and also started a vineyard to grow around his imposing Colonial-style house, which soon included a winery—he had clearly found success in his mining venture. Still, the valley's immediate future rested not with grapes but with hops.

By the 1890s, the Ukiah Valley had achieved modest fame for its vast hop fields. The town of Ukiah boasted two hotels, three livery stables, and 10 saloons. But traffic on its dirt streets kicked up clouds of dust in summer and churned up thick mud in winter. One especially wet year a two-horse wagon sank hub-deep in the middle of Main Street.

Most incoming travelers arrived by way of Fort Bragg on a stagecoach that left at 7:00 A.M. and made a loading stop at Mendocino, before rumbling over twisty, dusty, roads to Ukiah. Along the route, the stage stopped for a meal and change of horses, with passengers arriving in Ukiah about dinnertime. When the railroad finally arrived with service to and from San Francisco, it started a tourist boom. By then the hop fields had achieved notoriety, and travelers came from hundreds of miles away just to spend a weekend in the country.

For the hundreds of hop pickers, those trellised vines were less romantic. Pioneer Hazel Pittman recalled those days: "It was awfully hard work. We wore gauntlet gloves and still the hops would cut through with the stickers on them. You would perspire from the terrible heat and itch. But we made a penny a pound, and if you could pick a hundred pounds a day there was a whole dollar." (From *Mendocino County Remembered—An Oral History*.)

Other attractions arose to bring tourists. This was the age of the curative mineral bath, and the area boasted several. Most elegant was Vichy Springs, an upscale resort featuring such niceties as croquet, horseback rides, hunting safaris, and dancing under the stars. The water in the swimming pool was allegedly "charged with electricity and gas, a real Champagne Bath." Vichy Springs had a long fallow period, but in the late 1980s it was revived, reconstructed, and rejuvenated, and it is once again an elegant resort spa (see our Spas and Resorts chapter).

Meanwhile, in the early 1900s, grape-growing and winemaking started to become more serious. Dozens of small operations were producing wine in light volume; Zinfandel was the main product. Hardworking Italians planted grapes on the hillsides. For the most part, however, the wine industry in Mendocino County at this time involved growers shipping their fruit to other wine-producing regions for blending. Typical of early growers were the Malone family, who sold their grapes as reds and whites, with no varietal distinction.

In 1910, a census counted 5,800 Mendocino County acres in grape production, with 90,000 gallons of wine produced. Much of the activity stemmed from the arrival of the railroad, which opened up new markets. But for Mendocino County, as for the nation, wine production came to a halt when Prohibition became the law of the land. Today's wine industry is based not so much on quantity as on quality. And oenologists around the world now recognize the premier quality of Mendocino.

The Mendocino Coast

The jagged Mendocino Coast bears little resemblance to its southern relative, that stretch of beach that's lined with sunbathers from Santa Barbara to San Diego. Here the fog-festooned sand dunes are spotted with wild grasses, overwhelming in their lonely beauty. In springtime the hills are golden with Scotch broom, and in summer rhododendrons grow wild. Nowhere is nature more glorious.

It's a rugged coast, dotted with dog-hole ports (big enough only for a dog to turn around in), that prospered for two decades in the rush for building materials following the 1906 San Francisco earthquake. Many of these burgs have vanished or are greatly diminished. For some years, Point Arena was the largest, most active lumber port between San Francisco and Eureka. It was also a whaling station and regular port of call for passenger steamers. Today, its most impressive feature is its classic, soaring lighthouse, 115 feet up from the tip of a narrow, bleak, eroding rockbound point. It's the closest point to

Insiders' Tip

The town of Elk on the Mendocino coast actually has two names. Locals still call it Greenwood, after the brothers Greenwood who settled it. But when they tried to establish a post office, they were told the name Greenwood had already been chosen by a Gold Country town. Hence, Elk became the official address.

Headstones such as this one in the cemetery at Bodega offer a fascinating glimpse into the early settlers of California. PHOTO: JEAN SAYLOR DOPPENBERG

no holding back the tide. The history of the coast changed overnight.

Logging had been booming in Little River for 10 years when Silas Coombs selected it as one of the best-weather ports on the coast to build a mill. The mill wasn't memorable (it burned in 1910), but the mansion Coombs built lives on as Little River Inn, one of the coast's loveliest, with gabled windows and eaves festooned with wooden scrollwork. From the porch where Silas once spotted ship arrivals, visitors now can watch the annual migration of gray whales from cold Alaska to warm mating areas in Baja California (see our Spas and Resorts chapter).

There's another historic inn nearby. Heritage House is an old Victorian farmhouse dating to the 1850s. It was an early base for smuggling both liquor and foreign laborers and once was a hideout for 1930s gangster "Baby Face" Nelson. Today, it's a leisurely retreat with a commanding view of the craggy coast.

The Village of Mendocino

The picturesque town of Mendocino lies at the mouth of the Big River, on a rocky headland overlooking a small bay. In its heyday around 1870, it was a raucous, thriving port and lumbertown, often called "Fury Town" by locals. Nearly everything in Mendocino was and is built of wood, including the sidewalks and the water towers that stand on the skyline. The settlement was initially named Meiggsville for "Honest Harry" Meiggs, a San Francisco politician and wharf owner with a weakness for speculation. The town changed its name in 1854 after Meiggs got into financial hot water and had to flee the country. He recouped his losses by building the first railroad over the Andes in South America, but his partners in Mendocino were left facing bankruptcy.

Meiggs came hot-footing to Mendocino in the first place when a Chilean barque loaded with silks and spices wrecked nearby. The captain of the ship had lost his way to San Francisco and accidentally guided his vessel straight into the rocks at

Hawaii on the west coast. The light tower was built in 1870, then rebuilt after the devastating 1906 earthquake. For 36 years, it faithfully guided ships through the treacherous rocks, but today's visitors will see only seals, migrating gray whales, and cavorting sea lions.

The settlement called Elk, 18 miles north of the Point Arena light tower, used to be a lively port. The cove is heavily studded with craggy islets and tall, dome-shaped sea stacks. Steam schooners used to brave this navigator's nightmare to load lumber among the rocks.

Even before the 1906 quake, the Mendocino Coast had been turned into a lumberjack's paradise by the Gold Rush. San Francisco burgeoned into a bustling city in urgent need of lumber to build houses. At the time, the only lumber available came from the Sandwich Islands (now known as Hawaii) and was very costly. When news of the great redwood forest on the north coast trickled down, there was

Point Cabrillo. When Meiggs sent a salvage party, they found no silks but instead great forests of redwood. Meiggs, a born entrepreneur, rounded up a schooner, some mill equipment, and some partners and headed for the forested coast. Soon mills sprung up in every gulch, and mansions with leaded-glass windows rose up on hillsides filled with fine furnishings shipped around Cape Horn. Breweries, churches, and schools followed. On Steamer Day, when passengers came into port, carriages from eight hotels met ships from all over the globe.

When the forest had been cut and the mills closed down, Mendocino fell asleep and snoozed for a long while. In the 1960s, the town suddenly blossomed as a center for artists and bohemians seeking freedom of style and life on the cheap. William Zacha came up from the Bay Area to open an art gallery, then conceived the Mendocino Art Center, a rambling collection of buildings on a rise at the edge of town (see our Arts and Culture chapter).

It was this art colony that first attracted a more affluent breed of visitor, seeking escape from urban living. They came to stroll boardwalks and sniff ocean breezes. With them came a blossoming of gourmet restaurants and some uncommonly civilized inns. It is this ambience that sets Mendocino apart from other north coast villages. The fact that Mendocino looks a lot like the coast of Maine has not escaped the notice of filmmakers. Devotees of the television series *Murder, She Wrote* will recognize some "Cabot Cove" settings.

Fort Bragg

Only 8 miles north of Mendocino but seeming worlds apart, Fort Bragg is a hard-working town with a down-to-earth feel. There's the smell of sawdust in the air, and local talk often revolves around lumber or fishing. Noyo Harbor, a snug refuge just inland on the Noyo River, is the quintessential fishing port. In the predawn you can see the parade of boats heading down the river to the sea, their lights making an attractive scene.

Most visitors come to Fort Bragg to ride the California Western Railroad's Skunk Train, drawn by an old-time locomotive through 40 miles of dense redwood forest. The route from the town of Willits traverses over 31 bridges and trestles, through two deep mountain tunnels, and around sinuous switchbacks. It was a nightmare to build, and Chinese laborers did much of the work. While passenger travel is highly promoted, the Skunk—named for its coal-smoke aroma—still hauls lumber and other freight to stay in business.

Golden Gateway

It's common knowledge that "just passing through" San Francisco generally (hopefully!) means staying at least a couple of days and nights. An icon of the American West, the City (capitalized by locals) lives up to its legends. The classic old cable cars really do climb halfway to the stars (or at least as far as Nob Hill). Luminous fog does swirl around the Golden Gate Bridge. At eventide the golden glow of the setting sun glints from the windows of Alcatraz Island, making the old prison seem almost romantic, as errant sailors tack home against the late and misty sky. And taquerias in the Mission District, dim sum eateries in Chinatown, Italian coffeehouses in North Beach, to name just a few, make up a fascinating and tasty cultural mélange. Even the frequently chilling summer weather and traffic-snarled streets fail to diminish the multicultural excitement and avant-garde aura that pervade this town. It's a city with an irrepressible spirit, a noble grand dame on a hilltop throne, proud and resilient after the terrible earthquake of 1906 and the more recent Loma Prieta temblor of 1989.

So . . . if you had only two days in San Francisco, what places should you not miss? Everyone's tastes are different, but here are a few sites that most folks are sure to enjoy.

Nob Hill, at the top of California and Sacramento Streets, with its posh hotels, private clubs, and smart addresses, retains much of the glamour and gentility it possessed at the end of the 19th century, when men who had made fortunes in silver erected grand mansions for the world to envy on these unobstructed, commanding heights.

Fisherman's Wharf, with its picturesque views, pungent aromas, street performers, steaming crab pots, and fine restaurants, draws many visitors—it's all hustle and bustle during the summer tourist season. Fishing boats bob alongside the wharf, while seagulls float overhead and sea lions bask and bark on large rafts moored at the wharf's edge. Local gourmets (and commoners alike) consider West Coast Dungeness crab among the best seafood in the world. Walkaway shrimp cocktails are sold from the sidewalk, along with clam chowder and sourdough bread, and it's pleasant to nibble on a little seafood while watching the fishing boats return. Parking is available in public lots along Beach and North Point Streets.

Check out the Hyde Street Pier and look at the tall 19th-century ships permanently berthed there. Ghirardelli Square, a short walk uphill on Hyde Street, is one of San Francisco's most successful attempts to hang onto the transient past. Until 1964 it was a crumbling, abandoned factory that had once turned out Civil War uniforms and later served as a chocolate factory where Domingo Ghirardelli made cocoa. Within the rambling complex are a dozen fine restaurants, snug cafes, and almost 100 shops and galleries.

The Cannery, just down the street on Leavenworth, is where Del Monte once tinned fruit. Now it's a delightful and original collection of

Insiders' Tip

The elegant Curran Theatre on Geary Street had a starring role in the classic 1950 film *All About Eve*. Bette Davis, Marilyn Monroe, Anne Baxter, and Celeste Holm were all featured in several scenes shot inside the lobby and in the alley.

sprightly shops, art galleries, and restaurants; a place to buy French lingerie, English antiques, primitive art, and the newest in contemporary furniture. Often there's entertainment in the courtyard—small combo bands, magicians, and jugglers.

Alcatraz Island, once the end of the line and the beginning of hopelessness for federal prisoners, is now part of a national park. It can be reached by boats that leave several times a day from Pier 41 at Fisherman's Wharf. A cellblock tour gives some insight into life behind bars for men like Al Capone and Machine Gun Kelly, who lived out their days here without visitors.

An excellent audio tour narrated by former guards and inmates is full of fascinating anecdotes about some of the more notorious criminals, escape attempts, and the prison riot of 1946. Plan on staying at least a couple of hours on the island to soak in the history, and dress warmly. Same-day tickets are available at Pier 41 (you'll run into long lines in summer), or you can get them one month in advance by calling (415) 705-5555.

A $25 million renovation of Union Square, the heart of the city's shopping district, was completed in 2002. There are now more green spaces, light sculptures by R. M. Fischer, and a stage large enough to accommodate an orchestra. The underground parking garage beneath the Square, the first in the world, was also significantly renovated. It was originally built during World War II to serve as a bomb shelter. Around the Square or close by are Saks Fifth Avenue, Macy's, Neiman Marcus, Dior, and FAO Schwarz.

Chinatown is just a short walk up Grant Avenue from Union Square. This "city within a city" is home to more Chinese than any other place outside of Asia. Some 80,000 San Franciscans live, work, shop, worship, and play in Chinatown. It's packed with open-air markets, a variety of bakeries, restaurants, temples, souvenir shops, and, yes, people. Grant Avenue is touristy, but Stockton Street, a block west of Grant, offers a real taste of Chinatown. Tearooms, temples, Chinese schools, and shops lining the streets offer exotic produce and delicacies such as yellow croaker salted fish, and dried papaw, fish peel, and black fungus.

For a rare treat, stop for a dim sum lunch at one of the restaurants offering this unusual fare. Waitresses wheel different carts around the room, each offering a unique cornucopia of delights—some of it mysterious, all of it delicious. They call out their particular specialty in Chinese, and you order whatever you like. (Some restaurants sell their more popular items, such as steamed pork buns, in to-go bakery-style cases for those who want to savor this delicacy on the run.)

Between Chinatown and Fisherman's Wharf is North Beach, the Italian district of the city. Pasta, provolone, bocce, and dark, rich espresso are in abundance here, as are a wide variety of cafes, galleries, small theaters, and nightclubs. Beat poets Jack Kerouac, Allen Ginsberg, and William Burroughs chose North Beach as their principal hangout, contributing to San Francisco's international reputation as a funky, hip literary city. In 1953, Lawrence Ferlinghetti, then a struggling poet who later became a Beat legend, opened City Lights Books at 261 Columbus Avenue. It has since become one of the city's most cherished landmarks, as well as a leader among the many feisty independent booksellers that have staked their claim in the Bay Area. For the full Beat experience, wander through the little store's voluminous stacks, then take 10 steps across Jack Kerouac Alley to lift a tall, cool one at Vesuvio's Bar—a legendary watering hole that still draws the city's more colorful creative types.

If you're into museums, you'll appreciate the world-class offerings in San Francisco. The Asian Art Museum reopened in early 2003 in its new home at the Civic Center, filling 40,000 square feet of gallery space with $4 billion worth of Asian treasures. And the San Francisco Museum of Modern Art can always be counted on for spectacular shows. A recent coup for MOMA, at 151 Third Street, was "Yes Yoko Ono," the first comprehensive display in the United States of the artist's four decades of work.

When you get hungry in San Francisco, you're never too far from a restaurant. In fact, there's one on every corner. It's hard to make specific recommendations, but keep in mind that there are some 3,200 eating and drinking establishments in the city, which breaks down to about one restaurant for every 230 residents. Wherever you decide to dine, you're not likely to be disappointed.

Get the feel of the Pacific Ocean along the Great Highway. Start at Point Lobos Avenue and the Great Highway, then visit Cliff House, a once-famous resort area that overlooks the ocean and nearby Seal Rock. From there, the long windswept strand of Ocean Beach stretches to the great sand dunes to the south. Leave your bathing suit at the hotel, and stay out of the roiling surf, where the southbound tidal currents traveling at 12 mph have a habit of swallowing swimmers and surfers alike.

Along this highway you'll discover an entrance to Golden Gate Park, the city's great green retreat, bordered by the Great Highway, Lincoln Way, Stanyan, and Fulton Streets. When the park was built in 1887, it comprised 730 acres of dunes and 270 acres of arable land. Today, its 1,000 acres are lush with meadows, lakes, and 5,000 varieties of shrubs, flowers, and trees. Within its borders you can visit an aquarium, a planetarium, and a plant conservatory that looks a lot like Kew Gardens in London.

When the sun begins its slow descent into the ocean and the late afternoon fog snakes its tendrils over the hills and into the bay, the city takes on a more romantic feel. San Francisco may be a sightseer's paradise during the day, but it is also a great place to spend an evening. Ease into a silky-smooth night of jazz at the New Orleans room at the Fairmont Hotel, California and Mason Streets, and also inquire as to who's playing at the velvet-gloved and sedate Venetian room there. Give an amen for some soulful gospel music at Biscuits and Blues, 401 Mason Street, or enjoy an evening of comedy at Punch Line, 444 Battery Street. One of the best comedy shows in town is the long-running Beach Blanket Babylon at Club Fugazi, 678 Green Street. It's wacky, it's fun, and it's ever-changing—skewering whatever and whoever has recently shaken up our pop culture.

Of course, this listing of attractions only scratches the surface. It is said that everyone who visits San Francisco wants to come back again, and our tour leaves plenty more to see on a return trip. It would be nice, for instance, to take in the Cable Car Barn and Museum on Washington and Mason Streets to see the historic old paraphernalia and glimpse the innards of these machines in action. (Just how does that cable car work anyway?) Kids and parents alike should see the Exploratorium, Marina Boulevard and Lyon Street, which contains more than 600 interactive science exhibits.

Insiders' Tip

Though it seems as if it's been around forever, the fortune cookie is not an ancient Asian delicacy. It was invented in San Francisco about a century ago by Makota Hagiwara, who was a gardener at the Japanese Tea Garden in Golden Gate Park.

Spanning more than a mile of open water, San Francisco's Golden Gate Bridge is a must stop for any first-time visitor to the city. PHOTO: JOHN NAGIECKI

The city's Victorian architecture is almost as famous as its cable cars. Handsome and slightly irrational, painted brightly in all combinations of colors, these structures are certainly unique. Some of the best can be seen on Pacific Heights, particularly on these streets: Vallejo, Broadway, Pacific, Jackson, Washington, Pierce, and Scott, generally in blocks between 1600 and 3000.

One thing visitors should keep in mind is that San Francisco weather is, well, unlike what you would expect. True, temperatures don't often vary outside a range of 50 to 70 degrees, summer or winter. But sometimes January and February can be the sunniest, most glorious months. On the other hand, summer can be so cold that tourists who mistakenly thought California called for tank tops and flip-flops huddle in downtown doorways to keep warm. Mark Twain reportedly once said, "The coldest winter I ever spent was a summer in San Francisco." So you may want to have that sweater or jacket handy if you're walking about. What is the best time of year to visit? Locals will tell you the most pleasant months are September and October.

> ## Insiders' Tip
> San Francisco is home to one of the world's largest gay and lesbian communities. If you are visiting in the month of June, watch for the Gay Pride Day parade, one of the city's more popular and entertaining annual events.

Much like Manhattan and some quaint and compact European cities, San Francisco is best enjoyed by walking its many neighborhoods. Besides, driving a car in San Francisco—and then trying to park it here and there—can be an exercise in futility. But if you must drive, be prepared for the traffic idiosyncrasies you will encounter.

In negotiating the city by automobile, be aware of red-light-running fools, and expect traffic jams at any hour. On-street parking is virtually nonexistent—at best scarce—and those who overstay their legal welcome are subject to heavy fines and might even be clamped with "the boot," which immobilizes the vehicle. An impounded car is endless trouble to retrieve.

Fortunately there are a number of public parking facilities; one of the handiest offering underground parking is at Union Square. In hilly San Francisco, it is illegal to park a car on most hills (technically, those exceeding a grade of 3 percent) without setting your parking brake and turning the wheels into the curb. When parking uphill the wheels must be "heeled," with the inside front tire resting securely against the curb. Parking downhill, tires must be "toed"—turned in.

Complicated enough for you? We recommend letting your hotel valet park the car when you first arrive and forgetting about it until you're ready to leave town. You'll be glad you did.

So if you only have a day or, heaven forbid, even less, and you're still wondering what to do, our advice is this: Go out and simply walk. Enjoying yourself comes easy here. It costs nothing to breathe the fragrance of a vendor's flowers on Union Square, hike up Telegraph Hill—where rowhouses climb steep slopes—take in the breathtaking view from Coit Tower at the crest, stroll through Chinatown or Little Italy, or photograph the busy fleet at Fisherman's Wharf. And don't worry, you will be back.

Flora, Fauna, and Climate

Geology
Soil
Climate
Flora
Fauna

Upon arriving in the Santa Rosa area in 1875, famed horticulturist Luther Burbank could barely contain his excitement, declaring that "this is the chosen spot of all earth as far as Nature is concerned." Many Wine Country visitors have since echoed Burbank's sentiments, inspired by the bucolic scenery and the mild Mediterranean climate. From the marshes of San Pablo Bay to the mountains of Mendocino National Forest, and from the roaring Pacific to shimmering Clear Lake, the terrain is rarely less than wondrous. Few places on the face of the planet are so blessed with natural gifts.

Every season reveals a different facet of the landscape. In spring, a kaleidoscope of wildflowers lines the roadsides. In summer, the grapevines practically beam with verdant life. In fall, the fields are quilted in bright patches of red and orange. And in winter, always wet but not too harsh, a misty and mysteriously beautiful hush descends on the hills and valleys. But that's not all. Behind the Wine Country's ever changing beauty lies a fascinating natural history. Though we can't attempt to summarize all there is to tell, we have brought together a sampling of some more salient geologic, climatic, and ecological features.

Geology

A hundred million years ago, the Wine Country area was exceptionally poor as a grape-growing region. In fact, all of it was under water. It took a lot of tectonic activity—movement of the massive plates that together form the Earth's crust—to swing Napa, Sonoma, and environs eastward onto dry land. It was all part of the succession of north-south "island arcs" that violently, if patiently, crashed into the North American continent and sent California on the way to its modern-day topography, which includes the prominent Mayacmas Mountains—which divide Sonoma and Napa and Lake and Mendocino Counties—and the steep Coast Range.

Of course, the movement hasn't exactly stopped altogether, and you can feel their effects every now and then. The renowned San Andreas system, a massive network of strike-slip faults that forms the border between the Pacific and North American tectonic plates, runs the length of Sonoma and Mendocino Counties, sometimes on the mainland and sometimes beneath the sea. Several smaller, generally north-south faults lurk beneath the Wine Country, including the Rodgers Creek Fault, which caused some destruction in Santa Rosa with a 1969 quake that measured 5.7 on the Richter scale.

Things could be worse. In fact, they used to be. Much of the region was the scene of frightful volcanic activity three to four million years ago. Those eruptions, combined with unrelenting seismic activity, have given California's North Coast ranges a highly complex geologic profile. And this is of more than theoretical interest, for two of the lures that historically have drawn people to the region are direct results of geology.

The most obvious of these is geothermal activity. Sonoma and Napa Counties are pierced by fault "pipelines" that send water heated by magma 8 miles below the earth's surface percolating upward. In the Calistoga area you can pay to gawk at a burst of hot water (at the Old Faithful Geyser) or to soak in the stuff (at the many spas). And around one section of the Sonoma-Lake County border, geothermal sites are even used to generate electricity. In fact, the Geysers steam field weighs in as the world's largest complex (19 units) of geothermal power plants, owned and operated by the Calpine Corporation.

But the peculiar North Coast geology has spawned a lot more than mud baths. The second regional drawing card with its roots in plate tectonics is the mighty grapevine.

Soil

Soils reflect the rocks they used to be, so it makes sense that an area of convoluted geology will contain many types of soil. And because soil composition greatly affects the chemistry of a growing grape, it follows that precisely where you plant your vines has a lot to do with the quality of your wine.

The soil within a single vineyard can vary substantially. Red soil tends to produce soft wine; light, "fluffy" soils are known for hard, austere wines; and gravelly ground, which has a hard time holding water, tends to result in earthy wines. Moreover, wine made from hillside grapes usually is riskier and more robust than valley wine, because the grapes are smaller and therefore have a higher skin-to-pulp ratio. (The intense flavor is in the skin.) And some of the best vineyard soil in Napa Valley is found on the Oakville and Rutherford "benches"—broad, nutrient-rich alluvial fans that have been washed from the Mayacmas Mountains.

Of course, all of this is gross oversimplification. We provide more information on the whole business of "appellations"— slightly varied microclimates that produce grapes and yield wines with specific, refined characteristics—in our Wineries chapter, but sorting out such details is what separates a successful vintner from the rest of us guzzlers. The point is that, in a manner of speaking, the Merlot you're savoring today has been in the works for about 100 million years.

Climate

Northern California is one of five regions in the world that enjoys a Mediterranean climate, characterized by warm, dry summers and mild, moist winters. While the area's geographic location helps to shape its climate—Santa Rosa is about par with Athens on the latitude scale—local environmental influences are also important. Weather varies dramatically throughout the region, and you can often find a huge difference in conditions just by driving a few miles.

To understand what causes Wine Country weather, think of the Pacific Ocean as a giant climate-control device,

Insiders' Tip

Natural spas are not the only benefit of the Wine Country's abundant geothermal resources. If you're driving on a chilly morning north on U.S. 101 from Santa Rosa, you may notice several plumes of steam rising from the hills to the east. The steam is from Calpine Corporations's geothermal power plant, which generates 850 megawatts of power from the naturally occurring steam reservoirs located underground. Tours of the 30-square-mile facility are available (see our Attractions chapter). For more information call (866) 439-7377.

set on MILD. In general, the farther you stray from salt water, the hotter your summers will be and the colder your winters. Temperature variations along the coast are minuscule, and river towns such as Guerneville and Napa also are fairly mild. There's only about a 5-degree differential in the usual maximum winter high temperature on the Mendocino Coast (56 degrees) and the average summer high (the low 60s). Though coastal winter nights are cooler, they don't often see temperatures drop lower than 40. There is morning summer fog and evening sea breezes.

That is in stark contrast to places such as Ukiah, Calistoga, and Middletown, where hilly terrain serves as a barrier to ocean influences. Each of these towns can be uncomfortably still and hot in August. Inland Lake County reaches upward of 100 degrees regularly in summer, and its winters can dip well below the freezing mark. On the other hand, when it's hot, it qualifies as "dry heat." Californians tend to consider that phrase a meaningless cliche, but long-suffering Midwesterners and Easterners can immediately feel the difference. A 100-degree day is a test no matter how you look at it, but the night

air has a chance to cool considerably when humidity is low.

Rainfall, too, varies across the Wine Country. The Mendocino Coast gets about 39 inches, St. Helena about 34, and the Clear Lake Basin about 25. Regardless of volume, however, you can expect most of the rain between November and February, with residual storms in March and April. Summer and fall downpours are rare here.

In general, spring and autumn are the best months to visit. The weather is exceptional, and there is added color from wildflowers or turning leaves. Summer temperatures in Sonoma County usually edge into the mid-80s, but the nights are still comfortable (chilly even), with the mercury falling into the 50s.

Flora

A flora list from the Covelo Ranger District in Mendocino National Forest alone refers to 18 different coniferous trees, 13 varieties of oak, 6 types of willow, and 6 species of manzanita. So we won't try to construct any sort of comprehensive list here—it would be voluminous. We can, however, state a few generalities.

Two types of ecosystem—oak woodland and chaparral—dominate the rolling hills of Napa and Sonoma Counties. It's impossible to drive along U.S. 101 or Highway 29 without noticing the stolid oak trees, but the collection includes many varieties. Coast live oaks are perhaps the most impressive, with a single tree able to spread its branches up to 130 feet. These trees prefer moist locations, such as creek bottoms and north slopes. Canyon live oaks, with their exceptionally hard wood, thrive on steep hillsides. Blue oaks like hot, dry slopes, and California black oaks pop up on mesas with deep soil and gentle slopes.

Chaparral, made up of shrubs such as manzanita, ceanothus, and toyon, is more closely associated with the hills of southern California, but it is prevalent here too. It is an inhospitable environment for humans designed to burn—many of its

Insiders' Tip

The Napa Registry of Significant Trees was founded in 1995 to protect special trees on private properties in perpetuity until their natural death. To be listed on the registry, the tree must have historic significance and high public visibility, be native to Napa Valley, and be extraordinarily beautiful.

plant species have highly flammable oils in their bark and the underbrush can be thorny and impenetrable.

While most of the grapes are grown at lower elevation, the Wine Country counties include a lot of mountainous, forested topography. That's especially true in the upper half of Lake County and the northeast corner of Mendocino County, which form part of Mendocino National Forest.

The standout citizen of the damp, misty Coast Range forests is the coast redwood, the tallest tree in the world. Though Mendocino and Sonoma have several preserves devoted to redwoods (see our Parks and Recreation chapter), the biggest of all are found in Humboldt County (see "The Big Trees" section of our Day Trips chapter). You might also stumble on a redwood in steep, darker canyons along Wine Country streams. Other dominant trees include the ponderosa pine, with its arrow-straight trunk; the Pacific madrone, whose gnarled trunk will creep 50 feet horizontally to find sunlight; and the Douglas fir, the Western Hemisphere's premier lumber tree.

No matter which Wine Country microclimate you're in, you are likely to see wildflowers if your timing is sound. Somewhere between February and June, depending on elevation and intensity of sunlight, literally hundreds of shrubs and herbs burst into bloom. The most eye-catching include the California poppy—the bright orange state flower that pops up just about anywhere—and mustard, which lays a breathtaking yellow carpet in the early spring vineyards (and inspires all sorts of reverent celebrations—see our Festivals and Annual Events chapter). Other native wildflowers to look for include orchids, irises, monkey flowers, Indian paintbrushes, golden bushes, wild roses, lupines, violets, shooting stars, fiddlenecks, lilies, wild onions, and buttercups.

Fauna

It isn't exactly a jungle out here, but keen observers will spy a wide range of furry, feathered, or fishy creatures in the Wine Country.

Drive the scenic routes at dusk in summer and fall, and you are likely to see the omnipresent black-tailed deer nibbling scrub oak or buckbrush in the meadows. You are even more likely to see skunks, raccoons, and opossums, though it might be in the form of roadkill. They are among the most common of the region's mammals, especially in semideveloped areas. The more mountainous areas are home to all sorts of animals, including black bears, mountain lions, bobcats, coyotes, bats, diminutive gray foxes, porcupines, badgers, feral pigs, and even the occasional ring-tailed cat or tule elk. Many of them are nocturnal and all are elusive, but they are out there, trying to stay downwind of the humans. Once in a while, however, a bear or bobcat wanders into the eastern city limits of Santa Rosa, nestled along the western side of the Mayacmas Mountains, in search of some easy food and water. A mountain lion even startled commuters one afternoon when it strolled onto U.S. 101—a jungle of a different sort!—in the middle of the city. Though these sightings are rare, it serves to remind us that we are surrounded by wild and unpredictable beauty.

The rugged coastal areas have their own communities: seals and sea lions on the rocks; river otters in the estuaries; and gray whales offshore, migrating southward from the Bering Sea to Baja California between December and April. The nutrient-rich waters of the coastal areas also teem with a variety of benthic life, including eight species of the highly desirable—and highly endangered—abalone. River otters are found in much of the Wine Country's freshwater. The reptile and amphibian crowd includes alligator lizards, pond turtles, king snakes, rubber boas, skinks, and the ones you need to watch out for: western rattlesnakes.

The local waterways—primarily the Napa, Eel, and Russian rivers—are dominated by anadromous fish, that is, species that travel from the sea to spawn in fresh water. The three big fish in the Wine Country (as in most of northern California) are Chinook salmon, coho salmon, and steelhead—the latter are basically rainbow trout that have learned to migrate. Most of the good lake fishing is for bass (smallmouth

Distinctive abalone shells hang as ornaments around the yards of coastal homes. PHOTO: JOHN NAGIECKI

and largemouth) and catfish, though none of them are native sons. (See more on fishing in our On the Water chapter.)

Audubon Society chapters are active throughout the region, and they have plenty to catalogue. There are swallows and swifts, American robins, and northern mockingbirds, woodpeckers and warblers, finches and flycatchers. There are at least six species of hawk and seven species of owl, including the northern spotted, that rather harmless old-growth percher despised by a generation of loggers.

Golden eagles (the nation's largest raptor, with a wingspan of up to 7 feet), ospreys, kestrels, and peregrine falcons ride the thermals along high bluffs and cliff faces. Peregrines, with a maximum flight speed of up to 275 mph, have been known to overtake small airplanes. Herons and egrets poke about in swampy spots, such as the Napa-Sonoma Marshes Wildlife Area, south of those two towns, and we've got a varied collection of ducks and geese. And if jet lag and ambitious wine tasting have you feeling dehydrated and fatigued, don't fret too much about those California turkey vultures circling overhead. It's nothing personal—the hefty, red-faced scavengers are quite populous in the Wine Country.

Hotels, Motels, and Inns

Napa County
Sonoma County
Mendocino County
Vacation Rentals

Some folks love the bed-and-breakfast inn experience. Some don't. If you fall into the latter category, take heart: Not every guest room in Wine Country is swathed in Laura Ashley prints and crammed with antiques and teddy bears. In this chapter we will familiarize you with other options available for a good night's sleep. Some are full-service hotels that can be as charming and cozy as B&Bs (but with more amenities), and some are less expensive, basic motel rooms.

Our hotels reflect the dichotomy of this region: cosmopolitan, yes; metropolitan, no. Business people who come for conferences and meetings find themselves bedded down not in structures of glass and steel but in low-lying resort hotels with golf, tennis, swimming, horseback riding, and winery tours serving as relaxing options. Facilities may be ultramodern and services may match any big-city hotel, but the nation's business travelers share these accommodations with tourists from all over the globe.

For this chapter we define hotels and motels as structures that were built for the express intent of providing lodging. For our purposes, bed-and- breakfast inns are places with few guest rooms, places that may have started out as someone's residence. Everything else, especially anything with a staff and a dining room, is rated as a hotel or motel.

Unless we state otherwise, assume that hotels and motels take major credit cards and that pets are not welcome. Although California smoking laws are extremely stringent, many hotels listed provide rooms for their guests who smoke, but always inquire when calling for information. Expect that all entries will have color TV.

Hotels and motels are listed using the geographical sequence explained in our How to Use This Book chapter. We start with the Napa County accommodations, followed by those in Sonoma and Mendocino Counties. Afterward we give agencies specializing in vacation rentals.

Price Code

The schedule of dollar sign symbols shown below indicates the approximate price range for a one-night, weekend, double-occupancy stay, not including tax, gratuities, or other add-on amenities such as room service or premium movie channels.

$ . . . . Less than $80
$$ . . . . $81 to $120
$$$ . . . . $121 to $150
$$$$ . . . . $151 to $200
$$$$$ . . . . More than $200

Napa County

Embassy Suites Napa Valley $$$$$
1075 California Boulevard, Napa
(707) 253–9540, (800) 362–2779
www.embassynapa.com

In a valley where "business" usually takes the form of buying wine by the bottle and drinking it for lunch, this is as close as it comes to a high-end business traveler's hotel. A group of three-story, canary-and-burgundy buildings, the Embassy Suites offers a nice combination of corporate know-how and Wine Country charm. There are indoor and outdoor pools, wet and dry saunas, swans in the koi pond, and a soaring lobby with terra-cotta tiles and parlor chairs. Every guest unit is a two-room suite with extra pullout sofa, wet bar, and microwave. The tariff includes a full, cooked-to-order breakfast and an afternoon Manager's Reception with complimentary drinks. And if you really are here on business, Embassy Suites boasts eight meeting rooms (arranged around the Fountain Court), full conference facilities, and two-line phones with modem access in each room.

Napa Valley Marriott $$$$
3425 Solano Avenue, Napa
(707) 253–7433, (800) 228–9290
www.marriott.com

The 191-room hotel (including four suites) is just off Highway 29, north of the Trancas Street/Redwood Road exit. Each room has individual climate control, in-room pay movies, iron and ironing board, a work desk, and voice mail. The Harvest Cafe, specializing in steaks and California vegetables, serves breakfast and dinner; Character's Sports Bar & Grill serves lunch and dinner. For $10 extra, you can get breakfast along with your room. Amadeus spa offers massages, exfoliations, body treatments, and facials. (See the Web site at www.spame.com.) The Marriott also has a heated outdoor pool and Jacuzzi, lighted tennis courts, and a fitness center. And one entire level of the hotel gets down to business, with 8,500 square feet of flexible meeting space that can handle groups of 15 to 500.

Milliken Creek Inn $$$$$
1815 Silverado Trail, Napa
(707) 255–1197, (888) 622–5775
www.millikencreekinn.com

In its short life, this "boutique inn" set on the Napa River has become one of the valley's most luxurious and popular retreats for couples wanting to get away from it all. It's only two minutes to Copia (see our Attractions chapter) and downtown Napa's restaurants, yet you will feel far removed from city life. (The property dates from the 1800s, when the old carriage house was a stagecoach stop.) More than a bed-and-breakfast inn, but not a hotel or a spa resort, it's in a class by itself. Luxurious and inviting, it's in a tranquil setting, thanks to the natural expanse of the river wherever you look. (Don't forget to wave to the kayakers.) Enhancing the grounds are gardens, fountains, Adirondack chairs, and even a waterfall and koi pond.

The innkeepers, Lisa Holt and David Shapiro, have many years of experience in the upscale hotel industry, and it shows in their attention to detail. The guest rooms are elegantly noncluttered, in what Lisa calls "British campaign" design, but these rooms have modern amenities such as DVD players (there's a lending library of 200 movie titles), well-appointed mini-bars, telephones with modem hookups, and in-room continental breakfast service. Many of the rooms come with fireplaces and genuine spa tubs, Italian linens, and terry robes. There's even a pillow menu—soft or firm, feather or foam? In early evening guests can sip wine in the lobby while watching David tickle the ivories on the piano (he's an accomplished jazz musician). Massage and spa treatments, along with private yoga classes, are offered on-site. Needless to say, this inn is intended for the enjoyment of couples.

Napa River Inn $$$$$
500 Main Street, Napa
(707) 251–8500, (877) 251–8500
www.napariverinn.com

When the historic Napa Mill and Hatt Building were renovated along the Napa River in 2000, this hotel was the result. It offers luxury accommodations in 66 guest rooms and suites in various themes—from nautical to "California rustic" to vintage 1800s. All rooms feature large TVs, two-line data and voice ports, refrigerators, and in-room coffee. Many rooms have fireplaces, river views, and balconies. A full-service spa is nearby for use by guests, and restaurants and shops are handy right next door in the newly refurbished Hatt Market building. The room tariffs for weekends range from $225 to $500—slightly less during the week. All rooms are nonsmoking.

Wine Valley Lodge $$
200 South Coombs Street, Napa
(707) 224–7911, (800) 696–7911
www.winevalleylodge.com

South of downtown Napa, close to Highway 121, the Mission-style Lodge has 53 guest rooms. There is a heated pool in the motor court, and complimentary continental breakfast on summer weekends. Ask about the Elvis Presley and Marilyn Monroe suites, which run a bit higher in price and larger in size, each sleeping four adults comfortably. The stars stayed in these rooms at different times several decades ago—The King was making a movie nearby, but nobody seems to remember the reason Marilyn checked in.

Best Western Inn at the Vines $$$
100 Soscol Avenue, Napa
(707) 257–1930, (877) 846–3729
www.innatthevines.com

Best Western offers few surprises, which is probably why it's one of America's most popular chains. The Napa version has 68 rooms, including eight suites. Two of the suites are loft-style, with a bed upstairs and living room below; others are one-level units with sitting rooms. All rooms have cable TV and refrigerators. There is a heated pool and spa, a meeting room for up to 50 people, and a 24-hour Denny's restaurant on the property. This is a non-smoking hotel.

Hawthorn Inn & Suites $$$$
314 Soscol Avenue, Napa
(707) 226–1878, (800) 527–1133
www.napavalleyinns.com

One of Napa's newest hotels is this 60-room, three-story structure that focuses on comfort, with a nod to business travelers. The rooms are wired with two phone lines with voice mail and data ports, and there are irons, ironing boards, microwaves, refrigerators, and executive chairs with oversized desks. Business services, a daily newspaper, and a board room for meetings are also available. The deluxe suites have in-room Jacuzzis. Vacationers who like a little exercise will appreciate the hotel's swimming pool and spa, as well as the fitness

Insiders' Tip

Need help locating accommodations? Call Napa Valley Reservations Unlimited at (800) 251-NAPA or, within the area, at (707) 252-1985 or (707) 944-0709 or by visiting www.napavalleyreservations.com. They will assist you in selecting a hotel, motel, resort, bed-and-breakfast inn, or condo, and they won't charge you a cent.

center. A hot breakfast buffet is offered every morning from 7:00 to 9:00 A.M.

Napa Valley Downtown Travelodge $$$
853 Coombs Street, Napa
(707) 226–1871, (800) 578–7878
www.travelodge.com

If location is everything, the Travelodge has it all. The downtown Napa locale puts you two blocks from Riverwalk, four blocks from the Wine Train depot (see our Getting Here chapter), and a few steps away from shops and cafes. The 45-room motel has a heated pool. Each unit comes with a two-line phone with a fax port, individual air-conditioning, and a big-screen TV with VCR. Movie rentals are available through the motel.

Chardonnay Lodge $
2640 Jefferson Street, Napa
(707) 224–0789

The lodge offers convenient Napa centrality and beds of various proportions. The 20 rooms are air-conditioned, and they have phones and cable TV.

The Chateau $$$
4195 Solano Avenue, Napa
(707) 253–9300
www.napavalleychateauhotel.com

Somewhere between a budget motel and a major corporate hotel, The Chateau offers comfort and reliability, if not luxury. The 115 rooms are sizable, and each has a separate vanity dressing area and individual climate control. The two-story motel has six spacious suites too, with wet bars and fold-out couches. Also on the grounds are two conference centers that hold up to 500 people, and a swimming pool and spa. Kids 11 and younger stay free in the same room as their guardians.

The John Muir Inn $$$
1998 Trower Avenue, Napa
(707) 257–7220, (800) 522–8999
www.johnmuirnapa.com

We can't imagine John Muir, the naturalist who wandered through the Sierra Nevada range stocked with nothing more than a pocket full of biscuits, staying here at the intersection of Trower Avenue and Highway 29. But, hey, the inn that bears his name is very environmentally conscious. The hotel is a solid midpriced choice with a courtyard swimming pool and whirlpool spa, conference room, a 24-hour front desk, and free continental breakfast. About one-quarter of the 60 rooms have kitchenettes, and some have wet bars or private spas. Children 13 and younger stay free. There is no restaurant at the inn, but Marie Callendar's is within shouting distance. The entire property is a smoke-free environment.

Yountville Inn $$$$$
6462 Washington Street, Yountville
(707) 944–5600, (800) 972–2293
www.yountvilleinn.com

One of the midvalley's newest options is Yountville Inn, nestled against Hopper Creek. The rambling hotel has seven buildings and 51 bright and spacious rooms. Each unit boasts a fieldstone fireplace, French doors leading to a patio, a wood-beamed ceiling, and a refrigerator. All guests receive free continental breakfast. The inn also has a heated pool and spa, and is near the Vintners Golf Club (see our Parks and Recreation chapter). Should you be mixing business with pleasure, the elegantly comfortable Club Room facilitates groups of up to 60 people.

Vintage Inn $$$$$
6541 Washington Street, Yountville
(707) 944–1112, (800) 351–1133
www.vintageinn.com

This elegant, country-style inn is spread out on a large, landscaped lot. It has 80 units—basic rooms, mini-suites, and villas—divided between the outer court and the more protected inner court. Most have patios or balconies. All of them have fireplaces and come with a complimentary continental breakfast buffet, including California champagne. Vintage Inn offers room service, a 60-foot lap pool and hot tub, tennis courts, bike rentals in the summer, and a private limousine service. About 15 percent of the rooms are smoker-friendly, and you can even bring your dog if you don't mind handing over the $25 cleaning fee. The inn also has executive conference facilities that can handle 20 to 200 people.

Napa Valley Lodge $$$$$
2230 Madison Street, Yountville
(707) 944–2468, (800) 368–2468
www.napavalleylodge.com

If you've ever stayed at one of Woodside Hotels' Northern California establishments, you'll be keen to reserve a spot at this 55-room hotel at the north end of Yountville, which underwent a $3.5 million facelift in 2000. The exterior incorporates classic Tuscan-style architecture, with arched loggias, iron railings, and limestone details. Woodside is known for its gracious service and amenities, and Napa Valley Lodge is right in step—from the 400-book lending library and hearth in the lobby to the free champagne buffet breakfast to the Spanish-tile double vanities, duvet bed coverings, and reproduced vintage tapestries in the rooms. About three-fourths of the units have fireplaces, and all feature a balcony or terrace with views of vineyard or pool and gardens.

Besides the pool, the hotel has a spa, a redwood sauna, and a small exercise room,

Yountville's Vintage Inn is a luxury getaway, complete with room service, champagne breakfast buffet, lap pool, and private limo service. PHOTO: JEAN SAYLOR DOPPENBERG

and if they get your blood pumping, you can head to Chardonnay Golf Club (see our Parks and Recreation chapter), where guests receive a weekday discount on greens fees. Napa Valley Lodge does brisk corporate business—not surprising when you note the hotel's two warm, well-appointed conference rooms.

Rancho Caymus Inn $$$$
1140 Rutherford Cross Road, Rutherford
(707) 963–1777, (800) 845–1777
www.ranchocaymus.com

If Father Junipero Serra had built a really fancy mission to impress the folks back home in Spain, it might have looked like this. Rancho Caymus, a couple of blocks east of Highway 29 on Rutherford Cross Road (a.k.a. Highway 128), carries off the hacienda motif flawlessly, from the adobe-looking stucco to the tile roof. The rough-hewn white oak and pine beams were salvaged from an 80-year-old barn in Ohio; the parota wood chairs, tables, and dressers are from Guadalajara; and the wool rugs and wall hangings were made by indige-nous Ecuadorians. A central, tiled court-yard brims with flowers and small trees.

Most of the 26 nonsmoking units have fireplaces and a split-level layout, and five of them have kitchenettes. Continental breakfast is included, and the site includes fine dining at chef Ken Frank's La Toque restaurant (see our Restaurants chapter).

El Bonita Motel $$$$
195 Main Street, St. Helena
(707) 963–3216, (800) 541–3284
www.elbonita.com

The old neon sign and poolside layout point to this motel's roots as a classic 1950s roadside motor hotel, but there have been upgrades galore since then. The 42 rooms are nicely furnished and painted in subdued gray-green tones. About two-thirds have microwaves and refrigerators. Some allow pets for a small fee. There is a fireplace in the recently remodeled lobby, and each guest receives a continental breakfast. Flowers and fountains prolifer-ate in the lawn areas, while the pool is complemented by a sauna and a Jacuzzi.

Harvest Inn $$$$$
1 Main Street, St. Helena
(707) 963–WINE, (800) 950–8466
www.harvestinn.com

The Inn's reception building, the Harvest Centre, is built to evoke the English countryside, with its corkscrewed brick chimneys and oak-paneled great room. But "rustic" this place isn't. It is a sprawling, manicured complex that specializes in (but isn't limited to) corporate functions, with conference facilities accommodating as many as 60 captains of industry. Set between Sutter Home Winery and Sulphur Springs Avenue on the southern fringe of St. Helena, and bordering a sizable vineyard, Harvest Inn has 54 nonsmoking rooms. Most of them have king beds, brick fireplaces, wet bars, and dressing vanities, and some have patio balconies. There are two heated pools and whirlpool spas on the grounds, and all guests are served continental breakfast.

The Wine Country Inn $$$$
1152 Lodi Lane, St. Helena
(707) 963–7077, (888) 465–4608
www.winecountryinn.com

This hard-to-categorize accommodation does a good job of blending the comforts of a bed-and-breakfast with the convenience of a small hotel. The Wine Country Inn offers

Insiders' Tip
When figuring your travel budget, don't forget the occupancy tax, which varies from place to place. To take Napa County as an example, the charge is 12 percent of the bill if you are within city limits, 10 percent if you're in an unincorporated area.

a full buffet breakfast, afternoon appetizers and wine tasting, distinctive rooms filled with hand-picked antiques, a large pool and Jacuzzi, a well-trained staff, and easy parking. No matter how the inn is defined, Lodi Lane, about 2 miles north of St. Helena, is hard to beat for serenity. Immediately to the east is a working vineyard; almost all of the 20 rooms have private patios or balconies that practically sit on the trellises. Most units have fireplaces, and some even have private hot tubs. There are also four suites and five cottages. The hotel, popular with honeymooners, caters to adults rather than to families with children.

The Inn at Southbridge $$$$$
1020 Main Street, St. Helena
(707) 967–9400, (800) 520–6800
www.innatsouthbridge.com

This upscale St. Helena hotel, which opened in November 1995, looks something like a winery with its earth tones and creeping vines. The resemblance is no coincidence, as architect William Turnbull Jr. is known for his winery design. The Inn at Southbridge has 21 ample rooms (only two smoking units), each with a vaulted ceiling, fireplace, sisal-style carpets, and down comforter. French doors open onto a private balcony overlooking the courtyard. The rooms are set up for corporate clients, each having dual phone lines and a fax/modem port. The inn has a lap pool and a full-service health club with steam, weights, and stationary bikes. Guests also enjoy (paid) access to Meadowood resort's recreational facilities—the establishments are co-owned (see our Spas and Resorts chapter for more on Meadowood).

Hotel St. Helena $$$$
1309 Main Street, St. Helena
(707) 963–4388, (888) 478–4355
www.hotelsthelena.com

This restored hotel in the heart of downtown is quintessential St. Helena: immaculate, charming, and not cheap. It was an upscale hotel when it was built back in 1881, but soon deteriorated into a second-floor flophouse over the local Montgomery Ward. Now it has recaptured and redefined its glory. At ground level are shops and a flowery arcade, plus a wine and coffee bar in the lobby. Upstairs are 18 antique-filled rooms painted in combinations of subdued tones: burgundy, mauve, chocolate, dark tan, and pale gold. Four of the rooms share two baths; the rest have private bathrooms, some with old claw-foot tubs. There is a sitting room at the top of the stairs and a TV-equipped solarium overlooking the arcade. A large continental breakfast is included in the price. Don't bring your cigarettes—this is a nonsmoking property.

Calistoga Inn $
1250 Lincoln Avenue, Calistoga
(707) 942–4101
www.calistogainn.com

For a no-frills (okay, maybe a couple of frills), ambiance-thick stay in Calistoga, try the Inn, an old western-style hotel that dates back to 1882. The 18 second-floor rooms, connected by a creaking wood-floored hallway, sit over a restaurant and microbrewery/bar (see our Restaurants and Nightlife chapters). Each room has a sink and a queen or king bed, but there are central, shared bathrooms and showers, and no in-room TVs. At about $75 (mid-week) and $100 (weekends), including continental breakfast, these are some of the most affordable tourist digs in town.

Mount View Hotel $$$$
1457 Lincoln Avenue, Calistoga
(707) 942–6877, (800) 816–6877
www.mountviewhotel.com

This is the closest Calistoga comes to the Ritz-Carlton. The Mission Revival building, now a National Historic Landmark, was constructed in 1919 and served the area for years as the European Hotel, haunt of literary bigwigs and first ladies. (It is said that Mrs. Herbert Hoover planted the roses in the garden.) An elegant lobby takes you to either the hotel, Mount View Spa, or Catahoula Restaurant; all three are run separately and catalogued separately in this book. Mount View Hotel has 32 rooms, suites, and cottages, the latter being detached units (with private Jacuzzis) out by the pool. The other rooms are on the second floor, and some have antique furnishings. Con-

tinental breakfast is delivered to your room. No smoking is allowed anywhere on this property.

Hotel D'Amici $$$$
1436 Lincoln Avenue, Calistoga
(707) 942–1007
www.rutherfordgrove.com/hotelpage

If Calistoga had luxury apartment suites, they'd look something like this. Hotel D'Amici is downtown, perched on the second floor of a 1936 building once known as Green Hotel. (The "secret door" is just to the right of the Flatiron Grill entrance.) The hotel has four spacious, well-appointed rooms, two of which share a balcony over Lincoln Avenue, making them coveted spaces during the Fourth of July and its Silverado Parade (see our Festivals and Annual Events chapter). All have private baths and kitchenettes. The owners are the Pestonis, who run Rutherford Grove Winery. You pick up your keys there (1673 Highway 29 in Rutherford) and get a complimentary wine tasting. You also get a bottle of Rutherford Grove Chardonnay in your fridge at the D'Amici.

Comfort Inn $$$
1865 Lincoln Avenue, Calistoga
(707) 942–9400, (800) 228–5150
www.callodging.com

Only in Calistoga would the Comfort Inn have a mineral water swimming pool and whirlpool tub. It also has a sauna and steam room. Each of the 55 rooms (including a two-room suite) features HBO and individual temperature control; most are in the functional style Comfort Inn is known for. Continental breakfast is included in the price.

Stevenson Manor Inn $$$$
1830 Lincoln Avenue, Calistoga
(707) 942–1112
www.callodging.com

This motel is affiliated with Best Western. Stevenson Manor has a pool, a sauna, and a gazebo-sheltered central courtyard. The 34 rooms are done in subdued shades of green and burgundy. Four have private whirlpool baths, and seven are warmed by fireplaces; all of them are equipped with refrigerators, microwaves, and coffeemakers. Guests of the inn receive a 10 percent discount at the nearby Calistoga Village Inn & Spa (see our Spas and Resorts chapter). All rooms are nonsmoking.

Sonoma County

Southern Sonoma

El Dorado Hotel $$$$$
405 First Street W., Sonoma
(707) 996–3030, (800) 289–3031
www.hoteleldorado.com

On the northwest corner of Sonoma Plaza, the El Dorado has had a checkered history as a government office, college, winery, and hotel. Salvador Vallejo built the adobe between 1836 and 1846; subsequently, it was occupied by Bear Flag Party members (see our History chapter) as well as Gen. John C. Frémont during the opening days of the Mexican War. Today its 26 rooms have an Old World aura of casual elegance. It's definitely the right choice for those who really want to revel in the plaza's historical ambiance. Some rooms face the plaza with balconies that give a view of the city below. Other rooms face onto a garden courtyard and overlook flowers and trees. Continental breakfast is included in the room rate.

El Pueblo Inn $$
896 West Napa Street, Sonoma
(707) 996–3651, (800) 900–8844
www.elppuebloinn.com

Built of adobe brick, it is the classic L-shaped motel of the 1950s. El Pueblo has been in the same family since it was built in 1959 and is now run by the original owners' daughters. With a large, heated swimming pool, a new spa, and a grassy, shaded garden area around the 38-room complex, it is an excellent location for either families or singles. Cribs are available, and there's a coffeemaker in each room, plus cocoa for the kids.

Sonoma Hotel $$$$
110 West Spain Street, Sonoma
(707) 996–2996, (800) 468–6016
www.sonomahotel.com

Situated on the northwest corner of Sonoma Plaza, this fine old hotel was originally a town hall built in the 1880s. Rooms are furnished with antique furniture and one, the Vallejo Room, has a bedroom suite of carved rosewood once owned by Gen. Mariano Vallejo's family (see our History chapter). All rooms are furnished in keeping with the 19th century, and all have been given names to match their decor—Bear Flag room, Yerba Buena, and Italian Suite. In one of the rooms, author/poet/actress Maya Angelou holed up to write her third novel. All 16 rooms have private baths and air-conditioning. Breakfast of fresh pastries, coffee, and juices is served in a quaint foyer that retains the original fireplace and stained glass windows.

Best Western Sonoma Valley Inn $$$$$
550 Second Street W., Sonoma
(707) 938–9200, (800) 334–5784
www.sonomavalleyinn.com

This hotel is of recent origin (built in 1987), but it has been designed in California Mission-style architecture to match the ambiance of the town's early Mexican heritage. One of its great assets is its location: It's only two blocks from the city's plaza (see our Shopping chapter), yet away from city hubbub with rooms that face onto an inner courtyard. You park your car outside your room, motel-style, yet your view is of the swimming pool, spa, gazebo, and fountain. Most rooms have patios or decks for outdoor privacy. The spacious rooms feature either a fireplace or a Jacuzzi bath. Open the refrigerator in your room, and you'll find a complimentary bottle of wine. Children 12 and younger stay free. A laundry room is available, and continental breakfast is delivered to your room.

Sheraton Petaluma Hotel $$$$
745 Baywood Drive, Petaluma
(707) 283–2888
www.sheratonpetaluma.com

Opened in summer 2002, this marina-front hotel featuring Asian architectural details has 183 guest rooms, including three suites. (The grand staircase is a stunner.) The setting is convenient to U.S. 101, yet the hotel offers views of adjacent pro-

Petaluma's newest hotel is the Sheraton, set on the city's picturesque marina. PHOTO: JEAN SAYLOR DOPPENBERG

tected wetlands along the Petaluma River, about 300 acres' worth. The rooms are decorated in earth tones and include state-of-the-art phone systems, in addition to the usual amenities you would expect from a Sheraton. Meeting spaces total nearly 10,000 feet, including a 4,300-square-foot grand ballroom. Begin your day in the fitness center, equipped with men's and women's saunas and outdoor swimming pool and spa. End your day dining at Jellyfish, which leans toward a fusion of Asian and Mediterranean cuisine (see our Restaurants chapter).

Best Western Petaluma Inn $$
200 South McDowell Boulevard, Petaluma
(707) 763–0994, (800) 297–3846
www.bestwestern.com

Surrounded by two shopping centers, this Best Western on Petaluma's east side is right off U.S. 101. The motel is about 1 mile from the city's historic downtown area and the quaint Victorian homes of the west side. It's also about 2 miles from the Petaluma Village Premium Outlets (see our Shopping chapter). The 75 guest rooms are pleasantly furnished, and the

amenities include coffeemakers, hair dryers, iron/ironing boards, two phone lines, and a data port. A small meeting room can accommodate 40 persons. There's a Carrows restaurant and lounge on-site, too.

Quality Inn $$
5100 Montero Way, Petaluma
(707) 664–1155, (800) 228–5160
www.lokhotels.com

Built in 1985, the hotel comprises seven clustered Cape Cod-style buildings nestled amid landscaped grounds and redwood arbors planted with grapes. Its 111 rooms include 36 with in-room spas and four two-room suites with private spas. The outdoor pool is surrounded by a large sundeck with a sauna adjacent. Its location near Adobe Creek Golf & Country Club and its Robert Trent Jones–designed course makes it appealing to golfers (see the Golf section of our Parks and Recreation chapter), and shoppers will be glad to know it's the closest inn to Petaluma Village Premium Outlets (see our Shopping chapter). A full continental breakfast is served.

DoubleTree Hotel $$$$
1 DoubleTree Drive, Rohnert Park
(707) 584–5466, (800) 222–TREE
www.doubletree.com

Set on 22 acres between two golf courses, the hotel evokes Sonoma County's Spanish heritage with tiled roofs and arched windows. For business travelers, the DoubleTree offers every convenience and amenity necessary for successful meetings and full conferences, including 17,000 square feet of conference space; it's also conveniently located near U.S. 101 and offers express bus service to San Francisco airport. But those on business will also find, as do great numbers of tourists, that it's a very enjoyable resort, with 245 luxurious guest rooms and suites, a restaurant, a pool and Jacuzzi, and live entertainment.

Vineyard Creek Hotel, Spa & Conference Center $$$$
170 Railroad Square, Santa Rosa
(707) 528–4542, (888) 920–0008
www.vineyardcreek.com

This new hotel in downtown Santa Rosa opened its doors in summer 2002. The $30 million property with Mediterranean-inspired architecture and courtyards was built in a unique fashion: Its foundation is a combination of concrete and 2,000 plastic tubs, a revolutionary technique that allows the adobe clay soil of our region to expand and contract with the changing seasons. On top of those tubs are 155 plush rooms with upscale amenities and the extra touches business travelers appreciate: T1 lines and dual-line speaker phones with voice mail and complimentary domestic and international newspapers. Some rooms have fireplaces and whirlpools; all have deluxe mini-bars. The Seafood Brasserie is the hotel's fine dining establishment, focusing on French-inspired fresh seafood dishes (see our Restaurants chapter). You can get an in-room massage treatment, too. Facials, massages, bodywork, and treatments of many types are offered, including a warmed river-rock massage.

The 21,000-square-foot conference center is the largest in the area, with a multitude of meeting rooms, big and small. All this, and it's a two-minute walk to Railroad Square's restaurants and antiques stores.

Flamingo Resort Hotel & Fitness Center $$$
2777 Fourth Street, Santa Rosa
(707) 545–8530, (800) 848–8300
www.flamingoresort.com

Lush landscaping makes this resort hotel very appealing, both as a vacation spot and as a business center offering conference facilities for 600 people. For the harried executive or the tourist, there's plenty of physical activity available, including a heated Olympic-size pool, Jacuzzi, tennis courts, a lighted jogging path, basketball and volleyball courts, and table tennis. Also available for a modest fee is the Montecito Heights Health & Racquet Club. The Flamingo's golf package makes good use of the nearby Fountaingrove course, as well as other top Wine Country links. The 170 rooms are luxuriously appointed with elegant furnishings—some rooms also have copy machines and refrigerators. This is a favorite base camp for Hollywood moviemakers when they come to town. In fact, portions of the blockbuster *Bandits* were filmed at the Flamingo.

Fountain Grove Inn $$$$
101 Fountaingrove Parkway, Santa Rosa
(707) 578–6101, (800) 222–6101
www.fountaingroveinn.com

In harmony with the natural environment, the Fountain Grove Inn's design is all redwood and stone, sweeping low across historic Fountaingrove Ranch. The lobby, too, is far from ordinary, dominated by a large redwood sculpture of the legendary horse, Equus. Utmost restraint and understated elegance mark the inn's 125 rooms, which are almost Oriental in their simplicity. All rooms have separate dressing alcoves, double closets, and work spaces with modern dataports for traveling executives. The inn's pool, waterfall, and spa offer a charming view of the historic Round Barn, which sits atop a small nearby hill. Guests gather in the restaurant each morning for a generous buffet breakfast. The inn's restaurant, not surprisingly called Equus, carries out the theme, with the legendary horse etched in glass and redwood carvings.

Sonoma County Hilton $$$$
3555 Round Barn Boulevard, Santa Rosa
(707) 523–7555, (800) 445–8667
www.hilton.com

Just off U.S. 101 north of downtown Santa Rosa on 13 acres of Fountaingrove Ranch, this hotel has let stand the historic landmark known as the Round Barn to mark its entrance. This chalet-style hotel has 246 rooms and suites and boasts many amenities, including a state-of-the-art in-room phone system, business center, the award-winning Harvest Grill restaurant, an outdoor patio with a panoramic view of the Santa Rosa valley, a Junior Olympic-size swimming pool, and an on-site workout facility.

Vintners Inn $$$$$
4350 Barnes Road, Santa Rosa
(707) 575–7350, (800) 421–2584
www.vintnersinn.com

Your first vision at Vintners Inn may make you feel as if you've dropped into a charming European village. From the French country decor to the arched windows and wrought-iron railings, the hotel exudes Old World atmosphere—a group of three red-roofed buildings is arranged around a plaza and fountain, surrounded by 45 acres of vineyards. Many of the oversized rooms in this Provence-inspired inn have fireplaces, exposed-beam ceilings, and pine furniture, some of which dates back to the turn of the century. Ground-floor rooms have patios; second-floor suites have balconies with vineyard or courtyard views. On the premises is John Ash & Co., a nationally acclaimed restaurant serving some of the best cuisine in Sonoma County. Its wine list won the Sonoma Harvest Fair Sweepstakes Award three years running (see our Restaurants chapter).

Courtyard Santa Rosa by Marriott $$$
175 Railroad Street, Santa Rosa
(707) 573–9000, (800) 354–7672
www.marriott.com

Right on the edge of historic Railroad Square, this Marriott hotel has close access to enough antiques shops to delight any collector looking for bargains or the unusual. All the standard amenities are available in this 138-room inn. Kids will love the swimming pool, spa, and in-room movies, and adults may wander down for cocktails between 5:00 and 10:00 P.M., or to any of the wonderful restaurants located within walking distance. Kids younger than 12 stay free. There are wheelchair-accessible rooms.

Hotel La Rose $$$$
308 Wilson Street, Santa Rosa
(707) 579–3200, (800) 527–6738
www.hotellarose.com

A quaint and romantic hotel in Santa Rosa's historic Railroad Square, Hotel La Rose was reconstructed in 1985 and designated a National Historic Landmark. The hotel is graced with a charming English Country interior decor that belies the fact that this is a very modern hotel. The four-story hotel has elevator access to its 29 nonsmoking rooms, and the carriage house, added in 1985, has 20 additional guest rooms (three are designated for smokers) built around a lovely courtyard. A 1998 remodel included marbled bathrooms and a spa. One of the hotel's great assets is its proximity to the restaurants in Railroad Square, including its own, Josef's.

> **Insiders' Tip**
>
> For a room like no other, book one of the luxurious tent cabins at Safari West, an African-style wildlife preserve located between Santa Rosa and Calistoga. You'll get a king-size bed and private bath, and the sounds of exotic animals nearby. See our Attractions chapter for more details.

Northern Sonoma

Hotel Healdsburg $$$$$
25 Matheson Street, Healdsburg
(707) 431–2800, (800) 889–7188
www.hotelhealdsburg.com

The biggest thing to pop up in Healdsburg in quite some time is this three-story, 55-room, $21 million luxury hotel that overlooks the quaint plaza in central Healdsburg. Big, because it rises grandly on the west side of the plaza (and will forever change the small-town feel of the town square, some locals fear). Nonetheless, it's proven extremely popular with visitors, and made the list of "100 Great Escapes for 2002" compiled by Travel & Leisure magazine.

The rooms all feature oversized bathrooms with walk-in showers and soaking tubs, French doors opening to private balconies, wood floors with Tibetan rugs, bathrobes and fine linens, and the usual modern amenities for business travelers. Even more luxurious suites are available (there are six of them), if that's your pleasure. Room service is offered from the Dry Creek Kitchen (see our Restaurants chapter) and breakfast is delivered to your door. The lobby features a grappa bar, the garden has a 60-foot pool, and there's a cardio-fitness room for a quick workout. All this and a spa, too! You can get pampered to your heart's content here, from massages to facials to a couples room with a soaking tub for two.

Duchamp Hotel $$$$$
421 Foss Street, Healdsburg
(707) 431–1300, (800) 431–9341
www.duchamphotel.com

This contemporary European-style hotel is made up of 10 cottage suites that are all truly unique, with artist Marcel Duchamp as the inspiration and the namesake. Unlike any lodgings in Wine Country, six of the rooms are poolside and creekside "villas" that are nearly spartan in their luxurious opulence. The four "artist cottages" are named Man Ray, Mirô, Picasso, and Andy Warhol. The latter, once a small house, is now a tasteful salute to Andy's genius and style. All the rooms feature modern amenities, fireplaces, down comforters on king-size beds, and fabulous bathrooms with spa showers (the Warhol room has a sunken Japanese soaking tub, too). The complimentary breakfast will start your day off right, and the 50-foot pool and heated Jacuzzi beckon after wine tasting and sight-seeing.

No less than Conde Nast Traveller magazine proclaimed the Duchamp as "one of the world's top 25 new hot hotels." It's a great location, down a quiet side road off the main thoroughfare through Healdsburg, yet an easy two-block walk to the shops and restaurants on the town's plaza. This is a nonsmoking property that is unsuitable for children. English, German, and French are all spoken here.

Best Western Dry Creek Inn $$
198 Dry Creek Road, Healdsburg
(707) 433–0300, (800) 222–5784
www.drycreekinn.com

The distinguishing factor here is this motel's outstanding location for wine touring in the beautiful Dry Creek Valley. The 102 rooms (including some "executive mini-suites") are pleasant, in the standard motel style. A continental breakfast is included. There's a pool, whirlpool, and exercise room.

Travelodge/Vineyard Valley Inn Motel $$$
178 Dry Creek Road, Healdsburg
(707) 433–0101, (800) 499–0103
www.travelodge.com

Built in 1992, this is not your ordinary Travelodge. The Vineyard Valley Inn Motel has 23 rooms and suites that blend into the Wine Country setting, while still providing all the modern amenities that seasoned travelers have come to expect. Rooms are furnished with two double beds or one queen. A two-room suite is available with wet bar, refrigerator, and entertainment area.

Geyserville Inn $$$
21714 Geyserville Avenue, Geyserville
(707) 857–4343, (877) 857–4343
www.geyservilleinn.com

Situated at the north end of the town of Geyserville and surrounded by vineyards, the location of this hotel is ideal for visiting Dry Creek and Alexander Valley wineries, as well as hitting the bike trails that crisscross this rural countryside. It's also close to Lake Sonoma (see our On the Water chapter). The 38 rooms have a Wine Country feel, decorated in shades of vineyard green and the russet colors of autumn. Rooms are graced with various amenities—for example, patios or balconies and fireplaces—and guests can enjoy the swimming pool and spa. A continental breakfast is served each morning.

Sonoma Coast

Bodega Bay Lodge Resort $$$$$
103 Coast Highway 1, Bodega Bay
(707) 875-3525, (800) 368-2468
www.woodsidehotels.com

Luxurious and intimate on eight landscaped acres, the lodge overlooks wildflower-covered dunes, protected marshlands, the Pacific Ocean, and the gentle surf of Doran Beach. While it's close enough to enjoy the sound of the surf, the wood-shingled lodge is sheltered from coastal winds. All 84 spacious guest rooms have fireplaces, private balconies, and original artwork. Many feature vaulted ceilings, spa baths, refrigerators, wet bars, and coffeemakers. The 5,000-square-foot conference center is impressive, with high, arched ceilings supported by thick beams of polished oak. The Duck Club Restaurant can be counted on for imaginative cuisine. Complimentary wine is served in the late afternoon. An 18-hole Robert Trent Jones-designed golf course is next door at Bodega Harbour Golf Links (see our Parks and Recreation chapter).

Inn at the Tides $$$$
800 Coast Highway 1, Bodega Bay
(707) 875-2751, (800) 541-7788
www.innatthetides.com

Six coastal acres with natural landscaping surround this inn, which is actually an enclave of 12 separate lodges that appear to be part of the rumpled hills and tawny headlands. Each of the 86 guest quarters overlooks Bodega Bay, home port for one of the coast's most productive fishing fleets. Amenities include a heated indoor-outdoor pool, spacious spa, soothing sauna, and luxurious logo bathrobes. A continental breakfast is served, and gour-

In Bodega Bay, the Inn at the Tides has bay views from most of its rooms, as well as a relaxing pool/spa/sauna complex. PHOTO: JEAN SAYLOR DOPPENBERG

met cuisine is featured in the Bay View Restaurant (see our Restaurants chapter).

Fort Ross Lodge $$
20705 Coast Highway 1, Jenner
(707) 847–3333
www.fortrosslodge.com

Just north of historic Fort Ross State Park (see our History and Attractions chapters), the lodge is situated above a sheltered cove where seals lounge on rocky outcroppings. There's plenty of space in the guest rooms to stretch out and relax, or you can unwind in the hot tub and sauna. The 22 rooms are decorated in natural tones and hues. There's a barbecue on each deck and a country store across the highway. Children younger than 12 stay free. Intimate, secluded suites are available for adults only. And the lodge now offers a private two-bedroom home.

Salt Point Lodge $
23255 Coast Highway 1, Timber Cove
(707) 847–3234
www.saltpoint.com

This is a well-maintained, older motor lodge, with 16 rooms. Situated on a knoll overlooking the ocean, Salt Point Lodge includes a restaurant with a full bar. Lovely gardens surround the place, and it's open year-round. There are TVs and VCRs in the rooms, but no phones. Besides the nearby beaches, there are miles of hiking trails to explore.

Sea Ranch Lodge $$$$$
60 Sea Wall Drive, Sea Ranch
(707) 785–2371, (800) 732–7262
www.searanchlodge.com

On bluffs above the Pacific, this lodge features one of the best ocean vistas in the Wine Country. All but one of its 20 rooms face the sea, and cozy window seats offer front-row viewing for spectacular sunsets. If you're in need of a peaceful getaway, this is the place. Rooms are walled in knotty pine, and the aura is rustic. Hiking trails along the bluffs are well marked, and you can follow them down to the beach. A challenging 18-hole golf course is available, and there's a restaurant. Some units have fireplaces, and family units are available. All are luxuriously appointed.

West County/Russian River

Fife's Resort $$
16467 Highway 116 E., Guerneville
(707) 869–9500, (800) 734–3371
www.fifes.com

Among the most popular gay resorts on the Russian River, Fife's features 15 forested acres of towering coast redwood. The resort offers cabins that range from the basic one-room variety to an elegant two-bedroom, two-bath deluxe version with fireplace and hot tub. The restaurant at Fife's includes a fine selection of continental dishes with fresh local vegetables and house-made desserts. The resort is also walking distance to downtown Guerneville, where you can peruse the antiques shops, have coffee at a local cafe, or dance the night away at Club FAB (see our Nightlife chapter).

The Brookside Lodge Motel $$
14100 Brookside Lane, Guerneville
(707) 869–2470, (800) 551–1881
www.sonic.net/welcome

A charming family resort located at the edge of Guerneville's Korbel vineyards and bordered by Fife's Creek, the Brookside offers 36 newly redecorated spacious rooms, some with their own patio and kitchen. Amenities include a pool, sauna, Ping-Pong table, and satellite TV. The lodge also offers one- and two-bedroom cottages, some of which have a private hot tub and spectacular Wine Country views.

Mendocino County

U.S. 101

Days Inn $
950 North State Street, Ukiah
(707) 462–7584
www.daysinn.com

Yes, it's a chain, but the rooms are spacious and luxuriously decorated; the inn is comfortable and convenient, and the staff is professional. This Days Inn has 54 units, a swimming pool, and a restaurant. It offers free local calls, and pets are welcome. Breakfast is included in the nightly rate.

Discovery Inn $$
1340 North State Street, Ukiah
(707) 462–8873

This is the largest of Ukiah's motels, with 177 units, two heated pools, four indoor spas, a restaurant, and a conference room. A workout room is a recent addition, and guest laundry facilities are available. Complimentary breakfast is included.

Baechtel Creek Inn $
101 Gregory Lane, Willits
(707) 459–9063, (800) 459–9911
www.baechtelcreek.com

An attractive two-story hotel built in 1992, Baechtel Creek Inn has 46 rooms, a heated swimming pool, spa, and conference rooms. Baechtel Creek runs right past the inn, providing considerable entertainment for kids and grown-ups by attracting such wild creatures as rabbits, squirrels, deer, and an occasional turtle.

Mendocino Coast

Breakers Inn $$$$$
39300 South Coast Highway 1, Gualala
(707) 884–3200, (800) BREAKER
www.breakersinn.com

The 24 oceanfront rooms at the Breakers are designed to offer spectacular panoramic views of the dramatic coast through large picture windows and spacious decks. Enjoy incredible ocean sunsets and the sound of waves crashing on the shore. In winter and spring, the deck provides a front-row seat to the migration of gray whales. Each room is individually decorated in the theme of a country or state in a seacoast region, highlighting locations such as Cape Cod, Ireland, and Japan. All rooms except the three garden rooms feature decks, fireplaces, wet bars, and ocean views, and deluxe continental breakfast is included each morning. The Luxury Spa Room is near a picture window so you can soak and enjoy the view.

Gualala Hotel $
39301 South Coast Highway 1, Gualala
(707) 884–3441

Built in 1903, the Gualala Hotel has weathered a century of Pacific sun and storm. Yet the building's classic facade looks much the same as it did a hundred years ago, when travelers waited on its deck for the coastal stage to arrive. Five of the hotel's 19 rooms boast a beautiful ocean view and private bath—the remaining rooms share hall baths in the European style. Though some of the individual accommodations are a bit cramped, a large central sitting room, complete with sofas and a wood-burning stove, offers plenty of space to snuggle up with a good book or to enjoy a board game. A restaurant and saloon are on the premises—the latter features a mahogany bar where you can sip your favorite vintage or brew, while drinking in the local color.

Greenwood Pier Inn $$$
5928 South Coast Highway 1, Elk
(707) 877–9997
www.greenwoodpierinn.com

Perched atop a high bluff overlooking the sea, the Greenwood Pier Inn is a quiet, meditative spot, resplendent in colorful flower gardens. The inn's 12 rooms are located in several architecturally interesting buildings, such as the Cliffhouse, Garden Cottage, and North and South Sea Castles. The latter pair indeed resemble castle towers, and each has a tub in the uppermost level—perfect for soaking your weary bones while scanning the horizon

---

Insiders' Tip

The best place to observe seals is at the mouth of the Russian River at Jenner. If you want to climb down to the beach to get a close-up photo, you must stay at least 100 yards from the animals. Getting too close can result in a fine, so bring a good zoom lens.

Perched high above the Pacific Ocean, the Greenwood Pier Inn could be mistaken for a Zen Buddhist retreat. PHOTO: JOHN NAGIECKI

for whales. The Lighthouse Suite in the main house has a cupola that offers an even more lofty perspective on the mighty Pacific beyond. Other inn amenities include fireplaces, private decks, nearby hiking trails along the bluffs, and in-room therapeutic massage.

Albion River Inn $$$$
3790 North Coast Highway 1, Albion
(707) 937–1919, (800) 479–7944
www.albionriverinn.com

Six miles south of Mendocino, Albion River Inn occupies a prime oceanfront spot on 10 secluded acres of gardens and ocean bluffs. Guests are quartered in 20 cliff-side, New England-style rooms for two, most in duplex arrangements and all with spectacular ocean views. All have fireplaces and private decks, and many have a spa tub or tub for two. A full breakfast is included in the adjoining restaurant, which shares the view.

Hill House Inn $$$$
10701 Palette Drive, Mendocino
(707) 937–0554, (800) 422–0554
www.hillhouseinn.com

You'd swear you were on the New England coast. The Hill House Inn captures the essence of the coast of Maine in the spectacular and unspoiled land and sea along California's scenic Highway 1. Forty-four guest rooms feature brass beds with comforters, lace curtains, elegant wooden furnishings, and the convenience of private baths. Hill House not only attracts vacationers but also caters to seminars and small conferences, with rooms designed to accommodate up to 100 people. A chapel is available for wedding ceremonies.

Heritage House $$$$
5200 Coast Highway 1, Little River
(707) 937–5885, (800) 235–5885
www.heritagehouseinn.com

Sprawling across 37 private acres of pristine coastline, Heritage House is a classic country inn, opened in 1949 and still maintained by the same family. A total of 64 accommodations are mainly grouped in clusters of two, three, or four private rooms under a common roof, which imparts a cottagelike feeling. One of the favorites is the sumptuous Carousel set of suites, housed in a secluded building offering unobstructed ocean views, huge decks, and elegant furnishings. The Water Tower suite includes a spiral staircase leading to a sleeping loft. But the most requested rooms were built for the filming of the movie *Same Time Next Year*, which was written while author Bernard Slade stayed at the inn. Dining at Heritage House is a world-class experience (see our Restaurants chapter).

Stanford Inn by the Sea $$$$$
Coast Highway 1 and Comptche-Ukiah Road, Mendocino
(707) 937–5615, (800) 331–8884
www.stanfordinn.com

This elegantly rustic lodge has so many diversions that guests will find all they need here. A firm believer in preserving the health of our environment, owner Jeff Stanford offers guests bicycles for local transport and a fleet of canoes and kayaks for paddling up Big River. His terraced gardens are tended organically, and he also keeps grazing llamas, horses, and a few cats. Jeff serves vegetarian dishes in the Ravens restaurant, along with organic wines. Hors d'oeuvres are available in the evening, champagne with breakfast.

The site is stunning, sloping from a high meadow down to the sea. And the 33 accommodations have all the amenities expected of the finest hotels—wood-burning fireplaces, down comforters, ocean views, decks, refrigerators, VCRs. Some have kitchens. There's a heated indoor swimming pool and group Jacuzzi/sauna.

Mendocino Hotel $$$$
45080 Main Street, Mendocino
(707) 937–0511, (800) 548–0513
www.mendocinohotel.com

Built in 1878 the venerable Mendocino Hotel is an opulent Victorian jewel named "best small hotel in Northern California" by *Focus* magazine. Guests register at a teller's cage from an old bank and congregate for drinks in a front parlor replete with antiques, leaded windows, and Oriental rugs. The historic section offers suites with balconies overlooking the Pacific as well as rooms with shared baths in the European style. The garden suites, across the courtyard, are fully modern but still maintain the Victorian decor. Look for lots of solid wood paneling, leaded glass, brass, and walls papered in period fabrics in the 50 rooms in the main hotel and the garden suites. An elegant dining room features California cuisine and an extensive wine list. The Garden Cafe is open in the daytime, as is the Garden Bar. The Lobby Bar operates in the evening. Advance reservations are almost mandatory during the summer months.

Anchor Lodge Motel $
32260 North Harbor Drive, Fort Bragg
(707) 964–4283
www.wharf-restaurant.com

Located in the heart of Noyo Fishing Village, Anchor Lodge has been a focal point for visitors and locals for more than 40 years. You can't get much closer to the water without being in it. There are 18 rooms here, and guests have their pick of four options: economy (two persons), waterfront (two persons), or an apartment with kitchen for two or four persons.

Harbor Lite Lodge $
120 North Harbor Drive, Fort Bragg
(707) 964–0221, (800) 643–2700
www.harborlitelodge.com

This rustic redwood motel has balconies that overlook Noyo River and its fishing fleet. If you're awake in the early dawn, you can see the lights of the fleet as boats head out for the day's fishing, stretching in a colorful parade out to sea. In late afternoon, the parade reenters the harbor. The lodge has 79 comfortable rooms, some with wood-burning stoves. A meeting center for business or educational conferences has two large rooms accommodating 30 and 50 people, respectively. Complimentary coffee, tea, and cocoa are served in the lobby each morning.

North Cliff Hotel $$$$
1005 South Main Street, Fort Bragg
(707) 962–2500, (866) 962–2550
www.fortbragg.org

This is Fort Bragg's showiest hotel, perched at the entrance to Noyo Harbor. From your private balcony you can watch the fishing boats go out to sea in the morning, and then wave to them when they return at night—it's that close to the waterway. With all rooms facing the ocean, the views are mesmerizing (bring binoculars for scanning the horizon)—even as you take the waters in your private spa tub next to the window. All rooms have fireplaces, mini-refrigerators stocked with juice and water, microwaves, and plush bathrobes. A continental breakfast is left at your door each morning. Not all rooms have the spa tubs, but most rooms have king-size beds.

Hi-Seas Inn $$
1201 North Main Street, Fort Bragg
(707) 964–5929, (800) 990–7327
www.callodging.com

All 15 of the rooms here have a full ocean view. Just slide back the big glass door that leads to the deck. Between the deck and the ocean is a two-acre lawn. And right behind the Inn is a 10-mile hiking trail that goes through Fort Bragg and back into the nearby hills.

Pine Beach Inn & Suites $$
16801 North Coast Highway 1, Fort Bragg
(707) 964–5603
www.pinebeachinn.com

You can walk to a beach and cove from this 50-room hotel, which is on 12 acres of landscaped grounds in a majestic setting of redwoods. The beach is secluded, the private path is paved, and you'll enjoy breathtaking views all the way down to the mighty Pacific, as it thunders in against the high rocks and cliffs. The rooms (nine are suites) are large, decorated with fine furniture, and comforters and pillow shams adorn the beds; 24 of the units have ocean views. If you're in the mood for tennis, championship courts await, offering the chance to lob into the clear blue skies.

Seabird Lodge $$
191 South Street, Fort Bragg
(707) 964–4731, (800) 345–0022
www.seabirdlodge.com

One of the best-known features of this 65-room motel is a continuing package special that includes passage on the Skunk Train. The train, of course, travels between Fort Bragg and Willits (see our Attractions chapter), and most visitors find an overnight stay in Fort Bragg to be a favorable option. The package deal may vary (it seldom does), but it usually includes two nights' lodging, two Skunk Train tickets, breakfast each morning, and dinner one evening at your choice of three restaurants.

The Seabird will also shuttle you to and from the depot. The lodge has an indoor pool and hot tub, and there is a restaurant right next door.

Super 8 $
888 South Main Street, Fort Bragg
(707) 964–4003, (800) 206–9833
www.super8.com

This inn offers affordable accommodations, a convenient location, and old-fashioned hospitality. The 54 rooms have cable TV and private phones, and there is a full-service restaurant on the premises. Staff will be delighted to give a rundown on all the unique natural wonders to be explored in the vicinity—Mackerricher State Park, for instance, or Glass Beach or Pudding Creek Headlands—as well as family activities available on sea and land.

Vista Manor Lodge $$
1100 North Main Street, Fort Bragg
(707) 964–4776, (800) 821–9498
www.callodging.com

Located at the north end of Fort Bragg, about a mile from downtown, this Best Western motel features 55 units. There's an indoor heated pool, complimentary continental breakfast, and a coffeemaker in every room. All rooms have ocean views, and a nearby tunnel dips beneath Highway 1, giving you about five minutes to walk to the beach.

Vacation Rentals

Napa County

Napa Valley Cottages
(707) 963–5343
www.vineyardcottages.com

This service specializes in placing couples in rented cottages located on private estates, with short- and long-term rates available. Rates run from $175 to $750 per night, depending on the cottage you choose. But calling them "cottages" may be an understatement. For instance, the carriage house at the six-acre Bella Costa Sorrento estate is a secluded, two-story brick structure built in 1865. Upstairs are two bedrooms with their own bathrooms; the living room, kitchen, and dining room are downstairs. A private hot tub is hidden outside in the trees.

Sonoma County

Russian River Vacation Homes
14080 Mill Street, Guerneville
(707) 869–9030,
(800) 310–0804 (in California),
(800) 997–3312
www.riverhomes.com

Since 1975 this firm has provided a large selection of vacation rental homes throughout western Sonoma County at nightly rates ranging from $145 to $450; weekly rates from $550 to $1,600.

Russian River Getaways
14075 Mill Street, Guerneville
(707) 869–4560, (800) 433–6673
www.rrgetaways.com

This friendly rental company would like you to "experience getaway heaven in your very own home away from home." All the homes they offer are first-class, with many choices in size, location, and amenities. Picture yourself in a cozy hideaway for two in the redwoods or rendezvous with your family or friends in a beach house that sleeps 18. Or you might prefer an elegant lodge with a dramatic river view in the wine-tasting region. Many houses are dog-friendly, and there's only a two-night minimum. Prices range from $125 to $750 per night, $600 to $4,500 per week.

Sea Coast Hide-a-Ways
21350 North Coast Highwy 1, Jenner
(707) 847–3278, (800) 937–7546

You have a choice here of oceanside vistas or seclusion among the redwoods. Hot tubs and fireplaces are featured, with boat rentals available at Sea Coast's Timber Cove boat landing.

Rams Head Realty
1000 Annapolis Road, Sea Ranch
(707) 785–2427, (800) 785–3455
www.ramshead.com

More than 120 vacation rentals are offered from two-night stays to multiple weeks. Sites are available in the meadows, in the forest, or on the oceanfront. The most desirable oceanfront sites offer grand vistas and the dramatic crashing of the waves.

Mendocino County

Coast Getaways
10501 Ford Street, Mendocino
(707) 937–9200, (800) 525–0049
www.coastgetaways.com

If you're looking for a romantic studio for two or a large house that will hold your whole family, this service can match you up with one of more than 30 homes along a 20-mile stretch of the Mendocino County coastline from Albion to Cleone. Choose from oceanfront studios or bungalows nestled in the redwoods, with hot tubs or without—whatever appeals to you. Like the properties themselves, the fees are all over the map.

Mendocino Coast Reservations
1000 Main Street, Mendocino
(707) 937–5033, (800) 262–7801
www.mendocinovacations.com

Here you'll find listings of the finest in weekend and vacation lodging, from cozy cottages to oceanfront estates. Some are right in the village of Mendocino, some on the coast, some in the forest. In July and August, a three-day minimum is imposed. A wide range of rental fees varies due to weekly or weekend occupancy, time of year, size, and property amenities.

Bed-and-Breakfast Inns

Napa County
Sonoma County
Mendocino County

There's nothing quite like entering a rambling, antiques-filled home—with a grandfather clock tick-tocking in the corner and a scrapbook of family photos perched on a pedestal next to a marble fireplace—to make you turn off the cell phone and lose yourself in a crystal goblet of tawny Port. If this doesn't describe your own home life, we understand. In large part, that's probably why you're visiting Wine Country—to capture the serenity of another place and time. It's not only possible here, it's available in abundance. Scores of Wine Country lodgings fit the description above. They may not be exactly like grandma's house, but one of them might be the next best thing.

If you love bed-and-breakfast inns, you've come to the right place. In Wine Country you'll find them everywhere, from grand and historic to more modest and modern. Unlike hotels and motels, B&Bs are a throwback to a time when lodgings were small and homespun, offering travelers not just a bed and a basin but a social experience as well. That basic premise still holds here, but the B&Bs themselves and the amenities they offer are nothing like what travelers of yesteryear could have imagined.

In this chapter, a wide range of B&B styles and choices are offered, from easy-on-the-budget to top-of-the-line. Unless you read otherwise, you can expect that the inns listed feature rooms with private bathrooms. Unlike grandma's house, some have gone high-tech, complete with TVs, phones, and computer ports. Afternoon munchies of wine or port and hors d'oeuvres are usually offered. Oh, yes, and they serve breakfast—in most cases, a morning meal like you've never seen before. Be aware that nearly all innkeepers prohibit smoking in the rooms and do not allow pets. Many establishments also have a two-night minimum on weekends—always inquire when booking.

What about kids? B&Bs usually do not forbid children, and current California law apparently won't let them make any such prohibition. However, innkeepers acknowledge that many of their guests are attempting to get away from children for a few days. So, in general, assume that bringing the little ones along is not a good idea.

Price Code

Please refer to the dollar-sign code below for tariffs. Rates are for double occupancy on a weekend in high season (generally May through October). Most inns offer significant discounts for off-season or mid-week stays. Note that prices do not include taxes, gratuities, or services that are considered "extra."

$	Less than $120
$$	$121 to $150
$$$	$151 to $180
$$$$	More than $181

Napa County

The Blue Violet Mansion $$$$
443 Brown Street, Napa
(707) 253-2583, (800) 959-2583
www.bluevioletmansion.com

The Blue Violet Mansion won the Reader's Choice Award in 1996, outdistancing inns from all over North America. It isn't hard to see why. Every detail is celebrated with a flourish here, from the in-room Port (complimentary) and rack full of wine (pay as you go), to the brass door frame salvaged from the Bank of Italy, to the iron front gate reproduced to match the original. The Queen Anne Victorian home was built in 1886 by Emanuel Manasse, executive at Sawyer Tannery and pioneer of patent leather production. Manasse's trade is evident in a most distinctive feature—embossed leather wainscoting that runs through much of the house.

The Blue Violet Mansion has 17 rooms on three floors. Each of them has a king-size or queen-size bed and a modem jack. Two ground-floor rooms are equipped with Murphy beds, making them ideal for upscale corporate meetings. And upstairs is the Camelot Floor, four rooms painstakingly hand-painted in trompe l'oeil fashion. Book the Royal Suite and sip your wine from Arthur and Guinevere silver goblets. On the one-acre grounds you'll find a heated swimming pool, a spa, an herb garden, and roses.

Churchill Manor Bed & Breakfast Inn $$$$
485 Brown Street, Napa
(707) 253–7733, (800) 799–7733
www.churchillmanor.com

In the heart of the Fuller Park Historic District is a grandiose, three-story Second Empire mansion built in 1889 for local banker Edward Churchill. With close to 10,000 square feet of space (and that doesn't include the full basement or the pillar-supported, three-sided veranda), it was said to be the largest domicile in Napa Valley for decades. The interior is essentially unaltered. There are four grand parlor rooms with beveled and leaded glass and redwood moldings and fireplace frames.

Three of the inn's 10 guest rooms (all on the third floor) were undergoing major renovations as this book was being updated, with completion scheduled for spring 2003.

You get a full breakfast in the dining room, plus complimentary wine and cheese (and fresh-baked cookies) in the afternoon. Play croquet in the side garden, borrow a tandem bicycle, or just stroll around the acre of grounds and toast the fat wallet of Edward Churchill.

Cedar Gables Inn $$$$
486 Coombs Street, Napa
(707) 224–7969, (800) 309–7969
www.cedargablesinn.com

Chances are, you've never seen a house like this one. Designed by British architect Ernest Coxhead in 1892, it's an immense, brown-shingled home that you might expect to find on an estate in England's Cotswolds. In fact, the feeling here is decidedly masculine, making it a logical choice for not-better halves who begin whining when they hear the expression "bed-and-breakfast." Cedar Gables' nine guest rooms are sizable and brimming with period antiques. The Churchill Chamber, originally the master bedroom used by Edward and Alice Churchill, has a walnut-encased whirlpool tub to match the fireplace. Several of the rooms have old coal-burning fireplaces, converted to gas. Breakfast is served either at the long, formal dining room table or cafe-style in the adjacent sun room. Cedars, palm trees, and a cork oak shade the house in the summer.

Inn on Randolph $$$$
411 Randolph Street, Napa
(707) 257–2886, (800) 670–6886
www.innonrandolph.com

This modest, tasteful inn is on a quiet street in a neighborhood of historic

Insiders' Tip

If you want a bed-and-breakfast experience without the legwork, here are a couple groups that will help you select one. B&B Style covers our entire four-county area—reach them at (800) 995-8884 or (707) 942-2888. Wine Country Reservations is oriented toward Napa and Sonoma valleys; their number is (707) 257-7757.

homes. The main house, an 1860 Gothic Revival Victorian, has five rooms with seasonal themes (the fifth is called Equinox). Spring, for example, boasts intricate flowers painted on the walls and ceiling, and Autumn features a handcrafted bent-willow canopy bed. Five more expensive rooms are in the newly refurbished 1930s cottages. All of the cottages and some of the main-house rooms have gas fireplaces and two-person whirlpool tubs; some have private decks. Roses line the front walk, and the gardens are flanked by a common deck, a gazebo, and hammocks. The Inn on Randolph serves a full breakfast, and in-room massage can be arranged upon request.

The Beazley House $$$$
1910 First Street, Napa
(707) 257–1649, (800) 559–1649
www.beazleyhouse.com

On a row of rambling turn-of-the-century mansions, this house was originally built for local surgeon and politician Adolph Kahn in 1902, but he and his wife divorced and left the area seven years later. Subsequent owners included the Hanna Boys Center and San Francisco jet-setter Joan Hitchcock, who reputedly had an affair with JFK and for a fact had seven husbands.

The Beazley, the first B&B in the city of Napa, now has 11 rooms, 6 in the main house and 5 in the carriage house. The latter are large units, each with a fireplace and two-person spa tub. Ask for the Sun Room, a bright and nostalgic corner with a two-sided balcony and a 6-foot soaking tub. Full breakfast is served in the formal dining room. Children are permitted, and pets are assessed on a case-by-case basis.

Candlelight Inn $$$$
1045 Easum Drive, Napa
(707) 257–3717
www.candlelightinn.com

In the tradition of all good bed-and-breakfast inns, the Candlelight, an English Tudor–style mansion with 10 guest rooms, will pamper you with four-poster beds, French doors, private balconies, and a three-course breakfast. The Garden View room has a private entrance and deck, with—you guessed it—views of the garden and 30-by-60-foot swimming pool. Other rooms look out on the surrounding hills, and several rooms have Jacuzzi tubs for

Eleven comfortable rooms make up the Beazley House, Napa's first bed-and-breakfast inn. PHOTO: JEAN SAY-LOR DOPPENBERG

two and marble fireplaces. All rooms have TVs and phones.

Hennessey House $$$$
1727 Main Street, Napa
(707) 226–3774
www.hennesseyhouse.com

Adjacent to the Jarvis Conservatory on the fringe of Napa's turn-of-the-century downtown, Hennessey House is an East-lake-style Queen Anne built for Dr. Edwin Hennessey, one-time mayor of the town, in 1889. The 10 rooms (6 in the main residence, 4 in the carriage house) are air-conditioned, and most have canopy, brass, or feather beds. Some have claw-foot or two-person whirlpool tubs in the bathroom, and the carriage-house rooms have fireplaces.

Breakfast has been known to feature delights such as blueberry-stuffed French toast or basil-cheese strata. A hand-painted, stamped tin ceiling shelters the dining room. In the evening you can enjoy wine and cheese by the garden fountain.

Arbor Guest House $$$$
1436 G Street, Napa
(707) 252–8144
www.arborguesthouse.com

In the Napa neighborhood appropriately known as Old Town, the Arbor Guest House is a pretty, whitewashed Colonial with a porch swing in front and a shady garden in back. The house is compact, but the rooms—three units upstairs, two more in the original Carriage house—manage to be ample. Two of them have spa tubs, three have fireplaces, and the main-house rooms are cooled by a reliable cross-breeze (and air-conditioning, if things get serious). Breakfast is served in the dining room or the garden or, if you're staying in the carriage house, it is brought to your door with prior notice.

La Belle Epoque $$$$
1386 Calistoga Avenue, Napa
(707) 257–2161, (800) 238–8070
www.labelleepoque.com

In 1893 Napa's leading hardware dealer built this splendid Queen Anne for his infant daughter, who died shortly there-after. Tragic origins aside, La Belle Epoque

beams with class: multi-gabled dormers, Oriental carpets, divans, marble-topped dressers, and radiant stained glass, much of it transplanted from an old church. The inn has six rooms, with all the cozy alcoves and claw-foot tubs you would expect. You get your full breakfast in the formal dining room or on the garden patio.

The Old World Inn $$$$
1301 Jefferson Street, Napa
(707) 257–0112, (800) 966–6624
www.oldworldinn.com

This 1906 Victorian isn't as noisy as you might think, despite being situated on busy Jefferson Street (where it meets Calistoga Avenue). The inn is touched up in mellow pastel blue, rose, peach, and mint—colors inspired by Swedish artist Carl Larsson—and the interior walls bear hand-lettered quotations, most of which could be filed under the heading "Be Kind to Strangers." And they do practice what they preach.

You'll receive a complimentary carafe of local wine upon arrival, evening hors d'oeuvres such as smoked salmon or Moroccan eggplant on sourdough bread, and a late-night buffet of chocolate treats. Of course, you get a full, hot breakfast in the dining room. Some rooms have canopied beds; some have claw-foot tubs. Others have fireplaces and private Jacuzzis. There is also an outdoor Jacuzzi shared by all guests of the Old World Inn.

Brookside Vineyard Bed & Breakfast $$
3194 Redwood Road, Napa
(707) 944–1661

With seven acres of land, Brookside offers plenty of room for sequestering. Tom and Susan Ridley's homey spot is full of images and relics true to the house's Mission style. The three ground-floor guest rooms are off a long hallway, and each opens onto the garden. About half the acreage is devoted to vineyard, and visitors have been known to join the autumn crush. Elsewhere, fruit trees, California poppies, and Douglas fir Christmas trees abound, and a path descends to a creek-side clearing. (At least it's creekside when Redwood Creek is flowing.) Brookside has a swimming pool, and the largest bedroom has a dry sauna. The Ridleys accept personal checks, but no credit cards.

La Résidence $$$$
4066 St. Helena Highway N., Napa
(707) 253–0337, (800) 253–9203
www.laresidence.com

Is La Résidence a hotel disguised as a bed-and-breakfast inn or a B&B masquerading as a hotel? Does it matter when you're sitting in the elegant, sun-infused dining room at a table for two, eating a three-course breakfast from the fixed but ever-changing menu? La Res, as it is called, is a nice surprise within shouting distance of Highway 29. The 16 rooms and 4 suites, divided between the 1870 Gothic Revival mansion and the newer French Barn, are decorated in French Provincial style. Most include working fireplaces and patios or verandas. The inn sits on two and a half acres of heritage oaks, pines, and fledgling vines. There is a swimming pool, a separate Jacuzzi, and a small meeting room for up to 15 people. Smoking is prohibited in all rooms, and the place isn't really set up for children.

Oak Knoll Inn $$$$
2200 East Oak Knoll Avenue, Napa
(707) 255–2200
www.oakknollinn.com

The land around Oak Knoll Inn is part of Napa County's agricultural preserve, so businesses such as this are not allowed. Fortunately for its guests, the inn was here in 1984, before the prohibition. In effect, it has a virtual monopoly on 360-degree vineyard views. There is a big wooden deck outside the rooms, so you can spend all day looking at the Chardonnay and Merlot grapes before they head to Rutherford Hill, Beaulieu, or Trefethen, which is just down the road. Oak Knoll Inn has four units, each with a fireplace and private entrance. There is a heated pool and spa for common use. The place is known for its breakfasts; on one recent morning it included baked pears in cognac sauce, baked herbed eggs, and fresh muffins. But mostly the inn is renowned for the incredibly detailed itineraries that owner Barbara Passino customizes and prints out

for guests. This is not a good option for couples with children.

Maison Fleurie $$$$
6529 Yount Street, Yountville
(707) 944–2056, (800) 788–0369
www.foursisters.com

In the middle of Yountville (but a block away from most of the traffic) is this French-style country inn. The 100-year-old main building has 2-foot-thick stone walls, terra-cotta tile, and a gas fireplace in the brick parlor. Two other structures—the Old Bakery (a working bakery in the 1970s) and the carriage house—bring the total number of rooms to 13. You get a gourmet breakfast (or breakfast in bed if you'd rather) and a jar of homemade cookies in the lobby. There is a swimming pool, spa tub, and mountain bikes for guest use. Maison Fleurie is part of Four Sisters Inns, a group of nine bed-and-breakfast establishments, most of them on the California coast.

Bordeaux House $$$
6600 Washington Street, Yountville
(707) 944–2855, (800) 677–6370
www.bordeauxhouse.com

A mixture of new (1980) and old (1895) structures, this inn is a bit of a bargain for this neck of the woods. In the heart of Yountville, it is surrounded by lovely trees and gardens, and the world-class restaurants and shops of the whole town are within easy walking distance. (The French Laundry is just steps away, in fact.) The inn's newer, main building has five guest rooms with fireplaces and private patios or decks. Modern amenities are provided in each room; all have private exterior entrances. The Old Water Tower, overlooking the garden, is about 15 steps up and down. The inn's reception area is where you can enjoy your morning buffet breakfast and late afternoon Port and munchies.

Burgundy House Inn $$$
6711 Washington Street, Yountville
(707) 944–0889

Yountville's main drag may not be the place you'd expect to find an Old World country inn, but Burgundy House has the requisites. It's a durable cube with 22-inch-thick walls, hand-hewn posts and lintels, and lace curtains. Built as a brandy distillery in the 1890s from local fieldstone and river rock, it has also been a winery, a hotel, an antiques warehouse, and, now, a five-room inn. Buffet breakfast is served in the "distillery" or outside on the rose garden patio. Children older than 12 are permitted.

The Ink House $$$$
1575 St. Helena Highway S., St. Helena
(707) 963–3890, (800) 553–4343
members.aol.com/inkhousebb

If you have driven the length of Highway 29 a few times, you have no doubt taken notice of this remarkable house, a wedding-cake Italianate Victorian with a wraparound porch and a third-floor crow's nest. Built by Theron H. Ink in 1884, it's now a seven-room bed-and-breakfast inn where the highway meets Whitehall Lane. The Ink House has a formal parlor and dining room for guests. You get a full breakfast in the morning, appetizers and wine, usually poured by a local winery, in the afternoon. Tapestries and polished antiques abound, and paintings are hung with brocade.

The rooms are lovely but not huge—five have private baths; two share a bath. The observatory serves as the TV room. While taking advantage of the 360-degree panorama, you might pop in a video of *Wild in the Country*, an Elvis Presley romp filmed at the Ink House in 1960. The inn also offers 18-speed bicycles and an antique pool table in the basement. A steep staircase makes this an iffy choice for families with kids.

Shady Oaks Country Inn $$$$
399 Zinfandel Lane, St. Helena
(707) 963–1190
www.shadyoaksinn.com

The buildings are full of history at Shady Oaks, but it's the two acres of outdoor space that really sell the inn. On one side of the house is a working walnut orchard; on the other are grapevines. And in back, a twisted 100-year-old wisteria vine protects the patio. Shady Oaks offers two suites (each with private entrance) in a two-story, stone structure that operated as a winery from 1883 to 1887. Three

The third-floor observatory of The Ink House near St. Helena offers a spectacular 360-degree vista of the surrounding mountains and vineyards. PHOTO: JEAN SAYLOR DOPPENBERG

more rooms are found in John and Lisa Runnells' 1920s, Craftsman-style home. Each unit features its own small collection of antiques; particularly lovely are the beds, such as the brass and ivory king-size in the Winery Retreat. Three of the rooms have fireplaces, and the Sunny Retreat has an adjoining second bedroom.

Afternoon wine is served on the patio. Champagne breakfast, meanwhile, is a splendid affair likely to entail eggs Benedict or Belgian waffles served in elegant style. Besides advice on restaurants and attractions, they can usually set up private tours at lesser-known wineries. Please note that children are not recommended here.

La Fleur Bed and Breakfast Inn $$$$
1475 Inglewood Avenue, St. Helena
(707) 963–0233
www.lafleurinn.com

This is a classic Wine Country inn—an 1882 Queen Anne Victorian with vineyard views, on a quiet road in the heart of Napa Valley. Up a steep, curving staircase you'll find the guest units. All have private bathrooms. Four have old-fashioned tubs; four have fireplaces. The wonderfully bright Vineyard Room has a big balcony hanging over the vines. The inn is across the highway from V. Sattui (see our Wineries chapter) and next door to Villa Helena Winery, where guests are accompanied for special tours. A large buffet breakfast is served in the solarium or outside on the porch, depending on the weather. No credit cards.

Glass Mountain Inn $$$$
3100 Silverado Trail, St. Helena
(707) 968–9400, (877) 968–9400
www.glassmountaininn.com

Glass Mountain was named for its large deposits of obsidian, also known as "black glass." That obsidian is evident in the dining room of the Glass Mountain Inn, where guests can peer into a wine cave dug by Chinese laborers (originally for perishables, not Pinots) in the late 1800s. The house, with its wood shingles and steepled roof, isn't nearly as old as the cave. The inn has three large rooms with private baths, each room with individual strengths—the queen-size bed in the Mountain View Suite is framed by five arched windows; the Garden Suite has an oversized, oval whirlpool tub; and the Treetops Suite has a claw-foot tub and a private deck. Guests are greeted with a full breakfast each morning. Bring the children; they are welcome.

Cinnamon Bear Bed & Breakfast $$$$
1407 Kearney Street, St. Helena
(707) 963–4653, (888) 963–4600

The name accurately describes this inn at the corner of Kearney and Adams Streets in bucolic St. Helena. From the handmade quilts and floral wallpaper to the braided rugs to the army of antique teddy bears, it all adds up to cuteness. The ample, shingled Craftsman bungalow was built in 1904, a wedding gift for Susan Smith from her father. The man Susan married, Walter Metzner, later was mayor of St. Helena for 20 years. His former abode has been fabulously restored. Cinnamon Bear inn has three second-floor guest rooms, two with queen-size beds and one with a king-size. Proprietor Cathye Ranieri is a chef, so you can expect a complete and well-executed breakfast (on the porch if the weather is nice). Children 10 and older are welcome.

The Ambrose Bierce House $$$$
1515 Main Street, St. Helena
(707) 963–3003
www.ambrosebiercehouse.com

Ambrose Bierce was a novelist, a poet, an essayist, a cartoonist, and a noted misanthrope. He wrote *The Devil's Dictionary* before disappearing in Mexico in 1913. The 1872 Victorian home he left behind in St. Helena bears his name and offers visitors three lovely rooms and a covered balcony tucked next to a grand redwood tree. The entire inn was recently remodeled. The Ambrose Bierce Suite, secluded on the second floor, has a private sitting room (with a television) that can be converted into a second bedroom. All rooms have plush, raised beds; stools are provided to help you make your way up under the covers.

Like its sister bed-and-breakfast, Shady Oaks Country Inn (see write-up in this chapter), Ambrose Bierce House is guided by the Runnells family. A full champagne breakfast is served in the morning, premium wine and cheese in the evening. Each guest room is equipped with a crystal decanter of Port. Relax to classical music in the parlor, or soak in the home's hot tub. Parents, please note that children are not recommended here.

Forest Manor $$$$
415 Cold Springs Road, Angwin
(707) 965–3538, (800) 788–0364
www.forestmanorbandb.com

Six miles into the forest above St. Helena is this magnificent property with 20 acres of wooded trails and a huge 54-foot swimming pool. The six rooms are named for writers; the two honeymoon suites are the William Shakespeare and the Ernest Hemingway. All of the rooms have refrigerators and robes, and most have king-size beds, fireplaces, and Jacuzzis. A full gourmet breakfast is included in the tariff.

Scarlett's Country Inn $$$
3918 Silverado Trail, Calistoga
(707) 942–6669
www.members.aol.com/scarletts

A "country inn" can sometimes mean a suburban cul-de-sac and a large rose garden. But Scarlett's is the real thing, a bucolic acre midway between Calistoga and St. Helena, where guests share space with friendly dogs and chickens. The early-twentieth-century farmhouse now holds two of the three guest units—the Gamay Suite and the Camellia Suite, which actually can be opened into a full house for larger parties. Each room boasts a separate entrance, a queen-size bed, a TV, a microwave, and a fridge. But the outdoor space is the big selling point here: a hammock, a tree swing, an aviary with finches and canaries, a lush fig tree, a pine-protected swimming pool, and a spa. Guests can choose the time and place for their full breakfast—and you know where the eggs are from. Note that Scarlett's does not accept credit cards, though personal checks are all right. The inn is just south of Wermuth Winery.

Christopher's Inn $$$$
1010 Foothill Boulevard, Calistoga
(707) 942–5755
www.chrisinn.com

This inn proves the old adage that you can't judge a booking by its cover. The owner, an architect, joined an 80-year-old house with two cottages to make one large building. It's nice enough from the outside, but doesn't hint at the luxury held within the 22 rooms. Laura Ashley prints, exquisite antique desks, fresh flowers, and high, open ceilings—it's a tasteful experience. Some newly added rooms have private Jacuzzis. Breakfast—yogurt, baked cobbler, etc.—is delivered to your door. For those who must conduct a bit of business while relaxing in splendor, there are two small conference rooms with fax accessibility, and modem ports are available in most rooms.

Christopher's also has two voluminous flats in back, facing onto Myrtle Street, that sleep as many as five people. Children are allowed at the inn.

Wine Way Inn $$$
1019 Foothill Boulevard, Calistoga
(707) 942–0680, (800) 572–0679
www.napavalley.com/wineway

This bed-and-breakfast inn, opened in 1979, was the first in Calistoga. It's near Calistoga's busiest intersection, and the owners want you to know up front that there is some street noise. Nonetheless, from the solid oak front door with etched glass to the patchwork quilts in each second-story room, the owners have managed to create a pleasant environment in their circa-1915 home. In addition to the five interior rooms, the Calistoga Room is a detached unit—it's out by the multi-tiered deck that backs up to a wooded hillside. The breakfasts alternate daily between sweet and savory, with specialties such as frittata and tomato omelettes.

Falcons Nest $$$
471 Kortum Canyon Road, Calistoga
(707) 942–0758
www.falconsnestbb.com

The view is the attraction here. Sitting well above the valley floor, the many decks surrounding this inn offer spectacular panoramas of terraced vineyards and mountains. The seven-acre estate is nearly a mile off Highway 29 along a forested road. All the rooms have queen-size beds, private entries, and private baths. A Jacuzzi is available on the lower deck, and it makes an ideal spot for watching hawks and gliders circling overhead. A full breakfast is served each morning.

The Elms $$$$
1300 Cedar Street, Calistoga
(707) 942–9476, (800) 235–4316
www.theelms.com

A.C. Palmer, the first circuit judge of Napa and Sonoma Counties, went to France for his honeymoon sometime around 1870, and he and his bride returned to Calistoga with two important items: designs for a new home and a small number of elm seedlings. The house lives as The Elms, shaded by the now-towering trees. Without a doubt, it is one of the most impressive homes in the valley. Palmer ran a lumber yard just across the Napa River, and The Elms is full of richly detailed, hand-hewn wood. It's also brimming with antiques—mostly French— thanks to the current owners.

The inn has four rooms in the main house. Two of them face Cedar Street, while another (the one in which Audrey Hepburn once slept) gazes upon pretty Pioneer Park. At the rear of the property are three rooms in the refurbished carriage house, including the Honeymoon Cottage, a large unit with a two-person shower and views to the river. Five of the rooms have fireplaces, and all seven come with a TV, plus Port and chocolate. The Elms is not a good choice for those with children.

La Chaumiere $$$$
1301 Cedar Street, Calistoga
(707) 942–5139, (800) 474–6800
www.lachaumiere.com

La Chaumiere is a small, picturesque house with a pitched roof and an arched window that looks across the street to Pioneer Park. There are two well-appointed rooms in the house (one has a sitting room in addition to the bedroom), plus a detached cabin in the rear. The bathrooms are part of the attraction—one has antique lavender-and-black tile work, the other has a mirror framed by an old billiards cue-rack.

The log cabin, built in 1932, isn't exactly the kind Abe Lincoln grew up in. The whole-timber redwood uprights and crossbeams are complemented by touches of comfort, including a wood stove, a fireplace built of petrified wood, and a large kitchen. The outdoor common areas include a flowery patio and a treehouse built around the trunk of a redwood. You get a full breakfast in the morning, plus wine and cheese in the afternoon and Port in your room. La Chaumiere is just a block off Lincoln Avenue.

Scott Courtyard $$$
Chelsea Garden Inn
1443 Second Street, Calistoga
(707) 942–0948, (800) 942–1515
www.scottcourtyard.com

This small, six-suite bed-and-breakfast on the corner of Fair Way and Second Street tries for neither Victorian splendor nor designer finery. The hallmarks at Scott are service, comfortable outdoor space and, if you want it, privacy. Each unit has a sitting room, bedroom, and private bath; some have kitchen facilities. Children are allowed in some rooms, but are not really encouraged. Air-conditioning is provided in all rooms. There is a latticed courtyard, a pool and hot tub, a small aviary full of flitting finches, and an artist's studio that inspired guests are

Insiders' Tip

The last of the so-called Great Eight mansions built in Calistoga in the 1870s is now the Elms B&B, a Queen Anne Victorian Second Empire listed on the National Register of Historic Places.

allowed to use. (Local artists sometimes lead seminars there.) Breakfast, served in the bistro-style dining room or on the patio, tends to get rave reviews, with dishes such as banana-walnut pancakes and Thai chicken sausage.

Hideaway Cottages $$$
1412 Fair Way, Calistoga
(707) 942–4108
www.hideawaycottages.com

If you want a classic bed-and-breakfast experience without the breakfast, try this establishment on peaceful Fair Way. Look for the hedges and palm trees in front of a two-story gingerbread house. In back are 17 cottages facing onto a landscaped courtyard. Many of the rooms have full kitchens. Hideaway, an affiliate of Dr. Wilkinson's Hot Springs (see our Spas and Resorts chapter), has a large mineral pool and Spa Jet tub.

Wisteria Garden Bed & Breakfast $$$
1508 Fair Way, Calistoga
(707) 942–5358
www.bbinternet.com/wisteria

This circa-1910 Colonial Revival cottage, about halfway between Lincoln Avenue and the fairgrounds, takes its name from the 100-year-old wisteria vines that drape over the carport. Behind the house is an old valley oak that shades the two guest rooms. Both units have private baths, gas fireplaces, air-conditioning, refrigerators and microwaves, cable TV, and VCRs. Continental breakfast is served on weekends. While Wisteria Garden does not have an on-site pool, guests receive complimentary passes to take the plunge at a local spa.

Brannan Cottage Inn $$$$
109 Wapoo Avenue, Calistoga
(707) 942–4200
www.brannancottageinn.com

About 130 years ago, this spot had row upon row of one-story white bungalows, all with five-arched fronts, intricate gingerbread gable boards, wraparound porches, and scalloped cresting. Now only one of them remains on its original site, and it's a six-room inn. (Two of the rooms are out back in the carriage house.) The look of the place—the 11-foot ceilings, oak floors, and ceiling fans—whisks you right back to the days of Sam Brannan (see our History chapter). Each unit has a queen bed and a refrigerator. Full buffet breakfast is served in the dining room or on the patio. Children 12 and older are accepted.

Cottage Grove Inn $$$$
1711 Lincoln Avenue, Calistoga
(707) 942–8400, (800) 799–2284
www.cottagegrove.com

In stark contrast to the trailer park that occupied this space for many years, the Cottage Grove is decidedly high-end. That's appropriate, because long before the trailer park this was the promenade area of Brannan's Hot Springs Resort, the spa that gave birth to Calistoga (see our History chapter). The grove of Siberian elms was planted by Brannan in the 1850s, and today they form an effective visual barrier to the traffic of Lincoln Avenue.

Each of Cottage Grove's 16 private cottages has a wood-burning fireplace (and a basket of wood on the porch), a CD stereo system, TV and VCR, air conditioner, private bath with two-person Jacuzzi tub, Egyptian cotton towels, and an ironing board. Each has a theme, too, like the Music Cottage, the Audubon Cottage, and the Fly Fishing Cottage. Continental breakfast and evening wine and appetizers are served in the common room. The owners allow children age 12 and older.

Culver Mansion $$$
1805 Foothill Boulevard, Calistoga
(707) 942–4535, (877) 281–3671
www.culvermansion.com

Proprietor Jacqueline LeVesque has done a magnificent job of renovating this circa-1875 Victorian mansion to make it homey and inviting. The six guest rooms are nicely furnished with comfortable McRoskey mattresses, hand-made in San Francisco, and as Jacqueline explains it, "the choice of the Queen of England for a wonderful night's sleep!" There's a private pool, spa, and sauna out back, and a full breakfast is included in the tariff. The resident feline will make you feel right at home while you enjoy the sweeping views from the old-fashioned veranda. Children 16 and older are welcome.

The Wayside Inn $$$
1523 Foothill Boulevard, Calistoga
(707) 942-0645

This split-level, Spanish-style home, built in the 1920s, is more like something you would expect to see in an older Los Angeles neighborhood, but it seems right at home in Napa Valley. The living room has rough beams and a wood fireplace. The back yard is densely shaded by trees—a dogwood, English walnut, a loquat, and at least a dozen others. The three guest rooms are distinctly furnished and cooled by ceiling fans. One of them, the Camellia Room, has sole use of the home's original master bathroom.

The Pink Mansion $$$$
1415 Foothill Boulevard, Calistoga
(707) 942-0558, (800) 238-7465
www.pinkmansion.com

Alma Simic was a colorful character. She was the previous owner and longest resident to live in this stately home, and she had eclectic tastes in decorating, with a mixture of Victorian and Oriental influences. Fortunately for visitors, the current owners have made certain that Alma's sense of style remains intact. The six guest rooms are elegant and tasteful, and most have views. The Master Suite and Honeymoon Suites are large—900 and 800 square feet, respectively—and feature king-size beds, two-person Jacuzzis, and private decks and sitting rooms. By the way, the mansion has been pink since the 1930s.

Bear Flag Inn $$$$
2653 Foothill Boulevard, Calistoga
(707) 942-5534, (800) 670-2860
www.bearflaginn.com

Just northwest of the intersection of Highway 128 and Petrified Forest Road, this five-room bed-and-breakfast is a renovated farmhouse built in the 1930s. Purportedly, it was on this very site that Peter Storm constructed one of the flags used for the Bear Flag Revolt in 1846. The Bear Flag Inn sits on three acres, surrounded by vineyard and meadowed hillside. Four rooms are in the two-story house; the cottage is a detached unit with a sitting room. All have private baths, queen-size beds, robes, cable

TV and VCRs, and air-conditioning. There is a swimming pool and an outdoor hot tub for guests. A full breakfast is served, with wine and appetizers in the afternoon.

Foothill House $$$$
3037 Foothill Boulevard, Calistoga
(707) 942-6933, (800) 942-6933
www.foothillhouse.com

One of Calistoga's most renowned B&Bs sits in a woodsy setting on the northwest outskirts of town. Fountains and cascades lend a soothing air, and views to Mount St. Helena help to keep you oriented as you sit in the arbor or Jacuzzi. Each room includes TV and VCR, CD player, refrigerator, and fireplace or wood stove. Three of the four have whirlpool tubs. Each has its strengths, but the Quails Roost, a detached cottage just up the hillside, is clearly the palatial unit. Quiet and private, the Quails Roost has a full kitchen and a washer/dryer setup; guests have been known to rent it for a week and go into hiding. (If you are bringing children, please book the Foothill Cottage.) Doris, trained as a chef, oversees breakfast and the afternoon "wine appreciation hour."

Hillcrest B&B $$$
3225 Lake County Highway, Calistoga
(707) 942-0332
www.bnbweb.com/hillcrest

From Highway 29 (a.k.a. Lake County Highway) as it begins to wind up Mount St. Helena, look for the twin stone pillars and drive to the end of the rutted quarter-mile driveway. The owner, Debbie O'Gorman, is the great-great-granddaughter of Senator Tubbs, who constructed Chateau Montelena on the valley floor (see our Wineries chapter), and this property has been in her family since 1860. Debbie is happy to open her family photo albums—with century-old pictures—to show the old wineries of the region. Views from the house, especially from the big-paned windows of the living room, are superb.

The mood here is extremely casual. Guests come and go as they please and are often left with a free run of the premises. Hillcrest has a fishing pond, hiking paths, a swimming pool and outdoor Jacuzzi, and a barbecue area. There are six rooms—three have private bathrooms and balconies, one has a bathroom but no balcony, and two share both bath and balcony. All of them have fireplaces. Children and dogs are accepted. Credit cards are not, but you can write a personal check.

Sonoma County

Southern Sonoma

The Cottage Inn and Spa $$
302 First Street E., Sonoma
(707) 996–5220, (800) 944–1490
www.cottageinnandspa.com
Located on a quiet street a block off the plaza, the Cottage invites visitors into its courtyards, which include fountains and a seating area. A nearby six-person hot tub is available to all guests. Five of the seven rooms open onto the courtyards, five have their own private outdoor spaces, and five include fireplaces. The studio room has a cathedral ceiling.

Thistle Dew Inn $$$
171 West Spain Street, Sonoma
(707) 938–2909, (800) 382–7895
www.thistledew.com
This is a prime location for Wine Country visitors. Just a half-block off the Sonoma Plaza, the Thistle Dew puts guests within walking distance (or biking distance, if you want to borrow from the inn's stable) of fine restaurants, shops, wineries, and historic sites. The living room invites guests to sit by the fireplace, read a book, or work on a jigsaw puzzle. The six guest rooms manage to provide a feeling of seclusion and privacy in spite of the fact that the inn is on a busy street on the edge of downtown. Breakfast is served in the dining room looking out on Spain Street. All rooms have private baths, and some have whirlpool baths.

Victorian Garden Inn $$
316 East Napa Street, Sonoma
(707) 996–5339, (800) 543–5339
www.victoriangardeninn.com
It's a farmhouse built in 1870, but it's only blocks from the downtown plaza. The wraparound porch with wicker chairs could make you believe the past is present. But it's the gardens that make this inn unique. Lawns and paths wind through the trees and along the creek, with occasional spots to sit and contemplate.

The four guest rooms—one in the main house and the rest in a century-old water tower—have private baths and are elegantly decorated. Woodcutter's Cottage is a private retreat with a fireplace, clawfoot tub, and garden view. Breakfast is served in the dining room, on the patio, or in your room. The inn now offers professional massage services in your room or on the patio. A new business center—when duty calls—includes a copy machine, fax, printer, and Internet access. A three-night minimum stay is required on weekends.

Trojan Horse Inn $$
19455 Highway 12, Sonoma
(707) 996–2430, (800) 899–1925
www.trojanhorseinn.com
Rebuilt after a tragic fire in 1990, this inn has turned into a charming B&B decorated with English and French antiques. Each of its six rooms has a different

> ## Insiders' Tip
> California's Gold Rush brought an influx of new residents to the state, and with them came a variety of eastern U.S. architectural styles. For example, many of San Francisco's new Victorian homes were constructed in the Italianate style. An exceptional example can be found in St. Helena's Ink House, built in 1884.

theme, decorated individually. Especially popular is the room called Grape Arbor, boasting a fireplace and double Jacuzzi, but all rooms are furnished with antiques of the 1880s era, when the original house was built. Children older than 12 are welcome with advance notice. A full breakfast is served along the lines of French toast or banana pancakes, lemon chicken sausage, fresh fruit, and Starbucks coffee. Join other guests for complimentary wine and hors d'oeuvres between 6:00 and 7:00 P.M.

Above the Clouds $$$$
3250 Trinity Road, Glen Ellen
(707) 996–7371, (800) 736–7894
www.sonomabb.com/abovetheclouds.htm

The mountain road called Oakville Grade (up Trinity Road on the Sonoma side) straddles the Mayacmas Mountains that rise between the Sonoma and Napa valleys. Trinity Road sprouts from Highway 12 about 8 miles north of the Sonoma Plaza, and winds through thickets of manzanita and scrub oaks for 3 miles before reaching Above the Clouds bed-and-breakfast inn. When the fog rolls through the Sonoma Valley, this inn lives up to its name. It's a secluded mountain retreat that surveys forests and catches the sunset. Three guest rooms are furnished with antique iron or brass beds, and each has a private bath, queen-size bed, down comforters, and lots of pillows. Robes are provided for those who want to take advantage of the swimming pool and Jacuzzi spa. A gourmet breakfast is served. Two-night minimum is required. You should book well in advance. The inn is closed from mid-November to February.

Beltane Ranch $$$
11775 Highway 12, Glen Ellen
(707) 996–6501
www.beltaneranch.com

The place has an exotic—even romantic—past. The land was first settled in 1882 by Mary Ann "Mammy" Pleasant, whose exploits as a madam to San Francisco's upper crust (plus suspicions of a possible homicide in her posh establishment) had led to alarming headlines. It was said she conducted black magic sessions too. But Mammy had another side: She became known as "the western terminus" of the Underground Railroad, making frequent trips to the South to secretly help thousands of Blacks escape to Canada.

Beltane Ranch's architectural style suggests Deep South, with a stylish veranda set off with an elaborate gingerbread railing. But the Ranch's recent past is more mundane. In the 1920s it was the bunkhouse for a turkey ranch. Inside are six guest rooms (including one cottage), each with an individual outdoor entrance. The rooms are rustic but cozy, furnished with antiques. The 1,600 acres include a working vineyard, and the owner is happy to tour the grounds with you and explain what viticulture is all about.

A full breakfast is served, and it may include omelettes and homemade scones served on your own veranda or in the garden. This is a popular lodging place, and reservations are definitely recommended during the harvest season of August through October.

Gaige House Inn $$$$
13540 Arnold Drive, Glen Ellen
(707) 935–0237, (800) 935–0237
www.gaige.com

An elegant Italianate Victorian, restored from its original 1880s construction, Gaige House Inn has a prime location at the edge of the village of Glen Ellen in the heart of Wine Country. It has six guest rooms and one suite in the main house, and eight garden rooms with outside entrances. The signature room is the Gaige Suite, a spacious sunny room with large windows on three sides and a wraparound deck overlooking the garden. You'll awake in your four-poster bed and step into a bathroom that's larger than most bedrooms.

The Kenwood Carriage House is one of three cottages off-site also available for rent. It's a one-bedroom, second-floor accommodation with use of a private estate's swimming pool. Long stays are encouraged. The creekside setting includes a large swimming pool and Jacuzzi. A formal breakfast is included, as are afternoon hors d'oeuvres and beverages.

Glenelly Inn $$$
5131 Warm Springs Road, Glen Ellen
(707) 996–6720
www.glenelly.com

This is one of the few Wine Country bed-and-breakfast inns that was actually built as an inn. Visitors of the 1920s and '30s came by railroad and basked in the sun on the inn's long verandas. The long verandas are still there, now with wicker chairs to provide a perch to watch the sun set over Sonoma Mountain. Each of the eight rooms has a private entrance and is furnished in a country motif, with antique furniture and Scandinavian down comforters. The Jack London Room has a sleigh bed and wood-burning stove, and all rooms have claw-foot tubs and antique sinks. An outdoor spa is set amid native landscaping. In the morning, a full breakfast is served in the common room by a large cobblestone fireplace. It's a great experience, with hot entrees, homemade bread and muffins, fresh fruit, and fresh-squeezed orange juice. Children younger than 12 stay free.

Tanglewood House $$$
250 Bonnie Way, Glen Ellen
(707) 996–5021
www.tanglewoodhouse.com

On a quiet country road a mile from Glen Ellen, Tanglewood House is a retreat occupying more than an acre of park-like, secluded gardens. Only one room is available—a large luxurious suite that occupies an entire wing of this lovely house. It has its own private entrance and patio and a spacious sitting room with fireplace, cathedral ceiling, and color TV. A magnificent pool is available to guests, and there is a full breakfast in the morning.

Cavanagh Inn $
10 Keller Street, Petaluma
(707) 765–4657, (888) 765–4658
www.cavanaghinn.com

There's a feeling of turn-of-the-century elegance here that few modern houses achieve. It was built for lumberman John Cavanagh in 1902, a time when his company was known for providing some of the finest rare heart-redwood available.

His house paneling shows he picked the best of what he had for his residence. The mansion's four bedrooms are furnished in Victorian style, though one of them has a special addition Cavanagh wouldn't believe—a tub with a whirlpool ready to froth with bubble bath.

There's a three-bedroom cottage beside the main house, built for two Cavanagh sisters. Bedrooms here are less formal, furnished with wicker, and two of the three rooms share a bath. The inn is within walking distance of most everything you will want to visit, including Petaluma's historic district with its antiques shops. A typical breakfast might include pears in butterscotch sauce and fluffy scrambled eggs topped with crab and seafood sauce.

The Gables Inn $$$
4257 Petaluma Hill Road, Santa Rosa
(707) 585–7777, (800) 422–5376
www.thegablesinn.com

Built in 1877 at the height of Victorian Gothic Revival architecture, this home was built with 15 gables rising above some unique keyhole-shaped windows. There are seven rooms in the main house, five up a mahogany staircase, and two accessible to disabled guests, some of which include fireplaces, and all of which share central air-conditioning. Each room is furnished in unique decor that displays its history and character; each has a claw-foot tub in its private bath. An adjacent cottage is furnished with a kitchenette, TV with video library, stereo, woodstove, two-person whirlpool tub, and private phone/data port. A lavish country breakfast is served. A large sundeck looks out across acres of countryside just outside Santa Rosa.

Melitta Station Inn $
5850 Melita Road, Santa Rosa
(707) 538–7712, (800) 504–3099
www.melittastationinn.com

Once this was a busy railroad station; before that it was a general store and post office. Today it's a warm inn with six guest rooms (five if the two-room suite is occupied) furnished with antiques and folk art. The inn's former life is evident in its unique plank flooring and hand-sawed fir boards with the sawyer's strokes still well-marked. The style here is American antique, with lots of collectibles to admire. The setting is part of the charm: The inn is surrounded by state parks, hiking trails, and biking opportunities. A full buffet breakfast is served by the wood-burning stove in the large sitting room on the balcony.

Pygmalion House $
331 Orange Street, Santa Rosa
(707) 526–3407
www.bedandbreakfast.com

Built in 1880 down near Railroad Square, where Santa Rosa had its beginnings, this Queen Anne home has been restored to a bed-and-breakfast inn of five rooms, all with private baths featuring showers and claw-foot tubs. It's furnished with pieces that include Gypsy Rose Lee antiques and memorabilia. Decorated in the European style, the parlor has a fireplace, TV, and telephone. There's a private garden and parking behind the inn. A hearty breakfast and afternoon treats are served.

Northern Sonoma

Belle de Jour Inn $$$$
16276 Healdsburg Avenue, Healdsburg
(707) 431–9777
www.belledejourinn.com

This inn's hilltop setting is on six acres and looks out on rolling hills. The farmhouse, a single-story Italianate built around 1873, is the residence of the innkeepers, and it is here guests enjoy a hearty breakfast. Guests are quartered in five white cottages, all with fireplaces and some with decks. Each cottage is its own country experience. The Caretaker Suite, for instance, has a king-size, canopy bed and a fireplace in the sitting room. There's a sunny studio atelier room with a high, vaulted ceiling, and the grand Carriage House has everything, including views and a tub for two.

Camellia Inn $$$
211 North Street, Healdsburg
(707) 433–8182, (800) 727–8182
www.camelliainn.com

From November to May the inn is over-taken by blooming camellias, hence the name. Built in 1869, the house served at one time as Healdsburg's first hospital, and in fact, the room you rent might have been the lab. As a plus, the Camellia Inn is just two blocks from historic Healdsburg Plaza and its chic shops and boutiques. When you return to your room from your excursions you might recuperate from the rigors of shopping in your whirlpool tub for two, light up the gas fireplace if you're chilly, and have a lovely night's sleep in your four-poster bed. The Camellia Inn includes a family suite—unusual in an industry largely geared toward couples.

Breakfast is served buffet style, with a selection of entrees and breads that will keep your energy up until noon (maybe later). Sometimes it's quiche or breakfast custard, and it's always accompanied by fruit, cereal, sourdough toast, and home-made jam.

George Alexander House $$$
423 Matheson Street, Healdsburg
(707) 433–1358, (800) 310–1358
www.georgealexanderhouse.com

This historic house was built in 1905 by George Alexander, the 10th child of Cyrus Alexander. Cyrus was the first settler in the north county, and Alexander Valley is named for him (see our History chapter). There are four rooms in this lovely inn. The Alexander room has a fireplace and bay windows, while the Back Porch has a private entrance with a deck, whirlpool tub for two, and wood-burning stove. If you're hungry for a hearty breakfast, you'll be happy to see such menu items as ricotta pancakes with sauteed apples. Two spacious parlors are available to guests, as is the sauna in the garden. Stay two nights (a minimum on weekends) and get a bottle of wine.

Grape Leaf Inn $$
539 Johnson Street, Healdsburg
(707) 433–8140
www.grapeleafinn.com

Pssst! Don't look now, but there's a secret room behind that bookcase in the corner! Yes, this inn takes the B&B experience a step further with a hidden "speakeasy" just for guests. A gentle push on the bookcase and it swings open to reveal a secret wine cellar and gathering spot. Here you will find many local small-production wines available for tasting, sometimes poured by the winemakers themselves. Sherlock Holmes would be impressed. Elsewhere around the 1900 Queen Anne Victorian are 12 guest rooms ranging from masculine to feminine—there's a room for just about any taste. Some feature fireplaces and spa tubs. Expect a full gourmet breakfast that might include crab-stuffed herbed croissant French toast with mango-papaya salsa, or asparagus/parmesan cheese soufflé. Another plus: The inn is just a five-minute walk from the town plaza.

Haydon Street Inn $$
321 Haydon Street, Healdsburg
(707) 433–5228, (800) 528–3703
www.haydon.com

In a quiet residential area within walking distance of Healdsburg's historic plaza, this Victorian inn has nine charming guest rooms. One of the most popular is the Turret Room, tucked into the slope of the roof, with a step-down entrance to the sleeping level. Each of the other rooms is distinctively different in decor, from iron bedsteads and handmade rugs to French antique furnishings. Six of the guest rooms are in the main house, a 1912 Queen Anne structure, and three are in the adjoining two-story Victorian cottage. All rooms have private baths; those in the cottage also have double whirlpool tubs. If breakfast is your idea of the right start to the day, this is your place. You can get fired up for a full, energetic Wine Country adventure with scones slathered with orange butter, frittatas, croissants, French toast, quiches, fresh-baked breads, oven-roasted potatoes, meat side dishes, plus an aromatic house-blend coffee.

Healdsburg Inn on the Plaza $$$$
110 Matheson Street, Healdsburg
(707) 433–6991, (800) 431–8663
www.healdsburginn.com

The front entrance is unpretentious enough, but it opens onto a handsome art

Insiders' Tip

The Grape Leaf Inn in Healdsburg has a special "speakeasy" hidden behind a bookcase. Each evening, guests at the inn are treated to a generous pouring of Sonoma County wines in the secret hideaway.

gallery. Once a Wells Fargo building, the inn now rates high on the luxury scale. A staircase leads to the 10 antique-filled rooms—most with fireplaces, all with private baths, in-room phones, and TVs, and some with whirlpool tubs for two. A solarium in the roof garden is the common area where guests meet for breakfast and afternoon refreshments, when wine and fresh buttered popcorn, coffee, tea, and a bottomless cookie jar are available. A carriage house—complete with a kitchenette—is also available for rent.

Honor Mansion $$$
14891 Grove Street, Healdsburg
(707) 433–4277, (800) 554–4667
www.honormansion.com

The architecture, decor, and surrounding gardens give this inn a feeling of turn-of-the-century grace. You can almost imagine women in ankle-length frocks carrying on polite conversation with gentlemen in tennis sweaters as they stroll along the garden path. Its 11 guest rooms and suites are furnished with antiques and feather beds, and each has a private bath. The place has a fascinating history, and the innkeeper will be glad to regale you with the life of the Squire Butcher family over a breakfast of home-baked pastries and gourmet entrees. Spa services have been added to make your visit more enjoyable.

Madrona Manor $$$$
1001 Westside Road, Healdsburg
(707) 433–4231, (800) 258–4003
www.madronamanor.com

Tucked away in the lush Dry Creek Valley, Madrona Manor is an estate for which adjectives like elegant and majestic were invented. Originally built in 1880 by business tycoon John Paxton, Madrona Knoll Rancho, as it was then called, became one of the grandest showplaces in all the valley. Today it stands as a wonderful exponent of a bygone era of grandeur and refined taste. The Manor's accommodations include 21 rooms in four buildings on eight acres of wooded and manicured grounds. Seventeen of the rooms have fireplaces, and eight have a balcony or deck. A buffet-style breakfast is included. Need more elegance? World-class gourmet dining can be enjoyed each evening in a romantic candlelight setting (see our Restaurants chapter).

Midnight Sun Inn $$
428 Haydon Street, Healdsburg
(707) 433–1718
www.midnight-sun.com

Somewhat different from many bed-and-breakfast inns, Midnight Sun is decorated in a modern country style, with almost no antique decor. The linens are top-of-the-line, as are the beds and mattresses. There are three guest rooms in the main house: "Juliet's Balcony" invites a second-story stroll across the entire front of the house. Inside, there's a canopy bed to stretch out in. The other two rooms are the Enchanted Garden Room and the Safari Room. The latter has jungle-patterned sheets and mosquito net for atmosphere. There's also a cottage in the back yard; it has a Wine Country theme and is said to be the most romantic room of all. Both the Garden Room and Juliet's Balcony have Jacuzzis for two.

The Raford House $$$
10630 Wohler Road, Healdsburg
(707) 887–9573, (800) 887–9503
www.rafordhouse.com

Here's a Victorian inn with an expansive porch ideal for sipping wine. The Raford House sits on a knoll surrounded by vineyards and palm trees, and the view from the porch is worth the price. The structure dates from the 1880s, and is listed as a Sonoma County Historical Landmark. The six affordable guest rooms are fur-

One of Madrona Manor's guest houses, behind the main house, overlooks magnificent flower gardens.
PHOTO: JEAN SAYLOR DOPPENBERG

nished with queen-size beds and each has a private bath. A hearty breakfast is dished up every morning. The rooms are all nonsmoking, but puffing is allowed on the porch and in the gardens.

Villa Messina $$$
316 Burgundy Road, Healdsburg
(707) 433–6655
www.villamessina.com

The setting is unbelievable, with a 360-degree view of three exquisite valleys—Alexander, Dry Creek, and Russian River. The Italian villa-style inn was built in 1986 on top of the foundation of a former water tower. The inn's five guest rooms are furnished with antiques, and the floors are carpeted with Oriental rugs. All have private baths, plus TVs, VCRs, and phones. Some have Jacuzzis or fireplaces. For breakfast the chef prepares such treats as fresh-squeezed orange juice and blueberry pancakes with bacon. He also bakes his own breads. There is a swimming pool and hot tub.

Hope-Bosworth House $$
21238 Geyserville Avenue, Geyserville
(707) 857–3356, (800) 825–4233
www.hope-inns.com

Driving down Geyserville Avenue, you'll have no trouble instantly recognizing the Hope-Bosworth House—it's the Queen Anne with the picket fence covered with "roses of yesteryear" varieties that were popular when the house was built in 1904.

All the rooms are a step into the past. The original oak-grained woodwork is evident everywhere, from the sliding doors in the hallway to the upstairs bedrooms. Polished fir floors and antique light fixtures enhance the period furnishing. At 9:00 A.M. a country breakfast is served in the formal dining room and includes fresh fruit, egg dishes, homemade breads and pastries, and coffee or tea.

Hope-Merrill House $$$
1253 Geyserville Avenue, Geyserville
(707) 857–3356, (800) 825–4233
www.hope-inns.com

In its former life, it was a stagecoach stop of the 1870s. Now it's an enchanting inn, listed on the Sonoma County Landmarks Register. Anyone interested in architecture will recognize the squared-off look of Eastlake Stick Style, popular between 1870 and 1885. J.P. Merrill, who was a land developer, saw to it he had the best of everything for his house, and he built it entirely of redwood. The Inn has eight rooms, all with queen-size beds and private baths. Four rooms have fireplaces, two have whirlpool baths, and one has a sitting room. There's also a swimming pool. Please note the restored Victorian hand-screened wallpaper—it's stunning! Breakfast is superb, served in the dining room.

Abrams House Inn $
314 North Main Street, Cloverdale
(707) 894–2412, (800) 764–4466

A restored 1870s Victorian, Abrams House Inn offers four guest rooms, one of them a special suite with a four-poster bed and private porch. There are also three parlors, two with TV and VCR, the other a library/game room. A wicker-decorated upper deck gives a lovely view of a rose garden, gazebo, and deck with a hot tub. Breakfast is ample (to put it mildly), and in the evening you can enjoy a decadent dessert with Abrams House's own specially blended hot cocoa.

Mountain House Winery and Lodge $$
33710 Highway 128, Cloverdale
(707) 894–5683
www.mtnhousewinery-lodge.com

In its former life, Mountain House was a stagecoach stop and inn, flanked by a barn and some outbuildings. Now this 1890s-era homestead has been converted to a bed-and-breakfast inn, operating in conjunction with Mountain House's winery. Accommodations at Mountain House include four suites (all with fireplaces) at the top of the winery building, three suites in the inn, and five cottages next to a lake, three of them one-bedroom and one two-bedroom—a great bonus for families. There is a spa too.

In the morning, you can look forward to quiche or other hot breakfast specialties and fruit in season. This is a great place to get married or to have a conference, if that's your inclination. The banquet room and tasting room (with full kitchen available to caterers) provides a grand background for either occasion.

Vintage Towers Inn $$
302 Main Street, Cloverdale
(707) 894–4535, (888) 886–9377
www.vintagetowers.com

Mining executive Simon Pinchower had an unusual idea when he asked an architect to design a Queen Anne house in 1913. He wanted three towers, all built in different shapes—one round, one square, and one octagonal—so his house would be different from its neighbors.

Pinchower is long gone, but his legacy has given travelers a fine way to find their way to the seven-guest room Vintage Towers Inn. Each of the three tower suites has its own sitting area, sleeping quarters, and private bath. Three of the other rooms also have private baths, and two share a conveniently located bath. The wide front veranda's porch swing is a pleasant place to relax after a day of touring the countryside. A hearty breakfast can be expected.

West County/Russian River

The Inn at Occidental $$$$
3657 Church Street, Occidental
(707) 874–1047, (800) 522–6324
www.innatoccidental.com

This is the type of romantic getaway where you can just be together surrounded by the forested hills of western Sonoma County. Owner Jack Bullard is a lifelong collector of fine art and antiques, and each of the 16 rooms is decorated with meticulous care in a theme related to a specific piece of art. The effect is that of a gallery with beds. All rooms have a private bath, one room has wheelchair access, and all but one have fireplaces and decks. Several units have double spa tubs and views of the courtyard, and a two-bedroom guest house is also available. A full breakfast is included.

The Farmhouse Inn & Restaurant $$
7871 River Road, Forestville
(707) 887–3300, (800) 464–6642
www.farmhouseinn.com

In 1878 it really was a working farm, with a row of cottages off to the side for the workers. Now it's a country inn by the side of the road, and the workers' cottages have become charming private guest rooms with amenities the farm workers never dreamed could exist. All the rooms have jetted spa tubs, CD players, TV/VCRs, personal saunas, refrigerators, fireplaces, feather beds, luxurious linens, and European-style "rain" showerheads. Full concierge services are offered, as well as on-site massage and facials, which can be enjoyed poolside. (Farmhouse Inn was honored by Travel & Leisure magazine recently in its Top 30 Great Inns list.)

The Inn was set to launch a special series of "culinary adventures" for guests beginning in 2003. These three-day excursions will provide an up close and personal look into winemaking, a chance to pick your own vegetables for your evening meal, or visits to artisan cheesemakers, oyster farms, and more. Call the Inn for more details.

In addition, there's an events center on-site, where business affairs and weddings can be held. The facility and gardens can accommodate 300 guests.

Ridenhour Ranch House Inn $$
12850 River Road, Guerneville
(707) 877–1033, (888) 877–4466
www.ridenhourranchhouseinn.com

Louis Ridenhour came to this land in 1850 and began farming 940 acres of land along the Russian River. This house, however, was not built until 1906. What guests find today is a large living room overlooking redwoods, and eight guest rooms, each with a private bath. One of them, Hawthorne Cottage, has a fireplace and cozy window seat. Korbel Champagne Cellars is within walking distance (see our Wineries chapter), and the Russian River is five minutes away by foot. Breakfast is ample.

Applewood Inn $$$
13555 Highway 116, Guerneville
(707) 869–9093, (800) 555–8509
www.applewoodinn.com

Nineteen stylish rooms and suites fill three multistory Mediterranean-style villas set among apple orchards and redwood trees. Each is individually decorated,

One of the coziest spots in the town of Occidental is the porch of the Inn at Occidental. PHOTO: JEAN SAYLOR
DOPPENBERG

romantic, and formal, yet familiar—like the home of a wealthy great-aunt you may have visited. The newer rooms have fireplaces, sitting areas, private verandas or decks, and either couples showers or spa tubs for two. The common area is centered around a huge stone fireplace. The restaurant seats 50 (see our Restaurants chapter). The kitchen, once reserved for breakfast, now offers dinner Tuesday to Saturday. A full breakfast is served.

Fern Grove Cottages $
16650 Highway 116, Guerneville
(707) 869–8105
www.ferngrove.com

A small, quaint village of 22 romantic cottages, Fern Grove Inn provides a stylish country atmosphere and a base for exploring the back roads of the neighborhood. Cottages range from spacious one-bedroom suites to intimate guest rooms with sitting areas. All have a refrigerator; some have fireplaces, spas, or TVs. Stroll the gardens, swim in the pool, feel romantic in general! The buffet breakfast features homemade pastries. The shops of downtown Guerneville are within walking distance.

Mendocino County

Hopland Inn, A California Roadhouse $$
13401 South U.S. 101, Hopland
(707) 744-1890, (800) 266-1891
www.hoplandinn.com

In 2002, this historic 21-room hotel—like those you've seen in a hundred western movies—underwent a complete makeover, including a name change. No longer encumbered with velvet drapes and heavy furnishings, the former Thatcher Inn is now awash in sunlight, freshly repainted and decorated with a lighter touch. Without taking away from the inn's colorful role in Mendocino County history, the new owners have lovingly spruced up the old Victorian, which is listed on the National Register of Historic Places. The restaurant menu was upgraded as well, incorporating lighter California cuisine alongside traditional steak-and-potato entrees. Continental breakfast is served to hotel guests.

Fetzer Valley Oaks Bed & Breakfast $$
13601 Eastside Road, Hopland
(707) 744–1250, (800) 846–8637
www.fetzer.com

Located in the Fetzer Vineyards complex of tasting room and organic gardens is a charming 10-room bed-and-breakfast inn, housed in the ranch's original carriage house. Each room is beautifully appointed and features panoramic views of the surrounding vineyards (or organic gardens) from a private patio. The interiors are country casual, with overstuffed chairs pulled up to large coffee tables in the sitting rooms. All guests enjoy continental breakfast and access to a secluded pool. Two master suites have whirlpool tubs in their oversized bathrooms, separate bedrooms, large sitting rooms, and small kitchens. (For more on the Fetzer complex, see our Wineries chapter.)

Highway 128

Anderson Creek Inn $$
12050 Anderson Valley Way, Boonville
(707) 895–3091, (800) 552–6202
www.andersoncreekinn.com

This inn is a rambling ranch house set on 16 acres at the junction of two creeks, with views of the hills beyond. Each of its spacious and spotless five rooms offers a different view and feeling, and each has a private bath, king-size bed, and complimentary bottle of local wine. Two rooms have fireplaces, and one has a Franklin stove. The friendly family livestock includes llamas, sheep, horses, and a goat. Come in March and see the newborn lambs! Breakfast is a special event and is served in the courtyard, weather permitting.

Pinoli Ranch Country Inn $$
3280 Clark Road, Philo
(707) 895–2550
www.andersonvalley.org/b&b

A place for total peace and tranquillity, the inn is nestled on 100 acres with incomparable views of the entire Anderson Valley. Guests can cycle around the quiet country roads, ride horses, or visit some of the dozen or more wineries in the area. The inn has three guest rooms, two

with private baths. But the real draw here is the great outdoors. A country-style breakfast is served, and well-mannered children are welcome.

Mendocino Coast

Whale Watch Inn $$$$
35100 North Highway 1, Anchor Bay
(707) 884–3667, (800) 942–5342
www.whale-watch.com

Whales swim by to get a closer look at this stylish inn, perched on a cliff's edge 5 miles north of Gualala. This charming complex of five buildings is set on two acres of woods and gardens. There are 18 rooms and suites, most with whirlpool tubs and all with fireplaces, private decks, and awesome views of the rocky coast. The inn's decor slants toward contemporary rather than traditional, elegant instead of woodsy. Romance is the calling card here. Televisions and telephones have been banned from all rooms. Leave the laptop at home, and be prepared for some serious creature comforts. Breakfast is hearty: fresh seasonal fruits, freshly baked pastries, and an entree that changes daily, all delivered to your private deck.

Wharf Master's Inn $$
785 Port Road, Point Arena
(707) 882–3171, (800) 932–4031
www.wharfmasters.com

When Point Arena bustled with sailors hauling lumber and fish to supply California's Gold Rush, the wharf master had only to step onto his porch to make sure all was proceeding in an orderly fashion in the harbor below. The view is much more peaceful these days. The Victorian, built in 1865, and several newer buildings together form the Wharf Master's Inn, an accommodation that is hard to pigeonhole. All of the 23 rooms have feather beds, private baths, and TVs, and most have fireplaces and spa tubs. A continental breakfast is served.

Glendeven $$$
8205 North Highway 1, Little River
(707) 937–0083, (800) 822–4536
www.glendeven.com

Named for a Scottish grand estate, Glendeven consists of 10 rooms in three separate buildings, one containing an art gallery. The gallery is a showplace for 10 local artists and craftspeople. The central building was a farmhouse from 1867 until the late 1930s. The mood is of casual elegance. It's light and spacious, and all rooms have private baths and most have fireplaces. Wine and hors d'oeuvres are served by the fireplace in the sitting room, to the tinkling music of the baby grand. Breakfast is generous and will be delivered to your room should the fancy strike.

Rachel's Inn $$
8200 North Highway 1, Little River
(707) 937–0088, (800) 347–9252
www.rachelsinn.com

Rachel's Inn borders 2,500-acre Van Damme State Park and its wooded hills sloping toward the sea (see our Parks and Recreation chapter). The inn is surrounded by informal gardens and century-old cypress trees. Cliffs overlooking the ocean are just a stroll away. A lane behind the inn leads to the beach. Each of the 10 rooms is tastefully appointed but also different from the rest. The morning meal is also unique.

Seafoam Lodge $$
6751 North Highway 1, Little River
(707) 937–1827, (800) 606–1827
www.seafoamlodge.com

The lodge has eight separate buildings offering 24 guest accommodations and a conference center. A forested hillside provides the backdrop for the lodge, which is perched on six acres of coastal gardens and pines above the inlet of Buckhorn Cove. Guests can look forward to panoramic ocean views and breathtaking sunsets from every private room. Some rooms have kitchens, some have fireplaces, and all have VCRs. Two spas let you enjoy the outdoor space. The Crows Nest Conference Center, with its magnificent ocean view, will accommodate up to 50 guests—perfect for business meetings, seminars, family reunions, and wedding receptions. A continental breakfast is

delivered to your room each morning. Pets and children are welcome.

Stevenswood Lodge $$
8211 North Highway 1, Little River
(707) 937–2810, (800) 421–2810
www.stevenswood.com

There could scarcely be a more enchanting setting than this lodge enjoys, surrounded on three sides by 2,500 acres of Van Damme State Park forest. Leave your room and it's a short walk to the ocean, Fern Canyon, and the headlands. The mood here is decidedly upscale, with nine one-bedroom suites and one guest room (with handicapped access) that overlooks the gardens. All the room options have beckoning views, cozy wood-burning fireplaces, spacious private baths, and stocked honor bars. Breakfast is a gourmet delight to remember, and there is an on-site restaurant.

The Victorian Farmhouse $$
7001 North Highway 1, Little River
(707) 937–0697, (800) 264–4723
www.victorianfarmhouse.com

How charming is this bluff-top house south of Mendocino? Your heart could definitely end up here, on a two-acre parcel bordered by a creek on the south. The house was built in 1877 by John Dennen, whose grandson would later buy Pullen Farm and turn it into Heritage House (see our Spas and Resorts chapter). The Victorian Farmhouse does not have an ocean view; however, Buckhorn Cove—a public beach that feels quite private—is a five-minute walk. There are four rooms in the old structure, and six more split between two separate buildings. Seven of the units have fireplaces; two have double spa tubs. A full breakfast is served in-room, and co-owner Jo Bradley will cater to your dietary needs, adding to an overall feeling of attentive comfort.

Elk Cove Inn $$$$
6300 South Highway 1, Elk
(707) 877–3321, (800) 275–2967
www.elkcoveinn.com

Secluded high atop a bluff overlooking nearly a mile of coastline, the Elk Cove Inn captures the essence of peace and tranquility. Built in 1883 as an executive guest house for a lumber company, this beachfront retreat offers the quintessential "room with a view." Massive windows bring dramatic, panoramic views and the unspoiled beauty of the outdoors to each of the 14 large accommodations (six rooms, four cottages, and four luxury suites). A trail leads down to the beach, and an outdoor hot tub leads to tranquility. A multicourse gourmet breakfast is served daily in the oceanfront dining room.

Harbor House $$$$
5600 South Highway 1, Elk
(707) 877–3203, (800) 720–7474
www.theharborhouseinn.com

The main building of this inn was built in 1916 by the Goodyear Redwood Lumber Company as an executive residence and for the lodging and entertainment of company guests. Situated on a bluff overlooking Greenwood Landing, Harbor House is a sanctuary for relaxation and privacy that is reminiscent of a leisurely, romantic era.

The 10 guest rooms reflect the decor of those bygone days. A sumptuous breakfast and four-course dinner are included in the price. Products are all from local sources. In addition to homegrown vegetables, the cuisine includes naturally raised meats and cheeses from nearby farms. Rooms in the main building and adjacent cottages are individually heated and have private baths.

Sandpiper House Inn $$$
5520 South Highway 1, Elk
(707) 877–3587, (800) 894–9016
www.sandpiperhouse.com

In 1916 when the house was built, Elk was a bustling harbor, where schooners loaded with redwood set sail for the San Francisco market. The gray, shingled inn is decidedly unpretentious, though it was then one of the finest homes in town. Coffered ceilings and raised panel walls typify the craftsmanship of the era. Its five rooms are tastefully appointed in the style of a European country inn, decorated with antiques, comfy chairs, fresh flowers, and down comforters. All have private baths. Look

forward to breakfast served on a lace tablecloth that's brightened with a bouquet of fresh flowers. Children 12 and older are welcome, but no pets please.

Fensalden Inn $$$
33810 Navarro Ridge Road, Albion
(707) 937–4042, (800) 959–3850
www.fensalden.com

Once a Wells Fargo stagecoach way station, Fensalden rests on 20 tree-lined, pastoral acres on a majestic ridge crest. At this 400-foot elevation, the ocean and meadow views are spectacular. The inn's eight rooms are divided among the main house, the water tower house, and a separate bungalow, with three common rooms in the main building. One is a guest's office, one a parlor, and the third the Tavern Room, a namesake common for way stations in the raucous Old West lifestyle. (If you can't sense the history, check out the bullet holes that pock the original ceiling.) In the evening, wine and hors d'oeuvres are served in this room, while guests view the sunset over the Pacific. In the morning, a gourmet breakfast is also served there.

Brewery Gulch Inn $$$$
9401 Coast Highway 1, Mendocino
(707) 937–4752, (800) 578–4454
www.brewerygulchinn.com

The owner of this inn, Arky Ciancutti, bought the 10-acre property in 1977, then a few years later turned the original farmhouse into a small B&B. When he learned that a huge amount of virgin-growth redwood, cut a century earlier, had been discovered deeply buried in silt nearby, he found his inspiration to build a new inn. This "guiltless" redwood, mineralized by time, encompasses the major building blocks of this structure, crafted from 100,000 board feet of the nearly petrified redwood. The property was once home to a successful dairy and a brewery—hence the name. Now it's the gardens that dominate the scenery, with thousands of blooming flower bulbs amid ponds and streams, and a two-acre woodland garden with more than 600 rhododendrons and a thousand delicate ferns.

The 10 luxurious guest rooms feature ocean views, leather club chairs, fireplaces, phones, CD players, and TVs. Some have Jacuzzi tubs for two, as well as private decks. A gourmet breakfast is served (try the caramelized banana and praline pecan pancakes), and an evening wine hour is offered at the special tasting bar. There's also a library with a large selection of books and CDs and a telescope and binoculars for gazing at the stars or watching for whales. This nonsmoking property is aimed at couples seeking quiet romance.

Agate Cove Inn $$$
11201 North Lansing Street, Mendocino
(707) 937–0551, (800) 527–3111
www.agatecoveinn.com

Agate Cove Inn was built as a farmhouse in 1860, and for the past few decades it was a comfortably funky inn with spectacular views. With breakfast cooked on an antique wood-burning stove, its current incarnation still feels like a farmhouse. The views are still breathtaking too. Many of the eight cottages and two farmhouse units feature oversize tubs and showers for two, fireplaces, and huge beds with down comforters. Still down-home, however, are those breakfasts—hearty meals served with an unobstructed floor-to-ceiling view of the headlands and the waves crashing against the rocks.

Blair House $$
45110 Little Lake Street, Mendocino
(707) 937–1800, (800) 699–9296
www.blairhouse.com

This is perhaps the best-known home in Mendocino, because millions of people have seen it watching the TV show *Murder, She Wrote*. The show's producers used the exterior of Blair House as Jessica's Cabot Cove home. The house was built in 1888 for Elisha Blair, a railroad worker who graciously loaned money to his fellow workers, then turned his loan business into a career as a financier. The extensive use of virgin, clear-heart redwood, now prohibitively expensive, is probably what has kept the house so well-preserved. Four guest rooms are equipped with plush queen-size beds and handcrafted quilts. Angela's Suite is a two-room suite with 10-foot ceilings and bay windows that offer a view of both the village and ocean. Three other

guest rooms share a large bathroom in the hall. Breakfast is served on-site. Two-night minimum on weekends.

Inn at Schoolhouse Creek $$
7051 North Highway 1, Mendocino
(707) 937–5525, (800) 731–5525
www.schoolhousecreek.com

The amenity guests appreciate most about this coastal inn is its eight surrounding acres of outdoor space, replete with tall cypress trees and an open meadow. The east end of the property leads to Schoolhouse Creek itself, and for beach-goers, Buckhorn Cove is a short walk to the south. The Inn offers 15 accommodations—nine freestanding cottages, two suites, and four units in a small lodge. Some have ocean views. In every room you will find a TV/VCR, CD player, and phone. Families are welcome, and dogs are allowed in some rooms. The Inn has a hot tub on the property, situated at the top of the meadow and with a sweeping ocean view.

John Dougherty House $$$$
571 Ukiah Street, Mendocino
(707) 937–5266, (800) 486–2104
www.jdhouse.com

Historic John Dougherty House, built in 1867, is one of the oldest houses in Mendocino. The main house is furnished with country antiques of the 1860s. Two guest rooms are in the main house, six more are in the adjoining cottages or historic water tower. All are individually decorated, accented with dried flower wreaths and fresh flowers from the garden. The Captain's Room has a private veranda. Upstairs, the First Mate's Room has hand-stenciled walls and antique pine furniture. Some rooms have four-poster beds and village views (two boast spectacular vistas); most have a small refrigerator and a wood-burning stove; four feature jet tubs. Breakfast is served by a crackling fire in the New England–style keeping room.

Joshua Grindle Inn $$
44800 Little Lake Road, Mendocino
(707) 937–4143, (800) 474–6353
www.joshgrin.com

Situated on two acres, this lovely home was built in 1879 by Joshua Grindle, who came from Maine to enter the booming lumber business and stayed on to become the town banker. The house features unmistakably New England–style architecture, and the decor of the inn is a reflection of the same early-American heritage. There are five rooms in the main house, two in the cottage, and three in the water tower. Some have views of Mendocino and the ocean; others have woodburning fireplaces. All have well-lighted, comfortably arranged sitting areas and private baths. Breakfast is a time to enjoy a delicious morning meal as well as conversation with other guests around the circa-1830 pine harvest table. The inn has received many honors, including *Focus* magazine's Inn of the Year award.

Nicholson House $
951 Ukiah Street, Mendocino
(707) 937–0934, (800) 962–0934
www.nicholsonhouse.com

Nicholson House, built in 1905 and located in the heart of Mendocino, was home to three generations of Nicholsons until 1976, when it was converted to an apartment and office building. Now it's a bed-and-breakfast, preserving much of the history and charm of the original house. There are seven plush rooms in all, and throughout the property guests can enjoy great views of the coast. For the more reflective, there's a pond. Plus, you can rent the entire house for weddings or reunions.

Sea Gull Inn $
44594 Albion Street, Mendocino
(707) 937–5204, (888) 937–5204
www.mcn.org/a/seagull

Built in 1878, one of Mendocino's oldest standing houses is also one of its oldest continuous inns. The Sea Gull began welcoming tourists in the 1960s. It's a cozy place with a profuse flower garden, a holly tree shading the front porch, and a resident feline. It has nine rooms, some of which offer hints of ocean blue from the windows. All have private bathrooms, though the unit known as The Shed does not have bathing facilities. Two rooms accommodate children. One of those is The Barn, a funky, self-contained structure with a private deck and a secondary sleeping loft. This is the only unit with a television. Continental breakfast might include offerings from the Mendocino Cookie Company.

Sea Rock Inn $$
11101 North Lansing Street, Mendocino
(707) 937–0926, (800) 906–0926
www.searock.com

You might quibble with the Sea Rock's designation as a bed-and-breakfast inn. The inn's 15 units are spread among a complex of buildings, and the breakfast is a continental buffet. You will not, however, argue with the view. Every room has an ocean vista, on a continuum that ranges from "peek" to "spectacular." And the grounds include benches perched atop the bluffs, crashing waves, and barking sea lions far below. The Sea Rock comprises six private cottages, five deluxe suites, and four rooms in the refurbished Stratton House. Each unit is equipped with private bathroom, queen-size bed, cable TV, VCR, telephone, hardwood furniture, fine linens, and down pillows. Many have feather beds and/or Franklin fireplaces. Some have whirlpool tubs, and two rooms have an ocean view from the tub. Children are permitted under close supervision. The Sea Rock Inn is about a half-mile north of Mendocino.

Whitegate Inn $$$$
499 Howard Street, Mendocino
(707) 937–4892, (800) 531–7282
www.whitegateinn.com

The framework for this bed-and-breakfast inn is an elegant house dating from 1883. A cobblestone path bordered with primroses leads to a terrace and gazebo. Restored in splendid style, the house is furnished with a collection of French, Italian, and Victorian antiques. Award-winning gourmet breakfasts are served on bone china and sterling silver and include such offerings as caramel-apple French toast or eggs Florentine. Seven lovely bedrooms with private baths provide comforts from fireplaces to cable television. Guests receive a welcome basket and are invited to a wine and cheese serving at 5:00 P.M.

Annie's Jughandle Beach Inn $$
Gibney Lane and Highway 1, Fort Bragg
(707) 964–1415, (800) 964–9957
www.jughandle.com

This five-room Victorian-style inn built in 1883 sits midway between Mendocino and Fort Bragg. Guests enjoy private baths, spa tubs, fireplaces, and, in some rooms, ocean views. Jean LaTorre and his wife Shannon like to use the phrase "Louisiana hospitality and cuisine with the country charm of the Mendocino coast." Shannon, the chef, is the one from Louisiana, so meals at the Jughandle Inn tend to have a Cajun flair. The place overlooks the Jughandle State Preserve, and footpaths lead down to the ocean. There's access to plenty of hiking trails nearby, and in the springtime visitors can watch the whales right from the inn during breakfast—and all through the day.

Country Inn at Fort Bragg $
632 North Main Street, Fort Bragg
(707) 964–3737, (800) 831–5327
www.beourguests.com

Inside this 1890s residence, innkeepers Bruce and Cynthia Knauss' intention is to transport you back to "the carefree turn-of-the-century." The sloping ceilings, decorative wallpaper, and inviting fireplaces are part of the journey. Each of the eight rooms has its own theme, such as "Granny's Attic," with its clothing niche, walnut wainscoting framed by redwood molding, and old-fashioned bathtub. The Country Inn is a short walk from the beach and features a full breakfast, free newspaper, and afternoon wine and cheese.

The Grey Whale Inn $$
615 North Main Street, Fort Bragg
(707) 964–0640, (800) 382–7244
www.greywhaleinn.com

The first bed-and-breakfast in Fort Bragg, the Grey Whale has gathered a coterie of longtime admirers who come back time after time for the ambiance and cozy comforts of its spacious guest rooms. Twelve rooms on the first and second floors offer various amenities—some have gas log fireplaces, some have views of the coastline, some are in French country style, and one has an antique sleigh bed. Two rooms in the penthouse have private sundecks; one has a double-size Jacuzzi. All rooms have private baths. The recreation room has a pool table and VCR. Breakfast is lavish.

Lodge at Noyo River $$
500 Casa Del Noyo, Fort Bragg
(707) 964–8045, (800) 628–1126
www.noyolodge.com

The lodge overlooks Noyo Harbor, and suites are particularly spacious, with a solarium-style parlor and bedrooms with king-size or queen-size beds, window seats, and plenty of fluffy pillows scattered about. Most have fireplaces. There are seven guest rooms and suites in the main lodge (one is said to be haunted!) and nine in an adjoining modern building. All rooms have private baths, down comforters, and first-class bathroom amenities. In the evening you can watch pink sunsets over the Noyo bridge, then wake up in the morning to the far-off barking of harbor seals. A sumptuous breakfast is served in the wood-paneled dining room.

Old Stewart House Inn $
511 Stewart Street, Fort Bragg
(707) 961–0775, (800) 287–8392
www.oldstewarthouseinn.com

Stewart House is Fort Bragg's oldest, a pre-Victorian erected in 1876. The proprietors bill it as the perfect spot for families or honeymooners. A third-story deck overlooks the ocean. All six of Stewart House's rooms have a European flair. The most formal, the Queen Anne Room, has a gas fireplace and a bathroom with a big soaking tub. (There's a Jacuzzi tub room below the main house.) An outside cottage has a Greek theme. The carriage house is more of a family unit, with bunk beds for the kids, a minikitchen, and a separate room for mom and dad. Need another family amenity? Stewart House sits right across the street from the depot where the Willits–Fort Bragg Skunk Train arrives and departs. A two-night minimum is required on weekends.

Spas and Resorts

Enjoy playing in the mud? In addition to premium wine grapes, the region known as Wine Country has unlimited quantities of rich volcanic ash just below the surface, thanks to prehistoric eruptions of our resident inactive volcano, Mount St. Helena. The ash and the hot water that naturally percolates way down in the Earth's strata constitute the main ingredients of our legendary mud baths that attract visitors by the thousands.

Some of the nation's finest and famous full-service resort spas are here—heavyweights such as Auberge du Soleil and the Fairmont Sonoma Mission Inn—and most of them revolve around mud, steam, massaging fingers, and the like. There is variety, however. Silverado Country Club & Resort pampers with world-class spa services *and* provides a world-class golf course; Little River Inn on the Mendocino coastline has a front-row seat to the Pacific Ocean.

Now about that mud. The uninitiated may have a few questions. Yes, the mud is hot, thick, and heavy. Typically a mixture of volcanic ash, white clay, peat moss, and hot mineral water, it is warmed to a temperature of about 106 degrees. And yes, it is sanitary, in case you were wondering. After each use the tubs are refreshed with scalding mineral water at a temperature that zaps any and all germs. When the water is drained and the mud cools, it's ready for the next bather.

The one-hour mud bath procedure varies among spas, but in general resembles this: You are immersed and swathed in the gooey mixture up to your neck for about 12 minutes. Attendants watch closely and supply you with cold water and cloths soaked in soothing oils. When your time is up, you pull yourself out of the ooze and thoroughly rinse off. Follow that with a mineral Jacuzzi bath or five minutes in a eucalyptus steam cabinet. After steaming, you might retreat to a private room and be covered with light sheets for a brief nap. Then the choice is yours: massage, salt scrub, mini-facial, foot reflexology, or a combination of all.

Many of the facilities listed offer amenities and services above and beyond a standard lodging—places that will rub you, wrap you, soak you, feed you, and give you a bed in which to drop your newly detoxified body. Nearly all of these properties accept credit cards, welcome children but not pets, and prohibit smoking. Always ask about specifics before booking.

Don't be intimidated by all those dollar signs in these listings. You can still get exceptional spa services at the more affordable facilities in our list—or simply walk into one of the many day spas profiled at the end of this chapter.

Price Code

For room prices, refer to our dollar code below. Rates are for double occupancy on a weekend night in high season (generally May through October). Most spas and resorts offer discounts for off-season or mid-week visits. The tariff usually includes use of facilities such as tennis courts and gyms, if there are such things, but you will pay separately for spa services. The dollar code does not reflect taxes and tips.

$	Less than $100
$$	$101 to $150
$$$	$151 to $200
$$$$	More than $200

Resorts

Napa County

Silverado Country Club & Resort $$$$
1600 Atlas Peak Road, Napa
(707) 257–0200, (800) 532–0500
www.silveradoresort.com

It is hard not to be impressed by this mega-resort at the base of Atlas Peak. For one thing, it's big. Silverado comprises 1,200 acres and 280 cottage suites—every one of them a deluxe accommodation with living room, wood-burning fireplace, full kitchen, and a private patio or terrace. Most of the hubbub is centered around the two 18-hole, Robert Trent Jones Jr.–designed golf courses. But there is a slew of additional activity, including mountain-bike rentals, nine swimming pools, jogging trails, 17 plexi-paved tennis courts, and a 16,000-square-foot spa and gym. Check-in and concierge service is in the circa-1870s Colonial mansion, originally owned by Civil War Gen. John F. Miller. There you'll also find a conference center with 15,000 square feet of flexible meeting space (including a 5,200-square-foot grand ballroom) and a fully staffed catering and conventions department. Dining options include the Bar and Grill for breakfast and lunch and either Vintner's Court or the Mesquite-influenced Royal Oak for dinner (see our Restaurants chapter).

Villagio Inn & Spa $$$$
6481 Washington Street, Yountville
(707) 944–8877, (800) 351–1133
www.villagio.com

Here's an inn inspired by the colors and architecture of Rome and Tuscany. The images of nine Roman goddesses are in abundance to give this property a mythical atmosphere, complete with fountains, vineyards, and gardens galore. The inn comprises 112 rooms in two-story clusters of buildings; 26 of these are mini-suites. Each room comes equipped with fireplace, refrigerator, welcoming wine, TV, terry robes, and the usual modern amenities. Daily continental champagne breakfast is included; afternoon tea, coffee, and cook-ies are also served. Outside are two heated pools and two tennis courts.

The 3,500-square-foot spa features 10 treatment rooms where your epidermis will be delightfully recharged. They can do it all here: facials, massage, body scrubs, body wraps (including a grapeseed polish), and a Vichy shower treatment, too. Treatment packages include the Juventas (goddess of rejuvenation) at $230 and the Juterna (goddess of the healing waters) for $190.

Auberge du Soleil $$$$
180 Rutherford Hill Road, Rutherford
(707) 963–1211, (800) 348–5406
www.aubergedusoleil.com

What began as a restaurant in 1983 has blossomed into one of the Wine Country's most exclusive resorts, nestled among 33 acres of olive trees and chaparral. The whole operation exudes brightness and health, with terra-cotta tile floors, fresh bouquets, natural wood and leather furnishings, and Mediterranean color schemes. The 31 guest rooms and 19 suites all have private terraces, fireplaces, down comforters, and stereo CD systems. The sizable bathrooms have double sinks and huge tubs under skylights.

The recreational opportunities include three tournament-surfaced tennis

Insiders' Tip

Auberge du Soleil in Rutherford weighed in at Number 74 on the Top 100 "best overall" hotels in the world, as compiled by *Travel & Leisure* magazine in 2002. The resort also ranked Number 24 among the Top 25 small hotels in the world, those with 100 rooms or fewer.

courts, a swimming pool, a whirlpool tub, and an exercise room. There is a sculpture garden and three separate facilities for meetings, receptions, or special occasions. The Auberge du Soleil restaurant is profiled in the Restaurants chapter. The spa services are an attraction in their own right. You can get a facial, a body wrap, or a scalp treatment and choose from a variety of massage styles. The spa also delves into Ayurvedic treatments (a holistic approach developed in India some 5,000 years ago), yoga, and somatics, based on "neuromuscular retraining principles." Auberge du Soleil is not appropriate for children younger than 16.

Meadowood Napa Valley $$$$
900 Meadowood Lane, St. Helena
(707) 963–3646, (800) 458–8080
www.meadowood.com

In the 1800s, Chinese laborers harvested rice in the small valley known as Meadowood. (The 800-foot tunnel they built still drains the valley during heavy rains.) The full-service, Relais & Chateaux estate that now graces the area would have been beyond the wildest dreams of those immigrants. There are 85 suites, lodges, and cottages, spread among 250 acres and often tucked into the hillside scenery. All accommodations feature high-beamed ceilings, heated bathroom floors, private porches, and down comforters. If you're feeling active, choose among two pools, a whirlpool, saunas, seven tennis courts, two championship croquet lawns, a nine-hole golf course, and a 3-mile hiking trail. The Health Spa features a dizzying array of fitness classes, personal training, yoga, skin-care treatments, salt treatments, and body wraps.

Meadowood's staff of resident experts includes a wine director who leads Friday night wine receptions and a croquet pro—one of only two in America. The resort also has five private conference and event rooms with a total reception capacity of 200. Accommodations start at $375 and go up to nearly 10 times that: The lodges top out at $3,500. (See the Meadowood listing in our Restaurants chapter for even more decadence.)

White Sulphur Springs Resort & Spa $$
3100 White Sulphur Springs Road, St. Helena
(707) 963–8588,
(800) 593–8873 in Calif. and Nev.
www.whitesulphursprings.com

California's oldest hot-springs resort (established in 1852) retains its 19th-century charm, thanks to a laid-back management style and an idyllic setting. Take Spring Street west from downtown St. Helena; soon the town ends, but the road keeps going until you're tucked into a forest of redwood, fir, and madrone.

The 330-acre resort has 37 rooms—14 in the Carriage House (shared baths), 14 in The Inn (private baths), and nine creekside cottages. There is a warm (85 to 92 degrees) sulphur pool fed by a natural spring, and you can smell it anywhere in the main residential area. Children are okay in the cottages. The spa treatments involve massage therapy and aroma/thermo therapy, including herbal facials, mineral mud wraps, seaweed wraps, and herbal linen wraps.

Silver Rose Inn & Spa $$$
351 Rosedale Road, Calistoga
(707) 942–9581, (800) 995–9381
www.silverrose.com

The Silver Rose is building a reputation as the top-of-the-food-chain spa in the northern Napa Valley. The setting is quite pleasant—a quiet road just off the Silverado Trail, about a half-mile south of Calistoga. The inn has a total of 20 rooms divided between two buildings, Inn on the Knoll and Inn on the Vineyard. Most units face onto vines; some have vines planted right outside the windows. Each room is themed, e.g., the gold-accented Cleopatra Room and the Art Deco-inspired Hello Hollywood.

Guests are free to make use of the Jacuzzi, tennis courts, putting green, and wine bottle-shaped swimming pool, and breakfast is served in the tiled dining hall. There is also a state-of-the-art conference room. The spa services include massage, body and facial treatments, various water treatments, hydrotherm massage, and herbal body wraps (some available in-room). Prices range from $50 for a reflexology session to $249 for a three-hour-plus, all-purpose body reclamation project. No children younger than 15, please.

Dr. Wilkinson's Hot Springs $$

1507 Lincoln Avenue, Calistoga
(707) 942–4102
www.drwilkinson.com

This has been a Calistoga institution since John Wilkinson opened his spa in 1952, and it celebrated its 50th anniversary in a big way in 2002. More than a million people have passed through the doc's treatment rooms, and the facility has been profiled on *Lifestyles of the Rich and Famous* and *Good Morning America*. A perennial favorite for five decades, "the works"—mud bath, facial mask, mineral whirlpool bath, steam room, blanket wrap, and half-hour massage—is still the most popular package. But expect to pay about $99, rather than the original $4.50. Doc is a local legend who once served as the town's mayor. As often as not, this fit octogenarian can be found prowling the town's streets, serving as a walking billboard for his health treatments. His two children, Mark and Carolynne, now run the business.

Dr. Wilkinson's has 43 rooms, some with kitchens, all with refrigerators and private bathrooms. Rooms in the adjacent five-unit Victorian are slightly more expensive. Individual spa services start at $49 for a half-hour massage. Children must be 14 or older to take a mud bath. Doc also offers an on-site salon where you can get facial and skin-care treatments or select from a wide range of related products.

Indian Springs $$$$

1712 Lincoln Avenue, Calistoga
(707) 942–4913
www.indianspringscalistoga.com

If this collection of teal-and-white buildings evokes the heyday of the recuperative spa, it's appropriate. Indian Springs is on land that was once part of Sam Brannan's inspired attempt to make this town the Saratoga of the West. The bathhouse and Olympic-size swimming pool date to 1913, and most of the bungalows were built in the 1930s. The property has a scattering of squat buildings (most units are duplexes) and open vistas. In addition to the 17 studio and one-room units, Indian Springs offers the Merchant Bun-

Indian Springs is one of Calistoga's oldest spa resorts. PHOTO: JEAN SAYLOR DOPPENBERG

galow, a three-bedroom, two-bath suite that sleeps six and goes for $500 a night. The spa services include 100-percent volcanic ash mud baths starting at $75, mineral baths with a full massage for $140, facial or body polish treatments, and combinations thereof.

Calistoga Spa Hot Springs $$$
1006 Washington Street, Calistoga
(707) 942-6269
www.calistogaspa.com

Considering Calistoga Spa's services, excellent in both quality and quantity, this has to be considered something of a bargain. The spa is a block off Lincoln Avenue, set next to the old Gliderport runway and behind the Depot and other commercial buildings (on the site of the old Roman Olympic Pool). All 57 rooms come with kitchenettes (all the basics provided except an oven), air-conditioning, and cable TV; two suites have full kitchens. Guests are free to use the small but well-maintained gym (the only one in Calistoga) and four naturally heated mineral baths that range from 83 to 105 degrees. And then there is the typical lineup of spa services: mud baths, mineral baths, massage, and steam-and-blanket combos. Prices start at $16 for a basic steam-and-blanket; a mud dunk, mineral bath, blanket wrap, and one-hour massage go for $92. Calistoga Spa also has a conference room that accommodates as many as 40 people.

Insiders' Tip
The Olympic-size swimming pool at Indian Springs spa in Calistoga is one of the oldest and largest in California. Built in 1913, it is naturally heated by mineral water from nearby geysers.

Roman Spa $$$
1300 Washington Street, Calistoga
(707) 942-4441, (800) 250-2457
www.tales.com/romanspa

The Roman Spa is a straight-up motel, but you can get pampered next door at Calistoga Oasis Spa. The two establishments have the same owners, though they're run separately. Roman Spa, just a block from downtown Calistoga, has lily ponds; a large, heated outdoor pool; an indoor, hydro-jet therapy pool; and outdoor hydro-jet and Finnish-style saunas. The 60 rooms include everything from a single with a queen-size bed to a family suite with two full rooms. About a third of the rooms have kitchen facilities, and there are five smoking rooms. They do not take credit card reservations over the phone here; you'll need to send a check or show up in person.

Golden Haven Hot Springs $$
1713 Lake Street, Calistoga
(707) 942-6793
www.goldenhaven.com

This is a comparatively affordable spa in a quiet section of Calistoga. The exterior is nothing special, but the rooms are clean and full of conveniences, including air-conditioning, color TV, and refrigerators. All the soothing spa treatments are there if you want them. The lineup features mud baths (including private rooms for couples), herbal mineral baths, herbal facials, and massage. Those fees range from $45 for a half-hour massage to $159 for a mud bath, hour massage, and herbal facial package. Golden Haven also promotes a "European body wrap" guaranteed to take off 6 inches of unsightly fat. Guests use the swimming pool and hot mineral pool free. Children are allowed on weekdays only.

Calistoga Village Inn & Spa $$$
1880 Lincoln Avenue, Calistoga
(707) 942-0991
www.greatspa.com

Another of the town's older (post-World War II) spas, the Village Inn is a long row of whitewashed bungalows along the northern reaches of Lincoln Avenue, just before it hits the Silverado Trail. There are plenty of reasons to be semiclothed here: a swimming pool, a wading pool (children are welcome), a Jacuzzi, and a dry steam room. Among the numerous spa treatments are mud baths, massage, salt scrubs, facials, foot reflexology, and body wraps. The inn also offers 16 different types of mineral baths, including the aromatic seaweed bath, Dr. Singha's mustard bath, and the Moor mud baths. A package known as The Ultimate features a mud bath, salt scrub, mini-facial, and one-hour massage for $185. Guests of the inn receive a 10 percent discount for all of the above. The Village Inn has two conference rooms, 42 guest suites, and a restaurant, Headlines Bistro & Grill, which specializes in American cuisine.

Sonoma County

The Fairmont Sonoma Mission Inn & Spa
$$$$
18140 Sonoma Highway, Boyes Hot Springs
(707) 938–9000, (800) 862–4945
www.sonomamissioninn.com

The style is Spanish-influenced early California, a sprawling pink building with red tile roof, arcade, and bell tower. Lobby decor features heavy Spanish furnishings, grouped around a massive fireplace, where guests sip late-morning coffee on Sunday while reading the San Francisco *Chronicle* or the *Wall Street Journal*. It would be no surprise to see a Hollywood star or world leader—Mikhail Gorbachev and Liz Taylor have stayed here. The health and fitness program covers all bases—aerobics, aromatherapy, body sculpting, yoga, herbal wrap, seaweed sauna, and steam room. For total indulgence, ask for the $200, 100-minute Wappo Harvest Kur. To recharge after all this activity, two great restaurants—Sante, in the main building, and the nearby Big 3 Diner—both offer low-calorie cuisine (see our Restaurants chapter).

The Inn itself has a colorful history. The first spa was built in 1860 by an eccentric doctor who burned it down after a tiff with his wife. But it was rebuilt and by the 1890s San Francisco society was journeying north by rail and auto to "take the waters." The present inn dates to 1927, when it took shape in the style of a California mission. In 1985, a total renovation brought 70 new rooms and a conference center. The hot springs, however, lay dormant, lost in the earth until 1993, when the legendary waters were brought back to the surface from 1,100 feet below the Inn. And today, this spring water is the water that fills the two pools and whirlpools.

Further expansion totaling $36 million has taken place over the last couple of years, culminating in the inn's affiliation with Fairmont Hotels & Resort corporation.

MacArthur Place $$$$
29 East MacArthur Street, Sonoma
(707) 938–2929, (800) 722–1866
www.macarthurplace.com

One of the newer spa resorts in Wine Country, MacArthur Place began its life as a 300-acre horse and cattle ranch with vineyards. The two-story Victorian house dominating the former Burris-Good ranch was built in the 1860s. Constructed with wooden pegs and square nails, the house was home to David Burris and his family of nine children. Burris was also a banker; he founded Sonoma Valley Bank, still in business today, in the corner library on the home's first floor.

It became a luxury destination in 1997, when it was transformed into a 64-room hotel with full-service spa and a steakhouse restaurant called Saddles (see our Restaurants chapter). New cottages were also added and the gardens and landscaping generously enhanced and upgraded to include a swimming pool and whirlpool. Ten of the rooms are in the original stately home; the inn's 29 newest suites are luxuriously appointed with fireplaces, wet bars, flat-panel TVs with DVD players, and king beds.

The Garden Spa lives up to its name, using the herbs, flowers, and fruits grown on the property in its treatments. Most of the massages, facials, body polishes, and mud wraps (with grapeseeds) run about $100; a Lomi Lomi massage, practiced by Hawaiians for centuries, will set you back about $200. Several "signature" treatments, also about $200 each, utilize rose petals, grapefruits and oranges, and essential oils.

The Lodge at Sonoma $$$$
1325 Broadway Avenue, Sonoma
(707) 935–6600 (lodge),
(707) 931–2034 (spa)
www.thelodgeatsonoma.com,
www.raindancespa.com

Sonoma is a spa town, and this new world-class facility helps keep the town's reputation for hot water and luxurious body scrubs intact. The 182 spacious guest rooms are nicely appointed with fireplaces, balcony or patio, two-line phones, cable TV, and complimentary breakfast in the restaurant, Carneros (see our Restaurants chapter), or in-room.

Hot mineral waters flow right beneath the property, so the Raindance Spa is the perfect source for therapeutic bathing treatments. There are outdoor soaking and watsu therapy pools, and underwater massage is offered. The full-service spa has a dizzying array of massages, skin-care treatments, body wraps, facials, and an assortment of "kurs"—a series of treatments using mineral water, algae, therapeutic mud, and essential oils and herbs to detoxify and hydrate your overstressed bod. Prices range from about $100 for facials to $295 for a kur treatment. A full-day spa indulgence, with lunch too, costs about $475; a half-day is $275.

The Kenwood Inn $$$$
10400 Sonoma Highway, Kenwood
(707) 833–1293, (800) 353–9663
www.kenwoodinn.com

Intimate in scale with a peaceful, Old World charm, the Kenwood Inn offers the ambiance of an Italian country villa nestled in the heart of Sonoma Valley.

The inn is situated on a secluded hillside facing more than 1,000 acres of sloping estate vineyards. A recent expansion added 24 private suites to the existing 12, as well as two more courtyards. The suites contain feather beds, down comforters, European antiques and lush fabrics, private baths, and fireplaces. A complimentary bottle of wine greets guests on arrival. Breakfast is served either in the dining room or at outdoor tables in good weather. A full-service spa pampers guests and day visitors alike with different therapeutic massages, 11 special skin-care treatments and spa body treatments—such as clay and chamomile, seaweed body wrap—and ancient Ayurvedic body purification rituals. Half-day spa experiences are available, including the popular couples "togetherness massage," as well as the Faccia Bella facial. Spa treatments are priced individually.

River Village Resort & Spa $$$
14880 River Road, Guerneville
(707) 869–8139, (800) 529–3376
www.rivervillageresort.com

This newly renovated resort features 20 cottages clustered around two swimming pools, a hot tub, and two large decks in a courtyard on the edge of town. Owners Gary and Donna Klauenburch have lived in the area for more than 20 years and together have created a charming getaway that offers a wide range of rejuvenating and relaxing therapies. Services include Swedish, deep tissue, reflexology, and aromatherapy massage as well as salt scrubs, mud wraps, full facials, and herbal body wraps. The resort also features nutrition and diet counseling—from an herbalist and certified nutritional consultant and diet counselor. The location also affords relatively easy access to the nearby Russian River, where you can swim, canoe, kayak, or just bask in the sun.

Mendocino County

Orr Hot Springs $$
13201 Orr Springs Road, Ukiah
(707) 462–6277

The hot spring waters bubble up from the earth into a redwood tub and spill over into the swimming pool below. The spa has had a checkered history and at present could only be described as rustic. The first bath house was built in the 1850s and is now used as a dormitory. A 14-room lodge and three cottages serve as the main buildings today. During the 1970s the 26-acre hot-springs facility became a kind of commune. Today, the situation is informal;

you can bring a picnic lunch and store it in the communal kitchen. Besides the basic facilities (some of which have half-baths), camping is also an option. Day-use is another option. Another informality: Clothing is optional.

Vichy Springs Resort $$$
2605 Vichy Springs Road, Ukiah
(707) 462-9515
www.vichysprings.com

Named after the world-famous springs first discovered by Julius Caesar in France, the waters of Vichy Springs bubble up from deep within the earth and are virtually identical in chemistry to those of the French namesake. Available in abundance for bathing and swimming, the waters are naturally warm and effervescent (dubbed "champagne baths"), filled with minerals and energy renowned for healing and restorative qualities. Also restorative and soothing is the idyllic parklike setting of the resort—the oldest continuously operating mineral springs spa in California. Opened in 1854 and now a California Historical Landmark, it was a favorite retreat of Mark Twain, Jack London, and Presidents Ulysses S. Grant, Benjamin Harrison, and Teddy Roosevelt. Today, the resort is restored and renovated to tastefully combine its historic charm with modern comfort and conveniences. More contemporary visitors have included Wavy Gravy and Patch Adams.

Twelve individually decorated rooms with private baths have been created from the ancient, broken-down former facilities that date to the 1860s. There are also four cottages with kitchens, bedrooms, and living rooms. Just steps away from the accommodations are the renovated indoor and outdoor bathing tubs, therapeutic massage building, and mineral-water-filled, Olympic-size swimming pool. Offered at varying rates are therapeutic massage, Swedish massage, and herbal facial. Day visitors are also welcome to use the pool, baths, and the property.

Little River Inn $$
7751 North Highway 1, Little River
(707) 937-5942, (888) 466-5683
www.littleriverinn.com

Built in 1853 by Silas Coombs, a lumberman from Maine, this classic coastal resort once was the Coombs' family home. Eucalyptus trees, planted as a windbreak for the Coombs' orchard, now shelter a golf course. The wisteria-covered front porch of the original home, where Silas once spotted ocean freighters, now beckons guests into the dining room. In the music room, someone may be tickling the ivories on the Emerson square grand piano, which survived its trip around Cape Horn in 1850. The inn has a long tradition of hosting Hollywood celebrities—Joan Fontaine and a crew of 40; Jonathan Winters, who provided impromptu entertainment; Ronald Reagan, who sprawled on the floor to illustrate football plays. (All rooms are nonsmoking.)

The inn's Third Court Salon and Day Spa offers classic European facials, aromatherapy wraps, and a host of other body treatments, hydration skin treatment, and massage. Reservations are required year-round. There is no charge for children younger than 18. Sunday brunch and dinner are served.

Sweetwater Spa & Inn $$
955 Ukiah Street (spa), 44840 Main Street (inn), Mendocino
(707) 937-4140, (800) 300-4140
www.sweetwaterspa.com

The Sweetwater complex takes up most of the two blocks between Ukiah and Main Streets in the village of Mendocino, and that's not all. Besides the 22 units downtown, the company has six rooms in Little River and the cozy Redwood Cottage, a popular lodging about five minutes east of Mendocino.

For 14 years Sweetwater has maintained one of the premier massage staffs in Northern California. They offer a full range of massage and bodywork options. Sweetwater also has hot tubs and sauna, with prices that vary according to privacy and tub size. Kids are welcome.

Day Spas

Along with the destination spa resorts, you also have the option of luxuriating at one of several day spas. Spend a few rejuvenating hours sunk neck deep in mud, or enveloped in a stress-relieving hydro wrap, or soothed by the skilled hands of a masseuse, and then be on your way. Here are just a few of the many possibilities.

Napa County

Mount View Spa
1457 Lincoln Avenue, Calistoga
(707) 942–5789, (800) 772–8838
In the Mount View Hotel building (see our Hotels, Motels, and Inns chapter), but run separately, this spa is the ultimate in luxury. The tasteful furnishings, personalized service, waffle-weave cotton robes in the dressing rooms—all combine to set a mood of elegant decadence. Mount View offers five types of massage, from Swedish to reflexology; customized whirlpool baths with additives such as fango mud, mineral salts, powdered milk whey, and herbal bath oils; and body wraps. The latter include the herbal linen wrap, the stress-relief hydro wrap (a warm, aloe vera-based gel), and the Enzymatic Sea mud wrap, which is painted over your entire body like a dusky leotard. All of it is performed in private rooms. The massages cost $40 (for 25 minutes) to $95 (for 85 minutes). A bath treatment followed by a 55-minute massage runs $85; add an herbal wrap and a 25-minute basic cleansing facial and pay $170.

Lincoln Avenue Spa
1339 Lincoln Avenue, Calistoga
(707) 942–5296
www.lincolnavenuespa.com
Set in an old stone building in the heart of town, this spa is an upscale companion to Golden Haven Hot Springs (see the listing in this chapter). Lincoln Avenue specializes in the easygoing Swedish/Esalen style of massage, with rates ranging from $45 for back, neck, and shoulder work to $99 for a full body massage and a foot reflexology treatment. The mud treatments are longtime favorites too. Lie for an hour on a steam table while wearing a suit of herbal mineral body mud (with 34 herbs), sea mud (with kelp), or mint mud. If you're not allowed to play in the mud, try on the herbal wrap. The spa also offers facials and acupressure "facelifts." Packages are available, of course, such as the Ultimate Pamper Package, a four-and-a-half-hour slice of heaven that costs $259.

Lavender Hill Spa
1015 Foothill Boulevard, Calistoga
(707) 942–4495, (800) 528–4772
www.lavenderhillspa.com
This intimate retreat bills itself as "A Garden Spa for Couples," and, indeed, the verdant grounds in back of the bathhouses are a suitably romantic spot for postmassage reverie and sweet talk. Inside, Lavender Hill offers elegant trappings and a warm staff. Choose from four basic bath treatments: volcanic mud bath, seaweed bath, herbal blanket wrap, or aromatherapy mineral salt bath, all of which come with a facial mask and light foot massage. Other options include la stone massage, therapeutic massage, and foot reflexology. Prices range from $55 for a basic half-hour massage to $165 for a bath treatment with one-hour massage and mini-facial.

The Calistoga Massage Center
1219 Washington Street, Calistoga
(707) 942–6193
www.calistogamassage.com
The Massage Center is for connoisseurs of massage. They offer deep tissue and sports

massage, shiatsu, Thai, and esoteric methods called cranio-sacral and Jin Shin. Select a mode and a duration—it's $45 for 30 minutes, $80 for an hour, or $125 for 90 minutes. (Swedish/Esalen-based massage is a little less expensive, running $40, $70, and $100.) The center also offers massage for two ($130 for an hour each), massage instruction for couples ($240 for three hours), foot reflexology ($80 for an hour), herbal facials ($70 an hour), and various combinations of the above. Ask about discounts for students, seniors, upvalley residents, and anyone visiting Tuesday through Thursday.

Sonoma County

Sonoma Spa on the Plaza
457 First Street W., Sonoma
(707) 939–8770
www.sonomaspaontheplaza.com

When you've worked yourself into a tizzy shopping and dining in Sonoma, slip into this conveniently located spa for a relaxing tune-up. You'll find everything from specialty massages to body treatments and herbal facials, in package form or a la carte. Deluxe packages, lasting from two to five hours, run from $128 to $298. Three types of one-hour, mud-based body treatments are offered at $55 each.

Osmosis Enzyme Bath and Massage
209 Bohemian Highway, Freestone
(707) 874–1108
www.osmosis.com

Named the best day spa in America by *Travel & Leisure* magazine, Osmosis features a Japanese enzyme bath comprising fragrant cedar fiber, rice bran, and more than 600 enzymes. The action of the enzymes produces a special quality of heat that improves circulation and metabolism and cleanses skin pores and beautifies the skin. Massage treatments include Swedish/Esalen method and many others. If you like, you can have your massage outdoors under a pagoda near Salmon Creek. The enzyme bath is $75, with massage $150. Osmosis is located off Highway 12 in the small town of Freestone, about halfway between Sebastopol and Bodega.

A unique spa experience awaits visitors to Osmosis Enzyme Bath and Massage in Freestone. PHOTO: JEAN SAYLOR DOPPENBERG

A Simple Touch Spa
239 Center Street, Healdsburg
(707) 433–6856
www.asimpletouchspa.com

This lovely little spa in downtown Healds-burg offers aromatherapy baths, massage, facials, and body treatments. One of the specialty baths features detoxifying fango mud made from dehydrated volcanic ash. The body wraps range from fragrant herbal or rose petals—the latter wrap involves painting the body in rose whey and then wrapping it in a heat blanket—to the more common remineralizing sea-weed wrap. Several special packages are available that range from $70 for a bath and half-hour massage to the deluxe package for $210, which includes a bath, salt scrub, one-hour massage, herbal facial, and rose petal wrap.

Insiders' Tip

An enzyme bath at Osmosis in Freestone is preceded by a soothing enzyme tea ceremony. What's in the bath? Aromatic cedar fiber, rice bran, and more than 600 active enzymes.

Camping

Napa County
Sonoma County
Mendocino County

Prefer to end your day sipping Chardonnay by campfire light? Then you'll appreciate the wide variety of Wine Country campgrounds and RV parks. Here you can have the best of both worlds: relaxing under the stars at night and visiting wineries and other attractions by day.

If you desire more in the way of outdoor adventure, many campgrounds afford ample opportunities for backpacking, hiking, and fishing. Campgrounds in northern Mendocino County are generally among the most remote and primitive, where nary a wine taster is likely to be found.

If we don't say otherwise, assume that each campground has piped, potable water, a desirable part of any outdoor experience. If it doesn't, arrange to bring or pump your own. And please note that some of the listed sites are part of the region's state parks. In those cases we have provided all the basic camping information here, but for a more thorough description of the park, you should turn to our Parks and Recreation chapter.

To pitch your tent or park your RV, expect to pay from $12 to $25 nightly, depending on the location and the degree of development. (State park camping fees range from $8 to $12 per night.) Senior rates are also offered in many places, while some of the more primitive campgrounds are free.

Napa County

Napa Town & Country Fairgrounds
575 Third Street, Napa
(707) 253-4900
www.napavalleyexpo.com

The fairgrounds are just off Third Street in Napa, as it approaches the Silverado Trail. There are about 75 motor-home spaces, a group campground for 15 to 500. On-site are restrooms and showers, and close by are a laundry and a market. Pets are permitted on leashes. Note that Town & Country is closed to campers for the latter half of July and most of August.

Pleasure Cove Resort
Wragg Canyon Road, off Highway 128,
Lake Berryessa
(707) 966-2172
www.vacanet.com/pleasure.htm

This family-oriented campground is one of five around Lake Berryessa. Pleasure Cove has 105 sites for tents or motor homes, 20 with water and electrical hookups. The wheelchair-accessible sites have picnic tables and fire pits, and there

are restrooms, showers, ice, a restaurant and bar, propane, and groceries. Pleasure Cove also has a boat ramp if you're prowling for trout.

Spanish Flat Resort
4290 Knoxville Road, off Highway 128,
Lake Berryessa
(707) 966-7700
www.spanishflatresort.com

Another possibility for a recreational jaunt to Berryessa is Spanish Flat, which has 120 campsites for tents or motor homes, a few of them with partial hookups. Picnic tables, fire pits, flush toilets, and showers are provided. The hosts also have complete marina facilities, a boat launch, and rentals. A laundry and a restaurant are a short drive away.

Bothe-Napa Valley State Park
Highway 29, south of Calistoga
(707) 942-4575 (info),
(800) 444-PARK (reservations)
www.napanet.net/~bothe

While a million or so industrious tourists whiz by on Highway 29, you can lie next

109

to your tent and look up at the boughs of oaks and pines or at the stars of the Milky Way. The park has a first-rate campground along Redwood Creek, with 9 tent-only sites and 50 for tents or RVs up to 31 feet long. You get picnic tables and fire pits, toilets, and showers. Wheelchairs can be used here, and pets are allowed (campground only). There is a spring-fed swimming pool, where you can take the plunge for $1 (free for children). There are blackberries for the pickin' in summer.

Napa County Fairgrounds
1435 North Oak Street, Calistoga
(707) 942–5111

If you're going to pick a municipal campground, you could do a lot worse than Calistoga's. The scenery is nice, you can walk to restaurants and spas, and next door is Mount St. Helena Golf Course (see our Parks and Recreation chapter). There are about 60 drive-through campsites with electrical hookups, plus a small grassy area for tents.

Restrooms, showers, and propane are available, but campfires are not permitted. Pets are allowed on leashes. The campground is closed from mid-June through mid-July as the grounds are prepared for and cleaned up after the Napa County Fair (see our Festivals and Annual Events chapter).

Lower Hunting Creek
Knoxville-Devilshead Road, Knoxville
(707) 468–4000

This is one of the Wine Country's least-known campgrounds and, because of its isolation in the uppermost northern tip of Napa County, that isn't likely to change anytime soon. Located about 17 miles north of Lake Berryessa near the small community of Knoxville, Lower Hunting Creek has only five sites for tents or RVs, but it does have picnic tables, fireplaces, shade shelters, and vault toilets. Pets are permitted on leashes. Be forewarned that the campground is popular with off-road enthusiasts and hunters. From Berryessa-Knoxville Road, turn west on Devilshead Road and drive for 2 miles. A map of the area is available from the Bureau of Land

Management at the number listed. There is no charge for camping here.

Sonoma County

Southern Sonoma

Sugarloaf Ridge State Park
2605 Adobe Canyon Road, Kenwood
(800) 444–7275
www.parks.sonoma.net/sugarlf.html

This locale in the Mayacmas Mountains has 50 campsites for tents or motor homes up to 24 feet long. There is piped-in water and restrooms. In 1996, Sugarloaf Ridge State Park became the home of the largest observatory in the western United States that is completely dedicated to public viewing and education. Hiking is the main recreation at this popular state park (see our Parks and Recreation chapter). Pets are okay.

Spring Lake Regional Park
5585 Newanga Avenue, Santa Rosa
(707) 539–8092
www.sonoma-county.org

A group camping area and 30 family campsites (4 for tents only) at Spring Lake Park have centrally located restrooms and

Insiders' Tip

To reserve a campsite in one of California's state parks, you must go through the Reserve America booking service at (800) 444-PARK. Reserve America will add a one-time $7.50 surcharge to any reservation; get more details at www.reserveamerica.com.

shower facilities. Also available are 200 picnic sites, barbecue pits, a bikeway, a hiking trail, and equestrian trails. No electricity is available at this campground, which is open all week during the summer (the week before Memorial Day until the week after Labor Day) and weekends only during the winter. Please reserve at least 10 days in advance during high season.

Northern Sonoma

Windsorland RV Trailer Park
9290 Old Redwood Highway, Windsor
(707) 838-4882
www.gocampingamerica.com/windsorland/index.html

There are 66 sites here, with 56 full-hookup, pull-through sites. Windsorland also features a laundry, playground, a small store, showers, and restrooms. A pool is open seasonally. The park is open all year, and night registration is available.

KOA Kampground
26460 River Road, Cloverdale
(707) 894-3337
www.koakampgrounds.com/where/ca/05275.htm

This campground has 152 campsites (50 for tents), plus a swimming pool, recreation hall, store, minigolf course, stocked fishing pond, ball courts, and horseshoe pits. Located 1 mile from the Russian River on a hill overlooking the Alexander Valley, the Cloverdale KOA is open all year. There are also 14 Kamping Kabins for two (with no water or electricity).

Lake Sonoma–Liberty Glen
3333 Skaggs Springs Road, Lake Sonoma
(707) 433-9483
www.parks.sonoma.net/laktrls.html

Eleven miles northwest of Healdsburg, off Dry Creek Road, this Lake Sonoma park offers more than 17,000 land and water acres. Lake Sonoma facilities include a visitor center and fish hatchery (see our Kidstuff chapter), with 118 campsites available for tents or RVs up to 50 feet. There are two group sites for up to 50 campers (advance reservations required). In addition, there are 15 boat-in/hike-in

> ## Insiders' Tip
> Every summer, forest fires rage in various parts of California, some of them as a result of careless smoking by campers. Please use caution when smoking in our wilderness areas—which are tinder-dry by midsummer—and always make certain campfires are extinguished thoroughly.

primitive campgrounds around the lake, and a privately operated marina that offers boat rentals and a launch ramp. Piped water, flush toilets, solar-heated showers, and a sanitary disposal station are available in the developed area.

Sonoma Coast

Doran Regional Park
Highway 1, 1 mile south of Bodega Bay
(707) 875-3540
www.sonoma-county.org

Park facilities include 125 sites for RVs or tents, 10 tent-only sites, and 1 group camping area for tents only. There are tables, fire rings, and a trailer disposal site. What to do? Try fishing, beachcombing, clamming, boating, and picnicking.

A boat ramp and fish-cleaning station are available. There's an extra charge of $5.00 per vehicle and $1.00 per dog.

Stillwater Cove Regional Park
22455 Highway 1, approx. 15 miles north of Jenner
(707) 847-3245
www.sonoma-county.org

This 210-acre park comprises open meadow and coastal forest with spectacular

Forgot your corkscrew? The Stewart's Point General Store near Salt Point State Park on the Sonoma Coast is where campers fill their essential—and some not so essential—needs. PHOTO: JOHN NAGIECKI

ocean views from Stillwater Cove. There is also a half-mile trail leading to the historic one-room Fort Ross Schoolhouse. Twenty-three campsites serve most campers (large RVs and trailer campers should contact the park office to ensure that their vehicle will fit) and there is a hike-in/bike-in area. Facilities include pay showers, flush restrooms, and day-use parking.

Salt Point State Park
25050 Highway 1, approx. 20 miles north of Jenner
(707) 847–3221
www.parks.sonoma.net/coast.html

This 31-site campground offers picnic areas, hiking trails, diving, horseback trails, and the beautiful, adjacent Kruse Rhododendron State Reserve (see our

Parks and Recreation chapter). It's open all year, but there are no RV hookups. Piped water and flush toilets are available. In early winter this is headquarters for local abalone divers.

Gualala Point Regional Park
Highway 1, 0.5 mile south of Gualala
(707) 785–2377
www.sonoma-county.org

The 195-acre park is located near the coast, adjacent to the Gualala River. The overnight camping area is across the highway from the park's day-use facilities, and it contains tables and stoves. Water and restroom facilities are nearby. Recreation options for day-use or overnight campers include fishing, bike trails, hiking (one trail beside the bluff is especially good for bird-watching), and picnic areas. It's open all year and offers 19 family campsites for tents and motor homes up to 28 feet, 7 hike-in/bike-in campsites, and a trailer sanitary station.

West County/Russian River

Village Park Campground
6665 Highway 12, Sebastopol
(707) 823–6348

Village Park is open from May 1 to October 31 for overnight or weekly stays. Laundry facilities and restrooms with showers and hot water are offered, and children and pets are welcome.

River Bend Campground
11820 River Bend, Forestville
(707) 887–7662
www.campgrounds.com/ctpa/ca/regions/nc/39riv.htm

Eleven miles from U.S. 101, off the River Road exit, this campground has 65 sites, 35 with full hook-ups. Canoe rentals, volleyball, barbecue pits, and basketball courts are among the amenities. Other features include flush restrooms, hot showers, groceries, teepees for rent, and a huge Paul Bunyan statue. It's open all year.

Faerie Ring Campground
16747 Armstrong Woods Road, Guerneville
(707) 869–2746
www.russianriver.com/accommodations

Tucked away on 14 acres near Armstrong Redwoods State Reserve (see our Parks and Recreation chapter), this gay-friendly campground features 44 campsites—33 for tents, 4 full hookups—in either a sunny or shady location. Hot showers and flush toilets are available. It's near the Russian River, 1.8 miles north of Highway 116, and it's open all year. Faerie Ring also has a popular adults-only area. Pets allowed. No credit cards.

Schoolhouse Canyon Campground
12600 River Road, Guerneville
(707) 869–2311

This camping option lies adjacent to a 200-acre wildlife sanctuary, with tent and RV sites set in the redwoods. Hot showers, fishing and swimming along the nearby Russian River, hiking, and nature trails are among the attractions. It's open April through October.

Mendocino County

U.S. 101

Manor Oaks Overnighter Park
700 East Gobbi Street, Ukiah
(707) 462–0529, (800) 357–8772
www.mendonet.com/places/noframes/
camplist.htm

There are 53 motor-home spaces (15 of which are drive-through) with full hookups. Picnic tables, fire grills, restrooms, showers, and a swimming pool are provided. A laundry and ice are available, and right next door are the tennis courts and barbecue facilities of Oak Manor Park. Leashed pets are allowed in the campground. Manor Oaks is open year-round.

Quail Meadows Campground
23701 North Highway 101, Willits
(707) 459–6006

Most of the 49 motor-home spaces here have full or partial hookups, and there is a special section for tents only. Amenities include patios, picnic tables, restrooms, showers, and a sanitary disposal station. A laundry, propane, ice, and TV hookups are available. Pets are allowed on leashes.

Willits KOA
1600 Highway 20, Willits
(707) 459–6179
www.mendonet.com/places/noframes/
camplist.htm

There are 18 sites for tents only and 50 RV spaces (27 of which are drive-through) with full or partial hookups as well as 12 cabins. Piped water, flush toilets, showers, picnic tables, playground, swimming pool, and sanitary dump station are provided. And that's just the beginning. The Willits KOA has hiking trails, fish pond, petting zoo, minigolf, an arcade, weekend barbecues, and even seasonal horseback riding. A grocery store, laundry, and RV supplies are available, too. Pets are allowed on leashes.

Highway 128

Hendy Woods State Park
18599 Philo-Greenwood Road, Philo
(707) 937–5804
www.mcn.org/1/mendoparks/hendy.htm

The park campground offers 92 sites for tents or RVs up to 35 feet long, including 4 wheelchair-accessible sites. Piped water,

Insiders' Tip

Planning to snuggle up before a campfire? Many Wine Country stores sell firewood, as do private campgrounds (gathering firewood is generally not permitted). But remember that during the dry summer months campfires are often prohibited in some areas due to grass or forest fire danger. Check your campground bulletin board for details.

flush toilets, hot showers, a sanitary disposal station, picnic tables, and fire pits are provided. A grocery store and a propane gas station are available nearby. Pets are permitted.

Paul M. Dimmick Wayside State Camp
Highway 128, 6 miles east of Highway 1
(707) 937–5804
www.mcn.org/1/mendoparks/pmd.htm

Located about 6 miles inland from the Pacific Ocean, this campground features 30 sites for tents or RVs up to 35 feet long (no hookups). Restrooms, fireplaces, and picnic tables are provided, and pets are permitted, but there is no potable water. The nearby Navarro River is the highlight here. In summer it's a spot for swimming or canoeing; in late winter, the river gets a fair steelhead run. The state camp is open year-round.

Mendocino Coast

Manchester State Park
41500 Kinney Road, Manchester
(707) 937–5804
www.mcn.org/1/mendoparks/manchst.htm

Bordered by large sand dunes, this popular state campground offers 46 sites for tents and motor homes up to 30 feet long. It also includes a 40-person group site and 10 environmental camps. Most sites have piped water, chemical (nonflush) toilets, picnic tables, and fireplaces. The campground has a sanitary dump station. No pets are allowed.

Van Damme State Park
Highway 1, 3 miles south of Mendocino
(707) 937–5804
www.mcn.org/1/mendoparks/vandam.htm

Van Damme offers quiet rain forest groves and great ocean views, with 70 campsites for tents or motor homes up to 35 feet long. There are also 10 primitive campsites reached by a 1.7-mile hike, plus a group camp that accommodates 50 people. Piped water, flush toilets, a sanitary disposal station, hot showers, picnic tables, and fireplaces are provided in the

main campground. A grocery store, laundry, and propane are available nearby. Pets are permitted.

Russian Gulch State Park
Highway 1, 2 miles north of Mendocino
(707) 937–5804
www.mcn.org/1/mendoparks/russian.htm

Set near some of California's most beautiful coastline, this park offers 30 campsites for tents or RVs up to 30 feet long—as well as several hike-in/bike-in sites. There is also a wheelchair-accessible site and a 40-person group site. Piped water, hot showers, flush toilets, picnic tables, and fireplaces with cooking grills are provided. Pets are permitted. The campground is open April through October.

Jackson State Forest
State Department of Forestry, 802 North Main Street, Fort Bragg
(707) 964–5674

Pick up a camping permit and campground map at the Department of Forestry's Fort Bragg offices. There are 18 separate campgrounds scattered throughout this large state forest, with as few as 2 or as many as 24 campsites each. Open to both tents and RVs, this is a primitive area with no piped water available, but pit toilets, picnic tables, and fireplaces are provided. Pets are permitted. Two equestrian campgrounds are available (check that campground map). There is no fee at any of the campsites in this state forest. The surrounding redwood forest is an amazing attraction.

Mackerricher State Park
24100 Mackerricher Park Road, Fort Bragg
(707) 937–5804
www.mcn.org/1/mendoparks/macker.htm

There are 11 hike-in/bike-in campsites (for up to four people) and 143 sites for tents or motor homes up to 35 feet long—but no hookups—at this beautiful coastal park 3 miles north of Fort Bragg on Highway 1. One site is wheelchair-accessible. Piped water, hot showers, flush toilets, a dump station, picnic tables, and fireplaces are provided. Pets are permitted.

Some state campgrounds reserve sites specifically for hikers and bikers. PHOTO: JOHN NAGIECKI

Fort Bragg Leisure Time RV Park
30801 Highway 20, Fort Bragg
(707) 964–5994

The wooded setting is a highlight here for RV campers. There are 82 sites for tents or RVs, many with full or partial hookups. Restrooms, picnic tables, satellite TV, fire rings, coin-operated hot showers, and a sanitary disposal station are provided. A laundry is available, and pets are allowed on leashes.

Restaurants

We're beginning to think we should reclassify our region as "Wine and Food Country" because the cuisine in many cases threatens to outshine the wine. In fact, we've found that many visitors don't come here for the wine at all. They come for the experience of dining in world-class establishments, and the wine is a really nice bonus. If you've ever wielded a knife and fork in these parts, you know why.

Several Wine Country restaurants seem to consistently show up on the "top" lists in a variety of gourmet and travel magazines. They achieve this lofty distinction by inventing some of the most delectable dishes imaginable. For instance, just look at what a few of them can do with a single chicken: Wine Spectator Greystone Restaurant will spit-roast it with toasted orzo, olives, preserved lemon, and sun-dried tomatoes; Celadon will roast it Indian-style, with ginger and red curry, and serve it with saffron-basmati risotto; Compadres will turn it into arroz con pollo; Catahoula will take that little sucker and roast it with tasso potatoes and garlic-lemon escarole; Pacifico Restaurante will add chayote and potato and bury it all with mole sauce; the Calistoga Inn will marinate it in lime and crust it with Jamaican jerk sauce; and Auberge du Soleil will redefine it as rosemary-roasted petite poulet with artichoke-eggplant ragout.

Note that this chapter is organized a bit differently from the rest. It still follows our geographical method of listing Napa County first, followed by Sonoma and Mendocino Counties. But to make it easier to locate that famous greasy spoon you read about in *Bon Appetit* magazine, restaurants are listed alphabetically within their respective regions and cities.

As you read these entries remember that, unless we say otherwise, you can count on certain things: The restaurant serves beer and wine but does not have a full bar, it accepts major credit cards, it is wheelchair-accessible, and it takes reservations. Most of the upscale restaurants do not have children's menus, but the down-home places do.

Price Code

Refer to this price code as you peruse our Restaurants section. The dollar figure refers to the average price of two entrees only—no appetizers, no dessert, no drinks, no tax or gratuity. We don't actually expect you to eat that way—or forego the tip!—we just wanted to keep the calculations simple.

$	Less than $20
$$	$21 to $30
$$$	$31 to $40
$$$$	More than $40

Napa County

City of Napa

Bistro Don Giovanni $$$
4110 St. Helena Highway S., Napa
(707) 224–3300

Giovanni Scala's restaurant is "romantic." The subdued earth tones, the unpolished wood and the tiles, the vineyard views, the high ceilings, the fireplaces in and out—your date will be putty in your hands. Just make sure you can still concentrate on the food. Donna Scala does the cooking, favoring regional Italian dishes and tossing in a bit of Provence. The pan-seared salmon filet with buttermilk mashed potatoes is excellent, as is the grilled portobello mushroom appetizer. Side dishes not to be missed are the sautéed spinach with garlic or the house-marinated Mediterranean olives. The restaurant is also noted for its risottos and pastas. Don Giovanni is open seven days a week for lunch and dinner. The menu changes daily, and there is a full bar.

Celadon $$
500 Main Street, Napa
(707) 254–9690
Displaced by the Napa River flood project, a move became necessary for Celadon. Serving the same great food, it is now located at 500 Main Street in the Hatt Marketplace in a pleasant space that seats about 100 patrons. Chef Marcos Uribe might tempt you with crabcakes or flash-fried calamari, followed by a truffle-and-honey-glazed pork chop or braised Algerian-style lamb shank. Celadon is open daily for lunch and dinner, and reservations are accepted.

Cole's Chop House $$$
1122 Main Street, Napa
(707) 224–6328
When Greg Cole opened this classic American steakhouse in 1999, it was an immediate success. As its name implies, this is where one goes to get red meat—in huge portions. The menu's pricier steaks include the 21-day Chicago dry-aged New York strip or porterhouse, and a 2-inch-thick Black Angus filet mignon. For non-carnivores, there's plenty of fish and even a short stack of portobello mushroom caps.

Housed in a restored historic building dating from 1886, the restaurant, with dining rooms on two levels, features stone walls and a wood-beamed ceiling. The cozy booths are set with white tablecloths and copper-beaded lampshades over candles. It's elegant and masculine at the same time. Another draw here is the great old bar, where you can belly up for a classic Manhattan, martini, or cosmopolitan. Not surprising is the varied assortment of bold Napa Valley Cabernets on the wine list. Dinner is served Tuesday through Sunday, accompanied by live jazz on weekends.

Foothill Cafe $$$
2766 Old Sonoma Road, Napa
(707) 252–6178
Foothill Cafe sits in a nondescript little strip mall, an unlikely venue for a locally adored restaurant. Enter the cafe and your faith will be rewarded with food that relies heavily on fresh local produce and a hickory smoker in the kitchen. Nightly specials accent favorites such as baby-back ribs, seared ahi tuna with wasabi and ginger dipping sauce, or roasted free-range chicken breast with creamy polenta. The decor is frenetic, with objects from Baja California. Foothill Cafe is open for dinner from Wednesday through Sunday.

Julia's Kitchen $$$$
500 First Street, Napa
(707) 265–5700
www.copia.org
Named for Julia Child, who was one of the first diners when it opened its doors inside Copia (see our Attractions chapter), this eatery has about 20 tables and an open, active kitchen led by executive chef Victor Scargle. The decor is almost industrial-like, with a concrete floor and pea soup–green accents on the walls and chair cushions. Instead, the frills and the presentation are saved for the food, which is pleasing to the eye and the palate.

Start with a first course of sunchoke risotto with hazelnuts, garlic chives, and Parmesan cheese; or opt for the grilled quail with chanterelle mushrooms, foie gras, and herb vinaigrette. With your tastebuds thoroughly spoiled, move on to a second course of steamed Thai snapper with enoki and shiitake mushrooms, scallions, and mushroom consommé—unless you prefer seared dayboat scallops with pancetta, potato puree, and chanterelle mushrooms surrounded by a Port wine reduction sauce. For dessert, dig into the chocolate bread pudding (made with devil's food cake, not bread) or the caramel pear.

As you would expect from a restaurant inside a center for wine and food, the wine list is ample. The service is professional, caring, and friendly without being cloying. The acoustics keep the racket level high, so it's not the sort of romantic place where you can whisper sweet nothings. But if you prefer a lively, bustling atmosphere—with an international clientele all around—you'll feel right at home in Julia's Kitchen. In less than one year of its opening, Julia's Kitchen was named "Restaurant of the Year" by *Esquire* magazine in its 2002 listing of great new dining experiences in the United States.

You can dine at Julia's without paying admission into Copia; the restaurant is open for lunch and dinner in summer and for lunch only in winter. Needless to say, reservations are a must.

La Boucane $$$
1778 Second Street, Napa
(707) 253–1177

Housed in a Victorian building dating to 1885, this is a Napa Valley landmark. There is a white tablecloth, a red rose, and silver utensils on every table. Classical music strums in the background. And out comes the classic French cuisine: a Chilean sea bass Bretonne appetizer; lobster bisque; classic escargot; onion soup Lyonnaise; and crisp roast duckling with orange sauce for two.

La Boucane's wine list sticks exclusively to Napa Valley. And remember what it says at the bottom of the menu: "We will prepare any dish upon request, providing we have the ingredients on hand." The restaurant is open for dinner every night but Sunday.

Pairs Cafe $$$
4175 Solano Avenue, Napa
(707) 224–8464
www.pairscafe.com

This is the same Pairs that once resided in St. Helena. Brothers Craig and Keith Schauffel increased the size of their restaurant, from 50 to 150 seats, and moved it south, but the focus of the food remains the same: California cuisine with an Asian twist. The idea at Pairs is expressed in the restaurant's name: to pair food and wine to the advantage of both.

Each dish on the menu, even appetizers, comes with a varietal recommendation. For instance, Chardonnay is suggested for the lemon-fried calamari, Sauvignon Blanc for the vegetarian spring rolls, and Merlot for the grilled rosemary lamb chops. There are private dining rooms, an outdoor patio with water gardens, and an open kitchen and dining bar.

Pearl $$
1339 Pearl Street, Suite 104, Napa
(707) 224–1552
www.therestaurantpearl.com

Proprietors Nickie and Pete Zeller have created a comfortable bistro with soaring ceilings and lots of geometric artwork to ponder as you enjoy fresh oysters served in a multitude of ways. There are soups, pizzas, sandwiches, and chicken and beef dishes with Mexican, Italian, and even Asian influences. Try the triple-double pork chop with an apple-dijon brine, or a New York steak with blue cheese and roasted garlic butter. The wine list includes several obscure Napa Valley labels. Open Tuesday through Thursday for lunch and dinner; closed Sunday and Monday.

Piccolino's Italian Cafe $$
1385 Napa Town Center, Napa
(707) 251–0100
www.piccolinoscafe.com

Food has always meant comfort to Joe Salerno, who grew up stirring pots and making sausage with his extended Italian family in upstate New York. Salerno now does his best to create fond memories at Piccolino's, his unpretentious, child-friendly restaurant in downtown Napa. The cafe offers fresh fish dishes, house-made sausage, and four types of pizza. The pasta entrees are highlighted by the colorful fettuccine Calabrese, with its multitude of simple ingredients; and the lasagna, a family recipe that employs a light ricotta shipped in from the East Coast. Lasagna and spaghetti are available in immense family-style portions. The wine list is primarily Napan, though it does include a small line of Italians. Piccolino's is open daily for lunch and dinner, plus brunch on weekends. See our Nightlife chapter for information on live music.

The Royal Oak/Vintner's Court $$$$
Silverado Resort, 1600 Atlas Peak Road, Napa
(707) 257–0200
www.silveradoresort.com

Two separate restaurants are housed in The Mansion at Silverado. To the left of the main lounge is Vintner's Court, larger and more formal, with stolid, oak-sided walls and lots of glass. To the right is the more rustic Royal Oak, with its open beams and open kitchen. Vintner's Court serves fresh California cuisine with Mediterranean and Pacific Rim influences—for example, seared Chilean seabass with mango and jicama or Sonoma foie gras with endive, citrus relish, and honey vinaigrette. The Oak is more traditionally American, with big steaks and filet of salmon. Peter Pahk is executive chef for both restaurants. Both offer full bar service. The Royal Oak is open seven days a week for dinner. Vintner's Court is open Wednesday, Thursday, and Saturday for dinner off the menu, Friday night for seafood buffet, and Sunday morning for brunch.

Tuscany $$$
1005 First Street, Napa
(707) 258–1000

Guess the specialty: the cooking of northern Italy. Start with a traditional minestrone with a bevy of vegetables and pancetta. Follow that with risotto con quaglia, featuring walnuts and a touch of gorgonzola cheese topped with two roasted quail. Classic cannoli is the perfect finishing touch. The menu also includes pizzas from the wood-fired oven and rotisseried rabbit, veal, pork, and chicken. The open room features high ceilings and earthy colors, and a wine bar is separated from the dining room by a low partition. There's a counter with stools where you can watch the chefs preparing such fare as a halibut steak with roasted red and golden beets on the side. Open daily for dinner.

Yoshi-Shige $$$
3381 California Boulevard, Napa
(707) 257–3583

Good sushi restaurants are hard to find north of San Francisco. One of the best is Yoshi-Shige, now in business more than a decade, with Japanese decor and a menu of more than 60 sushi items, not to mention entrees such as chicken teriyaki and shrimp-and-vegetable tempura. Yoshi-Shige serves sake in addition to its beer and wine. It's open for lunch and dinner every day and night except Monday.

Yountville

Bistro Jeanty $$$
6510 Washington Street, Yountville
(707) 944–0103
www.bistrojeanty.com

Philippe Jeanty became head chef at Domaine Chandon a year after it opened, and over the next 20 years he turned it into a world-class restaurant. There was much local hand-wringing when Jeanty flew the coop in 1997. But his comfortable, two-room bistro opened in April 1998 and quickly occupied a niche that, Philippe explains, is part Paris, part French countryside. You won't find a single pasta on this small menu, no Caesar salad or hamburgers. Instead, be on the

Insiders' Tip
Yountville has restaurants aplenty—and two of them were singled out by *Gourmet Magazine* for inclusion in that publication's "250 Best American Restaurants" list in 2000. The winners? The French Laundry and Bistro Jeanty.

lookout for lamb tongue and potato salad, beef tournedos in black pepper cream sauce, cassoulet, and mussels steamed in red wine. The setting is just as authentic, with French furnishings and paintings by Guy Buffet. And the color of the walls? Dijon, of course. Bistro Jeanty is open for lunch and dinner seven days a week. It has a full bar; the staff calls the giant rooster that sits atop it "Philippe."

Bouchon $$$
6534 Washington Street, Yountville
(707) 944-8037

If you're looking for a place to have a late-night dinner, here's one of the few gourmet delights in Napa Valley that will serve you till the wee hours—closing time is 2:00 a.m. The fare here is classic French bistro ("bouchon" is the local term for "bistro" in Lyon, France.) But it's typically not the trendy stuff; instead, it's classics like mussels mariniéres and leg of lamb with flageolet beans. The appetizers can include terrine of foie gras and an extensive raw seafood bar. The sweets run to crème caramel or tarte Tatin. The wine list is terrific and the prices are down to earth.

The atmosphere is lively and loud, but that's part of the charm. The dining room is furnished with a zinc-plated bar and antique lighting fixtures, and the music is typically jazz from the 1930s. There's also al fresco dining. Because it keeps late hours, Bouchon is a favorite with local winemakers and staff from other restaurants. Open for lunch and dinner daily.

Brix $$$
7377 St. Helena Highway, Yountville
(707) 944-2749
www.brix.com

Grilled rare ahi tuna with tomatillo crème fraîche, chanterelles, and purple potatoes? Grilled salmon with sesame mustard sauce, crisp salsify, red chard, and pickled shiitakes? Hoison grilled rack of lamb with pearled barley, radicchio, and mint oil? What do you call this? "Asian fusion" if you're Brix, the restaurant just north of Yountville. Brix is surrounded by 10 acres of vineyard and a couple of acres of olive trees. They have a full bar, including what

the *San Francisco Chronicle* called an "Academy Award–winning wine list." Brix is open for lunch and dinner, seven days a week.

Compadres Mexican Bar & Grill $$
6539 Washington Street, Yountville
(707) 944-2406

Mexican fare is more than appropriate here, on a portion of the land grant deeded to Salvador Vallejo by the Mexican government in 1838. Compadres is a sprawling, 165-seat restaurant with both indoor and outdoor seating. There is depth to the Margarita list, which includes what *San Francisco Focus* magazine once ordained the best Margarita it had sampled. The food is wide-ranging, too, with traditional Jaliscan carnitas, seafood tacos, daily fish specials, and at least eight types of enchilada. Compadres is open seven days a week for breakfast, lunch, and dinner.

Domaine Chandon $$$$
1 California Drive, Yountville
(707) 944-2892
www.chandon.com

Parked against the hills west of Yountville, Domaine Chandon sits amid century-old oaks and the winery's own vineyards. The atmosphere is elegant, immaculate, and trés français. The menu changes weekly but returns to a few of chef Robert Curry's favorites, such as smoked trout or salmon, foie blond pâté, caramelized scallops, and local lamb. Domaine Chandon is open for dinner every night except Monday and Tuesday. It's open for lunch seven days a week. Note that reservations here should be booked well in advance.

The French Laundry $$$$
6640 Washington Street, Yountville
(707) 944-2380
www.sterba.com/yountville/frenchlaundry

What does Yountville have that Manhattan and Los Angeles don't? How about the best chef in America? That's what the prestigious James Beard Foundation called Thomas Keller in May 1997. In fact, this restaurant received its third James

Beard Award in 2001. Keller's restaurant is at the corner of Washington and Creek Streets in Yountville, in a century-old fieldstone house that was once, indeed, a French steam laundry. The French Laundry has been elevated to almost mythical status among foodies, many of whom have never come close to eating here, possibly because it's so difficult to procure a reservation. If you do make it in, congratulations. But be prepared for a very pricey experience. It's a prix fixe menu only: $80 per person for a five-course vegetarian offering; $105 for a more robust five-course meal; or $120 for the nine-course Chef's Tasting Menu. Keller, though a devotee of traditional French principles, is also known for his whimsical takes on common meals, like "macaroni and cheese" that turns out to be butter-poached Maine lobster with creamy lobster broth and Mascarpone-enriched orzo, or "coffee and doughnuts" that are, in fact, fresh-baked cinnamon-sugared doughnuts with cappuccino semifreddo. The French Laundry is open for dinner seven days a week and lunch from Friday through Sunday.

Mustards Grill $$$
7399 St. Helena Highway, Yountville
(707) 944-2424

Roadhouse meets fine dining at Mustards Grill. The restaurant is situated on Highway 29, and the casual dining room looks onto a beautiful swath of the Napa countryside. But the real action here is in the kitchen.

The menu changes seasonally, but classics like Mongolian pork chops (marinated, grilled chops with braised cabbage and garlic mashers) and hanger steak are available year-round. Everything is made from scratch here—don't miss the house-made ketchup served with paper-thin onion rings. The menu tends toward creatively reinvented American classics, with daily fish specials providing the haute end of the cuisine. After dessert you can order a cigar and retire to the smoking patio. Mustards has a full bar with a huge wine list and is open for lunch and dinner seven days a week.

Napa Valley Grille $$$
Highway 29 at Madison Street, Yountville
(707) 944-8686
www.calcafe.com/napavalleygrille

Like most chefs in Wine Country, chef Jude Wilmoth dishes up a changing menu that uses seasonal ingredients produced locally, described as California cuisine with Italian and French influences. A past award-winning dish here was the wild mushroom and pine nut raviolini, voted the People's Choice award in the 2002 Napa Valley Mustard Festival.

There are as many as 800 wine selections to choose from here, including rare and older vintages. The dining room looks out onto vineyards, and the exhibition kitchen adds interest. Lunch and dinner is served daily, with brunch on Sunday.

Piatti Restaurant $$$
6480 Washington Street, Yountville
(707) 944-2070
www.piatti.com

Dwelling on the Mediterranean end of Italy, the Piatti menu is filled with fresh herbs and seafood. Chef Peter Hall offers daily pizza, pasta, and fish specials. Some things remain constant, though, like the pappardelle "fantasia": wide saffron ribbons with shrimp, arugula, fresh tomato, and spicy lemon-wine sauce. The spice-rubbed rotisserie chicken is another favorite. Piatti has osso bucco and live music every Wednesday. The restaurant has a full bar (with many Italian wines) and is open for lunch and dinner seven days a week.

Rutherford

Auberge du Soleil $$$$
180 Rutherford Hill Road, Rutherford
(707) 963-1211
www.aubergedusoleil.com

Before Auberge du Soleil the inn, there was Auberge du Soleil the restaurant. It's known as one of Napa Valley's premier eateries, not just for the food but for the remarkable vistas from the dining terrace. Following a multi-million-dollar makeover, the dining rooms and kitchen reopened in early 2003. Chef Richard Reddington joined the restaurant in 2000 and transformed the menu from merely adequate to outstanding. His new cuisine has included marinated raw yellowfin tuna with baby beets, radish slices, and Meyer lemon oil; and Florida red snapper with sliced almonds and capers in cauliflower puree. The fixed-price, four-course dinner without wine is $75 per person. (Lunch choices might include grilled calamari with chick peas, red peppers, and lemon oil.) The restaurant is open for lunch and dinner seven days a week, and it has a full bar.

La Toque $$$$
1140 Rutherford Road, Rutherford
(707) 963-9770
www.latoque.com

French-inspired with occasional Asian influences—that's one way to describe this elegant restaurant recently listed among the Top 20 in America by *Wine Spectator* magazine. The decadent five-course prix fixe menu changes with the seasonal ingredients available locally, and can include fresh corn polenta with English peas and chanterelles for an appetizer, followed by chicken Ballotine with crayfish and black truffle; or a wild striped bass with spinach, Cabernet, and roasted red marble potatoes. But La Toque goes one step further in its pursuit of excellence with its annual truffle menus, when fresh white truffles come into season for a few months in the fall. When white truffle season slows down, out come the first black truffles. Season permitting, the black truffle menu options are available from January through Valentine's Day.

Rutherford Grill $$$
1180 Rutherford Road, Rutherford
(707) 963-1792

This restaurant is easy to spot by the large Phoenix date palm trees swaying in front. It's a casual "neighborhood" roadhouse that offers American comfort food in big portions. The mashed potatoes are legendary and make a yummy accompaniment to the rotisserie chicken, steaks, burgers, and prime rib offerings. (Start your meal with the Maytag blue cheese chips.) The decor is warm, with redwood walls made from old wine barrels. The huge outside patio is a great place to watch Wine Country visitors hurrying by on the highway. More than 100 Napa Valley wines are offered, with at least 30 available by the glass. Open daily for lunch and dinner.

St. Helena

Cindy's Backstreet Kitchen $$$
1327 Railroad Avenue, St. Helena
(707) 963-1200

Cindy Pawlcyn, renowned for her Mustard's Grill farther down Highway 29 in Napa Valley, has transformed her restaurant on Railroad Avenue once again, moving away from Latin American-influenced cuisine (when it was called Miramonte) and returning to the more traditional comfort food for which she is revered. The menu ranges from innovative salads (the curry chicken salad is delightful) to small plates such as shiitake mushrooms and asparagus, to spring pie, a twist on mom's classic potpie. This is a friendly place on two floors, with an inviting and comfortable bar. The wine list is equal opportunity, not devoted entirely to Napa Valley.

Gillwoods Restaurant $$
1313 Main Street, St. Helena
(707) 963-1788
1320 Napa Town Center, Napa
(707) 253-0409

You have to get up pretty early in the morning to beat the locals to Gillwoods, St. Helena's favorite breakfast spot. It's casual, intimate, and filled with good cheer and caffeine. The big draw always has been the scrambles—eggs and cream cheese mixed with various ingredients. (Our personal favorite: the salmon scramble with capers.)

The restaurant is open for breakfast and lunch seven days a week and does not take reservations. Gillwoods has a second location in Napa Town Center. The menu is the same there, except it includes dinner on Friday and Saturday nights.

Green Valley Cafe $$
1310 Main Street, St. Helena
(707) 963-7088

Small, cozy, and reasonably priced (i.e., exactly what you don't expect in St. Helena), Green Valley Cafe is the perfect place to sup before or after a film at Cameo Cinema. Green Valley offers daily fresh-fish specials, but otherwise sticks to a simple, well-executed menu. Locals tend to gravitate toward the lasagna (with tomatoes, ham, mozzarella, and basil), the braised lamb shank with polenta, or the melanzane-eggplant topped with tomato and bechamel sauces and Parmesan cheese. The wine list is a mix of Napa Valley and Italy. Green Valley Cafe is open for lunch and dinner from Tuesday through Saturday.

Martini House $$$$
1245 Spring Street, St. Helena
(707) 963-2233
www.kuleto.com/Martini.htm

Housed in a vintage California craftsman bungalow originally built by an opera singer, this restaurant has garnered fabulous reviews since opening in 2001. Famed restaurant designer Pat Kuleto teamed with chef Todd Humphries (formerly of the Wine Spectator Greystone Restaurant) to create a beautiful setting as well as a unique dining experience. Martini House excels in rare wines, with a Wine Cellar bar that includes a 600-bottle list. The menu changes with the seasons and the availability of local produce. Among the options may be seared Maine sea scallops, sautéed squab breast and leg confit, grilled prime beef tenderloin, or Atlantic striped bass. Save room for persimmon pudding with ice cream, maple cheesecake tart with pomegranate glaze, or a chocolate crepe soufflé.

The Restaurant at Meadowood $$$$
900 Meadowood Lane, St. Helena
(707) 963-3646
www.meadowood.com

Chef Steven Tevere had big shoes to fill at Meadowood, when chefs Didier Lenders and his wife, Pilar Sanchez, moved on to other culinary pursuits. Tevere has created such dishes as the terrine of Sonoma Moulard and Muscovy foie gras and the rack of lamb served with herbed potatoes and eggplant puree. Begin your meal with sweet corn flan or roasted eggplant soup; finish it with a raspberry soufflé or strawberry-rhubarb crisp.

And the wine list, by the way, is phenomenal. Sticking exclusively to Napa Valley, it represents nearly all of the county's wineries. The Restaurant at Meadowood has a full bar, and is open for dinner seven nights a week, plus Sunday brunch.

Model Bakery $
1357 Main Street, St. Helena
(707) 963-8192

You'd think it was a film set if those whiffs of fresh-baked bread didn't call you from the kitchen. The look is perfect for a small-town bakery, with a black-and-white checkerboard floor, and ceiling fans. The Model Bakery makes scones, croissants, danishes, bagels, and at least a half-dozen types of muffins. The repertoire includes six or so daily breads, plus regular daily specials. They bust loose on Friday with five specials: whole wheat, seeded, oatmeal, sour rye, and pumate-basil. The bakery also sells juices, soups, and prewrapped sandwiches and, as you would guess, coffee and espresso drinks. It's open every day but Monday.

Pinot Blanc $$$
641 Main Street, St. Helena
(707) 963-6191

A country bistro on the south side of St. Helena. Pinot Blanc has always-creative pasta, fish, and meat dishes complemented by a plat du jour. Monday it might be Bellwether Farms spring lamb with potato, fava beans, and truffle oil; Sunday it could be braised pig with herb-mustard spaetzle and red cabbage. Their fall menu features wild game, and the Liberty duck breast with celery root puree and fresh huckleberries is heavenly. This is hearty food in big proportions. Pinot Blanc is open seven days a week for lunch and dinner and features a full bar.

Roux $$$$
1234 Main Street, St. Helena
(707) 963–5330

The cuisine of chef Vincent Nattress is unforgettable. French-trained, he offers a fixed price, four-course tasting menu in addition to the nightly menu selections. Count on choices like delicious foie gras or scallop with artichoke appetizers, Muscovy duck with spaetzle, organic free-range chicken on braised escarole, and asparagus with morel mushrooms. There's a small wine bar and a courtyard patio for enjoying your meal when the weather is warm. It's dinner only here for the time being, Tuesdays through Saturdays (closed Sundays and Mondays).

Taylor's Refresher $
933 Main Street, St. Helena
(707) 963–3486

Retired traveling salesman and pharmacist Lloyd Taylor opened the Refresher for business in 1949. It's now owned by the Gott family, who spruced it up—but managed to retain the quaint atmosphere—in 1999. Taylor's cooks up lunch and early dinner seven days a week. The menu includes burgers, hot dogs, tacos, salads, and fountain treats. There are nice picnic grounds behind the eatery.

Terra $$$$
1345 Railroad Avenue, St. Helena
(707) 963–8931
www.terrarestaurant.com

Terra sits one block away from Main Street in a historic landmark, a hardy fieldstone foundry constructed in 1884. The open redwood-beamed ceilings in the two dining rooms give you the feel of a Tuscan villa. Chef Hiro Sone's one-page menu aims for southern France and northern Italy, though he admittedly takes a few geographic twists and turns. Two appetizers should give you an example of what to expect: the fried rock shrimp with organic greens and chive-mustard sauce and the terrine of foie gras with Belgian endive, walnuts, and Fuji apple salad. The most popular main course might be the broiled, sake-marinated sea bass with shrimp dumplings in shiso broth. Terra is open for dinner every night except Tuesday.

Tra Vigne $$$
1050 Charter Oak Avenue, St. Helena
(707) 963–4444

Chef Michael Chiarello scrambled to the top of the Napa Valley hall of fame on the strength of this cozy trattoria in St. Helena. The stone building is an old landmark, and Tra Vigne has become a contemporary one. The regional Italian menu encourages grazing, with a host of interesting small plates, pastas, and pizzas to complement the meats and fish. The restaurant is open for lunch and dinner seven days a week. There is a full bar and a wine cellar stocked with Italian reds and whites, plus a good selection of Californians.

Wine Spectator Greystone Restaurant $$$
2555 Main Street, St. Helena
(707) 967–1010
www.ciachef.edu/rest

Don't worry, eating at the Culinary Institute of America's restaurant doesn't make you a guinea pig for fresh-faced chefs-in-training. This branch of the CIA focuses on continuing education.

Insiders' Tip
The Culinary Institute of America in St. Helena hosts an annual "Service—You Deserve It" celebration to honor the servers, bussers, and other staff of Napa Valley hospitality businesses. Wine for the event is donated by local vintners, and the CIA staff cook up a great meal as a tribute to these hardworking folks.

One of the most popular restaurants in St. Helena is Tra Vigne, with award-winning regional Italian cuisine. PHOTO: JEAN SAYLOR DOPPENBERG

Chef de cuisine Pilar Sanchez, formerly of Meadowood, focuses on first-course small bites that she calls "temptations," which are designed to be shared by all at the table. These might include mussels steamed in Fritz Winery Melon, torchon of foie gras, or oxtail roulade. Second-course selections could be wild mushroom lasagna or a grilled pork chop with sage spaetzle, apples, braised escarole, and whiskey sauce.

Try not to dribble while craning your head around the dining room, with its cement floor and stone walls lightened by blues and yellows. Greystone has a full bar. It is open seven days a week for lunch and dinner.

Calistoga

All Seasons Cafe $$$$
1400 Lincoln Avenue, Calistoga
(707) 942-9111

If you read the food-and-wine magazines, you've probably been introduced to All Seasons. It has been profiled in *Gourmet*, *Wine Spectator*, and *Wine Country Living*, among others, and its high standards haven't faltered a bit over more than 16 years of operation. Mixing the quaint and the luxurious, the cafe has a wine bar that makes use of a truly exceptional wine list—it ranges far beyond the valley and is especially deep in Pinots and Zinfandels. The menu changes often, but you can expect "seasonal California" dishes along the lines of grilled rib-eye steak with Cabernet glaze and creamy horseradish sauce; or English pea risotto with asparagus, spring garlic, tomato, and mushrooms. The chef is Kevin Kathman, who honed his skills at The French Laundry. All Seasons is open for lunch and dinner daily.

Brannan's Grill $$$$
1374 Lincoln Avenue, Calistoga
(707) 942-2233
www.brannansgrill.com

Brannan's is physically arresting both inside and out, with refinished trusses and ironworks (all original to the 1911 building, long used as a motor garage) and windows that open onto Lincoln in warm weather. Most notable is the bar, a mahogany Brunswick design that was shipped around the Cape in the late 1800s. The food is regional American, decidedly carnivore. Try the grilled hanger steak with potato leek gratin and roasted portobello mushrooms or the blue cheese and walnut-crusted filet mignon. Brannan's has a full bar. It's open seven days a week for lunch and dinner in high season, but lunch is Friday through Sunday in the winter.

Cafe Sarafornia $$
1413 Lincoln Avenue, Calistoga
(707) 942–0555

Calistoga's most popular breakfast spot playfully incorporates the other half of Sam Brannan's legendary malapropism: "I'll make this the Calistoga of Sarafornia." The busy, sun-infused dining room has a central counter and sidewalk booths. Regulars swear by the cheese blintzes, the Brannan Benedict (two poached eggs with guacamole, bacon, and Cajun cream on toast), the chicken-apple sausage, and the Wildcat Scrambler (three eggs scrambled with mushrooms, Italian sausage, spinach, and choice of cheese). The burgers are good at lunchtime. The cafe does not take reservations, which makes it easy to spot on Sunday morning—it's the place with the line out the door.

Calistoga Inn & Restaurant $$$
1250 Lincoln Avenue, Calistoga
(707) 942–4101
www.napabeer.com

Popular any time of year, business at this restaurant really booms in the summer, when dining moves to the delightful creekside patio. (The meat is even grilled outside, over hardwood.) Regional American cuisine is served here. The marinated Australian lamb sirloin, the Jamaican jerk half-chicken, and the tri-tip sirloin finished with blue cheese butter are all winners. There are fish specials too. The Inn is open for lunch and dinner every day of the year but Christmas. The restaurant has a full bar, including an extensive wine list and its own line of beers.

Calistoga Roastery $
1631 Lincoln Avenue, Calistoga
(707) 942–5757

This place must be doing something right: Half the inns and restaurants in the vicinity boast about serving Roastery coffee. Owners Clive Richardson and Terry Rich roast almost 20 varieties of beans—sometimes right on the spot in a preserved 1919 Probat roaster, the oldest of its kind in the nation. If the regular house coffee isn't exciting enough for you, there is a selection of espresso drinks, frappes, and ice cream mochas, not to mention iced teas, Rocket Juices, and Italian sodas. Yes, there are fresh-made baked goods too: bagels, croissants, scones of various stripes, banana bread, granola, and more. The Roastery opens at 6:30 A.M. every day and doesn't close its doors until 6:00 P.M. It's an atmosphere designed for lounging, so bring a newspaper. No credit cards.

Catahoula Restaurant & Saloon $$$
1457 Lincoln Avenue, Calistoga
(707) 942–2275
www.catahoularest.com

Chef/owner Jan Birnbaum hails from Baton Rouge (the catahoula hound is the state dog of Louisiana), but he admits to taking creative liberties with his native Cajun cuisine. Birnbaum cooks up wonderful gumbos, but the menu also includes interesting combinations such as a pork porterhouse steak with red-eye gravy and "soft sexy grits" or grilled lavender squab with Calvados figs and garlic spinach. Dessert is an event here. How about a chewy molasses cookie and chicory-Kahlua ice cream sandwich with fresh peaches? Both restaurant and saloon are housed in the historic Mount View Hotel building (see our Hotels, Motels, and Inns chapter). Catahoula serves dinner nightly and breakfast, lunch, and dinner on weekends. There is full bar service.

Flatiron Grill $$
1440 Lincoln Avenue, Calistoga
(707) 942–1220
www.flatirongrill.com

Hungry for steak? Slip on in to the Flatiron Grill, which beckons with a bovine-inspired sign outside. The stylish cow theme continues inside in the artwork. You can usually count on the house specialty, the Flatiron steak (boneless shoulder steak), roast chicken, grilled salmon, pork chop, seafood pasta, and maybe stuffed roast quail and beef brisket. And here's something you don't see every day on a menu: $150.95 for New York steak, potato gratin, fresh veggies, and a bottle of 1998 Opus One. Or skip the wine and buy the steak dinner for $19.95. Open daily for lunch and dinner.

Hydro Bar & Grill $$
1403 Lincoln Avenue, Calistoga
(707) 942-9777

In a town where the sidewalks sometimes roll up at dusk, the Hydro is the restaurant that doesn't sleep. It offers dinner until 11:00 p.m. on weekdays and midnight on weekends, then greets you for breakfast the next morning. (It's closed only for lunch on Thursday.) Hydro is an affordable complement to its sister restaurant across the street—All Seasons Cafe. It does daily fish specials and top-notch hamburgers, and the crispy skin boneless chicken with warm white Tuscan beans, grilled red onions, arugula salad, and herbed pan jus might be just the ticket after a relaxing mud bath. The full bar has 20 carefully selected microbrews. They don't take reservations.

Pacifico Restaurante Mexicano $$
1237 Lincoln Avenue, Calistoga
(707) 942-4400
www.pacificorestaurant.com

Calistoga isn't your typical small town, so why should Pacifico be your typical Mexican restaurant? Instead of mountain ranges of rice and beans, the kitchen cooks up traditional specialties from Jalisco, Veracruz, and Oaxaca. The restaurant is especially noted for its fish dishes, such as grilled fish tacos with avocado tomatillo salsa or camarones a la diabla-sautéed prawns with garlic, onion, arbol chilies, and lime.

There is a full bar, and the Margaritas won't let you down. Pacifico is open seven days a week for lunch and dinner. It's also popular for Saturday and Sunday brunch.

(The morning favorites are Huevos Benito and Huevos Pacifico, Mexican eggs Benedict with a mulato chili hollandaise.) The restaurant takes reservations for parties of seven or more.

Soo Yuan $
1354 Lincoln Avenue, Calistoga
(707) 942-9404

The Fang family opened its first restaurant in Taipei in 1974, and they have operated in Calistoga since 1985. The tried-and-true favorites include the pepper-sauce spareribs, the asparagus with prawns, and the mu shu pancakes. If you can't reach a decision, go for the multi-course Soo Yuan Special Dinner. Soo Yuan is open daily for lunch and dinner.

Wappo Bar & Bistro $$$
1226 Washington Street, Calistoga
(707) 942-4712

One of the few Calistoga restaurants not found on Lincoln Avenue, the compact

Wappo Bar & Bistro offers indoor and outdoor dining in an informal setting in Calistoga. PHOTO: JEAN SAYLOR DOPPENBERG

Wappo Bar is easy to miss—and that would be a big mistake. The scene is fairly informal and always gratifying, especially in the summer when the arbor-protected brick patio takes center stage. The inside features copper-topped tables and a wine bar with redwood interior; in the warmer months, ask for a table next to the fountain outside.

Signature dishes include the chili relleno with walnut pomegranate sauce; a paella of chorizo, rabbit, prawns, clams, and mussels; and the Chilean sea bass with Indian spices. And ridiculous as it sounds, you have to try the table water here—"marinated" with citrus, cucumber, and mint, it is highly addictive. The Wappo Bar is open for lunch and dinner six days a week (closed Tuesdays).

Sonoma County

Sonoma

The Big 3 Diner at The Fairmont Sonoma Mission Inn $$$
18141 Sonoma Highway, Sonoma
(707) 939–2410, (800) 862–4945
www.sonomamissioninn.com

This is a great place for breakfast—the eggs Benedict with rosemary potatoes will draw you back time after time. Since this is connected to the Mission Inn Spa (see our Spas and Resorts chapter), the menu also includes dishes for the calorie-watcher that are equally good—especially apple oat cakes with walnuts and crème fraîche. Lunch and dinner are also served each day, with a fine wine list and full bar. Service is friendly but not intrusive.

Carneros at The Lodge at Sonoma $$$$
1325 Broadway, Sonoma
(707) 935–6600
www.carnerosrestaurant.com

This restaurant can be found within the hotel/spa complex The Lodge at Sonoma (see our Spas and Resorts chapter), but you needn't be a guest at the lodge to enjoy dining here. Executive chef Brian Whitmer has developed some interesting

dishes that change with the seasons, as do the menus of many Wine Country restaurants. Here are a few examples of what you might expect to find: wood oven-roasted whole fish with baby artichokes, horseradish pappardelle with short rib ragu, rotisserie ribeye with caramelized shallots, and Sonoma lamb offered with braised fennel or slow-roasted with tomatoes and lemon thyme. The atmosphere is relaxed and casual. It's open for breakfast, lunch, and dinner daily.

Della Santina's $$
133 East Napa Street, Sonoma
(707) 935–0576
www.sterba.com/sonoma/santina/

This intimate, no-frills Italian trattoria-pasticceria faces onto the main street, and the food is authentic Italian prepared from recipes inspired by owner Dan Santina's grandmother. All dishes are made from scratch, using a rotisserie to contain the flavors of all the herbs and spices used in such dishes as locally raised chicken, rabbit, and duck. The menu offers traditional northern Italian dishes such as lasagna bolognese, pressed squab, and all sorts of antipasti. One of the best entrees—maybe the best in all of Wine Country—is pollo allo spiedo, a traditional Italian roast chicken. Della Santina's serves lunch and dinner every day. Because the restaurant is small, reservations are advised.

Depot Hotel Cucina Rustica $$$
241 First Street W., Sonoma
(707) 938–2980
www.sterba.com/sonoma/depot/

Located in a historic stone building a block from the plaza, this was once a hotel, but it is now a delightful restaurant serving northern Italian cuisine. The chef does wonders with such dishes as ravioli al bosco (shiitake mushrooms and herbs sauteed with white wine and shallots) and hand-stuffed tortellini. One of the real delights of the restaurant is its garden, with Roman fountain and poolside dining. Vegetarian dishes and heart-healthy choices are also offered. The wine list is strictly from the Sonoma and Carneros valleys and has won *Wine Spectator* magazine's Award of Excellence several times. Lunch is available Wednesday through Friday and dinner is served Wednesday through Sunday.

Deuce $$$
691 Broadway, Sonoma
(707) 933–3823
www.dine-at-deuce.com

You can count on one thing at this restaurant: fresh ingredients from the garden of chef Richard Whipple. Start your dinner with a first course of warm Laura Chenel goat cheese on a bed of arugula, or smooth duck rillette with croutons, or possibly even sweetbreads with mushrooms and fava beans. Main courses range from salmon to pork chop, game hen, veal chop, and flank steak. The desserts are exceptional, with more to choose from than the usual fare found in fine restaurants, such as pumpkin cake, gelato, Marjolaine torte, and Meyer lemon mascarpone cheesecake. There's even a bar menu of sensational offerings, from grilled portobello mushroom to barbecued spare ribs. You can pop in just about any time—the restaurant is open seven days a week for lunch and dinner.

The General's Daughter $$$
400 West Spain Street, Sonoma
(707) 938–4004
www.thegeneralsdaughter.com

It could win a contest for "prettiest little restaurant in the county" hands down. Erected in 1864 for Gen. Vallejo's daughter (hence the name), the house had been standing dilapidated and unappreciated for years until Suzanne Brangham undertook its renovation in 1994, transforming it into a first-class restaurant. The place is gorgeous, set in lush landscaping with an interior decor of antiques and lively murals (the Honduran mahogany bar is a standout). Lunch is served on the wide front porch in fair weather. The food is traditional Californian. For lunch, you might want to try the jambalaya with blackened prawns, sausage, chicken, tomatoes, and baby spinach. Or consider the warm peach tart Tatin with a ginger crème anglaise for dessert. Lunch and dinner are served daily, with brunch on Sunday.

The Girl & the Fig $$$$
110 West Spain Street, Sonoma
(707) 938–3634
www.thegirlandthefig.com

The name conjures up a sensual experience that's slightly naughty. Perhaps it's because the food is sinful, the service attentive, and the decor awash in pastels. On the ground floor of the Sonoma Hotel on the Plaza, the Girl & the Fig promises and delivers country-style Provençal-inspired cuisine. Figs figure prominently in some of the dishes, especially the signature fig salad with goat cheese, pancetta, pecans, and arugula. Several cheese cart and charcuterie selections are offered (a goat cheese sampler, for instance), mushroom ragout, and ravioli of butternut squash, raddichio, and blue cheese. The owner, Sondra Bernstein, emphasizes local seasonal produce, so the menu selections will vary. Also a nice touch in a town that rolls up the sidewalks early: a late dinner menu from 9:30 to 11:00 P.M. on Fridays and Saturdays.

La Casa Restaurant $$$
121 East Spain Street, Sonoma
(707) 996–3406
www.lacasarestaurant.com

In a town dedicated to Italian cuisine, La Casa's smashing Mexican food is as welcome as a breeze in the heat of summer. The ambiance is as close to authentic as

> ## Insiders' Tip
> Most Wine Country restaurants are not picky about how you dress for dinner. Blue jeans are almost always acceptable, and "casual" is the byword, as long as you're well groomed.

you can get north of the border, with Mexican woven leather chairs and a tiled bar. The nachos are sensational, the salsa and chips addictive. For a view of the Mission and Barracks (see our Attractions chapter), ask for a window seat. Or choose to eat outdoors on the patio facing onto El Paseo de Sonoma courtyard. Fiesta hour (from 4:00 to 6:00 P.M. Monday through Friday) is popular among the locals, thanks to the ambiance and the great Margaritas.

Ristorante Piatti $$$
405 First Street W., Sonoma
(707) 996-2351
www.piatti.com

You enter Piatti from either the El Dorado Hotel lobby or the door on West First Street. Either way, you'll soon be enveloped by the marvelous aromas from the open kitchen at the back of the dining room. Alfresco dining is also available amid the trees on the gorgeous patio courtyard off the dining room. While you're looking over the menu, you'll be served fresh breads with a saucer of olive oil, balsamic vinegar, and garlic dipping sauce. The menu features the best of Tuscany pastas, pizzas, and grilled meat and fish. Piatti is the winner of numerous Sonoma Valley restaurant awards. A full bar features select Sonoma Valley wines at lunch and dinner seven days a week.

Saddles $$$$
29 East MacArthur Street, Sonoma
(707) 933-3191
www.macarthurplace.com

Within the classy MacArthur Place hotel and spa (see our Spas and Resorts chapter), this restaurant exudes a rustic, bunkhouse feel, because it's in the original barn on the property. It has a cowboy motif—with real saddles made into chairs in the lobby and the wait staff in denims—but don't expect beans and boiled coffee here. What you will find is plenty of red meat and fixins, primarily Midwestern corn-fed, mesquite-grilled USDA prime beef. For lighter appetites, there's salmon, ahi, and chicken entrees. Start your meal with the cornmeal onion rings—a crunchy, tasty bit of heaven. The wine list

runs about 70 labels strong and there's a Martini Bar that offers 14 different over-sized libations. Saddles is open daily for lunch and dinner, with a weekend brunch to boot.

Sante at The Fairmont Sonoma Mission Inn $$$$
18140 Sonoma Highway, Sonoma
(707) 938-9000, (800) 862-4945
www.sonomamissioninn.com

If you're ready to go upscale, walk to the main building of the Inn for a Sunday brunch overlooking the pool, or have lunch or dinner in an ambiance that has country-club class—elegant but not stuffy. This is a spa, after all (see our Spas and Resorts chapter), so there are two types of cuisine here: the spa menu for those who really are here to get healthy (a four-course, prix fixe meal for $50), and the menu for those who must have their foie gras and crème brûlée (also $50 for four courses). The award-winning wine list features 300 selections from Napa and Sonoma vineyards. Reservations are recommended for dinner. Sante is open daily.

The Swiss Hotel $$$
18 West Spain Street, Sonoma
(707) 938-2884
www.sterba.com/sonoma/swiss/

It's a wonderful old building—a remarkably preserved adobe that was once the home of General Vallejo's brother, Salvador, who built it in 1850. It became "The Swiss" when a stagecoach operator bought it and changed the name. Today it is easily recognizable by the Swiss flag flying over the door.

For decades the restaurant was patronized largely by local families who came for the generous family-style Italian dinners. The barroom was a hangout for locals as well, who came to meet and greet friends. It even drew a few celebrities: Herb Caen is said to have tippled there, as have Tommy Smothers, Jim Corbett, and even the late Charles Kuralt.

The menu is a bit upscale from the days of the massive Italian feasts, but the pastas are still served al dente, and the pizzas are turned out of wood-burning brick ovens. It's open daily for lunch and dinner.

Glen Ellen

Garden Court Cafe & Bakery $
13647 Arnold Drive, Glen Ellen
(707) 935–1565
www.gardencourtcafe.com

This popular eaterie moved from the highway outside of Glen Ellen into the heart of the town, and its bright green awning is easy to spot. Breakfast is the big draw here, with eggs Benedict in three varieties leading the popularity list and a variety of omelettes following close behind. The cafe is open for breakfast and lunch seven days a week, and dinner is served on the second Wednesday of each month.

The Girl & the Gaucho $$$$
13690 Arnold Drive, Glen Ellen
(707) 938–2130
www.thegirlandthegaucho.com

No, you're not seeing double. Sondra Bernstein owns two restaurants in the Sonoma Valley: the one described in the Sonoma listings, and this one, which moved into the space previously occupied by that fig girl. They are a few miles apart in distance and even further apart in cuisine. Gaucho is all about South American culinary experiences. There are small plates (tomatillo guacamole and fried yucca or jicama and quinoa slaw) and large plates (grilled ribeye, roasted swordfish, half-chicken), all with a Latin flavor. Make a meal of several small plates, or choose a large plate selection with side dishes influenced by Spain, Mexico, Chile, Argentina, or Brazil. For your ears there's Latin American jazz and salsa music; for your eyes there's an eclectic collection of art from Latin countries. Open daily for dinner.

Glen Ellen Inn Restaurant $$$$
13670 Arnold Drive, Glen Ellen
(707) 996–6409
www.glenelleninn.com

Set inside a Cape Cod–style cottage, this tiny restaurant delivers one delight after another. You have three choices of where to eat—the indoor dining room, the sun porch, or the patio. The chef learned his skills in New York and uses local ingredients to cook with a French accent. Particularly impressive is the Voodoo Jambalaya—prawns, bay shrimp, chicken, sausage, and honey-smoked ham simmered with cayenne, vegetables, and tomato sauce on a bed of basmati rice. The desserts are truly decadent. If you can manage two, go for the Bailey's Irish Cream mousse scented with chocolate and the French vanilla ice cream rolled in toasted coconut and drizzled with caramel sauce. The restaurant is open for dinner every night except winter Wednesdays.

Kenwood

Kenwood Restaurant $$$$
9900 Sonoma Highway, Kenwood
(707) 833–6326
www.sterba.com/kenwood/restaurant/

The parking lot is always full—a sure sign of the restaurant's well-deserved popularity. The chef makes an extraordinary bouillabaisse, using seafood from Bodega Bay in a flavorful broth. The roast duck, using local fowl, is crispy on the outside, tender inside. And the prawns in succulent sauce with puff pastry are sheer inspiration. *Gourmet* magazine once voted this one of the top 20 restaurants in the entire Bay Area. One of the real pleasures of dining here is the opportunity to drink in the exquisite view as the late-afternoon sun hits the peaks of Sugarloaf Ridge. The scene is particularly rewarding from the deck. The wine list is acclaimed for featuring the best wines produced in Kenwood (bar drinks are also available). Lunch and dinner are served Wednesday through Sunday.

Insiders' Tip
Smoking is no longer permitted in California restaurants. However, a few Wine Country establishments have set up separate smoking rooms mainly for the enjoyment of cigar aficionados.

Petaluma

Jellyfish $$$
745 Baywood Drive, Petaluma
(707) 283–2900
www.sheratonpetaluma.com

Despite being named for a poisonous sea creature, the small restaurant in the Sheraton Petaluma Hotel is remarkably appealing. Begin by perusing the list of specialty cocktails, or order from the sake menu, then take a look at the impressive wine list, which offers 30 wines by the glass and 14 half-bottles. The cuisine is Asian fusion, and the negamake (asparagus and scallions wrapped in beef) and the Hog Island oysters are reportedly sensational. There's also ravioli, sea bass, Petaluma Liberty duck breast, lamb loin chops, and much more.

McNear's Saloon and Dining House $$
23 North Petaluma Boulevard, Petaluma
(707) 765–2121
www.mcnears.com/index.htm

It's friendly, funky, and great fun. Every square inch of the walls is covered with historic memorabilia and old photographs, including old sleds, skis, street signs, flags, and banners. The name McNear looms large in Petaluma history, stretching back to 1856 when John McNear came to town, creating a business empire and becoming the first owner of the McNear Building. The goal of the present-day owners is to provide a meeting, eating, and entertainment spot for locals and fun-loving visitors. Barbecue is the house specialty, with an extensive menu to back that up; the saloon is well stocked. The dining room is large, but the sidewalk cafe in front is the popular place to sip espresso on Sunday morning. McNear's is open for lunch and dinner every day of the week, plus breakfast on Sunday.

Twisted Vines $$$
16 Kentucky Street, Petaluma
(707) 766–8162
www.twistedvines.com

This is something a little different—a combination wine shop and restaurant. The local restaurant reviewer gives it five stars, for both food and wine. Fresh fish is flown in from Hawaii every day, and mahi mahi is one of the most popular features on the menu. They take pride in using only the best ingredients, including the local poultry, which they transform into their special, half-roasted chicken. You can select a wine off the racks to enjoy with your food (paying only retail plus a $5.00 corkage fee), or you can buy it by the glass.

It's a tiny place, so it's best to call ahead. The restaurant is open for lunch and dinner Tuesday through Saturday. Look for it in the Lanmart Building.

Volpi's Ristorante $$$
124 Washington Street, Petaluma
(707) 765–0695

There's a lot of Old World charm in this place run by the Volpi family; it's been on the local scene since 1925—in a building that was once a speakeasy. This is family-style dining in an unhurried atmosphere. The cuisine is Italian, created by chef Glen Petrucci, who specializes in homemade pastas, veal, and seafood. The fully stocked bar serves tavern and restaurant patrons. If you're up to it, you can listen

Insiders' Tip

Wine lists can be confusing if not intimidating at times, with many obscure labels from boutique wineries unfamiliar to the average diner. Don't hesitate to ask a restaurant's sommelier for help in making your selection. These wine experts can recommend a good, reasonably priced bottle to complement your meal.

to live accordion music Friday and Saturday evenings. Lunch is served Wednesday, Thursday, and Friday; dinner Wednesday through Sunday.

Santa Rosa

John Ash & Co. $$$$
4330 Barnes Road, Santa Rosa
(707) 527–7687, (800) 421–2584
www.vintnersinn.com

John Ash is no longer there, but the cuisine he created carries on, with each entree made a masterpiece of taste, texture, color, and design. Nothing here is ordinary. The fare is "Wine Country cuisine," i.e., California cuisine using only the freshest produce from local farmers and local goat cheeses—the signature dish is the Dungeness crab cakes. Large, arched windows give an open airy feeling to the dining room. The wine list is one of the best, with a good selection sold by the glass. John Ash & Co. is adjacent to Vintners Inn, a Provençal-style hotel arranged around a central plaza and fountain, all set in a 45-acre vineyard (see our Hotels, Motels, and Inns chapter). The restaurant and bar are open for dinner seven days a week, but John Ash & Co. does not serve lunch on Monday.

Equus $$$$
101 Fountaingrove Parkway, Santa Rosa
(707) 578–6101
www.fountaingroveinn.com

Because this is the restaurant for Fountain Grove Inn (see our Hotels, Motels, and Inns chapter), the decorating theme is horses and honors Equus, the legendary horse. The menu changes with each season, and one lovely dish to try is grilled Hawaii Walu with grilled vegetables and pancetta/parsley mashed potatoes. You may choose to sink into a spacious booth or dine center stage under the coffered mahogany ceiling. Take time to examine the Gallery of Sonoma County Wines, a display of nearly 300 premium wines, chosen personally by each winery's own winemaker. Lunch is served from Monday through Friday and dinner is served daily.

La Gare French Restaurant $$$
208 Wilson Street, Santa Rosa
(707) 528–4355
www.sterba.com/sro/lagare/

La Gare has been voted "most romantic" and "best restaurant" by *The Press Democrat* newspaper. *The Bohemian* also has awarded La Gare its "best restaurant" award for the past few years. Tucked away in Santa Rosa's historic Railroad Square, it's a favorite of the locals, who come for hearty, country-style, traditional French cooking. Romantic it is, with lace curtains, soft lighting, and stained glass. It is one of the few places in Wine Country that you are offered (gasp!) French wines. La Gare ("railway station") is open for dinner Wednesday through Sunday.

Lisa Hemenway's Restaurant $$$$
612 Terrace Way, Santa Rosa
(707) 526–5111
www.sterba.com/sro/hemenway/

The atmosphere is cozy and romantic, with the warm, intimate feel of a European bistro. Lisa Hemenway was a protege of John Ash and has traveled six of the seven continents to add to her cuisine knowledge. You might want to try her bouillabaisse with rouille or hamburger stuffed with herb cream cheese. Meals are hearty here. All are made with fresh, locally grown ingredients. There's a daily fish entree, freshly caught, along with daily pasta and salad specialty. Don't miss the perfect orange-currant scones! There is a full bar and award-winning wines. Lisa's is open for lunch and dinner every day but Sunday.

Mixx $$$
135 Fourth Street, Santa Rosa
(707) 573–1344
www.sterba.com/sro/mixx/

Billed as an American bistro, the atmosphere is intimate and elegant without being stuffy. (Julia Child has even dined here.) Chef Dan Berman takes an ethnic melting-pot approach to California cuisine, shaping it into Cajun, Indian, Italian, and straight Californian. One house specialty is ravioli, but Berman also does wonderful things with fish. Berman's wife is responsible for the desserts. Dinner is served nightly except Sunday; lunch is offered Monday through Friday.

Omelette Express $
112 Fourth Street, Santa Rosa
(707) 525–1690
www.sterba.com/sro/omelette/

If you happen to be walking around Santa Rosa's Railroad Square on a weekend morning, you'll see as many people on the sidewalk waiting to get into this restaurant as there are patrons inside. The menu lists 48 different varieties of the humble omelette—both plain and fancy, including vegetarian and seafood. The choices for lunch include two dozen "Pullman Car" sandwiches. You might want to bite into the Hot Express Special—grilled onions, mushrooms, melted jack and cheddar cheese, served open-face on dark rye. The restaurant is open seven days a week and most holidays.

The Seafood Brasserie $$$
170 Railroad Street, Santa Rosa
(707) 636–7388
www.vineyardcreek.com

Vineyard Creek is one of two major new hotels that opened in Sonoma County in 2002. Surprisingly, both of the restaurants at these hotels are well above average. The Seafood Brasserie leans toward seafood, and lots of it. There are dishes revolving around swordfish, scallops, Sacramento Delta crayfish, Dungeness crab, Alaskan halibut, and Hawaiian opah. The wine list is heavy on Sonoma County selections, with reasonable prices. The service in particular is very good.

Zazu $$$
3535 Guerneville Road, Santa Rosa
(707) 523–4814

When it was the Willowside Café, loyal droves from as far away as San Francisco came to partake of the cuisine. Reincarnated in the same location, Zazu offers familiar food with a twist. Local produce features prominently in many dishes, including Bellwether Farms cheeses. There's a tomato soup and grilled cheese sandwich served as an appetizer that you will not recognize from the days when mom served it up.

Healdsburg

Bistro Ralph $$$$
109 Plaza Street, Healdsburg
(707) 433–1380

Bistro Ralph offers a somewhat formal, but unstuffy, atmosphere, featuring American country French cuisine. The place is plain enough, with white-linen-covered tables lined up along one wall in an arrangement reminiscent of earlier San Francisco Italian restaurants. The food is prepared with an imaginative touch and fresh ingredients. Chef-owner Ralph Tingle can be seen at the farmer's market Saturday mornings, selecting from the seasonal bounty of vegetables that will be on his menu that night. The smoked salmon starter with an unusual focaccia pastry is a good choice. Enjoy a bottle of local wine or beer with your meal or the specialty of the house: a dry martini. The Bistro is open for lunch and dinner on weekdays and for dinner only on weekends.

Dry Creek General Store $
3495 Dry Creek Road, Healdsburg
(707) 433–4171

It's an old-time grocery store that looks as it it's been there forever, but if you've been cruising the Dry Creek vineyards for hours and your tummy says it's picnic time, you'll love the simple, delicious homemade sandwiches and salads, the wine selection, and the gourmet food section. Take your purchases to any one of the many wineries in the area, buy yourself a bottle of their best, and settle in for a beautiful picnic. The store is open seven days a week, from 6:00 A.M. to 6:00 P.M. The bar adjacent to the store is open from 3:00 to 8:00 P.M. weekdays and 3:00 to midnight weekends.

Dry Creek Kitchen $$$$
317 Healdsburg Avenue, Healdsburg
(707) 431–0330
www.hotelhealdsburg.com

Maybe you've heard of Charlie Palmer. He was named New York City's best chef in

Like an old western outpost in rural Sonoma County, the Dry Creek General Store has been in business for more than a century. PHOTO: JEAN SAYLOR DOPPENBERG

1997. His restaurant ventures include Aureole, with locations in New York and Las Vegas; Alva American Bistro in Manhattan; and Charlie Palmer Steak at the Four Seasons Hotel in Las Vegas. Now he's brought his award-winning way with cuisine to Wine Country, in the restaurant of the Hotel Healdsburg (see our Hotels, Motels, and Inns chapter).

Charlie hired Mark Purdy to lead the kitchen here, and Mark follows Charlie's approach of presenting American cooking with European influences and doing it spectacularly with a hearty heaping of locally grown organic produce. Expect fabulous flavors and presentations around duck, salmon, beef—to name a few—and appetizers and desserts to die for. There's also a fixed price seven-course tasting menu. To accompany your meal, you're sure to find just the right vino among the eight-page wine list. The dining room is delightful, with soft lighting, fine art, and views of the leafy Healdsburg Plaza. Lunch is served until 3:00 P.M. daily; dinner begins at 5:00 daily and lasts a bit later than most places—10:00 P.M. on weekdays and 10:30 on weekends.

Felix and Louie's $$$
106 Matheson Avenue, Healdsburg
(707) 433-6966

Located on Healdsburg's charming downtown square, Felix and Louie's offers fine Italian cuisine in a large, often bustling, dining room. If the tables are all taken, grab a stool at either the fully stocked bar or the counter overlooking the wood-fired pizza ovens. Chefs turn out extraordinary pizzas here, topped with the familiar pepperoni and bell peppers or the more exotic caramelized onion and gorgonzola. Open for dinner every night and Saturday and Sunday for brunch and lunch.

The Geyser Smokehouse $$
21021 Geyserville Avenue, Geyserville
(707) 857-4600

If you get the munchies while wine tasting in Alexander Valley, this is a good place to take a load off. It's popular with the local population, as well as the winery and vineyard workers. Chef-owner Jeff Mall (Zin Restaurant in Healdsburg) opened this Texas-style barbecue emporium to offer more family-style fare such as sandwiches, burgers, salads, and chili, but you can count on these items being jazzier than at the usual barbecue joint. The priciest thing on the menu is $17.95 (a full slab of pork ribs), but most of the dinners average about $11.00; lunch sandwiches top out at 10 bucks. There is a full bar, with eight beers on tap and a decent selection of wine by the bottle or glass. The Smokehouse is open daily for lunch and dinner.

Healdsburg Bar & Grill $$
245 Healdsburg Avenue, Healdsburg
(707) 433-3333
www.hbg4fun.com

Is it a restaurant, or is it a bar? It's both, and the proprietors handle the food and drink equally well. The cuisine isn't gourmet or snooty, but it's well above the standard fare you might expect. There's an adequate wine list, too, with many available by the glass. For dinner, choose from a blackened snapper sandwich, lamb chops, or salmon sautéed with radicchio and coarse grain mustard sauce. (The kids have their own menu here, but when dinner is done, it's 21-and-over only.) Top off your meal with crème brûlée or mousse, then stick around for the live entertainment (see our Nightlife chapter) and be prepared to do some dancing. The atmosphere is friendly and upscale, and there's an outdoor patio when the weather turns warm. Hotel Healdsburg is just steps away.

Lotus Thai Restaurant $$
109-A Plaza Street, Healdsburg
(707) 433-5282

Here's where Bangkok meets Healdsburg. Open for lunch and dinner six days a week (excluding Monday), the chef has managed to strike a near-perfect balance between authentic dishes of Thailand and the tastes and desires of Californians. His is arguably the most succulent chicken

satay with the best peanut sauce north of the Golden Gate. It's a neat, clean, and well-lit storefront restaurant. Service is unobtrusive and adequate.

Madrona Manor $$$$
1001 Westside Road, Healdsburg
(707) 433-4231
www.madronamanor.com

Nestled on a wooded knoll surrounded by lush vineyards, Madrona Manor is a majestic sight, its mansard roof rising three stories into the treetops (see our Bed-and-Breakfast Inns chapter). The dining room is opulent, the atmosphere romantic. Chef Jesse Mallgren specializes in New California cuisine, using the freshest produce and ingredients available in Sonoma County. He might create an appetizer of crab with ruby red grapefruit, avocado, arugula, and pancetta vinaigrette; and an entree of roast venison loin with carrots, leek risotto, nectarine-rosemary brochettes, and vanilla sauce.

A fixed price menu is offered daily and two gourmet tasting menus as well. There's also an extensive a la carte menu Sunday through Thursday. It's open daily for dinner, but prior to eating, you might want to stroll through the delightful eight-acre gardens. Long story short: Madrona Manor is everything you love about Wine Country.

Manzanita $$$$
336 Healdsburg Avenue, Healdsburg
(707) 433-8111

Manzanita opened in the spring of 2001 with standard Wine Country menu selections such as cassoulet and roast sea bass—California cuisine with European influences. But what chef Bruce Frieseke has created is an outstanding example of what makes a restaurant great: food with flair, combined with terrific service in pleasant surroundings. The first-course options are exceptional—baked black mussels, a truffled beet salad, carrot soup—and the entrees include grilled rabbit set off with polenta, sweet cooked prunes, and black chanterelle mushrooms. There's a small wine bar, and the wine list is impressive. Dinner is served Wednesdays through Sundays until 10:00 P.M.

Ravenous $$$
420 Center Street, Healdsburg
(707) 431–1302

Once a tiny restaurant next to the Raven Theater, with just a few tables and many people milling about outside waiting for those coveted tables, Ravenous has moved up in the world. It's now a full-size restaurant not far from the old place, and the food is better than ever. Chef Joyanne Pezzolo serves generous portions of amazing cuisine that defies categorizing. You can order Liberty duck legs that are steamed and roasted, presented atop noodles, and accompanied by grilled white and black eggplant; or choose the beef brisket braised in red wine. It comes with potato fritters and tasty vegetables, too. It's dinner only here, Wednesdays through Sundays.

Zin $$$$
344 Center Street, Healdsburg
(707) 473–0946
www.zinrestaurant.com

Why name a restaurant after a wine varietal? Why not? Zin delivers great food and offers lots of great Zinfandels, too. Much of the cuisine is created to be enjoyed with Zinfandel and features an all-American accent. You might find St. Louis–style ribs one night and roasted chicken with polenta on another night. Chefs Jeff Mall and Scott Silva call their cuisine "New American"—updating classic American dishes with more interesting flavors and imagination. The dining room is simple, with big bouquets of flowers and soothing paintings. You can get dinner here every night but Tuesday and lunch on weekdays (except Tuesday).

Sonoma Coast

Bay View Restaurant $$$$
800 Highway 1, Bodega Bay
(707) 875–2751
www.innatthetides.com

Bay View is part of Inn at the Tides, one of the most relaxing hostelries at Bodega Bay (see our Hotels, Motels, and Inns chapter). The restaurant features a menu that changes weekly and goes well beyond the local catch. Look for grilled ahi tuna on the menu, bouillabaisse, scaloppine of veal, duck breast, and rack of lamb. Cocktails are served in the lounge, a romantic setting as the sun goes down over the Pacific. The restaurant is open for dinner Wednesday through Sunday.

Lucas Wharf Restaurant & Bar $$$
595 Highway 1, Bodega Bay
(707) 875–3522
www.lucaswharf.com

This is a cozy, romantic place, with a vaulted ceiling and a fireplace to warm you when the weather cools (as it often does on this coast). Seafood will never be fresher than it is here, for this is a commercial fishery that supplies grocers and the public with fresh Pacific catch. The chef's special of the day is based on the best of the day's catch—salmon, halibut, crab, calamari, and oysters. Bask in the glow of the setting sun while you enjoy your meal or watch sea birds cavort as fishermen deliver their bounty at the pier. Lucas Wharf is a great place to pick up fresh cracked crab or custom-smoked fish. The restaurant is open for lunch and dinner seven days a week. Fresh crab season is mid-November through June, and fresh salmon season is mid-May through September.

River's End Restaurant $$$$
11048 Highway 1, Jenner
(707) 865–2484
www.rivers-end.com

From its position on a bluff where the Russian River flows into the Pacific, River's End has an extraordinary view. Menu offerings have left local seafood far behind and moved on to upscale comfort foods with a European flair. Here you can have beluga caviar for an appetizer, whiskey-marinated lobster for the fish course, and roasted rack of lamb filled with oysters for the entree. The house specialties sound almost as exciting—say, beef Wellington or medallions of venison. Either way, it's open for breakfast, lunch, and dinner, Friday through Sunday.

Starfish $$
1400 Highway 1, Bodega Bay
(707) 875–2513

When the Tides and Lucas Wharf restaurants in this seaside town are a little too crowded, keep winding north on Highway 1 until you spot the sign for Starfish. This intimate eatery offers pleasant surroundings and affordable entrees, such as prawn and vegetable brochettes, stuffed snapper, and fried calamari. A nice touch is the genuine mashed potatoes. The wine list features 37 wines, with 12 available by the glass.

The Tides Wharf & Restaurant $$$
835 Highway 1, Bodega Bay
(707) 875–3652
www.innatthetides.com/tideswharf.com

If the setting looks familiar, it's because you saw it in Alfred Hitchcock's film, *The Birds*. If you didn't see the movie, you can get a taste of the action through a poster on the wall. Aside from the renown that has come from Tippi Hedren fending off birds, the restaurant has earned its own fame as the long-standing favorite of regulars who have been popping in since the place was a one-room affair. A very nice lunch can be made of the special seafood chowder, some sourdough bread, and a glass of Chardonnay. The restaurant is open every day for breakfast, lunch, and dinner, and it offers full bar service. You might want to pick up some cracked crab in the marketplace as you leave, if it's in season.

West County/Russian River

Alice's Restaurant $$$
101 South Main Street, Sebastopol
(707) 829–3212

This small, cozy restaurant—with comfortable upholstered chairs and fresh flowers on every table—is friendly and inviting, and the food is among the best in town. The chicken Caesar salad is excellent, and we like the sound of fresh pumpkin rigatoni with grilled chicken-apple sausage, sautéed Mayan sweet onions, and sugar snap peas in nutmeg cream sauce. North Coast labels predominate on the wine list, many available by the glass. Alice also serves locally produced Ace Pear Cider, and her desserts

are made on the premises with Ghirardelli chocolate. Another plus: Alice's is open every day from 9:00 A.M. to 9:00 P.M., with dinner beginning at 5:00 P.M.

Applewood Inn & Restaurant $$$$
13555 Highway 116, Guerneville
(707) 869–9093, (800) 555–8509
www.applewoodinn.com

Snuggled among the redwoods just south of Guerneville, Applewood Inn is famed for its sophisticated meals. It's one of those special places you want to keep to yourself, but you can't stop talking about it. The fire-lit dining room serves 60 at individual candlelit tables with windows facing the redwoods on three sides. The restaurant does wonderful things with a crisp duck breast set off with corn and bing cherries, stuffed pork loin cured in spiced black tea and basmati rice, or roasted salmon with mushrooms and chive-caviar butter. Leave room for the blueberry and fromage blanc cheesecake in semolina cookie crust. Applewood is open for dinner Tuesday through Saturday.

Cape Fear Cafe $$
25191 Main Street, Duncans Mills
(707) 865–9246

If you can, try to visit this restaurant for one of its weekend brunches, when the chef's phenomenal menu of Benedicts is available. The cooking here is a mixture of California cuisine with a southern bent, so expect such dinner entrees as Carolina chicken (with bourbon and pecans) or pork tenderloin with mahogany ginger sauce. But it's those Benedicts that steal the show. Instead of English muffins, the poached eggs are served on peppered grits. Similar to polenta, the grits are cooked, cooled, mixed with cheese, and then grilled.

Chez Marie $$$
6675 Front Street (Highway 116), Forestville
(707) 887–7503
www.chezmarie.com

Chez Marie offers a cozy, unpretentious atmosphere, exceptional food, a glowing fireplace on cool nights, and French country-kitchen and Mardi Gras decor.

Thursday through Sunday the restaurant features Cajun-Creole dishes done in an authentic New Orleans style—the chef's hometown—and French-continental cuisine. The rotating menu includes such items as escargots, cassoulet, bouillabaisse, lamb chops, étouffée, and gumbo. From the homemade bread served hot from the oven to the elegant desserts, all items are prepared to order. The outdoor patio, which borders the restaurant's herb and flower garden, offers a charming setting in which to enjoy a meal.

Chez Peyo $$$
2295 Gravenstein Highway S., Sebastopol
(707) 823–1262
www.sterba.com/chezpeyo/

A charming restaurant in a beautiful garden setting, Chez Peyo features the cuisine of the French Basque nation. Its name comes from the owner, Pierre Lagourgue—"Peyo" is Basque for "Pierre." The menu is heavy on traditional French cooking with its grand sauces, but there is also California-French, using fresh herbs and lighter sauces. Produce is garden fresh, utilizing baby greens and baby spinach for salads. Fresh fish and seafood figures frequently on the menu, one of the most popular dishes being baked mussels. But for a real treat, one must try Peyo's paella, made in the Basque fashion with mussels, clams, shrimp, scallops, linguica (a Basque sausage), chicken, and ham tossed with saffron rice. It's sensational. Peyo's is open for lunch and dinner Wednesday through Sunday and serves a Sunday brunch.

The Farmhouse Inn $$$
7871 River Road, Forestville
(707) 887–3300
www.farmhouseinn.com

The bed-and-breakfast service has now been expanded to include dinner, and the Farmhouse restaurant is open to visitors as well as guests. The dining room seats no more than two dozen, but the chef does a terrific job on a varied menu of fish, beef, pasta, and poultry. The entrees include sea bass sautéed with sweet pepper, scallions, and an orange sauce. Save room for dessert because the chocolate pecan pie is the best you'll ever taste. Open for dinner Thursday through Sunday (see our Bed-and-Breakfast Inns chapter).

Negri's $$
3700 Bohemian Highway, Occidental
(707) 823–5301

It's a toss-up whether the hungry folks of Sonoma County head first for Union Hotel or Negri's—they're both terrific purveyors of great Italian meals. Negri's has been cooking pasta since 1940. Its fame is well-established, as is the expertise of the family that has been running the place since it opened. A family-style meal starts out with a tureen of minestrone that's so popular people come in to buy it by the bucket. The pasta list is long, including vegetarian spaghetti, penne, and homemade ravioli. After that, if you choose, you can order some of their other specials, such as deep fried calamari, grilled red snapper, and prawns—wash it down with a drink from the fully stocked bar. Open for lunch and dinner every day.

Sparks $$
16248 Main Street, Guerneville
(707) 869–8206

California is vegetarian heaven, and this small but hip gourmet eatery serves extraordinary fare that seems sinful, but it's not. Like San Francisco's renowned Millennium Restaurant, the menu is 100 percent vegan, meaning absolutely no animal products. Owner/chef Alex Bury studied at New York's avant-garde Culinary Institute of America, and it shows. Even ruthless carnivores will enjoy such dishes as the rich, smokey "sausage" and potatoes (made with protein-rich wheat gluten), the polenta torte (made with layers of spinach and tomato polenta and a garlic-tofu ricotta), or the tempeh vegetable loaf. Add a glass of local organic wine and it's the quintessential California experience. Open for breakfast, lunch, dinner, and weekend brunch; closed Tuesdays.

Stella's Cafe $$$
4550 Gravenstein Highway N., Sebastopol
(707) 823–6637

Set in an unassuming building in outer Sebastopol, Stella's Cafe is where locals go to enjoy a revolving menu of creative delicacies, whipped up by chef-owner Greg Hallihan. Items such as the steamed half artichoke stuffed with a scoop of purple-black niçoise olive tapenade, the hearty lentil-carrot soup, the lamb kabob, or the pan-roasted chicken with truffled mashed potatoes—not to mention the mocha crème brûlée and other luscious desserts—keep this place packed on most nights. If you are too stuffed for dessert, buy a Gravenstein apple pie to-go at Mom's Apple Pie Shop, a Sonoma County institution, located right next door. Open Wednesday through Monday for dinner, and lunch on Sunday.

Sweets River Grill and Bar $$
16251 Main Street, Guerneville
(707) 869-3383
www.sweetsrivergrill.com

In the mood for grilled ostrich fillet, venison tenderloin, or a little Cajun alligator sauté? Then head for Sweets River Grill in the heart of downtown Guerneville, just a few miles from Korbel Champagne Cellars. Along with these more exotic items,

Sweets features more familiar fare, including New York steak, herb-roasted chicken, and citrus-glazed pork tenderloin. The outdoor patio is shaded and pleasant, and the dining room is highly informal but still elegant. The wine cellar offers a good selection of local vintages, and the fully stocked bar can shake up your favorite libation. Open for dinner every night, lunch Monday through Friday.

Union Hotel Restaurant $$
3731 Main Street, Occidental
(707) 874-3555
www.unionhotel.com

It seems like the Union Hotel dining room has been there forever, housed in a building that goes back to 1879. It's not been around quite that long, but the same family has run it since 1925. The great fame of the place comes from the huge portions of pasta that are served family-style—it's known far and wide for the heaping helpings. The portions are outsized, and the family really knows how to cook pasta. But there are other great items on the menu, chicken cacciatore for one. The establishment has its own bakery and makes great croissants and muffins to serve in its cafe. The restaurant is open for lunch and dinner every day, serving family-style meals and drinks from the saloon.

Mendocino County

U.S. 101

North State Cafe $$
263 North State Street, Ukiah
(707) 462-3726

The logo says it all: "A Casual Experience in Fine Dining." The atmosphere here is that of a fine restaurant, without being too dressy—somewhere between tank tops and neckties. The fare, known as "California Italian," features fresh local ingredients.

Ukiah is not a town with a heavy influx of tourists, and the Cafe's clientele is estimated to be about 95 percent local—much of the patronage coming from the staff at the nearby courthouse. The Cafe is open for lunch Monday through Friday from 11:00 A.M. to 2:00 P.M., and for dinner

Wednesday through Saturday from 5:00 to 9:00 P.M.

Valley Oaks Deli $
Fetzer Vineyards, Highway 175
and Eastside Road, Hopland
(707) 744–1250
www.fetzer.com

This gourmet deli is in the visitor center of Fetzer Vineyards (see our Wineries chapter) and offers an extraordinary selection of fresh salads and sandwiches, all made daily with organic vegetables, fruits, and herbs grown in Fetzer's adjacent Bonterra Garden. You might like to try a grilled vegetable sandwich on focaccia with jambalaya pasta salad. For dessert, go for a cappuccino and the "devil's triangle," if you're a chocolate lover. If you are on your way to a picnic, Valley Oaks will supply you with a special gourmet bag lunch, created to fit your needs. The deli is open daily from 9:00 A.M. to 5:00 P.M. and adjoins the tasting room—you may want to pick up some of Fetzer's best and take it all out to a table on the patio.

Mendocino Coast

Albion River Inn Restaurant $$$$
3790 North Highway 1, Albion
(707) 937–1919, (800) 479–7944
www.albionriverinn.com

A spectacular ocean view, California cuisine, and an award-winning wine list combine to make this an especially romantic dining place. There's seafood, sure, but lots of other options, too, such as roast breast of duck with lentils and carmelized bacon, or pasta with rich Bavarian cambozola cream sauce.

Dinner is served nightly seven days a week: 5:30 to 9:00 P.M. Monday through Friday, and 5:00 to 9:30 P.M. Saturday and Sunday. Reservations are essential. (See our Hotels, Motels, and Inns chapter for more information on this inn.)

Heritage House $$$$
5200 North Highway 1, Little River
(707) 937–5885, (800) 235–5885
www.heritagehouseinn.com

The dining room is opulent, the ambiance elegant. Quite simply, dining at Heritage House is a world-class experience. Chef Velasquez (named one of America's 10 best new chefs by *Food and Wine* magazine) uses only the freshest local ingredients and premier quality foods, personally selected for his seasonal menus. The swordfish with wasabi gnocchi and braised oxtail is just one example. The view from the dining room is of the spectacular Pacific. Breakfast and dinner are served daily (reservations are advisable for dinner), and brunch is a weekend tradition. Heritage House is closed in midwinter. (See our Hotels, Motels, and Inns chapter for more on Heritage House.) There is a full bar.

The Ledford House Restaurant $$$$
3000 North Highway 1, Albion
(707) 937–0282
www.ledfordhouse.com

If you've ever been to Provence, in southern France, you'll recognize the style and ambiance of this restaurant. The expansive windows look out on the Pacific. Add candlelight and music and you've got the basis for a most romantic evening. The food is Mediterranean, and the menu changes monthly. Regulars are rack of lamb, steak, Pacific salmon, and a selection of vegetarian entrees. But you might want to be adventurous and try the tiger prawns flamed in vermouth for dipping in a smoky hot-and-sweet mustard sauce. Dinner is served Wednesday through Sunday from 5:00 P.M., and reservations are advisable.

Little River Inn $$$$
7750 North Highway 1, Little River
(707) 937–5942, (888) 466–5683
www.littleriverinn.com

Unlike most coastal restaurants, the menu here is not partial to seafood, but leans to classics like leg of lamb filet, Cornish game hen, and grilled pork chops. Salads are made from locally grown lettuces and greens. Desserts too may feature local items—don't fail to leave room for the ollalieberry cobbler. The restaurant at Little River Inn is open every day for breakfast and dinner and also offers Sunday brunch. (For more on the inn, see our Spas and Resorts chapter.)

Pangaea Cafe $$$
250 Main Street, Point Arena
(707) 882–3001
www.pangaeacafe.com

Walls are lined with paintings by local artists, giving the small restaurant a feeling of serenity. The food is distinctive, based on the chef's long experience living in other parts of the world (the Middle East, Portugal, Spain), and a changing menu reflects the global influence. Breads are baked fresh in a brick oven every day. Mendocino County wines are featured, often from small, offbeat wineries that don't get much attention. When it comes to desserts, you've hit the culinary big time with the chocolate cake with brandied cherries. Pangaea is open for dinner Wednesday through Sunday.

Mendocino Village

Cafe Beaujolais $$$$
961 Ukiah Street, Mendocino
(707) 937–5614
www.cafebeaujolais.com

It was once a Victorian farmhouse, then at the edge of town. But the town has expanded and engulfed the farm. The ambiance inside is not overwhelming—two dozen well-spaced tables occupy a rather plain room. But the food! It's been praised by restaurant critics for more than two decades and remains something of a legend in Mendocino. Borrowing from France, Italy, Asia, and Mexico, the menu features local produce and free-range poultry as much as possible. Entrees run from sturgeon with truffle sauce, for example, to boneless veal roast. During good weather, there is the option of dining on the large deck out back, which faces onto a beautiful garden. Another option: Call and ask what the menu is for the evening, pick up the entire meal at the "call window," and dine in your hotel room. Dinner is served nightly.

MacCallum House Restaurant $$$$
Grey Whale Bar & Cafe, 45020 Albion Street, Mendocino
(707) 937–5763
www.maccallumhousedining.com

Daisy MacCallum's 1882 Victorian house is one of the earliest of Mendocino's lumber era. Now a bed-and-breakfast inn, the MacCallum House has a dining room open to the public, and the Grey Whale Bar & Cafe offers cafe fare served at friendly prices on the sun porch or parlor. The dining room is more formal, warmed by a stone fireplace. The menu emphasizes fresh local seafoods and organic produce from neighboring farms. You might consider grilled portobello mushrooms or pan-seared duck breast. Dinner is served nightly, and a Sunday brunch is available after 11:00 A.M. The restaurant is closed from the first of January to mid-February.

Mendocino Hotel Restaurant & Garden Room $$$
45080 Main Street, Mendocino
(707) 937–0511, (800) 548–0513
www.mendocinohotel.com

Perhaps it's the graciousness of the hostess, or maybe it's the welcoming decor of this Victorian dining room, but somehow just being here is a pleasant experience. California cuisine is the specialty for dinner, and it is influenced considerably by local seafood. Service is warm but not intrusive. Breakfast and lunch are available in the Garden Room, a large, airy room with a skylight ceiling that really was a garden at one time. (See our Hotels, Motels, and Inns chapter.)

The Moosse Café $$$
390 Kasten Street, Mendocino
(707) 937–4323
www.theblueheron.com

Take a seat on the deck, relax, and gaze at the sea, then order some delicious food—maybe an eggplant sandwich or smoked salmon pâté. If the weather is inclement, the indoor cafe is warm and casual and the service agreeable, with beer and wine available. For the most part, the menu features fresh regional ingredients. Try the velvety-smooth chicken and potato soup, for instance. The salmon sandwich and portobello mushroom sandwich on foccacia bread are exceptional lunch options. Open seven days a week for lunch and dinner.

The Moosse Café is one of the best reasons to dine in Mendocino. PHOTO: JEAN SAYLOR DOPPENBERG

955 Ukiah Street Restaurant $$$$
955 Ukiah Street, Mendocino
(707) 937–1955
www.955restaurant.com

Located in what was once an artist's studio down a garden path next door to Cafe Beaujolais, this may be one of the major reasons visitors from California and the rest of the country like to come to this coast. Basing its fame less on elegance per se than on memorable meals, the restaurant offers a wide-ranging menu and uses local products whenever possible. Options include steaks, roast duck, lamb, and pasta. The restaurant is open every day but Tuesday from 6:00 P.M.

Fort Bragg

Egghead's Restaurant $$
326 North Main Street, Fort Bragg
(707) 964–5005
www.eggheadsrestaurant.com

It's known as the local's favorite, and yes, the locals do brag that there are no better omelettes or eggs Benedict in the entire United States. Beyond that, Egghead's

features some 40 varieties of crepes, specialty pancakes, and waffles for breakfast. For lunch, there are creative salads, unusual sandwiches, and many unique vegetarian treats. The restaurant is distinguished by another feature: a yellow brick road that runs from the front door to the kitchen (here it's known as Oz). Open seven days a week.

Mendo Bistro $$$
301 North Main Street, Fort Bragg
(707) 964–4974
www.mendobistro.com

Upstairs in the Company Store complex of shops along historic Main Street is a fine dining experience in a town not generally known for its gourmet cuisine. Mendo Bistro has changed Fort Bragg's reputation by creating a delightful environment with plenty of large picture windows looking out over the town. Entrees might include seared sea scallops on avocado with citrus dressing, grilled beef tenderloin, and herb-crusted Diestel turkey with risotto. Lighter appetites and thinner wallets might appreciate having the freedom to choose a meat (or portobello mushroom or tofu), have it cooked any way you choose (roasted to fried), then topped with one of seven sauces.

The Rendezvous $$$
647 North Main Street, Fort Bragg
(707) 964–8142
www.rendezvousinn.com

California continental-style seafood, poultry, veal, and steak are served in cozy, comfortable surroundings in one of Fort Bragg's classic early homes. Chef Kim Badenhop studied under master chefs in Switzerland and France, and much of the food served at the Rendezvous reflects the labor-intensive European style of cooking. Seasonality is important to him, and his menus reflect this—in winter he works with wild game and Dungeness crab; in summer, fresh vegetables and king salmon figure strongly on his menu. Dinner is served Wednesday through Sunday, and reservations are advisable.

The Restaurant $$$
418 Main Street, Fort Bragg
(707) 964–9800

Like the meeting place of the friends on television's *Seinfeld*, this place is simply called The Restaurant, and it has been for the past two decades. It offers light meals such as grilled polenta with mozzarella and sautéed mushrooms, and a delightful chicken piccata cooked in fresh lemon and white wine sauce. But whatever you eat, save room for the desserts because they're memorable—especially the tiramisu. The Restaurant presents live jazz on Friday and Saturday. It's open for dinner Thursday through Tuesday and for Sunday brunch. Reservations are recommended for Sunday brunch.

Wharf Restaurant $$$
32260 North Harbor Drive, Fort Bragg
(707) 964–4283
www.wharf-restaurant.com

The Wharf is a favorite spot for both locals and travelers, as it has been for more than 40 years. Relax as you enjoy a cocktail or specialty of the house, watching the boats bring in the catch of the day or head out for some night fishing. The chef's pride is the menu of fresh seafood, with steaks as an alternate. Open for lunch and dinner seven days a week.

Nightlife

Bars and Clubs
Movie Theaters

Though most towns around here start rolling up the sidewalks after sundown, there are a number of popular music venues and dance hot spots to keep your toes tapping well into the night. Napa and St. Helena have a few options, and the downtown areas of Petaluma and Santa Rosa can be relied upon for several good shows on the weekend. Guerneville, too, gets lively in the summer, especially in the town's thriving gay bars. And Lake County's Konocti Harbor Resort is always kicking up its heels in an environment dedicated to mixing music with water sports.

So, if after eating gourmet meals and drinking wine all day you are still looking for more decadent fun, here are a few Wine Country music halls, bars, and clubs where you can look for after-hours entertainment. Some of the smaller establishments don't collect a cover charge, but many do. In general, expect to pay from $2.00 to $5.00 to watch local talent, more if someone of greater renown is taking the stage. Guidelines for pricier show tickets are given in the listings.

The bar and club listings are followed by movie theaters in the region. Check a local newspaper for more up-to-date information.

We don't want to nag about this too much, but one thing bears repeating, especially in this chapter: Please observe the same common sense about drinking and driving that applies anywhere. California's legal blood-alcohol threshold is a stringent .08, so taking to the road after more than one drink can be expensive and embarrassing, as well as extremely dangerous. If you need a taxi, consult our Getting Around chapter.

Bars and Clubs

Napa County

Downtown Joe's
902 Main Street, Napa
(707) 258–2337
www.downtownjoes.com

This riverside microbrewery offers a variety of rock, pop, and blues bands every Thursday, Friday, and Saturday. Sunday evenings are for karaoke, and Tuesdays are open-mike night.

Silverado Country Club & Resort
1600 Atlas Peak Road, Napa
(707) 257–0200
www.silveradoresort.com

A classy joint indeed, Silverado features jazz piano from 5:00 to 9:00 P.M. on the patio terrace, Wednesday through Saturday. On Friday and Saturday nights the

soloist is followed by a band that plays from 9:00 P.M. to 1:00 A.M. The regular act of late has been the five-piece Paul Martin Band.

Piccolino's Italian Cafe
1385 Napa Town Center, Napa
(707) 251–0100
www.piccolinoscafe.com

On Friday and Saturday evenings, this centrally located restaurant provides jazz accompaniment, perhaps spiced with a little R&B or salsa. Hours are generally 5:00 to 9:00 P.M.

Pacific Blues Cafe
6525 Washington Street, Yountville
(707) 944–4455

This popular restaurant and watering hole sits right outside the east entrance of the Vintage 1870 shopping complex. In addition to serving what they call "Maverick American" cuisine, they spice things

145

up with live blues on Saturdays in summer from 5:00 to 8:00 P.M.

Ana's Cantina
1205 Main Street, St. Helena
(707) 963–4921

This tropical-themed Mexican restaurant heats up from 9:30 P.M. to 1:30 A.M. most Friday and Saturday nights, with a stream of bands that run from Latin-Mediterranean to jazz to rock to reggae. Wednesday and Sunday are karaoke nights. Thursday is open-mike night.

1351 Lounge
1351 Main Street, St. Helena
(707) 963–1969
www.1351lounge.com

A small club with a capacity for packing 'em in, that's 1351. It's usually live blues or rock on weekends, and there's always a cover charge. Acoustic singer-songwriters can be found there on the occasional weeknight.

Calistoga Inn & Restaurant
1250 Lincoln Avenue, Calistoga
(707) 942–4101
www.calistogainn.com

The bartender slings Napa Valley Brewing Company beers here, and every Saturday from 8:30 to 11:00 P.M. (and often on Tuesdays and Fridays), live music fills the small oblong bar. The material varies but tends toward intimate, singer-songwriter stuff. Wednesday is open-mike night.

Hydro Bar & Grill
1403 Lincoln Avenue, Calistoga
(707) 942–9777

Calistoga's late-night eatery is a perfect spot for everything from swing music to rock 'n' roll.

Sonoma County

Murphy's Irish Pub
464 First Street E., Sonoma
(707) 935–0660

This pub keeps sleepy Sonoma awake, usually every Thursday through Sunday night. The genre is hard to predict. It could be blues one night, traditional Celtic the next. Or it could be folk ballads followed by a melodious string ensemble. There is no cover, but expect a two-pint minimum.

Copperfield's Cafe
140 Kentucky Street, Petaluma
(707) 762–8798
www.copperfieldscafe.com

Sonoma County's hippest bookstore chain goes one step further at this Petaluma branch, laying down folk music on Wednesday nights.

Kodiak Jack's
256 North Petaluma Boulevard, Petaluma
(707) 765–5760
www.kodiakjacks.com

On different nights, there is West Coast swing dancing, two-step, line dancing, "beginner couples," power country, and honky-tonk. You can take lessons every night. There's a restaurant (Sundance Steakhouse) with cuisine to match the country theme. Call for cover information.

Mystic Theatre & Music Hall
23 North Petaluma Boulevard, Petaluma
(707) 765–2121
www.mcnears.com

Not as big as Konocti Harbor, not as polite as the Luther Burbank Center, the Mystic Theatre might be the Wine Country's coolest venue. Built in 1911 in the historic McNear Building, it's a vaulted, double-decker palace that wouldn't be out of place on the Sunset Strip. Much of the music is classic rock of all shades and tones, from Warren Zevon to Tower of Power, Richard Thompson to Tommy Castro, Emmylou Harris to Todd Rundgren. A few years back, Van Morrison even recorded one of his live albums here. Stand-up comedy passes through from time to time, featuring jokers like Will Durst. Tickets generally range from $15 to $30.

Tradewinds
8210 Old Redwood Highway, Cotati
(707) 795–7878
www.tradewindsbar.com

This small club has music most weekend nights. Expect a lot of blues and R&B, and

Like the Fillmore Auditorium in San Francisco, the Mystic Theatre & Music Hall in Petaluma has showcased a wide range of musical talent for many years. PHOTO: JEAN SAYLOR DOPPENBERG

watch for Derek and the Aces, the roots-rock band that used to be regulars here.

A'Roma Roasters and Coffeehouse
95 Fifth Street, Santa Rosa
(707) 576–7765

Come down to Railroad Square on a Friday or Saturday night for live music and a hot cup of chai or joe. A'Roma does a lot of folk music, plus some world beat, jazz, and blues. Shows start at 8:30 P.M.

Last Day Saloon
120 Fifth Street, Santa Rosa
(707) 545–2343
www.lastdaysaloon.com

This is the northern outpost of the venerable San Francisco nightclub that's been rocking the Bay Area for more than 30 years. On a busy corner in Railroad Square, Last Day is 8,000 square feet of music, Bloody Marys, and food, too. DJ music is provided three nights a week, with weekends dedicated to live music of all kinds—you're likely to hear Motown or disco, funk or new wave. Owner David Daher draws on

his three decades in the music business to bring in some terrific acts that might have previously overlooked Santa Rosa on their tour itineraries. Recent legends appearing in the main music room have included Elvin Bishop and members of the Grateful Dead. Sunday night is generally reserved for showcasing local rock bands. DJ nights usually carry a $5.00 cover; tickets for live shows can range from $10.00 to $20.00, depending on whether the artist is a household name. There's also a full menu of decent pub grub, and it's served until midnight—a nice bonus for late-night revelers.

Flamingo Resort Hotel
2777 Fourth Street, Santa Rosa
(707) 545–8530
www.flamingoresort.com

Sure, it's a hotel bar, but it's better than most. Count on soul and rhythm & blues bands on the weekends, and DJs spinning discs during the week. The dance floor is one of the best around, and it's always packed with hoofers of all ages.

The Cantina
500 Fourth Street, Santa Rosa
(707) 523–3663

Generation Next moves to its own beat at the Cantina, in the heart of downtown—upstairs from the restaurant of the same name. Thursday is college night during the spring and summer. Fridays and Saturdays, you get a mix of top 40, R&B, disco, house, and Latin beats.

Dance Central
3535 Industrial Avenue, Santa Rosa
(707) 545–6150

If you don't know how to dance, but want to learn, or if you are a rising star looking to improve your style, then this is the place for you. You can take lessons almost every night, and get to practice afterward during the nightly open dance parties. Tuesday it's ballroom dancing, Wednesday it's West Coast swing, Thursday is salsa night, Friday brings on the big bands and the Lindy, Saturday is variety night, and Sunday is West Coast swing. Call for prices and details.

Insiders' Tip
Nonsmokers, take note: You can dance up a storm in Wine Country's nightspots without your clothes reeking of smoke afterward. That's because smoking has been banned in bars and nightclubs in California since 1998. Smokers are still welcome to get in on the fun inside, but they must light up outside at least 6 feet from the establishment's entrance.

Sweetriver Saloon
248 Coddingtown Center, Santa Rosa
(707) 526–0400
www.sweetriver.com

Locating a comedy club in the middle of a mall should provide a lot of grist for the comics. Sweetriver makes you laugh every Friday and Saturday night, starting at 9:00 P.M. The cover is $7.00 (no joke).

Healdsburg Bar & Grill
245 Healdsburg Avenue, Healdsburg
(707) 433–3333
www.hbg4fun.com

Nightlife improved significantly in this sleepy burg when HB&G opened its doors. Expect live bands on weekends, usually rock-and-roll from established local groups such as the Remedies or the Pulsators. Occasionally, the owners pull out all the stops for a Sunday evening show with renowned artists such as Dan Hicks or Coco Montoya (with tickets in the $20 to $25 range).

Bear Republic Brewing Company
345 Healdsburg Avenue, Healdsburg
(707) 433–2337
www.bearrepublic.com

Another microbrewery that offers music, Bear Republic often has entertainment on Thursday and Friday nights. It might be blues; it might be surf music; it might sound like heaven after a couple of pints.

Jasper O'Farrell's
6957 Sebastopol Avenue, Sebastopol
(707) 823–1389

O'Farrell's keeps Sebastopol busy every night of the week—mostly blues, some rock, some soul, some original songwriting, and even the occasional Celtic group. Tuesday is open-mike night. It's very eclectic and very local.

The Powerhouse Brewing Company
268 Petaluma Avenue, Sebastopol
(707) 829–9171
www.powerhousebrewing.com

This brewpub-cum-night spot offers a mix of local as well as national talent, heavy on the blues. Sometimes there is no cover. Other times, the cost can be as much as $12 for acts such as the Nervis Brothers, those New Orleans boogiers.

Main Street Station
16280 Main Street, Guerneville
(707) 869-0501
www.mainststation.com

When Guerneville gets a little too hot, duck into the Station for some cool, breezy jazz. The Benny Barth Jazz Trio on Tuesdays have been regulars lately. Other hipsters blow in and out on Thursdays, Fridays, and Saturdays.

Rainbow Cattle Company
16220 Main Street, Guerneville
(707) 869-0206

It celebrated its 20th anniversary in October 1999, but the Cattle Company hasn't slowed down a bit. It's still where the Russian River's gay clientele gather for loud, uninhibited fun. The club has a DJ on Friday and Saturday nights and holidays.

Club FAB
16135 Main Street, Guerneville
(707) 869-5708
www.fabpresents.com

Proclaiming itself as the largest gay dance club north of the Golden Gate, Club FAB is housed in an old cinema in downtown Guerneville. Since opening its doors in 1998, it's been the most happening scene along the Russian River. When there's not a name act playing, the DJ revs up dancers on Friday and Saturday nights with foot-tapping rhythms.

Mendocino County

Greenwood Pier Cafe
5926 South Highway 1, Elk
(707) 877-9997
www.greenwoodpierinn.com

If you find yourself in the village of Elk, south of Albion on the rugged Mendocino coast, you might be surprised to hear the sound of guitar chords floating on the breeze. They will lead you to Greenwood Pier Cafe, which has music every Friday and Saturday from 7:00 to 9:00 P.M.

Insiders' Tip

In 2002, the brewmaster at Third Street Aleworks in downtown Santa Rosa took home three gold medals and a silver medal from the World Beer Cup held in Aspen.

Patterson's Pub
10485 Lansing Street, Mendocino
(707) 937-4782
www.mcn.org/a/pattersons

Beer and tall tales are paramount at Patterson's, but the pub also keeps your sports appetite satisfied with four TV sets. Live music is featured on occasion, though it is rare. Look for the old London taxi in the driveway. Patterson's is open daily.

The Caspar Inn
14957 Caspar Road, Caspar
(707) 964-5565
www.casparinn.com

It's a long way from San Francisco, but Caspar Inn has the same type of colorful rock-and-roll history as the Fillmore. This old (1906) roadhouse-style inn has been in business since Caspar was a booming logging town, and many a big name has stepped through its doors and onto the stage (Mose Allison, B.B. King). Today you can expect karaoke on Wednesdays and such diverse musical concoctions as Afro-Cuban salsa and cowpunk on weekends. Bonnie Raitt reportedly comes in now and then (she lives nearby) and just hangs out, singing along with the jukebox. Cover charges range from $5.00 to $10.00.

Headlands Coffeehouse
120 East Laurel Street, Fort Bragg
(707) 964-1987
www.headlandscoffeehouse.com

This is the epicenter of local culture in Fort Bragg, a hipster java joint where there's almost always something interesting to listen to as you stay wired. Sunday is classical music night: maybe a string trio, maybe a guitar-and-flute combination. On Friday there is usually a jazz piano trio. Beyond that you're most likely to encounter jazz or acoustic singer-songwriter stuff.

Movie Theaters

Napa County

Napa CineDome 8
825 Pearl Street, Napa
(707) 257–7700

Cameo Cinema
(occasional art movies)
1340 Main Street, St. Helena
(707) 963–9779

Sonoma County

Sebastiani Theatre
(historic building; occasional art movies)
476 First Street E., Sonoma
(707) 996–2020
www.sebastianitheatre.com

Sonoma Cinemas
200 Siesta Way, Sonoma
(707) 935–1234
www.cinemawest.com

Rohnert Park 16
555 Rohnert Park Expressway W.,
Rohnert Park
(707) 586–0555

Sonoma Film Institute
Sonoma State University, Darwin Theater,
1801 East Cotati Avenue, Rohnert Park
(707) 664–2606

Airport Cinema 8
409 Aviation Way, Santa Rosa
(707) 522–0330

Rialto Cinemas Lakeside
551 Summerfield Road, Santa Rosa
(707) 539–9770
www.rialtocinemas.com

Roxy on the Square
620 Third Street, Santa Rosa
(707) 528–8770

Roxy Stadium 14
85 Santa Rosa Avenue, Santa Rosa
(707) 522–0330

The Raven Film Center
415 Center Street, Healdsburg
(707) 433–5448
www.raventheater.com

Clover Cinemas
121 East First Street, Cloverdale
(707) 894–7920
www.cinemawest.com

Sebastopol Cinemas
6868 McKinley Street, Sebastopol
(707) 829–3456
www.cinemawest.com

Rio Theater
20396 Bohemian Highway (Highway 116),
Monte Rio
(707) 865–0913

Mendocino County

Noyo Theater
57 East Commercial Street, Willits
(707) 459–0280

Ukiah 6 Theatre
612 South State Street, Ukiah
(707) 462–6788

Arena Theatre
214 Main Street, Point Arena
(707) 882–3020

Coast Cinemas
167 South Franklin Street, Fort Bragg
(707) 964–2019

Sip Wine by Day, Lift a Pint at Night: A Guide to Wine Country Brewpubs

You know you've wandered into serious microbrewery territory when you can sip—at the source—satisfying suds that bear such colorful names as "Death and Taxes Black Beer," "Twist of Fate Bitter," "Hop 2 It," "Damnation," "Lunatic," "Bony Fingers Malt," "Rat Bastard Pale Ale," and "Workingstiff Red."

The Wine Country ferments much more than just grape-based beverages. If you prefer ambers and blacks to reds and whites, and put more stock in a drink's head than its legs, you'll feel right at home. Brewpubs are plentiful, and they have co-existed comfortably for many years alongside our more established emporiums devoted to vino.

Following are descriptions of several microbreweries in the Wine Country that craft unforgettable ales and lagers, serve upscale pub grub, and have found fame beyond our three-county region. After a day of sniffing, sipping, and chewing on Cabernets, these friendly establishments might be just the place to quaff a cold one. Many offer live entertainment, too, especially on weekends (see individual listings in this chapter for more information).

We begin lifting our glasses in Napa Valley and wrap up the journey in Mendocino County.

Downtown Joe's
902 Main Street, Napa
(707) 258–2337
www.downtownjoes.com
Pick a pint of Ace High Pale Ale or Golden Ribbon (or the Golden Thistle Very Bitter Ale, if your palate prefers that) and enjoy the view of the Napa River outside. Joe's has the standard pub fare (fish and chips, burgers, and sandwiches), with fancier dinner items that range from pancetta wrapped grilled chicken breast to a Virginia smoked pork chop.

Silverado Brewing Company
3020 St. Helena Highway N., Suite A, St. Helena
(707) 967–9876
www.silveradobrewingcompany.com
This is a full bar with six beers made onsite—and 30 wines by the bottle, if you just can't get enough of the grape. It's located about 2 miles north of St. Helena in the Freestone Abbey complex (watch for the sign—it can sneak up on you). We like the tap handle for the Blonde Ale—a blonde in a red dress—and the warm ambiance of the small bar. The extensive menu has something for everyone, including St. Louis–style ribs.

Calistoga Inn Restaurant and Brewery
1250 Lincoln Avenue, Calistoga
(707) 942–4101
www.napabeer.com
This may be one brewery where the food gets more attention than the brews. Choose from a wheat ale, a pilsner, red ale, or a porter on most nights, with some seasonal

recipes thrown in. To accompany your foamy brew, order the paella, a pork tender-loin, or pepper-crusted duck breast. Calistoga Inn can boast that it has "survived the Depression, periods of neglect, and five major wars." In other words, it's been around a few years.

Dempsey's Sonoma Brewing Company
50 East Washington Street, Petaluma
(707) 765–9694

This brewpub has been quietly serving Petalumans for more than 10 years, combining its Red Rooster Ale and Petaluma Strong Ale with hearty meals like a marinated pork chop. Much of the produce used in the cuisine is organically grown locally. When the weather is fine, take a seat on the outside patio on the Petaluma River. If you're overnighting in Petaluma, get ye to Dempsey's.

Third Street Aleworks Restaurant and Brewery
610 Third Street, Santa Rosa
(707) 523–3060
www.thirdstreetaleworks.com

There are lots of brews to choose from here, and the pub fare to go with it. Have a pint of Annadel Pale Ale or the Stonefly Oatmeal Stout, or sample one of the "occa-sional" ales, such as Drunken Weasel and Burgher's Kolsch. Use any of these fine brews to wash down English bangers and mash or a selection of pizzas. It's an ethnic menu here, with appetizers ranging from hummus to quesadillas. Burgers, too, of course.

Russian River Brewing Company
725 Fourth Street, Santa Rosa
(707) 545–2337
www.russianriverbrewing.com

This brewery had its humble beginnings at Korbel Champagne Cellars near Guerneville, but now it's gone uptown, or more precisely, downtown as in Santa Rosa, with a projected opening in July 2003. The hops are grown in Sonoma County, and the brews include an amber ale, a golden wheat ale (a gold medal winner at the 2001 Great American Beer Festival), a pale ale, and a porter. Pizza rules the menu, but cal-zones and foccacia are included, too.

Bear Republic Brewing Company
345 Healdsburg Avenue, Healdsburg
(707) 433–2337
www.bearrepublic.com

There are usually 11 beers and ales on tap for sampling, most of them award winners (try the Red Rocket or Black Raven and see why). If you like what you taste, you can usually get a one-gallon reusable box of your favorite to go. (For the kids, there's homemade root beer and cream soda.) In the shadow of Hotel Healdsburg, the patio is a relaxing spot to nosh on calamari fritti, a huge chicken sandwich called "The Press," or such specials as chicken Parmesan, lobster bisque, or chicken potpie.

Powerhouse Brewing Company
268 Petaluma Avenue, Sebastopol
(707) 829–9171
www.powerhousebrewing.com

Housed in a National Historic Landmark powerhouse building in downtown Sebastopol, the aptly named establishment is probably more renowned locally for its live entertainment than its beer and food. Yet the brews have garnered several awards, especially the Blonde Ale and Strong Ale. There are seven ales and lagers on tap. The pub grub includes beef burgers, turkey burgers, red beans and rice, and veggie specialties.

Mendocino Brewing Company
13351 U.S. 101, Hopland
(707) 744-1361
www.mendobrew.com

This is the oldest microbrewery in California, established in 1983. Red Tail Ale is its best-known label, but it also produces Peregrine Pale Ale, Black Hawk Stout, Blue Heron IPA, and a seasonal offering such as Yuletide Porter. A 100-year-old brick building is where you'll find the pub; the beer itself is made about 12 miles away in Ukiah. An outdoor beer garden trellised in hops is the place to get great food at reasonable prices (quesadillas, smoked pork chops, steaks, hamburgers, and the like).

Ukiah Brewing Company
102 South State Street, Ukiah
(707) 468–5898
www.ukiahbrewingco.com

In another "first" for California, this establishment is the only certified organic brewpub in the nation. Six brews are on tap, all made from organic grains and hops. Try the Sun House Amber, or go all out with an Emancipator (8.3 percent alcohol content). In addition, all the food is chemical-free and certified organic—it's only the second restaurant in the nation to receive this distinction. There are vegan offerings as well as beef dishes, such as Flemish pot roast and shepherd's pie.

Anderson Valley Brewing Company
1770 Highway 253, Boonville
(707) 895–2337
www.avbc.com

Mosey on up to the Buckhorn Saloon for some vittles and a foamy brew. The brewhouse is about a mile away, but the saloon—on the same site the original saloon occupied 125 years ago—pours the brewery's many offerings. There's Boont Amber Ale, Barney Flats Oatmeal Stout, and Deep Enders Dark. Have a burger, then check out the gift shop.

North Coast Brewing Company
444 North Main Street, Fort Bragg
(707) 964-3400
www.ncoast-brewing.com

Wow, but we do love that Scrimshaw Pilsner. The Red Seal Ale and the Blue Star are nifty, too, as are the Acme Pale Ale, Acme Brown Ale, Old No. 38, and Old Rasputin Russian Imperial Stout. In 1998, this brewery was ranked by the Beverage Testing Institute as one of the world's 10 best breweries. The food is well above average, and the service friendly. The grilled salmon with dill butter is always a favorite, as are the Cuban hanger steak, Bahia escolar, and seafood etoufee. There's also a daily pasta special.

Wineries

A Taste of Each Region
Wineries to Visit
Wine Shops

This is the chapter that gave us the excuse to create this book in the first place. In our little galaxy, the wineries are the sun around which all of our other attractions seem to orbit. And just as the grape varietals we grow here are dramatically different from one another, so too are the wineries that produce them. If you take time to drop in at more than a few, you'll discover each place has its own special story to tell.

So when you visit Wine Country, set aside at least a day or two for a sampling of the region's wineries. On the outside, they can range from rustic barns to grand estates resembling castles. On the inside, you are warmly welcomed by genial guides and tasting room hosts who will gladly explain the mysteries of the craft.

Whatever you do, please refrain from rushing through Wine Country. There's nothing to be gained from sprinting between tasting rooms. Take the time to learn about the winery, the winemaking process, and especially its people. Usually they are as mellow and unhurried s the wines themselves.

A Taste of Each Region

So...with hundreds of wineries within the region, where does one begin? First, we'll give you a taste of what separates our coverage area from the rest of the winemaking areas of California and the world—qualities that have given our region the undisputed title of California's Wine Country. Next, we'll provide a brief overview of the wine and wineries of each of the counties in our coverage area. Then comes the part where you get to pick and choose: detailed listings for more than 120 individual producers throughout Wine Country.

Despite the number of wineries here and the number of acres under viticulture, it's interesting to note that Wine Country's grape harvest represents only a relatively small contribution to California's total wine production. The annual grape harvest of Sonoma County adds up to a minuscule 4 percent of the state's total volume, about the same as neighboring Napa County. This deceptively small percentage stands in stark contrast with the lofty reputation Wine Country's vintages have deservedly attained.

There are scores of wineries here, but they are not the oil-refinery-scale tank farms of the jug wine, bulk business. With a few exceptions, nearly all our wineries are small- to medium-sized operations, often family-owned. This is as good a reason as any to visit—you will nearly always find a tasty vintage to call your own personal discovery. Pour another glass of your favorite red, and read on about the climatology of fine wines.

Understanding Appellations

Understanding appellations is this simple: The quality of the grapes is the key to the quality of the wine. Where grapes are grown makes up almost 80 percent of the characteristics of a specific wine. The mellow in your Merlot? The zest in that Zinfandel? The panache of a particular Pinot Noir? It all can be traced back to the grapes, the climate that fostered their growth, and the soil from which they emerged.

Areas with hot days, warm nights, and deep, peat-rich soils might be good for growing corn and other vegetables (and even table grapes), but they produce wine grapes that are too high in sugar content and, therefore, not good for creating fine wines. A cooler, dryer climate and the volcanic soils so common in Napa, Sonoma,

Mendocino, and Lake Counties lead to the production of ultrapremium wines.

Within this four-county area, there are also many microclimates. Each of these areas has specific characteristics that affect the wine grapes grown there. In the wine industry, these special growing regions are called "American viticultural areas" (AVAs). Around here we refer to them as "appellations," a French word you will run into frequently in this guide, but which is not used officially by the Bureau of Alcohol, Tobacco, and Firearms (BATF), the agency of the federal government that monitors these things. How important is the term *appellation*? Some grapes grow better in one appellation than in another. Also, the same grape varietal grown in one appellation may produce a wine that is distinctly different from one made with the same grade of grapes grown in another appellation.

There are 12 AVAs in Sonoma County alone, and another 14 (and a 15th pending approval) in Napa County. In addition, the two counties share one—the aforementioned Carneros, a cool region bordering San Pablo Bay at the southern reaches of both the Napa and Sonoma valleys. At first, it may sound to the novice as if the wine snobs are splitting hairs. But the differences in the wines from different appellations (and different winemakers within the same appellation), when tasted side by side, are distinct and remarkable.

Appellations also are important economically. A wine labeled with a certain appellation name must be produced using a minimum of 75 to 85 percent of grapes from that region. For example, a "Sonoma Valley" Zinfandel must take at least 85 percent of its Zinfandel grapes from the Sonoma Valley AVA. Such distinctions add value to the wine and raise the shelf price. By comparison, a Zinfandel with the appellation "California" on the label means that the grapes could have come from anywhere in California. These wines often are produced with grapes from less-prestigious growing areas such as the San Joaquin Valley, where the long, hot summers allow production of massive quantities of grapes that are used primarily for jug wines and the so-called "fighting vari-etals" (wine industry jargon for lower-priced varietals).

The generally dryer and cooler micro-climates of Napa, Sonoma, Mendocino, and Lake Counties produce fewer grapes, but they are of a much higher quality for making fine wine. Grapes from these regions are more expensive (often as much as four to five times higher per ton), and they are in high demand.

Of course, grapes are not the only element that goes into making a fine wine. The object of the winemaker's craft—a blend of skill, experience, science, art, taste, and inspiration—is to take the special qualities of certain grapes and maximize their potential. Without getting too high-falutin' about it, a tour of Wine Country can include the dimension of a search for the perfect blend of the region's finest grapes and the winemaker's skill.

Napa County

When people hear the words "California Wine Country," they first think of Napa, where the wines have been established as the yardstick by which other American vintages are measured. Even the French have taken notice of this world-famous source. Compared to Europe, however, where vineyards have flourished for centuries, Napa Valley is still in its infancy. Yet it has grown quickly, and with approximately 250 wineries, it is believed to be the world's most densely concentrated winery region. Because of this, there is some concern that traffic and crowds will destroy

Insiders' Tip

It is estimated that 80 million gallons of wine (90 percent of it from California) was exported out of the United States in 2001. The wine was valued at approximately $541 million.

Where'd That Come From?

Wines labeled with a certain appellation name must be produced using a minimum of 75 to 85 percent of grapes (depending on the varietal) from that specific region. Below are the recognized appellations (American viticultural areas) of the four counties in Wine Country. Note that the North Coast AVA is a broad one, applying to wines from several different counties including Napa, Sonoma, Mendocino, and Lake.

Napa County

Atlas Peak, Chiles Valley, Diamond Mountain, Howell Mountain, Los Carneros, Mount Veeder, Napa Valley, North Coast, Oak Knoll District (pending), Oakville, Rutherford, Spring Mountain District, St. Helena, Stags Leap District, Wild Horse Valley, Yountville

Sonoma County

Alexander Valley, Chalk Hill, Dry Creek Valley, Knights Valley, Los Carneros, North Coast, Northern Sonoma, Rockpile, Russian River Valley, Sonoma Coast, Sonoma County Green Valley, Sonoma Mountain, Sonoma Valley

Mendocino County

Anderson Valley, Cole Ranch, McDowell Valley, Mendocino, Mendocino Ridge, North Coast, Potter Valley, Redwood Valley, Yorkville Highlands

Lake County

Benmore Valley, Clear Lake, Guenoc Valley, North Coast

Sources: *Wine Country Living* magazine; Mendocino Wine Growers Alliance; Lake County Visitor Information; Bureau of Alcohol, Tobacco and Firearms; The Wine Institute

---

the bucolic landscape, particularly in summer when tourist count is high.

Motorists who know the region well are inclined at such busy times to abandon the main highway through the valley, Highway 29, and turn onto the Silverado Trail, which runs parallel to the east. From there, they can cross over, using any of several connecting lanes that bind the two north-south roads. Silverado Trail is a delight in itself, winding between meadows and wooded slopes to the east and vineyards to the west. Its slight elevation produces some striking vineyard panoramas, eminently suited to photography. (For more on negotiating the byways of Wine Country, see our Getting Around chapter.)

Napa Valley boasts so many tasting rooms it is almost impossible to classify them as a group. They range in style from quaint to elegant, sparse to cluttered, disarmingly casual to alarmingly commercial. But beyond atmosphere and physical trappings, the valley's tasting rooms provide the makings of a truly unique wine experience. In these pockets of hospitality you will find an abundance of wines rivaling any in the world.

Those with a nose for business and an affinity for columns of numbers will appreciate these digits: The wine industry in Napa Valley accounts for about $4 billion (yes, billion) of the $33 billion California wine industry. In 2001, the Napa Valley winegrape crop set an all-time record, reaching a value of $359 million, including a $22 million increase in the value of the Cabernet Sauvignon crop alone. Approximately 126,400 tons of red and white grapes were produced. That's how important wine is to our area's overall economy.

At its widest, Napa Valley is no more than 3 miles across. It is 27 miles from north end to south end, framed on both sides by hulking mountains. Most of the valley's two million annual visitors come to see its 35,000 acres of groomed vineyards—some newly replanted, some ancient, with gnarled vines that stand like regiments of old soldiers.

Food-and-wine pairings are staged in several wineries, and many have picnic grounds that give new meaning to the great outdoors. Artesa has a charming museum with some 17th-century winemaking casks and paraphernalia from its home country of Spain. And several wineries have elegant and eerie caves open for exploring (see our Close-up "Holy Merlot, Batman!" in this chapter).

Sonoma County

The Napa and Sonoma valleys are separated by the Mayacmas Mountains, but much more distinguishes these two prime grape-growing regions. Napa, which enjoyed early prestige as a wine-growing region, is often considered the glitzier cousin of the more down-home Sonoma. Yet, beneath Sonoma's rural charm is an elegance and sophistication that you can sample in both the wine and local culture.

But when people say they are going to visit "Sonoma," just which Sonoma do they mean? Are they talking about Sonoma County—one-and-a-half times the size of Rhode Island? Or are they referring to the smaller Sonoma Valley, Jack London's famed "Valley of the Moon," where Count Agoston Haraszthy fathered the California wine industry? Maybe they simply mean the town of Sonoma, the historic little pueblo nestled in the southeast corner of the county, and site of the state's last mission. (See our History and Area Overview chapters for more on all these incarnations of Sonoma.)

Sonoma County is home to at least 12 distinct wine-growing appellations and shares a 13th, Carneros, with Napa County. Saying that a wine comes from Sonoma doesn't really say enough to those who know their wines. There are differences—sometimes subtle, sometimes dramatic—among the same types of wine produced by different Sonoma County vintners in different appellations.

With the exception of the bluffs overlooking the Pacific and the cool redwood forests, grapes grow in almost every corner of Sonoma County. Major grape-growing areas include the Russian River, where ocean fog makes the climate ideal for Pinot Noir and Chardonnay and for an exceptional Sauvignon Blanc; Los Carneros, where wind and fog from San Pablo Bay create conditions that produce intensely flavored Pinot Noir and Chardonnay; Sonoma Valley, whose many microclimates are suited to many grape varieties; Alexander Valley, known for its Cabernet Sauvignon and Sauvignon Blanc; and Dry Creek Valley, where the wines have been earning much publicity and numerous gold medals of late. Wineries here range from small, family-operated enterprises where bottle labels still are applied by hand, to huge corporations where ageless winemaking skills are blended with computerized technology.

If you have only one day to tour Sonoma County, you can't go wrong if you start in the Sonoma Valley. It is the closest of the premium wine-growing regions to San Francisco, only 45 minutes from the Golden Gate. Your tour might well begin with a stop at the Sonoma Valley Visitors Bureau (which is also the office of the Sonoma Valley Vintners and Growers Association) on Spain Street. It's next to the Sonoma State Historic Park headquarters, across the street from the lovely central plaza in the town of Sonoma (see our Attractions and History chapters). For an easy mix of shopping and browsing and wine tasting, walk around the square before taking a free trolley 3 blocks east for a winery tour and tasting at Sebastiani Vineyards.

If you are eager for some serious wine tasting, there are more than a half-dozen small- to medium-sized wineries within a 15-minute drive of the plaza. These include Ravenswood, known for its excellent Zinfandels; Buena Vista, which also has a tasting room on the plaza; Gundlach

Bundschu; and Bartholomew Park Winery (all are listed in this chapter). If you are headed south to San Francisco from the town of Sonoma, you will travel through the Carneros region with its many wineries. Stop in at Viansa (which also has an outstanding deli) and Cline Cellars. If you are able to visit and taste the wines of even half the places mentioned, you will have had a full and enjoyable day. The big-name producers in the county include Sebastiani, Glen Ellen, Clos du Bois, and Korbel, but don't neglect the smaller wineries: Benziger, Kenwood, Foppiano, Hop Kiln, Martinelli, and so on.

Besides the wine itself, touring Sonoma County offers the sheer pleasure of driving along winding roads with views of vineyards and farms that alternate between the dramatic and the sweetly rural. From some mountaintops and parts of the Carneros district at the southern border, the skyline of San Francisco is visible on clear days (and nights).

Mendocino County

While not as well known as Sonoma or Napa, Mendocino County is gradually getting the word out about the Anderson Valley's extraordinary wines—originally an area of orchards and sheep and cattle ranches. Discovered during the 1970s as a fine growing area for wine grapes, this rolling land, drained by the Navarro River, has quickly become braided in long rows of Pinot Noir, Chardonnay, Gewurztraminer, and Zinfandel grapes.

To prove to the world that Anderson Valley is the finest but least recognized Pinot Noir–producing region in the country, vintners there held the first annual "Pinot Noir Weekend" in May 1997 and promised annual renewals. Participating wineries offer vineyard and winery tours, a look at the history of growing Pinot Noir, and lots of tastings from both barrels and bottles.

If anyone deserved to be called the grandfather of Mendocino wine success, it would be Adolph Parducci. From Prohibition times until the end of the 1960s, Parducci Wine Cellars in Ukiah was one of the few—and at times the only—wine producer in the county. Parducci launched his operation in 1918, when fear of Prohibition was driving everyone else out of the business. He bought some casks, a crusher, and some elementary equipment and began making wine in an old barn in Cloverdale. He survived the Prohibition years in part because the law allowed home winemakers to have 200 gallons of "juice" for their own use.

By 1927 Parducci had pulled together enough money to buy some land in Ukiah Valley (now fondly called the Home Ranch) and planted 100 acres of grapes. From that time on, he and his four sons tended the vineyards, harvested the grapes, and built a winery. With the repeal of Prohibition in 1933, they opened a small tasting cellar in the basement of their home. Soon the charming family winery became a favorite stopping place for tourists. They'd sample from the spigot, have their jugs filled, and watch as the Parducci label was pasted on the bottle.

Another major player in Mendocino County wine is Fetzer, just off U.S. 101 in Hopland. In the 1950s, Bernard Fetzer bought vineyards in the Redwood Valley that had been established a century earlier by gold miner Anson Seward. Some of the vines actually dated back to Seward's earlier planting. During the next 10 years, Fetzer experimented with some Bordeaux-type varietals with considerable success, selling his Cabernet Sauvignon and Semillon wines by air freight to home consumers all over the country. The Valley Oaks Ranch, purchased by the Fetzer family in 1984, is now their headquarters.

If Parducci and Fetzer are the most easily recognized names, by no means do they stand alone. There are more than 35 other wineries in the Mendocino County area, producing an abundance of award-winning vintages. Of the county's 2.25 million total acres, just 14,000 acres are planted to vineyards—25 percent of that acreage is certified organic. Mendocino's wine regions are divided into six valley areas, each noted for the different varieties of grapes produced under slightly different climatic conditions. In the southeast areas of Sanel and McDowell valleys look for the wines of Fetzer, Milano, McDowell, Jepson, and Duncan Peak. Ukiah Valley lies farther north along U.S. 101, and it's here that some of the county's largest and oldest vintners make their home. Look for Hidden Cellars, Dunnewood, Parducci, Alambic, Fremont Creek, Mendocino, Whaler, Domaine St. Gregory, and Zellerbach.

The Redwood and Potter valleys—the northern frontier of California's commercial grape-growing territory—are home to Redwood Valley Cellars. The Anderson Valley, featuring some of the most pleasingly quaint countryside in the state, is where you'll find Navarro, Husch, Greenwood Ridge, Christine Woods, Lazy Creek, Brutocao, Yorkville, Handley, Roederer, Claudia Springs, and Pepperwood Springs.

Wineries to Visit

Where to begin? To make your decision easier, we have not listed wineries that limit their hospitality to "appointment only." All the wineries we include are open regularly to the general public, although some do require appointments for tours.

Tasting room hours at wineries generally range from 10:00 A.M. to 5:00 P.M. daily, but some have shorter hours. If there's a particular winery you absolutely must visit, call ahead to find out how early or late you can arrive.

Most—but not all—Napa Valley wineries charge a small fee for tasting, as well as some Sonoma County and Mendocino County establishments. The fees can range from about $3.00 to $10.00—prices fluctuate depending on the wines being poured. (Reserve wines and library wines, if offered, run a bit higher.) The tasting fee can be applied toward the purchase of a bottle, and you usually get to keep the logo glass. Many wineries also have picnic areas for enjoying munchies you bring along or buy onsite, but please purchase a bottle of the winery's own product to go with your food. It's just good manners.

As done throughout the book, we arrange the winery listings in the geographical sequence explained in our How to Use This Book chapter. We begin with

Napa County wineries, followed by those in Sonoma and Mendocino Counties. (See the Lake County chapter for information on its wineries.)

Napa County

Domaine Carneros
1240 Duhig Road, Carneros
(707) 257–0101
www.domaine.com

This imposing winery was inspired by the Louis XV-style Chateau de la Marquetterie in Champagne, country estate of the Taittinger family, which founded Domaine Carneros in 1987. The atmosphere is elegant and trés française, with a looming portrait of Madame de Pompadour in the main lobby. You can enjoy your beverage ($6.00 to $10.00 per glass, with complimentary hors d'oeuvres) in the salon or on the patio, which is swept by breezes off San Pablo Bay. Domaine Carneros offers three types of sparkling wine (Brut Cuvée, Blanc de Blancs, and Brut Rose) and its Famous Gate Pinot Noir. Free winery tours are at 11:00 A.M., 1:00 and 3:00 P.M. during the week, and hourly from 11:00 A.M. to 4:00 P.M. on weekends. On dry Friday mornings at 11:15, the winery offers vineyard tours that explain layout, planting techniques, and vine care. Cost of the vineyard tour is $10 and includes a tasting.

Carneros Creek
1285 Dealy Lane, Carneros
(707) 253–WINE
www.carneros-creek.com

San Franciscan Francis Mahoney started a trend in 1972 when he established the first winery in Carneros after the repeal of Prohibition. Carneros was little more than lonely cattle land then, but its Bay-cooled hills are now coveted by grape growers. Carneros Creek is a modest, homey facility, with arbor-covered picnic tables in back that offer a view to magnificent Artesa. The winery's reputation is steeped in Pinot Noir, which still makes up 85 percent of its production. (It also produces Chardonnay.)

Looking as if it arrived brick-by-brick directly from France, Domaine Carneros perches majestically on a hillside in the Carneros region. PHOTO: JEAN SAYLOR DOPPENBERG

Artesa Winery
1345 Henry Road, Carneros
(707) 224–1668
www.artesawinery.com

For a moment, if you can, forget Artesa's rich history and its world-class champagnes. Forget the 270-degree views of the Carneros hills and the small on-site museum with its 500-year-old wine casks. Those factors are more than enough to recommend Artesa, but the physical presence of the winery takes precedence. The building was designed by Barcelona architect Domingo Triay. Dug into the top of a hill, with native grasses planted over its sloping walls, it looks like a half-unearthed Mayan ruin—until you get inside, where the breezy central atrium and reflecting pools are nothing but modern elegance. Artesa is owned by Codorniu, one of the world's biggest producers of champagne, or cava. The Raventos family has been making wine since the 16th century (a Codorniu married a Raventos in 1659) and making methode champenoise sparkling wine since 1872.

The Napa outpost bottles three varieties, including the limited Reserve Cuvée, and also offers Chardonnay, Cabernet Sauvignon, and Pinot Noir. There are two free tours daily, and reservations are recommended.

Monticello Vineyards
4242 Big Ranch Road, Napa
(707) 253–2802, (800) 743–6668
www.corleyfamilynapavalley.com

Proprietor Jay Corley is a big fan of Thomas Jefferson. So big, he named his winery Monticello and built a small-scale "Jefferson House," patterned after the founding father's Virginia mansion, to serve as the company's offices and culinary center. It's a pretty setting on Big Ranch Road, which heads north out of Napa city about halfway between Highway 29 and the Silverado Trail. There is a vivid rose garden and a shady picnic area called The Grove. Monticello makes Cabernet, Chardonnay, Merlot, Pinot Noir, champagne, and, weather permitting, a late-harvest Semillon.

Trefethen Vineyards
1160 Oak Knoll Avenue, Napa
(707) 255–7700
www.trefethen.com

When Capt. Hamden McIntyre built the Eshcol winery in 1886, the three-story, wooden, gravity-flow architectural design was standard. Grapes were crushed on the third floor, fermented on the second, and stored at ground level. Today the old Eshcol building is the centerpiece of Trefethen Vineyards, and it's the last gravity-flow winery building in Napa Valley. Trefethen is a throwback in another way too: All of its grapes come from the surrounding vines, making it the valley's largest contiguous vineyard under single ownership. There are 600 acres of Chardonnay, Cabernet Sauvignon, Riesling, and Merlot plus gardens, walnut trees, and oaks. It was Eugene Trefethen, an executive for Kaiser (the massive construction firm responsible for, among other projects, Hoover Dam and the San Francisco-Oakland Bay Bridge), who bought the estate in 1968. His son, John, and John's wife, Janet, started the winery five years later.

The Hess Collection
4411 Redwood Road, Napa
(707) 255–1144
www.hesscollection.com

The "collection" is a stunning assemblage of modern art (see our Arts and Culture chapter). The Hess is Donald Hess, the Swiss millionaire whose holdings include Valser St. Petersquelle, one of Switzerland's most popular mineral waters. Hess keeps it simple as far as the wines go, with Chardonnay and Cabernet Sauvignon, bottling both under The Hess Collection label and a second, lower-priced label called Hess Select.

Clos Du Val
5330 Silverado Trail, Napa
(707) 259–2200
www.closduval.com

Clos Du Val is French in more than name only. Founder John Goelet is descended from a distinguished Bordeaux wine merchant family, the Guestiers, and president/winemaker Bernard Portet is a sixth-generation vintner from the same French region. They crushed their first Napa Valley harvest together in 1972, and their ivy-covered, stone tasting room opened in 1983. Clos Du Val now produces seven wines, including its signature Reserve Cabernet Sauvignon. Almost as much as for its vintages, the winery is known for the series of whimsical, wine-related illustrations it commissioned from famed graphic satirist Ronald Searle in 1977. Tours are given by appointment, and you can picnic on the grounds.

Chimney Rock Winery
5350 Silverado Trail, Napa
(707) 257–2641, (800) 257–2641
www.chimneyrock.com

At the foot of the hills east of the Silverado Trail—including the outcrop from which it draws its name—is Chimney Rock, a stately white structure of Cape Dutch style, cloaked (in the summer) or picketed (in the winter) by a row of poplars. Ask if you can see the wine cellar, where resides a faithful reproduction of the Ganymede frieze depicting the gods' cup bearer atop a fierce eagle. The winery makes Fume Blanc, Chardonnay, and Cabernet Sauvignon.

Stag's Leap Wine Cellars
5766 Silverado Trail, Napa
(707) 944–2020
www.cask23.com

Stag's Leap founder Warren Winiarski was a liberal arts lecturer at the University of Chicago, but his destiny should have been clear: In Polish, "winiarski" means "from wine" or "winemaker's son." Founded in 1972, Stag's Leap was a little-known family winery until 1976, when it outshone the best of French Bordeaux in the famous Bicentennial tasting in Paris (see our Close-up "California Is 'Discovered' in 1976" in this chapter). Since then it has been a Napa Valley landmark. The winery produces several types of wine, red and white, under both its own label and Hawk Crest, a line of accessible, reasonably priced wines crushed at other facilities. Its reputation, however, is staked

Holy Merlot, Batman!

Some of the wine-aging caves in Wine Country are so spectacular—with their chandeliers, velvet couches, artwork, and antiques—even millionaire Bruce Wayne would feel right at home. The tomb-like stillness of others may put you in mind of Poe's "The Cask of Amontillado"—minus the bones. Some caves swallow up entire wineries, such as Napa Valley's Jarvis Winery, carved into the Vaca Range some 1,000 feet over the valley floor. It is built entirely into the mountainside, and all winemaking functions take place underground.

But one thing is certain—more and bigger wine caves are on the way.

Many wineries have taken advantage of what nature left behind five million years ago: volcanic formations ideal for sculpting underground aging caves. The natural coolness of the rock maintains a temperature of 58 to 65 year-round, with humidity levels at 90 percent or above.

Napa Valley's first wine "caves" were actually tunnels excavated in the 1870s for Schramsberg Vineyards and a couple of decades later for Beringer Winery. Chinese laborers did most of the work, and these underground passages are still in use today for the wine-aging process.

Caves are now an essential part of winemaking at many wineries, and excavating bigger and longer tunnels and caves is becoming a more common component of the business plan in Wine Country. But caves don't just open up in the hillsides—they must be made. And that takes money, manpower, and lots of evil-looking machinery.

The "roadheaders" that typically crunch the rock are 32-ton behemoths with massive drilling heads that can carve out a tunnel 18 feet wide and 13 feet high in just one pass. Multiple passes are required for larger caves. The process requires patience, as it can be agonizingly slow. Some days the drills may make a dent of only 2 feet, depending on the soil type. When the rock just won't give, especially if big boulders are standing in the way, dynamite charges are set.

In general, cave construction goes something like this: The roadheaders chew up the rock, the debris is moved out (and usually recycled in some fashion), and "shotcrete"—a mixture of cement, pea gravel, and sand—is liberally applied several inches deep on the tunnel walls and ceilings to keep out excess moisture. Steel frames are placed around entryways and exits. More shotcrete is heaped on. Electrical wiring is installed, then hidden by more shotcrete. The coating is then waterproofed and the cave is ready for barrels and visitors—usually in that order.

Some caves remain spartan and basic, while others get the Batman-meets-Baroque treatment.

In addition to the expanded storage space for aging wine, the caves hold a fascination for most visitors, and they make an exotic location for special events such as weddings and wine auctions. The aroma of oak and wine fermenting together adds drama and a heightened sense of privacy and exclusivity to what might otherwise be an ordinary affair.

On the practical side, caves save wineries a bundle in air-conditioning costs, and the naturally high humidity discourages the water from evaporating from the barrels as it transpires alcohol into the air. That means the barrels stay fuller and more productive for the three years, on average, they are stacked underground.

The 32,000 square feet of caves at Kunde Estate Winery & Vineyards perform double duty: storage for approximately 6,000 barrels of wine and a spacious tasting and dining room used for special events.
PHOTO: COURTESY OF KUNDE ESTATE WINERY & VINEYARDS

The aforementioned $20 million Jarvis Vineyards facility is truly unique. The grapes are brought from the vineyards and taken underground into the 45,000-square-foot facility for crushing and fermenting. They will not be exposed to daylight again. The nectar is mixed, the barrels are stored, and the wine is bottled—all in the caves. This underground engineering phenomenon has more than 4 miles of tunnels and features a man-made river and waterfall to pump up enough humidity to rival a rain forest. One of the special events rooms is made entirely of quartz crystal and can accommodate up to 150 people. The winery is open for tours by appointment only; call (707) 255–5280 to inquire about visiting.

The caves at Clos Pegase Winery feature an extensive kitchen and a raised stage for special events. Even 12th- and 13th-century antiques are on display in specially designed cavities. The intent was to create a fully functioning wine-aging facility that also resembles an ancient museum. Mission accomplished.

Jumping to Sonoma County, one of the best spots for cave-dwelling is Kunde Estate Winery & Vineyards. On the mountainside just a short walk from the tasting room, the cave doors open to reveal a long entryway that invites visitors to mosey back to the dining room and take in the aroma and ambience of the fermenting wine. This cave gained some notoriety a few years back when it was rented as part of the high-profile $1 million Wine Country weekend wedding extravaganza of an Academy Award–winning actress and her movie director fiancè. Though the locals still talk about that glitzy weekend—and the fabulous time had by all at the lavish cave wedding dinner—the marriage didn't age as well as the wine and ended shortly thereafter.

upon Cabernet Sauvignon, especially the versions made from the Stag's Leap and Fay vineyards, including the world-renowned Cask 23. (Note: Stag's Leap Wine Cellars is not to be confused with Stags' Leap Winery or the Stags Leap District, all of which get their name from the rock outcropping that overlooks the scene.)

Pine Ridge Winery
5901 Silverado Trail, Napa
(707) 253–7500, (800) 575–9777
www.pineridgewinery.com

The pines aren't only high on the ridge. There is a grove of them surrounding the picnic area, making for a cool experience on a hot Valley day. Owner-winemaker Gary Andrus has been growing grapes since 1978. Pine Ridge currently produces Chardonnay, Chenin Blanc-Viognier, Cabernet Sauvignon, Cabernet Franc, Malbec, and Merlot. If you can't fit a tour into your schedule, investigate the Pine Ridge Demonstration Vineyard adjacent to the winery. It displays various combinations of rootstock, clone, and trellising apparatus—all you need to distinguish your Geneva double curtain from your traditional French double guyot.

Steltzner Vineyards
5998 Silverado Trail, Napa
(707) 252–7272
www.steltzner.com

Dick and Christine Steltzner started making wines for bulk sale in 1977, and they opened their Silverado Trail winery in 1983. (The current structure was built in 1992.) Steltzner is noted for its reds, as are all labels within the Stags Leap appellation. Its wines include Cabernet Sauvignon, Claret, and a South African varietal called Pinotage.

Silverado Vineyards
6121 Silverado Trail, Napa
(707) 257–1770
www.silveradovineyards.com

This is no Mickey Mouse winery, despite ownership by Walt Disney's daughter, Diane Disney Miller, and Diane's husband, Ron Miller. (Walt's widow, Lillian, died in 1997.) It isn't a '90s-style corporate take-over, either, as the Millers are longtime Napa Valley denizens. Silverado offers great views above the Trail and a winery crafted of native stone and redwood. It made its reputation with Chardonnay but probably is best known these days for its estate-grown Cabernet Sauvignon.

Robert Sinskey Vineyards
6320 Silverado Trail, Napa
(707) 944–9090, (800) 869–2030
www.robertsinskey.com

This is another multigenerational operation, with founder Robert Sinskey, M.D., having passed the reins to his son, Rob. Sinskey Vineyards, which has been crushing grapes since 1986, is known for tackling Merlot and the tricky Pinot Noir, grown in the winery's Carneros vineyards. ("Heathens in the land of Cabernet," as they describe themselves.) Winemaker Jeff Virnig also creates small quantities of a half-dozen other varieties, including a Stags Leap District Claret and a Pinot Blanc. The cathedral-like winery combines Napa Valley stone and California redwood.

Domaine Chandon
1 California Drive, Yountville
(707) 944–2280
www.chandon.com

Domaine Chandon, child of world-renowned Moet-Hennessy, is a trendsetter. It was California's first French-owned winery (established in 1973), and the first to use the Champagne varietal Pinot Eunier in sparkling wine. It welcomes visitors to Le Salon, an open, terraced, cafe-style tasting room where you get samples of their cuvées as well as complimentary hors d'oeuvres. Chandon's renowned tours run every hour (on the hour, except for opening and closing times), and they pretty much tell you everything you need to know about fermentation, aging, riddling, and disgorging. The scenic winery produces several types of sparkling wine plus brandy and pear liqueur. See our Restaurants chapter for information on Chandon's exclusive eatery, or call the phone number listed to inquire about upcoming musical events.

Goosecross Cellars
1119 State Lane, Yountville
(707) 944–1986, (800) 276–9210
www.goosecross.com

Goosecross Cellars likes to refer to itself as a microwinery, and the feeling is unquestionably intimate on this lonely lane off the Yountville Cross Road. The winery was established in 1985 by college buddies David Topper, the CEO, and Geoff Gorsuch, the winemaker. ("Goosecross" is an Old English derivation of Gorsuch.) They produce Chardonnay and Cabernet Sauvignon, in quantities that barely surpass 7,500 cases a year. If you have some free time Saturday from 11:00 A.M. until about 12:30 P.M., sign up for the acclaimed Goosecross Wine Basics class, a hands-on crash course designed to remove the "snobbery and mysticism" from grape appreciation. The free class includes a full tour of the vineyard and winery.

Cosentino Winery
7415 St. Helena Highway S., Yountville
(707) 944–1220
www.cosentinowinery.com

Mitch Cosentino crafts a variety of wines and sells them in an affable, low-key setting right next door to Mustards Grill (see our Restaurants chapter). Cosentino's Meritage reds stand out, as do his Merlots and Zinfandels. He also is no stranger to dessert wines. The winemaker prides himself on his "punched cap fermentation" process, a traditional, labor-intensive technique that involves continually dunking the floating grape skins (the cap) into the juice during fermentation.

Silver Oak Cellars
915 Oakville Cross Road, Oakville
(707) 944–8808, (800) 273–8809
www.silveroak.com

Wine & Spirits' 1996 poll of restaurants determined that Silver Oak produced the most popular Cabernet Sauvignon in America. Their secret? Do one thing and do it well. Silver Oak is all Cabernet, all the time. Silver Oak was founded in 1972 by Ray Duncan and Justin Meyer, who had recently abandoned his post as the Christian Brothers' Napa Valley winemaker. His company has two winery sites: one in Napa Valley at the site of the Oakville Dairy, and another in Alexander Valley in the old Lyeth Winery. The Oakville facility has a tasting room in an impressive masonry structure. Tours are by appointment only, and because the tasting room can get swamped on summer Saturdays, the winery suggests arriving early or calling ahead on those days.

Robert Mondavi Winery
7801 St. Helena Highway S., Oakville
(707) 226–1395, (888) RMONDAVI
www.robertmondaviwinery.com

Here it is, the Yankee Stadium of American wineries, with Bob himself playing the part of Babe Ruth. More than any other individual, Robert Mondavi is credited with educating the world about the virtues of California wine. His innovations are prolific. He took a disregarded varietal known as White Pinot, changed the fermentation, and released it as Chenin Blanc; sales quintupled the next

Insiders' Tip

Some of Wine Country's back roads beckon bicycle enthusiasts, particularly the two-lane country roads of the Dry Creek and Alexander valleys in Sonoma County. In Napa County, Silverado Trail is ideal for bikes—the road is level, the shoulders wide, and a multitude of small side roads invite exploration. (See our Parks and Recreation chapter for more on bicycling in Wine Country.)

California Is "Discovered" in 1976

In 1976, it was a rare vintner who hung up a sign and opened a tasting room in Napa Valley. Who would stop, except to use the restroom? Still, le vin de Californie had its fans, and one of them was Steven Spurrier, an Englishman who had become one of Paris' most influential wine merchants. His Cave de Madeleine wine shop was highly regarded, and the courses offered at his Academie du Vin were standard curriculum for the French Restaurant Association's chefs and sommeliers.

That spring, Spurrier had visited dozens of wineries in Napa and Sonoma Counties and tasted scores of labels. He then proceeded to go out on a limb by proposing a blind taste test matching the best of France against the best of the United States. Many of Spurrier's chosen vintages had not even been tasted outside of California, much less on the East Coast, and some were barely known outside the Bay Area.

And yet on May 24, 1976, on a patio of the Hotel Intercontinental in Paris, six California Pinot Chardonnays (as they were called at the time) stood ready to butt bottles with four white Burgundies, and six California Cabernet Sauvignons stared down four Bordeaux reds.

The nine assembled judges were the crème de la crème in their line of work. Each jurist held before him or her a score card and a hard roll with which to clear the palate between entries. The judges were immediately able to distinguish between wines from either side of the Atlantic—or so they thought.

"That is definitely California. It has no nose," one judge proclaimed after downing a Batard Montrachet '73.

When all of the whites had been evaluated, the top-rated Chardonnay was a 1973 made by Chateau Montelena. It was everything the French deplore in a wine. Not only were the grapes picked from young vines, it was a blend of fruit from two different districts—blatant disregard for France's strict appellation code.

Still, the mood remained jovial when the white results were announced, for it is red wine that courses through the heart of French culture. Then came the shocking news: The number-one Cabernet was a 1973 from Stag's Leap Wine Cellars.

For the moment, Napa Valley occupied the highest point on the global landscape of wine.

Two weeks later, word began to circulate among vinophiles about the competition, and wine stores and collectors swarmed Montelena and Stag's Leap in search of the victors.

Nobody in Napa Valley got rich right away, but a small snowball had begun to roll down the slope of popular consciousness. California wines were about to enter a new age. In the mid-1970s producers earned about $150 million a year from non-jug wines; today it's more like $2.5 billion.

In May 1996, the Smithsonian's National Museum of American History created a display to document the Paris tasting. One bottle each of Stag's Leap Wine Cellars' 1973 Cabernet Sauvignon and the Chateau Montelena 1973 Chardonnay are now part of the Institution's permanent collection.

year. He almost single-handedly popularized Sauvignon Blanc by producing a drier version that he renamed Fume Blanc. Mondavi still actively promotes the industry, but sons Michael (president and CEO) and Timothy (wine grower) run the winery.

Robert Mondavi Winery is known for its wine-and-food programs, art exhibits (displayed in the Vineyard Room), and jazz and classical concerts. But most of all, it is known for its tasting tours. The most popular is the Vineyard and Winery Tour, offered several times daily at $10 per person. Other tours concentrate on educating visitors on the wine-growing and wine-making processes; these are in-depth, three- or four-hour tours that cost from $35 to $95 per person (including a picnic or sit-down luncheon) and require advance reservations. Tastings are available in three different rooms, including the new To Kalon Room, with historical photographs of the valley on display.

Opus One
7900 St. Helena Highway S., Oakville
(707) 944–9442
www.opusonewinery.com

When Robert Mondavi and Baron Philippe de Rothschild announced this joint venture in 1979, it created quite a stir in the wine world. But it also added credence to what the French had recently discovered: California wines are among the best in the world. Though the Baron died in 1988, the business went forward and groundbreaking on this architectural masterpiece took place in 1989.

As you might expect from such a team of wine royalty, this is an elegant winery that produces one pricey product. Opus One is a big red wine—a blend that's predominantly Cabernet Sauvignon—that sells for $140 per bottle. You can try this hearty drink for $25 a taste in the winery's Partners' Room. A concierge greets you at the door and ushers you to the tasting room. Calling ahead is strongly recommended, as this showplace is frequently booked for private functions.

Turnbull Wine Cellars
8210 St. Helena Highway S., Oakville
(707) 963–5839, (800) 887–6285
www.turnbullwines.com

The winery is located just north of the Oakville Cross Road, and its vineyards are primarily contained within the Oakville Viticultural Area. Turnbull's production is about 10,000 cases per year, with most of it in Cabernet Sauvignon, along with Merlot, Syrah, Sauvignon Blanc, and Sangiovese.

Oakville Ranch Winery
7850 Silverado Trail, Oakville
(707) 944–9500

This group has been making wines since 1989 but has been in the hospitality business only since August 1996, when it purchased a 100,000-case facility on the Silverado Trail. (Oakville Ranch produces only about 4,500 cases per year; the site is also rented for custom crush.) The winery bottles under two labels: Oakville Ranch Vineyards, made 100 percent from estate fruit, is the premium line, while Oakville Ranch Cellars is a group of less expensive wines made from purchased grapes and sold only from the tasting room. The estate vineyards are at 1,000 feet, the highest in the Oakville appellation. Oakville Ranch produces many types, including award-winning Cabernets, fine Chardonnays, and Robert's Blend, a Cabernet Franc and Sauvignon composition named for Robert Miner, the winery's late founder and also a founder of Oracle Corporation.

St. Supéry Vineyards & Winery
8440 St. Helena Highway S., Rutherford
(707) 963–4507, (800) 942–0809
www.stsupery.com

More than its intriguing historical setting and its rich lineup of wines, St. Supéry is known for its Wine Discovery Center. You can wander through the display vineyard and the exhibit gallery (the SmellaVision display is a "must-see") or sign up for a free guided tour. St. Supéry (named for a one-time owner of the property) has a lengthy list of wines, with all the standards plus surprises such as a dessert Moscato and a Zinfandel Rosé sold only at the winery. Skalli also produces kosher Chardonnay and Cabernet under the Mt. Maroma label.

Peju Province Winery
8466 St. Helena Highway S., Rutherford
(707) 963–3600, (800) 446–PEJU
www.peju.com

Everything may look familiar as you head into Peju Province, as Herta Peju's prolific flower beds have been photographed for numerous garden magazines. Husband Tony sticks to winemaking, and his Cabernet Sauvignon has been winning awards. (He also makes Chardonnay, Cabernet Franc, Colombard, Merlot, a dry rosé and, occasionally, a late-harvest Chardonnay.) The Pejus opened their French Provincial-style facility in 1991 and produce about 15,000 cases a year.

Niebaum-Coppola Estate Winery
1991 St. Helena Highway S., Rutherford
(707) 968–1100
www.niebaum-coppola.com

Yes, it's that Coppola, a winemaker almost as long as he has been a film-maker. Francis and his wife, Eleanor, purchased a lavish Victorian and prime acreage in 1975, then discovered the story behind the locale. The house was built in 1881 by Gustave Niebaum, a Finnish sea captain who founded Inglenook, perhaps the most respected winery in California before corporate raiders used the name to sell jug wine. Enchanted by the history, Coppola used the substantial profits from his film *Bram Stoker's Dracula* to reunify Niebaum's original estate in 1995. The purchase included the original chateau, which the director renovated (check out the staircase made from exotic Belizean hardwoods). It now houses the tasting room and a museum of wine and film. Coppola's five Oscars stand at attention on the second floor, along with the Don's desk and chair from *The Godfather,* an authentic Tucker automobile, costumes from the aforementioned *Dracula,* and other memorabilia from his work in film. Niebaum-Coppola releases several wines under the Francis Coppola Family Wines label, but is best known for Rubicon, its Cabernet Sauvignon-Merlot-Cabernet Franc Meritage that is made to last 100 years.

ZD Wines
8383 Silverado Trail, Rutherford
(707) 963–5188
www.zdwines.com

ZD might be last on the alphabetical list, but it has been first elsewhere, such as the Los Angeles County Fair, where the 1996 Chardonnay was named Best of Class. And the label is clearly bipartisan—it has been served at the White House during three presidential administrations. ZD got its start in Sonoma County in 1969, then moved to Napa County a decade later. Today it makes primarily Chardonnay, Pinot Noir, and Cabernet Sauvignon.

Mumm Napa Valley
8445 Silverado Trail, Rutherford
(707) 942–3434, (800) 686–6272
www.mummnapavalley.com

The setting in Mumm's tasting salon is one of the most soothing in the valley, with a long wall of glass that faces uncluttered vineyard. (It's definitely the place to bring a date.) Their Pinot Noir and Chardonnay are available only at the winery for tasting. They offer tours of the winery on the hour; the last stop is the photo gallery, which is reason enough to make a pilgrimage (see our Arts and Culture chapter). Mumm Napa Valley was launched in 1979, a co-venture between G. H. Mumm of France and Joseph E. Seagram and Sons of New York. The winery currently bottles three Bruts—Blanc de Blancs, Blanc de Noir, and Brut Prestige—and a vintage sparkler, DVX, its prestige cuvée.

Beaulieu Vineyard
1960 St. Helena Highway S., Rutherford
(707) 967–5230
www.bvwine.com

The oldest continuously producing winery in Napa Valley? It isn't Charles Krug or Beringer. It's Beaulieu, which was founded by Georges de Latour in 1900 and survived Prohibition by turning out sacramental wines. By 1940 Beaulieu might have been the nation's most famous winery, a status no doubt aided by de Latour's recruitment of young, Russian-born enologist Andre Tchelistcheff, who was more or less the Luther Burbank of the wine industry. The winery's Napa Series is made up of Cabernet Sauvignon, Chardonnay, Pinot Noir, Sauvignon Blanc, Zinfandel, and Merlot; the Signet Collection includes everything from Viognier to Pinot Gris. (The Georges de Latour Private Reserve Cabernet, hunted by collectors, remains BV's benchmark product.)

Grgich Hills Cellar
1829 St. Helena Highway S., Rutherford
(707) 963–2784, (800) 532–3057
www.grgich.com

The Grgich is Miljenko Grgich. The Hills, you might be surprised to learn, is a reference not to the rugged terrain around Rutherford, but rather to Austin Hills of the Hills Bros. coffee family. Hills added his business acumen to Grgich's winemaking skills back in 1977, and they have been making tasty wines ever since. Grgich Hills is known for its buttery, creamy Chardonnay, though it also produces Sauvignon Blanc, Zinfandel, Cabernet Sauvignon, and a late-harvest dessert wine. Visitors may purchase library wines, which are available only at the winery.

Villa Mt. Eden Winery
Conn Creek Winery, 8711 Silverado Trail, St. Helena
(707) 963–9100, (800) 793–7960
www.villamteden.com, www.conncreek.com

You can break two bottles of wine with one stone here. The Silverado Trail tasting room houses Villa Mt. Eden and Conn Creek, sister wineries owned by Stimson Lane Vineyards of Woodinville, Washington. Villa Mt. Eden is descended, however tenuously, from Mt. Eden Vineyards, established in 1881 as the 11th bonded winery in Napa Valley. It now produces seven basic varietals, including Cabernet Sauvignon, Chardonnay, Zinfandel, and Pinot Noir. Volume increased after the purchase of more than 400 vineyard acres, 237 in the Stags Leap area and another 192 in Monterey County. Conn Creek bottles a tiny amount of reserve wines, primarily Cabernet and a Meritage.

Beaucanon Winery
1695 St. Helena Highway S., St. Helena
(707) 967–3520

If this built-in-1987 winery looks like it was transported from Bordeaux, with its vaulted ceilings and unpartitioned interior, it's no accident. Beaucanon is owned by the de Coninck family, which owns some 15 chateaux in France. Siblings Louis and Chantal de Coninck run the California operations, bottling Chardonnay, Cabernet Sauvignon, and Merlot under two lines, Beaucanon Napa Valley and La Crosse Napa Valley.

Franciscan Oakville Estate
1178 Galleron Road, Rutherford
(707) 963–7111
www.franciscan.com

This is part of the spreading Franciscan Estate empire, which also includes Mount Veeder Winery and Quintessa in Napa County, Estancia in Sonoma and Monterey, and Veramonte in the Casablanca Valley in Chile (the homeland of owner Augustin Huneeus). Outside the winery, which is right off Highway 29, you'll encounter the Rutherford Bench, a tongue-in-cheek reference to a local geologic feature. Inside the newly renovated visitor center you can taste wine from Franciscan and Mount Veeder. Franciscan specializes in Cabernet Sauvignon, Merlot, and Cabernet Franc, with all the grapes for Magnificat (a Meritage blend) coming from its 240-acre estate in the heart of the Oakville appellation. It also sets itself apart through its experiments in "wild" yeast fermentation, using the native yeast of each vineyard to help ferment those particular grapes. The winery's Cuvée Sauvage Chardonnay is 100 percent wild yeast, barrel fermented.

Rutherford Hill Winery
200 Rutherford Hill Road, Rutherford
(707) 963–7194, (800) MERLOT–1
www.rutherfordhill.com

Rutherford Hill produces numerous varietals (including a Zinfandel Port), but the name has become nearly synonymous with Merlot. It's also known as one of the most pleasant places to visit, with picnic grounds amid shady oaks and olive trees, and stunning views of Napa Valley. (Because of its popularity, you might think about calling ahead to reserve a table.) Rutherford Hill's wine caves are said to be some of the most extensive in America, with nearly a mile of tunnels, galleries, and passageways.

Rutherford Hill hosts a regular "Blending in the Caves" class for small groups to learn the basic principles of making wine. In fact, you get to create your very own blend to take home in a bottle. It's offered by reservations only, so call ahead to inquire about dates.

Raymond Vineyard & Cellar
849 Zinfandel Lane, St. Helena
(707) 963–3141, (800) 525-2659
www.raymondwine.com

Raymond has a strong reputation for Chardonnay and Cabernet Sauvignon, though it also bottles Sauvignon Blanc, Merlot, and Pinot Noir. It produces under four distinct brands: Amberhill, Raymond Estates, Raymond Napa Valley Reserve, and Raymond Generations. The winery's Napa Valley vineyards are supplemented by a large Chardonnay plot in Monterey County, on the Central Coast. All told, Raymond owns more than 500 acres.

Milat Vineyards
1091 St. Helena Highway S., St. Helena
(707) 963–0758, (800) 54–MILAT
www.milat.com

This is another intimate, family-run winery, 2 miles south of St. Helena. The Milats have been growing and selling grapes to Napa Valley wineries since 1949, and in 1986 they finally decided to affix their own label. Milat bottles Chardonnay, Chenin Blanc, Zinfandel, Cabernet Sauvignon, and a blush table wine called Zivio, selling the bulk of their production from the tasting room.

V. Sattui Winery
1111 White Lane, St. Helena
(707) 963–7774
www.vsattui.com

If you have made a few trips to Napa Valley, you probably know V. Sattui as the place with all the picnickers. It's a favorite for itinerant eaters, primarily because of an ample, shady picnic area and well-stocked deli featuring homemade items. The current wine list is immense, with two Chardonnays, two Johannisberg Rieslings, two Zinfandels, four Cabernet Sauvignons, and many others—all of them sold exclusively at the winery.

Whitehall Lane Winery
1563 St. Helena Highway S., St. Helena
(707) 963–9454
www.whitehalllane.com

As wineries go, this one is a youngster in Napa Valley. The Leonardini family of San Francisco purchased Whitehall Lane Winery from foreign investors in 1993 and brought in new equipment, a new barrel program, and plans for expanding production and acquiring vineyards. It now owns more than 100 acres of vineyards in Napa Valley and produces award-winning Sauvignon Blanc, Chardonnay, Merlot, and Cabernet Sauvignon. There's even an orange muscat dessert wine, Belmuscato.

Heitz Wine Cellar
436 St. Helena Highway S., St. Helena
(707) 963–3542
www.heitzcellar.com

The winery you visit is not the current Heitz facility, but rather the original facility opened by Joe and Alice Heitz in 1961. The winery built its reputation on Chardonnay, though now it is known more for its Cabernet Sauvignon. Three special Cabs are vineyard-designated: Martha's Vineyard (near Oakville), Bella Oaks Vineyard, and Trailside Vineyard (both near Rutherford). Heitz also makes Zinfandel and Napa Valley's only Grignolino, a light red.

Prager Winery & Port Works
1281 Lewelling Lane, St. Helena
(707) 963–PORT, (800) 969–PORT
www.pragerport.com

Prager makes Chardonnay and Cabernet but is really known for its Port, which accounts for about 85 percent of production. One of the top sellers is the Royal Escort Port, produced from Petite Sirah grapes. Prager's facilities are inside an old carriage house, part of the John Thomann Winery and Distillery, constructed in 1865. The intimate tasting room is plastered with money donated by visitors—everything from Indonesian rupiah to Toys R Us Geoffrey dollars.

Sutter Home Winery
277 St. Helena Highway S., St. Helena
(707) 963–3104
www.sutterhome.com

What was once a small, family-run winery is now a gigantic family-run winery, the nation's fourth-largest (and the number-one table-wine brand name), thanks to unqualified marketing genius. The facilities date back to 1874, the name to 1906, when the new Swiss-American co-owner named it after her father, John A. Sutter (not to be confused with the California pioneer of the same name). Sutter Home has been owned by the Trincheros since 1947, and the family gets credit (or blame, depending on your outlook) for inventing White Zinfandel—which it originally called Oeil de Pedrix, "Eye of the Partridge"—in the 1970s. Sutter Home has numerous vineyards in Napa and Lake counties but grows the bulk of its grapes in the Sacramento Valley, Sacramento Delta, and Sierra foothill regions. The company produces nine varieties of wine beyond the Zinfandel plus Fre, the best-selling nonalcoholic wines in America.

Louis M. Martini Winery
254 St. Helena Highway S., St. Helena
(707) 963–2736, (800) 321–WINE
www.louismartini.com

Louis M. was an Italian immigrant, born near Genoa, who founded the L. M. Martini Grape Products Co. in Kingsburg, California, in 1922. The "Grand Old Man" built his Napa Valley winery 11 years later. The company's vineyards are far-flung, stretching from Sonoma Valley to the Russian River Valley to Lake County to Chiles Valley to Pope Valley (two areas in eastern Napa County). The winery makes a wide range of wines, from Cabernet Sauvignon to Barbera to Merlot. It also produces cream sherry and dry sherry.

Merryvale Vineyards
1000 Main Street, St. Helena
(707) 963–7777, (800) 326–6069
www.merryvale.com

Merryvale is hard to miss, as it sits in Sunny St. Helena. That's not a reference to the town, but to the old winery that dates back to the 1930s. The stolid stone structure took new life when it was founded as Merryvale by four partners (the same four who started San Francisco's Pacific Union Realty) in 1983. And then Merryvale was purchased by the Swiss family Schlatter in 1996. The facility produces several varietals, including Chardonnay, Cabernet Sauvignon, Merlot, and a dessert wine called Antigua. There are no tours, but Merryvale does offer wine component tasting seminars every Saturday and Sunday at 10:30 A.M. Cost is $10, and reservations are recommended.

Beringer Vineyards
2000 Main Street, St. Helena
(707) 963–7115
www.beringer.com

Just as you pass through the "Row of Elms" that forms a canopy over Highway 29 just north of St. Helena, what you'll see to the west is Beringer Wine Estates, arguably the most majestic of all Napa Valley wineries. Beringer produces a half-dozen wines that vary from high-quality to high-volume. The tours, which run every half-hour and last about 45 minutes, are extremely popular. They include an excursion into the wine caves tunneled into the hillside, and a finale in the tasting room, where you receive mouthfuls of three or four different wines. The winery's Rhine House, the impressive structure that grabs your attention from the highway, is a preserved historical landmark built by Jacob and Frederick Beringer in 1876. The tasting room, with its pine floors and slate roof, was Frederick's mansion.

Charles Krug Winery
2800 Main Street, St. Helena
(707) 967–2200
www.charleskrug.com

There is a lot of history working at this 19th-century structure. It was Napa Valley's first winery, founded in 1861 by the eponymous Prussian immigrant, political theorist, and editor of *Staats Zeitung*, the Pacific Coast's first German-language newspaper. Charles Krug, the winery, also shares the history of the Mondavi family, that dynasty of California winemaking. Cesare Mondavi bought Krug in 1943; his wife, Rosa, took over upon Cesare's death in 1959, and their son, Peter, became general manager in 1966. Now Peter's sons, Marc and Peter Jr., oversee most of the winery's operations, including the winemaking, marketing, and sales. Charles Krug bottles at least 10 varieties of wine, including the full-bodied Vintage Selection Cabernet Sauvignon and Generations, a traditional Bordeaux blend.

Markham Vineyards
2812 St. Helena Highway N., St. Helena
(707) 963–5292
www.markhamvineyards.com

The fortress north of St. Helena, with its fountains and eucalyptus trees, has seen a lot of change in its 120-plus years. It was built of stone quarried from nearby Glass Mountain by Bordeaux immigrant and failed prospector Jean Laurent in 1874, but it was used for bulk wines until 1977, when the winery was purchased by Bruce Markham. He sold the business 11 years later to Mercian, Japan's largest wine company. And in 1993, the winery officially reopened after a multimillion-dollar renovation that included restoration of Markham's 6,000-square-foot stone cellar. The tasting is not in the old structure, but rather in a new addition on its north side. Markham's Merlot, Sauvignon Blanc, and Chardonnay all, at various times, have been rated number one in the state by *Wine Spectator*. Their less expensive Glass Mountain Quarry wines have also received accolades.

St. Clement Vineyards
2867 St. Helena Highway N., St. Helena
(707) 967–3033, (800) 331–8266
www.stclement.com

The St. Clement winery is eye-catching anytime, but especially at night, when the pristine Victorian is bathed by floodlights. The house dates to 1878, when it became Johannaburg winery, the eighth in Napa Valley. It was a private residence for most of the 20th century, until Dr. Bill Casey started St. Clement in 1975. The winery bottles five varietals and is best known for its Carneros Chardonnay and Cabernet Sauvignon. If you are feeling flushed as you leave, use it as an excuse to sit on the porch swing on the veranda—you'll want to stay there all day.

Freemark Abbey Winery
3022 St. Helena Highway N., St. Helena
(707) 963–9694, (800) 963–9698
www.freemarkabbey.com

No, Freemark Abbey was never home to a group of wine-mad monks. The name comes from a triumvirate that purchased the winery in 1939: Charles Freeman, Markquand Foster, and Albert (Abbey) Ahern. Long before that (starting in 1886, to be exact), the winery was known as Tychson Hill, named for California's first female vintner, Josephine Tychson. The winery concentrates on several varietals: Cabernet Sauvignon, Chardonnay, Merlot, Petite Sirah, Sangiovese, Viognier, and Johannisberg Riesling. Among those are three esteemed single-vineyard wines—Cabernet Bosche, Sycamore Vineyards Cabernet Sauvignon, and Carpy Ranch Chardonnay. You also should keep an eye out for the Edelwein Gold, a Sauterne-like dessert wine made only when conditions are right (10 times since 1973).

Folie à Deux Winery
3070 St. Helena Highway N., St. Helena
(707) 963–1160, (800) 473–4454
www.folieadeux.com

Give this one extra credit for a sense of humor. "Folie à deux" is a French term that means "shared madness of two." It's a psychiatric diagnosis that the original owners, two mental health professionals, found appropriate. They even requisitioned a logo that resembles a Rorschach inkblot. You don't have to be not-all-there to enjoy Folie à Deux's wines, however. The broad selection includes Sangiovese, Cabernet Sauvignon, Muscat, and a special Amador Zinfandel from the oldest Zin vines in California, those of the 1870s Grandpere Vineyard.

Rombauer Vineyards
3522 Silverado Trail, St. Helena
(707) 963–5170, (800) 622–2206
www.rombauer.com

If the name rings a bell, think of food, not wine. Vintner Koerner Rombauer's great aunt, Irma Rombauer, has been in practically every kitchen in America: She's the author of *The Joy of Cooking*. Koerner makes six types of wine, including two—a Cabernet Franc and a Zinfandel—sold only from the tasting room. Rombauer is at the end of a long, steep driveway, and its views of the Napa Valley floor are hard to match—you should think about taking advantage of the picnic tables.

Frank Family Cellars
1091 Larkmead Lane, Calistoga
(707) 942–0859

This one isn't as gargantuan as some of Napa's other champagneries, but it's a treat for visitors: a sublime spot on one of the valley's less-traveled crossroads, a charming picnic area behind the 1906 stone building, on the National Registry of Historic Places, and sparkling and still wines sold only on the premises. The winery was known as Larkmead Cellars back in the old days, when it produced still wines, then was operated as Hans Kornell Champagne Cellars. The champagne line includes Blanc de Blancs, Blanc de Noirs, Brut, and Rouge.

Schramsberg Vineyards and Cellars
1400 Schramsberg Road, Calistoga
(707) 942–4558
www.schramsberg.com

When Richard Nixon and Chinese Premier Chou En-Lai raised a glass of bubbly for their "Toast to Peace" in 1972, it was a 1969 Schramsberg Blanc de Blancs they sipped. That was only one of the historic milestones marked by a one-of-a-kind winery. German immigrant Jacob Schram founded the business on Diamond Mountain in 1862, planting the first hillside vineyards in Napa Valley. Schram developed a good reputation, but the operation had crumbled by the time Jack and Jamie Davies (and their investors) purchased the property in 1965.

Jack and Jamie set about restoring Schram's old house and gardens and, most importantly, devoting the winery to champagne production. They were the first Californians to use Chardonnay and Pinot Noir grapes, the traditional Champagne varietals, in their sparkling wines, and their place in Wine Country history is now cemented. Schramsberg makes six types of champagne, including the world-renowned J. Schram prestige cuvèe. To find Schramsberg turn onto Peterson Drive from Highway 29, about 3 miles south of Calistoga.

Dutch Henry
4300 Silverado Trail, Calistoga
(707) 942–5771, (888) 224–5879
www.dutchhenry.com

The two families that own Dutch Henry, Chafen and Phelps, run it like a mom-and-pop winery. (There is no relation to famous vintner Joseph Phelps—"unfortunately," says winemaker Scott Chafen.) They pour in the cellar, and a tour consists of looking in different directions while you get the lowdown. The winery, named for nearby Dutch Henry Canyon, produces only about 3,000 cases a year, and its line includes Chardonnay, Zinfandel, Merlot, Cabernet, Syrah, and Pinot Noir. Dutch Henry does no distribution away from the winery.

Sterling Vineyards
1111 Dunaweal Lane, Calistoga
(707) 942–3345, (800) 726–6136
www.sterlingvineyards.com

The Napa uninitiated can be forgiven for unfailingly asking, "Is that a monastery up on the hill between St. Helena and Calistoga?" Not exactly. It's Sterling Vineyards, with its white stucco, Ionic-style architecture and knoll-top regality. Wine tasting here literally has been elevated to an event. A gondola takes you to the top of the hill, where you are free to sip samples and wander on a self-guided tour. Wide-angle views of the valley are worth the trip up the hill. It's $10 for adults for the whole experience. Most of Sterling's production falls among four wines—Cabernet Sauvignon, Chardonnay, Sauvignon Blanc, and Merlot, including several vineyard-designated versions. It also bottles small lots of lesser-known wines that it sells only at the winery, such as Malvasia Bianca and Charbono. Sterling was founded by English paper broker Peter Newton in 1964, sold to Coca-Cola in 1977, then to Joseph E. Seagram and Sons in 1983. Newton left behind a Brit legacy—the old bells of St. Dunstan's Church, which chime on the half-hour.

Clos Pegase
1060 Dunaweal Lane, Calistoga
(707) 942–4981
www.clospegase.com

Jan Shrem's winery is named for Pegasus, the winged horse whose hooves are said to have unleashed the Spring of the Muses, bringing both wine and art to the masses. Shrem, who built his fortune publishing reference and technical books in Japan, is preoccupied with both wine and art. His collection of sculpture and painting is profiled in our Arts and Culture chapter, and his wines—Cabernet Sauvignon, Chardonnay, Merlot, and Petite Sirah Port—are some of the best in the valley. The winery itself, designed by renowned Princeton architect Michael Graves (who was commissioned to build a "temple to wine"), is a stark, modern landmark of earth tones, angles, and curves.

Cuvaison Winery
4550 Silverado Trail, Calistoga
(707) 942–6266
www.cuvaison.com

When Silicon Valley engineers Thomas Cottrell and Thomas Parkhill started a small upvalley winery in 1969, they called it Cuvaison, a French term for the fermentation of wine on the grape skins. The winery is particularly known for

Clos Pegase winery south of Calistoga is renowned for its striking architectural style and eclectic collection of modern sculpture. PHOTO: JEAN SAYLOR DOPPENBERG

Chateau Montelena outside of Calistoga features an imposing castle-like façade. PHOTO: JEAN SAYLOR DOPPENBERG

Chardonnay. Cuvaison gets more than 90 percent of its grapes from its 400-acre vineyard in Carneros. The winery has a pleasant picnic area, shaded by 350-year-old oak trees.

Graeser Winery
255 Petrified Forest Road, Calistoga
(707) 942–4437, (800) 898–4682
www.graeserwinery.com

Want to get a feeling for the Napa Valley wine industry circa 1890? Take a drive to Graeser, about 2 miles northwest of Calistoga. The tasting room is in an 1886 home. If no one answers, ring the doorbell, a rope attached to the bell tower over the house. It's a bucolic setting once known as La Perlita del Monte ("The Little Pearl of the Mountain"), and Richard Graeser can genuinely claim a unique mountainside microclimate for his grapes, which are the traditional Burgundian varietals: Cabernet Sauvignon, Cabernet Franc, and Mer-

lot. Richard will even autograph your bottle of wine, if you ask nicely. Ask about their Adopt-a-Vine program.

Chateau Montelena
1429 Tubbs Lane, Calistoga
(707) 942–5105
www.montelena.com

Montelena was one of the two Napa Valley wineries—Stag's Leap being the other—that rocked the French establishment at a famous blind tasting in Paris in 1976 (see our Close-up "California Is 'Discovered' in 1976" in this chapter). It was a Chardonnay that prevailed that day, and the winery still makes one of the valley's best, along with top-notch Cabernet Sauvignon and Johannisberg Riesling (the latter grown in northward Potter Valley and sold only in the retail room).

Chateau Montelena's name and origins go back much further than 1976. The winery was started by Alfred L. Tubbs in the late 1800s, but no wine had been produced for 50 years when new owner Jim Barrett filled the barrels again in 1972. The building, nothing short of a hilltop castle with walls 3 to 10 feet thick, dates back to Tubbs' day, and a subsequent owner added Jade Lake and its Chinese gardens, a must-see if you're seeking an oasis of tranquility.

Sonoma County

Southern Sonoma
Bartholomew Park Winery
1000 Vineyard Lane, Sonoma
(707) 935–9511
www.bartholomewparkwinery.com

Formerly the Hacienda Winery, the winery and adjacent park have been renamed for Frank Bartholomew, former foreign correspondent with United Press International (later its president). The winery's picnic sites, set among native oaks, are unequalled, with tables overlooking vistas of vineyards. The winery sponsors a Punch Down Club, whose members get to "punch down" the relatively thick cap of skin that floats to the top of barrels during the fermentation process—the skin must be pushed down four or five times a day. Participants in this somewhat messy operation receive a bottle of "their" wine when it has aged.

Buena Vista Winery
18000 Old Winery Road, Sonoma
(707) 938–1266, (800) 926–1266
www.buenavistawinery.com

Huge shade trees surround Buena Vista, the oldest premium winery in California, established in 1857 by Count Agoston Haraszthy (see our Close-up "The Father of California Viticulture," in our History chapter). The fountain courtyard, a lovely picnic spot, is home to a self-guided historic tour, but there's also a guided historic presentation daily at 2:00 P.M. (plus one at 11:00 A.M. during July, August, and September). Two of the winery's stone buildings are registered as state historic landmarks. Chinese laborers dug long tunnels into the hillside for wine aging, and Buena Vista's buildings are made from the salvaged rock. The Press House, built in 1862, houses a gift shop, displays a fine collection of art, and offers complimentary tastings. Today Buena Vista supplies wine to all 50 states and 30 nations around the world, an accomplishment that would not surprise the enterprising count. Buena Vista has a second tasting room in downtown Sonoma, at the southeast corner of the plaza (494 First Street E.) in Pinelli's Corner Store (once the historic Pinelli Mission Hardware Store). Both the winery and the downtown Sonoma tasting room feature wines by Buena Vista, Robert Stemmler, and Haywood.

Cline Cellars
24737 Highway 121, Sonoma
(707) 935–4310, (800) 546–2070
www.clinecellars.com

After spending his childhood learning farming and winemaking from his grandfather Avaleriano Jacuzzi (of spa fame), Fred Cline founded Cline Cellars in 1982 on the sandy soils of Contra Costa County. His brother Matt joined him in 1991 as winemaker, and they relocated to the Sonoma Valley. The tasting room is in an 1850s farmhouse with a large, old-fashioned porch. Picnic grounds surrounded by 1,100 rose bushes make for a very pleasant lunch stop, with sweeping views of the Sonoma Valley on a site that was once a Miwok village. Complimentary tastings feature Rhône-style red wines—Syrah, and Mouvedre—as well as several white wines. Facilities are available for special events and weddings.

Gloria Ferrer Champagne Caves
23555 Highway 121, Sonoma
(707) 996–7256
www.gloriaferrer.com

The vineyards stretch across the hills, and from the hillock above, the Spanish-style winery overlooks the estate vineyards and the rolling Carneros hills. This is one of seven wineries owned and operated by the Ferrer family of Barcelona, which has produced methode champenoise sparkling wine for more than 100 years. You can tour the facility with its state-of-the-art caves and learn the secrets of the class methode champenoise process. Others may choose to linger on the vista terrace, noshing gourmet appetizers and sipping sparkling wine. Picnic tables are available for those who buy a bottle of wine to go with the comestibles. There is often musical entertainment on weekends, and there's plenty of banquet and meeting space.

Gundlach Bundschu Winery
2000 Denmark Street, Sonoma
(707) 938–5277
www.gunbun.com

Jacob Gundlach and his brother-in-law, Charles Bundschu, established this winery in 1858 on land east of Sonoma that they called Rhinefarm. The enterprise gained international fame in the late 1800s and survived the 1906 earthquake. It suffered under Prohibition—its owners were reduced to selling grapes to other vintners. The resurrection of the winery began on Halloween 1970, when Jim Bundschu, great-great-grandson of the founder, decided to turn his winemaking hobby into a viable business. Operating on a shoe-string budget, he and his brothers-in-law converted a dairy's milk tanks into fermentation vats and squeezed grapes with a muscle-wrenching, hand-operated basket press. Today Gundlach Bundschu produces 50,000 cases of premium, award-winning wines a year, specializing in Merlot, Pinot Noir, Chardonnay, Cabernet, and Zinfandel. Picnic tables are in a grove of oak trees overlooking a lake.

Jim Bundschu's lighthearted humor is legendary, and local residents like to drive out to the tasting rooms occasionally just to see the wacky posters he creates as part of his marketing plan. In one, Bundschu's mother, behind the wheel of a 1947 Kaiser on the edge of the family vineyards, is exchanging words with a motorcycle cop who says, "If you can't say Gundlach Bundschu Gewurztraminer you shouldn't be driving."

Ravenswood Winery
18701 Gehricke Road, Sonoma
(707) 938–1960, (888) 669–4679
www.ravenswood-wine.com

The advertising copy says it all: "Ravenswood's hand-crafted releases possess a unique vintage and vineyard identity in addition to an intense, powerful ('gothic,' as one wine critic wrote) character with which the winery has come to be associated. These attributes arise from what can only be called stubborn and impractical Old World enological practices." Ravenswood produces some of the best Zinfandel

in the world—and accounts for 70 percent of the winery's production. This winery also features picnic facilities and a barbecue in the vineyard every weekend from May through September.

Roche Winery
28700 Arnold Drive, Sonoma
(707) 935–7115, (800) 825–8475
www.rochewinery.com

This small, family-operated winery is the first you see as you enter the Sonoma Valley from the south, just north of Infineon Raceway. Owners Joseph and Genevieve Roche started with 10 acres in 1982, expanded to 25 acres in 1987, and plan to remain a small winery with carefully crafted estate wines. Housed in a modified barn at the top of a small hill, the setting commands a sweeping view of the valley, the bay, and the lights of the communities beyond. The tasting room features free sips of Chardonnay, Pinot Noir, Muscat, and Merlot, or a small fee for glasses of reserve wines.

Schug Carneros Estate Winery
602 Bonneau Road, Sonoma
(707) 939–9363, (800) 966–9365
www.schugwinery.com

This lifelong dream of owner-winemaster Walter Schug spans four decades and two continents. A native of Germany's Rhine River valley and a graduate of a prestigious German wine institute, Walter left for California determined to find success with his Pinot Noir, which has since been proclaimed no less than world-class by critics in both the United States and Europe. The winery, built in 1990 of post-and-beam architecture, reflects the Schug family's German heritage. Schug still maintains close ties to Europe (one-third of Schug wines are sold there), and it's a likely possibility you'll meet European neighbors while you're in the tasting room to enjoy complimentary sips.

Viansa Winery and Italian Marketplace
25200 Arnold Drive, Sonoma
(707) 935–4700, (800) 995–4740
www.viansa.com

When Sam Sebastiani visited the homeland of his grandfather in Italy, he was

A Wine Tasting Primer

During your enological experience, remember that the pleasure of wine comes from several senses—sight, smell, taste, and touch. Here are a couple of suggestions to keep you from feeling completely lost during your first winery adventures. (Rest assured that you will learn much more as you travel from one tasting room to another).

Sight: Hold the glass to the light and enjoy the wine's color.

Smell: Swirl the wine gently in the glass to release its fragrances. Sniff sharply to carry the aroma to the nerve ends high in the nose.

Taste: Take a drink and roll it in your mouth to reach all the taste bud areas. Connoisseurs learn to draw in air over the wine still in their mouth. It looks silly, but it carries fumes to the nasal cavity, where most of the subtle olfactory differences emerge. Try to pick out tastes that are familiar to you, such as berry or pepper.

Touch: Chew the wine, just as if you were munching on some mashed potatoes. Note the amount of astringency present and get its "feel."

Aftertaste: Swallow the wine and note the taste sensations remaining, also known as "the length." The aftertaste should always be pleasant, though it's often quite different from your first impression upon sipping.

astounded to see that Franetta, Italy, looked exactly like the Sonoma Valley. "It looked so much like Sonoma I damn near fell over," he said. The winery that Sam and his wife, Vicki (Viansa combines "Sam" and "Vicki"), established is about as Italian in aura as you will find this side of the Atlantic. Olive trees were imported from Italy, the architecture is Italian, and the garden paths that wind between levels of the winery are in Tuscan style.

The wine tasting room (sips are complimentary) is also a tasting room for some stunning gourmet foods—a manifestation of Vicki's longstanding interest in hospitality. (Her cookbook is on sale at the gift shop.) Visitors can wander about, picking up samples of olive-anchovy pesto, hot sweet mustards, blood-orange vinegar, and other aromatic foods. Vicki and her kitchen staff have also developed some unusual specialties that are available at the food counter, such as focaccia, sandwiches, and fine salads—all splendid foods for a picnic. Plenty of tables are available at various patio levels overlooking Sonoma Valley and Sam's award-winning wildlife preserve. Sam Sebastiani adheres to his loyalty to Italian-style wines; his winery features Piccolo Toscano (a Chianti type of grape), Sothena (a Dolcetto grape), and Nebbiolo (the name of the grape and the wine) plus 40 other varieties. The winery also offers specialty wine and food tasting programs, such as Tuscan Wine and Food Pairing, a private guided tour with wine and gourmet food tasting.

Sebastiani Vineyards
389 Fourth Street E., Sonoma
(707) 938–5532, (800) 888–5532
www.sebastiani.com

One of the few original family wineries still remaining, Sebastiani is extremely proud of its wines and its Italian heritage. Founder Samuele Sebastiani learned winemaking from the monks in Farneta, Italy, before he came to America in 1894 at the age of 19 and went to work hauling cobblestones. In 1904 he bought the old Sonoma Mission vineyard, where the padres had been making altar wines for 80 years. He sold his first vino to local Italian stonecutters in demijohns the size of beach balls.

The winery is 3 blocks east of Sonoma Plaza, set amid the vineyards from which Sebastiani produces its special Cherry-block Cabernet wines. A great convenience for visitors is the winery's trolley, which allows people to park at the winery and catch a shuttle back to the plaza. The visitor center underwent renovation in 2001. Tastings are also available at Sebastiani on the Square at 40 West Spain Street in Sonoma, on the northwest corner of the plaza.

Arrowood Vineyards & Winery
14347 Sonoma Highway, Glen Ellen
(707) 938–5170, (800) 938–5170
www.arrowoodvineyards.com

It had been the philosophy of Richard Arrowood to make only reserve-quality Chardonnay and Cabernet Sauvignon. But he has been unable to resist experimenting with unusual varietals, so his portfolio has now expanded to include limited quantities of Merlot, Viognier, and Pinot Blanc. Hospitality and personal service are a top priority at Arrowood. Visitors also can savor the spectacular view from the vineyard veranda.

Benziger Family Winery
1883 London Ranch Road, Glen Ellen
(707) 935–3000, (800) 989–8890
www.benziger.com

You could easily spend an entire day at the Benziger Family Winery, which is perched on the side of Sonoma Mountain high above the Sonoma Valley floor and the town of Glen Ellen. Guests can picnic in the redwood grove, visit an experimental vineyard, enjoy complimentary wine tasting, and take in a one-of-a-kind educational vineyard tour aboard a motorized tram. The Benzigers emigrated from White Plains, New York, to their mountain ranch next to Jack London State Park (see our Parks and Recreation chapter). They have since built a reputation for grape-growing innovation that produces award-winning wines in the Imagery series—Merlot, Chardonnay, and an unusual Bordeaux varietal, Cabernet Franc.

Wellington Vineyards
11600 Dunbar Road, Glen Ellen
(707) 939–0708, (800) 816–9463
www.wellingtonvineyards.com

Operating a small, family vineyard winery producing just 6,000 cases a year, John and Peter Wellington nevertheless produce a wide range of wines, concentrating on reds like Zinfandel, Merlot, and Cabernet. They also produce a couple of unusual wines unique to the area, including a Rhône-style blend, Côtes de Sonoma. The winery and tasting room are surrounded by vines, some as old as 100 years.

Kunde Estate Winery & Vineyards
10155 Sonoma Highway, Kenwood
(707) 833–5501
www.kunde.com

Louis Kunde arrived in California from Germany in 1884 and founded his ranch in 1904. Four generations of Kundes have worked the ranch, which stretches for 1.5 miles along Sonoma Highway and extends from the valley up into the mountains above. Today's tasting room is a replica of Louis Kunde's old barn, built on the site of the original. The Kunde family ages its wine in 30,000 square feet of caves dug into the hillside, providing an ideal environment for natural aging. Timbers from the old barn were used to handcraft tables and benches. Picnic grounds are surrounded by scenic vineyards. There's a nice gift shop inside, and tours are available Friday through Sunday. Chardonnay vineyards surround the tasting rooms, where samples are complimentary.

Insiders' Tip
Although many of the showcase wineries in California are owned by large corporations, most of the state's approximately 850 commercial wineries are family-owned and operated businesses.

st the tranquil slopes of
e, Chateau St. Jean (named
for former owner Ken Sheffield's sister
and pronounced "gene") was founded in
1973. An elegant chateau on the grounds
of this 250-acre estate was built in 1920
and is now a showplace surrounded by
beautiful gardens. It's a lovely spot for
picnicking. Chateau St. Jean's Cabernet
Sauvignon has been served at the White
House, and Queen Elizabeth has sipped
their Chardonnay.

Family Wineries of Sonoma Valley
9200 Sonoma Highway, Kenwood
(707) 833–5504
www.familywineries.com

It has been the lifetime dream of real
estate broker Henry Mayo to own a home
in the vineyards of Sonoma County and
to raise his own grapes. Now he has
achieved both goals. His first grapes were
planted in 1989, harvested in 1993. Using
the Mayo real estate offices on the main
highway through Kenwood (now on the
upper floor), they have turned the main
floor into a tasting room and have rented
tasting-room space to six other winery
owners who join them in pouring their
wines. Each winery owner takes one day
to pour the wines of all, so there is always
a knowledgeable owner on duty. The
wineries represented, along with the
Mayo family's, are Sable Ridge Vineyards,
Nelson Estate Winery, Sunce Winery,
Noel Winery, Meredith Winery, and
Deerfield Ranch Winery.

Smothers Remick Ridge Vineyards
9575 Sonoma Highway, Kenwood
(707) 833–6131, (800) 795–9463
www.smothersbrothers.com,
www.the-wine-room.com

The tasting room is filled with Smothers
Brothers memorabilia, including gold
records adorning the walls. Tommy
Smothers (the goofy one in the act)
bought 110 acres of vineyard land in
1972, and his brother, Dick (the straight
man), bought a home and 30 acres of
vineyard in the Santa Cruz mountains
two years later. When Dick added Vine
Hill Vineyard next to Tom's acreage, the
Smothers Winery was born. The famous
brothers had their first crush in 1977 and
opened the tasting room in 1985. Dick
has since sold out to his brother. Now
Tommy grows the grapes, but the wine is
made in Glen Ellen by Richard Arrowood.
They produce Chardonnay, Cabernet, and
a small amount of Merlot. This is also a
tasting room for smaller production
wineries such as Kaz, Moondance Cellars,
and Adler Fels.

Kenwood Vineyards
9592 Sonoma Highway, Kenwood
(707) 833–5891
www.kenwoodvineyards.com

When the Pagani brothers founded this
winery in 1906, Jack London lived on the
estate next door. Both estate owners are
gone now, and the winery was bought by
three college chums, all wine lovers, in
1970. The grapes they use are still grown
on the London ranch, and the label on a
special bottling shows a picture of Jack
London's signature and a wolf, Jack's
nickname. The tasting room is rustic, the
sips are complimentary, and the atmosphere is charmingly informal. Kenwood is
known for its Sauvignon Blanc, Zinfandels, and Cabernets.

Landmark Vineyards
101 Adobe Canyon Road, Kenwood
(707) 833–0053, (800) 452–6265
www.landmarkwine.com

Perhaps the most spectacular aspect of
this Spanish Mission–style winery is its
expansive interior courtyard, facing onto
dramatic, hulking Sugarloaf Mountain.
The hospitality center at Landmark is a
magnificent facility, featuring a granite
tasting bar, a warm fireplace for chilly
days, and a full-wall mural by noted
Sonoma County artist Claudia Wagar.
The pond-side picnic area is a picturesque
location for lunch or for just lounging
and watching the clouds drift by. A tower
conference room offers a 360-degree view

Located off Highway 12 near Santa Rosa, the courtyard at Landmark Vineyards is peaceful and serene.

PHOTO: JEAN SAYLOR DOPPENBERG

that must be distracting to those attending the meetings held there. Landmark's production focuses on Chardonnay, and three labels have won awards: Overlook, from Sonoma County vineyards; Damaris Reserve, from Alexander Valley appellation; and Two Williams Vineyard, from southern Sonoma Valley.

St. Francis Winery and Vineyards
100 Pythian Road, Santa Rosa
(707) 833–4666, (800) 543–7713
www.stfranciswine.com

Joseph Martin, who left the corporate world in 1971 to become a vintner, named his winery after St. Francis of Assisi and San Francisco de Solano Mission in Sonoma. His first harvest came in 1979 with production of 4,000 cases. Today his benchmark varietals are Chardonnay and Merlot, rich with character and complexity, but the portfolio also includes Cabernet Sauvignon and Zinfandel. The visitor center is a beauty, with terrific views and a huge gift shop and special reserve wine tasting bar.

Ledson Winery & Vineyards
7335 Sonoma Highway, Santa Rosa
(707) 833–2330
www.ledson.com

When this 16,000-square-foot French-Normandy structure was first erected, it seemed ideally suited to be a fancy haunted castle, set far back from the highway and with rocky mountains as a mysterious backdrop. But that all changed when the winery opened and the warmth and beauty of the place became apparent. Owned by the Ledson family, long-time Sonoma Valley farmers, the winery has three tasting rooms, a clothing and gift boutique, and a terrific gourmet market. But what really sets it apart is the picnic grounds, where on any given weekend in summer there might be a jazz combo or an art show to add to your wining and dining experience.

Construction on the winery, which was originally intended as a private home, began in 1993. The Ledsons soon realized the emerging castle was getting too much attention for their liking, so they decided it would work better as a winery open to the public. Ledson wines are sold only at the winery and have garnered some great reviews in *Wine Spectator* while amassing a variety of awards. They are known for their Merlot and Chardonnay, but also produce Sauvignon Blanc, Johannisberg Riesling, and Orange Muscat.

Matanzas Creek Winery
6097 Bennett Valley Road, Santa Rosa
(707) 528–6464, (800) 590–6464
www.matanzascreek.com

On the face of it, Bill and Sandra MacIver were unlikely candidates to succeed in the wine business. He had a 20-year military career behind him; she had no experience but a vision of creating a perfect wine. In 1978 they came together as partners in marriage and business, and today Matanzas Creek Winery is recognized as one of the country's best.

Ensconced at the base of Bennett Mountain, the environmentally friendly winemaking facility boasts one of the most sophisticated research laboratories in California. There, Matanzas Creek's winemakers have conducted more than 100 experiments in progressive winemaking. In the early 1990s, Matanzas released a new wine, Journey, made in a radically progressive winemaking program. Although its $70 price raised some controversy, the first 1990 Chardonnay sold out on release and was hailed by critics as the finest Chardonnay ever produced in America. Picnic facilities are available as well as a self-guided garden tour that includes one of the largest plantings of lavender in Northern California. Look for handmade lavender products in the gift shop.

Paradise Ridge Winery
4545 Thomas Lake Harris Drive, Santa Rosa
(707) 528–9463
www.paradiseridgewinery.com

Welcome to Paradise! For Walter and Marijki Byck, Paradise came to be on the day in 1994 when they opened the doors to their new winery, a California-style structure with breathtaking views from the decks. In fact, the view is so exciting the winery stays open late on Wednesday evenings just so visitors can catch the

sunset. After purchasing a 156-acre ranch adjoining the old Fountain Grove Winery, the Bycks planted 18 acres of Sauvignon Blanc and Chardonnay grapes, determined to produce the finest wines possible. In addition to their award-winning wines, they also feature a historical exhibit and world-class sculpture garden.

De Loach Vineyards
1791 Olivet Road, Santa Rosa
(707) 526–9111
www.deloachvineyards.com

Cecil and Christine De Loach have established a reputation as leading producers of premium wines and professional leaders in the industry ranks. He has served on the board of directors of the Wine Institute, and she is past president of the Sonoma County Wineries Association, both positions of prestige. Together, they cultivate 800 acres of vineyards in the Russian River Valley, producing Pinot Noir, Chardonnay, and Gewurztraminer as well as some remarkable Zinfandel from vines that were planted more than 100 years ago. The winery also makes Sauvignon Blanc, Merlot, and Cabernet Sauvignon plus a distinctive White Zinfandel. Picnic facilities are on the lawn in front of the winery, which is situated among the vines.

Northern Sonoma

Armida Winery
2201 Westside Road, Healdsburg
(707) 433–2222
www.armida.com

Tastings here are charmingly casual (and complimentary), and the setting is spectacular. Built on the side of a hill, the winery looks out on the Dry Creek and Russian River valleys, with Alexander Valley, Geyser Peak, and Mount St. Helena to the east and south. High on the hillside, three geodesic domes house the winery, lab, and administrative offices. If you've been looking forward to a game of Italian bocce ball (or if you'd like to learn what it is), visit the bocce ball court near the picnic grounds. Vineyards are south of the winery, producing Amida's five varietals: Merlot, Gewurztraminer, Chardonnay,

Pinot Noir, and the recently added Zinfandel.

Roshambo Winery
3000 Westside Road, Healdsburg
(707) 431–2051
www.roshambowinery.com

Architecture along Westside Road was shaken up when this sleek structure opened its doors. Roshambo is operated by the third generation of the Johnson family, longtime grapegrowers in Sonoma County. It specializes in estate wines, and its 2001 Imago Chardonnay walked off with the sweepstakes prize for white wine in the 2002 Sonoma County Harvest Fair judging. Winemaker Paul Brasset also creates memorable Sauvignon Blanc, Syrah, Pinot Noir, Zinfandel, and Merlot. The tasting room has a beautiful view of Russian River Valley vineyards, and you can count on rotating art exhibits that lean toward the unusual.

Belvedere Winery
4035 Westside Road, Healdsburg
(707) 433–8236, (800) 433–8296
www.belvederewinery.com

This winery, in the coastal foothills of the Russian River Valley, takes its name from the Italian word for "beautiful view." A trip to the winery reveals just that. Taste world-class wines while you enjoy a picnic on the sunny deck or under an oak tree in a beautiful garden setting. The picturesque vineyards of the Russian River Valley will spread out before you. Belvedere specialties are Zinfandel, Chardonnay, Merlot, and Cabernet Sauvignon from their premium vineyards in the Alexander, Dry Creek, and Russian River Valleys.

Foppiano Vineyards
12707 Old Redwood Highway, Healdsburg
(707) 433–7272
www.foppiano.com

This is the oldest family-owned winery in Sonoma County, whose history reaches back to 1896. Founded by John Foppiano, a disenchanted gold miner who decided to get back to his farming roots, the winery is now being run by fourth-generation Foppianos, producing 200,000 cases a year of Cabernet Sauvignon, Petite Sirah, Zinfandel, Merlot, Pinot Noir, Chardonnay, and Sauvignon Blanc. Some of the producing vines are 100 years old.

Kendall-Jackson Winery
Wine Country Store, 337 Healdsburg Avenue, Healdsburg
(707) 433–7102, (800) 769–3649
www.kj.com

The hugely successful Kendall-Jackson operation encompasses several wineries. The largest of these is Kendall-Jackson itself. The company describes the others—Edmeades, Camelot, Calina (Chile), La Crema, and Robert Pepi—as "Artisans and Estates."

To learn more about each winery and the wide span of varietals Kendall-Jackson produces, the Healdsburg store is the place to visit. The friendly folks at the K-J store will be happy to direct you to their other location: Kendall-Jackson Wine Center, 5007 Fulton Road, Fulton, (707) 571-8100. The Wine Center on Fulton Road features a viticulture exhibit, where students from Santa Rosa Junior College—and visitors—can become acquainted with 26 varietals and 19 trellising systems.

Insiders' Tip
Shared tasting rooms are popping up all over Wine Country, pouring wines of small wineries that typically are not open to the public. Family Wineries of Sonoma Valley on Highway 12 in Kenwood is one example; in downtown Napa, check out the Vintner's Collective at Main and Clinton Streets.

Martinelli Winery
3360 River Road, northwest of Santa Rosa
(707) 525–0570, (800) 346–1627
www.martinelliwinery.com

This family-run winery tends more than 350 acres of vines in the Russian River Valley, which it uses for its own wines and sells to other vintners. The winery specializes in Zinfandel—the Jackass Hill variety from the vineyard of the same name is considered by experts to be extraordinarily complex. They also produce a fine Sauvignon Blanc, Gewurztraminer, Chardonnay, and Pinot Noir. The winery is housed in an old hop kiln, just a short hop from U.S. 101 off the River Road exit.

Mill Creek Vineyards
1401 Westside Road, Healdsburg
(707) 431–2121, (877) 349–2121
www.mcvonline.com

This beautifully landscaped winery is set on a rise above the vineyard, which has been operated since 1975 by the Kreck family. The tasting room, complete with working waterwheel and a mill pond, is in an air-conditioned two-story redwood building. The bar top, trusses, and beams are all made from one redwood tree from the Kreck ranch on Mill Creek Road. A 3,000-square-foot picnic deck overlooks the Dry Creek Valley, Fitch Mountain, and Mt. St. Helena.

Rodney Strong Vineyards
11455 Old Redwood Highway, Healdsburg
(707) 431–1533, (800) 678–4763
www.rodneystrong.com

In 1959, long before Sonoma County was "discovered" as a premium grape-growing region, Rodney Strong began an exhaustive search for the very best vineyards. Ultimately, he selected several vineyards in the Chalk Hill, Alexander Valley, and Russian River Valley appellations. The winery, a low-lying building with a roof spreading across it like the wings of a giant eagle, is situated among acres of prime vineyards. The winery's estate wines are named after the individual vineyards where the grapes grow—for example, the Charlotte's Home, a Sauvignon Blanc, and Alexander's Crown, a Cabernet. Picnic areas are available. For special occasions there's a garden area adjacent to the vineyards (contact the vineyard for availability).

Windsor Vineyards Tasting Room
308-B Center Street, Healdsburg
(707) 433-2822, (800) 204-9463
www.windsorvineyards.com

Windsor offers a wide variety of wines that have brought home several awards. In 1959, Windsor was one of the first wineries to stake a claim to Sonoma County. Vineyards were set out in three valleys—Alexander, Dry Creek, and Russian River.

All wines are sold direct to the consumer through one of the three tasting rooms (Healdsburg, Tiburon, and Marlboro, New York).

Dry Creek Vineyard
3770 Lambert Bridge Road, Healdsburg
(707) 433-1000, (800) 864-9463
www.drycreekvineyard.com

Dry Creek Winery started in 1972 when ex-Bostonian David Stare began turning an old prune orchard into an award-winning winery. A trip he took to France in 1970 apparently inspired him to leave Boston and head for the University of California at Davis, where he studied viticulture and enology. Stare's was the first new winery in Sonoma County's Dry Creek Valley since the days of Prohibition, and it led to a dramatic wave of change in this long-neglected grape-growing region.

Stare now owns 135 acres of vineyards and also buys grapes from local growers to produce Fume Blanc, Chenin Blanc, Cabernet Sauvignon, and other wines, including his estate-bottled Meritage (a Bordeaux blend). The gray stone winery he built resembles a French country wine chateau. The tasting room, voted among the top 10 in Sonoma County by a local magazine, is casual and informal. When the weather turns cool in October, there's a warm fireplace. When the sun spreads warm yellow patches on the lawn, a picnic lunch in the gardens is a perfect idea.

Ferrari-Carrano Vineyard & Winery
8761 Dry Creek Road, Healdsburg
(707) 433–6700, (800) 831–0381
www.ferrari-carano.com

The Wine Shop at Villa Fiore (the name of the chateau that houses the Ferrari-Carrano operation) is one of California's friendliest and most enchanting wine country destinations. Visitors will discover magnificent gardens, critically acclaimed wines, and unique gifts. The spectacular underground barrel cellar where the wines of Don and Rhonda Carrano age are also a favorite. Among the wines poured at the wine shop are Fume Blanc, Chardonnay, Merlot, and a late harvest dessert wine called Eldorado Gold.

Lake Sonoma Winery
9990 Dry Creek Road, Geyserville
(707) 473–2999, (800) 750–9463
www.lakesonomawinery.com

The newest member of the Korbel family (obtained in 1996), Lake Sonoma Winery is notable for its breathtaking view of Dry Creek Valley and Warm Springs Dam. Gourmet picnic fare is available in the deli and can be enjoyed on the wooded picnic grounds with a bottle of Chardonnay, Cabernet, Zinfandel, or Cinsault. The winery is adjacent to Lake Sonoma Recreation Area.

Lambert Bridge Winery
4085 West Dry Creek Road, Healdsburg
(707) 431–9600, (800) 975–0555
www.lambertbridge.com

Established in 1975, the winery takes its name from a neighboring landmark bridge that spans Dry Creek. Many of the wines of this small, high-quality winery are available only in the charming tasting room, where the wine-stained tasting bar was made from oak casks. A crackling fireplace cheers frosty days, and on sunny days Lambert Bridge's picnic grounds may be the most elegant in Dry Creek Valley. The tasting room also features gourmet mustards to complement the winery's wines, which include Viognier, Merlot, and Zinfandel.

Pezzi King Vineyards
3805 Lambert Bridge Road, Healdsburg
(707) 431–9388, (800) 411–4758
www.pezziking.com

Pezzi King Vineyards is family owned and operated. The name represents the blending of two important family names and honors the mothers of owners Jim and Jane Rowe. The Rowes use "balanced and sustainable" viticulture techniques—which include vast additions of organically composted materials and the planting of nitrogen-fixing cover crops—to produce intensely flavorful varieties without sacrificing style, finesse, and balance. The James Rowe family released its first Zinfandel and Cabernet Sauvignon in March 1996, and they also produce a fine Chardonnay. Six picnic pavilions with redwood trees for shade offer panoramic views of Dry Creek Valley.

Preston Vineyards
9282 West Dry Creek Road, Healdsburg
(707) 433–3372, (800) 305–9707
www.prestonvineyards.com

According to the folks at family-owned Preston Winery, "Having fun is no scandal." They take pride in being known as the alternative winery: the place to go when you want something different and delicious. Not only can you taste some unusual wines, but you can also enjoy some freshly baked bread and picnic among flowers, herbs, vegetable gardens, and olive trees. If that's not enough fun, you can play a game of bocce ball on the house courts.

Preston is slightly off the beaten path, but with so much going for it, the adventure is worth it. The 115 acres of grapes grow without insecticides and produce flavorful, eccentric wines such as Viognier, Moscato Curioso, Barbera, Syrah, and Marsanne.

Quivira Vineyards
4900 West Dry Creek Road, Healdsburg
(707) 431–8333, (800) 292–8339
www.quivirawine.com

For centuries, European explorers searched for the legendary New World

Bored with Cabernet? Weary of Chardonnay?

Wine Country is busy experimenting with many winegrape varietals beyond Chardonnay and Cabernet that are changing the climate in the wine world and soon will be more noticeable at your favorite wine shop.

Leading the pack of white varietals taking the industry by storm is actually an old favorite: Sauvignon Blanc. "A lot of people had been predicting it, and now there's an interesting rebirth of Sauvignon Blanc and Fume Blanc going on in Napa Valley," says Clay Gregory, president of the board of directors of the Napa Valley Vintners Association and former general manager at Robert Mondavi Winery. "Frankly, consumers are getting a little tired of oaky Chardonnays."

To illustrate his point, Clay says many acres of Chardonnay grapes grown north of the Carneros region are being pulled out in favor of other varieties that grow more successfully in the warmer valley air. He adds that the cooler Carneros appellation, shared by both Napa County and Sonoma County, is better suited to Sauvignon Blanc grapes than Chardonnay, although Chardonnay will continue to be grown there. "But a lot of wine people now prefer Sauvignon Blanc," he says.

Nick Frey, executive director of the Sonoma County Grape Growers Association, agrees with Clay. "The movement now is toward Sauvignon Blanc rather than Chardonnay," says Nick. "Sauvignon Blanc is produced without oak, and it bursts with clean, crisp fruit. It's a food-friendly wine and a good value."

Among other white varietals, Viognier has been receiving its share of attention in the last couple of years, says Clay. "Viognier is very floral and aromatic—it smells like it's going to be sweet but it's actually dry." Yet instead of being "the next big white wine," as had once been predicted, Nick believes Viognier will likely be used more for blending, especially with Sauvignon Blanc. Also flashing brightly on the wine industry radar are Pinot Gris, Marsanne, and Roussanne.

In red wines, Syrah (or *Shiraz*, as Australian vintners spell it) is generating the most excitement, says Clay. "Cabernet Sauvignon is king in Napa Valley for the foreseeable future, but Syrah is coming up fast as the next big variety to plant. It grows well in many climates, the wines have a lot of character, and it's not as 'intellectual' as Cabernet." Nick agrees: "Syrah is going to be a very important wine very soon."

Bordeaux varieties getting more buzz these days include Petit Verdot, Cabernet Franc, and Malbec, while another old favorite, Zinfandel (not *White* Zinfandel) is making a welcome comeback. "There are still many old Zin vines around here that produce terrific wines, and most were planted by Italian immigrants," says Clay. Another small-production grape, the Spanish varietal Tempranillo, is likely to be a "next generation" wine, he adds.

Clay reminds wine lovers that, as in other kinds of perennial agriculture, ramping up to produce new varietals can take time. "But one of the hallmarks of Californians is our constant experimentation and desire to try new things."

land called Quivira. It was thought to be on the Pacific Coast in the region now known as Sonoma County. Three centuries ago European mapmakers placed it just about where the Quivira Winery is located now. Whatever else you find out here about the legends of Quivira, you will also encounter some excellent Sauvignon Blanc, Zinfandel, and a Rhône-style blend. This is a great place for a picnic, complete with terrific views.

Clos du Bois
19410 Geyserville Avenue, Geyserville
(707) 857–3100, (800) 222–3189
www.closdubois.com

Clos du Bois got its start in Sonoma County as a vineyard operation in the early 1970s, with 590 acres of vineyards in the Alexander Valley. Today, it is one of Sonoma County's most honored wineries, located on a 40-acre site in the heart of the beautiful Alexander Valley, and with approximately 1,000 prime acres of vineyard in Alexander and Dry Creek valleys. The winery produces Sauvignon Blanc, Chardonnay, Gewurztraminer, Pinot Noir, Merlot, Zinfandel, and Cabernet Sauvignon. With such a roster, it's remarkable that they seem to do all of them well, some superbly. In addition, they produce an exceptional Winemaker's Reserve Cabernet Sauvignon, and their reserve Chardonnay from the Flintwood vineyard is impressive.

Canyon Road Winery
19550 Geyserville Avenue, Geyserville
(707) 857–3417, (800) 793–9463
www.canyonroadwinery.com

A warm and friendly tasting room serves Canyon Road's Cabernet Sauvignon, Sauvignon Blanc, Merlot, Reisling, and Chardonnay, as well as wines of the Venezia and Nervo labels. A country deli and gift shop makes it easy to sit down for a picnic with a shared bottle of Canyon Road wine.

Canyon Road's wine club, known as the Roadies Club, uses a newsletter to announce opportunities to join in the autumn crush and do a little grape stomping. Other benefits of Roadie membership include a seminar on wines in the spring, a chance to visit with the winemaker, and an opportunity to receive shipments of select wines at discount prices.

Chateau Souverain
Independence Lane at U.S. 101, Geyserville
(707) 433–8281, (888) 809–4637
www.chateausouverain.com

This architecturally striking winery is one of the few with a restaurant—the Cafe is open daily for lunch and Friday, Saturday, and Sunday for dinner. Chateau Souverain's "room with a view" tasting room features a host of award-winning wines, such as Cabernet Sauvignon, Merlot, Zinfandel, Viognier, and Sauvignon Blanc made from selected vineyards within the Alexander Valley, Dry Creek, and Carneros appellations.

Field Stone Winery
10075 Highway 128, east of Healdsburg
(707) 433–7266, (800) 544–7273
www.fieldstonewinery.com

Eleven miles east of Healdsburg in the Alexander Valley, Field Stone Winery was built of large native cobblestones and is partially dug into a small knoll, creating a wine cellar in the European style. Beautiful picnic grounds under spreading oaks are the setting for summer events, including concerts, Shakespearean plays, and dinners. The estate-bottled wines include Cabernet Sauvignon, Merlot, and Petite Sirah, as well as three stylish whites—Sauvignon Blanc, Chardonnay, and Gewurztraminer.

Geyser Peak Winery
22281 Chianti Road, Geyserville
(707) 857–9400, (800) 255–-9463
www.geyserpeakwinery.com

One of the fastest-growing wineries in Sonoma County, Geyser Peak now distributes wines throughout the United States, as well as Switzerland, Germany, and Hong Kong. Though particularly known for its Chardonnay, Geyser Peak produces a number of fine varieties, including Merlot, Cabernet Sauvignon, Zinfandel, Sauvignon Blanc, California Riesling, and Gewurztraminer.

You might want to consider joining the winery's Cellar Door Club for discount opportunities on select wines and a chance to attend special events. A lovely picnic area overlooks the Alexander Valley, and the Panoramic Trail—winding up behind the winery—and the Margot Patterson Doss Trail—named for a well-known San Francisco walker and writer—will appeal to hikers.

Hanna Winery
9280 Highway 128, Healdsburg
(707) 431–4310, (888) 426–6288
www.hannawinery.com

Dr. Elias S. Hanna, a Marin County surgeon who was born and raised on a farm in Syria, founded Hanna Winery in 1985. His winery now produces about 34,000 cases of Sauvignon Blanc, Chardonnay, Cabernet Sauvignon, Merlot, and Pinot Noir annually. You can taste Hanna wines at two hospitality centers, one at 5353 Occidental Road in Santa Rosa and the other on Highway 128 in Alexander Valley. The patio of the visitor center in Healdsburg is a lovely place for a picnic, with panoramic views of the Alexander Valley and Hanna's magnificent hillside vineyard. It's also a grand setting for weddings or corporate events.

Johnson's Alexander Valley Wines
8333 Highway 128, Healdsburg
(707) 433–2319
www.johnsonwines.com

From time to time, the tasting room resonates with the mighty sound of a 1924 theater pipe organ. Tom Johnson makes the wine; Jay Johnson repairs old organs. This is a small, family winery producing seven varietals (Zinfandel and Cabernet are two) from family vineyards, all exclusively sold at the winery or on-line. Picnic tables are available, and you may enjoy an informal tour hosted by a member of the Johnson family.

Pedroncelli Winery
1220 Canyon Road, Geyserville
(707) 857–3531, (800) 836–3894
www.pedroncelli.com

John Pedroncelli, a native of Lombardy, Italy, bought the vineyard property that was to bear his name in 1927—the vines planted there had been yielding grapes for more than 20 years. During Prohibition, the winery sold grapes to home winemakers; after the repeal, it sold wine in bulk to other wineries. Today, Pedroncelli is run by John's sons, John and James, using grapes harvested from the Dry Creek Valley to produce excellent Cabernet, Zinfandel, and Pinot Noir wines. Tucked 2 miles up Canyon Road from U.S. 101, the charmingly rustic Pedroncelli Winery offers picnic tables for a pleasant lunch. Ask about getting on the winery's mailing list for its newsletter.

Simi Winery
16275 Healdsburg Avenue, Healdsburg
(707) 433–6981, (800) 746–4880
www.simiwinery.com

In 1881 two Italian immigrant brothers, Guiseppe and Pietro Simi, bought a winery near the grain depot in Healdsburg for $2,250 in gold coins. They built a magnificent, hand-hewn stone winery, and their business soon doubled. Then, in the midst of success, both brothers died, and Guiseppe's teenage daughter Isabelle took over. Prohibition was a blow for her, but when it ended, she had one of the winery's enormous redwood tanks rolled outside and created a retail tasting room. Isabelle could be found there until her late 80s, still selling Simi wines. The winery is

Insiders' Tip
In 2002 Gallo opened its first tasting room, located in Healdsburg at 320 Center Street facing the town's Plaza. The tasting room staff pours wines under the Gallo of Sonoma label, the large winemaker's top-of-the-line products made from Sonoma County-grown grapes.

now owned by the French company Moet-Hennessy, which has turned Simi's distinctive wines into part of a winemaking estate of worldwide recognition.

Trentadue Winery
19170 Geyserville Avenue, Geyserville
(707) 433–3104, (888) 332–3032
www.trentadue.com

Founded in 1969, family-owned and operated Trentadue has achieved an outstanding reputation not only for rare and unusual wines, but also for highly regarded, better-known varieties. Visitors are offered complimentary tastings of the many varieties (including Petite Sirah, Cabernet, and Sangiovese) and can spend time browsing through a fine collection of wine-related gifts, fine crystal, and china personally selected by Evelyn Trentadue. A gourmet food shop supplies items to snack on in the picnic area.

West County/Russian River

Davis Bynum Winery
8075 Westside Road, Healdsburg
(707) 433–2611, (800) 826–1073
www.davisbynum.com

Believing that there is "something of a spiritual union between the organic farmer and his soil and his vines," Davis Bynum has cultivated 22 acres of vineyard in accordance with California organic farming standards. To increase the ecological diversity and health of his fields, Bynum has also mixed in 130 olive trees, 120 mandarin trees, caper berries, sea berries, lavender, plums, kiwis, pomegranates, avocados, guavas, and figs in with his vines. The cool, coastal Russian River Valley gives Bynum's wines an intense varietal character. They include Fume Blanc, Zinfandel, Chardonnay, Pinot Noir, Merlot, and Cabernet Sauvignon. With the winery perched on a hillside, the picnic grounds offer a most pleasant view.

Hop Kiln Winery
6050 Westside Road, Healdsburg
(707) 433–6491
www.hopkilnwinery.com

Housed in an old stone building that was once a hop-drying kiln, the tasting room at Hop Kiln displays a fine collection of winemaking tools and a gallery of old photos showing the history of the hop

The distinctive turrets of Hop Kiln Winery near Healdsburg were originally constructed to process hops for beer. PHOTO: JEAN SAYLOR DOPPENBERG

industry, which bustled in Sonoma County during the early 1900s. The Hop Kiln was declared a state historic landmark in 1977 and has been the setting for several motion pictures, including *The Magic of Lassie* and the TV show *Homeward Bound*. The tasting room is cool, rustic, and pleasant and serves complimentary samplings of Zinfandel, Chardonnay, and two popular blends, Marty Griffin's Big Red and Thousand Flowers. Owner and community activist Dr. Marty Griffin—a retired internist who founded the winery in the early 1970s—is less involved in Hop Kiln's winemaking these days and more intent on saving the nearby Russian River from run-off degradation and mining. Hop Kiln's grounds are a great place to have a picnic and reflect Griffin's love of nature. A picturesque pond inhabited by local wildfowl sparkles next to the tasting room, and trees provide plenty of shade around the outdoor tables.

Martini & Prati Wines
2191 Laguna Road, Santa Rosa
(707) 823-2404
www.martiniprati.com

This is what wineries used to be! It's a unique experience—the only place in Sonoma County where you can fill a jug of Vino Rosso straight from the tank. It is said to be the oldest winery in continuous operation in the county, and it's still owned by the Martini family who opened it. If you have a picnic in mind, visit Elmo's Groceria and Italian Country Store, which is on-site. The Italian family tradition is reflected in the handcrafted style of wines produced—exceptional Sangiovese, Barbera, Vino Grigio, Muscato, and Port. To add to a lovely day, take a stroll through the landscaped grounds, which include an acre of lavender.

Topolos at Russian River Vineyards, Winery & Restaurant
5700 Gravenstein Highway, Forestville
(707) 887-1139 (winery), (800) 867-6567 (orders), (707) 887-1562 (restaurant)
www.topolos.com

This small, family-owned winery, established in 1963, has won awards not only for its exceptional wines, but for its unique, environmentally sound agricultural methods. In 1999, Topolos was named "Environmental Business of the Year" by the Sonoma County Conservation Council. Prior to this distinction, owner Michael Topolos was named "biodynamic farmer of the year." Biodynamics is a method of farming based on the philosophy of Rudolf Steiner and follows a chemical-free, spiritual approach. Topolos's vineyard was the first in the nation certified as biodynamic—it is also certified according to California organic farm standards. Visitors can sample complimentary sips of Zinfandel and Chardonnay and browse the gift shop.

Korbel Champagne Cellars
13250 River Road, Guerneville
(707) 824-7000, (800) 656-7235
www.korbel.com

When the three Czech Korbel brothers emigrated from Bohemia, they settled in a redwood forest along the Russian River, tried several different enterprises—including cigar box manufacture—and finally resolved to become winemakers. They built their handsome, brick winery in 1886, including a quaint turreted tower at the south end. The story behind this tower is a fascinating one. Before leaving Prague, the youngest Korbel inadvertently fired his pistola in the midst of the townfolk, who had gathered to hear the news called out by the town crier. He was jailed briefly, and upon his release the three brothers fled the country. The tower of the winery is a sentimental duplicate of the jail where young Joseph spent his last days in his home country.

Korbel has an excellent tour of both the champagne cellars and the antique rose garden that surrounds the old summer house. The champagne is produced in the methode champenoise, the traditional French method in which the second fermentation takes place in the same bottle.

Mendocino County

The wineries of Anderson Valley are clustered along a 6-mile stretch of Highway 128 near Philo. Morning fog off the

Pacific, afternoon breezes, and sunny hill-side vineyards make Anderson Valley a special place to grow cool-climate wine grapes, notably Pinot Noir, Chardonnay, and Gewurztraminer.

Farther north along U.S. 101, the Ukiah Valley is where the county's grape-growing began. Today it's where some of Mendocino's oldest and largest vintners make their home.

U.S. 101

Fetzer Vineyards
13601 East Side Road, Hopland
(707) 744–7600, (800) 846–8637
www.fetzer.com

Bernard Fetzer, a lumber executive, purchased the winery's Redwood Valley Home Ranch in 1958 as a place to raise his large family and grow fine grapes for home winemakers. The family began making wine commercially in 1968. In 1981, Fetzer's 11 children took over and helped the winery grow into one of the leading varietal wine producers in the world. Fetzer wines have won critical praise and tons of gold medals, especially for their Chardonnay.

The tasting room and visitor center, located 1 mile east of Hopland, features intimate vineyard and garden tours and offers tastings of new releases as well as older wines. A full-service deli with a spacious picnic area is also open to the public. The 50-acre Valley Oaks Ranch is home to vineyards, dozens of old barns, a dining pavilion overlooking Lake Fume, and the 5-acre 100 percent organic Bantera Garden, which includes countless varieties of fruits, vegetables, herbs, and flowers, both edible and decorative. All grapes and plants are grown organically, without use of pesticides or synthetic fertilizers. Also on the property is a charming seven-room bed and breakfast inn (see our Bed-and-Breakfast Inns chapter).

Jepson Vineyards
10400 South U.S. 101, Ukiah
(707) 468–8936, (800) 516–7342
www.jepsonwine.com

In addition to producing Chardonnay, Merlot, and Sauvignon Blanc, and some sparkling and dessert wines, Bob and Alice Jepson, along with winemaker Kurt Lorenzi, have created a special niche by producing Alambic Pot Still brandy, estate-grown and bottled.

Milano Family Winery
14594 South U.S. 101, Hopland
(707) 744–1396, (800) 564–2582
www.milonefamilywinery.com

In the early 1900s, Vincenzo Milone came to Mendocino County with his father, discovered some agriculturally rich land near Hopland, and planted grapes. They also built a hop kiln at the foot of Duncan's Peak, near their home. Today that hop kiln is the tasting room for Milano Winery. The kiln is one of the few left over from the days when the nearby village of Hopland was earning its name growing and curing hops.

Parducci Wine Cellars
501 Parducci Road, Ukiah
(707) 462–9463, (888) 362–9463
www.parducci.com

Since 1932, Parducci Wine Cellars has made wine according to a simple philosophy: Wine is an honest, natural product that should never be overprocessed, never be masked by too much oak, and never have its essential flavor and aroma filtered away. Parducci is Mendocino's oldest operating winery, but it is dedicated to contemporary consumers, using modern winemaking techniques and evolving wine styles. Parducci's conviction is that whites should be fermented cold and bottled cold to retain the liveliness, crispness, and freshness of the varietals. Parducci white wines produce a slight spritz from carbon dioxide, a natural retainer of the varietal flavors for which Parducci wines are famous.

Redwood Valley Cellars
7051 North State Street, off U.S. 101,
Redwood Valley
(707) 485–0322
www.redwoodvalleycellars.com

This is actually a tasting room for Barren-Pauli Winery in Petaluma. Redwood Valley Cellars also produces wine from grapes grown in Potter Valley. Located

A Vineyard Timeline

Wine Country vineyards are buzzing with activity just about any time of the year. Here's a brief wrap-up of what happens and when.

March and April: Leaves begin to emerge during bud break in mid-March, followed in April by the full unfurling of leaves. Buds resembling miniature bunches of grapes begin to appear.

May and June: Vines continue to send out shoots or "canes" that will create the vine's leaf canopy. (Shoots become canes as they mature.) Most vines have completed their bloom by the end of May, though the floral show is rather bland. Good weather is essential during this time—not too much rain or heat—to allow the successful self-pollination of the grapes. Care is also taken to prevent threat of frost. This is achieved through the use of wind machines, smudge pots, and sprinklers.

July and August: Grapes grow to their full size by mid-July and begin to change color and soften, in a process known as *veraison.* Red wine grapes begin to turn red, blue, or black, depending on the varietal; whites become translucent yellow. For most varieties, the proper sugar levels required to make great wine are still several weeks away. However, harvest begins in August of Chardonnay and Pinot Noir grapes used for sparkling wines, as they reach their optimum sugar levels before other varieties.

September and October: Harvest (also referred to as the "crush") intensifies to a fever pitch. Following the picking of Chardonnay and Pinot Noir grapes, Sauvignon Blanc, Zinfandel, and Merlot are harvested. Usually the last to mature, Cabernet Sauvignon brings the harvest to an end by late October.

November and December: Following harvest, vines take on the colors of fall. White wine varietals turn yellow and gold, while red wine varieties turn crimson. Cooler weather and winter rains trigger the vines into dormancy. As the quiet time of year settles over the vineyards, experienced workers begin methodically pruning the vines to cut back wood that bore fruit the previous year. Winter rains of between 24 and 40 inches will be needed to replenish the groundwater that will carry the vine through the next growing season.

January and February: Expert pruning continues through the wet months, setting the stage for early spring and the new burst of growth to come.

Source: Sonoma County Grape Growers Association

---

between Ukiah and Willits, at the West Road exit off U.S. 101, Redwood Valley Cellars offers complimentary tastings.

Highway 128

Greenwood Ridge Vineyards
5501 Highway 128, Philo
(707) 895–2002
www.greenwoodridge.com

Allan Green, a graphic artist turned winemaker, has crafted a lovely Anderson Valley winery and tasting room with a wraparound deck and a view of the hilltop ridge where his vines grow. On one wall of the tasting room are the ribbons his wine received for its excellence—White Riesling, Late Harvest Riesling, Sauvignon Blanc, Chardonnay, Zinfandel, Pinot Noir, Merlot, and Cabernet Sauvignon. Three Greenwood wines have been included in the *Wine Spectator*'s annual list of the "Top 100 Wines of the World." In another corner of the tasting room (samples are complimentary, by the way), you'll see Green's collection of 5,000 wine corks, arranged innovatively into a sculpture.

Handley Cellars
3151 Highway 128, Philo
(707) 895–3876, (800) 733–3151
www.handleycellars.com

Fermentation science is a natural interest for Milla Handley, the winemaker and owner who is also the great-great-granddaughter of brewing giant Henry Weinhard. After receiving her degree in enology and working six years in the wine industry, she and her husband, Rex, founded Handley Cellars in the basement of their home near Philo. Today's tasting room is a far cry from that basement winery. As visitors sip wine, they are surrounded by the Handley family's collection of folk art from around the world. Located 6 miles northwest of Philo, the tasting room offers samples of their unusual Pinot Menieur, as well as an excellent Pinot Noir. Complimentary hors d'oeuvres are presented along with the wines the first weekend of every month.

Husch Vineyards
4400 Highway 128, Philo
(707) 895–3216, (800) 554–8724
www.huschvineyards.com

Farming has been the occupation for three generations of the Oswald family, owners of Husch Vineyards. Theirs is the oldest winery in Anderson Valley and still contains some of its first varietal plantings. Originally planted in 1969 and bonded in 1971 by the Husches, it was purchased by the Oswalds in 1979. Currently, three members of the Oswald family are involved in the winery: Hugo, Miles, and Ken. All Husch wines are made from grapes grown only on the family-owned vineyards, including the original 21-acre block of Pinot Noir, Gewurztraminer, and Chardonnay.

Navarro Vineyards
5601 Highway 128, Philo
(707) 895–3686, (800) 537–9463
www.navarrowine.com

Ted Bennett has been making Anderson Valley Gewurztraminer since 1973, and over the years he has developed a successful formula for this grape, which requires a long growing season. His wife, Deborah, serves guests in the tasting rooms. "We're not a big corporate winery," she says. "We're the '70s homesteaders who happened to like wine." Navarro Vineyards seeks to make a fine wine but doesn't forget about "the guy in a camper van with three kids who just wants to enjoy a bottle," says winemaker Jim Klein, whose efforts produce 30,000 cases a year.

Roederer Estate
4501 Highway 128, Philo
(707) 895–2288
www.roederer-estate.com

The wines created by the European firm headed by Madame Orly-Roederer have been world-famous for 200 years. Now they are being produced in the Anderson Valley under the direction of her grandson, Jean-Claude Rouzard, who came here in 1981 in search of the perfect appellation. To create the perfect wine, Roederer uses only the first juice, pressed from the pulp with minimal skin contact. Subsequent pressings are not used, and even the first pressing is further critiqued, with 30 percent later discarded to be faithful to the Roederer style.

Yorkville Vineyards & Cellars
Highway 128 at Mile Marker 40.4, Yorkville
(707) 894–9177
www.yorkville-cellars.com

The 30-acre vineyard owned by the Wallo family lies at 1,000 feet above sea level, where sun-filled days and cool nights combine to create premium-quality grapes. Since its establishment in 1982, the Yorkville Vineyards estate has been farmed organically. Instead of pesticides and herbicides, they count on seasonal cover to serve as an alternative for insects to attack instead of the vine. The cover also provides a host environment for beneficial insects that prey on unwelcome ones. Yorkville Vineyards has been certified organic by the state of California every year since 1986. Yorkville grows seven Bordeaux varietals and makes at least one unusual wine—Eleanor of Aquitaine, a half-and-half blend of Sauvignon Blanc and Semillon, aged in French oak barrels only.

Wine Shops

As you would expect, they don't just make 'em, pour 'em, and sell 'em in the Wine Country—there is also a variety of stores dedicated to the display, presentation, storage, and properly outfitted enjoyment of wines. In addition, some shops offer amazing selections of wines from our region and beyond, along with all the decadent accouterments. So light up that fat, pricey cigar and take a look at a few of our favorite wine shops.

Napa County

J.V. Liquor Warehouse
426 First Street, Napa
(707) 253–2624, (877) 4–MY–WINE
www.jvwarehouse.com

Great bargains in wine can be found here. Napa residents tend to shop at this store for their premium vino, and there is much to choose from. Most are at discount prices, and they will pack up assorted cases and ship them home for you, too. It lives up to its reputation—and it's just across the river bridge from Copia.

The Vintage 1870 Wine Cellar
6525 Washington Street, Yountville
(707) 944–9070, (800) WINE–4–US
www.vintagewinecellar.com

Ironic that the stables of the old Groezinger Winery would end up as the one piece of the property expressly devoted to wine. Unlike most wine shops, this one is licensed for tastings—they pour about a dozen selections, all day long. On the shelves you'll find everything from $5.00 bottles to an imperial of Mondavi 1978 Reserve Cabernet Sauvignon that goes for $1,000. The Cellar also sells a few cigars.

St. Helena Wine Merchants
699 St. Helena Highway S., St. Helena
(707) 963–7888, (800) 729–9463
www.shwinemerchants.com

Across the road from V. Sattui Winery is this unpretentious purveyor of wines. The Merchants aim to carry the sort of small-availability labels that out-of-state visitors read about, but they can't find at home—Harlan, Dominus, and Maya come to mind as examples. Don't be surprised if you bump into a local winemaker or two during your visit.

Dean & DeLuca
607 St. Helena Highway S., St. Helena
(877) DEAN–WIN(E)
www.deandeluca.com

When those classy New Yorkers set up shop in Wine Country (see our Shopping chapter), it changed the face of retail wine sales in Napa Valley. D&D has the most extensive collection of California wines you could ever hope to see: 1,200 labels, and that's just 750-milliliter bottles. The wines are arranged alphabetically within varietal categories. Forget about trying to note every wine; by the time you make it to the last Zinfandel, they probably will have added a few more bottles.

Calistoga Wine Stop
1458 Lincoln Avenue, No. 2, Calistoga
(707) 942–5556, (800) 648–4521

Before you even get to the wine, there's a lot of history worth noting here. The Wine Stop is in The Depot, that big yellow wood building that was what it claims to be. Built in 1868, it's the second-oldest train station left in California (though no trains have stopped here since 1963). The wine shop itself is jammed inside a 19th-century boxcar, which limits the elbow room but somehow doesn't impair the Napa-Sonoma–concentrated selection. (Owner Tom Pelter estimates that 75 percent of his stock is made in those two counties.) Pelter is something of a Port aficionado, which explains the high density of Portugal's fortified wine in his store.

Enoteca Wine Shop
1345 Lincoln Avenue, Calistoga
(707) 942–1117

Discreetly cached on the second floor of Calistoga's 111-year-old I.O.O.F. building is this classy wine shop. ("Enoteca" is an Italian word meaning "wine cellar" or "wine library.") They tend toward artisanal vintners who produce hundreds of cases rather than tens of thousands. And they draw from all over the world, as evidenced by their affection for the likes of Chateau Musar in Lebanon.

Sonoma County

The Wine Exchange of Sonoma
452 First Street E., Sonoma
(707) 938–1794, (800) 938–1794

Looking for a more efficient way to sample local wines than driving from one place to another? Interested in a place that carries hard-to-find wines and will even ship them anywhere allowed by law? The Wine Exchange is the place for you, with some 800 premium wines and 280 beers in stock. It's opposite the Sonoma Plaza, with a tasting bar that features 18 wines and six draft beers.

Sonoma Wine Hardware
536 Broadway, Sonoma
(707) 939–1694, (866) 231–9463

Napa Valley Wine Hardware
659 Main Street, St. Helena
(707) 967–5503, (866) 611–9463

You just scored your first case of great Cabernet Sauvignon—now, how can you store it properly back home? Your next stop should be at one of these shops. The stores do not sell wine (they leave that up to you); their main focus is wine storage systems. Under the same ownership, both stores have similar inventories, but the Sonoma store features a slightly larger showroom and a larger library of wine books. On display in both are a multitude of cabinets, racks, and other "hardware" for storing and enjoying wine, and lots of accessories, too.

Taylor & Norton Wine Merchants
19210 Sonoma Highway, Sonoma
(707) 939–6611
www.taylorandnorton.com

Insiders' Tip
Many winery tasting rooms do double-duty as art galleries. For example, Roshambo near Healdsburg offers exhibits of modern art that change frequently, and Paradise Ridge Winery in Santa Rosa maintains a sculpture garden.

You'll have no trouble finding every local and regional wine you've been looking for in this wine shop. More than that, Taylor & Norton carries wines from other U.S. areas as well as wines from Europe and other foreign wine-producing regions. While shopping for wine, you might want to browse through a handsome selection of antique wine decanters and glasses, some from the Victorian era. They're pricey, but so beautiful you may not be able to resist taking home a souvenir.

The Wine Shop
331 Healdsburg Avenue, Healdsburg
(707) 433–0433

It's all wine here; in fact, it's a wine bar, meaning it's licensed by the state to serve and charge for full glasses of wine, not tastings. But the selection is enormous: The shop specializes in hard to find, small production wines worldwide, with more than 600 wineries represented. They will ship your selections, too.

Attractions

Main Events

Balloons, Planes, and Gondolas

Tours

So you've had a go at wine tasting, feasted on some fabulous food, and now you're ready for something completely different. This is your chapter. Sure, wineries, mud baths, and world-class restaurants are attractions in their own right, and all those selling points are detailed in other chapters. In this chapter, however, you'll find everything worth visiting that defies categorical lumping. That might be a culturally rich historical site (such as Fort Ross), a museum (such as the Sharpsteen Museum in Calistoga), a scenic jaunt (such as the Skunk Train), or even a good old-fashioned bit of fun (such as Infineon Raceway).

Price Code

The price code below reflects the admission price or fees for two adults in high season, not including gratuities, where appropriate.

$	Free or low cost
$$	$15 to $50
$$$	$51 to $150
$$$$	More than $151

Main Events

Napa County

Seguin Moreau Napa Cooperage $
151 Camino Dorado, Napa
(707) 252–3408
www.seguinmoreau.com

You've seen how the wine is blended, now take a good look at how the barrels get toasted. The only U.S. outpost of the famed French wine barrel makers, Tonnellerie Seguin Moreau Cooperage, is located in Napa. Watch the crew of skilled "coopers" bend, shave, and roast the oak staves over open flames in the floor, then hammer them together using steel hoops. It's a craft that has changed little in hundreds of years of winemaking. Admission is free.

Hakusan Sake Gardens $
1 Executive Way, Napa
(707) 258–6160
www.hakusan.com

Hakusan is one of only seven sake makers in the United States, and the only one in Wine Country. Sake, while comparable to wine in body and complexity, actually is brewed, like beer. It therefore is made to be refrigerated and consumed within a year, not aged. Hakusan, at the intersection of Highways 29 and 12, is open from 10:00 A.M. to 5:00 P.M. every day. There are self-guided tours, and for $1.00 you can sample about five varieties, both hot and cold. The brewery's offerings include cooking sake and sweet plum sake.

Copia: The American Center for Wine, Food and the Arts $$
500 First Street, Napa
(707) 259–1600
www.copia.org

In addition to overseeing the winery empire that bears his name, Robert Mondavi has spent his golden years getting this mega-project off the ground [see our Close-up "Copia: The World's Only Wine, Food, Art (and Fun) Center" in this chapter]. At a cost of $50 million, the 80,000-square-foot cultural museum and educational center features lively programs, classes, exhibitions, and demonstrations to bring together world-renowned chefs and home cooks, winemakers and wine lovers, and artists— from experts to amateurs.

Napa Firefighters Museum $
1201 Main Street, Napa
(707) 259–0609

This museum will give you a deeper appreciation of the folks who fight the flames. Inside you'll see a hand pumper and a steamer, hose carts, engines, ladder trucks, old fire equipment and uniforms, and photos from many eras of puttin' out fires. There is no admission fee, and the museum is open 11:00 A.M. to 4:00 P.M. Wednesday through Sunday.

Veterans Home of California $
California Drive, Yountville
(707) 944–4918

The museum in the old chapel of the Veterans Home features rotating displays of documents, photographs, models, uniforms, and weapons from various eras of U.S. military history. Unfortunately, it is open only on Friday and Saturday, noon to 2:00 P.M. However, just strolling around the manicured grounds of this Spanish Revival complex, much of which dates back to 1918, is a pleasure. Look for the signs on Highway 29 just south of Domaine Chandon.

Napa Valley Museum $
55 Presidents Circle, Yountville
(707) 944–0500
www.napavalleymuseum.org

A major capital project that was years in the planning, the nonprofit museum celebrates the artistic, historical, and cultural heritage of the valley, with a permanent exhibit called "The Land and People of the Napa Valley." Its central, permanent exhibition is "California Wine: The Science of an Art." Using music, the spoken word, and the power of technology (including 26 videodisc players and nine microcomputers), it effectively presents the winemaking process in near entirety.

The Napa Valley Museum is open Wednesday through Monday from 10:00 A.M. to 5:00 P.M. (until 8:00 P.M. on the first Thursday of the month). Admission is $4.50 for adults, $3.50 for students and seniors age 60 or older, and $2.50 for youth ages 7 to 17.

Silverado Museum $
1490 Library Lane, St. Helena
(707) 963–3757
www.napanet.net/vi/silverado

A California museum devoted to a Scottish novelist might seem a bit strange, but, hey, Robert Louis Stevenson did help immortalize the area with his *The Silverado Squatters*. He also penned classics such as *Treasure Island, Dr. Jekyll and Mr. Hyde,* and others you'll read all about at the museum. It has first editions, artifacts from the Stevenson home, personal letters and photographs, and a few original manuscripts (though most of those reside at Yale University). The museum is closed Monday but open every other day from noon to 4:00 P.M.

Bale Grist Mill State Historic Park $
3369 Highway 29, St. Helena
(707) 963–2236
www.napanet.net/~bothe

The friendly miller will tell you how this park is a working reminder of the days when "milling" involved more than driving to Safeway for a bag of all-purpose flour. Dr. Edward Bale built the wood-framed mill in 1846, and it has been painstakingly refurbished. The park is open 10:00 A.M. to 5:00 P.M. daily, but the best times to visit are weekend days at 11:30 A.M., 1:00, 2:30, and 3:30 P.M. That's when the park cranks up the wooden, 36-foot water wheel and gets those original quartz stones to grinding wheat or corn. Admission is $1.00 for adults; children under 16 free. From here you can hike to adjacent Bothe-Napa Valley State Park (see our Parks and Recreation chapter).

The Sharpsteen Museum in Calistoga is like no other small-town museum, featuring such diverse items as a genuine Academy Award Oscar statuette and a stagecoach. PHOTO: JEAN SAYLOR DOPPENBERG

The Sharpsteen Museum $
1311 Washington Street, Calistoga
(707) 942–5911
www.sharpsteen-museum.org

If every small town in America had a museum as lively and authentic as the Sharpsteen, maybe we wouldn't be so ignorant of history. The museum was founded in the 1970s by Ben Sharpsteen, who produced such films as *Fantasia* and *Snow White* for Walt Disney. (Sharpsteen's Academy Award "Oscar" statuette from his days with Disney gleams inside a special display case.) The crowning piece of his legacy is a 32-foot, scale-model diorama that lays out the grounds of Sam Brannan's Calistoga spa, circa 1860 (see our History chapter for more on Brannan). One of the original cottages from that spa serves as a museum annex.

The museum is open 10:00 A.M. to 4:00 P.M. daily from April through September and noon to 4:00 P.M. daily from October through March. There is no admission charge, thanks to the eager volunteer staff. They do, of course, accept donations.

Pedals Past Bicycle Museum $
1205 Foothill Boulevard, Calistoga
(707) 942–9469
www.pedalspast.com

Here's a museum that will make you feel like a kid again—a shrine to bicycles. Run by a couple of Napa Valley natives who traveled the United States for four years to gather together this collection, they claim it is the only museum of its kind on the West Coast. There are more than 60 bikes on display, and the exhibit changes every few months. Most bikes are American-made balloon tire two-wheelers from the pneumatic tire era (1933 to 1970), with all the major brands of the period represented—Schwinn, Monark, Shelby, Colson, Columbia, even Sears Roebuck and Montgomery Ward machines. Hours are generally 11:00 A.M. to 4:00 P.M. Wednesday through Saturday, or by appointment.

Old Faithful Geyser of California $
1299 Tubbs Lane, Calistoga
(707) 942-6463
www.oldfaithfulgeyser.com

About every 40 minutes on the yearly average (depending on how much water is in the aquifer), the earth gurgles, puffs, and blows a stream of boiling water (350 degrees hot!) about 60 feet into the air off Tubbs Lane. Welcome to Calistoga's geyser, one of only three in world that can call themselves "Old Faithful" without shame. There is a working seismograph in the entryway (the geyser is said to predict earthquakes), and outside near the erupting pond, for some reason, is a pen of Tennessee Fainting goats, a rare breed suffering from myatonia, which causes them to lock up and topple when startled. The Old Faithful complex is open from 9:00 A.M. to 6:00 P.M. daily in the warm months, 9:00 A.M. to 5:00 P.M. in the winter. Admission is $6.00 for adults, $5.00 for seniors, and $2.00 for kids ages 6 through 12.

Villa Ca'Toga $$
Off Tubbs Lane, Calistoga
(707) 942-3900
www.catoga.com

Italian artist Carlo Marchiori is one of the eminent trompe l'oeil artists in the world, and Villa Ca'Toga—a mansion and work-in-progress on the outskirts of Calistoga—is his vision come to life. Faux pillars, staircases, and hanging plants are painted in three-dimensional realism on two-dimensional walls. Alcoves end abruptly at painted backdrops, and surprises lie around every corner (even for the initiated—Marchiori is constantly adding new sculptures). The house is open Saturdays from May to October for a one-hour tour that begins at 11:00 A.M. Reservations are necessary, and you pick up your tickets and a map to the property at the Ca'Toga Galleria D'Arte at 1206 Cedar Street in downtown Calistoga (see our Arts and Culture chapter). Tickets are $20 per person, and children over 12 are welcome.

Sonoma County

Southern Sonoma

Depot Park Museum $
270 First Street W., Sonoma
(707) 938-1762
www.vom.com/~depot

This is more than a museum; it's an authentic piece of Sonoma city's history. Originally the depot was on the downtown plaza, much to the chagrin of Sonomans, who felt the plaza had been turned into a railroad yard, turntable and all. After some pressure, the depot was moved in 1890 to its present site. The museum now houses a terrific collection of historic memorabilia focusing on the 19th century. Several rooms are furnished in Victorian style, and a good deal of emphasis is placed on the life of General Mariano Vallejo (see our History chapter). Pioneer artifacts and exhibits of Native American culture are nicely displayed. Temporary exhibits shed light on specific historical periods, crafts, and events. The museum is open Wednesday through Sunday from 1:00 to 4:30 P.M. There's no admission, but donations are welcome.

Train Town $
20264 Broadway, Sonoma
(707) 938-3912
www.traintown.com

Train Town is the most well-developed scale railroad in America—a joy for anyone of any age. You climb into a miniature train, one-fourth the normal size, and chug your way through 10 acres of planned landscaped park filled with thousands of native trees, animals, bridges over lakes, tunnels, waterfalls, and replicas of historic buildings. Two miniature engines and handcrafted railroad cars take passengers on the 20-minute ride to Lakeville, a pint-sized, Western-flavored hamlet populated with geese and ducks. Along the way there's a stop to pet some llamas and goats. Trains operate daily in summer from 10:00 A.M. to 5:00 P.M. In winter they are on a shorter, weekend schedule. The

Copia: The World's Only Wine, Food, Art (and Fun) Center

When Robert Mondavi puts his mind to making a project happen, it usually happens. His newest high-profile venture in Wine Country—a must-see attraction—became reality in 2001 after 10 years of planning and more than two years of construction.

Copia: The American Center for Wine, Food and the Arts is described as "a cultural institution, museum, and educational center dedicated to the character of wine and food in close association with the arts and humanities, and to celebrating these as unique expressions of American life, culture, and heritage." That's the official version of the Copia vision, but it's really a fun house for foodies and wine enthusiasts, with fabulous art and exhibits to round out the experience. You can bet it's the only place like it in the world.

Built from private donations at a cost of about $55 million ($20 million from Mr. Mondavi alone), Copia is 80,000 square feet of stone, concrete, metal, and glass with gardens inspired by the 16th-century kitchen gardens at Villandry in France's Loire Valley. Rising along the banks of the Napa River, Copia, named for the goddess of abundance, is surrounded by three-and-a-half acres of organic culinary gardens ranging from olive to citrus orchards, to a collection of lavender shrubs from around the world, to groves of nut-bearing trees and beds of herbs and root vegetables.

Inside Copia are art exhibits and unique sculptures, an amphitheater for concerts and performances, an indoor theater for films and lectures, a rare books library, a demonstration kitchen, classrooms for learning about food and wine, a cafe featuring picnic-style fare, a gift shop, and gourmet dining and wine tasting.

Copia: The American Center for Wine, Food and the Arts includes a permanent display dedicated to food consumption in America. PHOTO: JEAN SAYLOR DOPPENBERG

A permanent exhibit, "Forks in the Road: Food, Wine and the American Table," takes a light-hearted look at the place of food and wine in American life today and features interactive exhibits that both kids and adults will find entertaining. There's more trivia than you can shake a ladle at: What sweet treat was named for a small Massachusetts town? The Fig Newton. What fizzy drink was originally called Lithiated Lemon? 7-Up! And where else will you see a display of food packets used by the astronauts or the war rations issued to soldiers (besides, possibly, the Smithsonian) or a collection of PEZ dispensers? You can leave behind a little piece of your life experience by recording your best tales of personal cooking disasters or favorite meals in a private kiosk for future visitors to watch and enjoy (remember to smile for the camera!).

A recent exhibit celebrated the "o-matic" world of kitchen gadgets, dominated by the Popeil products of TV infomercial fame.

Julia's Kitchen, the center's 75-seat, full-service dining room with an open kitchen, is named for Julia Child, the legendary food maven and an advisor in Copia's development for more than five years. (As an honorary trustee of Copia, she also donated her personal collection of copper cookware, used for several decades in her own kitchen, to be put on display.) The restaurant's executive chef is Victor Scargle (see our Restaurants chapter). The open kitchen allows visitors to watch distinguished American chefs and cooking teachers at work. For extra fun, ask for seats at the counter (there are only four), where you can watch the culinary action up close.

Copia is located at 500 First Street at the eastern edge of downtown Napa. Admission is $12.50 for adults, $10.00 for teens and seniors, and $7.50 for children. To learn more about this one-of-a-kind attraction, call (707) 259–1600 or visit www.copia.org.

fare is $3.75 for adults and $3.25 for children 12 and younger and seniors.

Vintage Aircraft Co. $$$$
23982 Arnold Drive, Sonoma
(707) 938–2444
www.vintageaircraft.com

You step back into the 1940s when you step onto the tarmac and check out Christopher Prevost's fleet of authentic, 1940 Boeing-built Stearman biplanes. One of the planes is a North American-built, World War II Navy SNJ-4, designed to train pilot candidates for the Air Force and Navy. Meticulously restored and maintained, the planes tempt thrill seekers to take one of several rides offered by Prevost. For the truly brave, Prevost offers a variety of aerobatic flights—the most intense is appropriately named "Kamikaze." Weekday flights are by appointment.

Infineon Raceway $$
Highways 37 and 121, Sonoma
(707) 938–8448, (800) 870–7223
www.infineonraceway.com

Each year you'll see some of the top names in the racing world compete here (formerly Sears Point Raceway) on the grueling road course, the rugged motocross dirt track, and the drag strip. Legends such as Mario Andretti, Al Unser (Sr. and Jr.), and Bobby Allison have all toured the track as well as Hollywood celebrities such as Paul Newman, Clint Eastwood, and James Garner. Annual events include NASCAR road races and sports car racing by the Sports Car Club of America with TRANS-AM, Formula Atlantic, and Pro Formula Ford entrants. Bike events include AMA motorcycle road races and several motocross races. Prices for events vary. (See our Spectator Sports chapter for more details.)

Historic Town of Sonoma $
Various sites

A national landmark and the largest square of its kind in California, the Sonoma Plaza evokes the feel of Old Europe. It is an ideal picnic spot, with numerous tables under nearly 200 trees, a playground, and a duck pond.

Surrounding the plaza are some of the buildings that marked the start of the village, then owned by Mexico and ruled by Gen. Mariano Vallejo. It makes a lovely walking tour, and one $2.00 ticket, available at any of the following sites, will give you access to the Mission, the Barracks, Vallejo's home, and the Petaluma Adobe.

Mission San Francisco Solano, founded in 1823 as the last of California's Franciscan missions, is diagonally opposite the plaza's northeast corner. Today's mission is a faithful re-creation of the original. Only the priests' quarters date from the founding. It's open daily from 10:00 A.M. to 5:00 P.M.

Sonoma Barracks, across from the mission, housed Vallejo's Mexican troops, sheltered the Bear Flag soldiers, and served as a U.S. military headquarters in the 1840s and 1850s. Today the Barracks are restored to their Mexican-era appearance, with exhibits inside and an attractive gift shop with California items. Grizzly bears once battled bulls in the enclosed courtyard behind the Barracks, while spectators gambled on the outcome. It's open 10:00 A.M. to 5:00 P.M. daily.

Salvador Vallejo Adobe (Swiss Hotel) has a bar and restaurant that have long been favorites of residents and visitors alike. The locally famous drink, "Bear's Hair" sherry, is served in the saloon. Originally the adobe was built for General Vallejo's brother, Salvador, in the 1840s. It has been known as the Swiss Hotel since the 1880s.

Salvador Vallejo Adobe (El Dorado Hotel), a Monterey Colonial adobe, has had a checkered history as a government office, college, winery, and hotel. Salvador Vallejo built it between 1836 and 1846. Subsequently it was occupied by the Bear Flag party members and U.S. General John C. Frémont during the opening days of the Mexican-American War. Presbyterian settlers operated Cumberland College at the adobe from 1858 until 1864.

El Paseo de Sonoma (Pinelli Building) is one of several plaza structures built of native stone. The building survived a 1911 fire when Augustino Pinelli let firefighters douse flames with his barrels of wine. Today several shops and restaurants can be found on the passageway behind First Street East and Spain Street. Blue Wing Inn, on E. Spain Street across from the mission, was once a rowdy gold rush-era saloon visited by future President U.S. Grant, Lt. William Tecumseh Sherman, Kit Carson, and notorious bandit Joaquin Murietta. This wisteria-covered, two-story adobe now contains shops and residences.

General Vallejo's Home (Lachryma Montis) is not on the plaza but 3 blocks down West Spain Street. General Vallejo built this Gothic Revival home at a cost of $50,000 in 1851 and named it Lachryma Montis ("tears of the mountain") because of a spring on the property. Abandoning Spanish-style architecture, he built a grand Victorian and furnished it with European imports. He had redwood lumber hauled in from the port at Vallejo, while bricks and marble mantels were shipped from Hawaii. Landscaping, a glass pavilion (now gone), and every convenience of the time were included. The Vallejos' 15th and 16th children were born at Lachryma Montis.

Vallejo's once-great holdings eventually were reduced to only the acreage around this home. Many of the original furnishings are still in place. The kitchen located in a separate building kept the heat of cooking away from the rest of the house. A charming little guesthouse remains on the property, and a short walk up the hill leads to the room of one of the Vallejo children. Picnic tables are set around a stream that runs through the property. Now a state historic park, Lachryma Montis is open 10:00 A.M. to 5:00 P.M. daily.

Jack London State Historic Park $
2400 London Ranch Road off Arnold Drive, Glen Ellen
(707) 938–5216
www.parks.sonoma.net/JLPark.html

Jack London called it his "Beauty Ranch," but he wanted to achieve more than aesthetic satisfaction here. His goal was to achieve a scientifically operated ranch where new techniques could be developed. Many buildings remain from his experiment in ranching: stone stables where he kept his prize horses, the last vestiges of his famous scientific piggery, and the farmhouse where he lived for five years and wrote most of his stories. In the center of the 1,400 acres is the rubble of Wolf House, the lava-stone mansion he had hoped to live in, burned to the ground in 1913. The half-mile trail to the Wolf House ruins passes through a forest of oak, madrone, and buckeye trees. Nearby is London's grave, marked only by a stone from the ruins of the house.

At the top of the hill, as you enter the state park, is the House of Happy Walls, built by London's wife, Charmian, after his death. It contains memorabilia of his life as a war correspondent, his abortive trip around the world with Charmian in a ship he designed himself, and a load of information about his writing life. Displayed are some of the 600 rejection slips he received, the first from the *Saturday Evening Post*. Seven miles of hiking, mountain biking and equestrian trails are available. The museum is open daily except for major holidays from 10:00 A.M. to 5:00 P.M., and admission is $3.00 per car ($2.00 when seniors are riding).

Petaluma Historical Museum $
20 Fourth Street, Petaluma
(707) 778–4398
www.petalumamuseum.com

A large, freestanding, stained-glass dome accents the beauty of this 1906 Carnegie Free Library—one of the hundreds that philanthropist Andrew Carnegie built and donated in the early 20th century. You'll find a 19th-century, horse-drawn fire wagon here, along with Native American artifacts, pioneer relics, and displays describing Petaluma's dairy and poultry beginnings. An exhibit about the Petaluma River illustrates how the town became an important manufacturing and trading hub when Petaluma was one of California's largest cities.

The museum offers brochures for self-guided walking tours of the city, featuring the famous Iron Front buildings and beautiful Victorian homes. In addition, docents costumed in Victorian attire lead guided tours of historic downtown on weekends. It's free, but donations are accepted. Admission to the museum is also free, and hours are 10:00 A.M. to 4:00 P.M. Wednesday, Thursday, and Friday, 11:00 A.M. to 4:00 P.M. Saturday, and noon to 3:00 P.M. Sunday.

Petaluma Adobe State Historic Park $
3325 Adobe Road at Casa Grande Road, Petaluma
(707) 762–4871
www.parks.sonoma.net/adobe.html

Once the headquarters of Gen. Mariano Vallejo's 100-square-mile Rancho Peta-luma, this enormous two-story adobe overlooking Petaluma stands as a monument to California's early history. A self-guided tour of the structure offers views of the period-furnished kitchen, the living quarters where the Vallejo family stayed when they spent their summer holiday at the rancho, and the guest rooms. The rustic chairs and candle sconces are of Spanish motif. Outside you will find replicas of the beehive ovens where cooks baked bread for rancho residents. Occasionally the ranger in charge may put in a loaf or two, using the same recipe the Vallejo servants used. The ranch is open daily (except Thanksgiving, Christmas, and New Year's Day) from 10:00 A.M. to 5:00 P.M. The $3.00 admission fee, $2.00 for children ages 6 to 12, entitles you to visit any of the sites on historic Sonoma Plaza (see previous listing).

Luther Burbank Home and Gardens $
Santa Rosa and Sonoma Avenues, Santa Rosa
(707) 524–5445
www.lutherburbank.org

During his 53 years in Santa Rosa, horticulturist Luther Burbank changed the plant world, improving and hybridizing more than 800 varieties (see our Close-up "Genius in the Garden" in this chapter).

This National Historic Landmark features Burbank's home, a carriage house, and the greenhouse where he performed his experiments. Outside you'll find a lovely garden filled with the plants Burbank introduced to the world. Docent-led house tours are offered on the half-hour Tuesday through Sunday from April through October. Tours, which are $3.00 for adults and free for children 12 and younger, run from 10:00 A.M. to 3:30 P.M. The gardens are open daily at no charge.

Jesse Peter Native American Art Museum $
Santa Rosa Junior College, 1501 Mendocino Avenue, Santa Rosa
(707) 527–4479
www.santarosa.edu/museum

Dedicated to arts and crafts created by Native Americans from the 19th century up to the present day, this museum contains an extensive assortment of baskets,

The Sonoma County Museum is located in downtown Santa Rosa. PHOTO: JEAN SAYLOR DOPPENBERG

including the extraordinarily beautiful baskets of the Pomo tribe. Most items displayed represent the work of California tribes, although beadwork of the Plains and Plateau tribes is on hand as well as some Eskimo art. There are replicas of a Southwestern pueblo, a Pomo roundhouse, and a Klamath River xonta (a family shelter). The museum is open Monday through Friday (except for school holidays) from mid-August through May. Admission is free.

Sonoma County Museum $
425 Seventh Street, Santa Rosa
(707) 579–1500
www.sonomacountymuseum.com

Housed in the old post office built after the 1906 earthquake, the museum was moved and restored as a part of local grassroots activities. The lower floor is devoted to an extensive collection of art exhibits, exhibits on the history and heritage of the county, and photographs of the local landscape and people. The second floor is given over to exciting temporary exhibits. Past ones have included

displays of cartoon art and a woodworking exhibit of bowls, boxes, and furniture. The Wild Oat Gift Shop has a particularly intriguing assortment of books and items on Sonoma County themes. The museum and gift shop are open Wednesday through Sunday year-round, from 11:00 A.M. to 4:00 P.M. A $2.00 donation is requested (students and seniors $1.00).

Redwood Empire Ice Arena $
1667 West Steele Lane, Santa Rosa
(707) 546–7147
www.snoopyshomeice.com

Outside of Charlie Brown, who will always be universally loved, the Redwood Empire Ice Arena may be the most appreciated gift Charles Schulz (1922–2000) has given Sonoma County. His career started in Minnesota and ballooned to fame, with his work appearing in more than 1,800 newspapers in 65 countries worldwide. Schulz was a resident of Santa Rosa, where he created many of his cartoons.

The arena offers a full range of skating, and many world champions have glided across the ice here. Open daily, but hours vary, with mornings reserved for special programs and classes. The cost is $5.50 for adults and teens and $4.50 for children younger than 12. Aside from the arena, visitors will delight in the gift shop with hundreds of items from the lives of the "Peanuts" gang.

Charles M. Schulz Museum and Research Center $$
One Snoopy Place, Santa Rosa
(707) 579-4452
www.charlesmschulzmuseum.org

"Peanuts" creator Charles Schulz didn't live long enough to see this museum dedicated to his legacy come to life (he died in early 2000), but he would be humbled by the result. Adjacent to Schulz's Redwood Empire Ice Arena (see previous listing), the $8 million museum opened in 2002. Within its 27,000 square feet are permanent and temporary displays of the cartoonist's 50-year body of work; a research library and archives for students, cartoonists, and scholars; and classrooms. Worth seeing is the 17-by-22-foot mural crafted from more than 3,500 individual "Peanuts" comic strips printed on ceramic tiles. Also on display is the wooden drawing board where Schulz drew his one-dimensional characters, in a recreation of his art studio. Admission is $8.00 for adults, $5.00 for seniors and children under 18, and free for toddlers.

Safari West $$$
3115 Porter Creek Road, Santa Rosa
(707) 579-2551, (800) 616-2695
www.safariwest.com

This is a little different than those drive-through safari parks where tourists outnumber perplexed animals by about 100 to 1. Safari West is a private preserve and working ranch dedicated to conservation and propagation of endangered species—the 400 acres of Safari West are home to 400 exotic mammals and birds. You can gaze at herds of zebra or watch a giraffe crane its mammoth neck to eat out of your hand.

Guests spend an unparalleled two-and-a-half hours on a unique educational trek through the rolling hills of the preserve. Accompanied by a naturalist, groups get the rarest of opportunities to photograph herds of antelope, eland, gazelle, zebra, and many more types of animals. Because the critters live in vast acreage, they are comfortable with vehicles and can be seen up close. (One group was even treated to the birth of an antelope.) Wear comfortable clothing and bring sunscreen and a hat. Oh, and the proprietors can customize tours if you have a particular interest in, say, springboks. Cost of a basic tour is $58 for adults and $28 for children 12 and younger. Safari West now includes overnight accommodations. The South African–made "tents" include hardwood floors, bathrooms, and king-size beds. Visits are by appointment only. Leave your pets at home.

Pacific Coast Air Museum $
2330 Airport Boulevard, Santa Rosa
(707) 575-7900
www.pacificcoastairmuseum.org

Located next to Sonoma County's Charles M. Schulz Airport, the Pacific Coast Air Museum was formed by local aviators interested in restoring and preserving retired military aircraft. The collection ranges from a Korean War-era RF-86 Sabre and Huey helicopter—which saw combat in Vietnam—to an F-16 Viper flown by the commander of the Navy's Top Gun flight school and an F-14A Tomcat that saw duty on several U.S. carriers. The museum is open every Tuesday and Thursday from 10:00 A.M. to 2:00 P.M., and every Saturday and Sunday from 10:00 A.M. to 4:00 P.M. On the third weekend of each month, museum staff unlatch the canopy of a featured aircraft and let visitors climb aboard to get a feel of what it's like behind the wheel of a war bird. The museum also sponsors a weekend air show—Wings Over Wine Country—each August (see our Festivals and Annual Events chapter).

Northern Sonoma

Windsor Waterworks and Slides $$
8225 Conde Lane, Windsor
(707) 838–7760

This recreational park offers welcome relief from hot summer days. Among the attractions are an inner-tube slide, speed slide, body slide, splash fountain with squirt guns, swimming pool and wading pool, large picnic area with barbecue pits, and an arcade. Kids can also play table tennis, horseshoes, and volleyball. The park's newest attraction is an inflatable ship on which children can bounce. A snack bar is available. The park is open every day from May through September from 11:00 a.m. to 7:00 p.m. The entrance fee is $13.25 for those 13 and older and $12.25 for kids ages 4 to 12. There's a special rate of $9.75 after 4:00 p.m. for the "afternoon splash." (See our Kidstuff chapter for more on this attraction.)

The Petrified Forest $
4100 Petrified Forest Road, Calistoga
(707) 942–6667
www.petrifiedforest.org

It's not as spooky as it sounds, unless you think too hard about the advancing wall of muddy volcanic ash that leveled these trees about 3 million years ago, following massive eruptions to the northeast. The trees lay unmolested until 1870, when a gent later known as "Petrified Charlie" Evans happened upon a rock-hard stump while tending his cows. The rest is tourist-industry history. A short loop takes you past all the highlights, including The Monarch, a petrified, 105-foot redwood with a diameter of 6 feet. The museum and store—open 10:00 A.M. to 6:00 P.M.— are housed in the big red Ollie Bockee House. Admission is $5.00 for adults, $3.00 for youngsters ages 12 through 17, and $2.00 for kids ages 6 to 11. Seniors 60 and over pay $3.00.

Healdsburg Museum $
221 Matheson Street, Healdsburg
(707) 431–3325
www.healdsburgmuseum.org

This museum is in a refurbished Carnegie library building and features both perma-nent and changing exhibits. The county's history is depicted from prehistoric times to the present, and displays include antique firearms, 19th-century clothing, tools, and an outstanding collection of Pomo basketry and crafts. The archives contain more than 5,000 historical photographs and newspapers dating back to 1865. Healdsburg Museum is open Tuesday through Sunday from 11:00 A.M. to 4:00 P.M. Admission is free.

West County/Russian River

Luther Burbank Gold Ridge Experiment Farm $
7781 Bodega Avenue, Sebastopol
(707) 829–6711
www.wschs-grf.pon.net/bef.htm

On this 18-acre experimental farm, horti-culturist Luther Burbank built a cottage and worked to perfect Gravenstein apples, plums, cherries, grapes, and lilies. Although he lived and worked in Santa Rosa, this is where he conducted his horticultural research between 1895 and 1926. Free guided tours, available by appointment from April through mid-October, explore Burbank's gardens and visit his restored cottage. The gardens are open for free self-guided tours year-round.

West County Museum $
261 South Main Street, Sebastopol
(707) 829–6711
www.wschs-grf.pon.net

A restored railroad depot houses the collections of the Western Sonoma County Historical Society. The Triggs Reference Room contains books, photographs, magazines, newspapers, audiotapes, and videotapes on local history. West County Museum is open Thursday through Sunday from 1:00 to 4:00 P.M. There is no admission fee, but donations are welcomed.

Children's Bell Tower $
2255 Highway 1, Bodega Bay
(707) 875–3422
www.nicholasgreen.org

In 1994, Nicholas Green, a seven-year-old boy from Bodega Bay, was tragically shot and killed by robbers during a vacation with his family in Italy. Nicholas' parents bravely chose to donate his organs to seven sick Italians, who were given a new chance to live a full life. The heartbreaking yet life-affirming tale received worldwide media attention and was turned into a movie. It also gave birth to this moving monument dedicated to the memory of Nicholas and the positive aftermath of his death. Families, schools, and churches around Italy donated all of the 140 bells that ring the 18-foot-high tower. The large bell in the center, blessed by Pope John Paul II, is inscribed with the names of the seven recipients of Nicholas' organs. The memorial is behind the Bodega Bay Community Center, at the north edge of town on the ocean side of the highway. Park in the small lot behind the center and stroll down to the tower. (Nicholas is buried in Bodega, a short distance inland. His grave is also an inspirational sight.)

Fort Ross State Historic Park $
19005 Highway 1, north of Jenner
(707) 847–3286
www.parks.ca.gov

On a grassy, windswept bluff north of Jenner stands a ruddy, wooden stockade, its main gate facing out over the Pacific Ocean. The 14-foot walls are made of weather-beaten redwood. Inside is a small chapel, dedicated to St. Nicholas and topped with an orthodox cross. In another building, seal and otter pelts hang on the walls above casks marked in Cyrillic characters.

Now part of a State Historic Park, Fort Ross provides a fascinating glimpse into the history of the settlement founded with the aim of providing food for the fledgling Russian colony in Alaska, where Russia's eastward push ended in the early 1800s (see our History chapter). The museum in the visitor center exhibits Russian and Native American artifacts, and the gift shop offers crafts made by the local Pomo tribe as well as goods imported from Russia.

Join more than 100 costumed participants for the annual Living History Day—held on the third or last Saturday of July—to get a taste of what life was like for the Russians nearly 200 years ago (see our Festivals and Annual Events chapter). The park is open daily from 10:00 A.M. to 4:30 P.M. There is no entrance fee for cyclists or hikers. Vehicles pay $2.00 for parking.

Berry's Saw Mill $
Highway 116 and Cazadero Highway, Cazadero
(707) 865–2365

This authentic sawmill offers visitors an opportunity to see trees sawed, split, and planed into usable lumber. Visitors can explore the mill on an informal basis—guided tours are not offered. It's open at no charge Monday through Friday from 7:45 A.M. to 4:30 P.M.

Mendocino County

Real Goods Solar Living Center $
13771 U.S. 101, Hopland
(707) 744–2100
www.realgoods.com

This shop is a giant demonstration project for residential energy efficiency and alternative earth-friendly designs. The large main building at the center is built of straw bales, and it's powered entirely by solar panels and wind turbines. You can shop from a wide selection of environmentally conscious products such as solar panels, hemp goods, and water filtration systems and enjoy a tour of the 12 acres of beautiful, permaculture organic gardens and ponds. For the kids, there's a special area for playing and learning, including a unique solar calendar; they call it a 21st-century Stonehenge. The Solar Living Center is open daily from 10:00 A.M. to 6:00 P.M. Each August the center sponsors a solar festival that features environmental activists—Julia Butterfly and Ralph Nader spoke here in 2000—and music (see our Festivals and Annual Events chapter).

Grace Hudson Museum and Sun House $
431 South Main Street, Ukiah
(707) 467–2836
www.gracehudsonmuseum.org

Grace Hudson Museum is an art, history, and anthropology museum focusing on

Genius in the Garden

Luther Burbank (1849–1926) knew plants not just for what they were, but for what they could become. The nation's most renowned and prolific horticulturist, he dedicated his life to the propagation of new plant varieties, many of which are still valued today for their extraordinary beauty and utility.

Born in Lancaster, Massachusetts, Luther's career began at the age of 21, when he accidentally discovered a potato that had sprouted a seed ball on his farm. At the time, the European potato blight had recently spread to the United States and farmers were in danger of losing their crops. From the 23 seeds he found in the seed ball, Luther developed a hardy, high-yielding variety of potato, the "Burbank potato," which eventually became the predominant type grown in the United States—today's russet potato is a descendant of the Burbank variety.

But this was only the beginning for a man whose name would become associated with nearly a thousand other new plants. Perhaps sensing his destiny, Luther quickly

The Luther Burbank Home and Gardens in Santa Rosa stand as a testament to the nation's greatest horticulturist. PHOTO: JOHN NAGIECKI

sold the rights to his new potato for $150 to a local seed dealer and used the proceeds to finance a trip to Santa Rosa, where his brother had been living.

Inspired by his brother's letters describing a gardener's paradise, Luther had dreamt of California for years. When he finally set foot in Santa Rosa in 1875, he found it beyond even his expectations. Yet, like most people who believe they have stumbled upon the Promised Land, Luther wanted to keep it a secret. Fearing that should the news leak out "all scuffs would come out here, get drunk, and curse the whole country," he warned his family back east to avoid speaking favorably about California.

It wasn't long before Luther acquired some land near "downtown" Santa Rosa— then a jumble of 726 houses, 6 hotels, 7 churches, and 22 saloons—and began his work. Though he had achieved some notoriety through early efforts, it wasn't until 1893, when he published his catalog "New Creations in Fruits and Flowers," that he achieved widespread fame. At the time, the propagation of new plant varieties was a slow, tedious process, and such a large offering—more than a hundred varieties—by a single individual was a surprise, if not downright shocking. Among individuals and groups who believed that God alone could "create" a new plant, Luther was considered an infidel.

But the results quickly trumped the skeptics. Gardeners from coast to coast and abroad bought Luther's plants, which were exceptionally hardy and high yielding. The catalog turned Luther into a popular hero, and his stature ranked with such greats as Thomas Edison and Henry Ford—Edison and Ford both personally admired Luther and visited him at his home in Santa Rosa.

Luther's plant varieties are legion, and it is difficult to do justice to the breadth and inventiveness of his creations. Varieties such as elephant garlic, plumcot (a cross between a plum and apricot), and the ubiquitous Shasta daisy are still popular today.

Luther had a genius for detecting desirable qualities in young plants and nurturing them into new strains. Having had no formal training, he relied more on intuition than rigorous scientific methodology and employed his unique gifts on a large scale in thousands of simultaneous experiments. At the time of his death in 1926, he had more than 3,000 experiments underway and was growing more than 5,000 species.

Throughout his long career, Luther sought to produce high-quality plant varieties that would help increase the world's food supply. But, more importantly, his work was inspired by a deep love of beauty. "The urge to beauty," he wrote, "and the need for beautiful and gracious and lovely things in life is as vital as the need for bread."

"I firmly believe, from what I have seen, that this is the chosen spot of all this earth as far as Nature is concerned." —Luther Burbank

the life works of Grace Hudson, who painted more than 650 oils, primarily of the local Pomo people. She was already a talented painter when she married ethnologist Dr. John Hudson, and focused her art on Native American subjects. The museum displays Hudson's portraits of Pomos, exhibits of Native American arts and crafts, and changing shows by local artists. Sun House, which shares the site, is a charming Craftsman bungalow that served as the Hudson residence. The museum is open Wednesday through Saturday from 10:00 A.M. to 4:30 P.M. and noon to 4:30 P.M. on Sunday. Tours of the Sun House are offered on the hour, noon to 3:00 P.M.

Held-Poage Memorial Home and Library $
Mendocino County Historical Society,
603 West Perkins Street, Ukiah
(707) 462–6969
www.pacificsites.com

A treasure trove of historical information, the library holds 4,500 books on county, state, and national history. Along with 13,500 historical photographic negatives and microfilms pertaining to Northern California history, the library also offers documents, maps, scrapbooks, genealogies, and more. Researchers from all over the United States contact the society for assistance. All this information is housed in the historic Queen Anne-style Victorian home built in 1903 for William D. Held and Ethel Poage Held, who were dedicated to the collection of archival materials about California. The home is open every day but Sunday from 1:00 to 4:00 P.M. Closed holidays. Donations are welcome.

Pomo Cultural Center $
Marina Drive, Lake Mendocino, Ukiah
(707) 485–8285, (707) 485–8685 (gift shop)

This small museum was built by the Army Corps of Engineers and is operated by the local Coyote Tribal Council. The round shape of the center is modeled on the Pomo ceremonial dance house, where cultural knowledge was passed down through the generations. On display are examples of Pomo basketry, a demonstra-

The Point Arena Lighthouse and Museum overlooks rocky bluffs and the wide sweep of Manchester State Beach along the Mendocino County coastline. PHOTO: JOHN NAGIECKI

tion of clam-shell money-making, and a hands-on exhibit of different animal skins. Admission is free. The museum is open 9:00 A.M. to 5:00 P.M. Wednesday through Sunday, June through October and is closed in winter.

Mendocino County Museum $
400 East Commercial Street, Willits
(707) 459–2736
www.co.mendocino.ca.us/museum

This large, modern museum displays artifacts and interpretations of the cultural history of the county, with a particular focus on local Pomo and Yuki tribes. A fascinating aspect is the collection of oral history interviews from Mendocino citizens. It's open Wednesday through Sunday from 10:00 A.M. to 4:30 P.M. Admission is free, but donations are gladly accepted.

Anderson Valley Historical Society Museum $
Highway 128, 1 mile north of Boonville
(707) 895–3207

In a century-old schoolhouse on the side of the road, this museum showcases Anderson Valley pioneer life. Displays include a sheepshearing shed, a blacksmith shop, Pomo Indian basketry and tools, and antique agricultural and lumber industry equipment. There is also an exhibit devoted to "Boontling," the valley's unique folk dialect. Open Friday through Sunday from 1:00 to 4:00 p.m. When the flag is flying, the museum is open.

Point Arena Lighthouse and Museum $
Lighthouse Road, Point Arena
(707) 882–2777, (877) 725–4448
www.mcn.org/1/palight

The lighthouse, originally built in 1870 and rebuilt after the 1906 earthquake, still shines a warning to keep ships off the dangerous rocks and shoals. The light is now automated, and the old Coast Guard facilities have been turned into a maritime museum, with several guest cottages run by a local nonprofit organization. Visitors may climb the light tower and view the broad terraces that run down to the sea or admire the ancient Fresnel lens that remains in place in the light room at the top. Offshore, scuba divers enjoy the Arena Rock Underwater Preserve, an area of abundant marine flora and fauna, as well as the sunken wreck of a freighter. The lighthouse museum is open daily from 11:00 A.M. to 2:30 P.M. on weekdays and 10:00 A.M. to 3:30 P.M. on summer weekends and holidays. Admission is $4.00 for adults and teens and $1.00 for kids younger than 12.

Greenwood State Park Visitors Center $
Highway 1, Elk
(707) 937–5804
www.mcn.org/1/mendoparks/greenwd.htm

This small history center tells the story of the tiny coastal town of Elk, from its founding by the Greenwood brothers in the late 1800s through its history as a logging and lumber town. Housed in the former L. E. White Lumber Company office—which was in operation from 1884 to 1916—the center includes a large mural depicting how lumber was transported down the steep cliffs to waiting ships. The visitor center is open on Saturdays and Sundays, March through October, from 11:00 A.M. to 1:00 P.M.

Ford House Museum $
735 Main Street, Mendocino
(707) 937–5397

The Ford House, built in 1854, was originally the residence of Mendocino lumber mill owner Jerome Bursley Ford. Today it serves as a museum and visitor center for Mendocino Headlands State Park. This is where to find out everything you need to know for your visit to the charming village of Mendocino and the wild shores off the Headlands. During the whale migrations from January through March, there are docent-led whale-watching walks on Saturday. At the height of the wildflower season in late spring, knowledgeable docents lead walks through a riot of color and tell about the flowers. Ford House is open daily from 11:00 A.M. to 4:00 P.M.

> **Insiders' Tip**
>
> Inside the new Charles M. Schulz Museum is a wall from a Colorado house where the cartoonist briefly lived, on which he painted some of his early cartoon characters in 1951. The artwork was later discovered under layers of paint, and the wall carefully removed and shipped to Santa Rosa in 2002 for display in the museum.

Admission is free, as are the docent walks, though small donations are encouraged.

Kelley House Museum $
45007 Albion Street, Mendocino
(707) 937–5791
www.mendocino.org

The house looks like a home transplanted from a Maine coastal town, a reflection of the fact that many New Englanders did come to Mendocino in earlier times. Its walls display a collection of historic photographs of days when redwood logs were loaded onto waiting ships via chutes and long piers. Displays tell the story of the logging and shipping industries that turned a wild, lonely coast into a thriving, driving city. The house is open Friday through Sunday from 1:00 to 4:00 P.M. during the months September–May. During the summer months it is open daily 1:00 to 4:00 P.M. There is a $2.00 (suggested) admission fee.

Anchor Charters $$$
Noyo Harbor, North Harbor Drive, Fort Bragg
(707) 964–3854
www.anchorcharterboats.com

Once on the endangered species list, the gray whale has made a comeback and can be seen traveling between the Bering Sea and Baja California from late November through late April. Although whales can be seen from shore, it is exciting to board a charter boat and see them directly in the waters they inhabit. Dress for any weather because it can change quickly from sunny and warm to cloudy and cool. Bring along a camera with a telephoto lens, a telescope (just like the old mariners), or a pair of binoculars. Other whale-watching excursions leave from Noyo Harbor as well (see our On the Water chapter). Anchor Charters cruises last approximately two hours and are $25 per person. They also offer fishing excursions for salmon, rock fish, and albacore tuna.

Mendocino Coast Botanical Gardens $
18220 North Highway 1, Fort Bragg
(707) 964–4352
www.gardenbythesea.org

This 47-acre delight is one of only three botanical gardens in the United States sit-uated oceanside. Founded in 1961, the gardens were purchased by grants from the California Coastal Conservancy and have been operated as a nonprofit public trust since 1992. The collections here are divided into garden "rooms" of perennials, rhododendrons (which grow wild in great abundance in this county), heathers, succulents, ivies, fuchsias, dwarf conifers, and other native species. Two creeks flow through the gardens, and more than 3 miles of trails provide easy access to the coast and opportunities for visitors to enjoy and learn about plants and nature.

A favorite haunt of local painters, the grounds include picnic tables tucked in quiet spaces for those who have had the foresight to bring lunch. Two miles south of Fort Bragg, the gardens are open daily from 9:00 A.M. to 5:00 P.M. from March to October and 9:00 A.M. to 4:00 P.M. from November to February. Admission is $6.00 for adults, $5.00 for seniors, $3.00 for children 13 to 17, and $1.00 for kids 6 to 12.

Footlighters Little Theater $$
245 East Laurel Street, Fort Bragg
(707) 964–3806

A Gay Nineties night of family theater since 1943, Footlighter plays are written by the cast and performed by most of the same people year after year. There's a little light can-can, a chance to hiss the villain, and plenty of laughs. The audience sits around tables drinking coffee, beer, or soft drinks and munching on pretzels. The cast makes its own costumes, and nobody is paid. In fact, they pay dues to belong! Performances are every Wednesday and Saturday at 8:00 P.M., Memorial Day to Labor Day.

Triangle Tattoo Museum $
356-B North Main Street, Fort Bragg
(707) 964–8814
www.triangletattoo.com

It's one of only a dozen places in the world dedicated to the documentation and preservation of tattoo history. The museum displays thousands of images of skin art, including those from several different nations and different periods in history. Several color prints of New Zealand's

Fort Bragg's history is expertly displayed at the Guest House Museum, in the historic downtown area of the city. PHOTO: JEAN SAYLOR DOPPENBERG

Maori people show both men and women with the cultural markings called Moko. Other tattoo portraits highlight designs from Borneo, Samoa, Japan, India, Burma, Zaire, and Native American tribes. The museum is open noon to 6:00 P.M. from Sunday through Thursday, noon to 8:00 P.M. on Friday and Saturday. Admission is free. Five tattoo artists are on hand, and international guests have been known to stop by.

Guest House Museum $
343 North Main Street, Fort Bragg
(707) 961–2840

Much of Fort Bragg's history is displayed here. Built entirely of redwood for the Fort Bragg Redwood Company in the 19th century, the building later became the guesthouse for friends and customers of C. R. Johnson, founder of Union Lumber Company. Along with a wonderful collection of photographs and artifacts the museum displays historic equipment such as steam donkeys, rigging blocks, locomotives, and high wheels once used in log harvesting. The museum is open Friday from 1:00 to 4:00 P.M., and Wednesday, Thursday, Saturday, and Sunday from 10:00 A.M. to 4:00 P.M. during summer. Admission is $1.00.

California Western Railroad (Skunk Train) $$$
Laurel Street Depot, Fort Bragg
(707) 964–6371
www.skunktrain.com

Named the Skunk Train by locals who did not enjoy the aroma emitted by the former gas locomotive engines, this pioneering logging railroad connects Fort Bragg on the coast with inland Willits. The 40 miles of serpentine track runs through scenic, dense redwood forests, across more than 30 bridges and trestles, and through two deep mountain tunnels. In 1885 the railroad was established to haul logs to the mill, and it still does today when it's not hauling passengers. Northspur, the halfway point, serves as a picnic stop, where you can relax under redwood trees and enjoy a snack from the outdoor grill. The fare for the full-day round trip is $45 for adults and $25 for children 3 to 17. The half-day trip is $39 for adults, $18 for children, though check on family packages. Reservations are recommended.

Balloons, Planes, and Gondolas

It's hard to find a Wine Country brochure that doesn't include a photo of a multicolored hot-air balloon drifting over vine-scored hills. Somewhere along the way, ballooning became part of the everyday lexicon here. It is a natural fit. Hot-air balloons are splashy, even extravagant, but in a way that celebrates the physical environment rather than tramples it.

The flying machines are quite safe, and most pilots are FAA-certified; feel free to ask about their qualifications when you phone. It is true that balloon pilots have limited control over the direction of their rigs, except on a vertical scale. This means there is always a chance you'll make an unscheduled stop in an open field, but it will likely be a gentle one, and the company's chase team will be right on your heels.

As for capacity, the balloon gondolas accommodate anywhere from 4 to 16 passengers. Those of average size hold 6 to 8 people. Dress in layers when riding in a balloon—the shifts in altitude, the breezes, and the heat from the fire make it hard to predict what level of clothing will be comfortable. And if you are a tall person, be sure to bring a cap—radiant heat from the burner can be unpleasant after an hour or so.

Napa County

Balloons Above the Valley $$$$
5091 Solano Avenue, Napa
(707) 253–2222, (800) GO–HOT–AI(R)
www.balloonrides.com

Launching from a variety of sites near Yountville, this company will take you on a drifting, one-hour flight and throw in a champagne brunch for $175 per person.

The Wine Plane $$$$
P.O. Box 4074, Napa 94558
(707) 747–5533, (888) 779–6600
www.wineplane.com

It had to happen eventually—first there was the Wine Train, now there's the Wine Plane, for the ultimate tour of the air over Wine Country. Jim and Kim Higgins gave up the corporate life in San Francisco to pursue their passions: flying and wine. There's a myriad of flights and prices, starting at $79 per person for a 35-minute tour, to the "Ultimate Sunset" ($199) that includes a prolonged buzz over the Golden Gate and a slow climb over the coast. Most tours include complimentary round-trip BMW livery service from your hotel or favorite winery. The FAA-certified and -inspected aircraft are a Cessna Centurion 210 and a Piper Navajo Chieftain. Jim flies the planes (he's FAA certified too), and Kim is the flight attendant, pouring vino while she acts as tour guide.

Gondola Servizio $$$
Main Street, Napa
(707) 257–8495, (866) 737–8494
www.gondolaservizio.com

With the addition of more tourist attractions in downtown Napa and the beautification project along the Napa River, it was a natural to include—gondolas! Come aboard for a gentle float on the river and experience the art of voga alla Veneziana (Venetian rowing). Your host, Angelino Sandri, will sing songs (in Italian) for special occasions, or love songs for lovers. Prices and duration of trips vary; the least expensive ride is $55 for two—or add extra time, wine, and a picnic meal for about $125. The service was expected to dock in spring 2003 in a new location at Hatt Market near the Napa River Inn, but please call to verify.

Adventures Aloft $$$$
Vintage 1870, Yountville
(707) 944–4408, (800) 944–4408
www.nvaloft.com

Insiders' Tip

Highway 12 (Sonoma Highway), once an old stage road between Sonoma and Santa Rosa, is a state-designated scenic road and is marked as such with signs depicting an orange California poppy on a blue background.

These experienced balloon pilots charge $185 for adults, $150 for youth ages 6 to 16. They will shuttle you to the launch site from anywhere in Napa Valley for no extra charge, with coffee and pastries served upon arrival and a sparkling wine breakfast afterward. You have the option of helping to blow up the balloons (no, your cheeks won't get tired) before your one-hour flight. Reservations are required.

Napa Valley Balloons, Inc. $$$$
P.O. Box 2860, Yountville 94599
(707) 944–0228, (800) 253–2224
www.napavalleyballoons.com

This is a scenic ride before you ever leave the ground. The company launches from Domaine Chandon at dawn, after a continental breakfast. Postflight, you get a champagne brunch at Napa Valley Grille and a color photo of the occasion. In between you'll spend an hour in the air (three to five hours for the entire experience). Meet the van at the southwest corner of Washington Square. It costs $175 per person. Reservations are required.

Bonaventura Balloon Company $$$$
Rancho Caymus Inn, 1145 Rutherford Cross Road, Rutherford
(707) 944–2822, (800) FLY–NAPA
www.bonaventuraballoons.com

Bonaventura works "the heart of the valley," from Oakville to St. Helena. The balloons take off at sunrise and stay aloft for 60 to 90 minutes. The company never rushes a flight (only one per balloon each day) and never puts more than six people in the basket. The price, $165 to $195 per person, includes breakfast at either Rancho Caymus or Meadowood Resort.

Sonoma County

Aerostat Adventures $$$$
P.O. Box 2082, Healdsburg 95448
(707) 433–3777, (800) 579–0183
www.aerostat-adventures.com

Aerostat enjoys an exclusive launch site out of the Rodney Strong vineyards near Healdsburg. The location affords spectacular views of the Dry Creek Valley, Alexander Valley, and Russian River wine regions. Upon touchdown, passengers can look forward to a big champagne brunch. Cost of the flight and brunch is $195.

Air Flambuoyant $$$$
250 Pleasant Avenue, Santa Rosa
(707) 838–8700, (800) 456–4711
www.airflambuoyant.com

This is the largest and most experienced family-owned balloon company in North America, flying since 1974. Their specialty is small groups, though they also take large groups.

The flight lasts one hour, followed by a grand breakfast. Flights depart early to take advantage of favorable early-morning weather conditions. They leave from the Healdsburg area and fly over the wine valleys of Dry Creek and Russian River. Flights are individually planned and start at $175 per person. Ask about group packages and special offers.

Tours

Napa County

Napa Valley Holidays $$$$
(707) 255–1050
www.napavalleyholidays.com

Eli and Laura Glick's company customizes tours for parties of any size. Napa Valley Holidays' basic fee is $350 for two people, and that's an all-day commitment—perhaps four to six wineries, lunch, and an on-board docent brimming with behind-the-scenes information and anecdotes. The Glicks also are happy to help visitors with recommendations and reservations for dinner, spas, and the like.

Napa Valley Bike Tours $$$
4080 Byway E., Napa
(707) 255-3377, (800) 707-BIKE
www.napavalleybiketours.com

You feel the breeze, you burn the calories, but someone else wrestles with the logistics. Sound all right? These winery tours begin at 9:30 A.M., end about 3:00 P.M., and cost $95 per person. Along with a bicycle and helmet, you'll get a fully catered picnic, a friendly guide, and a support van to lug bottles of wine (and bodies of worn-out riders). Group size is limited to 10 to ensure safety and individual attention. You can also arrange half-day group tours of 10 to 40 cyclists for $65 per person. Napa Valley Bike Tours also rents cycles by the hour ($7.00) and day ($22.00)—tandems run $12.00 and $38.00.

Wine & Dine Tours $$$$
345 La Fata Street, Suite D, St. Helena
(707) 963-8930, (800) WINE-TOU(R)
www.wineanddinetour.com

A full-service company? Wine & Dine does everything but brush your teeth for you. In addition to guided tours, they handle restaurant reservations, accommodations, ground and air transportation, corporate meetings and event planning, balloon flights, spa treatments, and golf—for any number from 2 to 2,000. A typical day tour might include transportation, tours, and tastings at three wineries and an elegant lunch at one of the wineries. Rates vary, but figure on $400 total for a car (1 to 6 people) plus $45 per person for lunch.

Napa Valley Tours and Trail Hikes $$$
315 Clark Way, Angwin
(707) 965-2000, (800) 964-4142
www.napanet.net/tourism/tours/nvtth

These folks give you no shortage of options for getting outdoors and getting informed in Napa. They not only do winery tours but also offer an overlook hike with a gourmet picnic lunch and a Mount St. Helena hike. They now offer van service to the peak too. Small backpacks are

provided, but it's up to you to wear sensible shoes. Tours range from $79 for a half-day winery circuit to $198 for an all-day, one-on-one trek.

Destination: Napa Valley Tours $$$
295 West Lane, Angwin
(707) 965-1808
www.tournapavalley.com

If your tastes are more highbrow than hedonistic, this might be the package for you. Destination: Napa Valley Tours offers chauffeur-driven private tours of wineries, but goes far beyond that to incorporate local lore and wine industry history. Prices for a full-day experience range from $65 to $100 per person, depending upon location of pickup and return. (They'll go all the way to San Francisco to get you.)

Getaway Adventures & Bike Shop $$$$
1117 Lincoln Avenue, Calistoga
(707) 942-0332, (800) 499-BIKE
www.getawayadventures.com

Getaway will rent you a bicycle anytime you drop in, but they can do a lot more than that upon request. They do winery tours: six varied wineries, a champagne cellar visit, and a shady picnic lunch for $89 (which includes basic tasting fees). They conduct an all-day Mount St. Helena extreme: a 4,000-foot, off-road descent for $89. And they even arrange kayak trips: Lake Berryessa, Lake Hennessy, or the Russian River for $109.

Sonoma County

Bikeman Bicycle Touring $$$$
18503 Sonoma Highway, Sonoma
(707) 938-0453, (888) 525-0453
www.bikemantours.com

Bikeman offers daily guided Wine Country bicycle tours for beginning and intermediate cyclists, with stops at several outstanding wineries in the Sonoma and Kenwood areas. Every rider is supplied with a new 21-speed mountain bike and helmet, and a van shuttle is on hand to carry winery booty or to give weary cyclists a lift. Rates (including an elegant catered lunch) are $89 per person. Tours run from 10:30 A.M. to 3:30 P.M., Monday through Saturday.

Carriage Occasions $$$$
530 Irwin Lane, Santa Rosa
(707) 546–2568
www.thebridalpath.com

Limousines and antique cars simply not ostentatious enough for you? How about a horse-drawn carriage? This company will meet you in Napa, Sonoma, or Alexander Valley and customize a two- to three-hour winery tour. Prices vary from town to town. You must book in advance.

Festivals and Annual Events

In Wine Country, every season brings its share of gala events. From January to December, there's always some kind of music, food, or farm celebration going on. In autumn, we have the "crush" and a slew of harvest fairs, and when spring blossoms begin to appear—whether apple, pear, or the venerated mustard blossom—we salute them in grand style.

Wineries play a major role in this celebratory milieu, sponsoring concerts and other major cultural events. Their lovely courtyards, grand estate lawns, and unique wine caves are some of the best places to listen to music, whether it's a symphony, chamber music, or jazz.

We couldn't possibly list all the festivals and events that occur throughout the year. We've selected some of our favorites to get you started. For more information, check with the local chambers of commerce listed in our Area Overview chapter.

January

Sonoma County

Sonoma Valley Olive Festival
Various locations, Sonoma
(707) 996–1090
www.olivefestival.com

In case you didn't know, we grow lots of olives in Wine Country (see our Close-up "Our Other Nectar" in our Shopping chapter). So holding a shindig to salute the mighty olive seemed like a natural thing to do. The First Annual Sonoma Valley Olive Festival took place during winter 2001–2002, with a variety of oil tastings, special dinners, demonstrations of olives being turned into oil, a visual arts contest with olives as the theme, and more. The Feast of the Olive and Founders Dinner is the most expensive event, at $150 per person; the remaining festivities vary in price. The whole affair begins in early December and ends in late February.

Old-Time Fiddle Contest
Cloverdale Fairgrounds, 1 Citrus Fair Drive, Cloverdale
(707) 894–9550
www.cloverdale.net/visit/fiddleco.htm

Sixty or more contestants, novice to pro, gather at the fairgrounds on Citrus Fair Drive for an old-fashioned fiddling contest. But some of the best action is not on the stage; it's in a side room where curious visitors can look in on some wild, free-form jamming. This free event is sponsored by the Cloverdale Historic Society on the fourth Saturday of January. The indoor event usually draws a festive crowd of about 1,200. The 2002 contest was the 27th annual.

Mendocino County

Mendocino Crab & Wine Days
Various locations, Mendocino County
(800) 726–2780, (800) 466–3636
www.mendocinocoast.com,
www.gomendo.com

This is a 10-day festival in late January dedicated to our two favorite delicacies: premium wine and Dungeness crab. You can count on a series of winemaker dinners, cooking classes, and various crab-and-wine tastings up and down the Mendocino coastline. There's also Crab Louie lunches, Dungeness crab specials nightly at most area restaurants, commercial crabbing demonstrations, and a crab-cake cook-off in the village of Mendocino. Bibs optional.

February

Napa County

Mustard Magic
The Culinary Institute of America
at Greystone, 2555 Main Street, St. Helena
(707) 259-9020
www.mustardfestival.org

This grand fête officially launches the annual Napa Valley Mustard Festival on a Saturday in late January or early February. The focus is on the arts, including an exhibition and silent auction of entries in the Mustard Festival Fine Art Contest. Other pleasantries include hors d'oeuvres and desserts created by prominent local chefs, ultrapremium wine tastings, and music (live opera in 2000). Admission to Mustard Magic is $75 to $95 in advance, $125 at the door.

Blessing of the Balloons
Domaine Chandon, 1 California Drive,
Yountville
(707) 944-8793

Only seven or eight balloons usually ascend to mark the first weekend of the Mustard Festival, but the Blessing draws anywhere from 200 to 400 people. You must convince yourself to leave your warm and cozy B&B pretty darn early to catch the action, which begins at 6:45 A.M., but it's worth it.

Chocolate Cabernet Fantasy
Sterling Vineyards, 1111 Dunaweal Lane,
Calistoga
(707) 942-0680

Looking for a little decadence? Nero might have been attracted to this three-hour get-together off Dunaweal Lane, about 2 miles south of Calistoga. The Soroptimists fix the desserts (mostly chocolate), Sterling donates its renowned Cabs, and you take care of the rest. There is dance music too. The Fantasy is held on a Friday or Saturday night around Valentine's Day. Tickets are $20, with all proceeds going to charity.

Sonoma County

Japanese Cultural Festival
Rohnert Park Community Center, Snyder Lane and Rohnert Park Expressway, Rohnert Park
(707) 584-4851

Spend the first Saturday in February immersing yourself in the culture of the Japanese courtesy of the City of Rohnert Park. Practice the art of paper-folding known as origami, listen to taiko drummers, and observe the formal, elaborate, ancient art of the tea ceremony. It happens at the city community center, and it's all free except for food booths and trinket vendors.

Citrus Fair
Cloverdale Fairgrounds, 1 Citrus Fair Drive, Cloverdale
(707) 894-3992
www.cloverdale.net/citrusfa/citrusfa.htm

Here's how to brighten up winter. On the weekend nearest President's Day, the citizens of Cloverdale come together in a jolly event organized by the Citrus Fair Association. It starts off with a downtown parade then moves out to the fairgrounds, with square dancing, country-western dancing, line dancing, and regular dancing. There is a carnival for young people and beer tasting and wine tasting for grownups. On Sunday you can attend a concert by a popular western music group such as Smokin' Armadillo. Admission is $6.00 for adults, $3.00 for seniors and kids ages 6 to 12.

Mendocino County

St. Mary's Mardi Gras
Redwood Empire Fairgrounds, 1055 State Street, Ukiah
(707) 462-3888
www.redwoodempirefair.com

For Ukiah, it's the biggest money-raising event of the year, a two-day celebration on a weekend in mid-February that raises money for St. Mary's Elementary School. On Saturday night there's a dinner and dance held at Carl Purdy Hall at the fairgrounds, with live music by one of the local bands. But Sunday is given over to family fun, with carnival rides and game booths for children. For adults, a wine auction gives bidders a chance to vie for bottles of the vintners' best or for weekend getaways contributed by hotels or resorts. Entrance to the event is free; carnival tickets cost varying amounts.

March

Napa County

Mustard on the Silverado Trail
Various locations
(800) 686–6272
www.mustardfestival.org

The wine producers that line Napa Valley's "other" north-south artery, the Silverado Trail, demand overdue attention on a weekend in early March. About 15 wineries—including Mumm Napa Valley, Round Hill, Rutherford Hill, Sterling, and ZD (see our Wineries chapter)—go above and beyond the call of duty, offering special tours, wine-and-food pairings, entertainment, barrel tastings, and so forth. It's a great way to familiarize yourself with the "quiet side" of the valley, and it's free of charge. The two-day open house series is part of the Mustard Festival.

Napa Valley Classic Irish Festival
Kolbe Academy, 1600 F Street, Napa
(707) 255–6412
www.kolbe.org

Nobody dyes the Napa River green for St. Patrick's Day, but the folks at Kolbe Academy (see our Education chapter) do a fine job of celebrating from 2:00 to 5:00 P.M. on an afternoon near the holiday. Food, including wine and ales, is inside the school. The entertainment is in the yard (weather permitting), and includes bagpipes, singing, and traditional Irish dancing. Figure on $25 for adults, $15 for children ages 4 to 12. This is the academy's one major fundraiser each year.

The Awards
Various locations
(707) 259–9020
www.mustardfestival.org

Lest your springtime excursions begin to convince you that mustard is merely a treat for the eyes, here is an evening that pits Napa Valley's best chefs in a spread-off. Guests get to taste the entries, along with food and wine. There is live music as well. The event, which moves each year and costs $75 in advance ($100 at the door), is held the night before The Marketplace (see next listing).

The Marketplace
Napa Valley Exposition, 575 Third Street, Napa
(707) 259–9020
www.mustardfestival.org

This is the Mustard Festival's signature event. The Exposition's halls and open spaces come alive with cooking demonstrations by celebrity chefs, wine and mustard tastings, gourmet food products, microbrews, fine art, local crafts, horse-drawn carriage rides, eclectic musical offerings on three stages, historical displays, and barrel-making demonstrations. It's a two-day event (11:00 A.M. to 5:00 P.M. both days) on a weekend in mid-March. Admission is $7.00 for adults, $2.00 for children 12 or younger. Net proceeds benefit a wide range of nonprofit groups.

A Taste of Yountville
Washington Street, Yountville
(707) 944–0904
www.mustardfestival.org

Come on down! Yountville likes to boast that it has "more gourmet restaurants and premium wineries than any other town of comparable size." So on the third weekend in March, the hamlet sets up a solid-mile gauntlet of food, olive oil, vinegar, mustard, wine, and beer for the sampling public to prove it. Local merchants get into the act with fashion shows, tours, furniture restoration displays, and even tips on table setting. Most demonstrations are free, and tasting tickets are reasonable (around $1.00). Even if you are beyond temptation, it might be worth your time to stroll the 6 blocks through downtown just to hear the live music and watch the entertainment. This is a Mustard Festival event.

The Photo Finish
Mumm Napa Valley, 8445 Silverado Trail, Rutherford
(707) 259–9020
www.mustardfestival.org
With this grand finale, the Mustard Festival usually leaves 'em longing for more as it heads into hibernation for a year. Mumm's hallways and visitor center are filled with lovers of photography, food, wine, and music (doesn't leave many of us out, does it?) on the last Saturday in March or the first in April. The food is by Napa Valley chefs, the wine is primarily from Silverado Trail labels, and the camera work is by the contestants in the annual Napa Valley Mustard Festival Photography Contest. Awards are presented in the tasting room at about 9:00 P.M. Tickets to the Photo Finish cost $65 in advance or $75 at the door.

Sonoma County

Russian River Barrel Tasting
Alexander, Dry Creek, and Russian River Valleys
(800) 723–6336
www.wineroad.com
This annual event sponsored by the Russian River Wine Road Association is a weekend festival of tasting, entertainment, and viticulture education. The tasting focuses on unreleased wines from wineries located in the Alexander, Dry Creek, and Russian River Valleys, offering participants the opportunity to taste

wines straight from the barrel and to purchase "futures." And it's free.

Mendocino County

Whale Festivals
Mendocino and Fort Bragg
(707) 961–6300, (800) 726–2780
www.mendocinocoast.com
One of the best reasons to visit the Mendocino Coast in winter is to watch the gray whales cut through the choppy seas during their annual migration, a 12,000-mile round trip from the Arctic Circle to Baja California. It's a cause for celebration, and there are festivals in two cities— in Mendocino the first weekend in March and in Fort Bragg on the third weekend— to welcome the migrating mammals. Whale-watching cruises set out from Noyo Harbor (various prices). There's music, marine art exhibits, discussions about whales at state parks, and samplings of wine, beer, and chowder all over the towns (pay as you taste) and more.

April

Napa County

April in Carneros
Various locations
(707) 938–5906, (800) 825–9475
www.carneroswineries.org
The Carneros area, in the bay-cooled hills between Sonoma and Napa, has emerged as the Wine Country's next great appellation. You can judge for yourself over one weekend in mid-April, when 20 or more wineries open their doors and stage special events. About a quarter of the participating producers are normally open by appointment only, and others don't even have proper wineries there—guests are welcomed instead to production facilities. New vintages are released, accompanied by barrel tastings, food pairings, music, and even cigar-smoking demonstrations (inhaling optional). Maps are distributed at the open houses, and there is no charge for attending. The circuit tends to be less crowded on Sunday.

Kitchens in the Vineyards Tour
Various locations
(707) 578–5656, (707) 967–0835
www.napavalleymusic.com

The emphasis is on food during this all-day affair in late April or early May that gives you a peek into one-of-a-kind kitchens, dining rooms, and gardens from Yountville to St. Helena. The event benefits Music in the Vineyards' Chamber Music Festival held in August. Tickets are $40 in advance, $45 the day of the tour.

Sonoma County

Sheepshearing at the Adobe
Petaluma Adobe State Park, 3325 Adobe Road, Petaluma
(707) 762–4871
www.petaluma.org

On a Saturday in mid-April, 4-H'ers and docents gather at the adobe building that was once the ranch home of General Vallejo (see our History chapter) to demonstrate the arts of wool cleaning, weaving, and sheep-shearing. It's all done to pay homage to an age-old craft. Looms are available for those who want to try their hand at the craft. Bring along a picnic and make a day of it. There's no charge for the event, but park admission is $3.00 per adult ($2.00 for ages 6 to 12).

Butter and Egg Days
Various locations, Petaluma
(707) 762–2785
www.petaluma.org

Petaluma celebrates its storied past through this popular event. Once known as the world's egg basket, Petaluma is now largely dairy country, thus the hometown Butter and Egg Days parade. This includes an egg toss in downtown and a parade of marching bands and (best of all) residents dressed as chickens and pats of butter. The "Cutest Little Chick in Town" contest adds to the fun. It all happens the last complete weekend in April, and there are also food booths, other entertainment, and an antiques fair.

Apple Blossom Festival
Various locations, Sebastopol
(877) 828–4748
www.sebastopol.net

It's a weekend in April, and it's a salute to the apple and its snow-white blooms. Festivities include the crowning of the Apple Blossom Queen, a mile-long parade down Main Street, and two days of good time partying with plenty of blues, country, and gospel music. There's an art show, crafts made by local artisans, and plenty of products made from apples. The festival is sponsored by the local chamber of commerce, and events are held in Ives Park (282 High Street) and at the Veterans Memorial Building next door. Admission is $5.00 for adults, $2.00 for seniors and children ages 11 to 17.

Bodega Bay Fishermen's Festival
Westside Park, Bodega Bay
(707) 875–3422
www.bodegabay.com

This annual event takes place at Westside Park during a weekend in April. It features foot races, the Blessing of the Fleet, a boat parade, and a bathtub race that includes tubs crafted out of anything that floats—from Styrofoam to milk cartons. Directions to the park are well-posted. A $3.00 donation is requested.

May

Napa County

MaiFest
Napa County Fairgrounds, 1435 North Oak Street, Calistoga
(707) 942–5356
www.napacountyfairgrounds.com

Upvalley's wurst festival is one of its best. Watch traditional German folk dancing. Sway to the soothing oom-pah-pah of Ottmar Stubler and His Pretzel Benders. More to the point, eat and drink in the robust style of Bavaria. Spaten is the most-requested brew at this all-day Saturday event in late April or early May, though Napa Valley Brewing Company offers its competent lineup of microbrews along with three or four wineries. Tickets are $10 in advance, $12 at the gate. Food and beverages are extra (though reasonable), as are raffle tickets. First prize is two round-trip airline tickets from San Francisco to Munich. MaiFest bankrolls a scholarship fund for Calistoga High School.

Hidden Gardens Tour
Various locations
(707) 255–1836, (888) 255–1836
www.napacountylandmarks.org
This is an organized, go-at-your-own-pace afternoon walking tour of pocket gardens and historic homes on a weekend in May or June. Explorers hit about 10 gardens, and then enjoy an outdoor reception. It costs $20.00 on tour day. If you buy tickets in advance, it's $8.00 for members of Napa County Landmarks and $15.00 for non-members. Landmarks also offers self-guided walking tours on 10 Saturdays between May and September. Call for details.

Merlot in May—International Merlot Conference
Sterling Vineyards, 1111 Dunaweal Lane, Calistoga
(707) 255–7667, (800) 709–7667
www.sterlingvineyards.com
This conference featuring Merlot producers from around the world is now open to the public (over 21 only, please). If Merlot is your drink, you'll be in heaven. Sample a huge array of the red stuff from as many as 50 producers during a two-hour afternoon consumer tasting. Tickets are $25 and sold in advance only.

Picnic Day
Fuller Park, Napa
(707) 253–0376
On the Friday before Memorial Day, normally serene Fuller Park becomes a squirming, squealing square full of toddlers and preschoolers. Community Resources for Children sponsors this free event. There is ice cream and oodles of activities and games, from face-painting to bubble-blowing to lamb-petting. To get to Fuller Park from Highway 29, take the Downtown Napa exit (Second Street), turn right at Jefferson Street, and proceed 2 blocks.

Sonoma County

Luther Burbank Rose Festival and Parade
Various locations, Santa Rosa
(707) 545–1414
www.lutherburbank.org
Find a spot along Santa Rosa's streets on a mid-May weekend to watch a parade that dates back to 1894 and now draws more than 20,000 people. Floats created with thousands of roses are the highlight of the parade, which begins in front of Burbank's home on Santa Rosa Avenue and winds its way through town to the Veterans Memorial Building. The event honors the world-famous horticulturist who improved 800 plant varieties, including the Santa Rosa rose, while living in Santa Rosa (see our Attractions chapter). Other festival events take place at various sites in the downtown area and include street fair exhibits, food booths, performances by singing groups, carnival rides, folk dancing, an antiques fair, a firefighter's competition, and displays of firefighting equipment. There's an awards ceremony to honor the best of the parade floats.

Sonoma Country Fair and Twilight Parade
Various locations, Healdsburg
(707) 431–7644
www.sonomacountyfair.com
Scheduled for the last weekend in May, this is the longest-running event in Healdsburg and the only fair in California that's nonprofit. The Future Farmers of America sponsor this event, in which everything's free except the food. There's a parade on Thursday, a livestock show and auction on Friday, and kids' activities on Saturday. Food and game booths are run by local youth organizations.

Mendocino County

Willits Celtic Renaissance
Lenore Street S., Willits
(707) 459-7910
www.renaissance-faire.com

The Celtic Faire is a throwback to 16th-century Scotland. For two days on the third weekend in May, Recreation Grove is filled with guild booths, where vendors dressed in period costume sell jewelry, swords, and weaponry of a bygone era. The event draws some 1,500 people a day to live Scottish life as it was 400 years ago and to enjoy events where javelins are hurled and water balloons catapulted. Jugglers juggle, and wenches walk about selling tidbits of food. The money collected goes for scholarships for local high school students on their way to college. Admission is $6.00 for adults, $3.00 for seniors and free for kids younger than 12.

Great Rubber Ducky Race
Wages Creek, Westport
(707) 964-2872
www.mendocinocoast.com

Westport is the northernmost town on the Mendocino Coast. It's isolated, and the residents like it that way. But the locals have a sense of humor, proven by their annual Great Rubber Ducky Race. It takes place on Mother's Day and is held on the wide, white sand beaches of Wages

Insiders' Tip

The men-only Bohemian Grove encampment of some of the world's most powerful leaders and household names, held annually in west Sonoma County near Monte Rio, was lampooned in a 2002 film called *Teddy Bear's Picnic*—the creation of actor/comedy writer Harry Shearer.

Creek just north of the town. Anyone who wants to enter can simply bring a rubber ducky from home (some people fancy them up a bit), launch it in the creek and wait to see how long it takes to float downstream to meet the ocean. Meanwhile, the barbecue coals are lighted (the menu is beef, not duck). Everyone is cool and laid back, watching the clouds float across the blue sky and keeping an eye on the fleet of ducks bobbing downstream.

The event is organized by the Westport Village Society to preserve the headlands as open space. The sunshine is free; race entry combined with the beef dinner is $10.

June

Napa County

Napa Valley Wine Auction
at Meadowood Napa Valley
900 Meadowood Lane, St. Helena
(707) 942-9775, (800) 982-1371
www.napavintners.org

Napa Valley's glitziest annual event, not to mention one of the nation's eminent charity auctions, takes place the first Thursday-through-Sunday block in June (see our Close-up in this chapter). Thursday features barrel tastings followed by gatherings organized by local vintners, such as intimate Thursday-night dinners or Friday luncheons. Saturday's live and silent auctions set world records, with astronomical bids for the most coveted of beverages (in 2000, a collector paid $500,000 for a single imperial of wine, a 1992 Screaming Eagle Cabernet Sauvignon). On Sunday, most Napa Valley wineries have open houses. All this, and more, for just $2,500 per couple.

Berryessa Lions Annual Lizard Races
Pleasure Cove, Lake Berryessa
(707) 966-2172

People can get pretty hot-blooded watching these cold-blooded creatures scamper across indoor-outdoor carpet on the first Saturday in June. Show up with a blue-bellied lizard and a feather and you, too, can enter the fray. (The feather is to be used only if your racer stalls.) There is no entrance fee, and the champions leave with nothing more than blue ribbons. Lizard "owners" are divided by age group, giving the adults a chance to win too. You reach Pleasure Cove via Highway 128—about 5 miles east of Highway 121, turn left on Wragg Canyon Road.

Vintage 1870 Father's Day Invitational Auto Show
Vintage 1870, 6525 Washington Street, Yountville
(707) 944-2451
www.vintage1870.com

When Dad begins to rebel against loud ties and cheap cologne, take him to a car show for Father's Day. The north parking lot of Vintage 1870 will be double-parked with 85 to 90 cars—from Vipers to DeSoto Coupes and from a 1939 Packard limousine to a boss old Woody. While you examine the cars, you can eat, drink (everything from Calistoga water to margaritas), and listen to music. The show runs from 11:00 A.M. to 4:00 P.M. and is free to the public, excluding food.

Wine Country Kennel Club
Napa Valley Exposition, 575 Third Street, Napa
(707) 253-4900
www.infodog.com

The dog days of summer start a little early in Napa—on a weekend in late June, to be exact. That's when some 2,000 well-groomed pooches strut around the halls and grounds of the Exposition. There are separate shows on Saturday and Sunday, each from 8:00 A.M. until about 6:00 P.M. There are eight age-and-experience classes (including two puppy classes) and seven dog groups: sporting, hound-working, terrier, toy, nonsporting, herding, and miscellaneous breeds. The animals vie for points, ribbons, trophies, and the ever-popular pat on the head. There is no charge to spectators. The Lions Club provides food, including a pancake breakfast.

Beringer Celebrity Golf Classic
Chardonnay Golf Club, 2555 Jamieson Canyon Road, Napa
(707) 255-0950

Tired of being ignored as you scream at televised sporting events? The last Wednesday in June is your chance to bend the ear of a famous athlete or coach. Bay Area luminaries such as Jim Plunkett, Bill Walsh, and Vida Blue have been spotted at recent Beringer Classics. Corporate groups pay a $1,500 entry fee; individuals pay $375 (just $300 if they don't feel the need to be paired with a big shot). It's expensive, yes, but the price includes a pregolf dinner at Beringer. More important, the event funds about half the annual athletic program at Justin-Siena High School, the only Catholic high school in Napa County.

Sonoma County

Ox Roast
Sonoma Plaza, Sonoma
(707) 938-4626
www.sonomavalley.com

For more than 30 years, the first Sunday in June has been marked by aromatic smoke rising from the town's central plaza. The annual Ox Roast is one giant picnic with barbecued beef, corn on the cob, and plenty of beer and wine. You'll pay $3.00 to $9.00 for the meal (beer and wine are extra, and there's also a vegetarian plate), and it all goes to benefit the local community center.

Health and Harmony Music and Arts Festival
Sonoma County Fairgrounds, Santa Rosa
(707) 547-9355
www.harmonyfestival.com

For more than two decades, loyal throngs of locals have been buying hemp clothing, eyeing belly dancers, and pounding the drums of world-beat music at this Sonoma County institution. For some, the annual affair in mid-June is like returning to the hippie days of 1967—but the hippies all sport gray ponytails these days. There's always plenty of free music on several stages (Jefferson Starship one year, for example) and a huge number of vendors selling everything from holistic health products to Indian cottons. Be sure to check out the Eco Village, where everything is solar-powered. Women have their own place to hang out—the Goddess temple, featuring female performers and themes. Admission is about $20 in advance, $25 at the door.

Cloverdale Heritage Days
124 South Cloverdale Boulevard, Cloverdale
(707) 894–4470
www.cloverdale.net

The citizens of Cloverdale close off the main boulevard of town once each year to celebrate the memory of days past. Events include wine tasting, cow-chip tossing (the local Boys & Girls Club collects the cow chips), a Gold Rush foot race, and a barbecue from 5:00 to 7:00 P.M. There's also country music and dancing outdoors on the plaza. It's all free except the food.

Stumptown Daze
Main Street and Rodeo Grounds, Guerneville
(877) 644–9001
www.russianriver.com

This is a great treat for Dad on Father's Day weekend. A parade, with school bands and preschool kids on bikes, starts at 11:00 A.M. Saturday and follows a route that's subject to local politics, so you might want to call in advance to find out where to park your folding chair. After the parade everyone heads over to the town of Duncans Mills, about 6 miles west of Guerneville on Highway 116. At 2:00 P.M. the rodeo starts, with all those events you expect—calf roping, bull riding, and barrel racing. On Sunday there's more free rodeo, and some horseback games. Where'd the name originate? Guerneville gained the moniker "Stumptown" in its early days when redwood trees were mercilessly chopped down, leaving only a forest of stumps.

Mendocino County

Spring Carnival
Redwood Empire Fairgrounds, 1055 North State Street, Ukiah
(707) 462–3884
www.redwoodempirefair.com

It's free to enter the gates to the spring fair, held the first weekend in June each year. Entrance to the carnival field is also free, with varying prices for individual thrill rides. Grandstand shows are held Friday and Saturday afternoons from 2:00 P.M. on and feature motor sports events such as stock car races. Admission to the grandstand is $10.00 to $12.00, and kids 10 and younger pay $8.00 to $10.00.

July

Napa County

Napa County Fair
Napa County Fairgrounds, 1435 North Oak Street, Calistoga
(707) 942–5111
www.napacountyfairgrounds.com

This brouhaha (during the Fourth of July weekend) features plenty of wine to taste, but there are also the usual assortment of carnival rides, livestock exhibits, arts and crafts, and cavity-creating snacks. The fair also includes one or two nights of sprint car racing and two nights of concerts, with recent headliners such as country heavyweights LeAnn Rimes, Toby Keith, and Faith Hill. Admission is $5.00 for adults; $2.00 for kids ages 6 to 12. Two separate events—the Miss Napa County Fair Pageant and the Champagne Art Preview—are held on the eve of the fair.

Fourth of July Celebrations
Napa (707) 257–9529
Calistoga (707) 942–6333

Veterans Park is the gathering place for a slew of activity in Napa, including food, carnival games, and wine tasting. Since 1995 the patriotism has expanded to include eight hours of music at the park by a lineup of five or six bands.

Serving as interlude to the Napa County Fair is a sublime slice of Americana. People come from miles around for Calistoga's annual Silverado Parade, placing lawn chairs along the route hours in advance. Past parades have featured the sparkling rigs of the volunteer fire department, horsemen, bikers, clowns, a kazoo corps, and floats ranging from sweet to absurd. The procession starts at 11:00 A.M. You do not want to miss it.

Bastille Day
Domaine Chandon, 1 California Drive,
Yountville
(707) 944–8844, (707) 944–2280
www.dchandon.com

More than 200 years after the fact, what does the revolutionary capture of Paris's most infamous prison mean to Napa Valley tourists? Party! French bands play folk songs or classic Parisian cafe music from 11:00 A.M. to 6:00 P.M., and the visitor center staff dresses up "French style." That phrase is interpreted liberally, so you have an equal chance of being greeted by a slinky French maid, Louis XIV, or a two-legged poodle. There is no admission fee, and you can "liberate" sparkling wine by the glass or bottle for the going rate.

Napa Valley Shakespeare Festival
Riverbend Performance Plaza, Hatt Mill,
500 Main Street, Napa
(707) 251–WILL
www.napashakespeare.org

To be or not to be … the question is, "Which night shall we attend?" The Bard's most popular works (and the creations of other notable playwrights) are performed over four weekends, beginning the weekend after the Fourth of July, on Friday through Sunday nights at 7:00 P.M. In 2002, *As You Like It* and *Othello* were presented. Tickets run about $18 for adults and $14 for seniors, students, and children under 12.

Meadowood Croquet Classic
Meadowood Napa Valley, 900 Meadowood Lane, St. Helena
(707) 963–3646, (800) 458–8080

This is no carefree backyard play day. Members of the U.S. Croquet Association flock to Meadowood in late July for a week of serious mallet-wielding. Guests at the resort may watch the preliminary competition for no charge during the week. On Saturday comes the finale: the championship round plus an auction (for charity) and an early-evening gourmet dinner. It's an elegant affair, with some 200 diners attired in natty whites and seated adjacent to the croquet courts. The finale package costs upward of $100 per person. During the rest of the year, Meadowood croquet pro Jerry Stark gives lessons in this rarefied sport of kings—ranging from $25 to $35 an hour.

Sonoma County

Old-Fashioned Fourth of July Celebration
Sonoma Plaza
(707) 938–4626
www.sonomavalley.com

You'd think someone rolled back the clock a few decades to see how Sonoma celebrates Independence Day. In fact, some Insiders say the Fourth of July is their favorite holiday here. Arrive early for a good place to watch the 10:00 A.M. parade that circles the Sonoma Plaza. After the parade, townsfolk assemble in the plaza for more band music, the singing of the national anthem, a patriotic speech, and the presentation of awards for parade entrants. Locals laze around the rest of the day, then reassemble at nightfall for the big finale—a fireworks display put on by the city fire department (partially funded by an appreciative public) in a large field next to the Vallejo Home.

World Pillow Fighting Championships
Plaza Park, Warm Springs Road, Kenwood
(707) 833–2440
www.kenwoodpillowfights.com

Like to get wet and muddy in front of hundreds of cheering onlookers? Approaching its 40th year, this annual event brings out a special breed of human—brave men and women who face each other one-on-one while straddling a slippery metal pole suspended over a mud pit. The opponents then vigorously swing pillows at one another. The one left on the pole is the winner. The men generally outnumber the women, but you can count on about 100 contestants. It's good, clean (well, sort of) fun on the Fourth of July that also includes a hometown parade, live bands, kids' activities, and plenty of food and drink. Admission is $5.00 for adults; free for children 12 and under.

Salute to the Arts
Sonoma Plaza
(707) 938-1133
www.salutetothearts.com

On the third or fourth weekend in July, the entire Sonoma Plaza in the heart of town is transformed into an elegant, lively outdoor setting, featuring five stages filled with theater troupe performances and a variety of music and dance. Fine art by Sonoma Valley artists, children's activities, and the best in local cuisine, wine, and handcrafted beers are available. Admission to the festival is free. Tickets for food and wine may be purchased for $1.00 per taste, or you can employ various package prices that include a souvenir wine glass and plate.

Fort Ross Living History Days
Fort Ross State Park, north of Jenner
(707) 847-3286
www.parks.sonoma.net/fortross.html

On the last Saturday in July, some 100 volunteers and staff participants don period attire and reenact a typical day at Fort Ross in the mid-1800s, during the days of Russian settlement when the commandant and his wife lived elegantly in the wilderness surroundings (see our History chapter). Bring a picnic! Coastal weather is unpredictable, so also pack a sun hat and warm clothes. Admission is $3.00 per vehicle.

Sonoma County Fair
Sonoma County Fairgrounds, 1350 Bennett Valley Road, Santa Rosa
(707) 545-4203
www.sonomacountyfair.com

This two-week event begins the last week in July and features carnival rides, a flower show, horse racing, livestock competitions, and a wide array of food and other vendors. This fair is a long-standing Sonoma County institution, and it is not to be missed. General admission is $5.00.

Mendocino County

Willits Frontier Days
Various locations, Willits
(707) 459-6330
www.willits.org

A three-day event during the Fourth of July weekend, it's claimed to be "the longest, continuous rodeo in California." Besides roping and steer riding, there is a Fourth of July parade, horseshoe pitching, dances, a carnival, cowboy breakfast, talent show, barbecue, and crafts show. Most of it happens in midtown or on the rodeo grounds.

August

Napa County

Napa Town and Country Fair
Napa Valley Exposition, 575 Third Street, Napa
(707) 253-4900
www.napavalleyexpo.com

You can join the 65,000-odd people who come to the Exposition over five days in early to mid-August—just don't call it a county fair. Napa's one and only official county fair is in Calistoga in July (see previous listing), but this is a more-than-reasonable facsimile. There are homemade jams and oversized zucchini, 4-H livestock, crowd pleasers such as a lumberjack competition, a high-diving exhibition, wine tasting, and a kiddie carnival. Headliners at this event have spanned the range from Chubby Checker to Chinese acrobats.

Admission is $7.00 for adults and teens and $4.00 for seniors and children ages 6 to 12. There is an additional charge for events in the grandstand, specifically a rodeo and a demolition derby.

Mostly Mozart
Various locations
(707) 252-8671

On a Sunday afternoon in August, the Napa Valley Music Associates occupy a local winery or landmark to offer tribute to that impish Austrian composer. This musical event usually begins with a "legacy," a series of dramatic vignettes and musical samplers from the life of Wolfgang Amadeus M., and possibly Schubert or some other classical giant. Tickets are about $30, and they include the legacy, the concert, a reception, and often a tour of the venue. All proceeds benefit NVMA's ongoing music programs.

Day for the Queen at Silverado
Silverado Country Club & Resort, 1600 Atlas
Peak Road, Napa
(707) 257-4044
www.qvhf.org

For one day in August, Silverado Country Club becomes a large, lush hat passed for Queen of the Valley Hospital (see our Healthcare chapter). The full bill includes a fashion show, tennis tournament and golf tournament, lunch, an evening barbecue, dancing, and a silent auction. The cost depends on how many events you mix and match. The fashion show and lunch are $45; golf and lunch are $130; golf, tennis, and the barbecue are $255; you get the idea.

Sonoma County

Wings Over Wine Country
Charles M. Schulz Sonoma County Airport,
2330 Airport Boulevard, Santa Rosa
(707) 575-7900
www.pacificcoastairmuseum.org

This two-day air show sponsored by the Pacific Coast Air Museum (see our Attractions chapter) showcases a variety of daredevil performances that will have you craning and squinting in disbelief. In addition to the aerial demonstrations by a variety of WW II aircraft and other vintage fighters, the event features an outstanding demonstration of an F-16 fighter jet in action, courtesy of the Air Force demo team. Bring your earplugs. Admission is $10.00 per day—children 12 and under are free and seniors are $5.00.

Sonoma County Folk Festival
Cinnabar Performing Arts Theater,
3333 Petaluma Boulevard N., Petaluma
(707)838-4857
www.socofoso.org

Renowned throughout the United States since 1986, this is a wonderful indoor music festival. It's a one-day event held in August, with a varied lineup of musicians. You'll hear everything from traditional and original acoustic music to blues, Caribbean grooves, country and '40s music. Instrumental workshops offer a chance to learn to play a variety of folk instruments from dulcimer to banjo, and there is a kids-for-kids concert.

Dixie Jazz Festival
DoubleTree Hotel, 1 Doubletree Drive,
Rohnert Park
(707) 539-3494

A late August weekend of solid jazz brings traditional purveyors of the genre from across the country. They play Dixieland and ragtime from 2:00 P.M. to midnight on Friday, 10:00 A.M. to midnight Saturday and 9:00 A.M. to 6:00 P.M. Sunday. Don't miss the gospel services Sunday morning. There are five venues at the DoubleTree Hotel at 1 DoubleTree Drive in Rohnert Park. For admission prices, which come in a variety of packages, call the above number.

Cotati Accordion Festival
La Plaza Park, West Silva Avenue and
Redwood Highway, Cotati
(707) 664-0444
www.cotatifest.com

On the weekend before Labor Day, accordion players from around the world descend on La Plaza Park. For them, this is a world classic—a two-day extravaganza with professionals playing tangos, Irish clogging music, and all else in between. The event's appeal is largely to a mature crowd, but on the morning of the second day, kid players show what they can do. Admission is $10 for one day, $18 for both. Kids 15 and under are admitted free.

Old Adobe Fiesta
Petaluma Adobe State Park, 3325 Adobe
Road, Petaluma
(707) 762-4871
www.petaluma.org

Costumed volunteers display craft demonstrations, food preparation, blacksmithing, and other period activities from 10:00 A.M. to 4:00 P.M. on this historic rancho (see our History chapter). There is also Hispanic music, Native American dancing, and a whisker contest. Enjoy food, kid games, farm animals and more. Park admission is $3.00 for adults, $2.00 for kids 6 to 12.

A young Mexican girl is ready to celebrate her nation's heritage at annual festivals in Wine Country. PHOTO: JEAN SAYLOR DOPPENBERG

Real Goods, a renewable energy retail store, hosts this annual environmental gala, where you can take a ride in an electric car, tour solar energy exhibits, attend an alternative energy workshop, or simply nosh and enjoy the music. Cost for adults is $6.00 per day or $10.00 for both days.

Redwood Empire Fair
Redwood Empire Fairgrounds, 1055 North State Street, Ukiah
(707) 462–3884
www.redwoodempirefair.com

Held the second weekend in August at the fairgrounds on N. State Street, it's a bang-up event (literally, if you consider the Destruction Derby) with a big carnival, country-western concerts, lots of livestock events, and plenty of family fun. Admission is $6.00 for adults and teens, $3.00 for kids 6 to 12, and free for those under 5.

Art in the Redwoods
Various locations, Gualala
(707) 884–1138
www.mcn.org/1/ga/

Held the third weekend in August, Art in the Redwoods includes fine art, crafts, food and beverage booths, games for children, and day-long musical and theatrical entertainment. The event is sponsored by Gualala Art Center, and the fun takes place at the center and Bower Park. There is a $5.00 admission charge.

Gravenstein Apple Fair
Ragle Road, 1 mile north of Bodega Highway, Sebastopol
(707) 571–8288
www.farmtrails.org/gravfair.htm

Traditionally scheduled for a mid-August weekend at Ragle Park in Sebastopol, the Apple Fair features local cuisine and food demonstrations, an animal petting zoo, arts and crafts, and, of course, lots of Gravenstein apples and plenty of pie. Music and kids' activities fill the day. Admission is $6.00 for adults, $4.00 for seniors and kids ages 6 to 16, and $1.00 for kids younger than 5. Pets not allowed.

Mendocino County

SolFest
Real Goods Solar Living Center, 13771 U.S. 101, Hopland
(707) 744–2100
www.realgoods.com

September

Napa County

Symphony on the River
Third Street Bridge, Napa
(707) 254–8520

The Napa Valley Symphony brings its music to the masses for one night a year—the Sunday before Labor Day. The action centers around the newly refurbished Third Street Bridge in downtown Napa, where the symphony performs between 7:00 and about 9:15 P.M. The show is followed by fireworks and preceded by a mixer at Veterans Park, where vendors sell food, wine, and crafts starting at about

3:00 P.M. It's all organized by Friends of the Napa River.

Music Festival for Mental Health
Staglin Family Vineyard, 1570 Bella Oaks Lane, Rutherford
(707) 944–0477
www.staglinfamily.com

Granted, it's not a very sexy title, but the event itself, staged in a big, open-sided tent overlooking the winery and Napa Valley, is rather divine. On a Saturday or Sunday in mid-September, guests arrive for a reception with wine and hors d'oeuvres. At 3:30, there is a classical concert directed by a celebrity guest conductor. Half the attendees then stay for a lavish dinner prepared by a renowned chef such as Wayne Nish, Charlie Trotter, or Traci des Jardins. Some 60 to 70 ultrapremium Napa Valley wineries pour their goods throughout. The base price is $250 per person for the reception, $1,000 if you stay for dinner, and the best tables are reserved for $10,000 to $50,000. Every penny funds much-needed research into mental illness, primarily through the National Alliance for Research on Schizophrenia and Depression. Nobel Prize winner John Nash, subject of the book and movie *A Beautiful Mind*, attended the 2002 event, which raised $2.4 million.

Sonoma County

Women's Weekend
Various locations, Guerneville
(877) 644–9001
www.womensweekend.com

This annual event is a big party that features a golf tournament, author readings, a great pool party, exotic and unusual crafts and other wares, and music and entertainment. There's also a serious side too, with proceeds from various events donated to West County health centers to fight breast cancer.

Exotic and unusual crafts are among the highlights of the annual Women's Weekend in Guerneville.
PHOTO: JOHN NAGIECKI

Wine Auctions for Charity:
From Ultrachic to Down-home

Napa Valley and Sonoma Valley are only a few miles apart, yet the two regions are worlds apart when comparing their annual wine auctions for charity. The Napa Valley Wine Auction is the big kahuna of charity wine auctions, the largest of its kind in the world. On the quieter side of the Mayacmas range, the smaller Sonoma Valley Harvest Wine Auction shares the same noble goal as its neighbor: to raise gobs of money for local charities.

In general, both auctions are three-day events in summer, with two days set aside for a whirlwind romp of winery dinners, open houses, and special wine and food tastings. Both weekends are capped off with their main attraction, the live auction, set on the grounds of their respective destination resorts: Meadowood in Napa Valley and the Sonoma Golf Club in Sonoma.

The number of lots (or packages) up for bid at auction reach about 150 at the Napa event and about 80 in Sonoma. The lots vary significantly; some are wine only, from one bottle to many, perhaps in custom-designed boxes. Or a single lot may be wine combined with a special event or culinary experience—say, 13 bottles of several varieties of Cosentino wines in big-bottle formats, plus dinner for six at the winery, and a specially handcrafted pendant from the collections of Carrera y Carrera in Madrid (winning bid at the Napa Valley event in 2001: $28,000). Bids like these (and the $650,000 paid for eight double magnums—that's 24 liters—of Screaming Eagle Cabernet Sauvignon) really add up: The 2002 Napa Valley auction raised more than $6 million.

At the Napa auction, 2,000-some attendees mill about and schmooze while sampling finger foods served by restaurants such as The French Laundry and Bistro Jeanty. The bright white tent where the bidding takes place seems large enough to conceal a 747, with closed-circuit TVs to help all those with bidding paddles stay connected to the action. Dress is "Wine Country casual" but there are plenty of colorful silk sundresses, summery hats, and designer duds, too.

You're likely to spot a show business celebrity here and there in the crowd, as well as celebrities from the world of wine. One year, Robin Williams took a turn at the podium, performing a frenzied 10-minute parody of the haughty and hefty auction catalog. In 2001 Robert Mondavi got up on stage dressed a la Vanna White to "spin the bottle." In sleeveless long gown, pearls, and flowing blond wig, the then 88-year-old wine baron was a sight to behold.

Food also figures prominently throughout the weekend. The evening before the live auction the big tent is filled to capacity for a black-tie gala and fabulous feast. (The 2001 dinner was created and overseen by Wolfgang Puck; entertainment in 2002 was by Lyle Lovett. The next day, when the last gavel falls after the auction, the crowd moves out of the tent and across the meadow to row upon row of white linen-topped tables for a "picnic" dinner and dancing. It's safe to say it's one of the most elegant and largest picnics you will ever experience.

The Sonoma Valley is no less refined when it comes to wine affairs and winemaking talent, but the Sonoma vintners long ago decided that their auction wouldn't be as big or as high falutin' as Napa's. Each year they set out to raise a serious pile of cash, just like Napa, but they have a lot of laughs doing it.

For instance, in 2001, the Napans dubbed their auction—its 20th year—the puffed-up "Ode to Napa Valley." The Sonomans, in their characteristic down-to-earth approach, chose "An Oasis of Irreverence" as their theme, and the vintners posed for their popular annual poster as island castaways gathered around a case of wine that's washed ashore. The caption? "Now all we need is a corkscrew."

Scaled down in size from its neighbor's event, the Sonoma live auction is also less stuffy, and the vintners provide the goofy entertainment and the stand-up comedy. Tommy Smothers, owner of Remick Ridge Winery in Sonoma Valley and half of the legendary Smothers Brothers, takes the stage frequently during the bidding to energize the audience and keep the fun and games moving along. As in Napa, dress is "Wine Country casual," but in Sonoma that means just about anything goes, from Hawaiian shirts and shorts for the men to sundresses for the ladies. And at the podium in 2001, there were plenty of coconut bras and grass skirts (on both sexes) to add to the hilarity. The 2002 event brought in more than $538,000.

Yes, the big bucks really do go to local charities. The beneficiaries in Napa Valley include 27 healthcare, youth, and housing nonprofit agencies. In Sonoma Valley, the good causes range from community health centers to vineyard workers' services to the regional Boys and Girls Club.

So how much will a bidding paddle at one of these auctions set you back? Napa's three-day event is $2,500 per couple; Sonoma's a relative bargain, at $800 per person. These prices are generally all-inclusive of the special dinners and tastings leading up to the auctions, but do not include accommodations or transportation. Anyone is welcome to request an invitation to attend these auctions, but it really helps if your credit rating is solid, you possess at least one platinum card, and you have spousal support to spend with abandon. You will walk away not only with some killer wine but also with the knowledge that you contributed significantly to improving the quality of life for the less fortunate, and you had a good time doing it.

You can learn more about these auctions—and request an invitation—by visiting their respective Web sites: www.napavintners.org and www.sonomavalleywine.com.

The tranquil grounds of Meadowood are transformed for the world-class Napa Valley Wine Auction.
PHOTO: FAITH ECHTERMEYER

Sonoma Valley Harvest Wine Auction
Various locations, Sonoma
(707) 935–0803
www.sonomavalleywine.com

Events during the Labor Day weekend occur at various wineries and vineyards and include a wine auction and dinner dance, celebrity-chef dinners, barbecue picnics, entertainment, and wine tasting panels. It's three days of irreverent fun and frivolity to raise money for various charities. Sunday's auctions culminate with an extravagant dinner buffet and live dance band. (See our Close-up in this chapter.)

Prices and package deals vary widely year to year as do the charities that benefit. Get information on tickets from Sonoma Vintners and Growers Alliance at the listed number.

Heirloom Tomato Festival
Kendall-Jackson Wine Center, 5007 Fulton Road, Santa Rosa
(800) 769–3649
www.kj.com

The lowly tomato is elevated to superstar status at this festival dedicated to the enjoyment of the juicy fruit that comes in many shapes and colors. In early September, at the height of the tomato harvest in local backyards, as many as 175 different varieties can be sampled in some fashion. For five hours, nearly 40 restaurants and purveyors of gourmet food offer tomato-inspired goodies in bite-size portions, along with cooking demonstrations, wine tasting, food and wine seminars, and even an art show. Amateur gardeners can enter their own tomato crop in a "beauty" contest with categories such as Ugliest Tomato. Tickets are sold in advance only for $40 per person.

Russian River Jazz Festival
Johnson's Beach, Guerneville
(707) 869–3940
www.sonic.net/rrjazz

At least eight internationally recognized jazz artists get together the first week in September for two all-day concerts on the Russian River. Food and drinks are available. Prices for jazz under the redwoods range from $33 to $75 for two days.

Valley of the Moon Vintage Festival
Sonoma Plaza
(707) 996–2109
www.sonomavalley.com

The 100-year-old Valley of the Moon Vintage Festival, held annually on the last weekend in September on the plaza in Sonoma, is among the oldest wine harvest celebrations in the country. It features a traditional Friday evening wine tasting party and a full weekend of historical pageants, the blessing of the grapes, parades, concerts, and wine and food tastings. The festival is easy to find—just drive to Sonoma, and it'll be smack in the center of town. If you want to attend the Friday night wine tasting event, however, you'll need to order tickets at least a month in advance—it's a sellout every year.

Mendocino County

Roots of Motive Power Festival
Mendocino County Museum, 400 East Commercial Street, Willits
(707) 459–9036, (707) 459–7910
www.rootsofmotivepower.com

This is a way to relive the excitement and dangers of everyday lumberjack work in the redwoods. In mid-September the Mendocino County Museum brings out some of the tools of the trade—antique locomotives and yarders and old steam donkeys (a steam-powered machine that replaced the donkey for pulling large logs). What really draws a crowd is the two-day lumberjack handcar race event, held in front of the Skunk Train railroad depot (see our Attractions chapter). Other than the race entry fee, the entire event is free.

Fiesta Patrias
Redwood Empire Fairgrounds, 1055 North State Street, Ukiah
(707) 463–8181
www.redwoodempirefair.com

To celebrate Mexican Independence Day on September 16, the Latino Club of Ukiah stages a Fiesta Patrias event to select a Latina queen. Actually the object is not so much a beauty contest as a way to raise money for a scholarship fund.

The contenders spend a lot of time and energy before the event in soliciting money from merchants, selling tamales and tickets, and other fund-raising endeavors. Each year some $10,000 is made available to help local students of Latin descent go to college. The festivities include fireworks and folk dancing.

Mendocino County Fair and Apple Show
14400 Highway 128, Boonville
(707) 895–3011
www.mendocountyfair.com

This is a traditional three-day family event held on a mid-September weekend and highlighted by a rodeo, sheepdog trials, rides for kids of all ages, and country-western dancing in the town of Boonville, located in the Anderson Valley. Admission is $6.00 for adults and $3.00 for children younger than 12.

Paul Bunyan Days
Various locations, Fort Bragg
(707) 964–8687
www.paulbunyandays.com

Held each year on Labor Day weekend, this community celebration is a tribute to Paul Bunyan, the legendary giant lumberjack and folk hero who seems to show up everywhere there's lumber, from the north woods of Minnesota to the forests around Seattle. Numerous events keep things hopping for four days. A Sunday logging show gives visitors a look at what professional loggers do in the way of very strenuous activity. Most events are free, and the location changes, so call for the current site.

Winesong
Mendocino Coast Botanical Gardens, 18220 Highway 1, Mendocino
(707)961–4688
www.winesong.org

More than 60 wineries and 50 restaurants participate in this wine tasting and auction, held at the delightful 47-acre botanical gardens in mid-September (see also our Attractions chapter). Winesong benefits the Mendocino Coast Hospital Foundation. The site is filled with native plants—rhododendrons, heather, fuchsia,

and dwarf conifers. It's a perfect site to sample Mendocino's famous wines. There's no entrance fee, but there is a charge for the wine.

October

Napa County

Southwest Art in the Wine Country
Lee Youngman Galleries, 1316 Lincoln Avenue, Calistoga
(707) 942–0585

If your idea of art is Native American spirit guides, dusty cowboys, fiery desert sunsets, and howling coyotes, don't miss this annual show at an upvalley winery. About 35 artists usually display varied works in late September or early October. Saturday is by RSVP only; Sunday is open to the general public, at no charge. A silent auction benefits the Boy Scouts of America.

Calistoga Beer and Sausage Festival
Napa County Fairgrounds, 1435 North Oak Street, Calistoga
(707) 942–6333
www.calistogafun.com/beer

You might think you have to speak in hushed tones when you discuss beer in the Wine Country, but this festival is well-regarded. (The 2001 event, the 18th annual, had its largest turnout ever.) The sudsfest features a chili cook-off, music, and samples from about 30 microbreweries (see the Close-up in our Nightlife chapter), not to mention sausage companies, and mustard makers. Twenty dollars gets you in the door and entitles you to a bottomless souvenir cup and borderless plate. It's a one-day affair in late September or early October.

Ghost Wineries Tour
(707) 252–3270
www.napalandtrust.org

Just as September in Wine Country brings on the crush, October hustles in the annual one-day Ghost Wineries Tour. Typically, five or six "ghost" wineries (some of the oldest forced to close during Prohibition) are revisited on a self-guided tour. Additional staff are on hand to greet visitors, and picnics are encouraged. Participants drive their own vehicles between the wineries at their own leisure.

Old Mill Days
Bale Grist Mill State Historic Park, 3369 North St. Helena Highway, St. Helena
(707) 942-4575
www.napanet.net/~bothe

The folks at the Grist Mill celebrate the end of harvest by partying like it's 1869. Coopers, weavers, storytellers, and old-time fiddlers don period costumes to lend a touch of authenticity to the 19th-century goings-on. The kids can make cornhusk dolls or dye wheat. And the park rangers offer nonstop tours of the mill, which will be busy grinding whole-wheat flour and cornmeal. It's a two-day event in mid-October. The cost is $4.00 for adults and $2.00 for children.

Napa Valley Open Studios Tour
Various locations
(707) 257-2117
www.artscouncilnapavalley.org

Come see real, live artists in their natural habitats! On successive weekends in mid- to late October, Napa Valley creative types throw open the doors to their studios and welcome the self-guided with refreshments. The format tends to be upvalley one weekend and downvalley the next. The Napa Valley Arts Council distributes maps prior to the free event; all you do is drive and gawk. At least 80 artists usually participate, including big names such as Earl Thollander, Catherine Anderson, Davis DeSelle, and Ann Hunter Hamilton.

Hometown Harvest Festival
Adams Street, St. Helena
(707) 963-5706

This festival, a one-day event on a Saturday in October, includes arts and crafts, a fun run, a carnival, wine tasting, and a canine Frisbee-catching contest. The highlight is the pet parade, an advancing column of dogs, cats, horses, llamas, roosters, and lizards. (One recent costume award went to a hamster.) Most of the action swirls around St. Helena Elemen-

tary School, on Adams Street between Oak and Stockton Streets. There is no admission fee, and most of the proceeds from vendor sales go toward building St. Helena a new community center.

Sonoma County

Sonoma County Harvest Fair
Sonoma County Fairgrounds, 1350 Bennett Valley Road, Santa Rosa
(707) 545-4203
www.harvestfair.org

This harvest festival on the first full weekend in October features a world-championship grape stomp, wine tasting, produce exhibits, food, arts, crafts, amateur beer and wine booths, music, and kids' exhibits. This bustling fair brings in droves of wine lovers from the Bay Area and beyond. Wine and food tasting tickets are extra, but you get a souvenir glass, and you will sip the top award winners in their specific categories—perhaps the only chance you'll get, because the wines are sometimes very limited production vintages. General admission is $5.00, but it's $2.00 for seniors on Friday and $2.00 for kids ages 7 to 12.

Mendocino County

Chainsaw Sculpture Championship
Fort Bragg
(707) 964-4251
www.fortbragg.org

Where else can manly men bearing chainsaws demonstrate their sensitive side? Leatherface would blend right in, as long as he can sculpt. Professional and novice chainsaw sculptors from around the nation gather every year in October to reduce a block of redwood or pine into a thing of beauty, based on certain themes (such as nautical, wine, and timber). In the process, they generate truckloads of sawdust over four days to complete their mission. Three winners are chosen from the pro, intermediate, and novice categories, and cash prizes are awarded. Later, the stately sculptures are auctioned off to benefit the Fort Bragg-Mendocino Coast Historical Society.

Wine bottles stand ready for their contents to be judged by throngs of willing tasters at the annual Sonoma County Harvest Fair. PHOTO: JEAN SAYLOR DOPPENBERG

November

Napa County

Napa Valley Wine Festival
Napa Valley Exposition, 575 Third Street,
Napa
(707) 253-3563

Encouraging kids to drink is not good, but encouraging kids through a drinking festival is another matter altogether. This gig on the first Saturday in November raises about $50,000 a year for the Napa Valley Unified School District. The fun includes a live auction, with about 50 valley wineries pouring and 1,000 guests sipping, student-provided music as a backdrop, and a pasta dinner for sustenance. Tickets are $30 in advance, $35 at the door.

Festival of Lights
Vintage 1870, 6525 Washington Street,
Yountville
(707) 944-2451

This isn't so much the lighting of a tree as the lighting of a town. At about 6:00 P.M. the day after Thanksgiving, all of Yountville flicks its switches and is bathed in fairy lights. Christmas is beckoned with singers, street performers, hayrides, and roasted chestnuts from 2:00 to 9:00 P.M. There is no admission fee, though you must buy tickets for food and wine. The extravaganza sets off a month of special dinners, musical performances, and the like around Yountville.

Sonoma County

Santa's Arrival
Petaluma Riverfront, Petaluma
(707) 769-0429
www.petaluma.org

On the last Saturday in November, Santa makes his way into Petaluma by boat. While awaiting his arrival, the children stay busy with a variety of entertainment options. As might be expected, Santa's first move is to start handing out candy canes. Then he steps into an antique wagon chosen from the collection at the county museum (considered the largest collection in North America) and leads a parade of beautiful wagons in a circular route around town. It ends in historic Petaluma, where merchants hold a "Share the Spirit" event with an array of treats for all.

Mendocino County

Thanksgiving Festival
Mendocino Art Center, 45200 Little Lake
Road, Mendocino
(707) 937-5818
www.mendocinoartcenter.org

A jolly festival at the Mendocino Art Center to survey the newest in professional arts and crafts occurs the weekend after Thanksgiving. Every inch of the center (and outside it, if the weather is cooperative) is filled with booths displaying crafters' works, from tie-dye to watercolors. A separate room has been reserved for kids to play, and there is always a visit from Santa.

December

Napa County

Carols in the Caves
Various Napa and Sonoma wineries
(925) 866–9559
www.carolsinthecaves.com

Local musician David Auerbach is a multi-instrumentalist likely to play two dozen musical devices including dulcimers, pan pipes, and psalteries. As you might guess, he specializes in unusual folk instruments, and he brings out the best of each in the flawless acoustic environment of wine caves. The Carols series consists of a minimum of eight simple, informal concerts, two or three per weekend between Thanksgiving and Christmas—and sometimes running into January for a Twelfth Night celebration. Locations vary from year to year and week to week. Cost for each show is about $30 per person.

Holiday Candlelight Tour
Various locations, Napa
(707) 255–1836

On the second Saturday in December, Napa County Landmarks (a local preservation society) organizes a 3:00 to 8:00 P.M. walking tour in a selected historic neighborhood. The stroll and open houses are usually in Napa but can turn up anywhere in the county. Many of the hosts put out cookies or cider, and there is a sweets-and-wine reception from 4:00 to 10:00 P.M. at a particularly fabulous building. Expect eight or nine stops, with strolling carolers and glowing luminaries along the way. The cost is $15 for Napa County Landmarks members, $18 for everyone else signing up in advance. It's $25 if you pay at the door.

Pioneer Christmas
Bale Grist Mill State Historic Park, 3369
North St. Helena Highway, St. Helena
(707) 942–4575

Ever wonder how Americans celebrated Christmas in the 1850s? What you can expect are Christmas carols sung to the accompaniment of mandolin and fiddle. You can string popcorn and cranberries, drink apple cider, and, for a nominal charge, decorate gingerbread cookies. Longtime miller George Stratton probably will be there giving tours and he may be grinding out fresh flour and cornmeal too. Adults pay $4.00; it's $2.00 for the kids.

Sonoma County

Sonoma Valley Olive Festival
Various locations, Sonoma
(707) 996–1090
www.olivefestival.com

December is the official kickoff month for this several-weeks-long annual event (see more details under the January listing).

Russian River Christmas Extravaganza
Various locations, Guerneville
(707) 869–9000
www.russianriver.com

Guerneville celebrates the holidays with a series of events guaranteed to raise everyone's spirits. The first is an evening open house with hors d'oeuvres and refreshments available free at many downtown businesses. The highlight of the evening is the lighting of the Christmas tree in Guerneville Plaza along with carolers and carriage rides throughout downtown. Next is the World Dance Celebration held at the Veterans Hall. This cultural music and dance exhibition features African, Irish, Scottish, Mexican, Caribbean, and other ethnic dance. The crowning event is the parade of lights, featuring trucks, horses, marching bands, antique cars, floats, and more, all decorated with Christmas lights. Check the Web site or phone number for exact dates and times.

Holiday Crafts Fair and Open House
Various locations, Cloverdale
(707) 894-4470
www.cloverdale.net

The first Saturday in December, Cloverdale shop owners host an open house with hors d'oeuvres and refreshments. The afternoon features the Parkside Chapel Singers performing in the downtown plaza. And there's Christmas cheer to be had at the Wine and Visitor Center.

Mendocino County

A Smalltown Christmas
Various locations, Ukiah
(707) 462-4705
www.ukiahchamber.com

Santa flies into the local airport, and from there he rides a fire truck around town to visit all the shopping centers. A music program is held in the downtown area and is followed by the "Truckers Light Parade." Kick off the Christmas spirit with this event, the first weekend in December.

Shopping

Like our award-winning nectar of the gods and the mouthwatering cuisine, the shopping possibilities in Wine Country are varied and fanciful. We are not overrun with mega-malls or endless discount outlet store complexes, though those that we have come in handy when you need to buy toothpaste or film or you require a huge assortment of apparel options.

Instead, what we spotlight in this chapter are the one-of-a-kind shops selling one-of-a-kind items in towns that are tucked amid sprawling vineyards or washed by the wild Pacific.

Wine Country shopkeepers are savvy and world-wise in their selection of merchandise, and you will fall under the spell cast by the picturesque streets of Healdsburg, St. Helena, and Calistoga. You may find yourself popping in and out of the shops and galleries clinging to the four sides of Sonoma's historic plaza. And a stroll among Mendocino's dozens of specialty shops is certain to bring the credit cards out of your jeans pocket.

Wineries add to the galaxy of possibilities. Drop in at one of the winery gift shops, and you'll see lots of things to bring home to friends. And if you're into antiques, you've come to the right place. Santa Rosa has devoted most of a city block to the sale of antiques. Tiny Sebastopol (population 7,700) has about 15 antiques shops, including one collective with more than 100 dealers. And those are just the big ones.

In this chapter, we detail the various specialty shops scattered throughout Wine Country that are unique to our area, and we follow that up with a breakdown of antiques stores and bookstores throughout the region. Expect these stores to keep reasonably regular hours—if operating times are particularly unusual, we'll let you know in the listings. It's always a good idea to make a call if you're not sure when a place is open.

Unique Shops

Napa County

Shackford's
1350 Main Street, Napa
(707) 226–2132

World-class restaurants necessitate a lot of chefs, and most Napa Valley kitchen whizzes do their shopping at Shackford's. So do the common cooks, and one step into the store will show you why. This is the nirvana of pots and pans. You'll find whole aisles of knives (Wusthof Trident, Sebatier, Forschner, and many more), pans (Calphalon, All-Clad, Look, etc., etc.) and cutting boards (wood, acrylic, poly, yada-yada-yada). The Kitchen Aid mixers are lined up like a Panzer division, and the pot racks hang like chandeliers. It's all priced competitively.

The Beaded Nomad
1238 First Street, Napa
(707) 258–8004

There aren't many stores where prices start at three cents. The Nomad stocks more types of beads than you thought existed on the seven continents of this world—beads of metal, thread, plastic, glass, wood, fimo (a polymer clay), ceramic, and even hemp. You can assemble your beads right there in the store (mixing is encouraged), and they'll provide design assistance and repair. The shop even offers classes in basic and advanced stringing. It also carries masks and jewelry from various exotic locales.

JHM Stamps & Collectibles
The Book Merchant and Sirius Bindery,
1330 Second Street, Napa
(707) 226–7511 (JHM),
(707) 259–1326 (Book Merchant)

Double your high-brow pleasure at one address housing two businesses. JHM, the only stamp shop within a 40-mile radius, has been on Second Street for more than 20 years. They have stamps from all over the world and a wide range of philatelic supplies—albums, refill pages, catalogs, and more. JHM also has boxes of blank postcards from every state in the union. The Book Merchant deals in antique and collectible books, especially those concerning local history. You might find a five-part library of Freemasonry, old pulp paperbacks, a 24-volume Dumas collection, signed first editions, or the complete work of Dickens in 20 volumes.

Inti
1139 First Street, Napa
(707) 258–8034

That this store was named for the Incan sun god tells you all you need to know about the business. It's a hodgepodge of imported multi-ethnic crafts popular with hippie kids—and anyone else looking for interesting decorations that won't devastate their checkbooks. Inti has jewelry, wood carvings, furniture, musical instruments, purses, candles, incense, batiks from Bali, and rugs from Peru. Oversized tapestries hang on the walls, and clothing from India and Indonesia hangs on racks.

Napa Valley Pianos
1141 First Street, Napa
(707) 224–5397

When a local winery or resort needs a grand piano for a one-night fête, it goes to Napa Valley Pianos. That's partly because this is the only piano store in Napa County, but also because of the shop's sterling reputation. They have both new and old pianos of varying sizes and new electronic keyboards too. All pianos are tuned twice—once in the store and again after delivery. One drawback: Few of them fit in the trunk of a rental car.

On the outside, Oakville Grocery Co. in Napa Valley's Oakville reminds you of grandmother's old general store. Inside, it's packed to the rafters with gourmet food and wine. PHOTO: JEAN SAYLOR DOPPENBERG

Overland Sheepskin Company
6505 Washington Street, Yountville
(707) 944–0778
www.overland.com

If it once bleated, you'll find it here. Overland's Jim Leahy began making sheepskin coats by hand in Taos, New Mexico, in 1973. Now the family-owned company sells its woolly wear at 11 locations around the nation, including this locale in Yountville. Try on the sheepskin slippers, or sit on a stack of amazingly plush rugs. Almost everything is 100 percent sheepskin, from the car seat covers to the coats (even the lining). Overland sells leather goods made by other manufacturers, including Australian outback dusters, hats, footwear, and water buffalo bags from India.

Mosswood
6550 Washington Street, Yountville
(707) 944–8151

When you have fully decorated your house and it's time to turn to the garden, Mosswood is here for you. This place has fountains, bird feeders, statuary, weather vanes, wind chimes, and more. The line of birdhouses is particularly impressive, with copper-domed, thatched-roof, and pebbled models. Mosswood also carries decorative interior accessories, including the Gracey Knight collection of bright, handpainted furniture, featuring dozens of different knobs and pulls.

Napa Valley Grapevine Wreath Company
8901 Conn Creek Road (Rutherford
Cross Road), Rutherford
(707) 963–8893
www.grapevinewreath.com
While most grape-growers are pruning, stacking, and burning vines in the winter, this company is building its inventory. The Wood family (a partner in the original Freemark Abbey investment group) trims its 80 acres of Cabernet Sauvignon plants, strips the leaves, and fashions the vines into decorative wreaths—and a whole lot more. They make dozens of styles of baskets, plus cornucopias, hearts, crosses, stars, wine carriers, even reindeer and magic wands. All of it is handmade, distinct, and highly durable.

Dean & DeLuca
607 St. Helena Highway S., St. Helena
(707) 967–9980
www.deandeluca.com
Twenty years after the first Dean & DeLuca opened in SoHo in 1977, the ultrapremium food purveyors brought their act to Napa Valley. And while the massive wine section (see our Wineries chapter) is what sets this one apart from the other four branches, there is plenty more to woo your senses. Such as jam and marmalade jars by the dozen and an ocean of olive oil compartmentalized into 16-ounce bottles. You can find dried beans and rice, dried fruit, tins of dried herbs, teas and coffees, cigars, chocolates, and sweetly packaged edibles you never knew existed. And you can complete the experience with a high-quality cooking utensil, a cookbook, or a basket. Dean & DeLuca has a sandwich-and-salad bar called Market Cafe, an espresso bar and bakery, fresh produce, and a central deli with no end of meats, cheeses, and olives. But most of all it has its reputation for service, a commodity delivered by a squadron of friendly attendants in white chef's coats. This is a great place for assembling a delicious feast to enjoy at your favorite winery's picnic area.

St. Helena Olive Oil Co.
Highways 29 and 128, Rutherford
(707) 967–1003
www.sholiveoil.com
Olive oil is as ancient a pursuit as wine, and it gets the same reverent treatment at St. Helena Olive Oil Co. This is one place where you can sample some of the best. Most of the fruit comes from the Central Valley, but the company contracted with a Napa Valley olive grower to produce the high-end Cask 85 line. St. Helena Olive Oil also imports balsamic vinegar from Italy and makes a few types of its own, including five flavored balsamics (with fresh berries) and a Cabernet vinegar. Everything is natural—no sugars or preservatives—and available in 60-ml., and 250-ml., or 375-ml. vessels.

Napa Valley Olive Oil Co.
835 Charter Oak Avenue, St. Helena
(707) 963–4173
For more than 50 years, this white clapboard barn has been distributing premier olive oil to Napa Valley and the world. The old mill and hydraulic presses are still here, but the olives are pressed in the Sacramento Valley now. Still, the Particelli family bottles and packages all of its oils in St. Helena (except for the extra virgin). That's a lot of bottling—about 100,000 cases per year. The oil is available in sizes ranging from pints to gallons.

Napa Style
801 Main Street, St. Helena
(707) 967–0405, (866) 776–6272
www.napastyle.com
Here are two words you'll be hearing a lot more of in the future: gray salt. It's the best type of salt for cooking, so says Michael Chiarello, and he should know. He founded Tra Vigne restaurant in St. Helena, among other achievements in the food world. Add this new business venture into the mix and he's a bit like the Martha Stewart of the West Coast (he has a TV show too). His retail store in St.

Helena and mail order catalog are devoted to entertaining with style—*Napa style*—and both feature glassware, table linens, and small appliances, along with staples such as gray salt (harvested from France's Normandy coast), olive oils and vinegars, pasta, and preserves. The store is at the corner of Charter Oak Avenue and Main Street.

Holly Golightly Goes to Italy
1350 Main Street, St. Helena
(707) 967–8881

When you enter this store, you're sure to utter "bellissimo!" It's the best word to describe the exquisite collection of Italian imports, from fabrics of all types, to bedspreads and lamp shades, to richly draped curtains and yards and yards of ribbon. Sprinkled throughout the store are delightful objects perfect for jazzing up your villa—chandeliers, ceramics, teapots, and old furniture. This is the type of boutique you might expect to see on *Lifestyles of the Rich and Famous,* though the prices and the proprietors are much friendlier. Named for owner Holly Wilkey (who runs the establishment with her partner Giondomenico Busato), it is one of only two Holly Golightly stores on the planet—the other is in Filasi del Lago, Italy.

Vanderbilt and Company
1429 Main Street, St. Helena
(707) 963–1010

"Barn" would be too pedestrian a word for this up-market emporium of home furnishings. But the effect created by the room's high open beams and skylights is not far removed. Inside are semi-enclosed alcoves devoted to, say, boldly painted Vietri tableware or the ornately muraled Wright Collection of furniture. Vanderbilt has glassware from Salas and Schott, a brimming Crabtree & Evelyn cupboard, linens and tablecloths, pillows and pillowcases, candles, baskets, and woven or twisted wine racks.

Calla Lily Fine Linens
1222 Main Street, St. Helena
(707) 963–8188

None of this "we sell a little bit of everything" here. Calla Lily inhabits a well-defined realm of linens, towels, rugs, and bathrobes, and only the best of each. The colors tend to be soft and muted, the prices steep, but the owners explain that some of the linens will last decades. Calla Lily also handles custom orders and offers select personal care products for the discriminating visitor.

Murray N' Gibbs
1220 Adams Street, St. Helena
(707) 963–3115

This store was founded by an interior designer, who has since retired. But the inventory collected by the new owners is much the same as before. It features the functional artwork of many valley locals, including drapery rods shaped like olive branches, colorful tissue boxes, and hand-painted tables. You'll also find jewelry, festive bowls, cups and plates, upholstered furniture by Lee and Shabby Chic, wall art and candles, plus enough picture frames to surround every head in Wine Country.

Tapioca Tiger
1234 Adams Street, St. Helena
(707) 967–0608

Not all kid stores are alike, as this one adeptly proves. Tapioca Tiger finds some items made just down the road and others manufactured overseas. The shop specializes in clothing (boys and girls, newborn to size 7) and toys. The clothes are highly original designs, everything from sweetly sophisticated European items to funky domestic lines. Many of the toys are handmade by small producers—items like wooden dinosaurs and dressable plush cats. Tapioca Tiger also features children's bedding and furniture.

Fideaux
1312 Main Street, St. Helena
(707) 967–9935

Greeting customers on a recent visit to this shop was a shirt that read, "I Kiss My Dog on the Lips." If that sentiment warms your heart rather than turns your stomach, this is the store for you. Dogs and cats are shaggy royalty here. Fideaux offers numerous squeeze-and-squeak toys, a wide selection of pet collars, collapsible dog dishes for hiking, pet futon beds (made for the Fideaux label), and even wine-barrel doghouses. They also stock the basics: shampoo, food, kitty litter, etc.

WilkesSport
1219 Main Street, St. Helena
(707) 963-4323
10466 Lansing Street, Mendocino
(707) 937-1357
www.wilkessport.com

The well-heeled crowd that buys its tailored suits from the Wilkes Bashford Company of San Francisco probably looks here for its weekend activewear. The shop has a small but flawless selection of pants, sport coats, shirts, shoes, and accessories, featuring fine Italian fabrics. Examples of the manufacturers are Zegna for men and Piazza and Sempione for women.

Amelia Claire
1230 Main Street, St. Helena
(707) 963-8502

Rene Sculatti's boutique specializes in sun hats, shoes, and accessories for those see-and-be-seen summer months. Name a color and a decorative twist for your head, and you'll probably find both here—and you may even find it at impulse-buying prices.

IMG Home
3431 St. Helena Highway N., St. Helena
(707) 963-4595
www.shopimg.com

One of several Bay Area furniture showrooms of IMG Home, this Wine Country outpost offers globally inspired furniture and home accessories. It's all contained in an old white house perched on Highway 29 north of St. Helena.

Hurd Beeswax Candles
1255 Lincoln Avenue, Calistoga
(707) 942-7410, (800) 977-7211
www.hurdbeeswaxcandles.com

Get your candles and wine here: This store combines the art of beeswax candle crafting with a tasting bar that pours wines produced by the same family that owns the candle business. There are all-beeswax candles by the score, in an end-less combination of sizes and styles. A demonstration beehive adds special interest, with the bees busy at work generating some of the raw material from which the two-legged artisans create their masterpieces. For an upclose look at the making of these fine candles, tours of the factory in St. Helena are offered; inquire at the numbers above.

Calistoga Pottery
1001 Foothill Boulevard, Calistoga
(707) 942-0216
www.calistogapottery.com

Sally and Jeff Manfredi run this pottery studio from the back of their home, and, while popularity has surged, in some ways it's all very similar to how it was in 1980. Everything is fired on-site. And they have remained loyal to a handful of rugged-looking glazes because their customers, in turn, have remained loyal to Calistoga Pottery. The company aims for utilitarian stoneware—platters, plates, pitchers, bowls, mugs, kettles, etc.—that complements food. (Sally used to be a painter, Jeff a chef.) Much of the work is made to order, but you can always find some pots for sale on the shelves.

Wexford & Woods
1347 Lincoln Avenue, Calistoga
(707) 942-9729, (800) 919-9729

If your mud bath is over, but you just can't stand the thought of ending your spa experience, rinse off and stroll into Wexford & Woods. Close your eyes, breathe in the mingled scents of innumerable skin- and hair-care products, then start exploring. You'll find triple-milled soaps from France, organic

Insiders' Tip
Not every state will allow interstate wine shipments into their territory, so ask your wine merchant in advance.

cleansers from Australia, and Dead Sea bath salts from Israel, not to mention soap bars of every possible size, color, fragrance, and ingredient—but all of one lofty quality. Nearly every line can be sampled, and most of it is 100 percent natural. Wexford & Woods also has a wide selection of baskets they will custom pack and gift wrap for you.

The Artful Eye
1333-A Lincoln Avenue, Calistoga
(707) 942–4743
www.theartfuleye.com

Several media are represented at this shop—ceramics, oil painting, iron—but what stands out immediately is the collection of colored glass, most of it mouthblown (often referred to as handblown). The vases, oversized wineglasses, and decorative flowers seem to writhe in the light as you look around the room. The Artful Eye also offers wearable art-like jewelry (from paper to gold) and clothing.

The Candy Cellar
1367 Lincoln Avenue, Calistoga
(707) 942–6990

If you have not just one sweet tooth but a whole mouthful of them, abandon all hope when you enter this place. You'll see barrels filled with saltwater taffy, jawbreakers, swirls, crunches, bubble gum, lollipops, and all the Jelly Bellies of the rainbow. Most of it is sold by weight, so you can mix and match. Anyway, you'll probably head straight for the award-winning fudge—10 to 15 flavors mixed right on the spot, including the likes of chewy praline, maple nut, rocky road, and caffe latte.

Sonoma County

Southern Sonoma

Along the dozens of buildings from yesteryear that rim the plaza in the town of Sonoma, visitors come to search out galleries, specialty shops, and fine boutiques to find the unusual, the elegant, the unexpected. Beyond the main streets are more shops tucked into El Paseo de Sonoma, a charming enclave behind the corner of East Spain and First Streets. The path down the Mercato leads to more wonderful shopping. The plaza is Sonoma's main shopping scene. Here are just some of the many retail establishments you can explore. Unless otherwise noted, they are all open seven days a week.

Spirits in Stone
452 First Street E., Sonoma
(707) 938–2200
www.spiritsinstone.com

Laura and Tony Ponter are on a mission: to import the best in elegant, simple sculpture from the Shona ("people of the mist") tribe in Zimbabwe and to demonstrate that "the spirit in stone" has much to teach us all about dignity, compassion, and peace. There is something almost magnetic about these profound sculptures—a feeling that you must reach out and touch them, and you are encouraged to do so. Large pieces are pricey, but the smaller sculptures are affordable and tempting for any lover of fine things. (See the gallery listings in our Arts and Culture chapter for more information.)

Viva Sonoma
180 East Napa Street, Sonoma
(707) 939–1904

How about a nice courtyard where you can sit among fruit trees or admire garden art while your companion shops? Viva Sonoma has taken up residence in Sonoma's second-oldest wood house (built in 1865 and located just a block east of the Plaza) and beautifully filled it with imported folk art, ceramics, linens, and more.

Sign of the Bear
435 First Street W., Sonoma
(707) 996–3722

Here's a great place to pick up handmade kitchen utensils, paella pans, cookie molds, madeleine pans, wooden bowls, immense Italian platters, and spaghetti drainers—all those things you need to feel like a professional chef or to make a friend who actually is one very happy.

Small specialty stores and restaurants beckon visitors into El Paseo de Sonoma, a quiet courtyard off Sonoma's Plaza. PHOTO: JEAN SAYLOR DOPPENBERG

Flag Emporium
20089 Broadway, Sonoma
(888) 438–3524
www.flagemporium.com

How often do you run into a store totally devoted to flags of the world? You'll find every flag here, including some in the category of "discontinued country." Owner Dallas Dutson is a leading authority on flags and has served as a consultant to the White House on the subject. The flags come in every size and every price.

Bear Moon Clothing
117 East Napa Street, Sonoma
(707) 935–3392

This is the place to go to find products that keep the environment in mind.

Brand names include S.F. City Lights, Royal Robbins, Mishi, and Woolrich Outdoor Wear. You'll find clothing and soft linens, cottons, tencel, and down-to-earth blends for life's simple pleasures. It's all natural. The store's motto, "quality clothing in natural fabrics with fashion and the environment in mind," pretty much sums up what Bear Moon is all about.

Sonoma Cheese Factory
2 West Spain Street, Sonoma
(707) 996–1931
www.sonomajack.com

This may be the most popular shop on the plaza. People see cheese makers produce this extraordinary local cheese and sample or buy one of the dozens of varieties of Jack or Cheddar cheese. There's an array of gourmet items to go with the cheese. You can take it all home or turn it into a picnic on the green plaza lawn. If you like, they'll make you a sandwich to eat at the sidewalk tables.

Vella Cheese Company
315 Second Street E., Sonoma
(707) 938–3232, (800) 848–0505
www.vellacheese.com

Some of the best cheese in the world is made on East Second Street, around the corner from the main drag, by Thomas Vella and his son, Ignazio. The family has operated out of the same 1905 rough-cut stone building since 1931; it's an architectural wonder in shaky, earthquakey California. The shop doesn't have the same exposure as the main street shops, but Vella Dry Jack has won international prizes, and the Cheddar is so sharp it makes your mouth pucker.

Milagros
414 First Street E., Sonoma
(707) 939–0834
www.milagrosgallery.com

Following the covered passageway called El Paseo, which winds between East Spain and East First Streets, you'll suddenly believe you've wandered into another country and another time. There before you is Milagros, a fabulous store of affordable fine Mexican folk art, featuring whimsical Oaxacan wood carvings, Spanish Colonial sconces, hand-crafted jewelry from all over Latin America, Talavera bowls, and wonderful masks. This shop also displays a rare collection of religious Mexican folk art. Milagros, which means "miracles" in Spanish, is named after the figures sold in front of churches in Mexico.

Sonoma Rock & Mineral
414 First Street E., Sonoma
(707) 996–7200

El Paseo courtyard has another shop worthy of a visit, particularly if you're interested in things lapidary. It's hard to believe the earth holds such wondrous rocks and stones. The display is professionally arranged in a spacious setting, with beautiful polished stones to buy.

The Legacy Gift Shop
452 First Street E., Sonoma
(707) 935–9447

If you love decorating your home, you'll go crazy here. Tableware and vases, chairs and umbrella stands, and candle holders in 100 shapes—they're all exquisite additions to the stylish home. The Legacy is also a great spot to find a memorable gift for a new bride. The shop is along the Mercato, the shop-filled promenade off First Street East.

La Villeta de Sonoma
27 Fremont Drive, Sonoma
(707) 939–9392
www.lavilleta.com

The beautiful handcrafted terra-cotta designer accessories in this unusual shop were all created by some of Mexico's best creative sculptors and ceramic artists. But what you see here won't remind you of Mexico; it will remind you of Portugal or Italy, Greece or Spain, even North Africa. The shop opened in mid-1997, and is a branch of a larger store in Guadalajara, where artisans respected in their fields turn out urns and plates, paintings, and furniture that are styled from the beautiful museum pieces of the Mediterranean. The shop is at the junction of Highways 116 and 121.

Other Southern Sonoma Shops
The Olive Press
14301 Arnold Drive, Glen Ellen
(707) 939–8900, (800) 965–4839
www.theolivepress.com

Inspired by the cooperatives of northern Italy, the Olive Press was created by a group of olive aficionados. Its purpose? To press olives for commercial producers, small-harvest growers, and hobbyists eager to make oil from homegrown olives. Visitors can sample a premium selection of olive oils, and during harvest season (October through March) they can view the pressing process. A bounty of olive-related specialty foods and gifts is available for purchase.

Snoopy's Gallery and Gift Shop
1666 West Steele Lane, Santa Rosa
(707) 546–3385
www.snoopygift.com

Snoopy's Gallery features a museum containing awards, drawings, and personal memorabilia from Peanuts creator Charles M. Schulz. The gift shop has the largest selection of Snoopy products in the world. The Redwood Empire Ice Arena is one block away on the right and the Charles M. Schulz Museum and Research Center is nearby (see our Attractions chapter).

Sonoma Outfitters
145 Third Street, Santa Rosa
(707) 528–1920, (800) 290–1920
www.sonomaoutfitters.com

For sports enthusiasts, this is the place to go. It's immense (more than 11,000 square feet), and the inventory is sure to cover everything you need for just about any sport. There's an enormous amount of boating and camping equipment—tents and sleeping bags, hiking boots and climbing shoes, canoes, rubber and plastic kayaks, ski clothing, in-line skates, you name it. It's sports equipment from wall to wall.

Northern Sonoma

The pretty plaza that makes Healdsburg so charming was built in 1852 by Harmon Heald, who sold lots for $15. Today, $15 will barely cover lunch, and the stores that sold harnesses and hardware in Heald's day are now occupied by charming shops filled with jewelry, books, fine art, clothing, and home furnishings. These shops are open every day.

The Irish Cottage
112 Matheson Street, Healdsburg
(707) 433-4850

If your passion is country decor, you'll want to dawdle here. The owner returns to her homeland in Ireland from time to time to find genteel Old Country pieces to add to her collection of distinctive pine tables, antique furniture, primitives, collectibles, and decorative accessories. But it's not all Irish, and it's not all antique. The cottage is cozy and cluttered, with plenty of linens, pillows, rugs, and textiles to warm up your home with country coziness.

Robinson & Co.
108 Matheson Street, Healdsburg
(707) 433-7116

Billed as "purveyors of fine coffees and cookwares," the store lives up to the claim. You encounter the aroma of coffee beans when you walk in, and there is a varied inventory of kitchenware. The shop is contemporary and glossy, filled with all the accoutrements you need to become a world-class chef, including the cookbooks that tell you how to go about it. David Robinson, the store's personable and welcoming owner, will be happy to acquaint you with a wide range of other products, including Italian porcelain, European and Australian pottery, French hand soaps, spices, and Williamsburg candles.

Oakville Grocery Co.
124 Matheson Street, Healdsburg
(707) 433-3200
7856 St. Helena Highway, Oakville
(707) 944-8802, (800) 736-6602
www.oakvillegrocery.com

The Healdsburg location is a branch of the same wonderful gourmet grocery store whose jam-packed shelves in the Napa Valley have attracted passersby for decades. At this location it has metamorphosed into a gentrified, glossy emporium of most everything gourmet and delicious. Here

Boutiques, antiques stores, and an assortment of other fine shopping opportunities can be found along the Plaza in Healdsburg. PHOTO: JEAN SAYLOR DOPPENBERG

you can stock your kitchen pantry with exotic mustards, duck pâté, caviar, Greek olives, and more. You can eat lunch here too, selecting salads, sandwiches, and yummy desserts to be eaten under umbrellas on the sun-drenched patio. Be sure to pick up a copy of their latest catalog—your mouth will water—that features custom gift packages for ordering by mail for yourself and others.

Working Gardener
330 Healdsburg Avenue, Healdsburg
(707) 473-9045

Owner Merede Graham has fashioned an inviting store for gardeners, stocked with everything from practical tools to luxurious gifts, including Tuscan-inspired planters and pots, lavender goodies, and a wide assortment of outdoor decor. She has so much to offer, it takes two floors to show it all off.

Seasons of the Vineyard
113 Plaza Street, Healdsburg
(707) 431–2222
www.seasonsofthevineyard.com

Here's a store that embodies all the gifts and decorative objects that can turn a house into a home. Owned by Rhonda Carano, of Ferrari-Carano Vineyards, it's a cornucopia of fabulous table settings, wreaths, furniture, linens, and other home accents. Rhonda also carries the locally produced Hare Hollow line of seasoned vinegars and olive oils. And don't forget to look up—the ornate tin ceiling dates from 1883.

Art and All That Jazz
119 Plaza Street, Healdsburg
(707) 433–7900
www.artandallthatjazz.com

Jessica Felix, whose works have been shown at the Smithsonian Museum as well as prominent galleries across the country, has been designing spirited jewelry since 1970. Her shop serves as a gallery that includes the work of others in art glass, ceramics, photography, collage, and an eclectic selection of jazz and Brazilian music.

West County/Russian River

Incredible Records & CDs
112 North Main Street, Sebastopol
(707) 824–8099

Forget the Rock & Roll Hall of Fame in Cleveland. Sonoma County has its own "museum" masquerading as a record/CD store in Sebastopol. Owner Jonathon Lipsin had a similar store in Toronto for many years, with much of the same priceless rock memorabilia on display. It's not exhibited in fancy museum-style; it's mostly a jumble of taped and push-pinned treasures, creating a mosaic of the weird and the wonderful, with no wall space left unused. There are vintage rock posters aplenty; a rare collection of early Beatles photos (including the proof sheets) taken by photographer Dezo Hoffmann, who accompanied the mop-tops around the world; The Who's contract to perform at Woodstock in 1969 (they earned $12,500, by the way); a

fringed vest worn by Steve Miller in the '60s; a guitar used by Randy Bachman in the '70s; and an assortment of odd pencil drawings made by Jim Morrison at the tender age of 14, which foretold his future legacy as the Lizard King. And that's just for starters.

Don't be surprised to find Carlos Santana or Tom Waits standing next to you at the racks—they pop in from time to time to do their music shopping.

California Carnivores
2833 Old Gravenstein Highway, Sebastopol
(707) 824–0433
www.californiacarnivores.com

It's been called "Little Shop of Horrors," but it's one of the most fascinating spots you'll see in a month of Sundays. About 550 carnivorous plants grow here, with about 120 varieties for sale. These are the meat-eaters of the plant world and are endless fun to watch. An unsuspecting fly circles above the Venus's flytrap and makes what will be its final landing. Other plants, like the pitcher plant or the bladderwort, are even more unkind to insects. The plants are easy to care for and inexpensive—you could get a dandy one for between $4.00 and $10.00 and perhaps be fly-free forever. If you'd like to send one to a friend, a mail-order service is provided.

Hand Goods
3627 Main Street, Occidental
(707) 874–2161
www.handgoods.com

Proclaiming a "distinctive mall-free experience," Hand Goods is located in the tiny hillside hamlet of Occidental. Since 1971, the shop has offered a wide variety of fine, locally made handcrafts, featuring the work of more than 100 artists. The ceramics encompass everything from functional tableware to ornamental sculpture, from painted oil lamps to Ikebana vases. You'll also find Shaker boxes and fine furniture, embroidered Thai jackets, and batik baby clothing. If it's jewelry you're looking for, Hand Goods offers a wide selection of local and imported earrings, necklaces, pins, and bracelets in every price range.

Handwoven Zapotec rugs from Oaxaca are a perennial favorite and come in all sizes and colors.

R. S. Basso Home
186 North Main Street, Sebastopol
(707) 829–1426
115 Plaza Street, Healdsburg
(707) 431–1925

Ron and Mary Basso began making custom sofas and chairs in the early 1980s in Sebastopol, and their presence has spread to one additional Wine Country location, plus others in Palo Alto and Danville. They also operate a fabric store. The Sebastopol store has been significantly expanded, with 28,000 square feet of retail space on two floors. The Bassos still manufacture the frames to specification in Sebastopol, and you can choose from thousands of fabrics to cover yours. They ship all over the nation, or farther—Ecuador on at least one occasion. R.S. Basso has fine art, floor and table lamps, figurines, wrought-iron chandeliers, and framed sketches and photos from eras past. And check out the magnificent mirrors, framed by embossed tin, inlaid stone tiger stripes, or handpainted Devonshire roses.

Studio Nouveau
25195 B Street, Duncans Mills
(707) 865–2461
www.studionouveau.com

Tucked behind the Cape Fear Cafe in a Hobbit-size cottage sits Studio Nouveau, which owner Andrea Record describes as carrying "objects of beauty." She has so much it spills out of the tiny store and onto a deck. Much of it she created herself, especially the pottery. There are also classic wooden wall hangings, candles, jewelry, scarves, and unique garden planters.

Mendocino County

U.S. 101

Real Goods Store
13771 South U.S. 101, Hopland
(707) 744–2100, (800) 994–4243
www.realgoods.com

Built as part of the Solar Living Center (see our Attractions chapter), Real Goods is both a retail store and educational center. A thousand items are available including a vast number of high-tech devices—from a laptop briefcase that doubles as a solar collector (yes, it will power your PC wherever you go) to a better mouse trap (it does not crush or kill its victims). Stop in (or order a catalog), buy some hemp socks or a solar-powered fountain, and learn to spurn bugs without noxious repellents. The array of innovative products they offer is mind-boggling, and makes you wonder why we keep burning fossil fuels.

Hoyman-Browe Studio
323 North Main Street, Ukiah
(707) 468–8835
www.earthenware.com

Trained in the European school of pottery making, Douglas Browe and his wife, Jan Hoyman, have established a studio in the traditional, old-time format—training apprentices and displaying their work. Much of the output from the studio is sold to restaurants across the country, but the showroom at the studio doesn't just have pots. There are tea sets, huge presentation platters, jardinieres, and 10-gallon flower pots, as well as tableware with bright designs of fruits, flowers, and vegetables.

Mendocino Bounty
200 South School Street, Ukiah
(707) 463–6711

This small shop is filled with food and wine made in Mendocino County and stuff for the kitchen. You'll find colorful bowls, linens, and gift baskets filled with products. If you wish, the basket can be custom-designed—let's say a pasta basket filled with grapeseed oil, organic herbs, and unusual pastas that are hard to find anywhere else. There's a breakfast basket with honey, local syrup, breakfast cakes, and a special waffle mix prepared by Mendocino's famous Cafe Beaujolais (see our Restaurants chapter).

Grace Hudson Museum
431 South Main Street, Ukiah
(707) 467–2836
www.gracehudsonmuseum.org

Grace Hudson's portraiture of Native Americans—particularly the Pomo tribe—brought her national recognition. The museum's gift shop collection of Native American crafts, books, and jewelry reflects that same fascination. A fine sampling of books explores all facets of Native American culture, and there's a nice selection of items for children. The gift shop is open Wednesday through Sunday. A jaunt through the museum is free, but donations are appreciated (see our Attractions chapter).

Mendocino Coast
Velvet Rabbit
38140 Highway 1, Gualala
(707) 884–1501

Shop to operatic music while you browse through the works of selected artisans in a variety of fields, from stained glass, bronze sculptures, carved stone, and wooden boxes from England, to china, crystal, hand-blown glass, and shells from all over the world.

The Courtyard
Kasten and Main Streets, Mendocino
(707) 937–0917

Here you'll discover all those kitchen gadgets that will make you wonder how you ever got along without them. The display of imported English teapots is large enough to convince you you're back in Sussex. Maybe you'll go home with a matching set of table linens and crockery. If you don't know how to cook, the shop will take care of that too—there is a large library of cookbooks.

Lark in the Morning Musique
10460 Kasten Street, Mendocino
(707) 937–5275
www.larkinam.com

If you have a passion for musical instruments, you shouldn't pass this one up. From alpenhorns to zithers, they fill every corner and hang from the ceiling—dulcimers, mandolins, banjos (with four or five strings), hurdy-gurdies, ukuleles, concertinas and accordions, harps, bagpipes, and drums of every size. There's barely enough room to turn around inside, but it's chockfull of fascinating instruments you've probably never seen before.

The Golden Goose
45094 Main Street, Mendocino
(707) 937–4655

Don't even think of saving this shop for the end of your shopping tour. They've got beds covered with down quilts and down pillows so fluffy you'll be overcome by the need to plop into bed and forget the rest of your stops. If you'd like to take home a bed full of luxurious sheets and down, it will probably run up a bill of about $1,500.

Panache
Kasten and Albion Streets, Mendocino
(707) 937–1234
www.panachegallery.com

You'll find art galleries all over town because Mendocino is artists' heaven. But it's worth stopping in here to see the metal sculpture of Don Quixote that's on

Wine Country's Fabulous Farm Trails

Wandering from one winery to another, Wine Country visitors are likely to come across green and white signs posted in some farmyards announcing "Farm Trails." Wine isn't the only thing this countryside turns out. Produce is our other forte.

Farm Trails was organized in 1973 by a group of farmers dedicated to the promotion and preservation of the agricultural heritage of the region. During the ensuing decades it has guided consumers through the spectacular countryside to "experience a farm," sample local fresh foods and wines, or select a rare plant from a specialty nursery. Maps and a guide have been printed to lead you to 100 farms open to the public, all eager to sell their goods directly to drop-in consumers. You can pick one up at a number of Wine Country visitor bureaus, hotels, fruit stands, and grocery stores.

The maps outline in fine detail the tranquil backroads and old-time farms that lie slumbering off the main thoroughfares. You'll never forget your first tangy bite of a Gravenstein apple picked right off the tree or the juicy you-pick-it strawberry you pop in your mouth. The product index includes other intriguing headings—hayrides, goats (pygmy), llamas and emus and pigs (Vietnamese), quails (and quail eggs), bees, wax, and pollen.

The produce of the Farm Trails group is as diverse as California's terrain and climate. From the fog-chilled valleys near the coast to the sunbaked fields inland, you'll find everything from smoked salmon to cacti and, best of all, have a chance to chat with the people who make their living from agriculture. Here you can learn the pleasures and pitfalls of an industry that's seldom showcased.

Locals always stick their necks out for visitors along the Farm Trails. PHOTO: JOHN NAGIECKI

exhibit front and center. It's like none other. Panache is also the place to buy the fruit and vegetable paintings of Gerald Stinski, who moved to Mendocino in 1991 to pursue his art dreams.

The Irish Shop
45050 Main Street, Mendocino
(707) 937-3133

Did you forget to pick up that fisherman's sweater last time you were in Killarney? You'll find it here, along with anything you might need from Scotland or Wales. The shop also carries high-quality food products such as the award-winning Christine and Rob's Old Fashioned Oatmeal, as well as Norwegian sweaters, Geiger jackets from Austria, men's caps, dolls, mohair afghans, and handmade Teddy bears.

Deja-Vu Hat Co.
10470 Lansing Street, Mendocino
(707) 937-4120, (800) 489-8125
www.dejavuhats.com

Who wouldn't want to see the largest selection of hats in Northern California? There's something for everyone who owns a head—felts, fine fur, straws, Stetsons, Akubras, Borsalinos, Panamas, and Deja-Vu's own dress hats.

Mendocino Coast Botanical Gardens
18220 North Highway 1, Fort Bragg
(707) 964-4352
www.gardenbythesea.org

This 47-acre showcase garden displays wondrous collections of rhododendrons, azaleas, heathers, and succulents. Some of these species can be purchased in the retail nursery that helps support the non-profit effort. Travelers might consider one of the sempervivum ("live forever") succulents, as a memento Northern California. They're inexpensive and travel well. There's also a gift shop with cards, vases, and so forth, as well as a shop for outdoor garden supplies. Admission prices are $6.00 general, $5.00 for seniors, $3.00 for juniors 13 to 17 and $1.00 for kids 6 to 12. (For more on the Mendocino Coast Botanical Gardens, see our Attractions chapter.)

Harvest Market
171 Boatyard Drive, Fort Bragg
(707) 964-7000
www.harvestmarket.com

Well, yes, it's a grocery store. But this is the one you wish was just around the corner from your kitchen. Homegrown produce, fresh local seafood, and fresh-baked bread are imaginatively displayed. The folks at Harvest Market will make you a picnic basket to go or fill your ice chest with the best foods in town.

Hot Pepper Jelly Company
330 North Main Street, Fort Bragg
(707) 961-1422, (800) 892-4823
www.hotpepperjelly.com

With 30 varieties of jelly to sample, you'll be licking your lips and fingers for hours. Don't neglect the old-time favorites, ginger pepper, Chardonnay conserve, or very cherry marmalade. For kicks, try the jalapeno pepper jam. All of Carol Hall jellies are handmade in small batches. They're sold nationwide, and the lineup also includes chutneys, dessert toppings, fruit syrups, mustards, vinegars, and salsa.

For the Shell of It
344 North Main Street, Fort Bragg
(707) 961-0461

Here you'll find pieces of the ocean, without the water. Long aisles hold everything from scallop shells for serving seafood to tiny shells made into earrings. But these are not local shells—remember that the state parks system discourages you from carrying any part of the beach away.

Fiddles & Cameras
400 North Main Street, Fort Bragg
(707) 964-7370

As befits a small community, sometimes retailers double up on their specialties. Fiddles and cameras are precisely what you can buy at this store. The stock runs to mostly stringed instruments of all types, instructional tapes, and sheet music and music books. But there's also a huge selection of cameras, and you can pick up binoculars for spotting whales, too.

Antiques

Napa County

The Neighborhood
1400 First Street, Napa
(707) 259–1900

Yes, it is almost big enough to be its own neighborhood. This showroom takes up half a block in downtown Napa, and inside it displays on two levels. Poke around and find everything from mission benches to barber chairs, framed photos of American Indians to ice sleds, and rough willow chairs to green bottles from the old Vichy Hot Springs in Sonoma.

Red Hen Antiques
5091 St. Helena Highway, Napa
(707) 257–0822

This is something of a local landmark about halfway between Napa and Yountville. It has been Red Hen since 1983, and it was the Napa Valley Garden Shop for many years before that. Look for the big chicken facing the highway. Inside you'll find a collective of 80 dealers peddling a wide range of goods.

Antique Fair
6512 Washington Street, Yountville
(707) 944–8440
www.antiquefair.com

This shop has been around for a long time (since 1971), but not as long as its merchandise. Antique Fair specializes in high-quality French antiquities from about 1890, la crème of Lyon and Paris estates. They have jewelry, statuettes, silverware, armoires, and bookcases. They're known for old beds they have converted to queen-size.

Erika Hills Antiques
115 Main Street, St. Helena
(707) 963–0919

Just south of St. Helena you will spy a line of statuary along Highway 29, and behind it, a former church that has been painted ocher and converted into an antiques store. This is Erika Hills, the namesake house of ancient delights. Inside you will find Limoges plates, Venetian glass, brightly accented Mexican chairs, baroque angels from Austria, and sturdy oak chairs salvaged right off the farm. Most, but not all, of the furniture is painted, and everything leans toward the high end.

St. Helena St. Helena Antiques
1231 Main Street, St. Helena
(707) 963–5878

This ultrahigh-end locale feels like a turn-of-the-century shop in London or New England. Customers are met at the door by two life-size, cartoonish "greeters"—a chef and a winemaker—carved from single trunks. (They're menu boards from the 1860s.)

If there is a specialty, it's wine-related items: corkscrews, bottles, racks, and practically anything that might have been salvaged from an old winery.

Lone Dog Fine Art & Antiques
1345 Lincoln Avenue, Suite A, Calistoga
(707) 942–1115

The shop is a relative newcomer, but proprietor Frederick Schrader has a wealth of experience in gathering artifacts. Lone Dog shares space with Enoteca Wine Shop (see our Wineries chapter) in the wonderfully restored I.O.O.F. building (also known as the Oddfellows building). It's the perfect setting for Schrader's collection, which includes framed lithographs of 19th-century local scenes, and wine-related tools and paraphernalia.

Sonoma County

Southern Sonoma
Country Pine Antiques
23999 Arnold Drive, Sonoma
(707) 938–8315
www.countrypineantiques.com

Looking for English and Victorian or Georgian pine designs and furnishings from the period 1820 to 1900? Country Pine Sonoma either has it or can obtain it for you. This is a one-of-a-kind showplace of unique pine antiques that would fit perfectly in the modern home.

Margaret's Antiques of Sonoma
472 West Second Street, Sonoma
(707) 938–8036

Tucked away in a cozy white cottage that dates to the 1870s and is now an historic landmark, Margaret's Antiques replaced the family that lived in the house for 100 years. The shop's specialties are art glass, china, furniture, dolls, pottery, and linens from the 1800s, although they do have a few collectibles that are more recent.

Cat & The Fiddle
153 West Napa Street, Sonoma
(707) 996–5651

With a storefront shop in the main plaza shopping area, this place gets a lot of exposure. The specialty here is French tables, armoires, and buffets, with some English and American antique pieces and gifts. New items to complement antique furnishings are also sold here.

Chelsea Antiques
148 Petaluma Boulevard N., Petaluma
(707) 763–7686

This is a collective that features a wonderful selection of decorative antiques, collectibles, and architectural and garden items in three buildings. Chelsea represents just about every field of antiques collecting.

Vintage Bank Antiques
101 Petaluma Boulevard N., Petaluma
(707) 769–3097

It's one of those wonderful old banks that has ceilings two stories high and a small window on the second level overlooking the bank floor—so the manager could monitor his tellers and cashiers. Today it's a collective for 48 dealers, giving you three floors to explore. What you'll find here is lots of jewelry, furniture, vintage clothing, porcelain, gentlemen's collectibles, dinnerware, and lots more.

Antique Marketplace & Annex
248 Petaluma Boulevard N., Petaluma
(707) 765–1155

It claims to have the finest and largest selection of antique furniture in Petaluma. Included is a large selection of pine and country furniture.

Kentucky Street Antiques
127 Kentucky Street, Petaluma
(707) 765–1698

Nine dealers display their collections here, showing everything from country to classic—furniture, china, glassware, toys, tools, old advertising, paper, and jewelry.

Whistle Stop Antiques
130 Fourth Street, Santa Rosa
(707) 542–9474

This is where it all began—Sonoma County's original collective, now more than 25 years old. With 10,000 square feet of space and more than 35 dealers, it's a collector's paradise with thousands of items from dishes to doorknobs. You'll also find clock repair, refinishing supplies, antique books, and a wonderful assortment of glassware, jewelry, furniture, and collectibles.

Railroad Square Basement Antiques
100 Fourth Street, Santa Rosa
(707) 569–9646

You enter this shop on Wilson Street. It features a fine collection of vintage furniture, glassware, pottery, kitchenware, china, and cookbooks. Closed Tuesdays.

Northern Sonoma
Mill Street Antiques
44 Mill Street, Healdsburg
(707) 433–8409

Look for the Big Blue Building, where more than 40 dealers showcase their wares in 20,000 square feet of space. You'll find furniture—classic to country—glass, china, silver, fine oil paintings by listed artists, plus some eccentric goodies that need a home, such as gas station collectibles, metal signs, and 1950s memorabilia.

Healdsburg Classics
226 Healdsburg Avenue, Healdsburg
(707) 433–4315

This is an enormous warehouse with a roster of some 20 dealers. It would be difficult to name something that isn't here, rather than what is. However, anyone looking for indoor-outdoor furniture or yard pieces will not be disappointed.

Antique Harvest
225 Healdsburg Avenue, Healdsburg
(707) 433–0223

Items range from country pine to Victorian, with lamps, brass, Art Deco furnishings, and Maxfield Parrish prints to boot. Meander through and check out the wares of more than 12 dealers.

Jimtown Store
6706 Highway 128, Healdsburg
(707) 433–1212
www.jimtown.com

Not only can you find American antiques, folk art, and primitives here, you can also have some "real food" (as they advertise) and a truly good cup of coffee.

Sonoma Coast

Wooden Duck Antique Shop
132 Bodega Lane, Bodega
(707) 876–3176

You'll spot the big yellow house (once a Druids hall) from the highway as you head toward the ocean. The store is open only Saturday and Sunday, but you'll find some fine 18th- and 19th-century furniture, plus a lot of Americana—pewter, glass, silver, whale oil lamps, plus some English Staffordshire china. There's also a fine collection of antique guns.

West County/Russian River

Llano House Antiques
4353 Gravenstein Highway S., Sebastopol
(707) 829–9322

Housed in the oldest wooden building in Sonoma County, Llano House Antiques deals mainly in American oak furniture, Depression glass, and kitchen collectibles.

Antique Society
2661 Gravenstein Highway S., Sebastopol
(707) 829–1733
www.antiquesociety.com

Antique Society is right when they claim "there's no place quite like" their collective. With more than 100 dealers, it is simply immense. You'll find just about

anything you're looking for here, and they claim to have "country prices."

School Bell Antiques
3555 Gravenstein Highway S., Sebastopol
(707) 823–2878

Housed in a charming old schoolhouse is a 24-dealer collective. The schoolhouse alone is worth the visit.

Sebastopol Antique Mall
755 Petaluma Avenue, Sebastopol
(707) 823–1936
www.sebastopolantiquemall.com

Want to take home a star? You'll find fabulous studio portraits and scene stills of yesterday's film stars—say, John Wayne, or Elvis—with autographs guaranteed authentic, all from the private collection of Laurel Proeme. A signed photo might be had for $75, with Elvis going for a little more. You'll find a lot more, and since

Insiders' Tip
Visitors to Wine Country farmers' markets may occasionally find a surprise nestled between the cukes and the arugula: a world-renowned chef signing copies of his latest cookbook. The French Laundry's Thomas Keller popped in at the weekly farmers market in Yountville one day and autorgraphed 58 books in just one hour. The first in line to get Keller's John Hancock was the mayor of Yountville.

this is a mall you can also stop for coffee, wine, or lunch at a gourmet cafe.

Mendocino County

Hopland Antiques
13456 U.S. 101, Hopland
(707) 744–1023

Much of the merchandise in this large building came from buying complete estates, so you'll find a lot of furniture, home accessories, and excellent estate jewelry.

Li'l Stinker Antiques
20029 North U.S. 101, Willits
(707) 459–2486

It's all furniture here—no small stuff. Some of it dates back to the 1830s. The store has been in business under the same owner since 1967.

Whistlestop Antiques
350 North Franklin Street, Fort Bragg
(707) 961–0902
www.the-whistlestop.com

Here they call about half the stock "temporary collectibles" and the other half antiques, on the assumption half the collecting community are "only temporary custodians." The extensive selection of elegant glassware includes Fostoria, Heisey, Cambridge, and many others, as well as Depression glass and Carnival glass. They also carry a fine line of American furniture.

Bookstores

Napa County

Bookends Book Store
1014 Coombs Street, Napa
(707) 254–7323
www.bookends-napa.com

Bookends counts a couple of big-chain book stores as neighbors in downtown Napa but manages to hold its own. How? With substantial sections on subjects such as computers, business, biography, self-help, crafts, children's books, and family (things like birth, child rearing, and weddings).

Bookends has plenty of magazines and fiction and a large collection of travel guides and maps, including a comprehensive set of Wine Country maps.

Copperfield's Books
1303 First Street, Napa
(707) 252–8002
www.copperfields.com

Wine Country literati have been relying on Copperfield's for years. The Napa edition, like its brethren in Sonoma County, is both well stocked and well staffed. This one sells new, used, and rare books.

Main Street Books
1315 Main Street, St. Helena
(707) 963–1338

This business has been around since 1983, but recently reinvented itself. Main Street Books is now an extremely small shop that emphasizes used items. (It's the only upvalley used-book store.) The cramped quarters and carefully selected titles are bound to remind you of a classic London book stall.

The Calistoga Bookstore
1343 Lincoln Avenue, Calistoga
(707) 942–4123

This bookstore, nicely set in the 19th-century Oddfellows Building, knows its audience. Catering largely to tourists, it has a large collection of oversized coffee-table books and Northern California travel guides. And because this is a spa town, Calistoga Bookstore gets into the act with material on massage, Reiki, reflexology, nutrition, yoga, and other healthful pursuits. It even goes one step further—into Celtic and Arthurian, New Age and Eastern religion, feng shui, and sexuality.

Sonoma County

Southern Sonoma
Sonoma Bookends Bookstore
201 West Napa Street, No. 15, Sonoma
(707) 938–5926
www.sonomabookends.com

It's a general interest bookstore with an eye toward tourists in the wide selection

Our Other Nectar

Color, bouquet, and taste—the words traditionally associated with wine tasting. But there's another nectar grown and bottled in Wine Country that is judged by foodies in much the same way: olive oil.

Color refers to the tinged green from the chlorophyll found in green olives or the yellow of mature olives. As the oil becomes oxidized, a red tint may appear.

Bouquet is determined by the volatile compounds in the oil, such as alcohols, ketones, and esters.

Taste involves the bouquet in combination with the four gustatory senses: salty, acid, bitter, and sweet.

Today's emphasis on improved health and better eating has brought a new appreciation for olive oil—not only the one- and three-liter bulk offerings found in most supermarkets but the hand-harvested, finely milled, flavorful, creatively bottled, and limited-availability artisan varieties found in places such as Wine Country.

Indeed, countless wineries now bottle their own brands and feature them prominently in their gift shops. The oils may be infused with many flavors, ranging from lemon to hot chili. Other creative combinations may blend orange and thyme, basil and chili, and mixed herbs and sun-dried tomato. And a meaty porcini mushroom-flavored oil is reputedly an aphrodisiac.

Olive oil production is not new to California. In fact, we've been at it since the late 1800s. But when lower-cost imports from Italy and Spain began eroding the market in the mid-1900s, olive orchards were abandoned for more profitable crops. Today, however, California accounts for approximately 99 percent of all the olive oil produced in the United States, amounting to about 325,000 gallons in 1998. Only a fraction of this output is gourmet-class extra-virgin, which sells for $10 to $40 per liter.

Olive trees are grown for oil production in all Wine Country counties, and the olives are generally harvested following the autumn wine-grape crush.

Harvesting is one of the most expensive operations in an olive orchard—accounting for about 45 to 65 percent of total production costs—because the best quality oils come from hand-harvested fruit.

Transforming olives into oil is not complicated. High-quality fruit is crushed in either stone grinders or metal hammer mills. The paste is then mixed until oil droplets begin to form, and then pressed in either single batch hydraulic presses or continuous flow spinning presses. The olive juice—containing both water and oil—is then separated in centrifuge separators similar to those used to separate cream from milk. From that, the "liquid gold" is revealed.

Newly pressed olive oils, which have the strongest flavors, are sometimes known as one- or two-cough oils. When the oil hits the back of your throat, the bitterness may produce an involuntary cough . . . or two—much like gulping down a shot of whiskey. But with olive oil, bitter is often considered a desirable trait.

Several Wine Country companies offer a peek into the production of their olive oil. In Sonoma County, the Olive Press in Glen Ellen (707–939–8900; www.theolive press.com) operates as a co-op for a handful of small-harvest producers to press at a common facility. Learn about the hammermill pressing technique and purchase an olive cutting to take home. The store is located at 14301 Arnold Drive. McEvoy Ranch near Petaluma (707–778–2307; www.mcevoyranch.com) runs a picturesque 70-acre orchard with approximately 11,000 organically-grown olive trees of the Tuscan varieties, and does custom crushing for other olive growers. Visits are by appointment only.

In Napa Valley, St. Helena Olive Oil Company (800–939–9880; www.sholive oil.com), located at the Rutherford Crossroads (the corner of Hwys. 29 and 128) has a retail showroom selling oodles of olive oil labels, wine vinegars, and other goodies. The store also features a demonstration press. Napa

There is no shortage of oil in Wine Country; distinctive home-grown olive oils dominate the shelves in most upscale groceries. PHOTO: LOREN DOPPENBERG

Valley Olive Oil Company (707–963–4173) now bottles its oils elsewhere but keeps the original press on display for visitors. The store is located at 835 Charter Oak Avenue, east of Tra Vigne restaurant, in St. Helena—look for the big white barn. For tastings only, try Tra Vigne's Cantinetta, where you can sample oils without an appointment. It's at Tra Vigne, on the corner of Highway 29 and Charter Oak Avenue in St. Helena.

of Wine Country books. The store's travel section focuses on California, but there's also a fine selection of U.S. Geological Survey maps.

Readers' Books
127 East Napa Street, Sonoma
(707) 939–1779
www.readersbook.com

Described by *Travel & Leisure* as a "honey pot" ("You can't help but get stuck there"), Readers' is a bookstore with many rooms, one of which is strictly for children's books and serves as a gathering room for youngsters. The store has gained some fame for its authors' readings.

Adobe Drug
303 West Napa Street, Sonoma
(707) 938–1144

It's a lot more than a pharmacy, with a fine gift section, a great collection of books by local authors, and plenty of good, old-fashioned friendliness. Closed Sundays.

Jack London Bookstore
14300 Arnold Drive, Glen Ellen
(707) 996–2888

Used and new books are sold here, with a special concentration of books dealing with the life of author Jack London. Closed Tuesdays.

Book Warehouse
2200 Petaluma Boulevard N., Petaluma
(707) 778–6981

This is a clearance bookstore tucked in the southwest corner of the Petaluma Village Premium Outlet. It sells the same range of books as any general bookstore, but all have been purchased from stock that has not been sold in other stores.

Insiders' Tip

Every Friday in summer in Napa, a chef's market takes place on First Street between Franklin and Main Streets, from 4:00 to 8:00 P.M.

Copperfield's Books
www.copperfields.com
140 Kentucky Street, Petaluma
(707) 762–0563
2316 Montgomery Drive, Santa Rosa
(707) 578–8938
650 Fourth Street, Santa Rosa
(707) 545–5326
138 North Main Street, Sebastopol
(707) 823–2618

Copperfield's has built its business on customer service and is highly respected in Sonoma County. The shelves are filled with general interest publications, and there's a great children's section with occasional special events for children (see our Kidstuff chapter). The Fourth Street store in Santa Rosa and the Petaluma store both deal in new and used books.

Lakeside Village Bookstore
4275 Montgomery Drive, Santa Rosa
(707) 538–0579

Both new and used books are sold here, and they buy and trade too.

Northern Sonoma

Toyon Books
104 Matheson Street, Healdsburg
(707) 433–9270
www.toyonbooks.com

Travelers looking for more information about Sonoma County's wineries will find a fine selection of wine-related books at the front of the store. The selection at Toyon Books is geared toward general

reading, but a group of books specializes in spiritual and self-awareness subjects.

Levin & Company
306 Center Street, Healdsburg
(707) 433–1118

It would be hard to find a more appealing bookstore—a large, airy room displays books on three large islands in the center of the store. Beyond that there's a cozy room with a comfortable couch in the mystery novel section, and then another cozy room with books on women's studies. A WPA-style mural spans one wall. There's also a children's room.

Levin & Company offers primarily new books—quality fiction, interior design, and garden titles. Upstairs in the loft, you'll find an art gallery displaying the works of some 15 local artists.

Sonoma Coast

Fort Ross Book & Gift Shop
19005 Highway 1, north of Jenner
(707) 847–3437

Located 11 miles north of the town of Jenner, the state park has a unique selection of books highlighting the Russian settlers and Native Americans, plus the natural history of the Fort Ross area (see our History chapter).

Mendocino County

U.S. 101

The Bookworm
202 South State Street, Ukiah
(707) 463–1901

With some 60,000 titles, the Bookworm sells both new and used books.

The Mendocino Book Company
102 South School Street, Ukiah
(707) 468–5940

It's billed as the largest bookstore between Santa Rosa and Portland, with special orders and mail orders welcome. It's a true family bookstore, featuring a special young readers room. In addition to books, there's an excellent selection of magazines and newspapers.

Leaves of Grass Bookstore
630 South Main Street, Willits
(707) 459-3744

Besides the books, this store has an excellent selection of U.S. Geological Survey topographical maps. Also available are educational games and toys for kids, plus books on tape for travelers.

Mendocino Coast

Gallery Bookshop & Bookwinkle's
Children's Books
Main and Kasten Streets, Mendocino
(707) 937-2665
www.gallerybooks.com

Here's a world-class bookstore stocking more than 25,000 titles, plus cards, magazines, and newspapers. The section on local history is comprehensive, and Bookwinkle's is a perfect place to shop for children's books.

Ford House Visitor Center
735 Main Street, Mendocino
(707) 937-5397
www.mcn.org

This is one of Mendocino's earliest residences as well as the headquarters of the State Historic Park (see our Attractions chapter). Here you can find out about beach walks and whale watches. The selection of books covers everything that ever happened to Mendocino and the people who have lived here. There are even books about the movies that have been filmed in Mendocino.

Cheshire Bookshop
363 North Franklin Street, Fort Bragg
(707) 964-5918

This full-service bookstore has been run by the same owner in Fort Bragg since 1973. The shop is spacious, uncrowded, and well organized.

Arts and Culture

Theater Companies and Venues

Music and Dance Organizations and Venues

Visual Arts Organizations, Venues, and Galleries

Writer Jack London, who arrived in the Sonoma Valley in the early 1900s, found a powerful muse here, writing most of the works that comprise his oeuvre, including *The Call of the Wild*. London was neither the first—nor the last—to be inspired by this land. Robert Louis Stevenson was perhaps the earliest wordsmith to arrive, making St. Helena his temporary home in the 1880s, and penning *The Silverado Squatters*.

The natural tranquility and abundant beauty of the place has stirred the soul and inspired the imagination of numerous writers, artists, musicians, and thespians. All sorts of creative types call this home. Don't be surprised to bump into blues guitarist and singer Boz Scaggs in Oakville or spy actor/director Robert Redford biking along

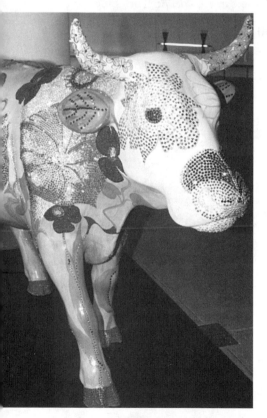

This bejeweled bovine is one of the many artworks on display at Copia: The American Center for Wine, Food and the Arts in Napa. PHOTO: JEAN SAYLOR DOPPENBERG

Highway 29. You might encounter the gravelly voiced entertainer Tom Waits while shopping in Sebastopol, see comedy legend Tom Smothers while dining in the Valley of the Moon, or come face-to-face with former Grateful Dead percussionist Mickey Hart as you stroll through Occidental—all are local residents.

For the haut monde set, the Wine Country offers a fine array of opera and theater choices. But while the performances themselves are often world class, don't expect the venues to necessarily resemble the upscale palaces of New York or Paris. The ambiance is generally more down-home, particularly in the smaller communities.

But the greatest of innovations may be in the use of the wineries themselves. Tasting rooms frequently double as art galleries, and the winery courtyards and surrounding grounds often serve as theaters and concert halls. Several examples are spotlighted in this chapter.

Here is a rundown of some of the Wine Country's best arts and culture, presented in three categories: theater, music and dance, and visual arts.

Theater Companies and Venues

Napa County

Dreamweavers Theatre
1637 Imola Avenue, Napa
(707) 555–5483
www.dreamweaverstheatre.org

This is Napa's only nonprofit live theater, supported by memberships, donations, and ticket sales—and completely staffed by volunteers. The troupe incorporated in 1987 and in 2000 renovated a former nightclub in the River Park Shopping Center. There is a main theater for big productions and a "black box" area for smaller shows. Dreamweavers has traditionally staged five shows a year for four weekends each, with smaller projects filling the gaps. Shows have included *To Kill A Mockingbird, Oleanna,* and *Steambath.* Tickets typically run $12 to $15. Dreamweavers also sponsors a young actors' theater, with performances by the kids.

Napa Valley College Theater
2277 Napa-Vallejo Highway, Napa
(707) 253–3200
www.napavalley.edu

The drama students of Napa Valley College stage several events at their campus theater during the academic year, August through May. Some examples of recent undertakings are *Amadeus, The Snow Queen, Oklahoma, De Donde, Noises Off,* and *The Servant of Two Masters.*

Prices range from $5.00 to $12.00; ask about student and senior discounts. See the Music and Dance section for more NVC productions.

Tucker Farm Center
1201 Tucker Road, Calistoga
(707) 942–9695

Nobody is trying to be facetious here. It really is a theater, but for most of its existence it has served as a working support center for local farmers. The stage company, mostly Calistogans, performs original works in the summer, fun musicals and comedies in the spring and fall. The theater building, which doubles as a meeting hall or whatever else the growers need it for, holds about 120 patrons for most performances. Admission is $10 to $20. The center is off Highway 29, just north of Bothe-Napa Valley State Park.

Sonoma County

Andrews Hall
276 East Napa Street, Sonoma
(707) 938–4626

A classic brick structure, Andrews Hall is a leftover from 1916, when it was the Sonoma Grammar School. More recently it achieved modest national exposure when it was selected as one of the settings for the hit movie *Scream.* It's a small theater that's now part of the Sonoma Community Center and will seat up to 299—it takes on no airs for being grand. There's a friendly hometown atmosphere about it, and it offers a surprisingly diverse assortment of talent, with five major performances staged each winter season using mainly local actors.

The stage is small, so plays generally run to those requiring few actors and uncomplicated sets such as *Mame, A Child's Christmas in Wales,* and murder mysteries. December usually brings a Christmas-themed production. Occasional musical evenings bring the internationally recognized Brass Works of San Francisco or a performance by the Baguette Quartet. The intimate, 50-seat Black Box Theater behind Andrews Hall stages one-act plays, sometimes written by local authors. Admission is set at $10 to $12 per event at Andrews Hall, or a season of five performances is $60.

The venue also puts on regular guest artist lectures, in conjunction with the ceramics and art department. Workshops in disciplines such as writing and painting also enrich Andrews Hall's calendar.

Avalon Players
Buena Vista Winery, 18000 Old Winery Road, Sonoma
(707) 938–1266, (800) 926–1266

This group has been performing Shakespeare's plays at Buena Vista Winery since

1980 and has become something of a tradition among theater lovers. A light-hearted spirit of fun prevails, and people come from Los Angeles and San Francisco—there are even some regulars from as far away as Texas—to watch the Avalon group perform. One group of 30 friends has come every season for the past several years. Whole families attend, kids and grandparents included. This is "Shakespeare with a twist"—the audience can expect an occasional actor to leave the stage and carry on his performance amidst the viewers. In 2002, the theater put on *Much Ado About Nothing*. Children are a part of the cast because the director, Kate Kennedy, also teaches acting to kids. The kids play demanding roles and often put in star performances.

Seating is at picnic tables and is on a first-come, first-served basis. It has become the custom among those who come often to bring some fanciful picnic fare and elaborate table settings. Buena Vista wine is available, of course. Tickets are priced at $18 for adults, $10 for kids.

Insiders' Tip

The Uptown Theater in Napa is being restored to its former glory. (It first opened in 1937 but fell into disrepair over the years and later closed.) Co-owner Francis Ford Coppola brought in technicians from New York to work on the stage and sound systems, and the theater's new seats are custom-created by a French chair maker. A summer 2003 reopening is planned.

Buena Vista Winery is at the eastern edge of Sonoma. Once on East Spain Street, follow the directional signs.

Sonoma State University
1801 East Cotati Avenue, Rohnert Park
(707) 644-2353
www.sonoma.edu/Depts/PerformingArts/

This university is one of 20 campuses in the California state university system (see our Education and Child Care chapter). Performing arts get top billing at Sonoma State, with works from the pens of local playwrights and international favorites performed year-round, along with dance recitals and musical concerts. The school's Everett B. Person Theatre seats 475, and it has featured such Broadway plays as *You're a Good Man Charlie Brown* and *Scapino*. A smaller theater seating 175 presents plays in the round, mostly student productions suitable for the more intimate stage. *Waiting for Godot* is a good example. There is also Warren Auditorium, which is devoted to music events throughout the year, from jazz to chamber music. Prices of tickets vary but generally run in the range of $5.00 to $25.00.

Spreckels Performing Arts Center
5409 Snyder Lane, Rohnert Park
(707) 588-3400
www.spreckelsonline.com

This is one Sonoma County building designed specifically for the arts. When the City of Rohnert Park was developed in the late 1970s, an $8-million performing arts complex of 35,000 square feet was included in the master plan. It is the home of the Pacific Alliance Stage Company, founded by Spreckels director Michael Grice, Smuin Ballet/SF, and Orchestra Sonoma.

The center houses two theaters designed and built exclusively for dance, music, and theatrical performances. The Nellie W. Codding Theatre seats 511 patrons and offers a variety of performances from nationally known arts groups. The innovative Bette Condiotti Experimental Theatre seats 175 and presents more unusual and creative programming as well as special productions by local arts groups, schools, and civic organizations. Codding productions include Broadway hits, an extraordinary ballet program featuring 12 of the Bay Area's most charismatic soloists, a performance of *The Nutcracker* at Christmas, and symphony performances. Main Stage ticket prices usually run $11 to $22.

The Santa Rosa Players
Santa Rosa
(707) 544–7827, (707) 579–8618

Santa Rosa's oldest theater group, so they say, stages musicals, tragedies, and comedies. Their venue is the Merlo Theater at Luther Burbank Center for the Arts. The 2002 season included performances of *Damn Yankees, Hello Dolly,* and *Once Upon a Mattress.*

Luther Burbank Center for the Arts
50 Mark West Springs Road, Santa Rosa
(707) 546–3600
www.lbc.net

This elegant center became a reality in 1981 when the Christian Life Center, a religious organization, was forced to sell the property as part of its bankruptcy proceedings. The Luther Burbank Foundation moved in and reopened it as a regional arts hub. It's still going strong, with concerts and cultural events of all kinds. It serves as host to many groups, including the Santa Rosa Players, the Actors' Theatre, the Redwood Empire Lyric Theatre, the Redwood Empire Ballet, Ballet California, the California Museum of the Arts, and the Santa Rosa Symphony.

Multilayered chandeliers light up the expansive 6,000-square-foot lobby, which is matched by the huge 1,500-seat main theater. Expect the finest in ballets, choral performances, symphonies, films, operas, and concerts of all kinds in this inviting setting. Tickets run from $15 to $100, depending on the event.

Other rooms at the Burbank Center include the East Auditorium, which seats 425; the Chamber Chapel, which seats 325 and has a spectacular, high-vaulted ceiling and stained-glass windows; and the Exhibit Hall, a 9,000-square-foot venue, which hosts trade shows, art exhibits, and wine tastings.

Santa Rosa Junior College Summer Repertory Theatre
11501 Mendocino Avenue, Santa Rosa
(707) 527–4343
www.santarosa.edu/srt

With 30 seasons under its belt, the SRT is a long-time local favorite. Running from mid-June into early August, plays rotate throughout the season and include musicals, dramas, and comedies. The 2002 lineup included *Little Shop of Horrors* and *Anne Frank Book of Days.* Performances are held variously at the college, Luther Burbank Center for the Arts (see previous listing), or local high schools. This is a professional training program geared to actors in graduate school, all of whom come on scholarships for summer work. Paid directors are well known and usually work on a rotating basis—six work each season. Ticket prices range from $8.00 to $14.00.

Sonoma County Repertory Theatre
104 North Main Street, Sebastopol
(707) 544–7278, (707) 823–0177
www.sonoma-county-rep.com

Once voted Sonoma County's "Best Theatre Troupe," Main Street Theatre was formed in 1991, then in 1996 teamed up with a sister company to form Sonoma County Repertory Theatre. The group offers an intriguing selection of fare—the 2002 season featured *Wait Until Dark, Parallel Lives,* and *Spinning into Butter.*

In addition, the theater offers year-round, multidisciplinary training for both children and adults, plus children's theater and a summer Shakespeare festival. Admission prices are generally $15; $12 for students and seniors.

Mendocino County

Ukiah Players Theatre
1041 Low Gap Road, Ukiah
(707) 462–1210
www.ukiahplayerstheatre.org

Offering an eclectic mix, Ukiah Playhouse stages five plays each season (October to June). In addition, the Playhouse offers readings for original, unproduced scripts, one of them eventually selected for pro-day through Sunday nights. The 2002 season presented *Dog Logic, Wit,* and *Lost in Yonkers.* Tickets are $10 to $15.

Gloriana Opera Company
721 North Franklin Street, Fort Bragg
(707) 964–7469
www.gloriana.org

Here's musical theater in grand style, featuring a full cast with lavish costumes, sets, and choreography. This group has been creating melodious magic since 1977, performing musical theater from *The Mikado* to *Fiddler On the Roof.* The company's new theater seats 150. The season is year-round, with performances Thursday through Sunday at 8:00 P.M. Tickets are priced at $10.00 and $8.00, with discounts available for series of shows.

Looking at theater from a different angle, Gloriana also has experimented with a series called Showcase Performances, designed to combine the highest values of musical theater with an elegant simplicity of production style, minimal sets, and simple costuming. Children's programs and workshops offer kids opportunities to express themselves in a creative environment through the skills and techniques of musical theater. For kids fourth grade and up, there are workshops in acting, singing, dancing, and makeup.

Another offbeat sideline is the Rent-A-Singer and Rent-A-Costume program. For weddings, parties, or other special events, Gloriana will send out a fully equipped theater company, a group of carolers, an a capella ensemble, or their children's chorus.

duction. These can be tricky presentations, as the audience must become accustomed to the fact that there is no action on stage.

Ukiah Playhouse has been producing plays since 1977, sometimes performing in rented spaces such as an abandoned 7-Eleven. It was reborn and revitalized in the mid-1980s when members of the company set out to build their own theater. The whole community came together, with everyone donating materials to the cause, landscaping included. The present structure seats 138 but will be enlarged to seat 198. Tickets for play productions are priced at $10 to $12—season passes are $50. The staged readings are $4.00 or $5.00.

Mendocino Theater Company
45200 Little Lake Street, Mendocino
(707) 937–4477
www.1mtc.org

The Mendocino Theatre Company has been offering high-quality theatre productions for nearly 25 years. The cozy 83-seat Helen Schoeni Theatre offers an intimate setting for a mix of comedies (*Picasso at the Lapin Agile*), drama (Eugene O'Neill's *A Moon for the Misbegotten*), and mainstream presentations. The theater adjoins the historic Mendocino Art Center (see listing under "Visual Art Venues and Organizations" in this chapter and our History chapter). The company produces six plays a year with shows Thurs-

Music and Dance Organizations and Venues

Napa County

Jarvis Conservatory
1711 Main Street, Napa
(707) 255–5445
www.jarvisconservatory.com

The Jarvis Conservatory was founded in 1973 as a nonprofit generator of scholarships for students of the performing arts. The corporation took a great leap in 1994 when it acquired its own educational facilities. And what facilities they are, centered around the Lisbon Winery, a registered historic landmark built in 1882. Performances are in a 221-seat theater in the acoustically superb, expensively equipped, stone winery building. The Conservatory's offerings feature a mix of students and visiting professionals. Recent artists have included the Jose Limon West Dance Troupe and pianist/conductor Donald Runnicles. The premiere Saturday of each month is opera night, and the specialty of the house is zarzuela, a splendidly costumed, melodramatic form of Spanish opera. Admission for all shows can range from $10 and $30.

Napa Valley Symphony
2407 California Boulevard, Napa
(707) 22–MUSIC
www.napavalleysymphony.org

The symphony, conducted by Asher Raboy, plays with an assurance and aptitude you might not expect to find in a city of 72,500. Its primary venue is the Lincoln Theater at the Veterans Home of California (see our Attractions chapter) in Yountville. The Napa Valley Symphony has tackled Beethoven, Tchaikovsky, and Mahler; Baroque chamber music; and jazzy compositions by Artie Shaw. It has welcomed guests such as pianist Ursula Oppens, clarinetist Todd Palmer, and violinist Amy Oshiro. And on occasion it leaves the Lincoln for special performances at Robert Mondavi Winery or St. John's Catholic Church in Napa. Single tickets in section A are $32 for adults, $16 for students and children younger than 16; in section B, prices are $26 and $13. You also can subscribe to a series of five Tuesday evening or Sunday matinee concerts. Adult series prices range from $85 to $150.

Napa Valley College Theater
2277 Napa-Vallejo Highway, Napa
(707) 253–3200
www.napavalley.edu

The college's esteemed music program puts on a variety of performances, such as orchestra and vocal recitals, even cabaret nights, during the August-through-May academic year. The theater also has lured independent groups, such as the North Bay Philharmonic Orchestra, the North Bay Wind Ensemble, and the Billy Browning Jazz Orchestra. Occasionally events are staged off campus, usually at wineries. Prices range from $5.00 to $10.00. Ask about senior and student discounts.

Chamber Music in Napa Valley
809 Coombs Street, Napa
(707) 252–7126
www.chambermusicnapa.org

This group brings the soothing sounds of chamber music to the Wine Country. Recent guests include Isaac Stern, the Prazak Quartet (a renowned group from Prague), and tenor James Morris. Most performances are at the First United Methodist Church in Napa, though the chamber music sometimes drifts to the wine caves of S. Anderson or Clos Pegase. The church performances are generally $15, while winery shows are $25 and include wine tasting.

Robert Mondavi Winery
7801 St. Helena Highway, Oakville
(707) 226–1395 ext. 4392
www.robertmondaviwinery.com

While Robert serves as unofficial wine ambassador to the world, his wife, Margrit Biever, does her part to make the winery a center of culture in the Wine Country. It seems as though there is always a note of music in the air here, whether it's the Preservation Hall Jazz Band kicking off the outdoor Summer Concert Series or Italian opera to benefit renovation of the Napa Valley Opera House. Mezzo-soprano Marilyn Horne gave a performance here in 2001. Call the winery for a schedule and admission fees.

Paulin Hall Auditorium
Pacific Union College, Angwin
(707) 965–7362
www.puc.edu

The forested heights of Howell Mountain might be an unlikely spot for the sweet melodies of classical music, but Pacific

Union College (PUC) is able to attract frontline talent to Paulin Hall. Recent performers have included soprano Marnie Breckenridge, Romanian-born pianist Eduard Stan, and Troika Balalaikas, an American trio that dresses in traditional costume and plays the folk songs of Czarist Russia. The Fine Arts series usually runs from October to April. The cost is $5.00 for adults and $3.00 for children per show, or pay $20.00 and $9.00, respectively, for five programs. There are numerous other events at Paulin that are not part of the Fine Arts series. Any shows requiring an organ take place in PUC's church sanctuary, home of the state's largest tracker pipe organ.

Sonoma County

Sonoma Valley Chorale
Veterans Memorial Building, 126 First Street W., Sonoma
(707) 935–1576
www.sonomavalleychorale.org
This professional-level, 140-member chorus, under the direction of Jim Griewe, has been singing together since the early '70s. Its annual concert series brings audiences to their feet with music that might be classical, sacred, or Broadway. The chorale has sung with the Napa Valley and Santa Rosa symphonies (see listings in this section) and even for the opening ceremony at a Giants baseball game. They've made two European tours, singing their way through France, Italy, and Great Britain—they toured Germany in 2001. Their regular venue is the Veterans Memorial Building auditorium, which has tiered, theater seating for 400. Tickets are $12 for adults and $10 for seniors and children.

Cinnabar Performing Arts Theater
3333 Petaluma Boulevard N., Petaluma
(707) 763–8920
www.cinnabartheater.com
In the summer of 1970, Marvin Klebe abandoned his career singing baritone with the San Francisco Opera Company, bought a 60-year-old, two-room schoolhouse on the outskirts of Petaluma surrounded by dairy cows and chickens, and began transforming the structure into a theater. Disenchanted with the usual regimentation of grand opera, Marvin's goal was to provide a stage for experimental works that would involve the local community.

Today Cinnabar Theater features an outstanding array of entertainers, performing everything from Bach to rock. Candlelight concerts give a rare and romantic opportunity to hear chamber music the way some of our ancestors did. Concerts are held not only at Cinnabar Theater, but also in some of Petaluma's loveliest gardens and mansions, intimate art galleries, and in the downtown Polly Klaas Theater (a school for young acting hopefuls). The Summer Music Festival presents the best in classical music, ethnic music, musical comedy, opera, and children's music.

In 1983 Marvin and his wife, Jan, created Cinnabar Children's Theater workshop. In the first year, the children mounted a musical production of *The Hobbit* that they wrote and publicized themselves. Children's programming and training play a role of growing importance at Cinnabar. Classes are packed. A free brochure outlining Klebe's many ventures is available. Performance tickets are $9.00 to $22.00.

Santa Rosa Symphony
50 Mark West Springs Road, No. 305,
Santa Rosa
(707) 546–8742
www.santarosasymphony.com

The Santa Rosa Symphony was founded by George Trombley in 1927. Thirty-two eager (and some talented) amateur musicians played for the first time at the local Elks Club. It is said that Mr. T (as his players called him) was fond of spirited selections. Under his direction the orchestra played Dvorak's *Slavonic Dance* at most concerts. These performances were enlivened by the gusto of Mr. T, who stomped his foot on the podium until the dust flew. Trombley's tenure lasted 30 years, when Maestro Corrick Brown took over the baton and held it for another 37 years.

The orchestra has long since left the Elks Club and now makes its home at the Luther Burbank Center for the Arts (see listing under "Theater Companies and Venues" in this chapter). Its conductor is Jeffrey Kahane, the world-renowned pianist, who assumed the podium in 1995. It is the only orchestra of its size and quality (there are 80-plus musicians) between Sonoma County and Eugene, Oregon. The concert season consists of seven three-day events plus a pops concert and picnic in June (table seating and lawn seating are available), a Redwoods Music Festival in August, and other special events in August and September. Kahane is particularly eager to work with young people and has established a Symphony Youth Orchestra, providing two free concerts for children (particularly popular with kindergarten through third-grade students). Adult ticket prices range between $17 and $30.

Mendocino County

Mendocino Ballet
209 South State Street, Ukiah
307 East Redwood Avenue, Fort Bragg
(707) 463–2290, (877) 354–5172
www.wildirisdesign.com/ballet

This regional dance company offers students the opportunity to demonstrate their talents in local dance productions. The ballet has been offering classical and contemporary works by local and guest choreographers, and it features regular performances of *Peter and the Wolf, The Dream of Sleeping Beauty, Sweet Coppelia,* and the *Nutcracker.* Founder Mary Knight operates a dance school to train the ballet company's performers. She instructs young children in ballet fundamentals and offers teenage students advanced training in a variety of choreography styles. The company also presents lecture demonstrations in schools throughout Lake and Mendocino Counties, offering an educational arts experience to thousands of children.

Visual Arts Organizations, Venues, and Galleries

To make it easier for you to skip from one gallery to the next one you will encounter, listings in this section are presented in the intra-county geographical sequence outlined in How to Use This Book.

Napa County

di Rosa Preserve
5200 Highway 121/12, Napa
(707) 226–5991
www.dirosapreserve.org

The subtitle of this collection is Art & Nature, and, indeed, many of the pieces are blended into the scenery of Carneros, that cool-climate grape-growing region on the north side of San Pablo Bay (see our Wineries chapter). Rene and Veronica di Rosa have been gathering artwork for more than 30 years, and their current display tends to the whimsical, even outrageous. All of it was produced in the Bay Area in the latter part of the 20th century. The indoor space includes a circa-1886 winery the di Rosas converted into their home, plus some contemporary galleries full of works of various media. Rene originally moved to Carneros to grow grapes, which he did as Winery Lake Vineyards until he sold the planted land to Seagram, the corporate beverage giant, in 1986. Admission is $10 and by guided tour only.

The Preserve offers two tours a day—9:25 A.M. and 12:55 P.M.—Tuesday through Friday from October through May, and Monday through Thursday from June through September. There are also Saturday morning tours at 9:25 A.M. and 10:25 A.M.

Jessel Miller Gallery
1019 Atlas Peak Road, Napa
(707) 257-2350
www.jesselgallery.com

On the road to Silverado Country Club, in a stately, vine-covered, white-brick building, is the studio of esteemed watercolorist Jessel Miller. The gallery shows the work of both emerging and established artists, in media from oil to collage to jewelry. It also offers public tours, lectures, and demonstrations. The gallery is open 10:00 A.M. to 5:00 P.M. daily.

Henry Joseph Gallery
2475 Solano Avenue, Napa
(707) 224-4356

This gallery is devoted to the California style—that spontaneous, impressionistic form spawned by a group of Californians in the 1930s. Painters such as Charles Surrendorf, Jade Fon, and Justin Faivre made the California style easily distinguishable from traditional English watercolor. The gallery also represents prominent Napa Valley artists like Roger Blum, Bill King, and Jay Golik. If you pop for an original, you can have it framed at the affiliated Napa Frame Studio. Hours of operation are 10:00 A.M. to 5:30 P.M. Tuesday through Friday and 10:00 A.M. to 3:00 P.M. Saturday.

Insiders' Tip
The first Friday of every month, Fort Bragg's downtown galleries and businesses open their doors with public receptions for visiting artists.

Napa Valley Art Association
1520 Behrens Street, Napa
(707) 255-9616

The Napa Valley Art Association was formed as a nonprofit corporation in 1953 to provide local artists with satisfactory facilities. At the association's once-a-month meetings (usually on the fourth Monday), guest artists demonstrate their skills and ideas. Those demonstrations are often videotaped for future observation. You can pay a $24.00 annual fee for membership or surrender a nominal $2.00 charge to attend a single meeting. The association hosts occasional shows of its members' work—everything from still lifes to portraits and landscapes to abstracts, in all sorts of media. Call the association for more information.

The Hess Collection Winery
4411 Redwood Road, Napa
(707) 255-1144
www.hesscollection.com

Donald Hess, the Swiss businessman who made his millions bottling water before he turned to wine, is a passionate art collector, and some of the best of his collection is here in Napa Valley. His three-story, 13,000-square-foot gallery is part of the winery and just as much of a draw to visitors. Hess collects only works by living artists, and the list is impressive: Francis Bacon, Frank Stella, Henri Machaux, and Theodoros Stamos, just to name a few. Some of the outstanding conceptual pieces include a group of oversized, headless figures fashioned by Polish artist Magdalena Abakanowicz and a vintage Underwood typewriter going up in flames, a work by Argentinian Leopoldo Maler. There is no charge to enter the museum, which is open 10:00 A.M. to 4:00 P.M. daily.

Images Fine Art
North: 6540 Washington Street, Yountville
(707) 944-0404
South: 6505 Washington Street, Yountville
(707) 944-0606

North and south have never been closer than at these twin galleries in downtown Yountville. The northern room came first; the southern was added in 1996. Neither has a specialty, just best-selling artists represented in a dramatic, two-story space with vaulted ceilings. Contributors include David Dodsworth, Guy Buffet, Roy Fairchild, and Pradzynski. Both galleries are open daily from 10:00 A.M. to 5:00 P.M.

RAKU Ceramics Collection
Beard Plaza, 6540 Washington Street, Yountville
(707) 944-9424

Raku, the process originally used to make bowls for tea ceremony in medieval Japan, involves using tongs to remove red-hot pots from the kiln, then cooling the ceramics quickly in the air or in water. Most of what you see here gets an additional copper-flashing technique. The pots, sprayed with copper, are covered with a pail after firing. When the pot is removed, the copper oxidizes and flashes in a rainbow of colors. RAKU has work by more than 75 ceramists, including Greg Milne, Ed Risak, and Tom and Nancy Giusti. Open daily from 10:00 A.M. to 5:00 P.M.

Mumm Napa Valley
8445 Silverado Trail, Rutherford
(707) 942-3434
www.mummnapavalley.com

Mumm's corporate owners, Joseph E. Seagram & Sons, have been appreciative of photographers, making the winery perhaps Napa Valley's premier venue for that industrial art. Luminaries such as Imogen Cunningham, Galen Rowell, Sebastio Salgado, and William Neill have been represented on the walls. But the rotating exhibitions have a hard time diverting attention from the winery's one permanent collection: "The Story of a Winery" by Ansel Adams. The legendary Californian was hired in 1959 to document construction of new wine cellars, care of the vineyards, and the process of winemaking from vine to bottle. The Smithsonian Institution circulated the best of the photos for three years, and now Mumm has dozens of gelatin silver prints. There is no admission charge to the galleries, which are open from 10:00 A.M. to 5:00 P.M. daily.

I. Wolk Gallery
1354 Main Street, St. Helena
(707) 963-8800
www.iwolkgallery.com

Ira Wolk's second-floor gallery is a definitive St. Helena establishment—tasteful art in a lovely, immaculate space. The gallery features everything from paintings and works on paper to photography and sculpture. It is open Wednesday through Monday from 10:00 A.M. to 5:30 P.M.

Art on Main
1359 Main Street, St. Helena
(707) 963-3350

One of St. Helena's most prominent and centrally located spaces, Art on Main focuses on, but is not limited to, images of vineyards and wine. It's primarily a venue for Northern California artists and traditional styles. An example is Gail Packer's extensive series of multiplate etchings, with frames designed by artist Hildy Henry. Other contributors include Garberville's Josh Adam and Hopland's Ray Voisard. Open daily from 10:00 A.M. to 5:00 P.M.

Rasmussen Art Gallery
Pacific Union College, Angwin
(707) 965-7362
www.puc.edu

Pacific Union College's stylish art gallery is largely a showplace for its own students, faculty, and alumni. It isn't limited to these groups, though. Other recent exhibitions have included the drawings of Samuel Fleming Lewis and the experimental photography of Cliff Rusch. Admission is free, and the gallery is open from 1:00 to 5:00 p.m. on Tuesday, Thursday, Saturday, and Sunday.

Clos Pegase Winery
1060 Dunaweal Lane, Calistoga
(707) 942-4981
www.clospegase.com

Art is everywhere at Clos Pegase, from the winery itself—something of a huge modern sculpture—to French and Italian carvings of Bacchus tucked into the wine caves. The variety is impressive, too, from granite sculptures to watercolors and collages. Clos Pegase offers a self-guided walking tour of the premises, as well as guided tours of the facility and wine caves at 11:00 A.M. and 2:00 P.M. (no reservation required). Among the pieces are a giant bronze thumb by Cesar Baldachini (designer of the "Cesar," the French equivalent of the Oscar); Michael Scranton's *Wrecking Ball*, an enervating installation in the Reserve Room; and a Henry Moore sculpture (*Mother Earth*) in the portico. In addition, a wine-in-art slide presentation, created by proprietor Jan Shrem, is given inside the caves at 2:00 P.M. on the third Saturday of each month (December and January excluded). The show is free.

Ca'Toga Galleria D'Arte
1206 Cedar Street, Calistoga
(707) 942–3900
www.catoga.com

Escape into a world of Renaissance, Baroque, and neoclassic styles of painting in Carlo Marchiori's fabulous gallery off Lincoln Avenue. You may recognize his work—he has been commissioned to produce murals found in the world's finest hotels and attractions, including San Francisco's Westin St. Francis and Tokyo's DisneySea. He also lives in Calistoga, and his Villa Ca'Toga outside of town is open for weekly tours in summer (see our Attractions chapter). The gallery is open 11:00 A.M. to 6:00 P.M. daily; closed Tuesday and Wednesday.

Lee Youngman Galleries
1316 Lincoln Avenue, Calistoga
(707) 942–0585, (800) 551–0585
www.leeyoungmangalleries.com

Owner Lee Love Youngman has long been surrounded by creative men. Her father, Ralph Love, was a painter from the Early California school who has work hung in major museums. And her husband, Paul Youngman, is noted for his contemporary landscapes, architectural renderings, and marines. Lee's gallery has a decidedly Southwest bent. It represents more than 60 full-time artists, including big shots such as Neil Boyle and Mark Geller. The gallery is open 10:00 A.M. to 5:00 P.M.

The classic creations of artist Carlo Marchiori can be found at Ca'Toga Galleria D'Arte in Calistoga.
PHOTO: JEAN SAYLOR DOPPENBERG

Monday through Saturday and 11:00 A.M. to 4:00 P.M. Sunday.

Sonoma County

Spirits In Stone
452 First Street E., Sonoma
(707) 938–2200
www.spiritsinstone.com

"Must touch to appreciate" is the byword when visiting this collection of Zimbabwe Shona sculpture. The form's sleek surface is beyond description. *Newsweek* has called Shona sculpture "the most important new art form to emerge from Africa this century." You can also find African photographs, paintings, and music at this museum-quality gallery, which is open daily from 10:00 A.M. to 6:00 P.M. (See our Shopping chapter for more on Spirits In Stone.)

Sonoma State University Art Gallery
1801 East Cotati Avenue, Rohnert Park
(707) 664–2295
www.sonoma.edu/ArtGallery

Changing exhibits of contemporary art are combined with works by artists known regionally, nationally, and internationally. The gallery is open Tuesday through Friday from 11:00 A.M. to 4:00 P.M. and noon to 4:00 P.M. on weekends. Admission is free.

Cultural Arts Council of Sonoma County
602 Wilson Street, Santa Rosa
(707) 579–2787
www.cacsc.org

Curating new exhibits every eight weeks, the council serves as a resource center for artists and provides a gallery for their work. A typical art competition commissioned by the Sonoma Land Trust challenged artists to portray imagery inspired by Sonoma County's agricultural environment. It's not just two-dimensional art. For five years the council has sponsored a gospel music concert, sharing a unique American art form in performances at Santa Rosa High School.

Sonoma Museum of Visual Art
Luther Burbank Center for the Arts,
50 Mark West Springs Road, Santa Rosa
(707) 527–0297
www.lbc.net/museummain.html

The only fine arts museum serving the Northern California coast and northern San Francisco Bay Area, the Sonoma Museum of Visual Art (MOVA) features local artists whose work transcends conventional painting, sculpture, photography, and architecture. An interactive salon is held at Sonoma MOVA on occasional Friday evenings throughout the year. These feature guest speakers from all walks of the artistic community. In the summer months, visitors can enjoy the outdoor Film Cafe, which pairs short experimental films with excellent local food and wine. Museum hours are Monday through Friday from 10:00 A.M. to 4:00 P.M. (later on Thursday, to 8:00 P.M.), and Saturday and Sunday from 11:00 A.M. to 4:00 P.M.

The Ren Brown Collection
1781 Highway 1, Bodega Bay
(707) 875–2922, (800) 585–2921
www.renbrown.com

Housed in a building with shoji screens and a small Japanese garden, this gallery is dedicated to showing contemporary art from both sides of the Pacific. The major focus is on modern Japanese prints by artists such as Shigeki Kuroda, Toko Shinoda, and Ryohei Tanaka, whose works often appear in prominent museums. The items shown at Ren Brown represent the largest selections of contemporary Japanese prints in California. Also featured are the works of several regional California artists. You'll see watercolor, sculpture in stone and bronze; acrylic paintings; as well as woodcut, silkscreen, mezzotint, and lithograph art. All in all, some 75 artists are represented on two floors of the gallery, which is open every day except Tuesday from 10:00 A.M. to 5:00 P.M.

Christopher Queen Galleries
John Orr's Garden, No. 4, Duncans Mills
(707) 865–1318
www.duncansmillscamp.com/christopher.htm

On Highway 116 in historic Duncans Mills, this gallery features nationally known wildlife artists, including Thomas Brenders, John Bateman, and Thomas Quinn. Serigraphs by John Powell and Don Hatfield also are on display. The Upstairs Salon features an extensive display of important early California artists. The galleries are open every day but Tuesday from 11:00 A.M. to 5:00 P.M., and by appointment.

Sea Ranch Lodge
North Highway 1, Sea Ranch
(707) 785–2371

Various artists and photographers display their work in the Sea Ranch Lodge's Fireside Room overlooking the ocean (for more on Sea Ranch, see our Real Estate chapter). New exhibits are posted each month, introduced with a reception of wine and hors d'oeuvres. Call for a list of upcoming exhibits.

Mendocino County

Gualala Arts Center
46501 Old State Highway, Gualala
(707) 884-1138
www.gualalaarts.com

In the early 1900s, Gualala was a lumber mill center, abandoned when sawmills closed down. But in the 1960s, the beauty of the area attracted artists and other creative people. They painted, photographed, wrote, acted, and watched whales. They attracted other talented people, and during the last three decades Gualala has become recognized as a center for the arts, drawing people from miles around to soak up the cultural atmosphere.

The focal point of all this art activity is a 15,000-square-foot arts center, established in 1997 and set in the forest. The scope of the center's activities is somewhat overwhelming. You'll find popular and classical music concerts, lectures, exhibits, youth and adult art classes, theater productions, and meeting space for artists, photographers, quilters, poets, weavers, and book groups. They do all this with one salaried secretary, a professional executive director, and a lot of volunteers.

The first Sunday of every month is given over to chamber music concerts (tickets are $15), but it's likely you will run into some kind of music event any time you happen to be in town. A wide variety of events—from theater presentations to lecture series—is held in the multipurpose room (seating capacity, 350). The mid-August Art in the Redwoods extravaganza (see our Festivals and Annual Events chapter) attracts more than 350 artistic entries and approximately 5,000 people attend each year.

Father Time and the Maiden, *a 19th-century statuary carved from a single block of redwood by mill worker Erick Albertson, sits atop the Masonic Lodge Building in Mendocino.* PHOTO: JOHN NAGIECKI

Now Starring in a Theater Near You: Wine Country

Ever since Alfred Hitchcock put sleepy Santa Rosa on the map in 1942, when he came to town to make his classic thriller *Shadow of a Doubt,* Hollywood moviemakers have returned again and again to Wine Country to capture its rural charms and natural beauty on film.

The list of movies partially or entirely filmed here over the past 50 years is lengthy and impressive. From simple love stories to mega-projects that lean to computer-generated imagery, nearly every genre of motion picture has featured Northern California locations in a starring role.

Here's a brief list of some better-known theatrical movies of the last three-plus decades—and more recent blockbusters—in which our three-county region served as a backdrop in one way or another:

American Graffiti
The Animal
Apocalypse Now
Bandits
Basic Instinct
Beverly Hillbillies
The Birds
Black Rain
The Candidate
Cujo
Flatliners
Die Hard 2
The Goonies
Grand Avenue (HBO)
The Horse Whisperer
I Know What You Did Last Summer
Inventing the Abbotts
It's a Mad Mad Mad Mad World
Lolita
Mumford
Peggy Sue Got Married
Phenomenon
Pollyanna
The Russians Are Coming, the Russians Are Coming
Scream
Tucker: The Man and His Dream
A Walk in the Clouds

In addition to full-length feature films, many made-for-TV movies and TV commercials are shot here. Particularly popular is the Sonoma County coastline—its ultra-green hills, rocky cliffs, and switchbacked highway make a snazzy setting for car commercials.

Alinder Gallery
39165 South Highway 1, Gualala
(707) 884–4884
www.alindergallery.com

Internationally respected authorities Mary and Jim Alinder manage this gallery. While specializing in original Ansel Adams images, the gallery maintains an excellent inventory of work by many other great photographers. Alinder Gallery is open Tuesday through Sunday from 10:00 A.M. to 6:00 P.M.

Mendocino Art Center
45200 Little Lake Street, Mendocino
(707) 937–5818, (800) 653–3328
www.mendocinoartcenter.org

This is an educational organization that features classes in everything from furniture making to bead artistry. Year-round courses in fine arts, ceramics, and children's art, conducted by paid artists-in-residence, draw students from around the country. A spacious gallery at the center features the work of established and emerging artists of local, regional, and national reputation. An additional showcase gallery is at 560 Main Street, open every day from 10:00 A.M. to 5:00 P.M. in spring and summer, 10:00 A.M. to 4:00 P.M. in winter.

Northcoast Artists Gallery
362 North Main Street, Fort Bragg
(707) 964–8266

This is a cooperative gallery with 22 artists showing their work. Started in 1986 with nine artists, it's now like a family, with four members of the original group still involved. Others come and go. Artists in oil paintings, ceramics, woodwork, and producers of silk-screens and fine paper products are featured. The gallery is open daily from 10:00 A.M. to 6:00 P.M.

Parks and Recreation

Parks

Golf

Bicycle Rentals

Bowling

Horseback Riding

Hunting

Swimming

Tennis

Ah, the great outdoors. We have it in spades in Wine Country, from majestic inland mountains to the crashing waves of an unspoiled and awe-inspiring coastline. If you're itching to hike, bike, or otherwise become one with nature, this chapter will point you in the right direction.

First we present the primary parks and recreation areas in the region, followed by separate sections on golf, bicycling, bowling, horseback riding, hunting, swimming, and tennis. There is no individual section on hiking, as almost all of the parks offer trails. While campgrounds and primitive camping sites are mentioned in these listings, more specific information may be found in our Camping chapter. If you break out in a rash at the sight of Winnebagos, or you're wanted by the California Park Service for absconding with a Chumash arrowhead in 1973, don't fret. There is plenty of recreational activity that goes beyond hiking and camping in the parks. If you still run out of things to do, turn to our On the Water chapter and read about a whole different order of activities.

Parks

Like the statewide system as a whole, the California state parks within the Wine Country offer an almost inconceivable diversity of ecosystems. While visitors to Mackerricher State Park are turning up their collars and waiting for the dense coastal fog to lift on a summer morning, folks are already in the water at Clear Lake State Park. See the grasslands of Austin Creek one day and the redwood canopy of Admiral William Standley the next, and try to convince yourself you're on the same planet. And that doesn't even address the historic parks, which are listed in the Attractions chapter.

Included in this section, along with the state lands, are major regional parks and recreation areas that offer more than a lawn and a playground. You're never far from one of them. (You're probably even closer to a municipal park—consult a local map or ask around.) Deciding where to go might depend on when you'll be there. Only the inland, northern entries, such as Mendocino National Forest, are likely to be affected by winter snow. But all the parks have a chance of being wet and dreary between November and February, while spring and autumn are always safe bets. Summer takes more thought. The coastal parks and state beaches are wonderful retreats from the heat, but some of the valley parks will put you right into the oven.

Unless otherwise stated, parks are open year-round and 24 hours a day. Most regional parks have no admission charge. Pets are welcome in campgrounds and picnic areas but usually not on trails or beaches.

With millions of jittery city folks visiting California's parks each year, the campgrounds are often filled to the brim, especially between Memorial Day and Labor Day. You can make reservations up to seven months in advance by phoning ReserveAmerica (see the number listed in the box in this chapter). All major credit cards are accepted.

In Sonoma County, several regional parks with camping facilities now take reservations. Because the nearly 200 camp-

When It's Time to Park It

Here are some helpful numbers and Web sites to keep in mind when considering a visit to one of the state parks.

California State Park Information
(916) 653–6995, (800) 777–0369;
www.parks.ca.gov

ReserveAmerica Camping Reservations
(800) 444–7275;
www.reserveamerica.com

ReserveAmerica Customer Service/
  Cancellations
(800) 695–2269

Special Services for the Handicapped
(916) 653–8148

Caltrans Road/Weather Information
(800) 427–7623

sites at the county's four coastal campgrounds are occupied by more than 100,000 people each year, this new reservation system is a welcome change. You can call (707) 565–CAMP (2267) to reserve a camping spot at these Sonoma County regional parks: Gualala Point, Stillwater Cove, Doran, and Spring Lake. (All are profiled in this chapter and in our Camping chapter.)

Napa County

Bothe-Napa Valley State Park
Highway 29, 4 miles south of Calistoga
(707) 942–4575
www.napanet.net/~bothe

A trail of cars crawls along Highway 29, but you can leave it behind by exploring this 1,900-acre retreat. Follow shady Ritchey Creek with its redwoods and maples, then venture deeper into terrain covered by oak, hazel, laurel, and madrone. From Coyote Peak you can gaze east into a rugged canyon—not a vineyard in sight. And in summer you can enjoy the cool, spring-fed swimming pool in the picnic area. There is a campground (see our Camping chapter) and a horse concession with guided rides. Bothe is just off Highway 29, between Calistoga and St. Helena. Parallel to the Highway runs a 1.02-mile trail that connects

Bothe with the Bale Grist Mill Historic Park.

Robert Louis Stevenson State Park
Highway 29 between Calistoga and Middletown
(707) 942–4575

Between Calistoga and Middletown, at the crest of Highway 29, is Stevenson State Park. Less than a mile from the trailhead rests a memorial to the noted author, who in 1880 spent his honeymoon squatting here and weathering a long illness. (His experience wound up as the basis for *The Silverado Squatters;* see our History chapter.) A steep 100 yards from the memorial, you will encounter a fire road/trail that winds 5 miles to the top of Mount St. Helena, offering brilliant views throughout. If you spin in a circle at the 4,343-foot summit, you'll probably be able to see the snow-capped Sierra Nevada Mountains to the east, the shining Pacific to the west, Mount Diablo to the south and, on good days, Mount Shasta, 192 miles to the north. The trail is highly exposed, so bring plenty of water and sunblock. The picnic area near the highway is lovely, although a bit noisy. Be advised there are no restrooms and parking is limited, but the vistas at the top are usually worth the trouble.

Sonoma County

Southern Sonoma

Sonoma Valley Regional Park
13630 Highway 12, Glen Ellen
(707) 565–2041
www.sonoma-county.org

A 162-acre spread just outside Glen Ellen, Sonoma Valley has a paved, 2-mile bicycle trail and about 5 miles of hiking trails through meadows and oak-dense terrain, plus a picnic area. Just across the Highway is Bouverie Wildflower Preserve. Open daily from sunup to sundown. Dogs must be leashed. Parking is $3.00.

Sugarloaf Ridge State Park
Adobe Canyon Road, 11 miles north of
Sonoma on Highway 12
(707) 833–5712
www.parks.sonoma.net/sugarlf.html

Standing at the summit of Bald Mountain, you don't have to choose between Sonoma and Napa valleys—you can see them both at the same time. It's a startling view that is aided by identifying signs. And speaking of distant vistas, Sugarloaf recently added an observatory with the most powerful publicly accessible telescope in the state. The park as a whole is rugged and steep, an adventurous contrast to the gentle valleys below. Look for deer, gray fox, and even bobcat and mountain lion. The chaparral can get hot in the summer, but you'll be shaded (sometimes by redwoods) if you stay next to Sonoma Creek.

Because day parking is limited, the road entering Sugarloaf Ridge tends to congest with spillover traffic, so try to arrive early on weekends. The 7-mile Bald Mountain loop is the highlight of the park's numerous and well-marked trails. The park is on Adobe Canyon Road, 9 miles east of Santa Rosa or 11 miles north of Sonoma on Highway 12.

Helen Putnam Regional Park
411 Chileno Valley Road, 1 mile southwest of
Petaluma
(707) 565–2041
www.sonoma-county.org

Just outside downtown Petaluma, 216-acre Helen Putnam Park has hiking, bik-

ing, and horse trails that lead to exceptional views of town and farmland. There is a playground and a picnic area with a gazebo. The park is open sunrise to sunset. From Petaluma Boulevard, go west on Western Avenue and turn left on Chileno Valley Road. Parking is $3.00. Dogs must be leashed.

Fairfield Osborn Preserve
6543 Lichau Road, east of Cotati
(707) 795–5069
www.sonoma.edu/Org/preserve

Formerly operated by The Nature Conservancy and now owned and managed by Sonoma State University, Fairfield Osborn is a jewel of a preserve that butts up against the western slope of 2,465-foot Sonoma Mountain, east of Cotati. The 210-acre holding has 6 miles of trails through oak woodlands, meadows, and riparian forest. The preserve is not open to the public on a daily basis. However, on Saturdays and Sundays in the fall and spring, naturalists lead hikes at 10:00 A.M. and 1:00 P.M. No reservations are required.

The cost is $3.00 for adults; children 12 and under are free. Please call for directions and exact dates.

Crane Creek Regional Park
6107 Pressley Road, east of Rohnert Park
(707) 565–2041
www.sonoma-county.org

No, Rohnert Park isn't made up entirely of Home Depots and Wal-Marts. This pleasant, 128-acre park is just east of Sonoma State University, in the foothills of Sonoma Mountain. It has a picnic area and 3 miles of trails open to people on foot, bicycles, and horses. Follow the creek past buckeye, oak, and maple. Crane Creek is on Pressley Road; take Roberts Road east from Petaluma Hill Road. The park is open sunrise to sunset. Parking is $3.00. Dogs must be leashed. Drinking water is not available in the park.

Annadel State Park
Channel Drive, southeast of Santa Rosa
(707) 539–3911
www.parks.sonoma.net/Annadel.html

One minute you're in Santa Rosa—largest city in the Wine Country—and the next

Though sightings and bitings are rare, signs like this warn hikers to keep their eyes open along Wine Country's remote trails. PHOTO: JEAN SAYLOR DOPPENBERG

you're hiking in the solitude of a 5,000-acre parcel of undulating meadow and oak woodland. Within Annadel, you'll find one large natural marsh and one man-made lake, Ilsanjo, stocked with black bass and bluegill. One of the best hikes is the Warren Richardson-Ledson Marsh Loop, a 7.5-mile outing that takes you to Ledson with its bulrushes, cattails, and bird life. Primary trail junctions are marked, but you should think about carrying a park map to help you sort out the details. There are several picnic sites in the park, which is open 9:00 A.M. to sunset daily. Get there by taking Montgomery Drive to Channel Drive on the east side of Santa Rosa.

Spring Lake Regional Park
Summerfield Road, Santa Rosa
(707) 539–8092
www.sonoma-county.org
Most of this 320-acre park is consumed by the central lake, popular with boaters and swimmers in the summer. Around the lake are a 2-mile bike path and a par-

course plus about 15 miles of hiking and equestrian trails. Spring Lake also has a developed campground, scads of picnic tables, and a visitor center that's open on weekends. The park is attached to the north end of Annadel State Park. The west entrance is on Newanga Avenue, off Summerfield Road in Santa Rosa; the east entrance is on Violetti Drive, off Montgomery Road.

Northern Sonoma

Lake Sonoma
Stewarts Point-Skaggs Springs Road, off Dry Creek Road, west of Geyserville
(707) 433–9483
www.parks.sonoma.net/laktrls.html
Lake Sonoma's primary recreational offerings are detailed in our On the Water chapter. However, the 18,000-acre park that surrounds the lake is filled with possibilities of its own, including more than 40 miles of trails with views of the lake. The visitor center has Pomo Indian artifacts, and the California Department of Fish and Game operates a nearby fish hatchery (see

our Kidstuff chapter). A self-guided nature trail begins at the center. Lake Sonoma also has a large developed campground and 15 primitive campgrounds around the lake. From Geyserville, go west on Canyon Road, turn right on Dry Creek Road and, after about 3 miles, bend left onto Stewarts Point-Skaggs Springs Road.

Sonoma Coast

Doran Regional Park
Westside Regional Park
Highway 1, 1 mile south of Bodega Bay
(707) 875-3540
www.sonoma-county.org

These two recreation areas are on the south and northwest sides, respectively, of ultraprotected Bodega Bay. The bay's water-based attractions are profiled in our On the Water chapter. But the parks also feature wavy sand dunes and, at Doran, a 2-mile stretch of beach. Each park has a campground, with 47 sites at Westside and 128 at Doran (see our Camping chapter). Each is reached from Highway 1. For Doran Park, turn west at Doran Park Road; for Westside Park, turn west at Bay Flat Road. Parking is $3.00 for day use. Dogs must be leashed.

Sonoma Coast State Beach
off Highway 1
(707) 875-3483
www.parks.sonoma.net/coast.html

The 100-foot bluffs, the ruinous offshore rocks and arches, the coastal scrub plateaus, the black-sand coves—it all adds up to a dramatic oceanside landscape. The park stretches 16.6 miles along the jagged coastline and offers three trails. The main attraction is Goat Rock, a large, wave-battered massif near the main parking lot. In spring, the bluffs are decorated with lupine, sea pinks, and Indian paintbrush. There is whale watching from Bodega Head and a seal colony at the mouth of the Russian River. Numerous marked and unmarked roads provide access to the beaches, some of them ending in parking lots, some not. All are found off Highway 1 between Bodega Bay and the high bluffs 4.8 miles north of Jenner—the town with the visitor center. There are two campgrounds, at Bodega Dunes and Wrights Beach. There also are two environmental camps; ask for a map at the visitor center. A final word: To get in this water, you'd have to be a lunatic, a harbor seal, or a surfer.

Stillwater Cove Regional Park
22455 Highway 1, approx. 15 miles north of Jenner
(707) 847-3245
www.sonoma-county.org

Even if you're not an abalone diver or a surf fisher, Stillwater Cove is a worthwhile stop. It has a picnic area and 5 miles of hiking trails amid the redwoods. It also has one developed campground with showers and flush toilets. In the park is a preserved, one-room schoolhouse from the 19th century. Day use parking is $3.00. Dogs must be leashed.

Insiders' Tip

A few rules to remember when encountering the California State Park system: (1) Do not disturb flowers, rocks, plants, animals, or artifacts—and, yes, putting something in your pocket is considered a disturbance; (2) Do not gather firewood; and (3) Hunting or possession of firearms (loaded or unloaded) is probably prohibited, so check with the individual park beforehand.

Salt Point State Park
Off Highway 1
(707) 847–3221
www.parks.sonoma.net/coast.html

Salt Point and neighboring Kruse Rhododendron State Reserve (see the following
listing) have a little bit of something for
everyone. Salt Point has about 10 miles of
rocky coastline featuring sea stacks,
arches, and tafoni—those eerily sculpted
knobs, ribs, and honeycombs that look
like they were crafted for horror movies.
The inland portion of the 6,000-acre park
has hiking trails through coastal brush,
Bishop pine, and Douglas fir, not to mention a ridge-top pygmy forest with half-
pint cypress, pine, and redwood. Salt
Point also boasts one of California's first
underwater parks, Gerstle Cove Marine
Reserve, a favorite for scuba divers (and
for fish, which are fully protected there).
The park has two campgrounds plus
walk-in campsites; see our Camping chapter for more on that. It straddles Highway
1, about 16 miles north of Jenner or 18
miles south of Gualala.

Kruse Rhododendron State Reserve
Off Highway 1 on Kruse Ranch Road
(707) 847–3221
www.parks.sonoma.net/coast.html

This 317-acre reserve near Salt Point State
Park was donated in 1933 by Edward P. E.
Kruse, whose family raised sheep, logged,
and harvested tanbark there. From April
through June, the pink and violet rhododendron blossoms brighten the shady
forest of fir and second-growth redwood.
Five miles of hiking trails offer great
opportunities to view the blooms. The
reserve is off Highway 1, toward the north
end of Salt Point, and is open sunup to
sunset

Gualala Point Regional Park
Off Highway 1, 1 mile south of Gualala
(707) 785–2377
www.sonoma-county.org

Located just south of the town of Gualala,
the park offers both seaside and riverside
environments. Anglers show up for saltwater and freshwater fishing. Hikers
enjoy 6 miles of trails. Picnickers have sev-

Waves of the majestic Pacific Ocean break along the rocky Sonoma Coast. PHOTO: JAN BLANCHARD

eral site options, some with barbecue pits. And campers are greeted by a developed area in the redwoods. The visitor center is open 10:30 A.M. to 3:00 P.M. Friday through Monday. Day use parking is $3.00. Dogs must be leashed and have proof of rabies vaccination.

West County/Russian River

Ragle Ranch Regional Park
500 Ragle Road, 1 mile north of Bodega Highway Sebastopol
(707) 565–2041, (707) 823–7262
www.sonoma-county.org

This 157-acre park offers the usual family-oriented facilities—baseball diamonds, playgrounds, a soccer field, a volleyball court, and picnic sites—but also claims hiking and equestrian trails through rugged oak woodlands and marshes. There is a parcourse too. Each August the park hosts the annual Gravenstein Apple Fair (see our Festivals and Annual Events chapter).The park is off Ragle Road, 1 mile north of Bodega Highway on the western perimeter of Sebastopol, and is open sunup to sunset.

Armstrong Redwoods State Reserve
Armstrong Woods Road, near Guerneville
(707) 869–2015
www.parks.sonoma.net/Armstrng.html

In the 1870s, lumberman Col. James Armstrong saw the errors of his clear-cutting ways and preserved a large chunk of old-growth redwood forest for posterity. Today it forms the core of 805-acre Armstrong Redwoods Reserve. Don't forget to say hello to two of the most impressive specimens in the park: the 1,400-year-old Colonel Armstrong Tree and the tallest tree in the area, the 310-foot Parson Jones Tree, (named for the Colonel's son-in-law). Next to the Jones Tree is a gigantic log cross section, whose growth rings chart the course of history back to the first millennium—unfortunately, the tree had been cut by vandals in the 1970s. To get to Armstrong from Guerneville, turn north off River Road onto Armstrong Woods Road and proceed 2.2 miles. The reserve is open daily from 8:00 A.M. to one hour after sunset.

> ## Insiders' Tip
> A great place to watch surfers—or catch a wave for yourself—is Salmon Creek Beach on the Sonoma Coast.

Austin Creek State Recreation Area
Armstrong Woods Road, near Guerneville
(707) 869–2015
www.parks.sonoma.net/austin.html

Directly adjacent to Armstrong Redwoods Reserve is 5,683-acre Austin Creek State Recreation Area. Austin Creek has miles of trails that hikers have to share with horses, which often come in large groups. (Mountain bikes are allowed only on paved roads and on a 5-mile dirt road called the East Austin Creek Trail.) Keep an eye open for deer, wild turkeys, raccoons, and possibly even world-famous ceramic artists. One of the latter, Marguerite Wildenhain, lived here, and her home and workshop—Pond Farm—are within the park, though off-limits since Wildenhain's death. There is a drive-in campground and four backcountry campsites within the recreation area. To get to Austin Creek, follow the directions for Armstrong Woods and, after reaching the entrance, continue another 3.6 miles to Bullfrog Pond Campground.

Mendocino County

U.S. 101

Lake Mendocino Recreation Area
Lake Mendocino Drive, off U.S. 101
(707) 462–7581
www.spn.usace.army.mil/mendocino.html

About as pretty as man-made lakes come, Lake Mendocino is surrounded by 1,800 acres of hills, vineyards, and pear orchards. There are 18 miles of riding trails and nearly as many of hiking trails. You can also take advantage of five day-use picnic areas and three developed campgrounds. (You can reach another 20 primitive campsites with a boat.) To get there, head east on Lake Mendocino Drive from U.S. 101, just north of Ukiah, or go south on Marina Drive from Highway 20 near Calpella. (See our On the Water chapter for more details.)

Montgomery Woods State Reserve
Orr Springs Road, north of Ukiah
(707) 937–5804
www.parks.ca.gov/default.asp?page_id=434
Here you can find all your major appliances, from microwaves to washers and dryers. Oh, wait, that's Montgomery Ward. Montgomery Woods is an isolated sanctuary northwest of Ukiah. The 2-mile nature trail not only guides you alongside giant trees, but also takes you right through them, with steps and passageways carved into toppled specimens. You'll visit five redwood groves along Montgomery Creek, including the splendid Grubbs' Memorial Grove. You can pick up a printed guide at the beginning of the trail. Montgomery Woods has one creekside picnic site and no water. It is open sunrise to sunset. From downtown Ukiah, take Orr Springs Road northwest for about 12 miles.

Insiders' Tip
Beware the western black-legged tick: Though the odds are slim of catching Lyme disease in Northern California, it has been known to happen. *Ixodes pacificus* is the bearer of the disease in this neck of the woods, so check yourself for ticks after hiking through grass or forests.

Admiral William Standley State Recreation Area
Branscomb Road, off U.S. 101, 14 miles west of Laytonville
(707) 247–3318
www.parks.ca.gov/default.asp?page_id=424
Admiral Standley's namesake is small (45 acres), hard to get to, and rarely crowded. It's a beautiful piece of forest, with virgin redwoods interspersed among Douglas firs, madrone, rhododendron, and mushrooms. It is also a popular salmon and steelhead fishing spot. There are no trails, however, so don't wander far from the parking area. From U.S. 101 in Laytonville, turn left on Branscomb Road, and drive 12 miles. The recreation area is set on either side of the road, and signs can be difficult to spot. It is open sunup to sundown.

Standish-Hickey State Recreation Area
U.S. 101, 1 mile north of Leggett
(707) 925–6482
www.parks.ca.gov/default.asp?page_id=423
This sizable park presents your basic gigantic redwoods plus access to the south fork of the Eel River. The Big Tree Loop starts at Redwood campground and ends near Miles Standish Tree, a 225-foot, 1,200-year-old giant that towers over its second-growth neighbors. Still visible on its side are the ax marks delivered—as the legend goes—by a 1930s evangelist who vowed to chop down the biggest tree he could find. Miles Standish lives on, while the evangelist has gone to that great lumber mill in the sky. In summer it's swimming that lures most visitors. The Eel is punctuated with deep pools formed by rock outcrops. The best is at the tail end of a wide bend, where the Big Tree Loop crosses the river. The pool is nearly 20 feet deep, with a sandy floor. There is no shade, so bring sunscreen and a hat. Standish-Hickey has three campgrounds and a picnic area.

Smith Redwoods State Reserve
U.S. 101, 4 miles north of Leggett
(707) 247–3318
www.parks.ca.gov/default.asp?page_id=427
Little more than a roadside attraction, this 665-acre park has no trails or picnic

facilities. It does, however, give you an up-close encounter with some of the largest trees in the world. Don't be shy, big fella, give that tree a hug. You can walk through two stumps. And if you're in need of a dunk, both a 60-foot waterfall (across the Highway) and the South Fork of the Eel River are close at hand. It is open sunup to sundown.

Highway 128

Mailliard Redwoods State Reserve
Fish Rock Road, off Highway 128
(707) 937–5804
www.mcn.org/1/mendoparks/maill.htm

There isn't much here for hikers or bikers, but if you're in the area, your eyes will appreciate the detour. Mailliard has 242 acres of virgin and second-growth redwoods along the headwaters of Garcia River. You can reach the park from Highway 128, 7.3 miles east of Boonville. Turn south on Fish Rock Road and proceed about 3 miles. There is one picnic area nearly a mile into the park. Open sunrise to sunset.

Hendy Woods State Park
Philo-Greenwood Road, off Highway 128
(707) 895–3141
www.parks.ca.gov/default.asp?page_id=438
There are campsites, a picnic area, and trails for hikers, mountain bikers, and equestrians. The Gentle Giants All-Access Trail is a surfaced path that accesses Big Hendy, Anderson Valley's last extensive grove of old-growth coastal redwoods. Another short trail leads to the hermit hut, a partially collapsed, thatched-roof lean-to that the Boonville Hermit used as his abode from the end of World War II (when he jumped his Russian ship) until he died in 1981. To get to Hendy Woods, take Highway 128 2.8 miles west of Philo and turn south on Philo-Greenwood Road.

Navarro River Redwoods
Highway 128, between Navarro and Highway 1
(707) 937–5804
www.parks.ca.gov/default.asp?page_id=435

Because this is America, you get to enjoy the beauty of Navarro River without leaving your rental car. The park straddles Highway 128 between Navarro and the coast, and the highway basically shadows the river. It's a shady corridor of second-growth redwoods, alders, and tan oak. There are plenty of turnouts if you want a breath of fresh air or a short stroll. In the fall, you'll likely see people fishing for steelhead. The river also has one overnight campground.

Mendocino Coast

Schooner Gulch
Off Highway 1, 3.5 miles south of Point Arena
(707) 937–5804
www.parks.ca.gov/default.asp?page_id=446

This park contains two beaches, separated by a bulging headland. The north lobe is Bowling Ball Beach, named for the perfectly spherical boulders revealed at low tide. (It might be worth it to consult a tide chart before visiting.) The cliffs abutting this mile-long strand of hard-packed sand are misshapen and interesting. The south lobe is Schooner Gulch, which is rockier and preferred by fishermen. The actual gulch feeds into the sea amidst a jumble of logs. There is no drinking water in the park, so bring your own. It's open sunrise to sunset.

Manchester State Beach
Kinney Road, off Highway 1
(707) 937-5804
www.parks.ca.gov/default.asp?page_id=437
Manchester's diverse topography encompasses rocky shore, dunes (both grassy and bald), marshes, a lagoon, and a coastal plain. It's a place where anglers, birdwatchers, and rowdy kids can find common ground. The avian wealth includes northern harriers, tundra swans, ducks, herons, and pelicans. The drift-log shelters along the 5 miles of beach attest to the relentless winds that buffet the area. There is a primitive campground and hiking trails, including the 5-mile Beach-Inland Loop. To reach Manchester from Highway 1, turn west onto Kinney Road and drive a little more than a half-mile.

Greenwood Creek State Beach
Highway 1, near Elk
(707) 937–5804
www.mcn.org/1/mendoparks/greenwd.htm

This park is quite small on the horizontal scale, but impressive on the vertical—it encompasses both the gravelly beach and the overlooking bluff, some 150 feet above. Most of the picnic sites are up top. From the shore you can see the three rock islands that punctuate the cove and watch for the bobbing heads of harbor seals. Greenwood Creek is west of Highway 1, adjacent to the town of Elk. The visitor center is Elk's original mill office (see our Attractions chapter). Greenwood Creek State Beach is open sunrise to sunset.

Van Damme State Park
Highway 1, 2.5 miles south of Mendocino
(707) 937–5804
www.parks.ca.gov/default.asp?_id=443

Don't worry, you aren't likely to be bothered by aggressive action-adventure heroes in this fascinating park. What you will get is a smorgasbord of redwoods, beach, underwater bounty, swamp, and pygmy trees. The Fern Canyon Trail is a 4.9-mile meander through a dark, cool fern forest. Separate mini-trails take you to the pygmy forest, with its 4-foot pines and cypresses, and a bog. Hikers and bikers share some trails, but not all. If you get claustrophobic in the woods, take a kayak tour of the small cove accessible at the Van Damme beach parking lot.

Van Damme has both developed campgrounds and hike-in tent sites, as discussed in our Camping chapter. It has a picnic area on the beach and an undersea preserve. And don't miss the re-created surge channel at the visitor center. The park is 2.5 miles south of Mendocino on Highway 1—turn east for the main park, west for the beach.

Mendocino Headlands State Park
Main Street, Mendocino
(707) 937–5804
www.parks.ca.gov/default.asp?page_id=442

This is the town of Mendocino's wraparound park on the bluffs, offering spec-

A stoic face carved into a stump looks out to sea from Mendocino Headlands State Park. PHOTO: JOHN NAGIECKI

tacular views of the sea on all sides. Spring brings wildflowers, winter ushers migrating gray whales, and summer draws sunbathers and hardy swimmers to Big River Beach, just south of the headlands. The miles of blowholes, arches, and craggy stacks are there year-round. There is a picnic area along Heeser Drive at the north end of town; in town is the Ford House Visitor Center with its fine historical displays. The Headlands Trail, 6 miles round-trip, skirts the edges of the bluffs. The park is open sunrise to sunset.

Russian Gulch State Park
Off Highway 1, 2 miles north of Mendocino
(707) 937–5804
www.parks.ca.gov/default.asp?page_id=432

Here you have the option of walking along the coast, where waves crash like giant cymbals, or wandering through the serenity of the forest. The Headland Trail offers two sideshow oddities: a blowhole fed by a sea cave and an inland punchbowl, connected to the sea by another hidden cave. The Fern Canyon Trail, meanwhile, takes you alongside Russian Gulch to a delicate, 36-foot waterfall. It's a 6-mile round-trip stroll through alder, California laurel, redwood and, of course, ferns. The park has campsites and a picnic area.

Caspar Headlands State Beach and Reserve
**Point Cabrillo Drive, off Highway 1, Caspar
(707) 937–5804
www.parks.ca.gov/default.asp?page_id=444**

These twin holdings are small (less than 5 acres between them) and highly regulated. You can visit the bluff-top reserve—with its far-reaching views—only with a permit, obtainable at the Mendocino District Office, 2 miles north of Mendocino. Get a map there, too, as the reserve interlocks with a private housing development, and it's easy to trespass. The beach, about a quarter-mile long, opens onto a square bay. It's popular with swimmers, divers, and anglers. This is no place for the meek. Caspar Headlands has no toilets, no picnic tables, and no water. Undeterred? From Highway 1 in Caspar, turn west on Point Cabrillo Drive. The park is open sunrise to sunset.

Jug Handle State Reserve
**Off Highway 1, just north of Caspar
(707) 937–5804
www.parks.ca.gov/default.asp?page_id=441**

This is another coastal park that gives you surf-and-turf options. One trail roams the soaring headlands, with views of Jug Handle Bay to the north and a similar inlet to the south. Look for sea stacks and an arch. The Ecological Staircase Trail is a 5-mile, round-trip tour of three marine terraces—a geologic showcase that displays about 250,000 years of elemental activity. The first terrace is meadow-transition habitat, the second is a mixed conifer forest, and the third is redwood-Douglas fir complex. At the end of the line, for no extra charge, is a pygmy forest.

The trails are for hikers only, and visitors should bring their own water. Jug Handle is open sunup to sundown.

Jackson State Forest
**State Department of Forestry, 802 North Main Street, Fort Bragg
(707) 964–5674**

Sprawling between Willits and the coast in the vicinity of Highway 20, this state holding has 50,000 acres of oak, pine, and redwood, not to mention a pygmy forest. There are 25 miles of fire road and two other trails suitable as footpaths. It's a mixed bag—as state forests often are—with some pristine areas and others that have been logged or mined. Jackson has campgrounds in two areas. One is near the hamlet of Dunlap, about halfway between Willits and the coast. The other, highlighted in our Camping chapter, is about 6 miles east of Highway 1.

Mackerricher State Park
**West of Highway 1, 3 miles north of Fort Bragg
(707) 937–5804
www.mcn.org/1/mendoparks/macker.htm**

Mackerricher is a prime slice of Northern California coast, with 8 miles of beach, large dunes, grassy headlands, and even freshwater Lake Cleone. Gray whales migrate offshore between December and March, and humans migrate to the headlands to watch them. If you're into cetacean anatomy, a 30-foot gray whale skeleton lies near the ranger station, just beyond the main entrance. The footpaths are varied. The Laguna Trail circles the lake and its marshy border. The Seal Point Trail leads to a (harbor) Seal Watching Station. And the Haul Road Bicycle Route is a one-time logging road that runs the length of the park, about 7 miles. It's closed to motorized vehicles and so is popular with cyclists and runners. Of course, you can simply walk down the beach for miles if you prefer. Mackerricher has two campgrounds and several picnic areas. The main entrance is 3 miles north of Fort Bragg, just west of Highway 1. The Pudding Creek Day Area is only a half-mile north of Fort Bragg.

Westport-Union Landing State Beach
Off Highway 1, just north of Westport
(707) 937-5804
www.parks.ca.gov/default.asp?page_id=440

North of the town of Westport is a series of four oceanside bluffs, separated by creek canyons and interspersed with beaches. Together they form this skinny park, with its 50-foot cliffs and craggy shoreline. It's a favorite haunt for storm-watchers, who can practically feel the spray from the angry waves.

Anglers come for spawning surf smelt in spring and summer. Pete's Beach and the sand below Abalone Point are fun to explore, but they don't offer much wiggle room, so watch out for sleeper waves—large, forceful waves that appear without warning. Westport-Union Landing has several access points off Highway 1, between a quarter-mile and 4 miles north of Westport. It offers open, grassy campsites but no water.

Sinkyone Wilderness State Park
County Road 431, west of Leggett
(707) 986-7711
www.parks.ca.gov/default.asp?_id=429

Wonder what the Mendocino Coast looked like before a certain bipedal mammal clogged up the scenery? Here's your answer. The Sinkyone Wilderness is part of the Lost Coast, a once-busy stretch of shoreline that has been isolated by its lack of contact with major roads.

There are two entrances to the park, one at the south end and another at the north. Between them lies a long expanse of unadulterated nature: forested ridges, rugged coast, black-sand beaches, and riparian ecosystem.

The Needle Rock Visitor Center is in a restored, turn-of-the-century ranch house; nearby is a short trail to Needle Rock Beach. There is a drive-in campground at Usal Creek (the south entrance) and walk-in sites near Bear Harbor in the north. To get to Usal Creek, follow Highway 1 west from Leggett and, 14 miles later, turn right on County Road 431 and proceed 5.5 miles. To get to Needle Rock, make your way to Redway, 2.5 miles west of Garberville and U.S. 101. Turn south on Briceland Road and continue past Whitethorn;

the road turns to gravel after 17 miles. Then, it's 7.2 miles to the visitor center.

Mendocino National Forest
(707) 983-6118

If we tried to present a detailed account of the options here, the book would be called "Insiders' Guide to Mendocino National Forest." This is an immense, million-acre tract of terrain in the North Coast Mountain Range that encompasses almost all of the upper half of Lake County and the northeast tip of Mendocino County, not to mention parts of Glenn, Tehama, and Trinity Counties. The forest boasts two wilderness areas (closed to motorized vehicles), 2,000-acre Lake Pillsbury, several smaller lakes, and various tributaries of the Eel River. Trails? Yes, more than 160 miles, including off-highway vehicle paths near Upper Lake and Stoneyford. Campgrounds? Ten developed sites (see our Camping chapter) and numerous primitive camps. There ae many routes into the forest. Perhaps the most prominent is Elk Mountain Road, which heads north from the town of Upper Lake. About a mile north of Upper Lake is a ranger station dispensing maps and advice. Another station is on Highway 162, where the route name changes from Covelo Road to Mendocino Pass Road (about 2 miles north of Covelo in Mendocino County). There is no charge for day use of the forest.

Golf

The Wine Country isn't a hacker's mecca in the way of a Scottsdale or a Myrtle Beach. On the other hand, the mild climate and the stunning terrain do lend themselves to the links, especially for those who consider walking from fairway to green a form of exercise.

The facilities in our coverage area range from nine-hole pitch-and-putts to manicured, PGA-caliber courses. All of them have some sort of refreshment option—either a snack bar or a full-service restaurant. And practically all of them have pro shops where you can stock anything you forgot to pack. Following are some basic descriptions of the public courses; private clubs (with one major exception that does facilitate play by nonmembers) are not included. Like airfares, greens fees are always fluctuating, but we give you some general figures in the listings.

Napa County

Silverado Country Club & Resort
1600 Atlas Peak Road, Napa
(707) 257–0200, (800) 362–4727
www.silveradoresort.com

Although part of a private club, the two 18-hole championship courses at beautiful Silverado—designed by Robert Trent Jones Jr. and opened in 1965—can be accessed by Wine Country visitors. Guests at the Silverado resort (see our Spas and Resorts chapter) receive extended golfing privileges, and reciprocal arrangements with selected clubs around the country are also honored. Some allowances are made for nonguests who make arrangements two days in advance. (In-house guests play for $140.) Call to find out more, and ask about special room-and-golf packages too.

Former PGA Player of the Year and NBC golf analyst Johnny Miller used to be the touring pro at Silverado and still plays the courses often. The north course is 6700 yards; the south course is 6500 yards. A $3.5 million renovation project was planned for the two courses during 2003.

Napa Golf Course at Kennedy Park
2295 Streblow Drive, Napa
(707) 255–4333
www.playnapa.com

With John F. Kennedy Memorial Regional Park and the Napa River to the west and the open spaces of Napa Valley College to the north, this is a nicely placed 18-hole, par 72 course that runs about 6730 yards. Fees range from $31 to $42. A cart is an additional $12 per person. Ask about the reduced senior rates. Napa Golf Club is easy to walk but quite difficult to shoot. This is a challenging course.

Chardonnay Golf Club
2555 Jamieson Canyon Road, Napa
(707) 257–1900, (800) 788–0136
www.chardonnaygolfclub.com

Southeast of Napa, where the cool breezes of San Pablo Bay keep the terrain lush and green, Chardonnay offers a public 18-hole, par 72, 6816-yard course called The Vineyards. The club also has a private course called The Club Shakespeare, a qualifying site for the 1998 U.S. Open. Rates for The Vineyards range from $60 to $90, depending on the season, and that includes a cart. There is a grass driving range, a bar and grill (Sandtrap), and tournament and banquet facilities. And only in Napa Valley would you have to abide by the rule, "Vineyards are out of bounds." Jamieson Canyon Road is another name for Highway 12 between Highway 29 and I–80. Proper golf attire is required.

Vintners Golf Club
7901 Solano Avenue, Yountville
(707) 944–1992
www.vintnersgolfclub.com

Napa County's newest golfing attraction is a nine-hole course with true, fast greens and a backdrop of the historic Veterans Home of California buildings. Total yardage is 2700; par is 34. Vintners is full of amenities, including a clubhouse that serves breakfast, lunch, and appetizers (including alcohol), and a full pro shop. A lighted, covered, 36-stall driving range has been joined by a smaller grass range. Here are your greens fees: $18 for 9 holes and $24 for 18 holes during the week; $28 for 9 holes and $36 for 18 holes on Saturday and Sunday. Rent an electric cart for 9 holes ($16) or 18 ($24).

Mount St. Helena Golf Course
Napa County Fairgrounds,
1435 North Oak Street, Calistoga
(707) 942–9966

The course itself is modest—nothing special, one might go so far as to say—but Calistoga's scenic situation, within a horseshoe toss of rugged hills, makes this a fine place to spend a few hours. Play all day for $12 during the week, $18 on weekends. After 4:00 P.M. the price dips to $7.00 during the week and $10.00 on weekends. The nine-hole course is 2748 yards and par 34 for men, 2647 yards and par 35 for "ladies," as they say in the golf world.

Sonoma County

Sonoma Mission Inn Golf Club
17700 Arnold Drive, Sonoma
(707) 996–0300
www.sonomagolfclub.com

Part of the Sonoma Mission Inn, the clubhouse is strictly modern, but Sonoma Golf Club dates back to 1926. It was designed by Sam Whiting and Willie Watson, the same duo that laid out the lake course at the Olympic Club in San Francisco, and it is beautiful. The facility has 83 sand bunkers, three lakes, and surrounding views of the Mayacmas Mountains. The course plays 6583 yards from the regular tees. Soft spikes are mandatory, as are collared shirts and slacks. The tab is $60 to $80 during the week, $70 to $100 on Friday and on weekends. That price does not include a cart.

Los Arroyos Golf Course
5000 Stage Gulch Road, Sonoma
(707) 938–8835

This nine-hole course is just southwest of Sonoma, adjacent to Highway 116. Weekend greens fees are $12 for 9 holes and $17 for 18. Play during the week for $10 or $15. Pull-carts are $2.00 and Los Arroyos has a snack bar.

Adobe Creek Golf & Country Club
1901 Frates Road, Petaluma
(707) 765–3000
www.adobecreek.com

Adobe Creek, designed by Robert Trent Jones Jr., is an 18-hole, par 72, 6986-yard course on the southeast edge of Petaluma (just south of Petaluma Adobe State Historic Park). It has a grass driving range, and greens fees range from $32 to $75 depending on time of the week and day. Carts are $13 to $26. Collared shirts and soft spikes are mandatory.

Rooster Run Golf Club
2301 East Washington Street, Petaluma
(707) 778–1211
www.roosterrun.com

Rooster Run opened in the spring of 1998 and has since become the Wine Country's supreme public-golf bargain. Situated across the street from Petaluma Airport, the course is subject to the same afternoon winds that bedevil its neighbor, Adobe Creek Golf Course. The front nine includes an island green on the par-3 number 6. You'll need an oasis after number 5—rated the course's most difficult. Rooster Run management likes to boast that the course includes "the toughest four finishing holes in Northern California golf." Believe it. Regular rates are $28 Monday through Thursday, $34 Friday and $45 on weekends; the corresponding rates for certified Petaluma residents are $22, $25, and $36. Seniors play for $15 Monday through Wednesday. Juniors pay $10 after 2:30 P.M. Monday through Thursday.

Foxtail Golf Club
100 Golf Course Drive, Rohnert Park
(707) 584–7766
www.playfoxtail.com

Extensive renovations on the two courses at this establishment now make for a more satisfying game. The South Course is a par 71, 6500-yard layout with new tees, contoured fairways, and 14 new bunkers. Meanwhile, the North Course, expected to reopen in May 2003, is getting all new or recontoured greens, more tees, and better drainage. Weekday fees range from $17.50 to $25.00; weekend fees are from $24.50 to $35.00. The cart fee is $11 per person.

Sonoma Fairgrounds Golf Center
1350 Bennett Valley Road, Santa Rosa
(707) 577–0755
www.empiregolf.com

This user-friendly facility sits inside the racetrack at the Sonoma County Fairgrounds. It's right off Highway 12, just east of U.S. 101, and it offers practice greens and a lighted driving range in case you feel like swinging after sundown. The nine-hole, par 30 executive course costs between $9.00 and $12.00, depending on tee time.

Bennett Valley Golf Course
3330 Yulupa Avenue, Santa Rosa
(707) 528–3673

Bennett Valley is the perfect place for a golf course, with the peaks of Annadel

State Park forming a backdrop to the east. It's an 18-hole, par 72 course that runs 6600 yards. You'll pay $25 on weekends, $18 during the week if you're an out-of-towner; residents pay $18 and $14. A cart costs an additional $22. Bennett Valley has a snack bar/restaurant.

The Oakmont Golf Club
7025 Oakmont Drive, Santa Rosa
(707) 539–0415 (West Course),
(707) 538–2454 (East Course)
www.oakmontgolfclub.com

This is one of the Santa Rosa area's premier facilities, with two 18-hole courses: the championship, par 72 West Course and the executive, par 63 East Course. Oakmont is just southeast of town, off Highway 12 where it starts to bend down toward the Valley of the Moon. Prices range from $30 to $45. Carts are $26 each. You can choose between a snack bar and a sit-down restaurant. PGA pro John Murray is the resident expert.

Wikiup Golf Course
5001 Carriage Lane, Wikiup
(707) 546–8787
www.golfwikiup.com

Wikiup is a cul-de-sac neighborhood just north of Santa Rosa, and the community pretty much revolves around the nine-hole, par 29 executive golf course. Weekday green fees are $11 for 9 holes, $16 for 18; on Saturday and Sunday it's $14 for 9 and $21 for 18.

Windsor Golf Club
6555 Skylane Boulevard, Windsor
(707) 838–7888
www.windsorgolf.com

This is a challenging and well-maintained facility—a par 72, 6169-yard championship course—that has hosted the Nike Tour on several occasions. Nontournament greens fees are $30 to $49. Twilight (after 2:00 P.M.) rates are several bucks less. A full cart will cost you $22 or $16 after 2:00 P.M. Windsor has a restaurant and a snack bar, and golf lessons are available. Because of the frequency of tournaments, call in advance for reservations.

Tayman Park Golf Course
927 South Fitch Moutain Road, Healdsburg
(707) 433–4275
www.taymanparkgolf.com

Sonoma County's oldest golf course (dating to 1923) has been significantly renovated over the past couple of years. New is a three-tiered driving range, and a clubhouse with some of the best views in the county. At the eastern edge of central Healdsburg, about a quarter-mile from one stretch of the Russian River and a half-mile from another, the course is a par 70 nine-holer. It's also one of the best golf bargains you'll find in the area: weekdays it's $11 for 9 holes, $17 for 18; weekends it's $13 and $19.

Bodega Harbour Golf Links
21301 Heron Drive, Bodega Bay
(707) 875–3538
www.bodegaharbourgolf.com

This seaside course offers wonderful salty breezes and ocean sparkle. Designed by Robert Trent Jones Jr., Bodega Harbour has rolling fairways, cavernous pot bunkers, native coastal rough, and marshlands. (Remember, players are prohibited from entering the marsh on holes 16, 17, and 18.) The 18th has been voted the best finishing hole in Northern California. The par is 70, and the yardage measures 5711 from the white tees. Greens fees are $60 Monday through Thursday, $70 on Friday, and $90 on Saturday and Sunday (all rates include cart rental). The clubhouse restaurant serves lunch daily, dinner on Friday and Saturday nights, and breakfast on weekend mornings. Bodega Harbour Golf Links has golf-and-lodging packages in conjunction with several hotels in Bodega Bay and with vacation rental agencies that offer private homes bordering the course. Contact Bodega Harbour for more information.

Sebastopol Golf Course
2881 Scott's Right-of-Way, Sebastopol
(707) 823–9852

This is your one and only option in Sebastopol. It's a 9-hole, par 66 for 18 holes course. Weekdays you'll pay $10 for 9 holes, $18 for 18 holes. Carts are $10 for 9 holes; $15 for 18.

Northwood Golf Course
19400 Highway 116, Monte Rio
(707) 865–1116
www.northwoodgolf.com

Set in an elbow of the Russian River and surrounded by redwood trees, this is one of the more beautiful Wine Country courses. The wind is almost always gentle and the temperatures are moderated by the tall trees. Northwood is a par 36, nine-hole course. Fees range from $16 to $38; carts are $12 to $24.

Mendocino County

Ukiah Municipal Golf Course
599 Park Boulevard, Ukiah
(707) 467–2832

Mendocino County's biggest city has its only 18-hole golf course, par 70 Ukiah Municipal. The 5850-yard course is known to be fairly forgiving. Greens fees vary, but generally work out to $20 on weekdays, $24 on weekends. Add $20 if you want a cart. Ukiah Municipal has a snack bar.

Little River Inn
7751 Highway 1, Little River
(707) 937–5667
www.littleriverinn.com

The Inn, a popular vacation retreat (see our Spas and Resorts chapter), also has a nine-hole, par 35 golf course. Actually, it has an 11-hole course, so if you play 18 holes (par 71, 5458 yards) you can experience two new greens. There is a driving range (off mats, not grass) and a putting green. The rates for nine holes are $20 on weekdays, $30 on weekends. For 18 holes you pay $30 during the week, $35 on weekends. Carts are $16 for 9 holes, $24 for 18 holes.

Bicycle Rentals

Napa County

Bicycle Trax
796 Soscol Avenue, Napa
(707) 258–TRAX
www.bikeroute.com/BikeTrax

Napa Valley Bike Tours & Rentals
4080 Byway E., Napa
(707) 255–3377
www.napavalleybiketours.com

St. Helena Cyclery
1156 Main Street, St. Helena
(707) 963–7736
www.sthelenacyclery.com

Palisades Mountain Sport
1330B Gerard Street, Calistoga
(707) 942–9687
www.palisadesmountainsport.com

Getaway Bike Shop
1117 Lincoln Avenue, Calistoga
(707) 942–0332, (800) 499–BIKE
www.getawayadventures.com

Sonoma County

Sonoma Valley Cyclery
20093 Broadway, Sonoma
(707) 935–3377
www.sonomavalleycyclery.com

The Goodtime Bicycle Company
18503 Highway 12, Sonoma
(707) 938–0453
www.goodtimetouring.com

The Bicycle Factory
110 Kentucky Street, Petaluma
(707) 763–7515;
195 North Main Street, Sebastopol,
(707) 829–1880

Rincon Cyclery
4927 Sonoma Highway, Suite H, Santa Rosa
(707) 538–0868, (800) 965–BIKE
www.rinconcyclery.com

Spoke Folk Cyclery
201 Center Street, Healdsburg
(707) 433–7171
www.spokefolk.com

Mendocino County

Catch a Canoe & Bicycles Too
Highway 1 and Comptche-Ukiah Road,
Mendocino
(707) 937–0273, (800) 320–BIKE

Fort Bragg Cyclery
579 South Franklin Street, Fort Bragg
(707) 964-3509

Bowling

Napa County

Napa Bowl
494 Soscol Avenue, Napa
(707) 224-8331

Sonoma County

AMF Boulevard Lanes
1100 Petaluma Boulevard S., Petaluma
(707) 762-4581

Double Decker Lanes
300 Golf Course Drive, Rohnert Park
(707) 585-0226

Continental Lanes
765 Sebastopol Road, Santa Rosa
(707) 523-2695

Windsor Bowl
8801 Conde Lane, Windsor
(707) 837-9889

Mendocino County

Yokayo Bowl
1401 North State Street, Ukiah
(707) 462-8686

Noyo Bowl
900 North Main Street, Fort Bragg
(707) 964-4051

Horseback Riding

Many of the trails in the state parks, state forests, and recreation areas of the Wine Country are open to horses. You did bring yours, didn't you? If it wouldn't fit in your overnight bag, there are a few outfits that will rent you a steed. You provide the cowboy hat and the harmonica.

Sonoma Cattle Co. & Napa Valley Trail Rides
P.O. Box 877, Glen Ellen 95442
(707) 996-8566
www.napasonomatrailrides.com

This is a private concessionaire that for nearly two decades has been leading groups into three Wine Country State Parks: Bothe-Napa Valley, Jack London, and Sugarloaf Ridge (see previous listings in this chapter). The Jack London rides—offered April through November—skirt vineyards owned by the author's descendants. The Bothe ride also is available for reservation April through November, offering the shade of Ritchey Creek and the peace of the Mayacmas Mountains. The company operates year-round in Sugarloaf Ridge, weather and trails permitting, and the views from the saddle are fabulous.

You can choose from a variety of forays, from a two-hour Sonoma Valley ride ($55 per person, $125 with winery stop and lunch) to a 90-minute Napa Valley trot ($57) to a half-day ride in Annadel State Park ($125 to $250). Reservations are a must. Riders must be at least eight years old. Open-toed shoes are not permitted, and the weight limit is 240 pounds.

Chanslor Guest Ranch and Stables
2660 Highway 1, Bodega Bay
(707) 875-3333
www.chanslorranch.com

You can lead a horse to the water, but you can't make him surf. Chanslor offers $50 beach rides from their inland property—over the dunes to Bodega Bay and back.

Insiders' Tip

Jack London State Historic Park became 600 acres larger in 2002 when property adjacent to the existing park was turned over to the state park system.

Bicycling

Greg LeMond, a three-time winner of the Tour de France, has stated that Sonoma County, particularly the Dry Creek and Russian River valleys, ranks among his five favorite scenic places to pedal in America. You can't go wrong with an endorsement like that. Wine Country roads are generally conducive to biking, with ample shoulders and side roads where traffic is often light. Still, you need to be mindful of other vehicles and always, always ride single file—cyclists who ride two abreast are simply asking for trouble.

Rentals are easy to find, and many of the establishments offer maps and sound advice. Not surprisingly, spring and fall are the ideal times to hop aboard. If you make a summer excursion, start early and take plenty of water. We have included a few popular off-the-beaten-path cycling areas and routes—this is but a scratch on the surface, meant to get you interested enough to dig deeper. In this chapter we also list shops that rent bikes. (Companies that offer special bicycle tours are listed in our Attractions chapter.) Call first to make sure the shop has what you want, i.e., a mountain bike or a road bike (some have tandems too). Expect to pay $10 to $15 per hour or $30 to $40 per day. Most shops throw in a helmet, plastic water bottle, and saddle bag, and some will even deliver your wheels to your hotel.

Promise us you won't be careless enough to leave the driveway or parking area without a helmet.

Las Posadas State Forest

This is one of Napa County's most popular mountain-biking areas, located in the hills near Angwin. Miles of trails—from single-track to fire road—crisscross the dusty, pine-covered landscape. You can stumble upon some nice views of Chiles Valley to the east. From Howell Mountain Road just south of Pacific Union College, turn east on Las Posadas Road and go nearly to the end of the road. (Look for the "Beware of Mountain Lions" sign, an ominous entry point.)

Annadel State Park

Annadel's miles of dirt and gravel roads let you customize your own combination of trails. A good one to start with is a double loop around Lake Ilsanjo and Ledson Marsh. Start from the parking area at the end of Channel Drive and take the Warren Richardson Trail up to the lake.

Skirt the lake counter-clockwise and turn left on the Rough Go Trail. Cross the dam and aim right at the next intersection, riding onto the Canyon Trail. Make a left at the Marsh Trail for a climb to Buick Meadows, then a descent to the marsh. Stay on the trail as it loops around the marsh, then make a right onto the Burma Trail, which will return you to the Warren Richardson Trail. It sounds complicated, but all intersections are well posted. The whole ride is about 12 miles. To get to Annadel from Highway 12 east of Santa Rosa, turn south on Los Alamos Road, make a right onto Melita Road, and merge onto Montgomery Drive. After 0.7 mile, turn left on Channel Drive and proceed into the park.

Van Damme State Park
If you are visiting Mendocino, you can ride south about 3 miles on Highway 1, an exhilarating romp with views of the spectacular coastline. After a nice downhill stretch to the park, turn left and follow signs to the Pygmy Forest. You'll be in Fern Canyon, on an old skid road used by ox teams to haul logs down to the mouth of Little River, site of a former lumber mill. After your only steep climb, on the Logging Road Trail, you'll reach the entrance to the Pygmy Forest. Dismount and do the nature trail on foot.

From here you can continue on to the Little River-Airport Road. Make a right and head back to the Coast Highway.

Pacific Coast Highway
Cyclists from around the world come to ride the two-laned Pacific Coast Highway, otherwise known as Highway 1. During the summer months you are likely to see long-distance riders on the route, some having pedaled all the way from Anchorage, Alaska—look for the especially lean-looking cyclists on bikes draped heavy with overstuffed panniers. If riding to Alaska sounds too gung ho, you can whittle it down to say 160 miles—the distance of the Mendocino-Sonoma coast.

A popular tour loop among Santa Rosa cyclists begins with a short Greyhound bus ride to Willits, followed by a half-day ride aboard the Skunk Train to Fort Bragg (see our Attractions chapter). They then ride the coast from Fort Bragg to Jenner, and turn inland at the Russian River, following it most of the way back to Santa Rosa. The round-trip tour (about 140 miles on the bike) can be comfortably done in a week, and fit riders can complete it in a few days. If you're thinking that maybe you'd like to try the trip in reverse, riding from Jenner to Fort Bragg, think again. The winds blow north to south along the coast, and cyclists headed north will be buffeted back by the gusty wind—those going south get an added boost.

One drawback to this route, no matter which way you go, is the preponderance of logging trucks and sightseeing RVs. These can become hazardous on curvy, shoulderless roads, which the road frequently is. Signs along Highway 1 periodically warn vehicles to beware of heavy bicycle traffic; nevertheless, not all drivers are wise or courteous enough to heed the warning.

There are other options, too: the one-and-a-half-hour Salmon Creek Trail ($50), which winds into a canyon and around much of the company's 730 acres; the one-hour Eagle View ride ($30), where you are likely to spot a couple of resident bald eagles; and a half-hour, $25 trek through the Wetlands Preservation Habitat.

Hunting

While some are out hunting for the perfect Zinfandel, others are combing the hills, rifle in hand, looking to bag something to complement their wine. The huge tracts of forested land within the Wine Country present numerous options for hunters. Below we offer an introduction to those options, highlighting the most popular areas and targets.

We stick primarily to public lands administered by the U.S. Forest Service, the Bureau of Land Management, the California Department of Fish and Game (DFG), and similar organizations. If you want to hunt on private land, be sure to obtain written permission from the landowner. And whether you're on public or private property, please don't leave any litter behind. It's the kind of behavior that gives hunters a bad name.

California's hunting license year runs from July 1 through June 30. You can pick up resident licenses and regulation booklets at most sporting goods stores or at the Region 3 DFG Headquarters at 7329 Silverado Trail, near Yountville in Napa County. Each resident license costs $29.95 if purchased directly from the DFG, slightly more from an agent (upland game bird and waterfowl stamps are additional). If you're visiting the area and just happen to have brought your rifle along, you can request a two-day, nonresident hunting license ($29.15) from the DFG. Call (707) 944-5500 or visit www.dfg.ca.gov for more details.

Napa-Sonoma Marshes
Wildlife Area, Department of Fish and Game
(707) 944-5500

On the west bank of the lower Napa River, where it widens out before dumping into Carquinez Strait, are 2,000 acres of public lands divided into six units. The hunting areas are accessible by boat via Mud Slough, Hudeman Slough, and Tolay Creek. Besides the abundance of waterfowl, you might scare up a pheasant or dove.

Cedar Roughs
Bureau of Land Management
(707) 468-4000

This little-known, 7,000-acre pocket west of Lake Berryessa is run by the BLM. The only public access to Cedar Roughs is a 1-mile foot trail that begins on Pope

Insiders' Tip

Stocking up on firewood for a camping trip? See if you can track down some Pacific madrone (a tree named by Father Crespi of the Portola expedition in 1769). The madrone makes a delightfully smoke-free fire.

Canyon Road, 3 miles north of the Pope Creek Bridge, which is at the lake. The trail rises steeply to a broad plateau of glades and forests that harbor deer, bobcat, bear, coyote, gray squirrel, rabbit, quail, dove, and pigeon.

Petaluma Marsh Wildlife Area
Department of Fish and Game
(707) 944-5500

This 1,900-acre tidal salt marsh along the Petaluma River, north of its confluence with San Antonio Creek, is accessible only by boat. (There are several public ramps along the river.) The marsh is a mecca for ducks, geese, and other waterfowl.

Lake Sonoma Wildlife Area
Department of Fish and Game
(707) 944-5500

The area around Lake Sonoma is leased by the California Department of Fish and Game from the U.S. Army Corps of Engineers. It is managed with the idea of providing special hunts for deer, wild pig, and turkey, especially for junior hunters. The hunts are by permit only. Call the DFG for specific information and dates.

Jackson State Forest
State Forest Headquarters
(707) 964-5674

Sizable Jackson State Forest, east of Fort Bragg in Mendocino County, is home to game animals such as deer, black bear, gray squirrel, rabbit, mountain and valley quail, and band-tailed pigeon. Check for possible road closures and firearms bans within the forest.

Knoxville
Bureau of Land Management
(707) 468-4000

Along the Napa-Lake county line, southeast of the town of Lower Lake, are 17,700 acres of public land in the Knoxville area. The rugged, isolated landscape tends to be hot in the summer and wet in the winter, but when did that ever discourage hunters? From Knoxville Berryessa Road south of the Homestake Mining Company, you'll see a signed access point. Follow the road and gun for deer, bobcat, gray squirrel, rabbit, quail, dove, or pigeon.

Boggs Mountain
State Forest Headquarters
(707) 928-4378
The State of California bought 3,460 acres on Boggs Mountain from the Calso Company in 1949 and turned them over to the state's Forest Service. If you hunt here, use extreme caution, as the area is popular with hikers and bikers in addition to deer, wild turkey, mountain quail, wild pig, and gray squirrel.

Swimming

If you are not fortunate enough to be staying (or living) next to any of the Wine Country's lakes during those summer hot spells, you might feel the need to jump into a different body of water—specifically, the rectangular, chlorinated kind. Here is a partial list of public swimming facilities. Call for more information on lessons, admission fees, and no-kids or kids-only periods.

Napa County

St. Helena Community Pool
1401 Grayson Avenue, St. Helena
(707) 963-7946

Sonoma County

Petaluma Swim Center
900 East Washington Street, Petaluma
(707) 778-4410

Alicia Pool
300 Arlen Drive, Rohnert Park
(707) 795-7265

Benicia Pool
7469 Bernice Avenue, Rohnert Park
(707) 795-7582

Ladybug Pool
8517 Liman Way, Rohnert Park
(707) 664-1070

Honeybee Pool
1170 Golf Course Drive, Rohnert Park
(707) 586-1413
Finley Aquatic Complex
2060 West College Avenue, Santa Rosa
(707) 543-3760

Ridgeway Swim Center
455 Ridgeway Avenue, Santa Rosa
(707) 543-3421

Healdsburg Municipal Swimming Pool
360 Monte Vista Avenue, Healdsburg
(707) 433-1109

Cloverdale Memorial Pool
105 West First Street, Cloverdale
(707) 894-3236

Ives Pool
7400 Willow Street, Sebastopol
(707) 823-8693

Mendocino County

Ukiah Municipal Swimming Pool
511 Park Boulevard, Ukiah
(707) 467-2831

Willits Municipal Swimming Pool
429 North Main Street, Willits
(707) 459-5778
In addition, many high schools open their pools to the public during summer vacation. To find out if such options exist in

your area, call the municipal recreation numbers listed in the Tennis section.

Finally, some spas permit walk-in (dive-in?) swimmers who pay for day use of their mineral pools. Search out the Spas and Resorts chapter for relevant information.

Tennis

If you think tennis is just the sort of vigorous-yet-natty sport that would flourish in the Wine Country, you're right on target. Because of the geographic enormity of the area, however, a complete list of available courts would be harder to handle than an Anna Kournikova first serve. Instead we provide a list of city recreation departments throughout the region. The folks on the other end of the line will tell you where the courts are— many of them are after-hours high school facilities—whether you need reservations, what it costs to play there, and whether the courts are lighted.

Napa County

City of American Canyon Recreation
(707) 647–4566

City of Napa Parks and Recreation
(707) 257–9529

Town of Yountville Recreation
(707) 944–8712

City of St. Helena Recreation Department
(707) 963–5706

City of Calistoga Parks and Recreation
(707) 942–2838

Sonoma County

Sonoma City Hall
(707) 938–3681

City of Petaluma Parks & Recreation
(707) 778–4380

City of Cotati
(707) 792–4600

City of Rohnert Park Recreation Department
(707) 588–3456

City of Santa Rosa Recreation & Parks Offices
(707) 543–3282

Town of Windsor Parks and Recreation
(707) 838–1260

City of Healdsburg
(707) 431–3300

City of Cloverdale
(707) 894–2521

City of Sebastopol Recreation Information
(707) 823–1511

Mendocino County

City of Ukiah Recreation
(707) 463–6237

City of Willits
(707) 459–4601

City of Point Arena
(707) 882–2122

Fort Bragg Recreation Center
(707) 964–2231

Lake County

Area Overview
History
On the Water
Wineries
Brewpubs
Attractions

Lake County is sometimes overlooked by Wine Country visitors because of its remoteness in relation to the concentrated wine valleys found in Napa and Sonoma counties. But if you are passionate about water sports, love live entertainment performed by household names, or embrace an appreciation for award-winning wine, Lake County is worth a side trip during your visit to our region.

Clear Lake, with its scenic shores and many water-related activities, brings tourists by the thousands. Likewise, Konocti Harbor Resort is a huge draw for Bay Area music lovers. For vinophiles, there are several tasting rooms to visit, including the historic Guenoc Winery. Read on for more about these attractions.

Area Overview

Lake County's economy is ruled mostly by agriculture. Its 803,840 acres burst forth with walnuts, kiwi fruit, wild rice, apples, wheat, barley, and Sudan grass—just to name a few. Other commodities include wool, milk, cheese, honey, beeswax, timber, and livestock. But pears are royalty here—and the Bartlett is king. Wine grapes also figure prominently in the overall agricultural picture, with the average annual wine grape crop hovering around $20 million.

The first town encountered in Lake County as you drive north on Highway 29 is Middletown, an old-fashioned country burg with a couple of hearty cafes along its truncated Main Street, as well as a thriving microbrewery. The Cobb Mountain resort area, north of Middletown via Highway 175, supports a series of tiny communities, with Cobb the foremost representative. The town sits at 2,500 feet, providing welcome breezes and pine-bough cover when the mercury rises during the summer.

Moving north you come to the many towns that ring Clear Lake like chairs arranged around a popular swimming pool. Lower Lake is the southernmost locality, with a quaint old downtown. Above that is Clearlake, the county's largest city (a whopping 13,000 people!).

It's largely a collection of small motels and old-style resorts that cater to anglers, boaters, and overheated families.

North of Clearlake, on Highway 20 and around a bend of the lake, is Clearlake Oaks. On the southwestern shore of Clear Lake is Kelseyville, a tidy community with a rural economy at the base of Mt. Konocti. It's one of the few towns in the area that doesn't actually cozy up to the lake, though it's only about 3 miles away.

Lakeport is a pleasant town of about 4,800 on the westernmost bulge of the lake. It has been the county seat since 1861, and today it is known as something of a retirement haven. Lucerne and Nice (pronounced like the French city, or your sibling's daughter, not the adjective) occupy the quieter, greener northern section of Clear Lake. Locals call Lucerne "Little Switzerland," and they have been known to don Alpine garb to prove the point. Finally comes Upper Lake, which is not on Clear Lake at all but about 3 miles due north of its uppermost shore.

Lake County's median household income ($27,295, according to the 2000 census) and its population (58,300) is the lowest among the counties that encompass Wine Country. Its cost of housing is about half that of the other three counties, and it is more remote and isolated. But the locals—many of them part-time residents with vacation homes—like it that way. Nonetheless, the California Employment Development Department forecasts that Lake County's population will nearly double during the next two decades.

History

For centuries Pomo tribes lived around Clear Lake, bathing in the hot springs and playing games on the small islands that dot the lake. Volcanic Mt. Konocti, with its eerie caves, was considered sacred ground.

The first white men at Clear Lake were probably Russian fur trappers from Fort Ross. Next came French-Canadian fur trappers and American mountain men. Then in 1836 General Vallejo's brother, Salvador, brought cattle and horses onto a newly acquired land grant. For the most part, Salvador ran the ranch from Sonoma headquarters, and the Pomo lifestyle was not interrupted.

But in 1847 Salvador sold out to two Americans, Andrew Kelsey and Charles Stone. They enslaved the natives, oppressed them, and starved them. In desperation, two of the Pomos were hired to steal a steer, but they bungled the job. Fearing a cruel reprisal, they decided to kill Stone and

Kelsey. Stone died from an arrow, Kelsey at the hands of a Pomo woman whose son had been tortured. Frightened settlers called in the military from Benicia. A battle ensued, and the Pomos, holed up on a Clear Lake island, were massacred, giving the name Bloody Island to the site. The island is no more, as farmers reclaimed the marshes around it. But the name of Andrew Kelsey lives on in Kelseyville.

In the early 1850s wagon trains began arriving and settlers started raising cattle and planting fields. By 1857 a county government had been set up in a tiny wooden courthouse, and Lakeport was on its way to being the county seat. A number of vineyards and wineries appeared, most of them clinging to the valleys around Clear Lake, as the rest of the county was quite rugged.

But wine would not be the real attraction in the area. That would turn out to be the hot springs that bubbled up everywhere. By 1880, 100,000 people had traveled to Lake County to partake of the beneficial waters and luxuriate in the elegant hotels adjacent to the mineral springs. Posh casinos, music halls redolent with gold leaf, and formal dining rooms gleaming with silver and crystal were just some of the luxuries offered during leisure hours, while the more energetic indulged in bowling, croquet, lawn tennis, and riding.

For generations many faithfully vacationed at these spas, not only for health benefits but also as a gathering place for the social elite. The undoing of this salubrious way of life was the invention of the combustion engine. With the advent of the automobile, people no longer lingered for weeks. Instead, they came for a few days and moved on to another spot. The fine old hotels degenerated, and most of them burned. It was the end of a gracious era that had lasted a half-century.

Of all the rich and famous who made their way to Lake County, none was more illustrious than the vibrant, graceful Lillie Langtry—famed actress and vivacious mistress of Britain's Prince of Wales, later crowned King Edward VII. She came to Guenoc Valley in 1887, weary of the acting

Insiders' Tip

If you're in Lake County in the spring, try something truly off the beaten path: a one-hour narrated wagon trip through the wildflowers of Bear Valley, followed by an authentic chuckwagon barbecue. Call the Eleven Roses Ranch at (707) 998-4471 to learn more.

This is the house that Lillie Langtry built when she came to Lake County in the late 1880s.
PHOTO: LOU ZAUNER

circuit and trying to get a divorce from her English husband. She bought a 4,000-acre ranch and intended to raise grapes and thoroughbred horses. With her was her celebrated lover, Freddie Gebhart, a wealthy horseman who had bought an adjoining 3,200 acres.

Langtry was enchanted with Lake County from the moment she arrived via jostling stagecoach from St. Helena at the end of the railroad line. In addition to raising cattle and horses, Langtry wanted to produce wine from her own grapes and winery. She decided that no one but a Frenchman could cope with this challenge, and she engaged a capable man from Bordeaux.

The vintage that resulted never reached market. "A new law putting liquor into bond for a period spoiled the sale of those bottles with a picture of myself on the label," she complained. Langtry stayed at the ranch a fortnight and eagerly looked to return after completing her committed engagements. However, she

never saw the ranch again, though she owned it 18 years.

When Prohibition dealt its death blow to winemaking, Lake County turned its land over to pears, walnuts, and grazing pasture. Not until the 1960s did the vineyards reappear. Now there are several top-rated wineries in operation, and one of them is Guenoc. From the winery's tasting rooms that rise above a small lake, one can see in the distance the house where Langtry lived, looking almost exactly as it did when she was there. And once again the wines of Guenoc are bottled with her portrait on the label.

On the Water

They don't call it Lake County for nothing. It has several significant wet spots, but Clear Lake takes the prize. Three things about Clear Lake are clear: It is big, it is shallow, and it is old. With 43,785 acres of surface area, it's the largest natu-

Phone Numbers for Lake County

Lake County Visitor Information Center
875 Lakeport Boulevard, Lakeport
(707) 263–9544, (800) 525–3743
www.lakecounty.com

Clear Lake Chamber of Commerce
4700 Golf Avenue, Clearlake
(707) 994–3600
www.clearlakechamber.com

Lakeport Chamber of Commerce
560 Lakeport Boulevard, Lakeport
(707) 263–5092
www.lakeportchamber.com

ral freshwater lake within California. And yet the volume of water contained therein is not staggering. That's because the average depth of the lake is less than 30 feet.

Scientists are convinced that lakes of some sort have existed at this site for some 2.5 million years, possibly making Clear Lake the oldest lake in North America. They figure the upper arm, between Lakeport and Lucerne, has been under water continuously for 450,000 years.

In terms of its importance to the identity of the county, Clear Lake is the undeniable hub. Almost all the towns in Lake County are clustered around the shoreline, and access for all is faithfully preserved. There are 11 public ramps around the lake, providing an array of launch points. (Permission is required for use of beaches and ramps not posted "public.")

Clear Lake is known as the Bass Capital of the West. Two-thirds of the fish caught here are largemouth bass, and spring is the season to reel 'em in, especially from docks or in pockets formed in the beds of tule reeds. Bass might be the most plentiful, but also swimming in these waters are channel catfish, bluegill, and crappie.

Wineries

Guenoc and Langtry Estate Vineyards
21000 Butts Canyon Road, Middletown
(707) 987–2385
www.guenoc.com

That charming countenance you see gracing bottles of Guenoc wine is Lillie Langtry—the "Jersey Lily," beloved stage actress of the late 19th century. Langtry ran the business from 1888 to 1906, and her palatial home is still the centerpiece of the property. The vineyards sit on the border of Napa and Lake counties in Guenoc Valley, the only federally approved appellation under single proprietorship. Grower Orville Magoon helps produce a wide range of wines, from Chardonnay and Cabernet Sauvignon to Petite Sirah, and even the occasional Port.

Ployez Winery
11171 South Highway 29, Lower Lake
(707) 994–2106
www.ployezwinery.com

You probably thought the only thing French in Lake County was the fries at Burger King, but along comes Gerald

Ployez, a fourth-generation winemaker from Champagne whose east-of-the-Atlantic family still bottles under the Ployez-Jacquemari label. Gerald opened this winery in 1997, and he concentrates mostly on Chardonnay and Sauvignon Blanc, though he produces three types of red, too.

Wildhurst Vineyards
3855 Main Street, Kelseyville
(707) 279–4302, (800) 595–9463
www.wildhurst.com

When Myron and Marilyn Holdenried started this winery in 1991, it was really just a case of diversification: Myron is a fifth-generation Kelseyville farmer. In fact, he had already been growing grapes and pears for 25 years. Wildhurst started at the site of the old Steurmer Winery in Lower Lake, then moved to Kelseyville in 1996; a year later it unveiled its tasting room in a refurbished Odd Fellows Hall. (The winery is 2 miles away, and not open to the public.) Wildhurst is primarily noted for its Merlot but makes three other reds and a couple of whites, all under the Clear Lake appellation.

Steele Wines
4350 Thomas Drive, Kelseyville
(707) 279–9475
www.steelewines.com

Kendall-Jackson was the pride of Lake County until it "went Sonoma" a few years ago. But Lake still can brag of its hold upon one of the men who nurtured that winery to prominence: Jed Steele. He dabbles in a number of varietals, but generally sticks to Chardonnay, Pinot Noir, and Zinfandel, with grapes from as far south as Santa Barbara County and as far north as Mendocino. You also might stumble upon a farmer's market if you arrive Saturday morning, or the Harvest Festival if you get there on the second weekend of October.

Brewpubs

Mount St. Helena Brewing & Restaurant
21167 Calistoga Street, Middletown
(707) 987–2106
www.mtsthelenabrew.com

As microbreweries go, this one has lots of gold and silver medals to show for its trouble. The beer menu includes Honey Wheat Ale, Palisades Pale Ale, Imperial Stout, an English style Brown Ale, India Pale Ale, and Belgian Wit. The food menu is extensive, with everything from pasta to house specialties of the red meat variety to a wide selection of pizzas. There's even a black bean burger or Thai noodles for vegetarians.

Attractions

Price Code
The price code below reflects the admission price or fees for two adults in high season, not including gratuities, where appropriate.

$	Free or low cost
$$	$15 to $50
$$$	$51 to $150

Konocti Harbor Resort & Spa $$$
8727 Soda Bay Road, Kelseyville
(707) 279–4281, (800) 660–LAKE
www.konoctiharbor.com

In a few short years, Konocti Harbor has managed to place itself among the top music venues in Northern California. In

Insiders' Tip

Bird-watchers, take note: Fall brings beautiful white pelicans to many areas of Clear Lake, along with western grebes, common mergansers, buffleheads, ruddy ducks, pied-billed grebes, and an occasional common loon.

With Mt. Konocti rising high in the background, Konocti Harbor Resort & Spa on Clear Lake beckons to boaters to throttle down and enjoy a tall cool one. PHOTO: LOREN DOPPENBERG

fact, the resort's Joe Mazzola Classic Concert Showroom was named by *Performance Magazine* as "America's No. 1 Small Concert Venue."

The resort actually has several different sites for performance. The Konocti Field Amphitheater, which operates between May and October, puts you under the stars for major concerts. This lakeside amphitheater seats 5,000, all within 200 feet of the stage. It pulls big acts, some contemporary, some revived. The lineup has included the likes of Wynonna, Vince Gill, Styx, Doobie Brothers, Cheap Trick, Don Henley, Journey, and Tim McGraw. Tickets usually range from $29 to $49.

Predating the amphitheater was the Classic Concert Showroom, a 1,000-occupancy dinner theater with two VIP balconies and tiered seating. The showroom tends to showcase stars more appropriate to an intimate setting, such as Ray Charles, B.B. King, Eddie Money, Ringo Starr, the Pretenders, and Bill Cosby. These tickets are in the $35 to $60 range, more if you include buffet dinner. Meanwhile, the Full Moon Saloon, right next to Clear Lake, has live entertainment Fridays and Satur-

days year-round, and seven days a week from June through Labor Day. The saloon has indoor and outdoor seating and a sizable dance floor. From time to time musicians from the big shows drop in to the saloon after their own performance and hop up onstage to jam with the house bands.

Most people know Konocti Harbor as a premier concert venue for post-40 rockers, but there's a lot going on here even after the last drum beat. The resort has 100 acres of lakefront property and 250 guest accommodations that range from basic rooms to apartment suites to beach cottages to fully equipped VIP suites. Many, but not all, of the rooms have views of Clear Lake. Basic rooms are $69 every night of the year; deluxe rooms with balconies vary in price according to season, but expect $119 on in-season weekends; Jacuzzi suites with fireplaces are $259. The price spectrum is wide, so call for more information.

Konocti Harbor bustles with activity. There is a tennis complex, gym, two swimming pools, two wading pools, shuffleboard courts, horseshoe pits, sand volleyball courts, and a softball field. And because the lake is primary among attractions, the resort has a 100-slip marina, launch ramp, and certified boat repair shop. It also offers a rental fleet (ski boats, Waverunners, etc.) and, believe it or not, a bass fishing pro. Konocti's Dancing Springs Spa features massage, herbal wraps, loofa treatments, facials, manicures, and more. If you must mix business and pleasure, the meeting facilities can handle groups from 10 to 700.

Guests with children, take note: Konocti Harbor caters to kids with its Kids Club, a supervised activity session for children 4 to 13 during big concert nights. While mom and dad boogie in the Classic Concert Showroom or the Amphitheater, the kids are entertained for up to six hours with games, movies, arts and crafts, and other distractions. Daytime hours are available too during summer; inquire when you call to book a reservation.

Calpine Geothermal Plant Tour $
15500 Central Park Road, Middletown
(707) 987–4270, (866) GEYSERS
www.calpine.com, www.geysers.com

Perhaps you've already indulged in a mud bath and had a soak in a hot mineral pool. Can you stand just a little more hot water? Steam, to be exact, as it comes out of the ground to generate electricity at The Geysers. Technically, they aren't geysers, but "fumaroles," and they can usually be seen boiling up out of a distant hillside on the Sonoma County/Lake County line. It's steam from subterranean cauldrons and it's being corralled by Calpine Corporation to make electricity. There are 19 power units at the remote site, with a total net generating capacity of 850 megawatts, or enough to turn on the lights in 850,000 homes.

We don't know of another geothermal power plant tour anywhere in the world, and you can't beat the price: it's all free. Buses depart from the visitor center in Middletown at 10:00 A.M., noon, and 2:00 P.M., Thursdays through Mondays. (Reservations are encouraged.) Each tour from beginning to end takes approximately 75 to 90 minutes, but you'll learn all about the colorful history of the site. The visitor center has a gift shop and picnic area, along with interactive displays about geothermal energy.

Clear Lake Queen $$
Library Park, Lakeport
(707) 994–5432
www.paddlewheel.com

This attraction is made to feel old. It's a 110-foot, triple-deck, paddlewheel boat that would look more at home in the Mississippi Delta. (Sorry, the wheel is just for show—the *Queen* is powered by two massive diesel engines.) You can watch the shoreline activity—we don't know if the animals or the humans will be more intriguing—while you eat lunch or dinner. High-season prices run from $16 to $18 for sightseeing only, to $28 for a two-hour lunch or brunch cruise, to $35 for a three-hour dinner. (The dining floors are warm and enclosed.) The *Queen* runs Wednesday through Sunday during the summer, Friday and Saturday during the winter, and features music and dancing once a month. The price goes up on those nights.

Outrageous Waters $
Highway 53 & Old State Highway 53, Clearlake
(707) 995–1402, (877) WE–BE–FUN

Beat the heat in Lake County by taking a long slide into a pool at this water park. Next to the slides is a fun center with vol-

> ## Insiders' Tip
> Take a deep breath: For more than a decade, Lake County has met or exceeded standards for air quality set by the California Air Resources Board. In fact, it's the only area in the state with such a record.

leyball courts and a video arcade. A grand prix race track features 15 cars with 9-horsepower engines maneuvering a professionally banked concrete track. Hardball and softball batting cages round out the energy-burning attractions. Outrageous Waters also has a food concession, storage lockers, and a kiddie pool. The water park is closed after summer, but the fun center is open all year. The park is open from noon to 7:00 P.M. daily in summer, and on Wednesday through Sunday in the off-season. Admission is $13.95 for adults, $9.95 for children shorter than 48 inches (children three and under are free), and

Insiders' Tip

Middletown's nickname "Steam City" comes from the Geysers steamfields in the hills above the town.

$3.95 for seniors 55 and older. ID-bearing Lake County residents get a discount, and the whole world gets one after 4:30 P.M.

On the Water

The Pacific

The Rivers

The Lakes

Provisioners:
  Charters, Watercraft,
  Lessons

Great rivers, fine lakes, and a spectacular ocean—take your pick. From all-day deep-sea fishing excursions to an afternoon swim in a lake, the variety of aqua activities and adventures available in the Wine Country will surprise and excite you.

The best place to begin is along the 150 miles or so of coastline that borders the Pacific in Sonoma and Mendocino Counties. If you're thinking palm-studded sandy beaches, you'll be surprised by what you find here. This section of California's coast bears little resemblance to its southern counterpart—that relatively mild stretch of oceanfront lined with sunbathers from Santa Barbara to San Diego. North of San Francisco the continent drops precipitously to the sea, with narrow crescents of beach occasionally flanking the rocky bluffs—you will not see a single high-rise hotel along this coast. And the ocean is rarely even-tempered here, alternating between violent fits of rage and quiet moods of calm. Its best times are during the summer months, when the sun burns through the morning fog and the wind is low.

Our rivers generally flow lazily through forests, meadows, and marshes, rarely achieving enough momentum to produce whitewater. A short section of the Russian River above Cloverdale and the portion of the Eel River in Mendocino County are two exceptions. When water volume is high, these stretches can get quite rough, reaching Class IV and V whitewater status. And of course, during the rainy winter months many Wine Country creeks—which are dry in summer—flow with gusto, some serving as spawning grounds for salmon and steelhead.

As for the lake situation, well, generally speaking, this is no Minnesota. Only in Lake County will you find natural lakes in Wine Country (see the previous chapter). There are a handful there, including Clear Lake and the Blue Lakes. All are teeming with fish and great for swimming and watersports.

So here's a rundown of the places and the ways to get wet.

The Pacific

Sonoma County

Sonoma Coast

The Sonoma coast feels wild and remote. It is hilly, almost mountainous at times, with coastal ranches stretching for miles along the bluffs. Bodega Bay, the county's largest coastal town, is home to approximately 300 commercial fishing boats. Its protected harbor is also an attractive spot for sporting activities. The shoreline on the west side of the harbor is great for windsurfing or launching a kayak. There's hardly a day when you don't see the fluorescent sails of a windsurfer darting about or the rhythmic movements of a kayaker plying the waters.

Surfers looking for the perfect wave will not be disappointed. Two of the most popular spots are Salmon Creek, just north of Bodega Bay, and Goat Rock State Beach, farther up the coast near Jenner. But it's always a good idea to contact a local surf shop for advice—it's a long coastline, and you can spend a lot of time looking.

Sportfishing is big at Bodega Bay. Charter boats sail every day, and, depending on the season, come back with a mix of rock cod, lingcod, halibut, salmon, albacore tuna, and crab.

North from Bodega Bay is a series of state beaches accessible from clearly marked parking areas. These are a part of the Sonoma Coast State Beach, and they are ideal spots for fishing, beachcombing, picnicking, and beach parties—unfortunately, the chilly waters are unsafe for swimming and there are no lifeguards. A ranger station, just north of Bodega Bay at Salmon Creek, is where you can get maps and information. Park rangers also offer whale-watching walks.

See our Parks and Recreation and Attractions chapters for more information on the Sonoma Coast State Beach and other coastal-area recreation sites, including Doran and Westside regional parks, Stillwater Cove Regional Park, Fort Ross State Park, Salt Point State Park, Kruse Rhododendron State Reserve, and Gualala Point Regional Park.

Mendocino County

Mendocino Coast

For sheer drama, nothing compares with the splendor of the view from the town of Mendocino, built on a rocky peninsula, where the sound of waves crashing against the cliffs is always in the air. The shoreline here is a labyrinth of rugged offshore spires and sea stacks, churning coves, and wave-sculpted arches and sea tunnels. This is one of the most soul-stirring settings in the state, with ocean views often mesmerizing visitors for hours. A popular activity here—aside from shopping—is to find a comfortable spot on the bluffs and simply watch wave after wave roll in.

Another favorite attraction along this scenic seashore is at Russian Gulch State Park, where a unique "punch bowl" was formed when a large sea cave collapsed. Waves enter through a tunnel in one side and crash around the interior of the bowl, letting go a distinctive array of throaty echoes. Russian Gulch State Park is just 2 miles north of Mendocino (see our Parks and Recreation chapter).

Fishing is a popular sport along the Mendocino Coast. Greenwood Creek State Beach, a day-use state beach near the town of Elk (at the intersection of Highways 1 and 128), is popular with picnickers and ocean anglers who want easy access to the beaches. Additional angling spots along the Mendocino Coast include Schooner Gulch State Park and Manches-

Bones from one of the planet's largest beasts are displayed in Bodega Bay. PHOTO: JEAN SAYLOR DOPPENBERG

ter State Beach, on Kinney Road off Highway 1, where there's a bonus of two creeks that run with salmon and steelhead during winter. (See our Parks and Recreation chapter for more on Manchester State Beach and Schooner Gulch.)

Abalone diving is a popular sport around these parts for the adventuresome, experienced diver. The abalone is a giant marine snail with a powerful foot that can lock a strong grip on rock surfaces. One of these mollusks can yield more than a pound of delicious white meat. Unfortunately, abalone is becoming an endangered species. Rules for abalone diving (including size limits) are strict. The mollusks can be harvested from April to December, excluding July, but check with the state Department of Parks and Recreation at any state beach for regulations—all abalone divers must have a valid fishing license bearing an abalone stamp. And above all, consult with park rangers and locals about the dangers of abalone diving. Every year brings its share of drownings—even among veteran divers—along this shoreline.

For more information on other popular recreational spots on or near the Mendocino Coast—including Van Damme State Park, Mendocino Headlands State Park, Jug Handle State Reserve, Jackson State Forest, Mackerricher State Park, Westport-Union Landing State Beach, and Sinkyone Wilderness State Park—see our Parks and Recreation chapter.

The Rivers

Napa County

Napa River

Though most of the Napa River's length snakes from Mount St. Helena to the town of Napa, the big-time angling is mostly confined to extreme points south, especially as the river broadens between the Butler Bridge (the airborne stretch of Highway 12/29) and Carquinez Strait. Summer fishing isn't great in these tidal waters, but autumn brings hungry striped bass and sturgeon. Try live bait, such as mudsuckers or bullheads for the stripers,

---

Insiders' Tip

The ocean along the Northern California coast is unsafe for swimming. It's cold, about 50 degrees, and the strong currents will whisk you off toward Japan before you can say sayonara. On top of that, large and powerful waves—called sleeper waves—also occur without warning, occasionally sweeping beachcombers off coastal rocks and sand shores. Take our advice, enjoy the view, build sandcastles that are high and dry, and stay clear of the breakers.

---

live bass shrimp or mud shrimp for the sturgeon.

The many sloughs that feed into Napa River in this marshy area are also good bets for striped bass. If you're looking for a full-service resort, try the Napa Valley Marina, (707) 252-8011, or Napa Sea Ranch, (707) 252-2799, both on or near Cuttings Wharf Road.

Sonoma County

Russian River

Called Slavyanka (Slavic girl) by Russian settlers in the 19th century, the Russian River begins in Mendocino County just above Ukiah. The East Branch of the Russian receives water diverted from the Eel River, which flows through an aqueduct cut through a hill. The diversion, which has been going on since 1908, has recently become controversial because of its impact on the Eel River's fisheries. Water from the Eel is used to feed the PG&E Potter Valley hydroelectric plant; it also helps to keep the Russian from being reduced to a trickle through the dry summer months.

Below Hopland, the Russian falls precipitously through a narrow canyon—alongside U.S. 101—and then slows to a more languid pace for the rest of the trip through Sonoma County. It rolls past small wineries, campgrounds, and several towns before reaching the sea at Jenner. During the summer months, canoeists, kayakers, rafters, and inner-tubists converge on the river. The more ambitious paddle the entire 70-mile stretch of relatively flat water below Cloverdale to Jenner, while most visitors opt for a one-day trip of about 10 miles—often between Forestville and Guerneville. April through September is the best time to canoe the Russian. It's a beautiful run through quiet waters among redwoods, past summer resorts, quaint old homes, and the occasional nude beach. (See our Provisioners listings in this chapter for information on area river outfitters.)

For more on Russian River area wineries, see our Wineries chapter. To find out about camping options, see our Camping chapter.

Mendocino County

Eel River

This river is a sight to behold, sparkling in emerald greens, turquoise blues, and foamy white as it tumbles over boulders, through narrow gorges, and past tall redwood and fir forests. The Eel begins in a cauldron formed by an ancient volcano in Mendocino National Forest, and then winds north for nearly 150 miles before spilling into the Pacific near Ferndale in Humboldt County. The third-largest river in the state (following the Sacramento and the Klamath), the Eel and its tributaries are home to chinook and coho salmon and steelhead, which migrate from the ocean to the river's spawning grounds each year. Though several dams, a hydroelectric plant, and the massive Russian River diversion—about 52 billion gallons annually—have all had an impact on the

fish population, the river still boasts one of the most abundant fisheries in the state and has a reputation for producing large, hard-fighting lunkers.

The Russian River water diversion has kept the Eel in near drought condition every summer and fall for almost 100 years. While it is hardly a boatable river during these times, it is great for swimming, particularly in the deeper holes. At other times of year, however, this is not a swimmer's river. During high water flows, the Eel becomes a roaring torrent, running hell-for-leather to the sea. The Mendocino County section offers some of the best whitewater in the state. It's a heart-thumping ride, featuring mile after mile of Class III and IV rapids. A word of advice and caution: This is a difficult whitewater river navigable by expert guides or highly experienced kayakers only—anyone else will certainly be ground to a fine pulp by the sharp rocks and churning waters. Inner-tubists, neophyte river rafters, or any other novice boater should head for the more placid waters of the Russian River.

Gualala River

Although the portion of the Gualala River most people see is the wide swath that spreads out where the river joins the Pacific (and where kayakers set out to sea), the Gualala does wind far into the interior of the county, through forests of redwoods and groves of ferns. In a good wet year, when winter rains have drenched the land and the river is full, it is possible to kayak almost 10 miles inland. That would be a rare year, but even paddling only a mile or so upriver is rewarding, giving a different view of the natural splendors of Northern California. With some luck, you'll witness soaring ospreys, great blue herons, and brown pelicans; catch a glimpse of the playful river otters; and watch the variety of birds that call the forest home.

Motorboats are not permitted on the river, but anglers in rowboats sometimes make their way upstream to cast a line in search of trout. During the winter rainy season, the river swells and roars out to sea, washing out beach sands that had accumulated near its mouth during the summer.

Navarro River

Motoring along the rolling hills of Highway 128 and into Anderson Valley, drivers suddenly encounter "a redwood tunnel to the sea" and their first look at the Navarro River. For first-time visitors and longtime residents alike, the redwoods along the Navarro River are a magnificent sight to behold. Second-growth redwood groves stretch along the river, making a home for riverbank denizens such as the belted kingfisher, along with families of raccoons and black-tailed deer. This is a great river for kayaking, and some of the kayak companies operating out of Sonoma County bring groups here (see our Provisioners listings for more information).

Insiders' Tip

Be advised that when water levels in streams and tributaries are running low, particularly in the fall, many are off-limits to fishing. To find out if angling is permitted in certain streams, call the Department of Fish and Game at (707) 944-5533 or (707) 442-4502 for a recorded update.

The Lakes

Napa County

Lake Hennessey

About 5 miles east of St. Helena is an 850-acre reservoir owned by the city of Napa and surrounded by rolling hills covered with grass and dappled with oak trees. Lake Hennessey was formed by the construction of Conn Dam. The Department of Fish and Game stocks Lake Hennessey with trout in the fall, winter, and spring, and you'll find a few bass, bluegill, and catfish as well. Motorized boats are allowed on the water if they don't exceed 14 feet and 10 horsepower; sailboats are permitted if they are 16 feet or shorter. Swimming and kayaking are prohibited. There is a $4.00 access fee for visiting the lake, and an additional $1.00 special fishing permit is also required. There is no particular place to pay for the fishing permit, so just be ready to fork over the buck if you see the Lake Hennessey caretaker.

Lake Berryessa

It was 40 years ago that Putah Creek was dammed, creating Lake Berryessa between two legs of California's Coast Ranges (and drowning the town of Monticello). The ragged perimeter gives Berryessa 165 miles of shoreline, more than surrounds massive Lake Tahoe. The north end of the lake is shallow, with gentle, grassy hills sloping down to the water. Contrast that with the south end and its steep, rocky terrain dotted with manzanita and oak. The eastern shore of the lake, meanwhile, is off-limits to the public.

The Bureau of Reclamation maintains three day-use facilities and a launch ramp at Capell Cove, plus picnic sites at Smittle Creek and Oak Shores. The trout and salmon fishing are great here in the spring; in the fall, the trout feed on shad near the surface early in the day. Cast between the dam and The Narrows, or troll in Markley Cove or Skiers Cove. Look for largemouth bass in the coves, smallmouth and spotted bass on the big island in the middle of the lake or at steep, jagged points in up to 40 feet of water. Bluegill usually hang out in the backs of shallow coves all around the lake, and catfish are plentiful at Capell Cove, Pope Creek, and Putah Creek.

There are several marinas along Knoxville Road and Highway 128. Keep in mind that this lake is heavily trafficked, especially in the summer. Berryessa welcomes more than 1.5 million visitors each year.

Sonoma County

Lake Sonoma

Designed to control Russian River flooding, the Warm Springs Dam has created some 3,600 surface acres of scenic recreational waters. Located 11 miles north of Healdsburg on Dry Creek Road, this is primarily a boating lake, although water-skiers and Jet Skiers are allowed in designated areas. Skiing is not always considered desirable because of the many large trees that have been partially submerged. Kayakers, however, have no trouble paddling their way through the treetops.

Fishing is the main recreational sport. Generally speaking, boat fishing is more successful than shore fishing, and the upper reaches of the lake usually produce the best results. Fish include smallmouth bass, red ear sunfish, green sunfish, and rainbow trout. A public boat ramp is available, as well as the full-service Lake Sonoma Marina. The fish hatchery is always great fun (see our Kidstuff chapter), and there's an interesting visitor center. Swimming is a possibility, but much of the shoreline is rocky.

Mendocino County

Lake Mendocino

Ten miles north of Ukiah off Highway 20, Lake Mendocino offers a variety of activities, including water-skiing, pleasure boating, sailing, windsurfing, and swimming. It's an aesthetically pleasing body of water and is popular in the Ukiah Valley, where summer temperatures can be sweltering.

Everything you could want for fun in the water can be rented here—Sea-Doos, Jet Skis, fishing boats, and pontoon boats. All you need is a swimsuit. The visitor center offers information about the lake, Pomo Indian culture, and the Coyote Valley. The Interpretive Cultural Center has exhibits of Pomo Indian crafts, pottery, jewelry, and decorative arts. This area is a great place for a summer picnic.

Provisioners: Charters, Watercraft, Lessons

Here's a sampling of Wine Country businesses that cater to the aqua-nut. You'll find information on renting everything from a Jet Ski to kayaks, and lots of these folks will either guide you along or teach you what you need to know to have a safe and enjoyable experience.

Napa County

A Wet Pleasure Jet Ski & Boat Rentals
5800 Knoxville Road, Lake Berryessa
(707) 966–4204

A Wet Pleasure has a full lineup of aluminum fishing boats (14- or 16-footers), ski boats, pedal boats, 24-foot patio boats, and Yamaha Jet Skis. Boat rentals cost $60 for eight hours.

Sonoma County

W.C. "Bob" Trowbridge Canoe Trips
13840 Old Redwood Highway, Healdsburg
(707) 433–7247, (800) 640–1386 (information and reservation line)
www.trowbridgecanoe.com

The company, named for the man who started it in 1953 (and whose granddaughter still helps run the shop), offers a wide range of canoe and kayak outings on the Russian River from April to October. You can choose from afternoon, half-day paddles for two to three hours; full days from four to six hours; or even a five-day canoe excursion.

Burke's Russian River Canoe Trips
8600 River Road, Forestville
(707) 887–1222
www.burkescanoetrips.com

Burke's provides your canoe, paddles, and life jackets for the day for a total of just $35 per canoe. Your trip begins at Burke's base near Forestville and ends 10 miles downstream at Guerneville. Burke's then shuttles you back to your car at Forestville. It's a leisurely four- to five-hour downstream paddle, with the opportunity for many stops on warm sunny beaches.

Bodega Bay Sportfishing Center
1500 Bay Flat Road, Bodega Bay
(707) 875–3344
www.usa.fishing.com/bodegabaysport fishing.html

These folks operate three charter boats out of Bodega Bay for either full-day or half-day fishing trips for bay or ocean fishing. You'll be going after rock cod, lingcod, salmon (April through November), halibut, and Dungeness crab. Fishing tackle is available. Whale-watching trips run from November to February. The center also specializes in evening cruises.

The cost of excursions ranges from $50 to $60 if you're going for the fish listed above, and you can fish for them in combinations. Going out 60 to 80 miles for salmon or halibut would require a negotiated cost. At the high end of the scale there's albacore tuna, and those trips will run you from $125 to $150.

The company also operates from another location, a boathouse called Fish and Chips and Fishing Trips, at 1445 Highway 1. It's the culinary extension of the business, with a sit-down restaurant that serves fish and chips, calamari, scallops, prawns, oysters, hot dogs, burgers, beer, and wine. Food is also available for takeout, and box lunches may be ordered.

Bodega Bay Surf Shack
1400 Highway 1, Pelican Plaza, Bodega Bay
(707) 875–3944
www.bodegabaysurf.com

Bodega Bay Kayak
1580 East Shore Drive, Blue Whale Shopping Center, Bodega Bay
(707) 875–8899
www.bodegabaykayak.com

These two shops are a must-stop for any visitor eager to glean the optimum amount of local surfing or kayaking knowledge. Bob Miller, the Surf Shack's friendly and welcoming owner, has been surfing nearby Salmon Creek Beach and other primo wave spots since 1984. His shop offers surfboards, wetsuit rentals, and surfing lessons. Bike rentals also are available, along with a great selection of

Scores of private seagoing vessels fill the marina along Bodega Head at Bodega Bay. PHOTO: JEAN SAYLOR DOPPENBERG

avail yourself of a High Tide public serv-ice, a continuous broadcast of the coastal weather report and surf conditions ema-nating from a not-so-loud speaker above the recessed doorway.

High Tide stocks a complete line of custom surfboards, body boards, skim boards, and accessories, plus a large selec-tion of wetsuits for men, women, and chil-dren of all sizes and shapes. Even if the surf isn't calling your name, there's a rack full of Hawaiian shirts and a good selec-tion of swimwear.

Windwalker Board Sports and School of Windsurfing
4347 Harrison Grade Road, Occidental
(707) 874-2331
www.wind-walker.com

Windwalker offers windsurfing lessons in Bodega Bay, where conditions are particu-larly favorable for learning the sport—a mile of 3-foot-deep water with consistent winds. The shop also rents wetsuits, boards, and sails.

Windwalker is unique in another respect: It offers bed and breakfast pack-ages in a variety of accommodations and a wide price range.

King's Sport and Tackle Shop
16258 Main Street, Guerneville
(707) 869-2156

You can buy just about anything you need for the outdoor life here. Whether you're a camping, fishing, or archery enthusiast, or you don't know a striped bass from a catfish, Steve Jackson, King's friendly and knowledgeable owner, can provide you with sportswear, footwear, camping gear and accessories, fresh and saltwater bait and tackle, and guns and ammo. He's also got custom, hand-tied flies, dry bags for river activities, and equipment for aba-lone diving.

King's also provides guide service for fishing on the Russian River during steel-head, salmon, and bass season. A local hunting guide is available to help you stalk wild boar, deer, and turkey. King's rents kayaks ($25 a day for one-person kayaks, $40 for two) and gives guided river tours at any time of year, weather permitting.

men's and women's beachwear and casual clothing. The nearby kayak shop offers single and tandem kayaks for half-day and all-day rental on sheltered Bodega Bay. More adventurous paddlers may want to consider signing up for the shop's guided tour of the coast.

High Tide Surf Shop
9 Fourth Street, Petaluma
(707) 763-3860
www.waveslave.com

Located in the McNear Building, part of Petaluma's historic downtown, High Tide is a relative newcomer, having arrived in 1992. If you should pass through "the crossroads to the beach," as proprietor Len Crain likes to call the neighborhood, don't expect his shop to be open before noon. Then again, you might want to

Mendocino County

All Aboard Adventures
Noyo Harbor, Fort Bragg
(707) 964–2079, (707) 964–1881
www.allaboardadventures.com

Hop aboard Captain Tim's *Sea Hawk* for salmon, rock cod, and lingcod fishing. Tim has been working charter boats for more than 20 years out of Fort Bragg, and the *Sea Hawk* is his newest purchase. Trips are at 7:00 A.M. and 1:00 P.M. daily. Deepsea fishing trips are between $45 and $55 (tackle kits are extra, rod and bait are included). During January through April, All Aboard features two-hour whale-watching excursions for $25.

Rubicon Adventures
9743 Highway 116, Forestville
(707) 887–2452
www.rubiconadventures.com

Owner Bill Mashek has been leading whitewater tours since 1971. He offers a one-day whitewater excursion on the Eel River for $45 per person during the months of April and May (wetsuits not provided). Bill brings the boats—deluxe seven-person whitewater rafts—rafting guides, and lunch and takes care of the shuttle arrangements. Call for details.

Tributary Whitewater Tours
20480 Woodbury Drive, Grass Valley
(800) 672–3846
www.whitewatertours.com

Tributary has been guiding whitewater tours on all the major California rivers for more than two decades. Its two-day Eel River trip in Mendocino County runs during the months of April and May, and costs approximately $200 per person (wetsuits and camping gear are extra). The company provides the boats—deluxe seven-person whitewater rafts—guides, and all meals. Though their headquarters is located near the Sierra Nevada Mountains, Tributary will rendezvous with clients for the Eel River trip at the take-out point at Dos Rios off Highway 162.

Spectator Sports

Baseball

Football

Basketball

Hockey

Soccer

Golf

Motor Sports

Marathons and
Running Events

Bicycle Road Races

Horse Racing

College Sports

The Wine Country approach to spectator sports varies from the occasional upscale PGA golf event to the more populist sprint-car racing. And professional-level happenings are always available in the Bay Area and Sacramento. No fewer than eight pro sports franchises take the field (or diamond, or court, or rink) within two hours of the Wine Country—each is covered in this chapter. Though the list goes on and on, we had to draw the line somewhere. Other Bay Area sporting events—from boxing matches to major golf and tennis tournaments—are not listed here.

Also note that some sports outings seemed more appropriately included in our Festivals and Annual Events chapter—the annual rodeo at the Sonoma County Fair is an example. And if the activity is more participatory than vicarious in nature, look for it in our Parks and Recreation or On the Water chapters.

The radio stations listed below every franchise name are the teams' English-language flagship stations, and the phone numbers are ticket sources. For major events you also can try TicketMaster at (800) 523-1515.

Baseball

San Francisco Giants
Pacific Bell Park, China Basin
(415) 468-3700, (800) 5-GIANTS
www.sfgiants.com
KNBR 680 AM

One of two franchises—the Los Angeles Dodgers being the other—to open major league baseball to westward expansion in 1958, the Giants have been a team of individual standouts but little collective success. The team has won several National League West championships and two pennants in its 40-or-so years in San Francisco, losing the World Series to the Yankees in 1962, to the Oakland A's in 1989, and to the Anaheim Angels in 2002.

Yet in this city, style points are almost as valuable as titles, and the Giants have had plenty of style. The 1960s squads had big clout from legendary center fielder Willie Mays, first basemen Willie McCovey and Orlando Cepeda, and the brilliant pitcher Juan Marichal.

The Giants of the 1970s and early '80s played hard but fell short of victory. Finally a slugging lineup that included Will Clark, Kevin Mitchell, and Matt Williams took the team to division titles in 1987 and 1989. Those three players are gone now; however, Barry Bonds continues to be a one-man draw. In 2001, Bonds went down in the history books for hitting 73 home runs during regular season play. He also set records for slugging percentage (.863) and walks (177). He continued to make headlines after the season was over when he re-signed with the Giants in a lucrative, five-year deal worth $90 million. Bonds hit his 600th career home run in 2002, joining an exclusive club of only three other players in the history of the game: Babe Ruth, Willie Mays, and Hank Aaron.

When the moody Bonds is focused on business, he is arguably one of the five best all-around players in major-league history.

The Giants do their thing at Pacific Bell Park. Designed by the renowned architectural group of HOK Sports Facilities, it's a nostalgic wonder along the lines of Baltimore's Oriole Park at Camden Yards and Cleveland's Jacobs Field. Pac Bell Park hugs San Francisco Bay—so close, in fact, that prodigious drives to right field end up in salt water, retrieved by a canine employee. The stadium includes a brew pub, a bayside promenade that allows fans to peek through the fence for no charge, and, unlike 3Com Park, ample public transportation options. Current Giants ticket prices range from $9 to $45.

Oakland Athletics
Network Associates Coliseum, off I–880,
about 5 miles south of I–980
(510) 568–5600
www.athletics.mlb.com
KFRC 610 AM/KVON 1440 AM

The Athletics' history in Oakland has been the steepest of roller-coaster rides. The A's had been unqualifiedly dreadful in Kansas City, but they immediately posted their first winning record in 16 years after moving to the Bay Area in 1968. Reggie Jackson hit the home runs and made the headlines, but the strength of the team was pitching, led by starters Jim "Catfish" Hunter and Vida Blue, and handlebar-mustachioed reliever Rollie Fingers. But Finley soon sold off his stars, and the Athletics sank into ineptitude. They played games in the late 1970s that drew fewer than 1,000 fans.

The A's became Major League Baseball's best team from 1988 to 1990. Dave Stewart won 20 or more games four straight years, Dennis Eckersley was reborn as baseball's eminent closer, Rickey Henderson returned to his hometown to steal bases and runs, and hitting giants such as Jose Canseco and Mark McGwire drove opposing pitchers into deep depression. Oakland was upset by the Dodgers in '88 and the Reds in '90 but flattened the Giants in 1989's "Bay Bridge Series," which was interrupted by the 7.1-magnitude Loma Prieta earthquake.

The renovated Network Associates Coliseum remains a delightful place to watch a ball game. The music is way ahead of the standard play list, there is a play room for bored kids, and rainouts are nearly as rare as no-hitters. (There were only 11 rain checks issued between 1978 and 1996.) The stadium lies south of downtown Oakland, right off I–880. The cheapest A's ticket is $3.00; the most expensive is $30.00, and all of them are half-price if you are younger than 15 or older than 60.

Football

San Francisco 49ers
The Stadium at Candlestick Point, off U.S.
101, about 1.5 miles south of I–280
(415) 656–4900
www.sf49ers.com
KGO 810 AM

Despite their recent implosion, the 49ers retain a firm grip on the hearts and minds of Northern California. The caps, the T-shirts, the bumper stickers, and the bar decorations are there to make sure you don't forget, not even for a minute, that

Insiders' Tip

If you're going to the Oakland Coliseum or the Arena for a game, consider taking BART, the Bay Area Rapid Transit system. You can park in Richmond, at the northwest tip of what is commonly called the East Bay, and take a train to the Coliseum's doorstep. Call (415) 992-2278 for schedules and directions.

The games have been sold out since 1981. Allow at least 90 minutes to Candlestick Point from either Napa or Santa Rosa, progressively longer from points farther north. And for heaven's sake, bring a jacket and a thermos of something hot.

Oakland Raiders
Network Associates Coliseum, off I–880,
about 5 miles south of I–980
(888) 447–2433
www.raiders.com
The Ticket, 1050 AM/KVON 1440 AM

That wasn't a tremor you felt in June 1995, it was the earth shifting back onto its proper axis upon the Raiders' return to Oakland—the first time a pro sports franchise had come back to a city it once fled.

So far, however, the homecoming has produced more political than playoff contention. The hastily brokered deal that brought the Raiders back to town has left the city of Oakland responsible for unsold "personal seat licenses," and this is a city with little financial cushion. Still, the East Bay fans have waited a long time for the return of "Raidah football" and they are generally forgiving.

The team's pinnacle was 1972 to 1976, when the blustery John Madden coached at least seven Pro Football Hall of Fame players: center Jim Otto, guard Gene Upshaw, tackle Art Shell, wide receiver Fred Biletnikoff, kicker George Blanda, linebacker Ted Hendricks, and cornerback Willie Brown (not to be confused with San Francisco's iconoclastic mayor of the same name).

Stars of the 1980s included soft-spoken quarterback Jim Plunkett, relentless defensive end Howie Long, and incomparable running back Marcus Allen. Davis' never-ending search for the right head coach continued in 1998, when he brought in young Jon Gruden, an offensive whiz kid from the Philadelphia Eagles. (But he's more than a whiz kid, he's also beautiful. He made *People* magazine's "50 Most Beautiful People in the World" list in 2001. Go figure.)

The Raiders' rich on-field history notwithstanding, the best reason to come to Oakland on an autumn Sunday always

the Wine Country is Niners country. It wasn't always this way, of course. The team had its core following for decades, but it wasn't until the harmonic convergence of Bill Walsh and Joe Montana that the serious adulation began.

The 49ers got their start in the All-America Football Conference in 1946, then became one of three AAFC teams (the Browns and Colts were the others) to join the NFL in 1950. From 1946 through 1980, the 49ers had no NFL title banners to fly.

That changed when Walsh, the academic head coach, and Montana, the uncanny quarterback, arrived in 1979. The 49ers were in the Super Bowl by January 1982, and they'd be back four times in the next 13 seasons. Along the way, Montana was replaced by scrambling Steve Young, now also retired from the game. Wide receiver Dwight Clark was replaced by Jerry Rice, maybe the best player ever to wear an NFL uniform. Even Walsh was replaced with protege George Seifert, who was in turn supplanted by Steve Mariucci in 1997. Through it all, the team hardly missed a beat—until 1999, when it sank to the bottom of the NFL. They took another hit in 2001, when Jerry Rice defected to the Oakland Raiders.

A few end notes: 49ers tickets are about $50, but good luck purchasing one.

has been the spontaneous circus that erupts in the parking lot and the cheap seats. It's a freak show of the highest order—not as physically dangerous as the version at the Los Angeles Coliseum, but more entertaining. Expect to see Darth Vaders, Grim Reapers, dangling bronco effigies, and more Harley-Davidsons and pirate tattoos than you can shake a cutlass at. Tickets are $41, $51, and $61.

Finally, take note that the Raiders moved their summer training camp to Napa in 1996. They practice on a field behind the Napa Valley Marriott Hotel at 3425 Solano Avenue, which runs parallel to Highway 29. Those sessions are closed to the public, but the team has an annual fan day in July—and perhaps a couple of open workouts—at Memorial Stadium, which is near the intersection of Jefferson Street and Pueblo Avenue.

Basketball

Golden State Warriors
The Arena in Oakland, off I–880, about 5 miles
south of I–980
(510) 986–2222
www.nba.com/Warriors
KNBR 680 AM

Born in Philadelphia in the 1940s, the Warriors moved west, becoming the San Francisco Warriors from 1962 to 1971, before floating across the bay to Oakland to become Golden State.

The team that brought Wilt Chamberlain from Philadelphia in 1962 has won only one NBA title on the West Coast. That came in 1975, when superstar Rick Barry and a gang of overachievers shocked the Washington Bullets in a four-game sweep. Big-time performers such as Nate Thurmond and Cazzie Russell came before 1974–75, Bernard King and World B. Free after, but no other Warriors team has gone all the way.

Things seemed to be looking up under coach Don Nelson in the early 1990s, but the situation blew up when Nelson feuded with star forward Chris Webber in 1994–95. Warriors tickets range from $10 to $113.

Sacramento Kings
ARCO Arena, near the northeast corner of I–5
and I–80
(916) 928–6900
www.nba.com/Kings
KHTK 1140 AM

Game after game, ARCO Arena is filled to the rafters with screaming, maniacal Kings fans. Finally, they've got something to shout about. In their first 13 seasons in Sacramento the Kings never had a winning season. But the love of hoops was unconditional here. Sellouts are practically a Sacramento city ordinance.

Existing franchises in various sports, including the Raiders and the A's, certainly have taken notice, making overtures to Sacramento in the recent past regarding possible moves. (Sacramento has been the Kings' home since 1985, but they've moved before—from Rochester, Cincinnati, and Kansas City.)

ARCO Arena is just north of Sacramento. From the Wine Country, take I–80 to Sacramento and turn off on I–5 north. Take the Del Paso Road exit and follow the signs. Tickets range from $10 to $115 per game, though all but the cheapest seats are snapped up by season-ticket holders. In fact, if you're after Kings tickets you are encouraged either to book weeks in advance or befriend a lonely corporate CEO.

Hockey

San Jose Sharks
San Jose Arena, off I–880
(415) 421–8497, (408) 287–4275
www.sj-sharks.com
KXBX 1270 AM

The Sharks made a reputation as giant-killers as they knocked off high-ranked opponents, Detroit and then Calgary, in the opening rounds of the 1994 and 1995 NHL playoffs. But the problem for San Jose has been getting to the playoffs. The Sharks have been known as the bottom feeders of the Western Conference, though Coach Darryl Sutter's 1999–2000 squad was eminently respectable.

San Jose Arena is a tidy venue smack dab in the middle of a tidy city, and professional hockey has been an incongruous hit in Silicon Valley. To get to the arena, exit I-880 at Coleman Avenue, turn left on Coleman, right on Julian, and follow the parking signs. The Sharks began play in 1991, and the arena opened two years later.

Be advised that San Jose is about 40 miles south of San Francisco or Oakland, so getting there and back from the Wine Country takes an investment of a full day or a long evening. Sharks tickets range from $18 for the most distant upper-reserved seats to $102 for sideline club seats. Many others are in the $35 to $72 range.

Soccer

San Jose Earthquakes
Spartan Stadium, off I–280
(408) 985–GOAL
www.sjearthquakes.com
KLIV 1590 AM

When Major League Soccer officially set up shop in spring of 1996, the fledgling league chose San Jose as the site of its inaugural game. The city had everything MLS was looking for: an established soccer tradition, a first-rate stadium, and a well-run organization headed by transplanted Englishman Peter Bridgwater. More than 31,000 fans crammed into Spartan Stadium on April 6, 1996, and the Clash (as they were then known) did not disappoint, leaving with a 1-0 victory over D.C. United.

Hope springs eternal in the heart of Silicon Valley for a team led by defender John Doyle and goalkeeper Joe Cannon. Midfielder Eddie Lewis was named to the U.S. National Team for '99 while gifted forward Ronald Cerritos played for El Salvador. In 2000 they meshed under the tutelage of Bay Area favorite Lother Osiander. The Earthquakes won the MLS Cup in 2001 over the L.A. Galaxy, on the winning goal of Cerritos.

Spartan Stadium is on the San Jose State University campus, accessible by I–280 in the heart of San Jose. Exit at Seventh Street, turn right on Seventh, and proceed about 1.5 miles to the stadium. (And please note the distance caveat stated at the end of the Sharks' summary.) Adult tickets range from $13 for behind-the-goal seats to $20 for the "premier" category. (Gold Club seats at midfield are sold out.) There are discounts for kids younger than 14 and seniors older than 60, beginning at $7.00 for the cheap seats. The Major League Soccer schedule runs from March through October.

Insiders' Tip
We can't emphasize this enough: If you intend to drive from the Wine Country to major-league sporting events in San Francisco and Oakland, be prepared to spend a lot of time in traffic getting to and from your destination. Leave early and please be patient.

Golf

The Napa Championship Presented by Beringer—Senior Golf Championship
Silverado Country Club and Resort, 1600 Atlas Peak Road, Napa
(707) 252–8687, (800) 286–GOLF
www.silveradoresort.com

The PGA Senior Tour returned to Napa's Silverado Resort in October 1999 for what was then called the Transamerica, a tournament that in 11 years raised more than $1.5 million for Napa Valley charities such as the Queen of the Valley Hospital Foundation and local Boys and Girls Clubs. The splendid 6632-yard, par 72 course, with its 1857 Colonial clubhouse, consistently lures the biggest names on the Senior Tour. Recent participants include Arnold Palmer, Lee Trevino, Chi Chi Rodriguez, Dick Stockton, Jim Colbert, and Tom Weiskopf.

Tom Kite won the 2002 event, completing the 54-hole tourney with a 12-under-par 204 total.

The weeklong event includes two practice rounds (free to attend the first day, $5.00 the second), a two-day Pro-Am competition ($13.00 each day to attend), and three rounds of serious golf ($18.00 the first day, $20.00 for each of the latter two). You also can choose from a series of packages that include subsequent admission to the tournament grounds and clubhouse. They run from $13 to $105. All of the noted prices are at the gate; you can save by ordering early. Parking runs $4.00 for a daily pass or $10.00 for a tournament pass. Silverado is northeast of downtown Napa, off Highway 121. This tournament is likely to be held at a new location in 2003 (not yet determined at the time this book went to press) while a $3.5 million renovation is underway on the courses at Silverado.

Motor Sports

Don't be surprised if the still air of your summer evening is suddenly torn apart by the growl of a 750-horsepower engine, the scent of ripening grapes replaced by a whiff of high-octane fuel. Love 'em or hate 'em, racing machines are here to stay in Wine Country. This section is divided by venue.

Calistoga Speedway
Napa County Fairgrounds, 1435 North Oak Street, Calistoga
(707) 942–5111

Calistoga is a gathering point for devotees of sprint cars, those miniature, winged beasts that evolved from old Indy 500 roadsters. Pound for pound, sprint cars pack as much power as modern-day Indy cars, and they seem to be as loud. They produce downward force, which helps the car grip the track; the larger one also happens to provide handy space for advertising.

Calistoga Speedway's half-mile dirt track hosts approximately seven sprint-car nights a year: four sanctioned by the Northern Auto Racing Club and a three-day event put on by the World of Outlaws. The NARC nights tend to be in early May, Memorial Day weekend, and July 4th weekend. The World of Outlaws event is Labor Day weekend. A typical program might include four 10-lap heat races, a feature-inversion dash, a 12-lap semi-main event, and a 25-lap feature event. Tickets run about $15 for NARC races and $80 for the Outlaws' three-day package.

Infineon Raceway
Highways 37 and 121, south of Sonoma
(800) 870–RACE
www.infineonraceway.com

Which event drew the largest crowd in the history of Northern California sports? It wasn't the 49ers vs. Dallas in the 1994 NFC Championship Game or one of the A's-Giants World Series contests in 1989. It was the NASCAR Winston Cup stock car race that drew 102,000 in May 1996. That event was staged at Infineon, formerly known as Sears Point.

If it's nitro-burning, rubber-ripping, and asphalt-grabbing, chances are you'll find it here. This might be the world's busiest raceway, with an average of 340 days a year of activity including 50 of 52 weekends. Much of that is devoted to the resident Russell Racing School, but there is plenty of competition among a variety of internally combusting machines.

Besides the twisting, 12-turn, 2.52-mile road course and the quarter-mile drag strip, Infineon offers 700,000 square feet of coexisting shop space and posh, tower VIP seats. The facility is in a beautiful corner of lush rolling hills at the southern tip of Sonoma County. If you just want a look, it's open to the public free of charge on weekdays. If you want to get truly revved, race tickets range from $15 to $100, with many in the $15 to $25 range.

A $50 million facelift over the last couple of years added more comfort for spectators: a new seven-story-high grandstand at the start/finish line with seating for 12,000, luxury boxes, and improved restrooms and concession stands, as well as two underground pedestrian walkways. The track and pit areas also underwent major renovations, and a new drag strip was built. About $1 million in landscaping improvements is currently underway.

Petaluma Speedway
Petaluma Fairgrounds, 100 Fairgrounds Drive
(707) 762–7223
www.petalumaspeedway.com

Check the notes about sprint cars listed in the Calistoga Speedway section and apply them here. NARC stages two events on Petaluma's three-eighths-mile, semi-banked track over the July 4th weekend and in early October. The fairgrounds are just west of U.S. 101 on East Washington Street. If you have to ask how far away it is, maybe this sport isn't for you. A 1996 survey showed that sprint-car fans traveled an average of 82 miles to each event.

Marathons and Running Events

Vineman Marathon
Northern Sonoma County
(707) 528–1630
www.vineman.com

This popular event—in its 13th year—attracts more than 2,000 participants from throughout the world. It is set mostly on the backroads of northern Sonoma County, with the swimming portion held in the Russian River at Guerneville. The full course includes a 112-mile cycle, 26.2-mile run, and 2.4-mile swim. A Half Vineman is also featured.

Napa Valley Marathon
Calistoga to Napa
(707) 255–2609
www.napa-marathon.com

Hey, if you're gonna torture yourself, you might as well do it in Eden. This is an unbeatable course: 26.2 miles due south along the Silverado Trail, hills hugging the left side of the road, and a yellow sea of blooming mustard to the right. Only the last half-mile, the approach to the fin-ish line at Vintage High School, is within any city limits. And after three moderate hills in the first 6 miles, the course offers a gently rolling descent. *Runner's World* magazine named this one of the top 20 marathons in America in 2002.

The Napa Valley Marathon usually takes place the first Sunday in March. The 2002 edition was the 24th annual. You can park at Vintage High and take a shuttle bus to the start line (just south of Calistoga on the Silverado Trail) but be punctual—the last bus leaves at 5:30 AM. Weather can vary, of course, but bet on lifting fog and temperatures in the mid-40s at start time (7:00 A.M.), progressing to warm sunshine later in the morning. Early entry costs $60, and it jumps to $75 on prerace Saturday.

The Relay
Calistoga to Santa Cruz
(415) 508–9700
www.TheRelay.com

The marathon doesn't present enough of a challenge for you? Try The Relay, a 199-mile trek that winds through seven counties and 36 cities from Calistoga to Santa Cruz, past cow pastures and redwoods and across the Golden Gate Bridge. The first Relay attracted exactly nine teams in 1995, but it has mushroomed to thousands of runners since then.

Everything about this race is unique, except for sore feet and sweaty bodies. Start times are staggered at the Calistoga Mineral plant. Teams of 12 competitors split up 36 3-to-7-mile legs, with vans leapfrogging runners to their next start position. The race heads south on the Silverado Trail, with competitors running through the night and the first finishers reaching the Pacific early the next morning. Several Silicon Valley companies have gotten involved, presenting more peculiarities. This was the first race in which runners wore bar codes and got scanned at checkpoints. The Relay's home page even offers a three-dimensional preview of each leg.

The Relay is run under a full moon in September or October. The entry fee is $40 per runner, climbing to $50 in August.

Individuals looking for a team have two options: Find one yourself at the Web site, or mark the appropriate box on your application and organizers will place you.

Bicycle Road Races

Cherry Pie Criterium
Napa Valley Corporate Park, Napa
(707) 224–2369, (707) 258–0663
The carbo-loading comes after the race at this event. Besides the $1,500 or so in prize money—including $600 for the Pro I-II division—the top three finishers in each class are awarded fresh cherry pies. The 2003 Cherry Pie is the 28th annual. The 1-mile course, which includes one modest hill, is bounded by Napa Valley Corporate Drive, Napa Valley Corporate Way, and Trefethen Way. The simplest way to find the start/finish line is to look for the famous Grape Crusher statue south of Napa. Between 300 and 350 racers split up into 11 divisions, including a recumbent category. It is run the second or third Sunday in February.

Napa Grand Prix
First and Main Streets, Napa
(707) 963–7736
This criterium (a timed road race, with the winner determined by number of laps completed) got its start only recently—in 1994—but its following is on the upswing. Hoping for a breeze off the Napa River in early August, the restaurants of downtown Napa put extra tables on the sidewalk so their customers can sip cool drinks and watch the colors go blurring by. The Master's race is a U.S. Cycling Federation district championship, and there are several other divisions including a 90-minute Pro race that draws about 80 riders. The 0.7-mile course is bounded by First, School, Second, and Main Streets.

Petaluma Criterium
8375 Lancaster Drive, Rohnert Park
(707) 795–6670
www.rahul.net/kpapai/westcoast
Sonoma County's West Coast Cycling Team organizes this race, which is held at

Oakmead Business Park on the southeast end of town, just off Lakeville Highway (a.k.a. Highway 116). The 0.7-mile course offers great spectator viewing, and all races last approximately one hour. The race is generally held in early May, and the entrance fee is between $15 and $20—the 2003 event will be the 15th. Expect 300 to 350 riders.

Wine Country Cycling Classic
Graton and Santa Rosa
(707) 528–3283
www.socobikes.com
What started as the Santa Rosa Criterium in 1984 has become a two-day road event, the largest of its kind in Northern California. The Classic takes place in late March or early April and includes a total field of nearly 1,500 riders. The first day features the Graton Road Race, staged on an 11-mile course that presents four short, rolling climbs and one certified calf-burner. The pro division race is 88 miles long and pays about $4,000. Graton is 3.5 miles north of Sebastopol, just west of Highway 116.

As many as 5,000 spokeheads turn out to watch the action on the second day on a flat, fast 0.7-mile course in downtown Santa Rosa. The racing is only part of a day of festivities that often includes a live band. The Senior I/Pro division competes for 90 minutes and splits about $3,500. The starting/finish line is on Sonoma Avenue. Take the Downtown Santa Rosa exit from U.S. 101 and head east on Third Street to Santa Rosa Avenue. Turn right and proceed two blocks. Dave Walters, who organizes the Classic, also stages a weekly criterium every Tuesday night from April through August. The first race starts at 6:00 P.M. at Corporate Center Industrial Park. Call for directions.

Horse Racing

Sonoma County Fairgrounds
Highway 12, east of U.S. Highway 101,
Santa Rosa
(707) 545–4200
www.sonomacountyfair.com
If the hoofbeat of the thoroughbreds

should happen to draw your attention in midsummer, heed the call to the colors. What you'll find at the Sonoma County Fair from late July through early August is one of the country's most entertaining 12-day horse racing meets. Top jockeys such as Russell Baze, Dennis Carr, and Rafael Meza guide the trainees of Jerry Hollendorfer, Brent Sumja, Lloyd Mason, and others as thousands cheer home the world's greatest four-legged athletes. Wagering on the competition is optional. First post is 1:15 P.M.

The Jockey Club
1350 Bennett Valley Road, Santa Rosa
(707) 524-6340
www.sonomacountyfair.com/jockey.asp

This is where Wine Country's wise guys and other hip handicappers amuse themselves when the shed rows across the street aren't booked with blood stock. It's a year-round off-track concession offering races live via satellite TV from major courses in California (e.g., Golden Gate Fields, Bay Meadows, Santa Anita, Hollywood Park, Del Mar), New York, and Florida.

Three bucks gets you through the door and into a well-kept room stocked with eight projection big-screen TVs, 70 monitors, a full bar, and complete food and beverage services. Friendly clerks will take your wagers, or you may purchase a voucher and have at the auto-tote self-serve screens yourself. Either way, remember: There's a winner in each race.

College Sports

With only three four-year colleges inside its borders, the expansive Wine Country isn't exactly a hotbed of collegiate sports. Again, the Bay Area might be the place to turn if you really feel like waving a pom-pom and belting out fight songs. Here is a brief look at your options.

Sonoma State University
1801 East Cotati Avenue, Rohnert Park
(707) 664-2701
www.sonoma.edu/athletics

With a couple of players in the NFL, including Pro Bowl guard Larry Allen of the Dallas Cowboys, the NCAA Division II Seawolves had reached a respected place among small football programs. That came to an end in 1997, when the university dropped football in the face of formidable travel expenses.

Sonoma State still has plenty of athletics, including seven women's and five men's teams (the student body is 60 percent female). Soccer is king and queen there: The women, who made it to the Division II championship game in 1998, enjoyed great success in the '90s, winning six straight Northern California Athletic Conference titles from 1990 to 1995 and a national championship in 1990. The men won five of seven NCAC titles between 1990 and 1996, and went on in 2002 to win the NCAA Division II national championship—the first ever for any SSU men's team. The Seawolves jumped to the California Collegiate Athletic Association in the 1998-99 sports year.

Pacific Union College
1 Angwin Avenue, Angwin
(707) 965-6344
www.puc.edu

Tiny PUC has to scramble to come up with funding for sports, but the NAIA Division II school does what it can. It fields men's and/or women's teams in soccer, volleyball, tennis, cross-country, basketball, golf, and softball, with all but tennis staged on campus. The Pioneers have produced recent California Pacific Conference champions in women's basketball and men's golf.

University of California
2223 Fulton Street, Berkeley
(800) 462-2327
www.calbears.fansonly.com

Known primarily for its academics and tradition of radical politics, Cal also has a rich sports heritage, with Rose Bowl victories dating back to 1921 (28-0 over Ohio State). The Golden Bear's football program, which produced such stars as Craig Morton, Steve Bartkowski, Wesley Walker, and Chuck Muncie, has seen better days. Coach Bruce Snyder took the Bears to strong conference finishes and a Citrus Bowl victory in the early '90s, but since then the program has floundered.

Bears basketball experienced a recent renaissance, begun by phenomenal point guard Jason Kidd (now an NBA star) in the early 1990s. In 1996–1997, first-year coach Ben Braun took over a team in disarray (and headed for NCAA probation, thanks to the misdeeds of his predecessor Todd Bozeman), lost leading scorer Ed Gray at the end of the Pac-10 schedule, and still managed to invade the NCAA tourney's Sweet Sixteen. There, the Golden Bears fell in a close game to North Carolina.

Stanford University
Stanford Ticket Office, Stanford
(415) 723–1021, (800) 232–8225
www.stanfordfanz.net
KVON 1440 AM

Stanford is acclaimed for its squeaky-clean (well, at least by today's standards) sports programs, but it still manages to attract professional-caliber talent. Historically, the Cardinal (singular, please) has been something of a quarterback factory, producing NFL passers from Frankie Albert to John Brodie to Jim Plunkett to John Elway. Lately, the basketball team has ascended under professorial coach Mike Montgomery. In 1998, Arthur Lee, Mark "Mad Dog" Madsen, and a group of no-names made it to the Final Four, where they lost their semifinal game in overtime to eventual champion Kentucky.

In the mid-'90s, Tara VanDerveer's women's basketball program earned most of the acclaim. The Cardinal women, building on the legacy of Jennifer Azzi and showcasing the graceful Kate Starbird (Class of '96) were an annual powerhouse that captured two Division I women's hoops titles early in the decade.

Kidstuff

Napa County
Sonoma County
Mendocino County
Outside the Wine Country

You've just exited your tenth tasting room of the day and have an impressive collection of souvenir glasses, coasters, and corkscrews from an assortment of winery gift shops. The kids are bored, but with energy still left to burn. If you don't find a suitable diversion for them soon, you'll have a full-blown mutiny on your hands.

No need to worry—you don't have to change your plans and head to Orlando. There are plenty of opportunities for pleasing the little ones while entertaining the big kids too. Many of the attractions in this chapter are reliable kid pleasers, guaranteed to put a smile on small faces.

In addition, check out our Attractions chapter, which features information on many other family-oriented fun stuff, such as Safari West and the Pacific Coast Air Museum. And read about great outdoor destinations for all ages in our Parks and Recreation and On the Water chapters.

Napa County

Napa Skate Park
Vajome and Clinton Streets, Napa
(707) 257–9529

If they're bouncing off the walls, just put a skateboard or a scooter under their feet and give 'em a gentle nudge. The skate park is just about what you'd expect: a cemented city block with an assortment of hills, dips, ramps, and pathways. This is a free, do-it-yourself attraction. Bring your own gear, supervise your own children, bandage your own knees. Roller skates and roller blades are welcome too.

John F. Kennedy Memorial Regional Park
Streblow Drive off Highway 121, Napa
(707) 257–9529

The largest of Napa's municipal parks at 340 acres, Kennedy has four group picnic areas, hiking and jogging trails, volleyball courts, a lighted baseball diamond, and a multiuse ball field. It also has a duck pond and playground for the really young ones, plus a boat ramp for family outings. It's a tranquil, breezy setting adjacent to the Napa River.

Paradise Miniature Golf
640 Third Street, Napa
(707) 258–1695

What would a family road trip be without a few rounds of miniature golf? Paradise is in the heart of Napa (which some would say is in the heart of Paradise). It has a 19-hole course and a snack bar with candy and soft drinks. A couple of favorites: the 5th hole, with its grand loop-the-loop and, best of all, the 17th—the Valley Fog Hole—which tests your bad-weather vision as well as your hand-eye coordination. The cost is $3.50 for adults, $2.00 for kids 12 and younger, and $3.00 for members of the "senior tour." Paradise is open from 3:00 to 7:00 P.M. Monday through Friday and 11:00 A.M. to 7:00 P.M. on Saturday and Sunday during the summer.

Playground Fantástico
Old Sonoma Road at Freeway Drive, Napa
(707) 257–9529

When a city the size of Napa can pull together more than 1,500 volunteers for an intensive six-day community project, you know the result will be something spe-

Giant sandbox animals become playmates at Playground Fantástico in Napa. PHOTO: JEAN SAYLOR DOPPENBERG

cial. In this case, the result is a world-class, 15,000-square-foot playground with an estimated worth of $2 million, built in 2002 entirely with donated materials and labor. There are two themed sandboxes, two castles, one area for tots and another for older children, a tree house, a train station, and much more. No shortcuts were taken in the quality of the materials and creativity—nearly everything is tastefully constructed from wood. At the entrance is a 22-foot-tall work of art described as "part Fred Flintstone meets the Michelin Man meets pick-up sticks" by one of the creative minds behind the project. It's fun, and it's free.

Carolyn Parr Nature Museum
3107 Browns Valley Road, Napa
(707) 255–6465

This modest facility a mile west of Highway 29 is sponsored by the Napa Valley Naturalists. People come here to see the museum's dioramas, which show five habitats: grassland, chaparral, marshland, riparian, and woodland/forest. Inside each diorama are examples of native plants and animal specimens,

from raccoons and wood ducks to king snakes and badgers. There is an extensive raptor display and a special kids' section with such hands-on items as pelts and skulls. Adults enjoy the Carolyn Parr museum too, but the small scale seems ideally suited to children. Admission is free. The museum is open from 1:00 to 4:00 P.M. Saturday and Sunday and for group tours by appointment (50 cents per head). It is at the entrance to Westwood Hills Park, a 111-acre green space with picnic facilities and a self-guided nature trail.

Learning Faire
964 Pearl Street, Napa
(707) 253–1024
www.learningfaire.com

This Napa toy store, under the same ownership for more than 20 years, prides itself on selectivity. All products are prescreened for safety, and they sell nothing that promotes violence. Learning Faire stocks Brio, Thomas wooden trains, Legos, plenty of other toys, and lots of games, puzzles, crafts, books, cassettes, and CDs. There are hands-on stations and the occasional market-research play day—when manufacturer reps bring new toys for kids to sample.

Fun & Games
3646 Bel Aire Plaza, Napa
(707) 257–1468

Tradition is important to the folks at Fun & Games. They stock no video games, no electronic games, and no weaponry. Instead you'll find marbles, Wiffle bats, and a colorful variety of yo-yos. (The store even hosts yo-yo events that draw nationally prominent, um, yo-yoers.) Fun & Games focuses on a handful of children's book publishers, including Scholastic and Random House. You'll find puzzles, timers, and games sitting out, waiting for tiny hands. And they have plenty of travel games, perfect for the drive home to Phoenix.

The Toy Cellar
Vintage 1870, 6525 Washington Street, Yountville
(707) 944–2144

Sprawling Vintage 1870 tends to be a lot more popular with moms than juniors. The antidote? Let them roam around The Toy Cellar with its books and Brio trains, its Beanie Babies and Playmobil, its Steiff bears and model rockets, its LGB German trains and old-fashioned metal jack-in-the-boxes. Meanwhile, Dad can pop down to the wine cellar (see our Wineries chapter).

Crane Park
Highway 29 and Grayson Avenue, St. Helena
(707) 963–5706

St. Helena families and kids of every stripe gather at this well-kept sanctuary. The 10-acre park has two baseball diamonds, horseshoe pits, lighted bocce courts and tennis courts, substantial picnic set-ups, a playground, and volleyball pits. On summer Fridays the Farmers Market is here.

Smith's Mount St. Helena Trout Farm and Hatchery
18401 Ida Clayton Road, Calistoga
(707) 987–3651

Smith's has been raising trout for private ponds for almost 60 years now. On weekends they open up their ¾-acre lake to the public, and locals have learned that it's one of the best diversions in the area for children. The proprietors provide poles and bait, and they even clean and bag the trout for you afterward. All you do is bait, cast, and reel. You pay only for the fish you take—$3.00 to $5.00, depending on size. From Highway 128 in Knights Valley, just north of Calistoga, go 7 miles north at the big sign for Smith's. On Saturdays and Sundays from February through October, the fun lasts from 10:00 A.M. to 5:00 P.M.

Sonoma County

Southern Sonoma
The Clubhouse Family Fun Center
19171 Sonoma Highway, Sonoma
(707) 996–3616

When's the last time you paid $4.00 for 18 holes of golf? The course is laid out to look like historic Sonoma, with ponds, fountains, and a lifelike City Hall. Not just for kids, it's a great place for teens. The Clubhouse also features a wide variety of the latest video games as well as sports games like air hockey, basketball, and football video games. To put an extra spin on a great family day, have a hot dog at the pond-side picnic area. The course and game room are open Monday through Thursday from noon to 8:00 P.M., Friday and Saturday to 10:00 P.M., and Sunday from 10:00 A.M. to 9:00 P.M. The rate for anyone older than five is $4.00 a game; kids younger than five play free. Special packages are available for family groups and birthday parties.

Train Town
20264 Broadway, Sonoma
(707) 938–3912
www.traintown.com

It's difficult to say who gets the most fun out of this train ride, kids or adults. The whole layout is so cleverly crafted that it's a marvel of dedication to the art of the train buff. The miniature train travels through scenic landscapes of trees, lakes, bridges, a 140-foot-long tunnel and a small-scale replica of a turn-of-the-century Sonoma Valley town called

Lakeville. While adults may feel they have arrived in Lilliput, kids seem right in tune with the tiny country they travel through. Midway along, the best part for many kids is the petting zoo. For five minutes the train stops and everyone hauls out to pet llamas, horses, and miniature goats and to feed the ducks and geese. Back at the station there's a carousel ride ($1.00) and some interesting mechanical exhibits. Trains operate 10:00 A.M. to 5:00 P.M. every day in summer. Winter hours are 10:00 A.M. to 5:00 P.M. Friday through Sunday. Trains leave every 30 minutes. Adult fare is $3.75; kids and seniors go for $3.25.

Morton's Sonoma Springs Resort
1651 Warm Springs Road, Kenwood
(707) 833–5511, (800) 551–2177
www.sonomasprings.com

One of the last of the natural mineral-water swimming holes, Morton's has three beautiful pools—for toddlers, for kids, and for the family. More fun can be had at the volleyball and basketball courts, horseshoe pits, baseball field, bocce ball court, and game room with all the latest video games. There are 11 naturally landscaped picnic areas (one by a stream) with barbecue pits and shaded tables. Morton's is well-known locally as a family gathering place and for hosting family and corporate picnics of up to 2,400 people. Parking is available at no extra charge. The snack bar is conveniently close to the pools with ice-cold drinks and a wide selection of hot dogs, hamburgers, chips, and all those picnic eats that make a family day so much fun. Morton's is open from the first weekend in May through most of September, from 10:00 A.M. to 7:30 P.M. on weekends and from 10:30 A.M. to 6:00 P.M. on weekdays. Admission is $10.00 for adults and $9.00 for children.

Early Work
141 Kentucky Street, Petaluma
(707) 765–1993
www.earlywork.com

Early Work was formerly a shop for teachers looking for educational materials, but it is now open to the public. It's a great

Insiders' Tip
A quiet redwood forest near the coast provides the perfect acoustics for the Cazadero Performing Arts Camp. It's a great place for young musicians—from middle school to high school—to refine their performance skills in a fun, social environment. Workshops focus on orchestra, jazz band, chorus, and other areas. Visit their Web site at www.cazpac.org or call (510) 527-7500.

favorite with children because of its selection of creative toys and learning materials. There's something for everyone here, from age 1 to 100. Toys and books cover art, science, math, and language. There's an event schedule that changes from month to month—call the store for times or check their Web site.

Jungle Vibes
163 Kentucky Street, Petaluma
(707) 762–6583, (800) 804–0007
www.junglevibes.com

They call it a nature and science store, but it's really an adventure where nature and science meet world culture. At this unique Petaluma store walking in the door is like entering another country. Imagine strolling from vendor to vendor amid gondolas and giant baskets heaped high with handmade textiles and artifacts. The sound of foreign tongues and the smell of strange new fruits converge. A taste of adventure and multicultural exploration goes a long way in our busy lives, and Jungle Vibes is set to help the community explore the world, using nature and science toys and books to complement an authentic collection of ethnic arts and sounds. This is the place to expand your child's world.

Victoria's Fashion Stables
4193 Old Adobe Road, Petaluma
(707) 769-8820
www.fashionstables.com

No, it's not related to that tantalizing fashion catalog. This place is pure, clean barnyard fun, featuring good stuff for good kids—small, medium, or large.

For the little ones, there's a petting zoo along with pony rides. This isn't your average petting zoo, though. You'll start by seeing clucking chickens and waddling ducks, proceed to greeting pygmy goats, potbellied pigs, and baby horses, and then go on to a lesson in how to milk a cow. Pony rides are suitable for even very small children—the staff will walk beside the horse and even hold junior steady if necessary. The stables are open every day except Tuesday. Appointments are preferred though drop-ins can usually be accommodated. Every October, there's a pumpkin patch here. Victoria's also operates a day-use and over-night campground, with fishing nearby. Wait, there's more: a horse and carriage service for weddings.

Cal Skate
6100 Commerce Boulevard, Rohnert Park
(707) 585-0500
www.calskate.com

Kids of all ages love to rollerskate here. The arena is open from 9:30 A.M. to 8:00 P.M., and it offers special sessions—such as the tiny tots session for kids eight and under. There is also plenty of open skating. Adult prices are $3.50 to $4.75.

Scandia Family Fun Center
5301 Redwood Drive, Rohnert Park
(707) 584-1398
www.scandiafunland.com

There's fun for everyone here: miniature golf, batting cages, go-carts, a video arcade, an Indy raceway, Tidal Wave bumper boats,

and a snack bar. It opens every day at 10:00 A.M. and stays open until 11:00 P.M. on weekdays and midnight on weekends. Prices vary by attraction.

Toobtown
6591 Commerce Boulevard, Rohnert Park
(707) 588-8100

This one is for children 2 to 12 and younger. Toobtown offers unlimited play in a four-story tube structure, plus a dinosaur-bounce and fun in the gym, three bumper boat rides in a pond, and lots of rides on horses and tortoises and spaceships. Socks are required by the dress code. Hours are 10:00 a.m. to 8:00 p.m. Sunday through Thursday, 10:00 a.m. to 9:00 p.m. on Friday and Saturday. Weekday prices are $4.95; it's $6.95 on the weekend.

Copperfield's Books
2316 Montgomery Drive, Santa Rosa
(707) 578-8938
650 Fourth Street, Santa Rosa
(707) 576-7681
www.copperfields.com

Voted best kids' bookstore by an independent Sonoma County readers' poll, Copperfield's keeps up a steady stream of events to get kids interested in reading. Book promotions are unusual: For the Cat in the Hat program, kids had a chance to get their picture taken with the Cat himself. Family Fun Night brought out Curious George and provided an opportunity to help the man in the yellow hat find his curious companion. Occasional get-togethers with balloons and storytelling give book reading a party atmosphere. (See the Bookstores section of our Shopping chapter for more on Copperfield's.)

Howarth Park
630 Summerfield Road, Santa Rosa
(707) 543-3425

One of 27 parks in Santa Rosa, Howarth is the big one, a 152-acre retreat into the world of nature. There's a 25-acre lake where families can rent canoes, rowboats, paddleboats, and sailboats and even take sailing lessons. Kids and parents also can fish for trout, bluegill, and bass through-out the year. In another part of the park, a simulated steam train follows a quarter-mile track over a bridge and through a tunnel. But wait, there's more: a carousel, pony rides, and Old Man Olson's farm, where kids can pet a variety of barnyard animals. Bring a picnic and have a great day! The park is open from 6:00 A.M. to 9:00 P.M. in summer and 6:00 A.M. to 6:00 P.M. in winter. Boat rentals (fishing is optional and subject to state regulations) and amusement rides are in operation Tuesday through Sunday from 11:00 A.M. to 5:00 P.M. during summer and on weekends in spring and fall.

Petrified Forest
4100 Petrified Forest Road, Santa Rosa
(707) 942–6667
www.petrifiedforest.org

The trees died a few million years ago, but they remain alive forever as stone sculptures of what they used to be. Paths wind in and out through the fossilized forest (see our Attractions chapter). Visitors can take a quarter-mile loop that requires about 20 minutes to stroll. Summer hours are 10:00 A.M. to 4:30 P.M. Admission is $5.00 for adults; $4.00 for kids and seniors. Almost as interesting as the forest is the museum and gift shop, where you can buy all kinds of good stuff—stones you've never seen before and pieces of wood turned to stone. There's also a good selection of books.

Redwood Empire Ice Arena
1667 West Steele Lane, Santa Rosa
(707) 546–7147
www.snoopyshomeice.com

Charles Schulz, famous for his Peanuts cartoons, grew up in Minnesota and never lost his love for ice skating. The rink he built in Santa Rosa is a beautiful venue compared to the outdoor rinks he knew in his youth. A full range of skating is offered, with mornings reserved for pro-grams and classes (many world champi-ons have trained here). The arena is open daily, but hours vary. The cost is $7.00 for adults and teens and $5.50 for children younger than 12. Aside from the ice arena, there's a wonderful Peanuts Gallery gift

Snoopy and Charlie Brown of "Peanuts" fame are forever young in this commemorative statue in Santa Rosa's Railroad Square. The late car-toonist Charles Schulz lived in Santa Rosa for most of his career. PHOTO: JEAN SAYLOR DOPPENBERG

shop that's appealing to all ages (see our Shopping chapter). You can also buy skates here, both ice and roller. (For more information on the arena and the Charles M. Schulz Museum next door, see our Attractions chapter.)

Riley Street Art Supplies
103 Maxwell Court, Santa Rosa
(707) 526–2416
www.rileystreet.com

This is a great place to pick up childrens' craft supplies, including face-painting kits, tempera paints, tattoo books, how-to-draw books, and build-your-own foam dinosaur kits. For one week each July (exact dates vary), a kids' art camp is held at the store from 9:00 A.M. to 1:00 P.M. at a cost of $120 per child. Youngsters get pro-fessional instruction in whatever medium is suitable for their age. This is a premier shopping spot for professional artists and craftspeople.

Santa Rosa Junior College Planetarium
2001 Lark Hall, 1501 Mendocino Avenue,
Santa Rosa
(707) 527–4371
www.santarosa.edu

Star-studded shows feature various astronomical phenomena, with the night sky projected (with special effects) onto the dome, using state-of-the-art equipment. Offered only during the school year, shows are scheduled at 7:00 and 8:30 P.M. on Fridays and Saturdays, and at 1:30 and 3:00 P.M. on Sundays. Cost is $4.00 for adult general admission and $2.00 for students and seniors, all on a first-come, first-served basis. Children younger than five are not admitted.

Northern Sonoma

Windsor Waterworks & Slides
5225 Conde Lane, Windsor
(707) 838–7360

The excitement begins 42 feet up, where you can pair up with a friend or go it alone on the big double-tube river ride. Or maybe you'd rather plunge down the speed slide for the thrill of a lifetime. Want more? Try King Richard's run, a giant of a slide, with double tubes that propel you through a tunnel of fun. The height requirement for those thrill rides is 45 inches. But the little ones (at least 36 inches tall) haven't been forgotten. There's a special body flume just for them. Between rides, there's time to swim, play volleyball, pitch horseshoes, or take a whack at Ping-Pong. Bring a picnic, or grab a pizza pocket or hot dog at Friar Tuck's. It's open 11:00 A.M. to 7:00 P.M. from May through September (weekends only until June 15). Adults and teens pay $13.25 for full use of the park, kids ages 4 to 12 are $12.25, and those younger than 4 are free. There is another option: an afternoon splash special running from 4:00 to 7:00 P.M. is only $9.75 per person.

The Toyworks
103-B Plaza Street, Healdsburg
(707) 433–4743
2759 Fourth Street, Santa Rosa
(707) 526–2099
6940 Sebastopol Avenue, Sebastopol
(707) 829–2003
www.sonomatoyworks.com

A store of educational toys, Toyworks claims 13,000 different items, from European toys, Lego blocks, and science and nature items to educational books and Lionel trains. Store hours are 10:00 A.M. to 6:00 P.M. Monday through Saturday and Sunday from 11:00 A.M. to 5:00 P.M.

Lake Sonoma Fish Hatchery
3333 Skaggs Springs Road, Geyserville
(707) 433–9483

Here's a chance to peek in on all phases of fish life, depending on the season. In summer you'll see the small, young fish; later in the season, from late October through March, you'll be able to watch the coho salmon and steelheads returning to spawn and climbing the fish ladder. The coho salmon will die after spawning, but the steelheads will live to return to the sea. Once the eggs have been laid and fertilized, the fish hatchery starts collecting eggs once a week—each Thursday at 10:30 A.M. Summer hours here are 9:00 A.M. to 5:00 P.M. daily; winter hours are 9:00 A.M. to 4:00 P.M., Wednesday through Sunday. There is no charge. Visitors also will enjoy a display of Native American artifacts, plus information on local geology.

West County/Russian River

Pet-a-Llama Ranch
5505 Lone Pine Road, Sebastopol
(707) 823–9395
www.pet-a-llama.com

You only need to look into a llama's soulful, gentle eyes and stroke its long, softly curving banana ears, to fall in love. The llama's long eyelashes are to be envied; their arched necks give them dignity. The place to get acquainted with these exotic animals is at Pet-a-Llama Ranch, where two dozen of them live and entertain visitors. School groups come during the week to learn about the animals' habits, to get up close and personal with them, and give them a snack. Saturday and Sunday, though, is open house from 10:00 a.m. to 4:00 p.m. from April to December. Kids will get a kick out of feeding them (it's 50 cents) and listening to the manager of the ranch tell what llama life is all about—where they come from, what they eat, and how they're used as pack animals in their native South America.

J's Amusements
16101 Neeley Road, Guerneville
(707) 869–3102

This small, affordable park is reminiscent of the amusement parks of yore—before the high-tech world invaded them. Rides include the tilt-a-whirl, go-carts, Roundup, bumper cars, water slides, and a roller coaster. No admission fee is charged. You pay as you enjoy the individual rides—most are $1.50, bumper cars cost $2.25, and $6.00 gets you unlimited use of the water slide. Summer hours (mid-June to mid-September) are 11:00 A.M. to 11:00 P.M. In winter the park is open on weekends from 11:00 A.M. to 10:00 P.M. Saturday and 11:00 A.M. until 6:00 P.M. on Sunday.

Mendocino County

Pomo Cultural Center
Marine Drive, Lake Mendocino, Ukiah
(707) 485–8285, (707) 485–8685 (gift shop)

The round shape of the center is modeled on the Pomo tribe's ceremonial dance house, where cultural knowledge was passed down through the generations. Kids will be intrigued with the games the Pomo played, will learn how clam shells were used as money, and will have the chance to hold animal skins in the wild animal exhibit. The gift shop, operated by the Pomo, has a fascinating collection of items made by local Native Americans. Admission is free. The museum is open from 9:00 A.M. to 5:00 P.M. Wednesday through Sunday, June through October and is closed in winter (see our Attractions chapter).

Mendocino Coast Recreation and Park District
213 East Laurel Street, Fort Bragg
(707) 964–9446
www.mcn.org/1/mcrpd/mcrhmpg1.htm

This county recreation program provides fun for kids the whole summer long. An indoor swimming pool is available for recreational swimming and for swim classes. Day use of the pool is $2.00 for

Kids leap for joy after riding Mendocino County's old-time Skunk Train. PHOTO: JOHN NAGIECKI

kids, $3.00 for adults, and $2.50 for seniors. A multiuse gymnasium provides a wide variety of other athletic activities including roller skating, available at $2.00 (75 cents for skates). Schedules vary by week and month, so it is necessary to call or drop by for activity information. A complete schedule is available by mail.

California Western Railroad
(Skunk Train)
Laurel Street Depot, Fort Bragg
(707) 964–6371
www.skunktrain.com

The "Skunk" got its name from the odor of earlier gas engines, but today the train is moved by steam (or sometimes diesel fuel).

It will take you all the way to Willits and back, but when you're traveling with kids, a more intelligent choice might be the trip to Northspur, at the halfway mark. There you can find food treats, cold juices, and soft drinks; then take the return trip on the next train. Fare for the full round-trip is $45 for adults and $25 for children ages 3 to 17. The one-way trip is $39 for adults and teens, $18 for children. Reservations are recommended. (For more on the Skunk Train, see our Attractions chapter.)

Triangle Tattoo Museum
356-B North Main Street, Fort Bragg
(707) 964–8814
www.triangletattoo.com

Here are some amazing examples of skin art among various peoples of the world and an opportunity to see the tools used and learn how tattooing is done. (See our Attractions chapter for more information.) The museum is open noon to 6:00 P.M. from Sunday through Thursday, noon to 8:00 P.M. on Friday and Saturday. Admission is free, and tours are given upon request.

Outside the Wine Country

Six Flags Marine World
Marine World Parkway, Vallejo, California
(707) 643–6722
www.sixflags.com/marineworld

Yes, it falls outside our "official" boundaries, but rare is the Wine Country parent who hasn't succumbed to the splashy fun of Marine World. Now run by the Six Flags Corporation, the park has occupied its present 160-acre spot since 1986. It's one of those places that is impossible to conquer in a day, though you can certainly try. The long bill of shows includes performances by whales and dolphins, sea lions, tigers, lions, and humans on water skis. The ongoing attractions are too numerous to mention—among them are Shark Experience, Walrus Experience, Butterfly World, Elephant Encounter, the Primate Play Area, and the Animal Nursery. And don't miss two recent additions: a 10-story roller coaster called Roar and the V-2 Vertical Velocity Spiral Coaster, one of only three like it in the world. One-day tickets are $44 for adults and teens, $27 for children 4 through 12, and $33 for seniors 60 or older (children 2 and under get in free). Two-day passes are available at significant discounts. Parking is $10 per vehicle. From Napa, go south on Highway 29, then east on Highway 37 for just more than a mile. Days and hours of operation vary by season, so call ahead.

Day Trips

Point Reyes National Seashore

The Big Trees

Lake Tahoe

Northern California is brimming with intriguing destinations, so it's understandable that Wine Country visitors might want to veer off the wine trail long enough to experience another taste of the Golden State. That's fine with us—we respect your right of wanderlust and encourage you to broaden your travel horizons. Fortunately, several exceptional locations are within a few hours' drive of Napa or Santa Rosa.

To the south, the Marin Headlands, part of the Golden Gate National Recreation Area, offers scenic drives and hikes and the best views (usually above the fog) of the Golden Gate Bridge and San Francisco. Nearby Sausalito is a charming burg, with bayside dining and interesting shops. Across the bay, Berkeley is still funky, and further east the Gold Country towns of the Sierra foothills are rich in history. All of these are suitable excursions, and so are the three areas outlined in this chapter.

Depending on where you start, the spots we're recommending may be enjoyed as day trips, but if you have the time, plan for an overnight or weekend getaway.

Point Reyes National Seashore

Just southwest of Wine Country, Point Reyes offers miles of windswept beaches and magnificent palisades. Walk along cliffside trails (not too close to the edge, please), roll down lofty dunes, explore tidal marshes, and wander through a foggy forest. You're equally likely to bump into a tule elk, a sea lion, or a cow.

Dividing Point Reyes from the bulk of Marin County is the long, skinny arm of Tomales Bay and the infamous San Andreas Fault—the active demarcation line between the Pacific and North American tectonic plates. Point Reyes is moving away from the rest of the mainland, heading toward Alaska at the rate of 2 inches a year.

To get to the park, take Petaluma-Point Reyes Road southwest from Petaluma for about 20 miles. A good place to start your excursion in the 71,000-acre park is the Bear Valley Visitor Center, a big barn of a building just off Highway 1 near Olema. Close to the center you'll encounter Morgan Horse Ranch, Kule Loklo, and several hiking trails. Morgan Ranch is the only working horse-breeding farm in the national park system. Kule Loklo is a re-creation of a Miwok village, with traditional domed shelters. If you visit in July, you might get to witness the

Insiders' Tip

Built 307 steps below the visitor center at the southern tip of the peninsula, the Point Reyes Lighthouse invites you to walk down for a closer look. But beware! The return climb up the narrow stairs is an aerobic challenge not intended for the meek. If you decide to venture down, pace yourself on the return and use the rest platforms provided by the park service along the staircase.

annual Native American Celebration, during which Miwok-descended basket makers, stone carvers, singers, and dancers bring the exhibit to life.

While some visitors simply want to flop down on the pearly sand for a good read or nap, others come to explore the diversity of fascinating natural attractions. Limantour Estero is an estuary where most of the bird-watchers flock; McClures Beach has excellent tide pools; the windy Great Beach, one of the longest in the state, gets high marks from beachcombers; and Drakes Beach (which, like Drakes Bay and Drakes Estero, is named for Sir Francis Drake, the English privateer who supposedly landed here in 1579) is a Northern California rarity: a safe swimming beach. Of course, hiking routes abound, including 70 miles of trails in a big chunk of park set aside as wilderness area.

Probably foremost among attractions is Point Reyes Lighthouse, built about 1870 to help prevent the many shipwrecks that had plagued the treacherous, rocky shoreline for centuries. It is also one of California's best spots for whale watching.

In the fall, gray whales migrate from Alaska to their breeding grounds in Baja, California. In spring, they return north with their young. The peak watching season is Christmas through the end of January, when it's not uncommon to see 100 or more spouts rise in a day. During this busy migration period, the park service runs a shuttle from Drakes Beach to the lighthouse.

In the southern end of the park, near the time-warped town of Bolinas, is the Point Reyes Bird Observatory—the first of its kind when founded in 1965. A rest stop on the western migratory superhighway, the aviary plays host to an incredible diversity of bird species, one of the largest in the continental United States. Nearly 350 varieties regularly show up in the Audubon Society's annual Christmas bird count. The observatory offers classes, interpretive exhibits, and a nature trail.

Even the villages are pretty here. Point Reyes Station and Inverness, in particular, have remained undisturbed by the masses of visitors. Note that the local microclimate is highly unpredictable—except at

The beach at Point Reyes invites a romantic stroll. PHOTO: JOHN NAGIECKI

A large coastal redwood measures nearly 15 feet in diameter. PHOTO: JOHN NAGIECKI

the actual Point, which is the foggiest place on the West Coast. For more up-to-date information, look for a copy of *Coastal Traveler*, a free quarterly published by the *Point Reyes Light*, the area's Pulitzer Prize–winning newspaper, or call the Point Reyes National Seashore at (415) 663-1092.

The Big Trees

California's legendary redwood forests have inspired poetry and major awe (and more than a little avarice) during the last 200 years. Though they are often confused with their inland cousin, the giant sequoia, the redwood—or coastal redwood as it is called—is a variety unto itself, with a coastal range that extends from Monterey to southwest Oregon. Santa Rosa considers itself the capital of the Redwood Empire, and several Wine Country parks are home to these noble giants (see our Parks and Recreation chapter). But if you really want to behold these extraordinary trees in all their grandeur you have to drive north to Humboldt County. There you will find the last large stands of California's coast redwoods.

Sequoia sempervirens covered some two million acres when Archibald Menzies first gave them botanical classification in 1794. The state government created several parks around individual groves in the 1920s, but by 1965 logging had reduced the redwood ecosystem to about 300,000 acres. This prompted the U.S. government to consolidate various state, federal, and private holdings into Redwood National Park in 1968.

More land was added to the park in 1978, after bitter wrangling between environmental and pro-industry groups and deterioration of virgin growth due to upstream logging along Redwood Creek. The 110,000-acre national park is the destination of many visitors, along with three remaining state parks: Jedediah Smith Redwoods, Del Norte Coast Redwoods, and Prairie Creek Redwoods. All four parks are adjacent and, in fact, comanaged by the National Park Service and the California Department of Parks and Recreation. The national park is a World Heritage Site, the only one on the Pacific coast of the United States. Prairie Creek, meanwhile, is home to the last herds of Roosevelt elk in California.

The 7,500-acre Headwaters Forest Reserve is the most recent entry in the list of protected ancient groves. The reserve, made famous by the tree-sitting, old-growth activist Julia Butterfly, came into being as part of a $480 million controversial deal struck between the U.S. government and the Pacific Lumber Company.

Farther south, between Garberville and Ferndale, is the famed Avenue of the Giants, a 33-mile stretch of roadway that parallels U.S. 101 and offers up the most majestic succession of trees on the planet. The Avenue follows the Eel River and cuts through 51,000-acre Humboldt Redwoods State Park, the largest state park in Northern California. Along the road you'll encounter a hollow redwood (The Chimney Tree), a redwood trunk made into a domicile (One-Log House), and a redwood you can bisect without leaving the car (Shrine Drive Thru Tree, one of the state's oldest surviving tourist attractions).

What are the big groves like? It's like walking into one of Europe's grandest old cathedrals, only with better ventilation. The huge trunks absorb every trace of sound, with the exception of the occasional notes of a Swainson's thrush or Wilson's warbler that float down from the branches above. The forest bed, soft with many layers of needles, crunches under your feet, and the lush fern understory lends a primordial feel to the place that goes to the bone.

The trees are indeed ancient, with the oldest dated at approximately 2,200 years. And big? Three of the six tallest trees in the world, including the grand-champion, 368-foot Howard Libby Redwood, are in the national park. What is the secret to their great size? Moisture, and lots of it. The 50 to 80 inches of annual rainfall that drenches coastal California quenches most of the redwood's tremendous thirst, while fog, almost a daily occurrence, keeps the trees damp and cool when the rains subside.

All the attractions mentioned here are accessed via U.S. 101 between Garberville and Crescent City, just south of the Oregon border. From Wine Country, simply continue north on U.S. 101 through Mendocino County; Garberville is about 10 miles past the county line. Admission to the state parks is $6.00, which will get you into all of them. There is no charge to enter the national park. Camping and hiking options abound. For more information, call the northern parks at (707) 464–6101 or Humboldt Redwoods State Park at (707) 946–2409.

Lake Tahoe

Nature has lavished on Lake Tahoe the bluest waters, the most majestic pines, the most handsome mountains, and the most brilliant cloud-studded skies you'll find anywhere—all that and keno, too! Mark Twain was the first travel writer to tour the Lake of the Sky. His awestruck descriptions have since been quoted by a thousand equally dumbfounded travel writers who can scarcely describe the indescribable. Photos simply don't capture this cobalt-blue beauty, nor do paintings. The colors are right, but oddly, they seem too perfect, too vivid.

Tahoe lies half in California and half in Nevada (the South Shore is a two-hour drive from Sacramento, on U.S. 50), which gives impetus for pilgrimages by a swarm of weekend gamblers. They head for our

Insiders' Tip

"Tahoe" is a Washoe Indian word for "lake," but the magnificent body of water on the California-Nevada border has gone by many other names since the arrival of Europeans. First it was Mountain Lake, then Lake Bonpland. And from 1852 to 1945 it was called Lake Bigler, after John Bigler, a California governor who had Confederate ties during the Civil War.

neighbor state and hope Lady Luck will smooch the slot machine or gaming table they've selected.

But Tahoe's best bet is the lake itself. At 12 miles wide and 22 miles long, it offers all the water-oriented fun one would expect from the largest alpine lake in North America (in the Western Hemisphere, only Lake Titicaca is larger). At 97 percent pure—the same as distilled water—Lake Tahoe is as clean as it is beautiful. Fortunately, the Sierra Club and other environmental groups are fighting to keep it that way.

Look out across the waters, and you'll see colorful hot-air balloons rising from a barge in the middle of the lake just as the sun makes its appearance over the edge of the Sierra Nevada Mountains. Two-masted sailboats cut a leisurely path across the waves, while yachts hurry on their way. Couples in canoes or kayaks paddle through the shallow waters. Anglers, waiting patiently for the trout to find them, sit in their fishing boats, unimpressed by the brave soul hovering above them, dangling from a rainbow-hued parasail.

In addition, the M.S. *Dixie II* takes passengers on two, sometimes three, cruises a day—an afternoon run that crosses the lake to Emerald Bay (with its turquoise waters), and a morning cruise that features a big breakfast while following the shoreline. Prices are approximately $20 for a basic cruise, $25 for a brunch cruise, and $35 for a dinner cruise.

For a look at the lake as a whole, nothing beats the spectacular 72-mile perimeter drive. It takes about five hours (with scenic stops) on a good weather day. Plan to begin your drive early. In summer, pack or buy a picnic lunch for a brief sojourn in an adjacent park. In winter, include a midday pit stop at a ski area.

Options exist for numerous side trips while traveling the highway that circles North America's second-deepest lake (maximum depth: 1,645 feet). If all the water were somehow released from the lake—and if water behaved very differently than it does in real life—it would cover the entire state of California to a depth of 8 inches.

Heading clockwise from South Lake Tahoe, you'll soon climb a steep grade to a point overlooking the breathtaking vistas of Emerald Bay State Park. Below is the 39-room Vikingsholm Castle, a 19th-century mansion built by Laura Knight, who fell in love with Norway and sent craftsmen there to copy museum pieces for her home. Tours are available to those who walk the half-mile down the hill, which is the only visitor access except by boat. Vistas along the entire west shore are so stunning, you'll be hauling your Nikon out of the car every few minutes. Heading northeast, you'll pass what has essentially always been the residential zone of Tahoe. San Francisco's early social elite spent their summers here, and millionaires put up huge estates. Hollywood has come calling more than once, and one of these homes figured prominently in the filming of *The Godfather, Part II*.

Tahoe's oldest permanent settlement is Tahoe City, on the northwest shores of the lake. Three shopping complexes and several condominium projects give this town a year-round population of 2,000. Near the site of the bridge over the Truckee River (called Fanny Bridge because of the people hanging over its floodgates), there's a wonderful collection of Indian lore at the Gatekeeper's Museum. Tahoe City is also the take-off point for three-hour rafting trips down the Truckee River, and it is a favored location for fishermen who head out to deep water with a guide in search of mackinaw and cutthroat trout.

The lake's north shore abounds with interesting geological formations—immense boulders and tiny carnelian stones. Along the north shore you'll cross the state line into Nevada, where gambling is legal. One of its more famous casinos, the Cal-Neva, once belonged to Frank Sinatra. Those were the days when Hollywood luminaries filled the lobby. At the northeast corner of the lake, you'll find Incline Village, with its shopping center, fine art galleries, craft shops, restaurants, and, for culture vultures, drama, opera, Shakespeare, and mime, courtesy of the North Tahoe Fine Arts Council.

South of Incline Village lies one of Tahoe's best beaches—Sand Harbor State Beach, strewn with giant boulders, the refuse of Tahoe's ice age. Paths climb to the

The tram at Heavenly Valley on the south shore of Lake Tahoe rewards visitors with a sterling view of the water and surrounding mountains. PHOTO: LOREN DOPPENBERG

top of one of the granite outcroppings, allowing a view down into turquoise waters so clear that submerged boulders as high as a house can be seen in full detail. Facilities for picnicking and barbecuing in a wooded setting are unusually pleasant. Also on the east shore you'll find Ponderosa Ranch, developed at the time the TV show *Bonanza* was popular. Some consider it corny, but kids have plenty of room to run around, and anyone who used to watch the show will recognize Ben Cartwright's office and accouterments.

Most of Tahoe's east shore is privately owned, but there is a small area (recognizable by a proliferation of parked cars) where sun worshippers thread their way down a footpath through the forest and spread out nude on the massive rocks to achieve that all-over tan. Zephyr Cove, meanwhile, is where you set sail on the *M.S. Dixie*. It's near the state line.

And there are other options for side trips. At Incline Village, for example, there's a junction with Highway 27 that will take you to Reno or to Virginia City, a lively ghost town recalling days when silver

taken from its mines built San Francisco and made millionaires whose names are still familiar. Its wooden plank streets and weathered buildings are surprisingly authentic, though the usual tourist shops line the street as well. (Look to the buildings' upper stories for a true feeling of the Old West.) Reno, calling itself the "biggest little city in the world," is rife with sleek, splashy gambling casinos. The city has achieved a modest fame among nearby California cities for its inexpensive hotel rooms. It is also home to the National Bowling Association, which is quartered in a massive complex of bowling lanes and offices.

In winter, some of the best skiing in the world can be had at South Lake Tahoe—specifically at Heavenly Valley. If you're not on hand during the winter months, take advantage of the tram anyway; ride to the top of the mountain and take a stroll along the path that skirts the rim. It's a breathtaking view, and you can sip wine and have lunch at the summit's inviting patio. Be sure to bring along a panoramic camera to freeze-frame the magnificent scenery for later enjoyment.

Real Estate

Napa County
Sonoma County
Mendocino County

The downturn in the national economy in 2001 and 2002 significantly cooled off the once-red-hot real estate market of the San Francisco Bay Area. Home prices and rental rates that had escalated wildly in the late '90s finally stabilized in the new millennium. Mind you, prices didn't drop—they just didn't skyrocket much higher.

Although some high-tech companies in Wine Country experienced financial setbacks and continued to cut staff in 2002, the agricultural base of the region remains strong and profitable. The real estate market here reflects this more stable and diverse environment.

Our goal with this chapter is to give you a glimpse of the market in each of the Wine Country counties, providing some average prices and broad descriptions. By no means take these quoted figures as gospel—always rely on a real estate agent for the most up-to-date prices and details. (See the Area Overview chapter at the beginning of this book for more county demographic data.) We've included information on a few real estate agencies in each county to get you started. Happy hunting!

Napa County

Like everywhere else in the greater San Francisco Bay Area, Napa Valley's real estate prices rocketed into the stratosphere during the 1990s. Make no mistake about it: You pay dearly for quality of life here.

Here's a bit of recent history: In the first six months of 2000, Napa Valley home prices increased by more than 21 percent. In August 2000, the median price of an existing house sold through the Multiple Listing Service was $285,000, up more than $50,000 from the previous year. (Median price means that half of the sales were at a higher price and half were lower.) In late 2002, the median price was hovering around $425,000. Today, single-family homes listing for under $200,000 are a distant memory, while listings for million-dollar-plus homes are setting records.

Bargain prices (if you can call them that) may still be found in American Canyon, just south of Napa. But as you head north on Highway 29, the meter on home costs begins to spin faster. As a general rule, Yountville is more expensive than Napa, the Oakville-Rutherford area is more expensive than Yountville, and St. Helena is the most expensive town in the valley. The price tags drop again in Calistoga, down to about the Yountville level. Along the way, you will find every sort of residence imaginable: new tract homes, spectacular Victorians, modest 1940s bungalows, mountaintop castles, Tuscan-inspired villas, and prefab structures.

But what you will see most as you travel Highway 29 is vineyards. That's because the whole of Napa County is a designated agricultural preserve, a decision ratified by the county Board of Supervisors in 1968. The designation put development decisions in the hands of the board and set a 20-acre minimum for any new subdivision of land—a dimension that later increased to 40 acres, and more recently to 160.

Before getting into specific areas, we can make a couple of generalizations about the valley. First, a dictum that applies here and just about everywhere else in the world: Property values tend to be directly related to elevation. In other words, the rich folks live on the hilltops. Second, the really ritzy places tend to be large holdings in the country.

In Napa, most of the Victorian splendor is in Old Town—located among the letter streets south of Lincoln Avenue

Vineyard acreage in Wine Country, such as this hillside planting in the Carneros appellation, represents some of the priciest cropland in America. PHOTO: JEAN SAYLOR DOPPENBERG

between California Boulevard and Jefferson Street—and the Napa Abajo/Fuller Park area. Fuller Park, in fact, is a Historical Preservation District. The boundaries of the preservation district are ragged, but it is bordered more or less by Jefferson, Third, Brown, and Pine Streets.

Another desirable locale, and much more expensive, is Silverado Country Club, where some of the massive homes (2,000 to 5,000 square feet) have listing prices ranging from $650,000 to as much as $1.3 million. Condominiums at Silverado can range from $498,500 to $765,000, while the last subdivision built at the country club (called the Highlands) fetches prices in the neighborhood of $600,000 to $800,000.

St. Helena is the burg that best typifies the Wine Country dream: charming, early-century stone-front buildings, modest scale, vineyard views, and well-kept flower gardens. Accordingly, the prices tend to be sky high here, especially on the west side. (The median price of a home in late 2002 was about $585,000.) Calistoga offers more of a mixed bag, but it does have

some wonderfully restored old houses, especially on Cedar and Myrtle Streets just northwest of Lincoln Avenue. But country estates are considered the true gems, especially if they have significant acreage.

Which brings us to the price of vineyard land. Thanks to the loyalty of wine lovers everywhere, prices for Napa Valley Cabernet Sauvignon grapes increased more than 40 percent over the past decade; Chardonnay grape prices were up 22 percent in the same period. As the value of the raw product is driven up, so is the value of the land upon which it is grown.

If you've fantasized about owning a hobby vineyard, investing in a few acres of grapes and living the life of a gentleman farmer, be prepared for sticker shock. Your name may not be Gallo or Gates, but you will still need a sizable bankroll to enter into the grape-growing business here. Vineyards in this region represent some of the most valuable agricultural land in America.

Skewing vineyard prices momentarily in late 2002 was vintner Francis Ford Coppola, who in a rare real estate transaction—

called "shocking" by industry insiders—paid a staggering $31.5 million for 60 acres of Rutherford vineyards planted to Cabernet Sauvignon and Merlot. The purchase was not expected to significantly alter the going rate for vineyard property elsewhere in Napa Valley.

Still interested in buying a vineyard? If you're willing to settle for a lower-quality parcel (less fruit density, old trellises, and no developable homesites), expect to pay at least $50,000 per acre. More modern and higher-density vineyards top out around $100,000 per acre. If your fantasy includes building a modest winery on that property, be prepared to wait about two years for approval of the use permits, at a cost of nearly $1 million. And that's all before you begin construction. Want a tasting room, too? Good luck. Napa County officials are saying "no" to many new winery proposals, especially those with big plans for tasting rooms and event centers.

Rentals

In late 2002, rent on a two-bedroom apartment in Napa was averaging about $1,100 to $1,300 per month; its St. Helena equivalent is fetching $1,450. The typical two-bedroom house in Napa can set you back about $1,300 per month; the price goes up to $1,500 and beyond for a three-bedroom, two-bath domicile, depending on location. A similar home in St. Helena starts at about $1,600, while some with more amenities rent for well over $2,000 per month.

In Calistoga, a studio apartment, if you can find one, might be around $750; a two-bedroom apartment is just shy of $1,000. Two-bedroom homes may be had for $1,110 to $1,250 per month.

Property Rentals Only Inc.
1612 Jefferson Street, Napa
(707) 252–6147
www.prorent.com

You can usually find 25 to 50 rental listings posted outside the Property Rentals Only office. If anything piques your interest, the company will hand you an application. You can then take the stack of paperwork they offer, drive by selected properties, and mark those that you feel may be appropriate. The majority of PRO's buildings are in Napa, but they handle Yountville, St. Helena, Calistoga and Sonoma County too. All they charge is a small fee for a credit check.

Real Estate Companies

Prudential California Realty
2015 Redwood Road, Napa
(707) 259–4900
www.prudentialnapa.com

Broker Ed Wickman now oversees this office. (His wife, Sally, manages the place.) With more than 20 realtors, Prudential California covers all of Napa County and

Insiders' Tip

If you are not from California, you should know that Golden State property transactions can get complicated. The standard real estate purchase contract runs eight tightly packed pages, and the buyers and sellers don't normally get together to sign papers in one sitting as they do in some other states. Also, California is very strict about disclosures—an obvious boon for buyers and a cautionary note for sellers.

all sorts of property. It also has a full-time commercial department, not to mention three outposts in neighboring Solano County.

Century 21 Alpha Realty
1290 Jefferson Street, Napa
(707) 255–8711
With 15 Realtors working the county, Century 21 has been one of the valley's premier offices since the early 1970s. Helen Johnson's crew focuses primarily on residential property, but also ventures into commercial space, acreage, and investment property. More services in the Century 21 portfolio: property management and real estate license training.

Coldwell Banker Brokers of the Valley
1775 Lincoln Avenue, Napa
(707) 258–5200
1289 Main Street, St. Helena
(707) 963–1152
6505 Washington Street, Yountville
(707) 944–0421
www.cbnapavalley.com
This is the county's biggest real estate office based on several parameters, not the least of which is its 80 agents (66 in the Napa office alone). The company covers the entire county and all variety of property, though it is particularly strong in the realms of vineyard and residential holdings. The latter extends to houses, condos, mobile homes, farms, and ranches. (The St. Helena office is known for properties valued at $500,000 or more.) Coldwell Banker also has the advantage of "preview" listings: expensive pieces that are advertised nationally or even internationally.

Continental Real Estate
743 First Street, Napa
(707) 257–1177
Shane (one name suffices, a la Cher) is the sole proprietor of this business, and she's a busy gal. She made more than 60 sales totaling in excess of $12 million in 1998, making her the most productive realtor in the county, according to independent research. Do-it-all Continental covers the whole valley but concentrates on Napa city. Shane also offers notary, appraisal, and consulting services.

RE/MAX Napa Valley
780 Trancas Street, Napa
(707) 255–0845
1407 Main Street, St. Helena
(707) 968–9600
www.remax-napavalley-ca.com
www.nvplatinum.com
There is plenty of experience at work here. RE/MAX has more than 30 agents, with hundreds of years of combined experience, working the length of the valley. They handle various residential and commercial properties, including large developments and subdivisions. Still, they stress that no job is too small.

Silverado Realty
1561 Third Street, Suite B, Napa
(707) 252–4755
www.silveradorealtyinc.com
Silverado does country, residential, and income property in Napa, including Silverado Country Club. The country club alone has many properties from which to choose. The office started in 1970 and has two realtors.

> ## Insiders' Tip
> The Viewshed Ordinance was passed by Napa County's Board of Supervisors in 2001 to camouflage new homes and buildings that go up on the valley's scenic hillsides. The ordinance came about in response to complaints about several enormous homes that can be seen from about 20 designated scenic roads. All new structures must now blend better into their natural environment.

Morgan Lane
1932 Sierra Avenue, Napa
(707) 252–2177, (800) 511–1030
1109 Jefferson Street, Napa
(707) 254–1100
6795 Washington Street, Yountville
(707) 944–8500
1350 Oak Street, St. Helena
(707) 963–5226
www.morganlane.com

This company doesn't want to exclude anyone, but it is clearly known for its high-end listings of vineyard acreage and estate homes. (If you want a serious case of house envy, gaze at their property board.) Morgan Lane has more than 30 realtors in Yountville, St. Helena, and Sonoma, covering all of Napa and Sonoma valleys. The company also is an official affiliate of Sotheby's, and as such has access to high rollers from San Francisco to Singapore and readers of publications such as the *New York Times* and the *Wall Street Journal*.

Arroyo Real Estate
1540 Railroad Avenue, St. Helena
(707) 963–1342
www.arroyorealestate.com

This is a small company that goes for luxury. Arroyo's agents are long-time residents of Napa Valley. The firm's realm stretches from Yountville to the north end of the county, and the listings are exclusive—fine country homes, vineyard estates, and similarly desirable acreage.

Frank Howard Allen Realtors
1316 Main Street, St. Helena
(707) 963–5266
1403 Jefferson Street, Napa
(707) 252–2290
www.winecountrygroup.com

One of Sonoma's most respected real estate offices moved into Napa Valley in 1998. They'll help you locate your dream home in either county. The St. Helena site has five realtors, including a woman who once was mayor of the town (plus her son and daughter-in-law). Frank Howard Allen handles a mix of residential, vineyard, and undeveloped land.

Up Valley Associates
1126 Adams Street, St. Helena
(707) 963–1222, (800) 326–6073
www.napavalleyrealestate.com

Up Valley has four brokers and two agents who cover the entire county, though they focus on, well, the name tells the story. The company does a little bit of everything, and they are also the exclusive Wine Country representative of Christie's Great Estates.

Pacific Union
1508 Main Street, St. Helena
(707) 967–1340, (707) 251–8805
www.pacunion.com

This team of 16 agents, a satellite office of the larger San Francisco-based real estate company, handles just about everything, from homes to land and other income property up and down the valley. They specialize in luxury estates and vineyard parcels. A recent listing: 700 acres of prime planted vineyards with plenty of room to build a winery with an asking price of $20 million.

California Properties
13 Angwin Plaza, Angwin
(707) 965–2485, (800) 788–0410
www.napavalleyrealestate.net

Connections? What can you say about a company whose lineup includes the former proprietor of historic Alta Vineyards and the director of the St. Helena Hospital Men's Chorus? California Properties, which started in St. Helena in 1983, has four agents who serve most of Napa County. They stick primarily to residential property but also handle a few vineyard sales.

Beck & Taylor
1406 Lincoln Avenue, Calistoga
(707) 942–5500
www.naparealty.com

Robert Beck's small shop is a general brokerage, but it has some specialties that set it apart in Calistoga. Beck & Taylor handles substantial property management and commercial space. In addition, one of its agents concentrates on the sale and purchase of bed-and-breakfast inns around Northern California. The company generally covers the entire Napa Valley.

Calistoga Realty Co.
1473-C Lincoln Avenue, Calistoga
(707) 942–9422
www.calistoga-realty.com

This is Calistoga's largest real estate company, with three licensed realtors and an office manager. They handle Napa Valley down to Yountville plus Knights Valley and a few other corners of Sonoma County. Calistoga Realty carries more listings than anyone in the immediate area, primarily residential and small land parcels.

Real Estate Publications

Wine Country Weekly Real Estate Reader
1921 Jefferson Street, Napa
(707) 258–6150
www.rereader.com

This is far more than a series of property listings. The *Reader*'s editorial format offers a comprehensive look at the region's real estate market, and beyond, highlighted by short articles on home-buying tips or new tax laws. It also lists a selection of open houses in the Wine Country and includes at least 10 pages of classified ads. The *Reader*'s sharpest focus is on estate vineyards, wineries, and farm and ranch property. The paper is distributed throughout the Wine Country, not to mention real estate offices, BART stations (rapid transit outposts), and supermarkets in nine Bay Area counties.

Distinctive Properties of Napa Valley
P.O. Box 2849, Yountville 94599
(707) 257–0803, (707) 944–0384
www.distinctiveproperties.com

When it comes to depth of listings, *Distinctive Properties* is the bible of Napa Valley. Make that the bibles: There are two versions of the publication. One is a monthly printed in black and white (inside, anyway) on newspaper stock. The monthly lists 500 to 600 different properties from the southern to northern tip of the valley, with a handy price index. The

other edition is a slick, color quarterly that focuses on estates, vineyards, and executive homes that go for $300,000 or more. Both publications are free, distributed throughout Napa and Sonoma valleys and around the Bay Area.

The Real Estate Book of Napa County
4086 Byway East, Napa
(707) 253–1284
www.realestatebook.com

This is a small, free booklet that has been publicizing a wide range of Napa and Lake County properties for about seven years. The *Real Estate Book* is distributed mainly in those two counties and to a lesser extent in Sonoma, Solano, and Marin Counties. Each issue includes listings from anywhere between 30 and 75 different real estate companies.

Sonoma County

The real estate market in Sonoma County made national headlines in 2000. For example, in its May issue that year, *Forbes* magazine listed the Santa Rosa area among the top three dynamic economic regions in the nation. A year later, Sonoma County ranked No. 6 on the same list. To help meet the explosion in housing demand, builders have been constructing new homes in Sonoma County, but not without resistance. Many residents have become increasingly fearful of losing their open spaces and associated quality of life and have been doing something about it. A county-wide sales tax was approved by county voters for use in preserving open space—the first of its kind in the nation—and most municipalities have instituted voter-approved growth restrictions. In spring 2003, high demand and low interest rates pushed the median price of a home in Sonoma County to $403,560.

Much of the county's growth is centered around the city of Santa Rosa. With a current population of about 147,600, it is the county's largest city. Here, as in most cities, home seekers will find neighborhoods of high-priced, handsome Victorian homes, a score of new modern housing developments (some still in progress), and a wide variety of medium and lower-priced homes.

In mid-2003, median prices in the northwest sector of Santa Rosa were about $356,900; in the southeast, $391,365; in the southwest, $339,500; and $470,000 in the northeast.

Prices vary in towns to the north along the U.S. 101 corridor. Median prices are $447,000 in Healdsburg and $330,000 in Cloverdale.

An interesting real estate situation exists in the town of Windsor. Until the late '80s, it was a sleepy village, but then it was "discovered" by housing developers. They just kept building and building. As a result, almost everything in the town is of recent origin. Now incorporated, Windsor is a fast-growing city—second only to nearby Cloverdale—with median home prices at about $405,000.

The area around the town of Sebastopol on the edge of Apple Country is, in a way, an anomaly in the county—a place where many homes are set on large acreage. People who live here like the idea of country living with amenities such as extra guest houses and plenty of room for dogs to run and horses to graze. Because of the super-large lot sizes, Sebastopol has among the highest housing prices in the county. Estate-size lots, rambling homes, and mini-ranches will often push or top the $1 million mark. The median home price is $574,500.

The southern reaches of Sonoma County are just 45 minutes from the Golden Gate, assuming, of course, there is no traffic on U.S. 101, which there usually is. Though San Francisco-bound commuters live in all parts of the county, most live in the southernmost reaches—a fact that has influenced average home prices there. Median home prices in the border towns of Petaluma and Sonoma in mid-2003 ranged between $430,000 and $480,000.

There is little residential property along the Sonoma Coast, which is one reason median home prices are about $600,000. The large, modern Sea Ranch development at the northeastern edge of the county offers homes on sites that range from a quarter-acre to three or more acres. Some of the oceanfront lots go for as much as $600,000. For people who love the ocean, life along the Sonoma Coast is indeed soul satisfying. Fortunately, it can

In recent years, residential subdivisions have popped up on the outskirts of Santa Rosa in all directions.
PHOTO: JEAN SAYLOR DOPPENBERG

also be rented. (See Rentals on the follow-ing pages.)

To help in your search for a home, local chambers of commerce are clearing-houses of information. Often, you can get more specifics about locations and indi-vidual real estate agencies through them. The Sonoma Valley Chamber of Com-merce is at 645 Broadway, Sonoma. Call (707) 996-1033 for assistance. Also, the North Coast Builders Exchange in Santa Rosa, (707) 542-9502, can help with infor-mation for individuals hiring contractors or building custom homes.

Rentals

Expect rental prices for apartments and duplexes in Sonoma County to be any-where from $700 (if you're lucky) to $1,500. The rent for a three-bedroom, two-bath midpriced apartment is about $1,500. You can generally find lower rents in the outlying areas. In Santa Rosa, where good jobs can be found, a newer, three-bedroom house will rent for a minimum of $1,300, while a simple two-bedroom house in the older section of town rents from $900 to $1,400. In the city of Sonoma, the favorable climate and pleas-ant ambiance have attracted retired folks. They come with their retirement funds and live in homes that cost upwards of $350,000. The rental picture reflects those real estate values.

Sonoma Management
662 Broadway, Sonoma
(707) 938-3177
www.sonomamanagement.com

Robert and Sylvia Bernard have operated this full-service rental agency since 1982, serving those moving to Sonoma from all walks of life. The office is in an historic home built more than 100 years ago. The Bernards provide listings throughout Sonoma Valley with no fee charged to the renter-client.

The Rental Connection
1220 Fourth Street, Santa Rosa
(707) 575-9652
www.rentalconn.com
Owner Cathy J. Romero provides a rental listing service that covers all of Sonoma County. Prospective renters pay a $50 serv-ice fee that gives them one month of access to a comprehensive list of rental properties tailored to their needs. The listings divide the county into 17 areas to offer thorough coverage in a convenient format.

West County Property Management
6380 Vine Hill School Road, Sebastopol
(707) 823-5700
Jim and Lynn Deis provide long-term rental services at no cost to the client. Rental prices vary, but you can bet that they will get snapped up quickly.

D&G Property Management
14080 Mill Street, Guerneville
(707) 869-0623
www.riverhomes.com
This firm offers permanent rentals in west-ern Sonoma County. You can expect to pay anywhere from $800 to $1,400 for a two-bedroom, one-bath unit, but a four-bed-room home might go as high as $1,800. Although much of D&G's clientele is look-ing for residential property, the company also offers business and commercial sites.

Vacation Rentals

If you are interested in a short-term rental for a vacation stay, Sonoma County has agencies that can help. Russian River Vacation Homes, Russian River Getaways, Sea Coast Hide-a-Ways, and Rams Head Realty all offer vacation rentals. See our Hotels, Motels, and Inns chapter for more details on these and other Wine Country agencies specializing in vacation homes.

Real Estate Companies

Prudential California Real Estate
101 Golf Course Drive, Rohnert Park
(707) 588–8900
326 Healdsburg Avenue, Healdsburg
(707) 433–4150
16315 Main Street, Guerneville
(707) 869–9011
www.pruweb.com

An award-winning team of seasoned pros covers everything from mobile homes to ranches and wineries in Sonoma County. Additional offices serve Northern California, but the Prudential is hooked into a network that is not just national but worldwide. Comprehensive relocation services can help you make the transition wherever you come from.

Frank Howard Allen Realtors
470 First Street East, Sonoma
(707) 939–2000
9200 Sonoma Highway, Kenwood
(707) 833–2880
905 East Washington Street, Petaluma
(707) 762–7766
460 Mission Street, Santa Rosa
(707) 537–3000
340 Center Street, Healdsburg
(707) 431–9440
6876 Sebastopol Avenue, Sebastopol
(707) 824–5400
www.fhallen.com

Frank Howard Allen Realtors has two corporate-owned offices and numerous independently owned firms operating as licensees. They handle all types of real estate, including residential, commercial, vacation, and business properties. In Napa and Sonoma Counties, they specialize in wineries and vineyards. In business more than 90 years, this is one of the Bay Area's largest independent, locally owned and operated real estate firms. Special relocation services can be arranged and coordinated from Frank Howard Allen's administrative offices in Novato.

Coldwell Banker
333 South McDowell Boulevard, Petaluma
(707) 762–6611
790 Sonoma Avenue, Santa Rosa
(707) 527–8567
www.cbnorcal.com

Claiming to be the nation's largest full-service real estate company, Coldwell Banker in Sonoma County handles all types of properties including homes, ranches, mobile homes, and land and investment property. Coldwell offers a free national relocation service, as well as a buyer-seller coupon booklet that gives discounts at Sears on home improvement items. Ask for their Best Buyer Guidebook to help find and finance your dream home. All Coldwell Banker offices are independently owned and operated.

RE/MAX Central
320 College Avenue, Santa Rosa
(707) 524–3500
371 Windsor River Road, Windsor
(707) 837–7800
www.santarosa-homes.com

RE/MAX has experts in transactions involving dwellings, business property, commercial developments, and agricultural real estate. Each RE/MAX office is independently owned and operated, assuring the dedicated service of personnel with local knowledge about the areas they cover.

> ## Insiders' Tip
> If you're one of those people who think electric ranges are for cretins, be sure to investigate when house hunting. Many ads proudly trumpet "AEK"—that's "all-electric kitchen," a common feature in Wine Country.

Old weathered fences that mark ranch boundaries are a familiar sight along coastal roads. PHOTO: JOHN NAGIECKI

Century 21
616 Petaluma Boulevard S., Petaluma
(707) 769–9000
1057 College Avenue, Santa Rosa
(707) 577–7777
107 North Street, Healdsburg
(707) 433–4404
114 Lake Street, Cloverdale
(707) 894–5232
www.century21.com

If you're attracted to a name you've seen elsewhere, Century 21 has a presence on the real estate scene that's recognized nationwide for its reliability and attention to clients. With offices covering strategic points in Sonoma County, Century 21 specialists offer knowledge of local residential markets.

Griewe Real Estate
141 East Napa Street, Sonoma
(707) 938–0916
www.griewerealestate.com

This independently owned firm started business in 1990 under the ownership of Jim and Linda Griewe and serves all of Sonoma Valley. Griewe is intimately familiar with the area and has a reputation for excellence and integrity. Griewe sale signs hang in front of many homes in the Sonoma Valley, but they also deal in vineyard properties.

Morgan Lane
500 Broadway, Sonoma
(707) 935–5777
www.morganlane.com

With seven offices throughout Sonoma County, Morgan Lane covers properties across Wine Country, as far north as Boonville in Mendocino County. (See previous listing under Napa County Real Estate Companies.)

Coralee Barkela & Company
1815 Fourth Street, Santa Rosa
(707) 542–9200
www.coraleebarkela.com

Coralee Barkela has been a top real estate professional in Sonoma County since the early 1970s, and in 1997 she opened her own office. With the help of five agents, her company covers all of Sonoma County. Highly knowledgeable about grape culture and wine making, she concentrates heavily on ranches and vineyards as well as high-quality residential properties.

Pacific Union Residential Brokerage
640 Broadway, Sonoma
(707) 939–9500
www.pacunion.com

Originally a Bay Area company specializing in commercial and estate-type property sales, Pacific Union now serves residential clients throughout the Sonoma Valley. The agents are all highly seasoned professionals, most of them brokers in their own right. Relocation services are offered.

Mid-Towne Realty, Inc.
709 Healdsburg Avenue, Healdsburg
(707) 433–6555
www.midtownerealty.com

This local, professional, and independent firm has been in business for more than 30 years. In addition to serving clientele in the Healdsburg community, the office also handles Russian River properties, both for sales and rentals. Relocation services are provided to purchasers from other areas.

North County Properties
21069 Geyserville Avenue, Geyserville
(707) 857–1728

Karen and Doug Waelde, a husband and wife team, have been in the real estate business for 17 years in Healdsburg and (for the last few years) in Geyserville, a favorable location between two beautiful wine appellations—Dry Creek Valley and Alexander Valley. They cover the area between Santa Rosa and Cloverdale, including the town of Windsor.

Sea Ranch Realty
Sea Ranch Lodge, Sea Ranch
(707) 785–2494
www.888searanch.com

Sea Ranch is a private community that extends 10 miles along the Sonoma Coast. Sea Ranch Realty provides infor-mation on existing home sales as well as building opportunities. Offices are right on-site at the lodge, and the company offers homes on ocean bluffs or grassy meadows.

Real Estate Publications

For more information about the Sonoma County real estate market, check the real estate section in the Friday edition of the *Sonoma Index-Tribune* or the Santa Rosa *Press Democrat*'s Saturday and Sunday real estate sections. You can also pick up the following free publications at area grocery stores, drug stores, or newspaper racks.

Distinctive Properties
www.buycoastal.com

Sponsored by the participating real estate firms, this publication comes out every other month in black and white, with a color version published quarterly. It covers only Sonoma and Napa Counties. Distribution is primarily in supermarkets, but locations that display free literature are also used as outlets. Range of properties included varies from mobile homes to million-dollar estates.

The Press Democrat Real Estate
Network Magazine
www.pressdemocrat.com

This publication, issued every other month, covers all Wine Country counties. Primarily black and white, with a few color photos, it presents advertising by individual real estate firms. Distribution is free at magazine racks at supermarkets, drug stores, and individual real estate offices. Properties are listed by individual real estate firms, but the magazine additionally provides maps and graphs and an indexed location guide.

The Prudential California Realty:
A Presentation of Wine Country Properties

This colorful quarterly presentation covers Sonoma Valley and the four Prudential California Realty offices. In addition to availability at Prudential offices, the magazine-format publication can be found at wineries, supermarkets, and drug store racks. All types of property, including commercial, are covered in a wide price range.

Real Estate in the Wine Country

This glossy real estate magazine, published weekly, colorfully presents properties in all counties of Wine Country. It's available at supermarkets, drug stores, and any available public-literature distribution point. Individual real estate firms advertise in the publication and present a full range of properties from mobile homes and residential ranches to acreage and vineyards.

Mendocino County

The rugged Mendocino coast stretches 120 miles along the Pacific from its southern point at Gualala to the King Mountain range on the north. Each of the small towns and hamlets that dot the coastline has its own unique identity and charm. And each has a different set of real estate values.

If you long for a view of the sea, it will cost you. But what it costs depends on where you want to settle. Fort Bragg, with a population of about 6,000, is basically a lumbering and fishing community, though tourism is on the rise. Most of Fort Bragg's homes are long established, but there is some new construction going on. Average price of single-family dwellings in the area is $200,000, though ocean views can go as high as $450,000.

Eight miles south in tiny Mendocino (population 1,000), the cost of housing rises steeply. A two-bedroom home in the village, without a view of the water, will likely be priced at $325,000. Add an ocean view, and the price jumps to $500,000 on average—these addresses top out in the millions.

In the inland valleys, a few modest-sized towns and hamlets cling to U.S. 101—Hopland, Ukiah, and Willits. The landscape is agricultural, and it is prime grape-growing territory. Nestled in the valley below the spectacular Coast Range is Ukiah, county seat and Mendocino's

> **Insiders' Tip**
>
> The slump in the national economy over the past couple of years affected the asking price of vineyard land. An acre that sold for $100,000 in 2000 can now be found down in the $75,000 to $80,000 range.

largest city (population 15,500). It's a blend of businesses, recreational opportunities, affordable housing, verdant vineyards and orchards, and untamed wilderness. The city's west side includes hundreds of historic homes and buildings shaded by a lush canopy of mature trees. Norman Crampton's *100 Best Small Towns* in 1993 named Ukiah the No. 1 small town in California.

Overall, housing in the Ukiah area presents the best of two worlds. In town one is close to everything—quiet, family-oriented neighborhoods are the city's primary feature. Just minutes from the city limits is the Yokayo Valley countryside. Dotted with orchards and vineyards, rolling green hills, and stands of oak and redwood, one can get away from it all and still be a quick 10-minute drive from the town's amenities. Average price for a three-bedroom home is $200,000, average home rental runs $1,000 a month, and apartments rent for $600 on average.

Known mainly as a railroad hub and lumber community, the town of Willits, 25 miles north of Ukiah, is at the western edge of the Little Lake Valley, 1,350 feet above sea level. The chaparral and oak glades characteristic of the southern part of the county give way here to thick redwood and fir forests that stretch to the Oregon border.

With a population of 5,000, the town itself is not very large; however, the surrounding area includes a surprising number of homes, bringing the greater Willits population to nearly 15,000. Home prices are more modest here, running between $85,000 to $200,000 for a three-bedroom home.

You'll find other information about the Mendocino market in the real estate pages of the *Fort Bragg Advocate-News*. Chambers of commerce often prove to be valuable resources as well. The Greater Ukiah Chamber of Commerce is at 200 S. School Street. Call (707) 462–4705 for assistance.

Vacation Rentals

If your stay will be short and oriented toward fun, or if you want a change of pace, you may want to rent a vacation home. Coast Getaways and Mendocino Coast Reservations offer vacation rentals. Details about these and other vacation rental agencies in Wine Country can be found in our Hotels, Motels, and Inns chapter.

Real Estate Companies

Wally Johnson Realty
3810 Eastside Calpella Road, Ukiah
(707) 485–8700, (800) 289–8542
www.wjrealty.com

Realtor Wally Johnson has served the Ukiah area since 1990, dealing in homes, income property, lots, and land sales as well as quality manufactured homes. He is a member of the Mendocino County Board of Realtors.

E. S. Wolf & Company
514 South School Street, Ukiah
(707) 463–2719
www.eswolf.com

This broker deals entirely in large properties—ranch lands, vineyards, and large estates. It is also the exclusive Mendocino representative for Sotheby's International Realty, handling the local end of that firm's national and international dealings.

Pacific Properties
36 South Street, Willits
(707) 459–6175, (800) 767–9546

This is the largest independently owned and operated real estate office in Willits, with 10 agents specializing in residential and county properties.

Mendo Realty
690 South Main Street, Fort Bragg
(707) 964–3610
1061 Main Street, Mendocino
(707) 937–5822
www.mendorealty.com

The Mendocino coast's oldest real estate firm, Mendo Realty covers the coast from Gualala to Westport. Most of their representatives have a lengthy tenure and they have accumulated firsthand knowledge of area history and trends in residential properties as well as commercial, business, ranch, and timber acreage.

Sea Cottage Real Estate
45120 Main Street, Mendocino
(707) 937–0423, (800) 707–0423
www.seacottage.com

The first certified residential specialist on the Mendocino coast, this firm has been in business since 1979. With six agents, Sea Cottage covers the entire Mendocino coast.

Retirement

Senior Services

Senior Centers

Retirement Housing
Options

Educational
Opportunities

Volunteer
Opportunities

In much the same way thousands of visitors flock to Wine Country for the vino, the cuisine, and the general ambiance that surrounds it, retirees have discovered that this region with its mild winters and laid-back ways makes an ideal place to spend their golden years.

Wine Country has become a happy haven for retirees, those young-at-heart oldsters who are aging with grace and style. They're a lively lot, this new breed of senior citizens. They're signing up for classes for everything from painting to wine tasting. And they have become volunteers—those essential citizens who move the wheels of progress in hospitals, learning centers, churches, libraries, and civic organizations.

In short, Wine Country is a place well geared to the 65-plus segment of our population (and those other lucky dogs who have been able to hang up the work togs at a younger age). In this chapter, we merely scratch the surface of living accommodations and lifestyle options for seniors.

We start the information rolling with listings of area senior services, which have grown right alongside the growth of the Wine Country's senior population.

Senior Services

We hope that most seniors who visit or choose to live in our region are spending their retirement years actively pursuing good health and happiness. Everyone, however, needs a little help and guidance from time to time to lead a satisfying life, and seniors are no different. Here are a few connections that should make it easier for seniors to find their way around in new territory.

Napa County

The Volunteer Center of Napa County
1820 Jefferson Street, Napa
(707) 252–6222, (707) 963–3922

The Volunteer Center does all sorts of good work in the county, and its Senior Services Program, funded by the Napa-Solano Area Agency on Aging (see listing in this section) and the United Way, is foremost on the list. Especially valuable is

the Senior Guide it publishes each year. It's a well-organized catalog of write-ups and phone numbers, with suggestions on topics ranging from health services and home care to housing and transportation.

Comprehensive Services for Older Adults
900 Coombs Street, Suite 257, Napa
(707) 253–4625, (888) 619–6913

This program, administered by the Napa County Health and Human Services Agency, offers in-home care to the aged, blind, and disabled who can't afford to fend for themselves. The manifold services include household tasks and shopping, nonmedical personal care when needed to ensure safety, alcohol and drug counseling, adult protective services, and psychiatric case management for seniors 62 or older who suffer from mental illness or Alzheimer's disease. Comprehensive Services also assists with procurement of food stamps and Medi-Cal (state-subsidized medical insurance) benefits.

Senior Class
Queen of the Valley Hospital, 1000 Trancas
Street, Napa
(707) 253–9000
www.thequeen.org

Queen of the Valley has targeted older adults for health promotion and education with this membership program since 1986. Members are offered a variety of classes, lectures, and health screenings, conducted by the hospital's able team of healthcare professionals. It's $15 to join and $10 a year thereafter, though nobody is turned away. (For more on Queen of the Valley, see our Health Care chapter.)

Napa Valley Dining Club
1500 Jefferson Street, Napa
(707) 253–6112, (800) 788–0124

This service cooks up hot, nutritious meals for people 60 years or older on a donation basis. When needed, the club will even transport guests to one of six Napa County sites or deliver food to homes. Call one day in advance for reservations.

Adult Day Services of Napa Valley
3295 Claremont Way, Suite 3, Napa
(707) 258–9087

The frail elderly and younger functionally impaired adults are the focus of this organization. Daily hot lunches, caregiver respites, social activities, and transportation assistance are all provided.

Napa Valley Committee on Aging
1500 Jefferson Street, Napa
(707) 224–5121

This is a referral service for seniors seeking in-home care or housekeeping. The committee also offers handyman service for minor home repairs. (The fee is negotiable.)

Garden Haven
2447 Old Sonoma Road, Napa
(707) 253–3425

Even the most devoted caregiver needs an occasional break, and here is a day center you can trust to watch over your elderly relative or friend, especially if they suffer from Alzheimer's or dementia. Activities include music, exercise regimens, crafts, cooking, and gardening. Wheelchairs are welcome. The center is open Monday, Tuesday, Thursday, and Friday from 10:00 A.M. to 3:00 P.M. The cost is $12.50 per day.

Napa-Solano Area Agency on Aging
1443 Main Street, Napa
(800) 510–2020

People 55 and older who are mentally and physically fit, and who are looking for a little extra cash, are encouraged to get in touch with this agency. They'll help you find part-time employment.

Sonoma County

Council on Aging
730 Bennett Valley Road, Santa Rosa
(707) 525–0143
www.councilonaging.com

This is the overall program that provides many of the benefits that are incorporated in member organizations such as the senior centers listed subsequently. Council on Aging provides dining rooms with a hot, healthy noontime meal at 10 locations in Sonoma County. The Meals on Wheels program delivers hot meals seven days a week to the homes of temporarily or chronically homebound seniors. Legal consultation services are provided, as well as money management programs, health insurance counseling, and door-to-door transportation for seniors with doctor visits. The council offers an excellent Senior Resource Guide available at senior centers or by calling the listed number.

AARP (American Association of
Retired Persons)
P.O. Box 662, Santa Rosa 95402
(707) 527–7282
www.aarp.org

AARP is a senior advocacy organization for people who have reached 50 years of age. Its mission is to promote the welfare and status of the country's elder population, and some of this work is carried on through local chapters. The agenda is likely to be the same for the different chapters—there's always a monthly meeting (call the numbers listed to find out

Weathered barns and decades-old vineyards are some of the many rural charms that attract retirees to Wine Country. PHOTO: JOHN NAGIECKI

which day and time), educational opportunities, insurance advantages, and travel information.

Meetings usually include speakers involved with state or local government, health organizations, Medicare, or widowhood. Some chapters organize social activities. The Santa Rosa chapter, for instance, has an annual picnic in July, featuring hot dogs and a potluck assortment of foods furnished by members. A nominal membership fee is charged ($12 per year), but anyone older than 50 is welcome to attend meetings.

AARP Senior Community Service Employment Program
2050 West Steele Lane, Suite E-1, Santa Rosa
(707) 525–9190

Partially government-sponsored, this is an AARP program to help low-income seniors get back into the work force through on-the-job training with organizations such as the American Red Cross and Goodwill Industries. It is also an employment office that can find jobs in the private sector after training.

AARP 55 Alive/Mature Driving
980 Ninth Street, Suite 700, Sacramento
(916) 446–2277

Sonoma County: Call (888) 227–7669 and leave your zip code and phone number, and an instructor will contact you. There is a $10 charge for the two-day course—four hours each day.

North Bay HI-CAP
3262 Airway Drive, Suite C, Santa Rosa
(800) 303–4477

The North Bay Health Insurance Counseling and Advocacy Program (HI-CAP) covers six counties north of the Golden Gate Bridge (including all in Wine Country). The center offers one-on-one counseling by trained volunteers registered by the California Department of Aging. They provide independent, unbiased information on health insurance, including Medicare and supplemental programs. They also help clients sort out their medical finances and make sure they are being billed appropriately for Medicare. There is no charge for this service.

Petaluma Ecumenical Project
1400 Caulfield Lane, Petaluma
(707) 762–2336

In 1977 three local ministers came together to find a way to provide low-cost housing for seniors. With community backing, the Petaluma Ecumenical Project sought out suitable building sites and developed architectural plans. The group has built and manages nine projects and is now supported by 11 churches and AARP contributions.

Jewish Seniors Program
3855 Montgomery Drive, Santa Rosa
(707) 528–4222
www.jcagency.org

The wide spectrum of entertainment and educational opportunities offered through this program includes musical events, folk dancing, autobiographical writing, book discussion, parties, and trips. Want to learn Yiddish? That's an option too! The group welcomes participants from all denominations.

Sons In Retirement
Sonoma
(707) 938–2643
www.sirinc.org

To join, you must simply be retired; there is no minimum age. Members meet once a month for lunch and to hear a speaker. Other than that there are few requirements, although you're expected to attend the meetings: Sonoma County has five groups of 125 each, offering various forms of entertainment—golf, bowling, computers, photography groups, and travel excursions, to mention a few. Bus tours to Reno or Lake Tahoe are frequent, and trips as far afield as Yellowstone and Canada are possible. SIR headquarters is in Sacramento.

Mendocino County

Multipurpose Senior Services Program
487 North State Street, Ukiah
(707) 468–9347

The Multipurpose Senior Services Program is a nonprofit community agency that strives to meet the needs of people with disabilities so that they can remain in their own homes and live an independent life of dignity. Some of the home-care services that MSSP helps obtain include personal care, home repairs, house cleaning, shopping, transportation, and home-delivered meals. The agency serves Ukiah, Willits, Hopland, Potter Valley, and the Fort Bragg/Mendocino area, plus Lake County.

Senior Centers

They're social centers, educational resources, service sources, and just plain fun places for seniors with leisure time. Most of the centers publish newsletters so everyone can find out what's in store. All have an extensive, varied program of activities, and all offer services such as blood pressure and hearing testing, legal counsel, and tax assistance on a regular basis.

Napa County

Senior Citizens Center
1500 Jefferson Street, Napa
(707) 255–1800

Older residents get one-stop shopping at this office. Nearly 60 clubs and organizations—including the Senior Friendship Club and Napa Grange—use the center as a meeting place. It's open Monday through Friday, from 8:00 A.M. to 4:00 P.M. Activities range from dances, bingo, and potluck dinners to arts and crafts and pancake breakfasts. Friday mornings welcome a diversity of guest speakers for Senior Seminars. Call for a monthly schedule of events.

Berryessa Senior Citizens
4380 Spanish Flat Loop Road, Berryessa
(707) 966–0206

The highlands surrounding Lake Berryessa sound like a nice place for retired folks—and, well, they are. The center has a strong lineup of health, educational, social, and recreational programs. If you call for a monthly schedule, you'll discover potluck meals, bingo, crafts, Adventure College classes, trips, dances, and more.

Sonoma County

Southern Sonoma

Vintage House
264 First Street E., Sonoma
(707) 996-0311

Staffed largely by senior volunteers, Vintage House is open Monday through Friday, serving more than 1,000 individuals each month with up to 70 classes and activities, most of them free or low-cost. The choices include art classes, line dancing, tap dancing, international folk dance instruction, canasta, bridge in several forms, exercise classes, and French, Italian, and Spanish at levels for beginner, intermediate, and advanced speakers. The Vintage House Singers, a choral group, is coached by a professional music director and performs twice a year. The Department of Motor Vehicles has a representative visit each month to administer driving tests, and the tax man cometh during his season. Lunch is served Tuesday, Thursday, and Friday in the dining room for a small fee.

Lucchesi Park Senior Center
(Petaluma Community Center)
211 Novak Drive, Petaluma
(707) 778-4399

This facility largely houses the recreational part of Petaluma's senior program—the local meal program is now administered by the adjacent Petaluma People Services Center. Line dancing events draw 25 to 40 participants each week, and ballroom dancing attracts 100 or more. Group exercise goes over big, along with the computer classes, eclectic discussion groups, art instruction, and creative writing classes. Many daytrips and extended trips are sponsored. The center also sponsors flu shots and blood pressure testing.

Rohnert Park Senior Center
6800 Hunter Drive, Suite A, Rohnert Park
(707) 585-6780

Active seniors as well as disabled persons who can manage on their own are welcome here to chat, play cards, and watch the once-a-month movie. General activities include line dancing, duplicate bridge, basketry, Spanish classes, a craft

Insiders' Tip

The Lifelong Learning Institute at Sonoma State University was established for students 50 years and older who want to learn new skills or pursue subjects that stir their fancy. The classes are intended for pure enjoyment, with no homework, no tests, and no grades. To learn more, please call (707) 664-2691.

shop, and a billiards table. Every other month an early-evening dance (held the second Tuesday of each month from 1:00 to 4:00 P.M.) brings out a lively crowd. In fact, it has grown so popular that the center had to move it to a larger facility—the Community Center on 5401 Snyder Lane. According to the director, seniors often claim this is the best center around, and it draws older folks from as far away as Ukiah. A noon meal is served daily.

Santa Rosa Senior Center
704 Bennett Valley Road, Santa Rosa
(707) 545-8608

Dancing is big here—afternoon ballroom dancing once a week, line dancing, and tap dancing. Bingo, bridge, whist, chess, and pinochle games are lively, and there are three billiards tables. Watercolor painting classes are a big draw, and there's creative writing, a poetry group, and Spanish instruction. The drama group puts on shows, and a choral group attracts those who like to belt out a tune. There are also clinics for blood pressure, allergy screening, chiropractic evaluations, and even toenail clipping. Once a month the Friendship

The Santa Rosa Senior Center on Bennett Valley Road is a popular gathering place. PHOTO: JEAN SAYLOR DOPPENBERG

Club organizes a potluck lunch. Meals are served Monday to Friday at 4:00 P.M. The Council on Aging also uses the center kitchen to prepare meals for delivery to the homebound.

Northern Sonoma

Windsor Senior Center
9231 Foxwood Drive, Windsor
(707) 838–1250

This center is surrounded by roses—45 varieties, in fact, in a lovely garden. In the artistic category, classes are available in oil and pastel painting and sculpture. Card players have a choice of pinochle or bridge, and seniors can learn to play the guitar, study genealogy, or join in a quilting bee.

For the athletic, the bocce ball court is an attraction, as is the horseshoe pit. But most popular of all is the swimming pool: Windsor tends to be hot in summer, and the pool is a terrific place to cool off. It is outfitted for the disabled, who can be lowered from wheelchair to water by a special lift device.

Healdsburg Senior Center
133 Matheson Street, Healdsburg
(707) 431–3324

Lunch is served here Monday through Friday, and a bus service is available to bring seniors to the center as well as to take them to shopping areas and other destinations around town. Crafts are popular here, with a group meeting once a week to work on a variety of handcrafts including the art of flower arranging. An unusually talented group of woodworkers has been awarded several honors for items created at the center. Bingo brings the lucky and unlucky to play each Thursday. Department of Motor Vehicles testing also is provided.

Cloverdale Senior Multi-Purpose Center
Main Street, Cloverdale
(707) 894–4826

Weekly blood-pressure screenings, visits by an optometrist, and hearing-aid maintenance are among the services offered in Cloverdale. Line dancing is offered one day each week, and an instructor comes in to help seniors create an autobiographical record of their lives. A newsletter keeps seniors apprised of coming attractions at the center, where lunch is served every weekday. The center was expected to move into a new, larger facility on Main Street, between Second and Third Streets, in mid-2003.

West County/Russian River

Sebastopol Burbank Senior Center
167 North High Street, Sebastopol
(707) 829–2440
www.seb.org/comm/seniorctr.html

This center receives laudable backing from the community, and several stores and bakeries bring in day-old products to distribute among the members. In addition, lunch is served in the dining room each weekday, and home-delivered meals are dispatched to those who cannot come in. Card games and bingo are regular sources of entertainment, and every once in a while, there's a special program by a harp and flute duo. Through a coalition of other senior service groups, a lively travel program has been developed in Sebastopol. Not only do seniors make short local trips—say, to Lake Tahoe, the San Francisco Zoo, the Golden Gate Bridge, and the Sonoma County Fair—but they have also taken journeys as far afield as Alaska and the Panama Canal.

Russian River Community Senior Center
15010 Armstrong Woods Road, Guerneville
(707) 869–0618

Both on-site lunch and Meals on Wheels are provided from this center, and because this is a rural area, limited transportation is provided. Afternoon field trips and picnics are ideally suited to this vacation spot with its many scenic locales. Writing autobiographies and exercise classes are among indoor activities.

Mendocino County

U.S. 101

Ukiah Senior Center
499 Leslie Street, Ukiah
(707) 462–4343

A lot happens here, and it would be hard not to have fun. There's line dancing, ballroom dancing, and dancing classes, plus a Saturday night dance to practice your lessons. You can play bingo, pinochle, bridge, Scrabble, or chess; learn to knit or crochet; or practice t'ai chi. The exercise class is on Tuesday, Wednesday, and Thursday. Legal help, tax assistance, and health screenings are available. Oh yes, lunch is served in the dining room each weekday.

Willits Senior Center
1501 Baechtel Road, Willits
(707) 459–6826

A noon meal is served at the center and delivered to shut-ins. Seniors enjoy movies and bingo twice a week and a dance once a month. Breakfast is served once a month, and special weekend dinners are staged monthly. A worthy program at Willits is Extra Hands—a plan to hire people to do chores like gardening, cleaning house, and shopping for seniors

Insiders' Tip

Bird-watching is a big draw at the leisurely one-mile-long loop trail at the Napa River Ecology Reserve. The trail meanders through tall grasses and valley oaks and offers shady places to rest along a trout-filled stream. The Reserve is located on the Yountville Cross Road between Silverado Trail and Highway 29. For more information, call the Napa Valley Visitor Center at (707) 226-7459.

who find these activities difficult. Drivers are provided to take people to medical appointments. The center is fortunate: there are 100 volunteers to help. Some funds are created by a thrift shop run by the seniors themselves. Says the director, "They have made the shop look like a real department store."

Mendocino Coast

South Coast Senior Citizens
140 Main Street, Point Arena
(707) 882-2137

Arts and crafts occupy part of the daily schedule in Point Arena. An abalone breakfast is served on the second Sunday a month, and a spaghetti dinner is served on the fourth Friday. Monthly bus trips are scheduled to visit various spots and happenings. The dining room here provides a noon meal twice a week and provides transportation so seniors can get to the center. Delivered meals also are provided on the same days.

Fort Bragg Senior Center

490 North Harold Street, Fort Bragg
(707) 964-0443

Seniors enjoy bingo twice a week and can take a course in writing provided by the College of the Redwoods staff. From time to time a four-week improvisation class gives seniors a chance to practice acting, and occasionally a professional writer comes to tell seniors how they can learn to write and sell their output. A hot meal is

Retirement Housing Options

In the city of Sonoma, more than one-third of the population is older than 60, and the situation is similar in most of southern Sonoma County. This means a wide assortment of housing arrangements for retired folks in that area.

Many retirees, of course, are simply absorbed into the general population. However, some choose to buy a home in one of the many active adult communi-ties, which are not much different from any other residential area except that resi-dents must have reached a certain age to live there. Usually there is a clubhouse and limited activities for homeowners. But mainly, there are no children.

Among the most popular of these communities in Sonoma are Temelec, Chantarelle, and Creekside. By far, the largest of these adult communities is Oak-mont. It lies between Valley of the Moon and Santa Rosa but is actually within the Santa Rosa city limits. Its population runs to 5,000, with amenities including two golf courses, bowling greens, several activ-ity rooms, and a sizable shopping center within the complex. It is possible to rent as well as buy at Oakmont.

Other popular options in Sonoma are adult mobile-home communities that limit residency to those over 55. These are generally operated by an on-site manager. They are practical, fairly inexpensive, and surprisingly spacious and appealing.

Although southern Sonoma County remains the setting for a large portion of Wine Country's adult mobile-home parks, they also are popular in other areas, par-tially because they are an inexpensive alter-nate to home ownership. Many are subject to rent control, which is adjusted annually by city government, and buyers should keep in mind that if rent control should cease, their home may be sitting on expen-sive property, making it difficult to sell and not so easy to move elsewhere.

With Wine Country in general showing every sign of becoming Northern California's retirement zone, senior housing facilities across the region are expanding to meet the demand. This is particularly true in the area of independent-living apartment complexes that provide housekeeping, meals, and laundry services, while allowing for complete freedom of movement and individuality. Following are examples of this type of retirement-living option (with a couple of other independent-living choices thrown in) within our area.

Napa County

The Meadows of Napa Valley
1800 Atrium Parkway, Napa
(707) 257-7885
www.meadowsofnapavalley.org

Three levels of personalized care are offered at this 20-acre residential retirement community. The apartments are available in one- and two-bedroom floorplans, augmented by the assisted living program and a skilled nursing center with rehabilitation services in a home-like setting. There's also a gift shop and beauty/barber shop on-site.

Aegis of Napa
2100 Redwood Road, Napa
(707) 251-1409
www.aegisal.com

Studio apartments, one-bedroom flats, and shared suites are offered at this community, along with "Life's Neighborhood," an Alzheimer's program. This facility's "Small Indulgences" program

Insiders' Tip
The California Department of Fish and Game offers a reduced-fee sport-fishing license for those aged 65 and older.

helps family caregivers by keeping track of each resident's favorite foods, flowers, and special treats.

Silverado Orchards
601 Pope Street, St. Helena
(707) 963-3688

In a quiet, green setting between St. Helena proper and the Silverado Trail is this popular retirement community. Silverado Orchards has 80 units all together—small studios, deluxe studios, one-bedroom apartments, and a couple of two-bedroom units. It's an active population that takes advantage of the immediate area's pleasant walking routes, plus twice-a-week exercise classes. They get a wealth of musical presentations in the multipurpose room. Because the proprietors are Seventh-day Adventists (the community itself is strictly nondenominational), residents can choose vegetarian meals if so desired.

Woodbridge Village
727 Hunt Avenue, St. Helena
(707) 963-3231

Several years ago this HUD-supported retirement complex won an award for best landscaping in St. Helena, and the park-like grounds have only improved since then, the managers say, thanks in part to some resident green thumbs. Woodbridge is a series of tidy one-bedroom, one-bathroom apartments, most of them grouped into fourplexes. Vineyards remain on one side of the property. HUD defines a senior as anyone age 62 or older.

Rancho de Calistoga
2412 Foothill Boulevard, Calistoga
(707) 942-6971

Yes, it's a mobile-home park, but if all of them looked like this, they would have a very different reputation. Centuries-old oak trees tower over the big lawn area out front, and the whole community is full of flowering plants. Rancho de Calistoga has a total of 184 lots. It also has a clubhouse, recreation building, pool, and spa. Oh, and activities? They include bingo twice a month, bridge, poker, exercise classes, quilting, potlucks, and Wednesday-morning brunch. The park is meant for seniors 55 and older.

Sonoma County

Westlake Wine Country House
800 Oregon Street, Sonoma
(707) 996–7101
www.westlakecompany.com

Billed as a "luxury congregate retirement facility," Westlake Wine Country offers one- and two-bedroom suites, fully carpeted (bring your own furniture), with a small kitchen, private deck, or balcony and three meals a day in a rather elegant dining room. Having guests? You can use one of the smaller dining rooms suitable for up to a dozen. You can also rent rooms for your guests in the complex for a nominal fee. The Westlake van takes residents to shopping or medical appointments, or you can use a parking space for your own car.

Westlake House Springs
4855 Snyder Lane, Rohnert Park
(707) 585–7878
www.westlakecompany.com

Although the Springs enjoys country views of rolling green farmlands, the property is near shopping, one block from a large medical complex, and a short putt to the nearest golf course. This complex is owned by the same company as Sonoma's Westlake Wine Country House (see previous listing), with accommodations slightly upgraded in price and style. You can participate in a wide range of activities, both in-house and away—wine-and-cheese socials, book reviews, college courses, pool tournaments, movies, swimming, library visits, exercise, and game-room fun. The complex consists of 176 apartments and 190 residents.

Valley Orchards Retirement Community
2100 East Washington Street, Petaluma
(707) 778–6030

No medical or nursing service is provided here, the manager says, "but from time to time the resident may contract for outside assistance for bathing or personal care, which makes it a good bit cheaper than

assisted living." Valley Orchards provides three meals a day, utilities, cable TV, transportation three days a week, housekeeping once a week, bathroom and bedroom laundry, 24-hour emergency assistance, and yard maintenance. Valley Orchard's 104 units are split between large studios and one- and two-bedroom apartments.

Friends House
684 Benicia Drive, Santa Rosa
(707) 538–0152
www.friendshouse.org

A Quaker institution, Friends House is composed of four interrelated programs for the older person: independent-living apartments and houses, an adult day-care center, an assisted-living facility, and a skilled-nursing facility. A large part of the six-acre Friends House site contains 60 garden apartments. People live in their own homes with their own belongings and garden space. One- and two-bedroom apartments are available, and recently some three-bedroom, two-bath homes were added to accommodate couples who want more space within the Friends House community. New residents must pay an entrance fee, and a monthly assessment covers housekeeping services. The dining room offers meals to residents for an additional charge. Cultural activities include visits to symphony performances, art galleries, libraries, and sporting events.

Renaissance at The Lodge at Paulin Creek
2375 Range Avenue, Santa Rosa
(707) 575–3722, (800) 900–HOME
www.renaissancesl.com

The Lodge is set in parklike grounds with inviting courtyards. Apartments are sunny and bright, with the charm of designer fabrics, art reproductions, and handmade quilts. They range from studios to three-bedroom, two-bath units. Some dining options are offered—you can either be served graciously in the dining room or serve yourself casually from the salad and hot entree buffet. Amenities include a pool, fitness trail, billiards room, an opportunity to garden, and a calendar of day trips.

Mendocino County

Redwood Meadows
1475 Baechtel Road, Willits
(707) 459-1616

In a lovely setting with walkways and green belts, Redwood Meadows is a senior apartment community open to active, independent seniors older than 55. The community center houses a game room, craft room, and community lounge. Because it is right next door to the Willits Senior Center (see listing in that section), the amenities of that group are easily accessible. Meals are not served, but the dining room is a center for potlucks, parties, movies, lectures, and other social events. Small pets are allowed.

The Woods
43300 Little River Airport Road, Little River
(707) 937-6132, (800) GO-WOODS
www.ncphs.org

Quality manufactured homes nestled among redwoods, pines, and rhododendrons make up this residential community for seniors. The Woods is on 37 sunbelt acres connected by winding roads that lead walkers to a heated indoor pool and spa, the clubhouse, library, and art room. State park beaches and golf courses are minutes away. Assisted-living facilities are also available.

Redwood Coast Seniors
490 North Harold Street, Fort Bragg
(707) 964-0443

This organization maintains a list of Fort Bragg senior housing. Entries are all clean, well-maintained apartments or detached houses, with rents on a sliding scale according to income.

Educational Opportunities

Several agencies and area schools offer opportunities for inquisitive, mature men and women to prove there is no age limit to new intellectual experiences. In addition to the resources listed, many senior centers throughout Wine Country offer classes in writing, foreign languages, computer skills, and other subjects.

Napa County

Napa Valley College Community Education
2277 Napa-Vallejo Highway, Napa
(707) 253-3070
www.napacommunityed.org

North Bay Driving School
1878 El Centro Avenue, Napa
(707) 252-2066

Pacific Union College Extension, Angwin
(707) 965-6311, (800) 862-7080
www.puc.edu

Sonoma County

Petaluma Adult Education Center
200 Douglas Street, Petaluma
(707) 778-4633
www.petalumachamber.org

Sonoma State University Gerontology Program
1801 East Cotati Avenue, Rohnert Park
(707) 664-2411
www.sonoma.edu

Lewis Adult Education Center
2230 Lomitas Avenue, Santa Rosa
(707) 528-5421

Santa Rosa Junior College
1501 Mendocino Avenue, Santa Rosa
(707) 527-4011
www.santarosa.edu

New Vista Adult Education School
6980 Analy Avenue, Sebastopol
(707) 824-6455

Volunteer Opportunities

A number of programs are available that put to use the skills, talents, and personalities of older individuals who choose to work full- or part-time for little or no remuneration. Here are a handful of options.

Retired and Senior Volunteer Program
264 First Street E., Sonoma
(707) 996–4644
17A Fourth Street, Petaluma
(707) 762–0111
1041 Fourth Street, Santa Rosa
(707) 573–3399
413 North State Street, Ukiah
(707) 573–3399 (ext. 215)

RSVP provides volunteer opportunities in more than 250 community agencies for people older than 55. This is an umbrella agency through which most volunteers work, whether they restock library shelves or send out mailings for Pets Lifeline.

Service Corps of Retired Executives
777 Sonoma Avenue, Suite 115-B, Santa Rosa
(707) 571–8342
www.score.org

Members of SCORE are retired business executives who volunteer their time and expertise without charge to advise and help people who are running or starting a new business. Sponsored by the Small Business Administration, it's open to any retired executive in any field of business.

Foster Grandparent Program
15000 Arnold Drive, Eldridge
(707) 938–6201
413 North State Street, Ukiah
(707) 462–1954

The Foster Grandparent Program is a nationwide volunteer program for those 60 years or older who choose to make a lasting connection with children with special needs (whether mental or physical). Forty hours of orientation are required to acquaint the grandparent with the facility and the child, but the rewards go both ways. The child forms a permanent loving attachment, and the grandparent/senior learns to know the child as a person in a close-knit relationship. It's not an easy commitment. The pair spends four hours a day together, five days a week. There is a modest stipend that goes with the work, in addition to transportation and lunch.

Education and Child Care

Public Schools

Private Schools

Two-Year Colleges

Four-Year Colleges
and Universities

Other Institutes of
Higher Learning

Child Care

Here's something most visitors to Wine Country don't know: This region is a great place to receive a formal education. The public school systems are solid, and residents have generously supported improvements and upgrades to school facilities. The rates of high school seniors matriculating to universities—though they vary from district to district—are frequently higher than national and state averages.

This chapter gives a thumbnail sketch of public and private schools in each county, followed by two-year colleges, four-year universities, and a sampling of specialty schools. At the close we briefly cover child-care options—perhaps the most important for those who are visiting the Wine Country for a short time.

Public Schools

Napa County

Anyone who questions Napa County's commitment to education would do well to look at the many charitable events devoted to private or public schools, some of them featuring ultrapremium wines generously donated by the biggest names in the valley for live and silent auctions. A recent fundraiser for Trinity Grammar and Prep School in Napa raised $60,000 in one afternoon. Among the big names donating items for auction were—in addition to scores of Napa Valley wineries—the Oakland Raiders, the Petrified Forest, and the Winchester Mystery House in San Jose. A baseball bat signed by Barry Bonds also went up for bid.

But Calistoga really goes all out. Every year, a special evening is set aside for an auction with generous donations from local vintners, restaurants, and dozens of sponsors. In 2000, about $180,000 was raised to benefit the Calistoga Joint Unified School District; in 2001, the tally dropped a bit, to $146,000, but was no less impressive. The money is used for field trips, art projects, and computer purchases, among other things.

In 2002, there nearly 20,000 pupils enrolled in Napa County public schools, dispersed among five districts: Calistoga Joint Union, Napa Valley Unified, St. Helena Unified, Howell Mountain, and Pope Valley.

Bilingual education is one of the many hot-button issues facing California schools. As with many areas of the state, a large immigrant population—in this case, almost wholly from Mexico—mingles with those of us who migrated earlier. Figures from a recent report about the Napa Valley Unified School District revealed that more than 24 percent of students are learning English as a second language and the percentage of Hispanic students has almost doubled in the past decade, to 32.6 percent.

On the academic side, Napa County's chartered performance remains relatively strong. SAT I scores are always well above the state average, and participation is usually high. In other testing, Napa County's students traditionally rank high on their Academic Performance Index (API) scores, with pupils in all grades showing improvement on the Stanford 9 tests that surpassed goals set for them by the State of California. In addition, a recent report about the Napa Valley Unified School District showed that three out of four high school graduates went on to college in 2001.

Other success stories abound: Ten school campuses in Napa County have recently received California Distinguished School Awards after evaluation of their curricula, test scores, school environments, parental participation, and special programs.

Progress has also been achieved through the New Technology High School, a Napa facility where students spend most of their time on-line or in-lab, with minimal teacher supervision. New Tech (www.techhigh.napanet.net), named a U.S. Department of Education Demonstration School for its technological advances, graduated its first senior class of future Silicon Valley moguls in 1998. Meanwhile, the only Waldorf-method charter school in Napa Valley opened in 2000.

Sonoma County

Sonoma County's schools have consistently ranked in the top half of the state, although they're funded at less than the state average. Thirty-eight of the county's schools have been named California Distinguished Schools, and four have been recognized as National Blue Ribbon schools. Within Sonoma County's 40 school districts, 154 schools serve students from kindergarten through 12th grade. There are 92 elementary schools, 20 junior high schools, 15 high schools, 29 special alternative schools, and 16 charter schools. Total enrollment in 2002 was nearly 74,000.

The growth in diversity among Sonoma County students is significant. Today, local schools are educating the most culturally, socially, academically, and linguistically diverse student population in the county's history. More than 7 percent of the county's students are limited in their ability to speak English, 8 percent are enrolled in programs for gifted students, and nearly 4 percent attend alternative programs such as independent study, home study, or continuation school.

Schools recognize an obligation to offer opportunities for success for all kids. Secondary school students receive the majority of efforts in this direction, because of larger student populations at the higher grade levels. For example, for

Educational facilities in Wine Country have come a long way since the days of the one-room school-house, like this historic building in west Sonoma County. PHOTO: JEAN SAYLOR DOPPENBERG

those who can't keep up, schools allow a home study arrangement. This demands that at least one parent be a stay-at-home presence. Students meet with teachers at specified intervals to review their progress.

Teenage parents also are offered a safety net. In the Petaluma School District, for instance, teens can leave infants and toddlers in a district-operated child-care center for the morning while they pursue their academic studies. The public school system also is working to address the needs of teens who have problems with alcohol or other drugs. Through programs such as Clean and Sober, the dropout rate for Sonoma County, at 2.8 percent, is considerably lower than the state average of 4.4 percent, and it continues to go down.

While attending to the needs of students with special needs, Sonoma County schools also consistently score in the top third of the state for every grade level and subject tested through the California

Assessment Program. Average SAT scores for the county are usually higher than state and national averages.

And things just keep getting better. New schools are being built, and older schools are being modernized and retrofitted for earthquake security. New libraries are being installed, and a system amphitheater is being built so students can perform outdoor plays.

Mendocino County

The size of this county is so immense and the geography so diverse—with its various communities separated by forests, mountains, and winding roads—that schools within the system operate almost independently of each other, relying on guidelines from the central offices of the county superintendent of schools. There are 12 districts that include 27 elementary schools, 15 middle schools, and 21 high schools (including continuation high schools). There are also 10 charter schools in the county. Enrollment in spring 2003 was 14,572.

Academic standards are high, with most schools posting average SAT scores at or slightly above national levels. About 35 percent of students go on to college, generally of the two-year community type. Special emphasis is put on vocational job training, with programs specifically aimed at jobs like firefighting (Mendocino County is heavily forested) and agriculture (since the area is mostly rural). This sort of training starts as early as grade nine for those who have no plans to go on to college and can benefit from learning a vocation.

There are other special programs. Preschool classes are offered, as well as classes for those for whom English is a second language. In addition, a staff member regularly makes the county circuit (racking up 100,000 miles a year) to assist with home-study programs and teach life skills to disadvantaged young people. The high school in Ukiah, the county seat, has classes at Juvenile Hall for young people who have run afoul of the law, as well as a Clean and Sober program for students with alcohol or drug problems.

Athletic programs are available, usually including basketball, baseball, softball, soccer, track, volleyball, and cheerleading and in some districts swimming, golf, and tennis. Fort Bragg High School is proud of its exemplary drama program that has given students an opportunity to work with acting and stage management. It has been extremely popular. Mendocino High School has an outstanding program called Windows to the Future, initiated in 1991, that links traditional studies in arts and sciences with computer technology. And here's a major advantage to having a widely scattered county population: Class sizes in Mendocino County schools are generally small, often having fewer than 20 students per teacher.

Private Schools

A wide variety of private schooling options exists in Wine Country. Individual school listings follow the geographical order for each county explained in How to Use This Book.

Napa County

Justin-Siena High School
4026 Maher Street, Napa
(707) 255-0950
www.justin-siena.com
Justin High School for boys was founded by the Christian Brothers of the San Francisco District in 1966, Siena High School for girls by the Dominican Sisters of San Rafael that same year. In 1972 the two schools merged to form Justin-Siena, a private, Catholic, coeducational high school that now serves about 615 stu-

> **Insiders' Tip**
> Napa County has the lowest high school dropout rate among the Bay Area counties.

dents in grades 9 through 12. Justin-Siena is widely regarded as one of the finest secondary educational facilities in Northern California. Ninety-seven percent of graduates go on to college, two-thirds of those to four-year institutions. The average SAT score for graduates attending a four-year college is 1,140.

The sports program has been quite successful; the school won 13 league championships in 1997-98, and the golf team won the Northern California championship. Justin-Siena also requires 100 hours of community service for graduation, including an annual Just-In Service day that involves all students and staff in a full day of activity.

Kolbe Academy
1600 F Street, Napa
(707) 256–4306
www.kolbe.org

"Absurdly simple" is how Kolbe's administrators describe the school's philosophy. It's a small Ignatian school (a total of 20 to 30 students in grades 1 through 12) that, unlike most modern Jesuit institutions, returns to the methods and objectives of Ignatius of Loyola, who founded the order

in the 1600s. Kolbe has three main goals: to help the student to speak, to write, and to act, and these are accomplished through a regimen of imitation and repetition. Oral presentations play a large role in the educational process here. There is a heavy emphasis on drama as well. Every pupil at the academy gets into character at some point.

The Oxbow School
530 Third Street, Napa
(707) 255–6000
www.oxbowschool.org

Further evidence of Napa's quest for consideration as a world-class arts hub is the Oxbow School, founded by Ann Hatch (who previously founded the Capp Street Project artist-in-residence program in San Francisco) and wine luminary Robert Mondavi. Set on three acres within a looping bend of the Napa River, the school offers a one-semester fine arts program for high school juniors or second-semester seniors. Students live in dormitories and earn marks through the portfolios they assemble. The focus is on studio art in four domains: drawing and painting, printmaking, sculpture, and new media (which include photography, video, and digital art). The Oxbow School takes only 48 students per semester.

Napa Adventist Junior Academy
2201 Pine Street, Napa
(707) 255–5233
www.najasda.com

Having celebrated its 50th anniversary recently, Napa Adventist Junior Academy (NAJA) has a lot to be proud of. Take the award-winning music program, for instance. Children learn the Kodaly Program in grades 1 through 4. Grades 4 through 6 have recorded a pair of compact discs—one Christian, the other Christmas songs—and grades 7 through 10 often perform at music festivals. The entire school (approximately 200 students) is wired for the Web, and the older kids play a variety of after-school sports. (NAJA, which resides on a 10-acre campus, is kindergarten through 10th grade—the traditional Adventist structure.)

St. John's Lutheran School
3521 Linda Vista Avenue, Napa
(707) 226–7970

This Christian-based school (in the Lutheran Church's Missouri Synod) was founded in 1937. It now sits in a pleasant grove of cedars north of Redwood Road. The approximately 275 students, ranging from preschoolers to eighth graders, are encouraged to develop beliefs and behavior consistent with Lutheran teachings, and to pass each grade with the requisite skills in communication, critical thinking, and analysis. St. John's offers some sports activities, a bit of arts and crafts, and after-school care.

Casa Montessori School
780 Lincoln Avenue, Napa
(707) 224–1944

"Respect" is the buzzword at this small (approximately 60 pupils) Napa school. Everyone must be treated with courtesy, and that goes for students as well as teachers. It is an ungraded elementary school, which means the kids progress at their own rate. The scope is preschool (age three) through sixth grade, but students can go far beyond that level if abilities dictate. In fact, administrators stress that most Casa students function about two years above the norm.

St. Apollinaris Elementary School
3700 Lassen Street, Napa
(707) 224–6525

The largest Catholic elementary/middle school (kindergarten through eighth grade) in Napa Country is in north Napa, near Trower Avenue. The academic program is rigorous, and there is a lineup of after-school sports for the more than 300 students who attend. The school was founded in 1959.

Foothills Adventist Elementary School
711 Sunnyside Road, St. Helena
(707) 963–3546
www.napanet.net/~foothilo

In 1902 the Elmshaven Seventh-day Adventist Church built a one-room schoolhouse for its pupils. That school, Foothills Ele-

mentary, now supports more than 175 students (grades K through eight) and is sponsored by four Adventist churches. Foothills balances religious training with lessons in reading, writing, math, social studies, science, technology, physical education, and music. Foothills also offers memorable field trips. Primary kids might spend a day combing tide pools at Point Reyes or climbing Mount St. Helena. The middle school pupils, meanwhile, might go to Catalina Island Marine Institute for five days of oceanography and marine studies or to the Marin Headlands Institute for a week of ecological training.

St. Helena Montessori School
1328 Spring Street, St. Helena
(707) 963–1527

This is Napa County's only Catholic Montessori facility, though it isn't affiliated with any one church. It's part of the Association Montessori Internationale, and its teachers must be accredited by that Amsterdam-based organization (founded by Dr. Maria Montessori in 1929). The school has about 75 pupils ranging from $2\frac{1}{2}$ to 12 years (sixth grade), and they are continually challenged to expand their abilities, though in a generally noncompetitive atmosphere. The youngest ones do tumbling and gymnastics, the elementary schoolers receive training in computers and foreign language, and all are exposed to the Orff-Schulwerk systematic music program.

St. Helena Catholic School
1255 Oak Avenue, St. Helena
(707) 963–4677
www.sthelenacatholicchurch.org/school

This school has been providing a Catholic education to Napa Valley residents since 1963. The sisters still aim for a well-rounded education for their economically and ethnically diverse student body. With 130 to 135 kids spread between kindergarten and eighth grade, multi-age classrooms are the norm (except for the kindergartners). The Boys and Girls Club of St. Helena meets on campus in the afternoon, making it easy for Catholic School kids to take part.

Sonoma County

Old Adobe School
252 West Spain Street, Sonoma
(707) 938–4510
www.wco.com/~kenwood/oldadobe

As the name suggests, Old Adobe School got its start in a historic adobe building—one believed to have been built by Gen. Mariano Vallejo 200 years ago. It has since relocated to its present location on the grounds of the First Congregational Church.

Old Adobe is private, nonprofit, and has no religious affiliations. It is managed by a board consisting of parents, teachers, the school director, and involved community members. It includes preschool as well as kindergarten (ages two through six), with extended day care available for both classes. Each child is encouraged to develop and express his total self, learning, discovering, and creating while growing. Cooperation rather than competition is stressed.

St. Francis Solano School
342 West Napa Street, Sonoma
(707) 996–4994
www.saintfrancissolano.org

The school's roots trace back to Presentation Academy, founded in 1882 as an adjunct of the Sisters of Presentation Convent in Sonoma. Many years after the convent school had closed for lack of financial support, wine patriarch Samuele Sebastiani funded a new school for the St. Francis parish. Today, St. Francis Solano School is housed in a building next to the church.

The school's reputation for academic excellence is well established, with its middle school students consistently winning national and state honors in competitions. Other values emphasized at St. Francis Solano include community service, the gospel message, social justice, and moral values. Enrollment is around 350 students.

The Presentation School
276 East Napa Street, Sonoma
(707) 996–2496
www.presentationschool.com

Believing Sonoma Valley needed more educational opportunities, several local families—led by Nancy and Don Sebastiani of the well-known winery family—founded the Presentation School in 1997. The K-8 school opened in temporary quarters at the Sonoma Community Center with an enrollment of 150 students. An independent Catholic school, Presentation's philosophy is, through education, "to build community, to proclaim the gospel message, and to reach out to the world in service." Its core curriculum, in addition to traditional subjects, includes religious studies, language arts, music, and physical education. With a limit of 20 students per grade, Presentation School offers "individualized instruction in a challenging, enriching, and nurturing environment." Students are required to wear uniforms.

St. Vincent de Paul High School
849 Keokuk Street (at Magnolia), Petaluma
(707) 763–1032
www.sonic.net/~svhs

This Catholic high school run by the St. Vincent de Paul parish takes pride in its prep school academic environment. It has won top national awards for physics and biology instruction, and 95 percent of the school's graduates go on to college. With an enrollment of slightly more than 400, the school places an emphasis on Christian values and academic excellence and attracts students, both Catholic and non-Catholic, from all over southern and central Sonoma County. St. Vincent's also has a full interscholastic athletic program for boys and girls and has won many league championships in the last decade in volleyball, football, and baseball.

Adobe Christian Preschool/Daycare
2875 Adobe Road, Petaluma
(707) 763–2012

Adobe school offers preschool and daycare for children from two to five years old, in a strong Christian environment. The curriculum stresses language development through the study of Bible literature and exploration of science and nature through gardening, animal care, and nature study.

There is also music, gymnastics, and computer play. The school's philosophy emphasizes enabling each child to experience the joy of playing, working, and learning with others. Child care is available from 6:30 A.M. to 6:00 P.M.

Ursuline High School
90 Ursuline Road, Santa Rosa
(707) 524–1130
www.ursulinehs.org

This Catholic school was started in 1880 in downtown Santa Rosa, but has been at its present location since 1957. The current population is more than 400 girls, who are required to wear uniforms. It's a college preparatory school—99 percent of the students go on to postsecondary school and 85 percent of those graduate from four-year colleges across the country.

Aside from strong academic requirements, students must also perform community service. Seniors must complete a special community research project focused on developing solutions to a local problem—performed with the help of a local mentor. Before graduation students must appear before a board to defend their project. The program has inspired many Ursuline students to become community leaders. The boys' school, Cardinal Newman High School, is just down the road, and although Ursuline freshmen and sophomores do not commingle, the girls in their junior and senior years share social activities with the boys of Cardinal Newman.

Cardinal Newman High School
50 Ursuline Road, Santa Rosa
(707) 546–6470
www.cardinalnewman.org

Unlike Ursuline High School—its girls' school counterpart—Cardinal Newman does not require uniforms for its 450 male students, but it does promote the same ideal of service to the community. Cardinal Newman is well known for its emphasis on sports, and the Santa Rosa school has had great success in basketball and football. However, there are plenty of other sports to choose from—baseball, wrestling, swimming, water polo, tennis, soccer, cross-country skiing, and track, to name a few. The school has a tradition of academic excellence, with more than 95 percent of students enrolling in four-year universities or two-year community colleges upon graduation.

St. Luke Lutheran School
905 Mendocino Avenue, Santa Rosa
(707) 545–0526
www.stluke-lcms.org

St. Luke serves the educational needs of Sonoma County children—from preschool through eighth grade—in a nurturing environment geared to touch and change young lives spiritually, academically, emotionally, socially, and intellectually. Faculty strive to provide a positive atmosphere in which students develop self-discipline, learn to understand what it means to be a child of God, and engage in healthy relationships with their teachers and peers.

Stuart School
431 Humboldt Street, Santa Rosa
(707) 528–0721

Believing that "success is the strongest foundation for academic growth," Stuart School works with children from prekindergarten through eighth grade and has done so since 1977. The downtown location is convenient for working parents and gives students opportunities for library and museum visits and athletic activities in the nearby park. The faculty stress fundamental education built on phonics, vocabulary, reading, composition, science, math, and yes, recess! Believing that active kids are better students, every class has plenty of moving-around time.

Merryhill Country School
4044 Mayette Avenue (Infants through junior kindergarten), Santa Rosa
(707) 575–7660
4580 Bennett View Drive (K–8), Santa Rosa
(707) 575–0910
www.nobellearning.com

The preschool program at Merryhill provides youngsters with a stimulating and creative environment. Focus is on activity-based learning, which includes counting, sorting, graphing, and playtime learning with paints, puppets, and music. The program for kindergarten through eighth grade is a strong, skills-based curriculum in math, literature, science, the visual arts, computer skills, and Spanish. Parent involvement is considered one of the significant reasons that children succeed. The school is supervised from 6:30 A.M. to 6:00 P.M. daily.

The Bridge School
1625 Franklin Avenue, Santa Rosa
(707) 575-7959

Offering a nurturing and educationally stimulating environment, this school's goal is to combine social development with academic growth. To that end, three programs are offered: Full Day Extended Care allows kids to experience this fun world from 7:30 A.M. to 5:30 P.M. Monday through Friday; Program Two offers either morning or afternoon half-day care; and Program Three is a flexible two- or three-day half-day program. The school emphasizes the importance of allowing children room for individual creativity within a safe and nurturing environment.

Little Angels Children's Center
4305 Hoen Avenue, Santa Rosa
(707) 579-4305
1363 Fulton Road, Santa Rosa
(707) 528-2933

Offering both day care and preschool, Little Angels aims to help children acquire readiness skills, increase their ability to express themselves, learn to get along with others through work and play, and accept responsibilities within a group setting. Although the school is owned and operated without church support, there are Bible stories, songs, and prayers. Other than that, the philosophy is to encourage children's eagerness, curiosity, and motivation.

Mendocino County

Mariposa Institute
3800 Low Gap Road, Ukiah
(707) 462-1016

With a successful record covering nearly 30 years of hands-on education for children from first through fifth grade, Mariposa School follows a tradition of social and academic learning in multiage classrooms. Youngsters pursue an academic program that integrates art, music, drama, Spanish, and social skills development. The country setting itself is beautiful—a place where children can play and learn amid oak woodlands.

Cozy Corner Children's Center
530 South Main Street, Ukiah
(707) 462-1251

Children in this school are mainly ages 2 through 5, though children up to age 12 are welcome. Half-day or full-day sessions are available, and drop-ins are accepted. The strong point here is the loving and nurturing environment, but teachers work with youngsters on academic readiness as well as learning to use the five senses. A dandy creative play area is augmented by a computer room to advance technological skills. The school usually has about 25 youngsters attending.

Melville Montessori School
4015 Second Gate Road, Willits
(707) 459-3100

Although this is a Montessori school, it operates more on the American Montessori plan, according to Athena Melville, a founder of the school in 1980. Its program is more holistic, covering every aspect of the child, not just the intellect. Emphasis is on impressive and expressive areas. The philosophy mixes dance, singing, making music, and having fun with a concentration on history, English, science, the humanities, and mathematics. With fewer than 24 students total in kindergarten through grade 12, the pupil-teacher ratio remains low at about 12 students per teacher. The school invites visitors on a drop-in basis, from 9:00 A.M. to 3:00 P.M. on school days.

Deep Valley Christian School
8555 Uva Drive, Redwood Valley
(707) 485-8778
www.deepvalleychristianschool.org

Not sponsored by any specific religious organization, Deep Valley Christian

School is committed to developing the best in every child, utilizing a back-to-basics curriculum that emphasizes individual responsibility. The student population runs to about 350 (grades K–12), with average SAT scores well above state and national levels. Situated in beautiful Redwood Valley, a region of vineyards and oaks, the school is growing so rapidly that new buildings are being added to house a science lab, computer lab, and gym. The athletic program includes both junior varsity and varsity football teams, volleyball, basketball, and track. A great deal of pride is also taken in the music program at Deep Valley—especially the band. There are about 30 students to a class at the high-school level, and the school receives the strong support of parents, who are required to put 25 hours of volunteer time into school activities each year.

Two-Year Colleges

Napa County

Napa Valley College
2277 Napa-Vallejo Highway
(Hwy. 221), Napa
(707) 253–3000, (800) 826–1077
www.napavalley.edu
Napa Valley College dates back to 1942 and has occupied its current site—180 tree-lined acres near the Napa River—since 1965. It's a two-year community college with about 9,000 students and associate degree programs in a spectrum of fields, including business administration, health care, and, not surprisingly, viticulture and wine technology. On-campus facilities include a Child and Family Studies and Services complex and an Olympic-sized swimming pool. The school has an Upper Valley Campus on the outskirts of St. Helena and a Small Business Development Center in Napa. It also shares a guaranteed transfer agreement with the University of California at Davis, Sacramento State University, and Sonoma State University. And in case you were interested, it's the sister college of Launceston College in Tasmania.

Sonoma County

Santa Rosa Junior College
1501 Mendocino Avenue, Santa Rosa
(707) 527–4011
www.santarosa.edu
The scholarship program at Santa Rosa Junior College is unique in all of America because of an association with the county-based Exchange Bank. In 1948 the bank's president, Frank P. Doyle, set up a trust that in the 1950–51 school year paid out $19,475 in scholarships to 95 students. In 2000–2001, dividends from the trust awarded more than $4.6 million in scholarships to approximately 4,000 students. Located on more than 100 acres, the college has a full-time enrollment of almost 7,000. Emphasis centers on general education, transfer education for students headed to four-year institutions, and occupational education in the fields of dental hygiene, radiologic technology, respiratory therapy, and many other areas.

The college's athletic teams (nicknamed the Bear Cubs) are part of the Bay Valley Conference, with the exception of the football team, which plays in the Nor-

> ### Insiders' Tip
> Napa Valley College and Santa Rosa Junior College both offer several courses—semester-long and shorter—in viticulture and winemaking. SRJC also offers classes such as Wine Industry Event Planning, Wine Marketing Fundamentals, and Media in the Wine and Vineyard Industry.

Cal Conference. Intercollegiate competition for men and women is offered in baseball, basketball, cross-country, football, golf, gymnastics, soccer, swimming, tennis, track and field, volleyball, water polo, and wrestling. A recent addition to Santa Rosa Junior College is an 87-seat planetarium. It has a dome 40 feet in diameter and 27 feet high. (See our Kidstuff chapter; see our Arts and Culture chapter for information on theater troupes and events at the school.) An additional 40-acre campus in east Petaluma offers occupational training, national park ranger training, police and fire technology, and public safety.

Empire College
3035 Cleveland Avenue, Santa Rosa
(707) 546-4000
www.empcol.com

Empire College offers four specialized associate degrees—in accounting, office technology, legal office administration, and medical assistance. Its School of Law awards juris doctor degrees in a four-year evening program. It also offers certificates to those studying to become legal secretaries, medical administrative/clinical assistants, medical transcriptionists, bookkeepers, and travel and tourism agents. A state-accredited college, Empire has operated since 1961 and now has some 500 students.

Mendocino County

Mendocino College
1000 Hensley Creek Road, Ukiah
(707) 463-3073
www.mendocino.cc.ca.us

The campus of Mendocino College occupies 126 acres and serves a rural area that encompasses 3,200 square miles. The school has additional educational centers at Willits and at Lakeport in Lake County. Founded in 1972 as a junior college, Mendocino provides the first two years of study for a four-year degree or confers an associate degree with vocational training in a wide variety of fields. There are programs in horticulture, agriculture, administration of justice, business administration, computer and information sciences, and premed and prenursing, to name a few.

One of the most stunning buildings on campus is the Center for Performing Arts, with its 400-seat theater and recording studio that houses programs in theater arts, music, arts, and textiles. The physical education program and the college's sports activities take place in an $8.2-million complex.

Both the Willits and Lake County centers provide administrative services and classrooms, plus counseling and financial aid assistance. Mendocino College has an additional facility at Point Arena, 50 miles southwest of Ukiah, which serves as a field laboratory for science classes in marine biology, geology and meteorology.

College of the Redwoods
1211 Del Mar Drive, Fort Bragg
(707) 962-2600
www.redwoods.cc.ca.us

The main campus of College of the Redwoods is at Eureka in Humboldt County. This is a two-year community college offering associate degrees, career training, and enrichment classes to residents of the north coast. Students receive top academic instruction in science, mathematics, and humanities courses, which transfer to Humboldt State University and other four-year colleges and universities across the nation.

The Fort Bragg site is beautiful, with low-lying buildings of natural-finish wood, an unobstructed view of the ocean, and a student population of 1,200. This campus is well known for courses in fine woodworking. It has a one-year program (though many sign up for a second year); its fame is such that students come to Fort Bragg from all over the world to study cabinetry and furniture-making. The college also offers a program that links art with computer technology to provide for study in photo transfer work and graphics communication. College of the Redwoods has no athletic program.

Four-Year Colleges and Universities

Napa County

Pacific Union College
100 Howell Mountain Road N., Angwin
(707) 965–6311, (800) 862–7080
www.puc.edu

PUC is a small (just more than 1,600 students), private, Seventh-day Adventist college surrounded by 1,800 acres of crops and forest on top of Howell Mountain, where it has been since 1906. The views are fabulous, and the education is highly regarded. *U.S. News & World Report* ranked the school the top liberal arts college in California in 1998, and the *Right College* places it in the top 10 in the nation for the percentage of male graduates who enter medical school. The student-faculty ratio is an appealing 12-to-1.

Pacific Union is most definitely a unique experience. The student body is ethnically diverse, the cafeteria is vegetarian (in line with Seventh-day Adventist practice), and the Abroad Program offers overseas study, including full-year programs in Argentina, Austria, France, Kenya, and Spain. Service is a big part of a PUC student's commitment. Many strike out on yearlong missions, and even more are actively involved with local homeless shelters, prison ministries, and the like. The college offers associate, bachelor's, and master's degrees in 19 academic departments. The 50-plus areas of study include all the usual subjects, plus such extras as digital media technology, fashion merchandising, and medical technology. Pacific Union is on the quarter system.

Sonoma County

University of Northern California
1304 Southpoint Boulevard, Suite 220, Petaluma
(707) 765–6400
www.uncm.edu

This new university, established in 1993, welcomes students from around the world. It aspires to become a premier engineering and scientific university with substantial programs in the liberal arts. Students enjoy small classes with ample individual attention from professors dedicated to quality teaching. About 50 full-time equivalent students attend the university, more than half of which are in graduate studies. Interdisciplinary studies are encouraged, and all academic programs emphasize the importance of effective communication for success in the modern world. The university focuses on programs in biological technology, and its early degree programs include the B.E., M.S., and Ph.D. in Biomedical Engineering and the B.A. in Engineering and in Languages and Linguistics.

Sonoma State University
1801 East Cotati Avenue, Rohnert Park
(707) 664–2880
www.sonoma.edu

This university was established on 270 acres of farmland in 1960. Today it offers undergraduate liberal arts and science curricula and 13 master's degree programs to a student population of about 7,000. Its computer engineering graduates walk directly into high-paying jobs, and similar results are expected for those completing the new wine business program. The school's Sonoma Plan is considered a model nursing program throughout America. In the fall of 2000, the university unveiled a new three-story, 215,000 square foot Jean and Charles Schulz Information Center. This elegant structure—named in honor of the renowned "Peanuts" cartoonist and his wife—is home to both the university library and the campus information technology department.

Performing arts get top billing at the campus, with plays from the pens of local writers and international favorites performed year-round, along with dance recitals and musical concerts (see our Arts and Culture chapter). Sonoma State ranks high in sports among the 23 campuses of the state system, particularly in men's and women's soccer, volleyball, women's basketball, and baseball. In all, the university has 16 intercollegiate teams. Its outdoor swimming pool is open to faculty, staff, and students and has access for the disabled.

One of the newest buildings on the Sonoma State University campus is the Jean & Charles Schulz Information Center. PHOTO: B.J. FUNDARO/COURTESY OF SONOMA STATE UNIVERSITY

Other Institutes of Higher Learning

Napa County

The Culinary Institute of America at Greystone
2555 Main Street, St. Helena
(707) 967-1100
www.ciachef.edu

This learning institution devoted to the gustatory arts is one of the perks of living in Wine Country. It is the only center in the world dedicated exclusively to continuing education for professionals in the food, wine, health, and hospitality fields—and it's a beauty.

It all began some years ago, when executives of the Culinary Institute of America, that factory of chefs in Hyde Park, New York, looked at some 50 potential sites to establish a West Coast center for continuing education. Their logical choice was Greystone, the majestic winery built in 1888 and used by the Christian Brothers to make sparkling wine from 1950 to 1989. After a massive gift from the Heublein Corporation (then owners of the property) and a $14 million renovation, the CIA opened for business in Napa Valley in 1995.

Inside, the facilities are almost as impressive as the 22-inch-thick tufa stone walls that frame Greystone's exterior. The third story is an immense teaching kitchen with 15,000 square feet of undivided floor space, 35-foot ceilings, and clusters of exquisite Bonnet stoves. In the middle of the space is a dining area where students sample the various assignments they and their cohorts have handed in.

The building also houses the EcoLab Theater, a 125-seat amphitheater used for cooking demonstrations and lectures; the Wine Spectator Greystone Restaurant (see our Restaurants chapter for more on that); The Campus Store with its preponderance of cooking equipment, books, and uniforms; and the DeBaun Food and Wine Museum, which displays a changing collection of wine-related artifacts. Outside the old winery are garlic and onion beds, seven terraces of herbs, an edible flower and herbal tea garden, and, off-site, 15 acres of Merlot grapes and an organic fruit and vegetable garden.

Courses vary in length from three days to the 30-week, two-semester Baking and Pastry Arts Certification Program. (The average class duration is one week.) The faculty is drawn from three sources: the small but talented core of resident instructors, visiting teachers from Hyde Park, and guest instructors.

Sonoma County

Western Institute of Science and Health
130 Avram Avenue, Rohnert Park
(707) 664–9267, (800) 437–9474
www.westerni.org

The Western Institute of Science and Health offers an Associate of Science program for physical therapist assistants and helps its students find employment in hospitals, outpatient clinics, public schools, and home-health agencies. The institute teaches students, through academic courses and clinical internship experiences, how to effectively treat patients who suffer from physical impairment. Graduates must pass a state examination given by the Physical Therapy Examination Committee before they may practice in California.

New College of California
99 Sixth Street, Santa Rosa
(707) 568–0122, (888) 437–3460
www.newcollege.edu/northbay/campus.htm

This alternative college's main campus is in San Francisco, where students can earn undergraduate and graduate degrees in subjects that range from women's spirituality to poetics. The north bay campus—located in a quaint brick building off Railroad Square—offers both BA and MA degrees in the subjects of culture, ecology, and sustainable community. The BA degree is a one-year weekend "completion" program designed for students who

Insiders' Tip

Even lifelong cooks who know their way around a good meatloaf and a hundred uses for cream of mushroom soup will enjoy an afternoon cooking demonstration at the Culinary Institute of America in St. Helena. For a small fee, you get to nosh on finger foods and wine, and receive a gift. Learn more and make reservations by calling (707) 967–2320.

are working and unable to attend traditionally scheduled classes. Applicants must have already acquired at least 45 units from another institution to enter the program. The college states that its program focuses on "the capacity to think globally and systematically, the capacity to clarify value conflicts as well as one's own motivations and learning styles, and the ability to plan and carry out a creative project which has been perceived in terms of its impact on the social ecology."

Mendocino County

Dharma Realm Buddhist University
City of Ten Thousand Buddhas, 5251
Kindness Avenue, Ukiah
(707) 468–9112
www.drba.org

State-approved Dharma Realm University offers year-round education to qualified students, with programs leading to bachelor's, master's, and doctoral certificates.

The emphasis is on Buddhist study and practice, including loyalty, felicity, humanness, and righteousness. Students are given the opportunity to develop their innate wholesome wisdom. At the same time, high standards of academic excellence are maintained. Degrees are currently offered in Buddhist studies and practice, translation, and Buddhist education. Full scholarships are available to qualified students.

Child Care

Whether you're visiting for a few days or putting down roots for a several years, finding qualified child care can be a daunting task. There are scores from which to choose, no matter where you're located in Wine Country, and each differs from the next in small ways. Some centers are church-affiliated, others purely secular; some are in charming, turn-of-the-century Victorians, others in office complexes; some provide transportation, others leave that to you; some accept infants, others don't; some are low-tech, others have computers; some aren't really "centers" at all, but licensed homes.

Each county has at least one organization that will help you sort out all the factors, free of charge. These agencies are able to quote prices, describe individual providers, and refer you to ones in which you might be interested. Here they are, by county.

Napa County

Community Resources for Children
5 Financial Plaza, Suite 224, Napa
(707) 253–0376 (general information),
(707) 253–0366 (referrals), (800) 696–4CRC
www.crcnapa.org

This nonprofit agency, funded primarily by the California Department of Education but supplemented by federal and private contributions, is an important friend to Napa County families. Community Resources for Children (CRC) is contacted most often for its free referrals to child-care centers and in-home providers.

It also gives financial assistance to qualifying families, trains prospective child-care providers, advocates for children and families in the community, provides low-cost car seats to eligible families, and maintains a lending library of toys, videos, books, and educational resources. CRC can help you find a continuing day-care center or a one-day baby-sitter. Se habla español.

Sonoma County

Community Child Care Council
396 Tesconi Court, Santa Rosa
(707) 544–3077
www.sonoma4cs.org

This service (known as 4Cs) helps parents find a suitable system of child care by providing names of licensed centers or homes near the parents' home or workplace. To assure that parents get the best from their search, the council provides a list of questions parents should ask when they call—such as what educational training is offered, whether the staff has CPR training, and any special programs offered. Another list indicates things parents should look for when they visit the facility. No recommendations are offered, but lists of licensed care centers and homes are extensive.

If parents prefer someone unlicensed to come into their home, such as a nanny or au pair, the council will give advice on that as well. It also can help with co-op parent participation, preschool planning, and organizing play groups, in which parents and children meet in one another's homes on a rotating basis.

River Child Care Services
16315 First Street, Guerneville
(707) 869–3613
www.sonic.net/~rccs

This service covers the area along the Russian River and West County as far as the coast, providing information on choosing child care and offering lists of licensed providers and home-based care. In addition to long-term regular care, they also can advise on baby-sitting services. The organization can provide parents with important information about prospective providers, such as methods of discipline used (spanking is not allowed), what happens if the provider is ill or the child is ill, and where meals are eaten.

River Child Care Services offers a list of workers interested in caring for children on a family-by-family basis. However, a referral does not imply a recommendation or a guarantee of quality. A brochure they publish gives some good hints on interviewing candidates by phone.

Mendocino and Lake Counties

North Coast Opportunities, Inc.
413 North State Street, Ukiah
(707) 462–1954
156 Humboldt Street S., Willits
(707) 459–2019
155 Cypress Street, Fort Bragg
(707) 964–3080
14130 Lakeshore Drive, Clearlake
(707) 994–4647
850 Lakeport Boulevard, Lakeport
(707) 263–4688

This valuable, not-for-profit organization is dedicated to offering referrals and resources to families in the largely rural and dispersed counties of Mendocino and Lake. Anyone who calls is given a free referral to one or more state-licensed child-care facilities. North Coast Opportunities also offers child-care subsidies, support services for both parents and providers, and a helpful food and nutrition program. If you have a general question about the service, call the Parent-Child Information Center at (707) 467–3211.

Insiders' Tip
Major upgrades worth about $9 million took place in 2002 on several Santa Rosa high schools and middle schools. Additional projects are planned for summer 2003.

Health Care

Walk-In/Prompt-Care Centers

Hospitals

Hospice Care

Alternative Health Care

The last thing you want to worry about while visiting Wine Country is a health crisis of some sort, but rest assured you'll be treated well by experts if it becomes necessary. No matter where you roam in this region, you're never too far from a clinic or hospital that can patch you up and have you back sipping Sauvignon Blanc in no time flat.

Considering that most of our region is rural, the population relatively sparse, and the towns small to midsize, health care is amazingly accessible and the quality is excellent. Hospital staffs (from the doctors on down to the volunteer helpers) are "small-town friendly" and more easy-going than their big-city counterparts. But their dedication to medicine is just as serious.

On the local level, zealous hospital benefactors have pitched in to provide state-of-the-art equipment and medical instruments. Several hospitals in the area have been competing keenly with one another for many years to acquire the best equipment, services, and physicians—leading to improved health care for all. Some of Northern California's finest doctors have traditionally gravitated by choice to this less stressful environment, while still providing the kind of technically current surgical and medical expertise that normally exists only in larger metropolitan areas.

However, the nationwide nursing shortage and other health care industry crises have also affected our medical facilities locally, with scaled-back services and shorter hours of operation at many places. The smaller community hospitals in particular have been hard hit by financial constraints and in response have reduced their services and trimmed staffs. Yet the larger facilities are expanding services, building new wings, and acquiring new and better equipment. Along the way, they are receiving accolades for their skills and expertise.

Twenty-four-hour emergency service is available throughout much of the area, so when you gash your finger while trying to master that new corkscrew from Dean & DeLuca, help is close at hand.

Walk-In/Prompt-Care Centers

Napa County

ExpressCare
Queen of the Valley Hospital
1000 Trancas Street, Napa
(707) 257-4008
www.thequeen.org

This walk-in center, an adjunct of Queen of the Valley's emergency room, is open from 10:00 A.M. to 10:00 P.M. daily and can address a variety of nonlethal illnesses, allergies, and injuries. Board-certified physicians are on hand to treat you, and they will make referrals or deliver follow-up care if needed.

Upper Napa Valley Urgent Care
1370 Railroad Avenue, St. Helena
(707) 963-4399

Upvalley residents gained a little peace of mind when this clinic opened in St. Helena in 1999. Urgent Care treats all nonlife-threatening ailments, including pain, migraine headaches, asthma, rashes, infections, allergies, and Homer Simpson-style, self-inflicted boo-boos. Appointments are preferred, but walk-ins are accepted too. The clinic is open Monday through Friday from 9:00 A.M. to 5:00 P.M., and on Saturday from 10:00 A.M. to 2:00 P.M.

Sonoma County

Rohnert Park Health Care Center
1450 Medical Center Drive, Rohnert Park
(707) 584–0674

Operated by the St. Joseph Health System—Sonoma County, this handy walk-in clinic is open 8:00 A.M. to 9:00 P.M. daily for treating minor injuries and illnesses. Health education, infusion services, and related services are also available.

Hospitals

Napa County

Queen of the Valley Hospital
1000 Trancas Street, Napa
(707) 252–4411
www.thequeen.org

Queen of the Valley is a well-respected facility with 162 beds. QVH has a community cancer center, a high-end imaging department, home-care services, maternity services (including an intensive-care nursery), occupational health services, a regional heart center where open-heart surgeries are performed, and a respiratory-care department. It also features an upgraded Vascular and Interventional Radiology Lab, an expanded maternity unit, and improved MRI technology.

Queen of the Valley is the designated trauma center for Napa County, with a 24-hour emergency room.

A couple of QVH services stand out. The Acute Rehabilitation Center offers comprehensive physical, occupational, and speech therapies for people who have experienced trauma (such as a stroke or spinal cord injury). And the hospital's community pharmaceutical services provide infusion capability, clinical monitoring, and computerized pumps for patients at home. Queen of the Valley is part of the St. Joseph Health System, which emphasizes dignity, service, justice, and excellence.

St. Helena Hospital
650 Sanitarium Road, Deer Park
(707) 963–3611,
TTY/TDD: (707) 963-6527
www.sthelenahospital.org

The address may conjure up lightning storms and strange goings-on in the basement, but don't be alarmed. This full-service community hospital, off the Silverado Trail about 3 miles northeast of St. Helena, dates back to the 1800s, when a sanitarium was a health resort.

St. Helena Hospital has 192 licensed beds and 36 beds for residential health-enhancement programs. It also has a wide range of specialties, including cardiac surgery, cardiovascular rehabilitation, pulmonary rehabilitation, mental health services, oncology, obstetrics, pain rehabilitation, and preventive medicine.

A member of the Adventist Health network of facilities, St. Helena is known for its sleep disorders clinic and, especially, its cardiovascular lab—a major heart center for Northern California. Add to the mix hospice services (through a joint venture with Queen of the Valley Hospital) and extensive adult mental health services, both inpatient and day treatment.

Insiders' Tip

St. Helena Hospital was founded as St. Helena Sanitarium in 1878 by Merritt Kellogg—Seventh-day Adventist, holistic-health maniac, and half-brother of cereal mogul Will Keith Kellogg. For an outrageously fictionalized account of Merritt's spa endeavors, rent *The Road to Wellville,* a movie starring John Cusack and Anthony Hopkins.

Finally, St. Helena has a Women's Center in downtown St. Helena, providing mammography, bone density testing, a health resource library, and a wide range of health education classes and support groups. The Women's Center is at 1299 Pine Street; call (707) 963–1912.

Sonoma County

Sonoma Valley Hospital
347 Andrieux Street, Sonoma
(707) 935–5000
www.svh.com

When Sonoma Valley Hospital was created in 1944, the vision was to combine the best of medicine with a warm and caring staff. Since then, tremendous advances in research and diagnosis have changed the face of medicine. But Sonoma Valley Hosptial remains a warm, caring, family-oriented hospital with the same small-town spirit that permeates the community from which it draws its patients.

Today's 83-bed facility serves 40,000 people in Sonoma Valley. The credentialed medical staff totals 136 active, consulting, and courtesy physicians involved in 25 different disciplines. The intensive-care unit has six private rooms staffed by experienced critical-care nurses. A full range of cardiopulmonary testing equipment is available, along with cardiac rehab programs. A Birth Center provides a comfortable, homey place where labor, delivery, recovery, and postpartum phases all take place in one room with the family at hand. Recently a state-of-the-art system was installed linking doctors instantly to patient information and test results.

Petaluma Valley Hospital
400 North McDowell Boulevard, Petaluma
(707) 778–1111
www.stjosephhealth.org

With 82 beds and 30 medical specialties from cardiology to urology, this facility, operated by the St. Joseph Health System—Sonoma County, is a busy place. The attractive two-story, 22-year-old hospital is also a genuine community resource. There's a full-service emergency department with a physician on duty 24 hours a day and a helipad for emergency helicopter air transport. The pharmacy is open and staffed seven days a week, 24 hours a day. Other features available to the community include home health care, a hospice, and an electronic telecommunications system called Lifeline that provides 24-hour emergency access to anyone who might need quick response at home.

Santa Rosa Memorial Hospital
1165 Montgomery Drive, Santa Rosa
(707) 546–3210
www.stjosephhealth.org

Memorial Hospital opened its doors in 1950 under the guidance of the Sisters of St. Joseph, founders of eight other hospitals on the West Coast since 1920. All services and programs are guided by the healing mission of the Sisters—service, excellence, justice, and dignity for all

A lifesaving helicopter arrives at the helipad at Santa Rosa Memorial Hospital, the designated regional trauma center for Sonoma, Lake, and Mendocino Counties. PHOTO: JEAN SAYLOR DOPPENBERG

members of the community. The hospital is the "flagship" facility for the St. Joseph Health System–Sonoma County, which operates several clinics and acute-care facilities throughout the region.

In 2000, Memorial Hospital was named the designated trauma center for Sonoma, Lake, and Mendocino Counties, making it the busiest and best-equipped hospital of its kind north of the Golden Gate.

In addition to cutting-edge surgical facilities and medical equipment, 192-bed Memorial Hospital has some unique services including the Mobile Health Clinic, which serves children 16 and younger from low-income families that have difficulty locating affordable health care. Care is provided by medical professionals who speak English and Spanish.

To give new parents extra peace of mind, the hospital partners with University of California–San Francisco Medical Center to operate an intensive-care nursery for ill newborns on-site.

Some of the other services in its facilities include physical and speech therapy and rehabilitation from brain injuries, strokes, spinal cord injuries, and comas. Home health care and preemployment physicals are also offered.

In 2000, the St. Joseph Health System added another dimension to its services: A Palliative Care unit, across the street from Santa Rosa Memorial Hospital. One of only two units of its kind in California, this acute-care service focuses on end-of-life pain management and improving the quality of life for those with life-threatening illness.

Sutter Warrack Hospital
2449 Summerfield Road, Santa Rosa
(707) 542–9030

Built in 1960, Warrack is a 69-bed hospital with four operating rooms. Its primary services cover intensive and coronary care, pediatric surgery, and diagnostic imaging. Emergency care is available 24 hours a day, with a physician always on duty.

Sutter Medical Center of Santa Rosa
3325 Chanate Road, Santa Rosa
(707) 576–4000

> ## Insiders' Tip
> If you are a Kaiser Permanente member staying in Wine Country, note that the hospital group operates a medical center in Vallejo, only 15 miles from Napa, and another in Santa Rosa.

This hospital was established in 1866 and has provided advanced health care services for Sonoma County and the adjoining communities for 137 years.

As a teaching institution affiliated with the University of California at San Francisco School of Medicine, Sutter is regionally recognized for its wide range of specialty services, including a high-risk maternity department, and an emergency trauma care program. It offers other special services too. The facility's major expansion in 2001 was to its cardiovascular services. The newly constructed Heart Center provides a complete range of cardiac services, from open-heart surgery to cardiac rehabilitation.

Healdsburg District Hospital
1375 University Avenue, Healdsburg
(707) 431–6500

Today the hospital is a far cry from the World War I-era, wood-frame building that burned to the ground in the 1930s. Amazingly, there was no loss of life, although patients had to be carried one-by-one down flights of stairs from surgery. Rebuilt during World War II when medical staff was virtually unavailable, the hospital was mainly operated by the director of nursing, who coped with staff shortages by hiring schoolgirls to do nursing chores while she slept on a gurney (on call) at night.

Today's hospital is a modern facility with 15 beds. Services include 24-hour emergency care, physical therapy and occupational medicine services, same-day surgery center, and a new respite care service.

Palm Drive Hospital
501 Petaluma Avenue, Sebastopol
(707) 823–8511
www.palmdrivehospital.com
Palm Drive's future as a small community hospital has been tested during the past few years. Currently it has 55 beds and one operating room, and its emergency room is staffed 24 hours a day.

Mendocino County

Ukiah Valley Medical Center
275 Hospital Drive, Ukiah
(707) 462–3111
www.uvmc.org
A member of the Adventist Health Corporation, this 116-bed hospital has offered a full spectrum of outpatient treatment and surgery since its inception in 1956, when it was known as Hillside Hospital. In 1979 it joined the 18-hospital Adventist Health group. This affiliation provides the advantage of being connected to a network of locations so that patients can be transferred quickly, by helicopter if necessary, to whichever Adventist Health hospital specializes in treating the particular problem.

The Adventist's university at Loma Linda is famed for being on the cutting edge of cardiac expertise, knowledge, and treatment. Hence, Ukiah Valley offers a high-quality cardiac specialty department.

Frank R. Howard Memorial Hospital
Madrone and Manzanita Streets, Willits
(707) 459–6801
www.howardhospital.com
Affiliated with the Adventist Health group since 1986, Frank R. Howard Memorial Hospital has been a part of the Willits community for 74 years. Willits is a small community (population 5,000) and also serves as a gateway to wide-open spaces to the north. That means the hospital serves a population in a wide area of wilderness and ranch and forest land as far north as the Oregon border. There is 24-hour emergency service. While the hospital is small (just 28 beds), its connection with the Adventist group gives it wide latitude in serving patients through larger hospitals in the group.

Redwood Coast Medical Services
46900 Ocean Drive, Gualala
(707) 884–4005
www.rcms-healthcare.org
In a town too small to accommodate a hospital, this federally qualified medical-service facility fills a gap with medical specialists that include an ophthalmologist, cardiologist, oncologist, and orthopedist. The office is open from 8:00 A.M. to 6:00 P.M. Monday through Friday and from 9:00 A.M. to 1:00 P.M. on Saturday. However, doctors are on duty 24 hours a day to treat injuries and medical emergencies for visitors and residents alike and can be reached for services after Redwood Coast closes.

Mendocino Coast District Hospital
700 River Drive, Fort Bragg
(707) 961–1234
www.mcdh.net
Its garden setting makes this lone hospital on the Mendocino coast very attractive. Created by the cities of the coastal community in 1971, it still maintains an attitude that locals call "neighbors taking care of neighbors." Patients from large cities often remark on this small-town support and warmth and on how amazingly caring the hospital personnel can be. With 54 beds, two operating rooms, and an outpatient surgery area, services offered include critical-care facilities, 24-hour emergency service, laboratory services, radiology, and cardiopulmonary care.

A very active ambulance service travels to coastal areas as far away as Westport, 16 miles north.

Hospice Care

Napa County

Hospice of Napa Valley
3299 Claremont Way, Napa
(707) 258–9080, (800) 451–4664

Safety in Numbers

Call 911 during any medical emergency. If an ambulance is not what you need, consider one of the following numbers. In the first group are lines that apply throughout the Wine Country. They are followed by county-specific numbers.

Throughout Wine Country
Poison Control Center
(800) 876–4766

National HIV and AIDS Information Service
English: (800) 342–2437;
Spanish: (800) 344–7432;

California HIV/AIDS Hotline
(800) 367–2437

Crisis Line for the Handicapped
(800) 426–4263

California Smokers Helpline
(800) 662–8887

Centers for Disease Control and
Prevention (Sexually Transmitted
Disease Hotline)
(800) 227–8922

Medical Board of California
(Central Complaint Unit)
(800) 633–2322

Dental Referral
(800) DENTIST

Napa County
Suicide Prevention
(707) 963–2555, (800) 784–2433

Napa County Health and Human
Services Department
(707) 253–4279

Napa Valley AIDS Project
(707) 258–2437

Napa County Alcohol and Drug Services
(707) 253–4412

Napa Emergency Women's Services
(707) 255-6397

Sonoma County
Sonoma County Department of Health
Services and Center for HIV Prevention
and Care
(707) 565–4620

Suicide Prevention
(707) 576–8181

Crisis Line for the Handicapped
(800) 426–4263

Department of Alcohol and Drug
Programs
(800) 879–2772

Mendocino County
Mendocino County Health Department
(800) 734–7793, (707) 463–4461

Mendocino County Suicide Prevention
(800) 575–4357

Community Care AIDS Project of
Mendocino and Lake Counties
(707) 462–3041

If the time comes to end the aggressive search for a cure and to focus instead on comfort and symptom alleviation as death approaches, hospice care is the appropriate choice. Hospice of Napa Valley, a nonprofit organization and a joint community service of St. Helena Hospital and Queen of the Valley Hospital, has been serving the county since 1979.

The hospice's provisions include round-the-clock, on-call nursing; short-term respite to reduce caregiver stress; medical equipment; oxygen; and intermittent visits from team members. That team includes a medical director, the patient's physician, registered nurses, medical social workers, home-health aides, chaplains, bereavement counselors, and volunteers. Hospice of Napa Valley accepts patients regardless of ability to pay. Grief education and counseling services are also available to community members.

Sonoma County

Hospice of Petaluma
416 Payran Street, Petaluma
(707) 778–6242

Memorial Hospice
821 Mendocino Avenue, Santa Rosa
(707) 568–1094
www.stjosephhealth.org

Working in tandem as part of the St. Joseph Health System—Sonoma County, these agencies provide support and care for persons facing life-threatening illnesses so that they may live as fully and comfortably as possible. Hospice of Petaluma (working with Memorial Hospice of Santa Rosa) benefits the community served by Petaluma Valley and Santa Rosa Memorial hospitals. A counseling and social work staff offer emotional support, counseling, and information about community resources. A hospice chaplain provides spiritual support. Nursing services include expert pain and symptom management, home visits, and 24-hour on-call family assistance. Trained volunteers provide companionship for family members. After the fact, there also is grief counseling, support, and education.

Alternative Health Care

Alternative forms of treatment and prevention proliferate and thrive in this region. Why? First of all, this is the Wine Country, where health and quality of life are paramount. And second, this is California, where people tend to be open-minded in their decision making.

So if you're in search of a less traditional cure for what ails you, you're in luck. Within a short drive you can find homeopaths and naturopaths, Ayurvedics and herbalists, acupuncturists and acupressurists, chiropractors and yoga gurus, reflexologists and hypnotists—and practitioners of Reiki, rolfing, and biofeedback. You can even find a few shaman healers if you try hard enough. The Sonoma County phone book alone lists approximately 65 acupuncturists, 46 hypnotists, 12 homeopaths, and a couple hundred chiropractors. If you want to verify a license, call the Medical Board of California at (916) 263–2635.

Now get out there and heal thyself.

Insiders' Tip
Local practitioners of holistic health swear by the *Share Guide*, which covers everything from psychic workshops to natural food products, and is circulated throughout Wine Country. It is available free at many newsstands in the area, in coffee houses, and at most other alternative lifestyle outlets. Visit its Web site (www.shareguide.com) to get the lowdown on New Age goings-on in the region.

Media

Daily Newspapers
Other Newspapers
Magazines
Radio Stations
Television
Cable TV

When you visit Wine Country, you're probably here to forget about the outside world for a few days, to escape from the daily onslaught of the media. Who can blame you? But when you do feel like plugging back into reality and picking up a newspaper, we've got the world covered.

In addition to local media, detailed in this chapter, it's easy to find one of the nation's largest newspapers, the *San Francisco Chronicle,* practically anywhere in the region, as well as the *New York Times* and the *Wall Street Journal.*

Along with hometown papers and regional TV and radio stations, in this chapter we also list specialized publications that cover niche markets.

Daily Newspapers

Napa County

The Napa Valley Register
1615 Second Street, Napa
(707) 226–3711, (800) 504–6397
www.napanews.com

Napa County's only daily dates back to 1863, though it has gone through a few changes of ownership since Abe Lincoln's administration. The paper is now a member of the Pulitzer Community of Newspapers. It had been the second-largest community paper in the Scripps chain (after Tucson's *Arizona Daily Star*) before Pulitzer gobbled up that group. Current paid circulation is about 20,500.

The *Register* ably handles the entire county, nodding to St. Helena and Calistoga in its "Upvalley" section. The paper uses wire-service reports but does a lot of local reporting, such as a multifaceted 1997 series about the valley's farmworkers that garnered much acclaim.

The *Register* is an afternoon paper during the week, switching to morning delivery on Saturday and Sunday. Also worth noting here is its monthly news-rack supplement: *Inside Napa Valley,* a tourist-aimed tabloid with better-than-expected features on art, food, wine, and coming events. The supplement is free.

Sonoma County

The Press Democrat
427 Mendocino Avenue, Santa Rosa
(707) 546–2020
www.pressdemocrat.com

For many Sonoma County residents, as well as readers in adjoining counties, the morning *Press Democrat* is the paper for local, national, and international daily news, with a circulation of about 93,000 (104,000 on Sundays).

The *P.D.,* as locals call it, is owned by the *New York Times* now but has been serving the Sonoma County area since 1857. Although the paper's name includes the word Democrat, the editorial stance is more middle-of-the-road.

A strong sports section features popular columnists such as Bob Padecky and Lowell Cohn. On the entertainment scene, local residents keep abreast of what's going on about town through a lively entertainment section called "Q." Columns by Chris Coursey, Chris Smith, and Gaye LeBaron also offer colorful, behind-the-scenes coverage of Sonoma County people, places, and happenings.

Mendocino County

Ukiah Daily Journal
590 South School Street, Ukiah
(707) 468–0123
www.ukiahdailyjournal.com

This newspaper's roots go back to 1860, when it was called the *Redwood Journal*. Former editor Robb Hicken plowed his way through 137 years of back issues to come up with a complete history of the paper, and in mid-1997 he published a three-page supplement to the *Daily Journal* to give readers a look at what was important news for Ukiah in other times. With a circulation of 8,500, the *Daily Journal*, now edited by K.C. Meadows, covers local and county news that the metropolitan dailies don't. Coverage includes sports, society news, club activities, high school events, and news from Mendocino College, located in the Ukiah foothills.

Other Newspapers

Napa County

Napa County Record/Positive Living
1320 Second Street, Napa
(707) 252–8877

The *Record* started as a monthly paper in 1946, went weekly, and in 1996 switched back to monthly, where it now comfortably abides. Distributed free on the last Friday of every month, it's a family-oriented community paper that covers topics such as business, automobiles, and hunting and fishing. *Positive Living* has two special editions: a program-style section dedicated to Symphony on the River (see our Festivals and Events chapter) and a seniors section that prints in February, July, and October (the last one focusing on the local Senior Games).

St. Helena Star
1328 Main Street, St. Helena
(707) 963–2731
www.sthelenastar.com

St. Helena's well-preserved Victorian charm even extends to its newspaper, the *Star*, which was recently purchased by Pulitzer Newspapers, Inc. The paper attempts to stay within the city limits, plus Angwin and its Howell Mountain environs.

The paper astutely covers the important local issues—growth, tourism, elections—and its wine coverage is getting more comprehensive. (There is a special wine edition every October.) George Starke, whose column concentrates on the human side of the wine industry, has ruffled a few feathers by breaking news on the buying and selling of vineyards. But even the editors will admit that the feature best known for reeling in readers is the precious Police Log. You don't really know St. Helena until you have studied this compendium of barking dogs, double-parked cars, and nosy neighbors.

The Weekly Calistogan
1328 Main Street, St. Helena
(707) 942–6242

This might be the only newspaper in the nation whose motto is longer than some of its features. And we quote: "Published at the Head of the Napa Valley, a Beautiful and Fertile Section of Country, Possessing a Climate that for Health and Comfort is Not Surpassed on Earth." Amen.

The *Calistogan* is owned by Pulitzer Newspapers, Inc., and like its sister paper, the *St. Helena Star*, comes out each Thursday. When publisher Paul Krsek shut down the *Weekly Calistogan* office and moved the staff to St. Helena (to share space with the *St. Helena Star*) in 1999, locals worried they were about to lose an institution founded in 1877. But the paper is still afloat, and its coverage of the local sports scene is about as thorough as you'll find in a small-town paper.

Sonoma County

The Sonoma Index-Tribune
117 West Napa Street, Sonoma
(707) 938–2111
www.sonomanews.com

Established in 1879, the twice-weekly *Sonoma Index-Tribune* has been in the same family since 1884. Current publisher Robert Lynch leads the family's third generation to own and operate the paper.

Serving the Sonoma Valley—a region approximately 18 miles long that extends from San Pablo Bay north to Kenwood—the paper publishes every Tuesday and Friday, with a paid circulation of 12,500. The *Index-Tribune* is an award-winning community newspaper, covering all aspects of local news—schools, city government, the fire and water boards, the wine business, prep and youth sports, adult recreational sports leagues, even bake sales and spaghetti dinners.

In May 1997, the *Index-Tribune* received five awards for excellence in the annual California Newspaper Publishers Association Better Newspapers Contest, including a coveted honor in the general excellence category.

Four times a year, the newspaper publishes *Sonoma Valley Magazine* as a supplement to the newspaper. It includes a variety of features and special stories on local people and institutions. The newspaper also publishes a number of supplemental journals, including the annual *Sonoma Valley Almanac* and the *Sonoma Valley Guide,* distributed each month to dozens of local hotels, motels, restaurants, and wineries.

Argus Courier
830 Petaluma Boulevard N., Petaluma
(707) 762–4541
www.arguscourier.com

Published each Wednesday, this publication (recently purchased by the *New York Times*) has been in business since 1855, making it the oldest paper in Sonoma County. Publisher John Burns and managing editor Chris Samson focus on Petaluma community news and information on arts and entertainment. Circulation is 8,500. About 12,000 nonsubscribing Petalumans receive a free weekly shopper each Wednesday.

The Community Voice
5625 State Farm Drive, Rohnert Park
(707) 584–2222

The *Community Voice,* published every Wednesday, is the local newspaper for residents of Rohnert Park and Cotati. It tells them what is going on in their schools and neighborhoods. Columnists write up the news about anniversaries, birthdays, and other small-town happenings. The paper's well-designed sports section covers local recreational activities—especially youth sports—with the intensity that city papers use to cover the major leagues.

The newspaper works closely with the Rohnert Park and Cotati chambers of commerce, is involved in promoting local business, and beats the drum for many local events and institutions. There is also a reporter covering Sonoma State University.

North Bay Bohemian
50 Mark West Springs Road, Santa Rosa
(707) 527–1200
www.metroactive.com/sonoma

Before becoming the *Bohemian* in 2000, this free weekly tabloid was known as the *Sonoma County Independent*—and before that it was the *West Sonoma County Paper*. In 1994 the paper joined a Bay Area group of alternative weeklies, Metro Newspapers. Formerly serving only Sonoma County, the *Bohemian* now covers Marin and Napa Counties, featuring news stories relating to civic issues—from an indy perspective—as well as a reliable culture and entertainment department. This weekly comes out each Thursday, with numerous distribution points in the three counties. On top of all this, there's great photography.

Sonoma County Herald-Recorder
1818 Fourth Street, Santa Rosa
(707) 545–1166
www.dailyjournal.com/public/home/home_
pub.cfm

Published twice a week with a readership of 5,000, the *Herald-Recorder* covers real estate, business, and legal news, with statistical information from the *Recorder's* Office and County Clerk plus news affecting local attorneys and real estate interests. The publisher is Christine Griego. The paper has been published since 1899.

Sonoma-Marin Farm News
870 Piner Road, Santa Rosa
(707) 544–5575
www.sonomacountyfarmbureau.com

The Farm Bureau has been distributing its monthly agricultural newspaper to the ranchers of Sonoma County and adjoining Marin County for 22 years. Editor Laurie Ferguson focuses on different laws and regulations that affect farm lands and disseminates information on wetlands and tree ordinances that apply to

vineyards and dairy and cattle ranches. There is also general farming and viticulture news. Circulation is 3,200.

North Bay Business Journal
5464 Skylane Boulevard, Suite B, Santa Rosa
(707) 579–2900
www.NorthBayBusinessJournal.com

The *Business Journal* publishes strictly business news, focusing on new startups, expansions of existing firms, and information on relocations. Circulation is more than 10,000. Usually the 40-page-plus journal will include a profile of a top-level executive describing the company, its history, and anticipation of future progress. Published weekly, it covers Sonoma, Marin, and Napa Counties. They also print a monthly wine industry *Business Journal.*

Healdsburg Tribune and Windsor Times
5 Mitchell Lane, Healdsburg
(707) 433–4451
www.sonomawest.com/healdsburg,
www.sonomawest.com/windsor

The *Tribune* has had different owners since its inception more than 130 years ago—it recently became a part of the Sonoma West Publishers newspaper group, which also publishes the *Sonoma West Times & News* (see below). The present editor, Ray Holley, puts out a well-rounded weekly, covering all the news of Healdsburg and Geyersville: community affairs and events, legal matters, and local personalities.

The paper also prints occasional special sections. Holley also edits the *Windsor Times.* This, too, is strictly locally oriented—and owned by the Sonoma West Publishers. Both the *Healdsburg Tribune* and *Windsor Times* print on Wednesdays. Together, the newspapers' circulation is approximately 9,000.

Cloverdale Reveille
207 North Cloverdale Boulevard, Cloverdale
(707) 894–3339
www.thegrid.net/reveille

This community newspaper is published on Wednesdays and covers community

---

Insiders' Tip

Truffles, anyone? The *Press Democrat's* Wednesday edition carries a "Tidbits" calendar that gives suggestions for food and wine fun for the current week. These may include hors d'oeuvres tastings, wine barrel tastings, or short cooking classes at such places as Ramekins Sonoma Valley Culinary School in Sonoma (their chocolate truffles workshop costs just $65).

and school news. Records stacked away in old files indicate the *Reveille* was first published in 1879. Present circulation of the *Cloverdale Reveille* is 2,400. Editor Bonny Hanchette is proud of the role of small newspapers in relaying local news to readers. "It's a special field that fills a niche that the larger mediums don't," she says.

Bodega Bay Navigator
1580 Eastshore Road, Bodega Bay
(707) 875-3574

A weekly newspaper established in 1986, with a circulation of 1,400, the *Bodega Bay Navigator* comes out on Thursdays and is distributed through most of West County. Publisher and editor Joel Hack focuses on both community news and global issues and has printed some controversial or unusual stories that other small papers often shy away from. For example, the *Navigator* has published stories on teen pregnancy services, violence, and the plight of the Navajo nation.

Sonoma West Times & News
130 South Main Street, Suite 114, Sebastopol
(707) 823-7845
www.sonomawest.com

Locally owned and intimately focused, this paper covers Sebastopol and the Russian River area. Publisher Rollie Atkinson says the *Times & News* is "about our families, our towns, about the guy next door." Those towns are primarily Sebastopol, Bodega Bay, and Guerneville. Look for the paper each Wednesday.

Mendocino County

Fort Bragg Advocate-News
450 North Franklin Street, Fort Bragg
(707) 964-5642
www.advocate-news.com

Mendocino Beacon
(707) 937-5874
www.mendocinobeacon.com

Publisher Sharon Brewer and managing editor Katherine Lee handle both of these weeklies. Both papers trace their roots to the heydays of the lumber industry that gave birth to the towns. The *Mendocino Beacon-News* came first in 1877, followed by the *Advocate News* in 1889—both are now owned by the Donrey Media Group. Early news coverage focused on forests and shipping and sawmills. Today the slant is local with a strong appeal to tourists. The *Advocate* and *Beacon* are based in Fort Bragg, which has a population of 7,000; the *Beacon* serves the village of Mendocino, with its population of 1,000. Each covers news of the community, the arts, school affairs, and local personalities. One of the most popular features in both papers is the calendar of events.

Independent Coast Observer
38500 South Highway 1, Gualala
(707) 884-3501
www.mendonoma.com

Stephen McLaughlin has been publishing and editing this weekly paper for nearly 30 years. It covers the coastal area from Jenner to Elk. This is strictly a visitors' publication, offering news of upcoming events, art exhibits (with a rundown on some of the artists), and reviews of musical groups performing in Mendocino and elsewhere in the area. There are 3,000 copies printed each week and distributed to restaurants along the coast. A free supplement, *Destination Mendonoma*, is published once a year, in May.

Anderson Valley Advertiser
12451 Anderson Valley Road, Boonville
(707) 895-3016
www.pacificsites.com/~ava

The *AVA*'s banner displays three quotes. "Peace to the cottages! War on the palaces," from the French Revolution. "Be as radical as reality," from Lenin. And Pulitzer's: "Newspapers should have no friends." Published weekly by Bruce Anderson, a "socialist unabashed," the *AVA* comes out on Wednesdays and covers news of Anderson Valley, an area largely devoted to farming and vineyards. But Anderson also gives in-depth coverage to political matters in the valley, particularly to the activities of the board of supervisors, and often challenges political policies. Because some of his views incite strong reactions, he claims to get more mail than the big daily newspapers in the area. Circulation of this paper is 3,000.

Magazines

Wine Country Living
489 First Street, Sonoma
(707) 935–0111
www.winecountryliving.net

This magazine underwent a name change from its former moniker, *Appellation,* but it's still a four-color publication that publishes every two months and has a circulation of about 100,000. Its primary function is to document what one would probably call The Good Life as it is lived up and down the wine regions of the western United States. What it does best is show people having a swell time with a bottle of wine, with the pages filled with food (including recipes and restaurant reviews), wine, travel destinations, personality profiles, and general finery. There's also a terrific Wine Country map.

Sonoma North Bay Biz
3565 Airway Drive, Santa Rosa
(707) 575–8282
www.sonomanorthbaybiz.com

Norman Rosinski publishes and edits this glossy monthly magazine, impressive with its well-designed cover and artistic inside pages. It has provided 25 years of business intelligence in Sonoma County. It covers technology, real estate, and wine and other industries. An annual issue identifies the top 500 industries in the county, ranked by gross revenues. The magazine's annual wine issue also doubles as the official program of the Sonoma County Harvest Fair. Circulation is more than 7,000.

Radio Stations

Station List
Adult Contemporary
KSAY-98.5 FM
KTDE-100.5 FM
KVYN-99.3 FM
KWNE-94.5 FM
KXBX-98.3 FM
KZST-100.1 FM

Christian
KLVR-91.9 FM
KNDL-89.9 FM

Country
KFGY-92.9 FM
KQPM-105.9
KRPQ-104.9 FM
KUKI-103.3 FM

Jazz
KJZY-93.7 FM

News, Talk, Sports
KPMO-1300 AM
KSRO-1350 AM
KVON-1440 AM
KZYZ-91.5 FM

Oldies, Standards
KMFB-92.7 FM
KXBX-1270 AM

Public Radio
KRCB-90.9 and 91.1 FM
KZYX-90.7 FM

Rock
KMGG-97.7 FM (Rock oldies)
KMHX-104.1 FM (Alternative)
KNTI-99.5 FM (Light rock)
KOZT-95.3 (Classic rock)
KRSH-95.9 FM (Classic rock and blues)

Insiders' Tip

A discount of $50 on a hot-air balloon ride! Don't underestimate the savings of coupons. Pick up copies of the many complimentary advertising handouts that proliferate in Wine Country and check out the deals. Hey, $50 is 50 bucks.

KSRT-107.1 (Classic rock)
KSXY-98.7
KXFX-101.7 FM, 1250 AM

Spanish

KBBF-89.1 FM
KDAC-1230 AM
KGRP-100.9 FM
KLLK-1250 AM
KRRS-1460 AM
KTOB-1490 AM
KUKI-1400 AM

Television

Station List

ABC: KGO Channel 7 (Napa, Sonoma, Mendocino, Lake)
CBS: KPIX Channel 5 (Napa, Sonoma, Mendocino, Lake); KOVR Channel 14 (Lake)
NBC: KNTV Channel 3 (Napa, Sonoma, Mendocino, Lake)
FOX: KTVU Channel 2 (Napa, Sonoma, Mendocino, Lake); KTXL Channel 12 (Lake)
PBS: KQED Channel 9 (Napa, Sonoma, Mendocino, Lake); KRCB Channel 22 (Sonoma)
UPN: KBHK Channel 44 (Napa, Sonoma, Mendocino) and Channel 11 (Lake)
Independents: KFTY Channel 50 (Sonoma, Mendocino)

Local Broadcast Channels

KFTY Channel 50 (Independent)
533 Mendocino Avenue, Santa Rosa
(707) 526-5050
www.newschannel50.com

Started in 1981 by Wichard Brown, then owner of the *Marin Independent Journal,* this station is now owned by Ackerley Broadcast Group, a Seattle-based advertising, sports, and entertainment conglomerate. KFTY serves the six counties just north of San Francisco (or, as they term it, "north of the Gate"). General programming includes news, movies, sitcoms, and public interest programs, with a special 30-minute North

Bay news program Monday through Friday at 7:00 P.M. and a one-hour news program at 10:00 P.M.

This station is intensely community-oriented and sponsors the Luther Burbank Rose Parade (see our Festivals and Annual Events chapter) each spring, along with a health, fitness, and safety series at the end of June.

KRCB Channel 22 (Public TV)
5850 Labath Avenue, Rohnert Park
(707) 585-8522

This public television station was started in December 1984 and now reaches the counties of Sonoma, Napa, Mendocino, and Lake, plus portions of Alameda, Marin, Solano, and Contra Costa Counties. It even broadcasts to San Francisco.

Programming is typical public television fare: *Sesame Street, Nova, This Old House,* news programs, a North Bay Journal featuring regional business news, and *Expressions,* which features local artists. It has pledge drives and an auction in November (its affiliate, KRCB-91.1 FM, is also listener-supported).

Cable TV

Napa County
Sonoma County

Comcast Corp.
(800) 945-2288
www.comcast.com

If you live in one of these two counties, this is your cable TV provider. Comcast (formerly AT&T Broadband) has the monopoly in a huge chunk of Wine Country, and reviews of its service are mixed. But there's no sign it will change anytime soon. Comcast offers standard cable and digital services in several packages. Digital packages begin at about $45 and go up to $75. Basic cable begins at about $37; add an "All-Star" package of several premium movie channels and the monthly bill jumps to around $67.

Mendocino County

Adelphia Communications
1060 North State Street, Ukiah
(707) 462–8737
1260 North Main Street, Fort Bragg
(800) 626–6299
www.adelphia.net

Adelphia provides two different levels of basic cable TV service with slightly varied channel lineups to customers in Ukiah, Willits, and Fort Bragg. Basic service runs about $28 per month; their digital service adds about 19 more channels to the basic lineup.

Central Valley Cable
38951 South Highway 1, Gualala
(707) 884–4111

This cable TV provider services the coastal region of Mendocino County, including Gualala, Point Arena, and Manchester, with some service to Sea Ranch residents in northern Sonoma County. Their basic cable service offers about 51 channels to subscribers; digital service is not an option at this time.

Worship

Every now and again some wise guy offers a variation on a witticism we've heard too many times before: "Give the United States a good shake-up, and everything loose will land in California."

We might not like the word "loose," but we are proud of the open-minded climate that has brought a wonderful diversity to California. It manifests itself in many ways—including the way we worship. Here in Wine Country, where a certain sense of spontaneity dominates the culture, an amazingly eclectic assortment of houses of worship has taken root and prospered. In Sonoma County alone, with a thinly spread population of about 458,600 (no larger than a good-sized American city), the Yellow Pages list nearly 80 different faiths.

That would be in line with figures gathered at the turn of the century, when it was revealed that Sonoma County had more churches than any other county in the state except San Francisco. The zeal of the early religious organizers and preachers sustained the pioneers and laid a firm foundation for the church-building of the future. Although the earliest religious activity had been the domain of the Spanish missionaries—particularly under the direction of Fr. Jose Altimira, who established the mission in Sonoma—that system broke down when the young republic of Mexico secularized the missions in the 1830s, leaving a religious vacuum (see our History chapter). But when the first American families started to move into the Sonoma and Napa valleys early in the 1860s to establish farms and businesses, organized religion moved apace. Some of the churches built in those times remain. Many have been designated historic landmarks, their congregations dedicated to keeping the coffers filled and the clapboard freshly painted.

Napa County

The story of spirituality in Napa County—or, more accurately, of European-rooted religion—is sprinkled with visionaries, hard knocks, and roustabouts. Fittingly, the tale more or less begins with the Gold Rush. Among the starry-eyed prospectors who gravitated to California in 1849 was James Milton Small, an ordained minister of the Cumberland Presbyterian Church. In the fall of 1850, Small gave up on gold and moved to Napa to save souls, preaching to early settlers in the dining room of a boarding house.

Three years later the national Presbyterian Board of Missionaries sent the Rev. J. C. Herron from Philadelphia to the Napa Valley. He sermonized in the old Court House, a trying experience according to church records.

It was in reaction to the poor conditions in the Court House that the Presbyterians built the first church in Napa city in 1855, at a time when white settlers were true pioneers. After the congregation moved its facilities a couple of years later, the old edifice was reduced to service as a paint shop. In 1858 it was purchased by a group of Black Methodists, who splintered from their white congregation, moved the structure to Washington Street, and called it the African Methodist Church. That church is gone, but a bell purchased for $600 by the main Presbyterian congregation in 1868 announces the hour of prayer even today, at the First Presbyterian Church at 1333 Third Street in Napa. Rev. Richard Wylie was the pastor of First Presbyterian when that bell was acquired, and he remained in the pulpit until 1921—a remarkable tenure of 54

The Sea Ranch Chapel is a tiny, nondenominational sanctuary for reflection and spiritual renewal. Built in 1985, the chapel has a cedar roof with a distinctive bronze spire that offers inspiration in a peaceful setting. PHOTO: JEAN SAYLOR DOPPENBERG

years, minus a couple of years he spent in Europe recuperating from illness.

Soon after the original Napa temple had been raised, the Presbyterians built a church in St. Helena. On July 26, 1873, somebody tried to burn it down, fastening bags saturated with coal oil up the length of the belfry rope and setting them ablaze. The fire was discovered and dampened before any real damage was done, but the relief was short-lived: The building was destroyed by fire in February 1874. Two years before that, a Presbyterian church had been erected in Calistoga.

Rev. S. D. Simonds is said to have been the first Methodist Episcopal preacher to reside in Napa Valley. That was about 1851. A year later Rev. Asa White delivered a sermon in a grove of redwood trees known as Paradise Park. The grove was part of the Tucker farm, about halfway between St. Helena and Calistoga, and it became the site of the first church in Napa Valley in 1853.

The Methodists built a separate church in Napa in 1856. The Rev. James Corwin, besides his evangelical duties, happened to be engineer at a sawmill north of St. Helena. The owner of the mill, Erwin Kellogg, donated use of his facility long enough for the Rev. Corwin to cut the logs and have them hauled to Napa for the new church. The Methodists also laid the foundation for a church in Calistoga in 1868, but construction didn't go much further. The railroad wanted the land, and there wasn't much the railroad didn't get. Sam Brannan donated another site to the congregation, and the church, Calistoga's first, was completed in 1869. It also served as the local primary school for a year.

In 1917 a new Methodist church opened in Napa. During the dedication service, it was reported that $31,000 had been raised for building the church—$5,000 short of the total cost. Addressing the congregation, Bishop Adna Leonard said, "A collection is now in order. This is a courteous congregation. I am going to ask you to remain until the benediction is reached." Leonard's lock-the-doors-until-we're-solvent strategy worked. He marked pledges on a blackboard and eventually reached the $36,000 goal. That building

stands today, a registered landmark of English Gothic architecture.

The Christian Church appeared in the valley in 1853, when J. P. McCorkle preached under a madrone tree in Yountville. His flock founded a church in Browns Valley in 1865, then moved to Napa in 1870, setting up shop in the building that previously had housed the town's first newspaper, the *Napa Reporter*. Later that year they purchased land at the corner of Pearl and Randolph Streets and built a proper church. (The American Legion Post is there now.)

The Roman Catholics held occasional services in Margaret McEnerny's boarding house on Main Street in Napa in the mid-1850s. (The priest would ride over from the Sonoma Mission.) Napa merchant George Cornwell, a non-Catholic, donated land on Main Street, and St. John the Baptist Church was erected in 1858. It's not the St. John's you see today, however. Father Slattery built a beautiful Gothic church in 1881. Unfortunately, that church was leveled in the 1960s. The current edifice was built in 1957.

The first Catholic Church in St. Helena was built in 1866; actually, it was the remodeled home of a Mrs. Sheehan at Oak Avenue and Tainter Street. When the local parishioners got a new church in 1878, they paid $72 for the old bell from the Napa Courthouse. It became the first bell in St. Helena. Separate Catholic parishes were formed in Calistoga in 1915 and Yountville in 1920.

The Seventh-day Adventist Church held its first meetings in 1873, in tents at the site of what is today known as Fuller Park in Napa, and a church was dedicated in the winter of 1873–1874. That building still stands, after many alterations, on the corner of Church and Second Streets.

In 1877, Dr. Merritt Kellogg was busy laying the groundwork for what would become the St. Helena Sanitarium. One of his builders, Frank Lamb, remembered hearing Ellen G. White remark at an Adventist meeting in Oakland, "We are going to have a health institution on the Pacific coast." The famed mystic (her visions in the 1860s called Adventists to adopt the message of health reform) didn't know exactly where, but "we had to go across water to get to it." Kellogg, in need of funding, immediately invited White and her husband to St. Helena for a view of his site. White said she had seen the terrain in her visions; this must be the place. She purchased eight acres next to Kellogg's and helped turn the area into an Adventist stronghold.

The history of Calistoga, meanwhile, is inexorably entwined with the Church of Jesus Christ of Latter-Day Saints, for Sam Brannan, that iconoclastic founding father and California's first millionaire, was a Mormon. After sailing around the Cape with a church group in the 1840s, Brannan hung onto the collected tithings. He wanted San Francisco to be the center of Mormon culture, not Salt Lake City. Brigham Young saw otherwise, and he eventually excommunicated Brannan for absconding with those funds.

The first LDS church in the valley was in St. Helena, adjacent to where that town's current Mormon church stands on Spring Street.

Other early arrivals included Christ (Episcopal) Church, organized in 1858. One of the church's earliest rectors was Rev. William Goodwin, inventor of the dry plate used in early photographic processes. Goodwin, it's said, helped make a multimillionaire out of George Eastman.

It wasn't just proper townsfolk who received the Lord's word, either. The Oat Hill Quicksilver Mine, in the rocky mountains east of Calistoga, offered diggers weekly church and Sunday school. Nor was worship confined to English speakers. Second-language services are a common occurrence today, but they aren't a recent invention. St. John Evangelical Lutheran Church gave sermons in German in the early 1900s. And even before that, in 1879, Napa was one of only two California cities to have a Chinese mission. Five evenings a week, local Chinese laborers were given instruction in English and Christianity, first in the chapel of the sponsoring Presbyterian Church, then in an old brick building on Franklin Street that was rented for $50 a year.

By 1963, Napa County counted some 37 separate churches, representing 20 denominations. Today, it's more like 70 churches and 40 denominations, not to mention the many spiritual individualists who defy traditional classification.

Sonoma County

A zealous young Spanish priest, Father Jose Altimira, was the first to bring Christianity to these parts. He came to what is now Sonoma County in 1823 to establish the Mission San Francisco de Solano, northernmost in a chain of missions spaced along California's coast. Despite the overthrow of the Spanish rulers in Mexico, Altimira was nothing if not enthusiastic, and he convinced his colleagues in the church that the area would be a better climate than San Francisco for the Native American converts.

Altimira's mission building was not impressive—a flimsy wooden structure that was swept twice by fire before achieving its present, fireproof adobe state. The Catholic Church's plan was to convey missions to the Native Americans they converted and trained, and within six years, Altimira claimed 1,000 converts.

The mission would not last (the Mexican government issued a decree in 1834 that all church properties were to be "secularized," or confiscated), but the influences of this early presence of organized religion are still evident today.

A small Russian Orthodox chapel was built on the coast in western Sonoma County about the time the Spanish secularized their missions. The small wooden chapel was a part of the Russian American Company's settlement at Fort Ross (see our History chapter). The Russians abandoned the fort in 1841, taking all the icons from the chapel with them, leaving behind only a large bell, candelabra, candlestand, and a lectern.

The chapel successfully withstood the ravages of time until the 1906 earthquake caved in its walls and reduced its foundation to rubble. The California legislature granted funds to rebuild the church in 1916, and timbers from some of the other remaining original buildings were used to reconstruct the chapel.

A Russian Orthodox priest arrives at historic Fort Ross to perform an annual consecration rite. PHOTO: JOHN NAGIECKI

The Russians had come and gone by the time other church activity began to stir in the established city of Sonoma. In approximately 1859, Congregationalists founded Cumberland Presbyterian College, a learning center where services were also sometimes held. But some distance from the village there lived a rancher named Edwin Sutherland who decided he would start his own church under the protecting branches of a large live oak tree on his property. He had five children, his sister across the road had six, and with the children of a few neighbors he established the Big Tree Sunday School in his own backyard.

Within three years, Sutherland began forming a church in the village. It would be called the First Congregational Church of Sonoma. That church still stands today, though in a different location, at 252 West Spain Street.

Conducting church services outside was actually not uncommon in those days of circuit-riding preachers. As early as 1852, on a ranch 6 miles from what would become Santa Rosa, the circuit-riding Rev. Stephen Riley helped form a congregation of Baptists, using the home of rancher Martin Hudson as a Sunday morning place of worship. When the congregation grew too large for the Hudson home, preacher and flock moved outdoors to the banks of a river, under the spreading branches of a large live oak. Winter rains and wandering cattle, however, helped take the luster off outdoor worship, and the congregation raised enough money to build a proper church, the Lebanon Baptist, which eventually merged with the First Baptist Church.

For years, one of the lesser known secrets about First Baptist Church was that it had been built out of a single 3,000-year-old redwood tree. The tree, 275 feet high and 18 feet in diameter, came from a ranch near Guerneville. The congregation had been unaware of the church's unique status until 1900, when a member, attorney Thomas Butts, told his story. He had been employed by a Guernevillle mill at the time the tree was felled. The mill's owner, knowing the intended purpose of the tree, personally monitored every step of the milling process to ensure the wood wasn't mingled with other lumber.

In 1939 Robert Ripley, a church member, featured the church in his "Believe It Or Not" column and gave it instant fame. For many years, the Church Of One Tree, at 492 Sonoma Avenue in Santa Rosa, housed the Robert Ripley Museum. Although it started as a Baptist church, One Tree became a church for many faiths, and on any given Sunday as many as 5,000 people worshipped there—as many as 10 services were offered there each week. Finally it was necessary to break up the flock. Two of today's Baptist congregations in Santa Rosa, the Community Baptist Church at 1620 Sonoma Avenue and the First Baptist Church at 3300 Sonoma Avenue, trace their roots to the church Ripley attended.

Members of a Petaluma Baptist church achieved fame of a different sort by installing a certain bell in their belfry, the legend of which still lingers. Having learned of a bell for sale in San Francisco,

a committee was dispatched to purchase what was said to be the sweetest-sounding instrument in the land. On arrival, they learned the bell had been used by vigilantes during Gold Rush days to announce the hanging of another lawless rascal, but the group bought it anyway for $550. It is said the bell's tolling could be heard for 12 miles.

The 1870s and 1880s saw tremendous expansion of church activity in Sonoma County. Denominations sprang up like dogs to the dinner bell, including Methodists, Baptists, Presbyterians, Episcopalians, and a sizable number of fundamentalist groups.

In the early days of frontier religion, most congregations were served by a circuit rider, a pastor who tended many flocks and spent most of his life on horseback. Pity the Rev. Isaac Owen, a Methodist minister, whose circuit included 10 congregations from Sonoma to Bodega and everything else up to the Russian River. One of the most renowned preachers of Sonoma County was the Rev. James Woods, who established a Presbyterian church in Healdsburg in 1858. His first congregation included Cyrus Alexander, who owned the entire valley north of Healdsburg and was himself a minister. In fact, it was Alexander who proposed that if the church could raise $1,000, he would put up $800 to secure the Methodist property on the plaza, which was up for sale. The lot was eventually purchased and the church was renovated and occupied.

The church remained there until 1932, when the Presbyterians and Methodists decided to join forces; one church had the building, the other had a large congregation. Together they created the Federated Church, which stands today at 555 Monte Vista Avenue in Healdsburg. At about the same time, the Church of Christ established a congregation in Healdsburg, followed by the Seventh-day Adventists and the Episcopalians.

In Santa Rosa, the first semblance of a Catholic church (a wooden building with eight pews) was erected in 1860 on a lot donated by one of Gen. Vallejo's relatives, Julio Carrillo. For the next 15 years, a priest came up from Marin County once a

Insiders' Tip

Twice each year, on Memorial Day and the Fourth of July, the Russian Orthodox Church conducts services at the chapel at Fort Ross. The events generally feature the extraordinary voices of a Russian choir from San Francisco and a colorful procession to the nearby cemetery to consecrate the graves of the old Russian settlers.

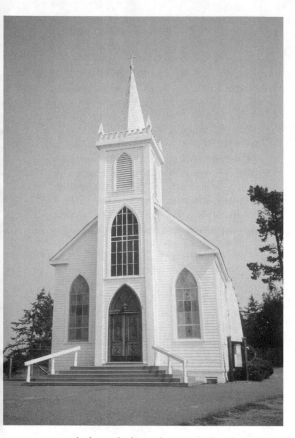

Perched overlooking the town of Bodega is St. Teresa's Catholic Church. PHOTO: JEAN SAYLOR DOPPENBERG

dist, Baptist, Catholic—have now splintered into dozens of churches. It started during the Civil War when Southern Methodists and Southern Baptists started their own congregations to denote their sympathies with the South. Today there are American Baptists, Independent Baptists, Fundamental Baptists, and GARBC Baptists. We have various branches of Presbyterians including Korean Western. We have Buddhist and Soto Zen centers, and we have Pentecostal, Orthodox Eastern, New Age churches, and a group called Metropolitan Community, plus a Church of God of Prophecy and the Foursquare Gospel.

If it is a similar upwelling of faith and devotion that resides in all these houses of worship, rest assured that the North Coast allows each of its citizens a unique way of describing it.

Mendocino County

A rough bunch of citizens populated the Mendocino Coast in 1854. The Gold Rush had waned and lumber was the new booming industry in need of lots of strong backs. Single men by the hundreds poured in from everywhere to work in the mills.

This was a hard-living breed, and any parson who sought to bring religion to them necessarily possessed a rare courage and tenacity. In 1854, the first Protestant services in this infant village on Big River took place in the cookhouse of the Mendocino Lumber Company. The first ministers who came to preach in Mendocino on an itinerant basis were Methodists, and it was four years before visiting ministers of any other persuasion showed up.

By 1859, eight determined members from the community had applied to the Presbyterian denomination for status as an established congregation, and a mere nine years later they built a church. It was a lovely little white church, in the Gothic style, designed by the same architect who designed the State Capitol in Sacramento. Today, the Mendocino Presbyterian Church is one of the first structures to catch your eye as you enter the village of Mendocino.

month to offer Mass at St. Rose. Finally, in 1876, a new parish formed that included Sebastopol, Healdsburg, Cloverdale, and Guerneville. The parish's most popular priest was Fr. John Conway, loved for his sense of humor. He stayed for 37 years.

Today, St. Rose parish serves as the mother church in Santa Rosa, with a seating capacity of 500. The church that was built in 1900—while Fr. Conway was there—still stands as a historic monument, but it is empty and unused, declared unsafe in earthquake conditions. Still grand, it is now surrounded by a new church that wraps around it like a boomerang. The new building at 398 10th Street is stunning, with walls of colored glass.

Churches that once fell neatly into a half-dozen denominations—mainly Metho-

Now a California Historic Landmark, the church also is listed in the Federal Registry of Historic Places. From its original eight charter members, it has grown to a membership of 230—this oldest of California's still-active Presbyterian churches is still vigorous and young. Guided tours are conducted on Saturdays between 10:00 A.M. and noon, from July 4 through Labor Day.

Perhaps the first church to be established in Fort Bragg was the First Baptist Church at the corner of East Pine and North Franklin Streets. Like most early churches, the congregation first met at a home in nearby Caspar, beginning in 1878. By 1887 a formal church with a handsome, tall steeple was under construction on land donated by the Fort Bragg Lumber Company.

That church is still there, though it would be hard to identify it. In 1911, the building was put on rollers, pushed farther back on the lot, and turned to face east instead of south. A new church was built right on top of the old. The original church now serves as a social room and Sunday school. One of the grand features of this early church was a beautiful, 1,200-pound bell, purchased in England and shipped around Cape Horn. It was said the bell rang so clearly you could hear it all the way to Caspar—several miles to the south—on a windy day. But by 1932 the clapper had worn out and had to be replaced—unfortunately by a clapper so heavy it cracked the bell. Another clapper, furnished by the fire department, would fit only upside down. At last the bell came down and was set behind the church, where weeds soon overgrew it. Rescued by a church member, it is now proudly displayed in front of the church with a plaque on it. The present church holds 300 people and is a rare example of a Protestant church built in the California Mission style.

The First Methodist Church at 270 North Pine Street in Ukiah originally served two congregations—one dating to 1850, the other to 1857. In 1926, they united and built a new church. When fire ravaged that building, they put another right on top of it—a brick building with grounds that spread out over a full city block. (They're still finding rubble from the old church under the sanctuary.) Its steeple stands out as you come into town on U.S. 101.

From the beginning, the great fame of this church came from the vesper chimes played high in the steeple. Every day someone mounted the stairs to play the chimes at 5:00 P.M., a welcome signal to office workers across town that it was time to go home. The chimes wore out (as chimes will), but have been replaced by a programmed version.

Perhaps the most beautiful of Mendocino's spiritual centers is the Sagely City of Ten Thousand Buddhas, set among 488 acres of groves and meadows in Ukiah's lovely Valley at Talmage. The campus consists of 70 buildings, including the Dharma Realm Buddhist University (see our Education and Child Care chapter), on approximately 80 landscaped acres. An atmosphere of quiet peace pervades the City of Ten Thousand Buddhas. Everyone shares a common goal: the sincere pursuit of spiritual truth and value, along with a desire to become wiser and more compassionate.

Incorporated in the United States in 1959, the Dharma Realm Buddhist Association seeks to spread the teachings of the Buddha in America. In 1966 the Most Venerable Master Hsuan Hua set up a center for Buddhist study in San Francisco. It has been moved to the Ukiah Valley to become one of California's foremost Buddhist centers. Serious-minded individuals from all walks of life may attend intensive recitation or bowing sessions and meditation retreats. The Dharma Realm Buddhist Association offers daily and weekly lectures and ceremonies, classes, vegetarian meals, and celebrations of Buddhist holidays.

Index

AARP 55 Alive/Mature Driving, 356
AARP (American Association of Retired Persons), 355–56
AARP Senior Community Service Employment Program, 356
Above the Clouds, 84
Abrams House Inn, 89
Adelphia Communications, 395
Admiral William Standley State Recreation Area, 284
Adobe Christian Preschool/Daycare, 371–72
Adobe Creek Golf & Country Club, 290
Adobe Drug, 259
Adult Day Services of Napa Valley, 355
Adventures Aloft, 214–15
Aegis of Napa, 362
Aerostat Adventures, 215
Agate Cove Inn, 95
Air Flambouyant, 215
airplane tours, 214
Airport Cinema 8, 150
airports, 18–20
airport shuttles, 20–21
air travel, 17–21
Albion River Inn, 68
Albion River Inn Restaurant, 141
Alice's Restaurant, 138
Alicia Pool, 297
Alinder Gallery, 276
All Aboard Adventures, 315
All Seasons Cafe, 125
alternative health care, 387. See also health care
Ambrose Bierce House, The, 78++79
Amelia Claire, 244
American Association of Retired Persons (AARP), 355–56
AMF Boulevard Lanes, 293
Amtrak, 21
Ana's Cantina, 146
Anchor Charters, 212
Anchor Lodge Motel, 69
Anderson Creek Inn, 92
Anderson Valley Advertiser, 392

Anderson Valley Brewing Company, 153
Anderson Valley Chamber of Commerce, 11
Anderson Valley Historical Society Museum, 211
Andrews Hall, 263
Angwin Airport, 19
animals, 51–52
Annadel State Park, 279–80, 294
Annie's Jughandle Beach Inn, 97
annual events, 218–39
Antique Fair, 254
Antique Harvest, 256
Antique Marketplace & Annex, 255
antiques, 254–57. See also shopping
Antique Society, 256
Antique Tours, 25
apartments. See rentals, housing
appellations, 154–55
Apple Blossom Festival, 222
Applewood Inn & Restaurant, 90–91, 138
April in Carneros, 221
Arbor Guest House, 75
area overview, 3–13
    Lake County, 299–300
    Mendocino County, 8–9, 12–13
    Napa County, 3–5
    Sonoma County, 5–8
Arena Theatre, 150
Argus Courier, 390
Armida Winery, 182–83
Armstrong Redwoods State Reserve, 283
A'Roma Roasters and Coffeehouse, 147
Arrowood Vineyards & Winery, 179
Arroyo Real Estate, 345
Art and All That Jazz, 249
Artesa Winery, 160
Artful Eye, The, 245
Art in the Redwoods, 230
Art on Main, 271
arts and culture, 262–76
    Mendocino County, 265–66, 269, 274–76

Napa County, 263, 266–68, 269–72
Sonoma County, 263–65, 268–69,
    272–73
attractions, 196–217
    Lake County, 303–6
    Mendocino County, 207, 210–13
    Napa County, 196–99, 214–15,
        215–16
    Sonoma County, 199, 201–7, 215,
        216–17
Auberge du Soleil, 99–100, 121–22
Austin Creek State Recreation
    Area, 283
automobile travel, 14–17
Avalon Players, 263–64
Awards, The, 220

Baechtel Creek Inn, 67
Bale Grist Mill State Historic Park, 197
Balloons Above the Valley, 214
balloon tours, 213–15
bars and clubs, 145–50
Bartholomew Park Winery, 175
baseball, 316–17. See also sports,
    spectator
basketball, 319. See also sports,
    spectator
Bastille Day, 227
Bay View Restaurant, 137
Beaded Nomad, The, 240
Bear Flag Inn, 82
Bear Moon Clothing, 246
Bear Republic Brewing Company,
    148, 152
Beaulieu Vineyard, 168–69
Beazley House, The, 74
Beck & Taylor, 345–46
bed-and-breakfast inns, 72–97
    Mendocino County, 91–97
    Napa County, 72–83
    Sonoma County, 83–91
Belle de Jour Inn, 86
Beltane Ranch, 84
Belvedere Winery, 183
Benicia Pool, 297
Bennett Valley Golf Course, 290–91
Benziger Family Winery, 179
Beringer Celebrity Golf Classic, 225
Beringer Vineyards, 171–72
Berryessa Lions Annual Lizard Races,
    224–25

Berryessa Senior Citizens, 357
Berry's Saw Mill, 207
Best Western Dry Creek Inn, 64
Best Western Inn at the Vines, 55
Best Western Petaluma Inn, 61
Best Western Sonoma Valley Inn, 60
Bicycle Factory, The, 292
bicycle rentals, 292–93. See also parks
    and recreation
bicycle road races, 323. See also sports,
    spectator
Bicycle Trax, 292
bicycling, 294–95. See also parks and
    recreation
Big 3 Diner at The Fairmont Sonoma
    Mission Inn, The, 128
Bikeman Bicycle Touring, 216–17
Bistro Don Giovanni, 116–17
Bistro Jeanty, 119–20
Bistro Ralph, 134
Blair House, 95
Blessing of the Balloons, 219
Blue Violet Mansion, The, 72–73
Bodega Bay Area Chamber of
    Commerce, 11
Bodega Bay Fisherman's Festival, 222
Bodega Bay Kayak, 313–14
Bodega Bay Lodge Resort, 65
Bodega Bay Navigator, 392
Bodega Bay Sportfishing Center, 313
Bodega Bay Surf Shack, 313
Bodega Harbour Golf Links, 291
Boggs Mountain, 297
Bonaventura Balloon Company, 215
Bookends Book Store, 257
bookstores, 257, 259–61. See also shop-
    ping
Book Warehouse, 259
Bookworm, The, 260
Boonville Airport, 20
Bordeaux House, 76
Bothe-Napa Valley State Park,
    109–10, 278
Bouchon, 120
bowling, 293. See also parks and
    recreation
Brannan Cottage Inn, 81
Brannan's Grill, 125–26
Breakers Inn, 67
Brewery Gulch Inn, 94–95
brewpubs, 151–53, 303

Bridge School, The, 373
Brix, 120
Brookside Lodge Motel, The, 66
Brookside Vineyard Bed & Breakfast,
    75–76
Buena Vista Winery, 175–76
Burbank, Luther, 208–9
Burgundy House Inn, 76–77
Burke's Russian River Canoe Trips,
    312–13
bus service, 21
Butter and Egg Days, 222

cable TV, 394–95. *See also* media
Cafe Beaujolais, 142
Cafe Sarafomia, 126
calendar, vineyard, 192
California Carnivores, 249
California HIV/AIDS Hotline, 386
California Properties, 345
California Smokers Helpline, 386
California State Park Information, 278
California Welcome Center, 10
California Western Railroad (Skunk
    Train), 213, 333–34
California Wine Tours, 26
Calistoga Beer and Sausage Festival, 235
Calistoga Bookstore, The, 257
Calistoga Chamber of Commerce, 10
Calistoga Inn & Restaurant, 59,
    126, 146
Calistoga Inn Restaurant and Brewery,
    151–52
Calistoga Massage Center, The, 106–7
Calistoga Pottery, 244
Calistoga Realty Co., 346
Calistoga restaurants, 125–28
Calistoga Roastery, 126
Calistoga Spa Hot Springs, 102
Calistoga Speedway, 321
Calistoga Village Inn & Spa, 102–3
Calistoga Wine Stop, 194
Calla Lily Fine Linens, 243
Calpine Geothermal Plant Tour, 305
Cal Skate, 330
Caltrans Road/Weather
    Information, 278
Camellia Inn, 86
Cameo Cinema, 150
camping, 109–15
    Mendocino County, 113–15

    Napa County, 109–10
    Sonoma County, 110–13
Candlelight Inn, 74–75
Candy Cellar, The, 245
Cantina, The, 148
Canyon Road Winery, 187
Cape Fear Cafe, 138
Cardinal Newman High School, 372
Carneros at The Lodge at Sonoma, 128
Carneros Creek, 159
Carols in the Caves, 238
Carolyn Parr Nature Museum, 327
Carriage Occasions, 217
Casa Montessori School, 370
Caspar Headlands State Beach and
    Reserve, 287
Caspar Inn, The, 149
Catahoula Restaurant & Saloon, 126
Catch a Canoe & Bicycles Too, 292
Ca'Toga Galleria D'Arte, 272
Cat & The Fiddle, 255
Cedar Gables Inn, 73
Cedar Roughs, 296
Celadon, 117
Centers for Disease Control and
    Prevention, 386
Central Valley Cable, 395
Century 21, 350
Century 21 Alpha Realty, 344
Chainsaw Sculpture
    Championship, 236
Chamber Music in Napa Valley, 267
Chanslor Guest Ranch and Stables,
    293, 295
Chardonnay Golf Club, 289
Chardonnay Lodge, 55
Charles Krug Winery, 172
Charles M. Schulz Museum and
    Research Center, 205
Charles M. Schulz-Sonoma County
    Airport, 19
Chateau, The, 56
Chateau Montelena, 166, 175
Chateau Souverain, 187
Chateau St. Jean, 180
Chelsea Antiques, 255
Cherry Pie Criterium, 323
Cheshire Bookshop, 261
Chez Marie, 138–39
Chez Peyo, 139
child care, 379–80

children's activities. *See* kidstuff
Children's Bell Tower, 206–7
Chimney Rock Winery, 161
Chocolate Cabernet Fantasy, 219
Christopher Queen Galleries, 273
Christopher's Inn, 79
churches. *See* worship
Churchill Manor Bed & Breakfast
    Inn, 73
Cindy's Backstreet Kitchen, 122
Cinnabar Performing Arts Theater, 268
Cinnamon Bear Bed & Breakfast, 78
Citrus Fair, 219
Clear Lake Queen, 305
climate, 49–50
Cline Cellars, 176
Clos du Bois, 187
Clos Du Val, 161
Clos Pegase Winery, 163, 174, 271–72
Clover Cinemas, 150
Cloverdale Heritage Days, 226
Cloverdale Memorial Pool, 297
Cloverdale Municipal Airport, 20
Cloverdale Reveille, 391–92
Cloverdale Senior Multi-Purpose
    Center, 359–60
Club FAB, 149
Clubhouse Family Fun Center,
    The, 328
clubs and bars, 145–50
Coast Cinemas, 150
Coast Getaways, 71
Coldwell Banker, 349
Coldwell Banker Brokers of the
    Valley, 344
Cole's Chop House, 117
College of the Redwoods, 375
colleges
    four-year, 376
    two-year, 374–75
college sports, 324–25. *See also* sports,
    spectator
Comcast Corp., 394
Comfort Inn, 59
Community Care AIDS Project of
    Mendocino and Lake Counties, 386
Community Child Care Council, 380
Community Resources for Children,
    379–80
Community Voice, The, 390
Compadres Mexican Bar & Grill, 120

Comprehensive Services for Older
    Adults, 354
Continental Lanes, 293
Continental Real Estate, 344
Copia: The American Center for Wine,
    Food, and the Arts, 196–97, 200–201
Copperfield's Books, 257, 260, 330
Copperfield's Cafe, 146
Coralee Barkela & Company, 350–51
Cosentino Winery, 165
Cotati Accordion Festival, 229
Cotati Chamber of Commerce, 10
Cottage Grove Inn, 81
Cottage Inn and Spa, The, 83
Council on Aging, 355
Country Inn at Fort Bragg, 97
Country Pine Antiques, 254
Courtyard, The, 251
Courtyard Santa Rosa by Marriott, 63
Cozy Corner Children's Center, 373
Crane Creek Regional Park, 279
Crane Park, 328
Crisis Line for the Handicapped, 386
Culinary Institute of America at
    Greystone, The, 377–78
Cultural Arts Council of Sonoma
    County, 273
culture. *See* arts and culture
Culver Mansion, 81
Cuvaison Winery, 174–75

dance and music, 266–69. *See also* arts
    and culture
Dance Central, 148
Davis Bynum Winery, 189
Day for the Queen at Silverado, 229
Days Inn, 66
day spas, 106–8. *See also* resorts
day trips, 335–40
    Lake Tahoe, 338–40
    Point Reyes National Seashore,
        335–37
    redwood forests, 337–38
Dean & DeLuca, 194, 242
Deep Valley Christian School, 373–74
Deja-Vu Hat Co., 253
Della Santina's, 128
De Loach Vineyards, 182
Dempsey's Sonoma Brewing
    Company, 152
Dental Referral, 386

Department of Alcohol and Drug Programs, 386
Depot Hotel Cucina Rustica, 128–29
Depot Park Museum, 199
Destination: Napa Valley Tours, 216
Deuce, 129
D&G Property Management, 348
Dharma Realm Buddhist University, 378–79
di Rosa Preserve, 269–70
Discovery Inn, 67
Distinctive Properties, 351
Distinctive Properties of Napa Valley, 346
Dixie Jazz Festival, 229
Domaine Carneros, 159
Domaine Chandon, 120, 164
Doran Regional Park, 111, 281
Double Decker Lanes, 293
DoubleTree Hotel, 62
Downtown Joe's, 145, 151
Dr. Wilkinson's Hot Springs, 101
Dreamweavers Theatre, 263
Dry Creek General Store, 134
Dry Creek Kitchen, 134–35
Dry Creek Vineyard, 184
Duchamp Hotel, 64
Dutch Henry, 173

Early Work, 329
educational opportunities for retirees, 364. See also retirement
education and child care, 366–80
    Lake County, 380
    Mendocino County, 368, 373–74, 375, 378–79, 380
    Napa County, 366–67, 368–70, 374, 376, 377–78, 379–80
    Sonoma County, 367–68, 371–73, 374–75, 376, 378, 380
Eel River, 310
Egghead's Restaurant, 143
El Bonita Motel, 57
El Dorado Hotel, 60
Elk Cove Inn, 93–94
Elms, The, 80
El Pueblo Inn, 60
Embassy Suites Napa Valley, 53–54
Empire College, 375
Enoteca Wine Shop, 194–95
Equus, 133

Erika Hills Antiques, 254
E. S. Wolf & Company, 353
Evans Airport Service, 20–21
Executive Limousine, 25
ExpressCare, 381

Faerie Ring Campground, 112–13
Fairfield Osborn Preserve, 279
Fairmont Sonoma Mission Inn & Spa, 103
Falcons Nest, 79–80
Family Wineries of Sonoma Valley, 180
Farmhouse Inn & Restaurant, The, 90, 139
Farm Trails, 252
fauna, 51–52
Felix and Louie's, 135
Fensalden Inn, 94
Fern Grove Cottages, 91
Ferrari-Carrano Vineyard & Winery, 185
Festival of Lights, 237
festivals and annual events, 218–39
Fetzer Valley Oaks Bed & Breakfast, 92
Fetzer Vineyards, 191
Fiddles & Cameras, 253
Fideaux, 243–44
Field Stone Winery, 187
Fiesta Patrias, 234–35
Fife's Resort, 66
film settings, 275
Flag Emporium, 246
Flamingo Resort Hotel & Fitness Center, 62, 147
Flatiron Grill, 126–27
flora, 50–51
Folie à Deux Winery, 172–73
football, 317–19. See also sports, spectator
Foothill Cafe, 117
Foothill House, 82
Foothills Adventist Elementary School, 370
Footlighters Little Theater, 212
Foppiano Vineyards, 183
Ford House Museum, 211–12
Ford House Visitor Center, 261
Forest Manor, 79
Forestville Chamber of Commerce and Visitors Center, 11
Fort Bragg
    history, 42

restaurants, 143–44
Fort Bragg Advocate-News, 392
Fort Bragg Cyclery, 293
Fort Bragg Leisure Time RV Park, 115
Fort Bragg Senior Center, 361
For the Shell of It, 253
Fort Ross Book & Gift Shop, 260
Fort Ross Living History Days, 228
Fort Ross Lodge, 66
Fort Ross State Historic Park, 207
Foster Grandparent Program, 365
Fountain Grove Inn, 62
Fourth of July Celebrations, 226
Foxtail Golf Club, 290
Franciscan Oakville Estate, 169
Frank Family Cellars, 173
Frank Howard Allen Realtors, 345, 349
Frank R. Howard Memorial
    Hospital, 385
Freemark Abbey Winery, 172
French Laundry, The, 120–21
Friends House, 363
Fun & Games, 328

Gables Inn, The, 85
Gaige House Inn, 84
Gallery Bookshop & Bookwinkle's
    Children's Books, 261
Garden Court Cafe & Bakery, 131
Garden Haven, 355
General's Daughter, The, 129
geology, 48–49
George Alexander House, 86
Getaway Adventures & Bike Shop, 216
Getaway Bike Shop, 292
Geyersville Chamber of Commerce, 11
Geyser Peak Winery, 187–88
Geyser Smokehouse, The, 135
Geyserville Inn, 64–65
Ghost Wineries Tour, 235–36
Gillwoods Restaurant, 122
Girl & the Fig, The, 129
Girl & the Gaucho, The, 131
Glass Mountain Inn, 78
Glendeven, 92–93
Glen Ellen
    history, 36–37
    restaurants, 131
Glen Ellen Inn Restaurant, 131
Glenelly Inn, 85
Gloria Ferrer Champagne Caves, 176

Gloriana Opera Company, 266
Golden Gate Transit, 24
Golden Goose, The, 251
Golden Haven Hot Springs, 102
Golden State Warriors, 319
golf, 288–92, 320–21. See also parks and
    recreation; sports, spectator
Gondola Servizio, 214
gondola tours, 214
Goodtime Bicycle Company, The, 292
Goosecross Cellars, 165
Grace Hudson Museum and Sun
    House, 207, 210, 251
Graeser Winery, 175
Grape Leaf Inn, 86–87
Gravenstein Apple Fair, 230
Great Rubber Ducky Race, 224
Green Valley Cafe, 123
Greenwood Creek State Beach, 286
Greenwood Pier Cafe, 149
Greenwood Pier Inn, 67–68
Greenwood Ridge Vineyards, 192
Greenwood State Park Visitors
    Center, 211
Greyhound Bus Lines, 21
Grey Whale Inn, The, 97
Grgich Hills Cellar, 169
Griewe Real Estate, 350
Gualala Arts Center, 274
Gualala Hotel, 67
Gualala Point Regional Park, 112,
    282–83
Gualala River, 310–11
Guenoc and Langtry Estate
    Vineyards, 302
Guest House Museum, 213
Gundlach Bundschu Winery, 177

Hakusan Sake Gardens, 196
Hand Goods, 249–50
Handicapped Special Services, 278
Handley Cellars, 193
Hannah Winery, 188
Haraszthy, Agoston, 31
Harbor House, 94
Harbor Lite Lodge, 69
Harvest Inn, 58
Harvest Market, 253
Hawthorn Inn & Suites, 55
Haydon Street Inn, 87
Headlands Coffeehouse, 149–50

Healdsburg Bar & Grill, 135–36
Healdsburg Chamber of Commerce, 10
Healdsburg Classics, 255–56
Healdsburg District Hospital, 384–85
Healdsburg Inn on the Plaza, 87
Healdsburg Municipal Airport, 20
Healdsburg Municipal Swimming
    Pool, 297
Healdsburg Municipal Transit, 24
Healdsburg Museum, 206
Healdsburg restaurants, 134–37
Healdsburg Senior Center, 359
Healdsburg Tribune, 391
Health and Harmony Music and Arts
    Festival, 225–26
health care, 381–87
    Mendocino County, 385, 386
    Napa County, 381–82, 382–83, 385,
        386, 387
    Sonoma County, 382, 383, 386, 387
Heaven on Wheels, 26
Heirloom Tomato Festival, 234
Heitz Wine Cellar, 170
Held-Poage Memorial Home and
    Library, 210
Helen Putnam Regional Park, 279
Hendy Woods State Park, 113–14, 285
Hennessey House, 75
Henry Joseph Gallery, 270
Heritage House, 68–69, 141
Hess Collection, The, 161
Hess Collection Winery, The, 270
Hidden Gardens Tour, 223
Hideaway Cottages, 81
High Tide Surf Shop, 314
Hillcrest B&B, 82–83
Hill House Inn, 68
Hi-Seas Inn, 70
Hispanic Chamber of Commerce of
    Sonoma County, 10
history, 28–42
    Lake County, 300–301
    Mendocino County, 39–42
    Napa County, 28–30, 32–33
    Sonoma County, 33–39
hockey, 319–20. See also sports,
    spectator
Holiday Candlelight Tour, 238
Holiday Crafts Fair and Open
    House, 239
Holly Golightly Goes to Italy, 243

Hometown Harvest Festival, 236
Honeybee Pool, 297
Honor Mansion, 87
Hope-Bosworth House, 89
Hope-Merrill House, 89
Hop Kiln Winery, 189–90
Hopland Antiques, 257
Hopland Chamber of Commerce, 11
Hopland Inn, A California
    Roadhouse, 91
horseback riding, 293, 295. See also
    parks and recreation
horse racing, 323–24. See also sports,
    spectator
hospice care, 385, 387. See also
    health care
Hospice of Napa Valley, 385, 387
Hospice of Petaluma, 387
hospitals, 382–85. See also health care
Hotel D'Amici, 59
Hotel Healdsburg, 64
Hotel La Rose, 63
hotels, motels, and inns, 53–71
    Mendocino County, 66–70
    Napa County, 53–60
    Sonoma County, 60–66
Hotel St. Helena, 58–59
hotlines, 386
Hot Pepper Jelly Company, 253
housing. See real estate; rentals,
    housing
Howarth Park, 330–31
Hoyman-Browe Studio, 250–51
hunting, 295–97. See also parks and
    recreation
Hurd Beeswax Candles, 244
Husch Vineyards, 193
Hydro Bar & Grill, 127, 146

I. Wolk Gallery, 271
Images Fine Art, 270–71
IMG Home, 244
Incredible Records & CDs, 249
Independent Coast Observer, 392
Indian Springs, 101–2
Infineon Raceway, 201, 321–22
Ink House, The, 77
Inn at Occidental, The, 90
Inn at Schoolhouse Creek, 95
Inn at Southbridge, The, 58
Inn at the Tides, 65–66

Inn on Randolph, 73–74
inns. *See* bed-and-breakfast inns;
  hotels, motels, and inns
Inti, 241
Irish Cottage, The, 248
Irish Shop, The, 253
Ives Pool, 297

Jack London Bookstore, 259
Jack London State Historic Park, 202–3
Jackson State Forest, 114, 287, 296
Japanese Cultural Festival, 219
Jarvis Conservatory, 266–67
Jarvis Vineyards, 163
Jarvis Winery, 162
Jasper O'Farrell's, 148
Jellyfish, 132
Jenner Visitors' Center, 11
Jepson Vineyards, 191
Jessel Miller Gallery, 270
Jesse Peter Native American Art
  Museum, 203–4
Jewish Seniors Program, 357
JHM Stamps & Collectibles, 241
Jimtown Store, 256
Jockey Club, The, 324
John Ash & Co., 133
John Dougherty House, 95
John F. Kennedy Memorial Regional
  Park, 326
John Muir Inn, The, 56
Johnson's Alexander Valley Wines, 188
Joshua Grindle Inn, 95–96
J's Amusements, 333
Jug Handle State Reserve, 287
Julia's Kitchen, 117–18, 201
Jungle Vibes, 329–30
Just D-Vine Limousine Service, 26
Justin-Siena High School, 368–69
J.V. Liquor Warehouse, 194

Kelley House Museum, 212
Kendall-Jackson Winery, 183
Kentucky Street Antiques, 255
Kenwood
  restaurants, 131
Kenwood Inn, The, 104
Kenwood Restaurant, 131
Kenwood Vineyards, 180
KFTY Channel 50 (Independent), 394
kidstuff, 326–44

Mendocino County, 333–34
Napa County, 326–28
outside the Wine Country, 334
Sonoma County, 324–33
King's Sport and Tackle Shop, 314
Kitchens in the Vineyards Tour, 222
Knoxville, 296–97
KOA Kampground, 111
Kodiak Jack's, 146
Kolbe Academy, 369
Konocti Harbor Resort & Spa, 303–5
Korbel Champagne Cellars, 190
KRCB Channel 22 (Public TV), 394
Kruse Rhododendron State
  Reserve, 282
Kunde Estate Winery & Vineyards,
  163, 179

La Boucane, 118
La Casa Restaurant, 129–30
La Chaumiere, 80
Ladybug Pool, 297
La Fleur Bed and Breakfast Inn, 78
La Gare French Restaurant, 133
Lake Berryessa, 311–12
Lake County, 299–306
  area overview, 299–300
  attractions, 303–6
  brewpubs, 303
  education and child care, 380
  history, 300–301
  phone numbers, 302
  water activities, 301–2
  wineries, 156, 302–3
Lake Hennessey, 311
Lake Mendocino, 312
Lake Mendocino Recreation Area,
  283–84
lakes, 311–12. *See also* water activities
Lakeside Village Bookstore, 260
Lake Sonoma, 280–81, 312
Lake Sonoma Fish Hatchery, 332
Lake Sonoma-Liberty Glen, 111
Lake Sonoma Wildlife Area, 296
Lake Sonoma Winery, 185
Lake Tahoe, 338–40
Lambert Bridge Winery, 185
Landmark Vineyards, 180–81
La Résidence, 76
Lark in the Morning Musique, 251
Las Posadas State Forest, 294

Last Day Saloon, 147
La Toque, 122
Lavender Hill Spa, 106
La Villeta de Sonoma, 247
Learning Faire, 327–28
Leaves of Grass Bookstore, 261
Ledford House Restaurant, The, 141
Ledson Winery & Vineyards, 181–82
Lee Youngman Galleries, 272
Legacy Gift Shop, The, 247
Levine & Company, 260
Lewis Adult Education Center, 364
Li'l Stinker Antiques, 257
limousine services, 25–27
Lincoln Avenue Spa, 106
Lisa Hemenway's Restaurant, 133
Little Angels Children's Center, 373
Little River Airport, 20
Little River Inn, 105, 141, 292
Llano House Antiques, 256
Lodge at Noyo River, 97
Lodge at Sonoma, The, 104
Lone Dog Fine Art & Antiques, 254
Los Arroyos Golf Course, 290
Lotus Thai Restaurant, 136
Louis M. Martini Winery, 171
Lower Hunting Creek, 110
Lucas Wharf Restaurant & Bar, 137
Lucchesi Park Senior Center, 358
Luther Burbank Center for the
    Arts, 265
Luther Burbank Gold Ridge
    Experiment Farm, 206
Luther Burbank Home and Gardens,
    203
Luther Burbank Rose Festival and
    Parade, 223

MacArthur Place, 103–4
MacCallum House Restaurant, 142
Mackerricher State Park, 114, 287
Madrona Manor, 88, 136
magazines, 393. See also media
MaiFest, 222–23
Mailliard Redwoods State Reserve, 285
Main Street Books, 257
Main Street Station, 149
Maison Fleurie, 76
Manchester State Beach, 285
Manchester State Park, 114
Manor Oaks Overnighter Park, 113

Manzanita, 136
marathons and running events,
    322–23. See also sports, spectator
Margaret's Antiques of Sonoma, 255
Mariposa Institute, 373
Marketplace, The, 220
Markham Vineyards, 172
Mark West Area Chamber of
    Commerce, 10
Martinelli Winery, 184
Martini House, 123
Martini & Prati Wines, 190
Matanzas Creek Winery, 182
McEvoy Ranch, 258–59
McNear's Saloon and Dining
    House, 132
Meadowood Croquet Classic, 227
Meadowood Napa Valley, 100
Meadows of Napa Valley, The, 362
media, 388–95
    Mendocino County, 389, 392, 395
    Napa County, 388–90, 394
    Sonoma County, 388, 390–92, 394
Medical Board of California, 386
Melitta Station Inn, 85–86
Melville Montessori School, 373
Memorial Hospice, 387
Mendo Bistro, 143–44
Mendocino, history of, 41–42
Mendocino Art Center, 276
Mendocino Ballet, 269
Mendocino Beacon, 392
Mendocino Book Company, The, 260
Mendocino Bounty, 251
Mendocino Brewing Company, 153
Mendocino Coast
    history, 40–41
    restaurants, 141
    water activities, 308–9
Mendocino Coast Botanical Gardens,
    212, 253
Mendocino Coast District
    Hospital, 385
Mendocino Coast Recreation and Park
    District, 333
Mendocino Coast Reservations, 71
Mendocino College, 375
Mendocino County
    area overview, 8–9, 12–13
    arts and culture, 265–66, 269,
        274–76

attractions, 207, 210–13
bars and clubs, 149–50
bed-and-breakfast inns, 91–97
camping, 113–15
education and child care, 368, 373–74, 375, 378–79, 380
health care, 385, 386
history, 39–42
hotels, motels, and inns, 66–70
kidstuff, 333–34
limousine services, 27
media, 389, 392, 395
movie theaters, 150
parks and recreation, 283–88, 292–93, 297–98
public transportation, 25
real estate, 352–53
resorts, 104–6
restaurants, 140–44
retirement, 357, 360–61, 364
shopping, 250–51, 253, 257, 260–61
towns and cities, 1
vacation rentals, 71
water activities, 308–9, 310–11, 312, 315
wineries, 156, 158–59, 190–93
worship, 402–3
Mendocino County Dial-a-Ride, 25
Mendocino County Fair and Apple Show, 235
Mendocino County Health Department, 386
Mendocino County Museum, 210
Mendocino County Suicide Prevention, 386
Mendocino Crab & Wine Days, 218–19
Mendocino Headlands State Park, 286
Mendocino Hotel, 69
Mendocino Hotel Restaurant & Garden Room, 142
Mendocino National Forest, 288
Mendocino Theater Company, 266
Mendocino Transit Authority, 25
Mendocino Village restaurants, 142–43
Mendocino Wine Tours, 27
Mendo Realty, 353
Merlot in May—International Merlot Conference, 223
Merryhill Country School, 372–73
Merryvale Vineyards, 171
microbreweries, 151–53, 303

Midnight Sun Inn, 88
Mid-Towne Realty, Inc., 351
Milagros, 246–47
Milano Family Winery, 191
Milat Vineyards, 170
Mill Creek Vineyards, 184
Milliken Creek Inn, 54
Mill Street Antiques, 255
Mixx, 133–34
Model Bakery, 123
Monte Rio Chamber of Commerce, 11
Montgomery Woods State Reserve, 284
Monticello Vineyards, 160
Moosse Cafe, The, 142
Morgan Lane, 345, 350
Morton's Sonoma Springs Resort, 329
Mosswood, 241–42
Mostly Mozart, 228–29
motels. See hotels, motels, and inns
motor sports, 321–22. See also sports, spectator
Mountain House Winery and Lodge, 89–90
Mountain View Hotel, 59
Mount St. Helena Brewing & Restaurant, 303
Mount St. Helena Golf Course, 289
Mount View Spa, 106
movie settings, 275
movie theaters, 150
Mumm Napa Valley, 168, 271
Murphy's Irish Pub, 146
Murray N' Gibbs, 243
museums. See attractions
music and dance, 266–69. See also arts and culture
Music Festival for Mental Health, 231
Mustard Magic, 219
Mustard on the Silverado Trail, 220
Mustards Grill, 121
Mystic Theatre & Music Hall, 146

Napa Adventist Junior Academy, 369
Napa Bowl, 293
Napa Chamber of Commerce, 10
Napa Championship Presented by Beringer—Senior Golf Championship, 320–21
Napa CineDome 8, 150
Napa County
area overview, 3–5

arts and culture, 263, 266–68, 269–72
attractions, 196–99, 214–15, 215–16
bars and clubs, 145–46
bed-and-breakfast inns, 72–83
camping, 109–10
day spas, 106–7
education and child care, 366–67, 368–70, 374, 376, 377–78, 379–80
health care, 381–82, 382–83, 385, 386, 387
history, 28–30, 32–33
hotels, motels, and inns, 53–60
kidstuff, 326–28
limousine services, 25–26
media, 388–90, 394
movie theaters, 150
parks and recreation, 278, 289, 292, 293, 297, 298
public transportation, 23
real estate, 341–46
resorts, 99–103
restaurants, 116–28
retirement, 354–55, 357, 362–63, 364
shopping, 240–45, 254, 257
towns and cities, 1
vacation rentals, 70–71
water activities, 309, 311–12
wineries, 155–57, 159–61, 164–65, 167–75
wine shops, 194–95
worship, 396–99
Napa County Airport, 20
Napa County Fair, 226
Napa County Fairgrounds, 110
Napa County Health and Human Services Department, 386
Napa County Record/Positive Living, 389
Napa Emergency Women's Services, 386
Napa Firefighters Museum, 197
Napa Golf Course at Kennedy Park, 289
Napa Grand Prix, 323
Napa restaurants, 116–19
Napa River, 309
Napa River Inn, 54
Napa Skate Park, 326
Napa-Solano Area Agency on Aging, 355

Napa-Sonoma Marshes, 296
Napa Style, 242–43
Napa Town & Country Fair, 228
Napa Town & Country Fairgrounds, 109
Napa Valley AIDS Project, 386
Napa Valley Art Association, 270
Napa Valley Balloons, Inc., 215
Napa Valley Bike Tours & Rentals, 216, 292
Napa Valley Classic Irish Festival, 220
Napa Valley College, 374
Napa Valley College Community Education, 364
Napa Valley College Theater, 263, 267
Napa Valley Committee on Aging, 355
Napa Valley Conference & Visitors Bureau, 10
Napa Valley Cottages, 70–71
Napa Valley Crown Limousine, 25–26
Napa Valley Dining Club, 355
Napa Valley Downtown Travelodge, 55
Napa Valley Grapevine Wreath Company, 242
Napa Valley Grille, 121
Napa Valley Holidays, 215
Napa Valley Lodge, 56–57
Napa Valley Marathon, 322
Napa Valley Marriott, 54
Napa Valley Museum, 197
Napa Valley Olive Oil Company, 242, 259
Napa Valley Open Studios Tour, 236
Napa Valley Pianos, 241
Napa Valley Register, The, 388
Napa Valley Shakespeare Festival, 227
Napa Valley Symphony, 267
Napa Valley Tours and Trail Hikes, 216
Napa Valley Transit, 23
Napa Valley Wine Auction, 224, 232–33
Napa Valley Wine Festival, 237
Napa Valley Wine Hardware, 195
Napa Valley Wine Train, 22–23
Napa Winery Shuttle, 26
National HIV and AIDS Information Service, 386
Navarro River, 311
Navarro River Redwoods, 285
Navarro Vineyards, 193
Negri's, 139

Neighborhood, The, 254
New College of California, 378
newspapers, 388–92. *See also* media
New Vista Adult Education School, 364
Nicholson House, 96
Niebaum-Coppola Estate Winery, 168
nightlife, 145–53
   Mendocino County, 149–50
   Napa County, 145–46, 150
   Sonoma County, 146–49, 150
955 Ukiah Street Restaurant, 143
North Bay Bohemian, 390
North Bay Business Journal, 391
North Bay Driving School, 364
North Bay HI-CAP, 356
North Cliff Hotel, 69–70
Northcoast Artists Gallery, 276
North Coast Brewing Company, 153
North Coast Opportunities, Inc., 380
North Coast Wine and Visitors
   Center, 11
North County Properties, 351
North State Cafe, 140–41
Northwood Golf Course, 292
Noyo Bowl, 293
Noyo Theater, 150

Oak Knoll Inn, 76
Oakland Athletics, 317
Oakland International Airport, 18–19
Oakland Raiders, 318–19
Oakmont Golf Club, The, 291
Oakville Grocery Co., 248
Oakville Ranch Winery, 167
Occidental Chamber of Commerce, 11
Odyssey Limousine, 26
Old Adobe Fiesta, 229
Old Adobe School, 371
Old Faithful Geyser of California, 199
Old-Fashioned Fourth of July
   Celebration, 227
Old Mill Days, 236
Old Stewart House Inn, 97
Old-Time Fiddle Contest, 218
Old World Inn, The, 75
olive oil, 258–59
Olive Press, The, 247, 258
Omelette Express, 134
Opus One, 167
Orr Hot Springs, 104–5
Osmosis Enzyme Bath and Massage, 107

Outrageous Waters, 305–6
Overland Sheepskin Company, 241
Oxbow School, The, 369
Ox Roast, 225

Pacific Blues Cafe, 145–46
Pacific Coast Air Museum, 205
Pacific Coast Highway, 295
Pacific Limousine, 26
Pacific Ocean, 307–9. *See also* water
   activities
Pacifico Restaurante Mexicano, 127
Pacific Properties, 353
Pacific Union, 345
Pacific Union College, 324, 376
Pacific Union College Extension,
   Angwin, 364
Pacific Union Residential
   Brokerage, 351
Pairs Cafe, 118
Palisades Mountain Sport, 292
Palm Drive Hospital, 385
Panache, 251, 253
Pangaea Cafe, 142
Paradise Miniature Golf, 326
Paradise Ridge Winery, 182
Parducci Wine Cellars, 191
parks, 277–88
parks and recreation, 277–98
   Mendocino County, 283–88, 292–93,
     297–98
   Napa County, 278, 289, 292, 293,
     297, 298
   Sonoma County, 279–83, 290–92,
     293, 297, 298
Patterson's Pub, 149
Paul Bunyan Days, 235
Paulin Hall Auditorium, 267–68
Paul M. Dimmick Wayside State
   Camp, 114
Pearl, 118
Pedals Past Bicycle Museum, 198
Pedroncelli Winery, 188
Peju Province Winery, 168
Pet-a-Llama Ranch, 332–33
Petaluma
   history, 36
   restaurants, 132–33
Petaluma Adobe State Historic
   Park, 203
Petaluma Adult Education Center, 364

Petaluma Chamber of Commerce, 10
Petaluma Criterium, 323
Petaluma Ecumenical Project, 357
Petaluma Historical Museum, 203
Petaluma Marsh Wildlife Area, 296
Petaluma Municipal Airport, 20
Petaluma Speedway, 322
Petaluma Swim Center, 297
Petaluma Transit, 24
Petaluma Valley Hospital, 383
Petaluma Visitors Program, 10
Petrified Forest, 331
Petrified Forest, The, 206
phone numbers
    health care, 386
    for tourists, 10–11
Photo Finish, The, 221
Piatti Restaurant, 121
Piccolino's Italian Cafe, 118–19, 145
Picnic Day, 223
Pine Beach Inn & Suites, 70
Pine Ridge Winery, 164
Pink Mansion, The, 82
Pinoli Ranch Country Inn, 92
Pinot Blanc, 123
Pioneer Christmas, 238
plane tours, 214
plants, 50–51
Playground Fantástico, 326–27
Pleasure Cove Resort, 109
Ployez Winery, 302–3
Point Arena Lighthouse and
    Museum, 211
Point Reyes National Seashore, 335–37
Poison Control Center, 386
Pomo Cultural Center, 210, 333
Powerhouse Brewing Company, The,
    148–49, 152–53
Prager Winery & Port Works, 171
Presentation School, The, 371
Press Democrat, The, 388
Press Democrat Real Estate Network
    Magazine, The, 351
Preston Vineyards, 185
prompt-care centers, 381–82. See also
    health care
Property Rentals Only Inc., 343
Prudential California Real Estate, 349
Prudential California Realty, 343–44
Prudential California Realty, The: A Pre-
    sentation of Wine Country
    Properties, 351–52

Pure Luxury, 26
Pygmalion House, 86

Quail Meadows Campground, 113
Quality Inn, 61
Queen of the Valley Hospital, 382
Quivira Vineyards, 185, 187

Rachel's Inn, 93
radio stations, 393–94. See also media
Raford House, The, 88–89
Ragle Ranch Regional Park, 283
Railroad Square Basement
    Antiques, 255
Rainbow Cattle Company, 149
RAKU Ceramics Collection, 271
Rams Head Realty, 71
Rancho Caymus Inn, 57
Rancho de Calistoga, 362–63
Rasmussen Art Gallery, 271
Raven Film Center, The, 150
Ravenous, 137
Ravenswood Winery, 177
Raymond Vineyard & Cellar, 170
Readers' Books, 259
real estate, 341–53
    Mendocino County, 352–53
    Napa County, 341–46
    Sonoma County, 346–52
Real Estate Book of Napa County, The, 346
real estate companies, 343–46,
    349–51, 353
Real Estate in the Wine Country, 352
real estate publications, 346, 351–52
Real Goods Solar Living Center, 207
Real Goods Store, 250
recreation. See parks and recreation
Red Hen Antiques, 254
Redwood Coast Chamber of
    Commerce, 11
Redwood Coast Medical Services, 385
Redwood Coast Seniors, 364
Redwood Empire Fare, 230
Redwood Empire Ice Arena, 204–5, 331
redwood forests, 337–38
Redwood Meadows, 364
Redwood Valley Cellars, 191–92
Relay, The, 322–23
RE/MAX Central, 349
RE/MAX Napa Valley, 344
Renaissance at the Lodge at Paulin
    Creek, 363

Ren Brown Collection, The, 273
Rendezvous, The, 144
Rental Connection, The, 348
rentals
    housing, 343, 348
    vacation, 70–71, 348–49, 353
ReserveAmerica Camping
    Reservations, 278
resorts, 99–106. *See also* day spas
    Mendocino County, 104–6
    Napa County, 99–103
    Sonoma County, 103–4
Restaurant, The, 144
Restaurant at Meadowood, The, 123
restaurants, 116–44
    Calistoga, 125–28
    Fort Bragg, 143–44
    Glen Ellen, 131
    Healdsburg, 134–37
    Kenwood, 131
    Mendocino Coast, 141
    Mendocino County, 140–44
    Mendocino Village, 142–43
    Napa, 116–19
    Napa County, 116–28
    Petaluma, 132–33
    Rutherford, 121–22
    Santa Rosa, 133–34
    Sonoma, 128–30
    Sonoma Coast, 137–38
    Sonoma County, 128–40
    St. Helena, 122–25
    U.S. 101, 140–41
    West County/Russian River, 138–40
    Yountville, 119–21
Retired and Senior Volunteer
    Program, 365
retirement, 354–65
    Mendocino County, 357,
        360–61, 364
    Napa County, 354–55, 357,
        362–63, 364
    Sonoma County, 355–57, 358–60,
        363, 364
retirement housing options, 361–64
Rialto Cinemas Lakeside, 150
Ridenhour Ranch House Inn, 90
Ridgeway Swim Center, 297
Riley Street Art Supplies, 331
Rincon Cyclery, 292

Rio Theatre, 150
Ristorante Piatti, 130
River Bend Campground, 112
River Child Care Services, 380
rivers, 309–11. *See also* water activities
River's End Restaurant, 137
River Village Resort & Spa, 104
Robert Louis Stevenson State
    Park, 278
Robert Mondavi Winery, 165, 167, 267
Robert Sinskey Vineyards, 164
Robinson & Co., 248
Roche Winery, 177
Rodney Strong Vineyards, 184
Roederer Estate, 193
Rohnert Park 16, 150
Rohnert Park Chamber of
    Commerce, 10
Rohnert Park Healthcare Center, 382
Rohnert Park Senior Center, 358
Roman Spa, 102
Rombauer Vineyards, 173
Rooster Run Golf Club, 290
Roots of Motive Power Festival, 234
Roshambo Winery, 183
Roux, 124
Roxy on the Square, 150
Roxy Stadium 14, 150
Royal Coach Limousine Service, 26
Royal Oak/Vintner's Court, The, 119
R. S. Basso Home, 250
Rubicon Adventures, 315
running events, 322–23. *See also* sports,
    spectator
Russian Gulch State Park, 114, 286–87
Russian River, 309–10
Russian River Barrel Tasting, 221
Russian River Brewing Company, 152
Russian River Christmas
    Extravaganza, 238
Russian River Community Senior
    Center, 360
Russian River Getaways, 71
Russian River Jazz Festival, 234
Russian River Region Visitors Bureau
    and Chamber of Commerce, 11
Russian River Vacation Homes, 71
Rutherford Grill, 122
Rutherford Hill Winery, 170
Rutherford restaurants, 121–22

Sacramento International Airport, 19
Sacramento Kings, 319
Saddles, 130
Safari West, 205
Salt Point Lodge, 66
Salt Point State Park, 112, 282
Salute to the Arts, 228
Sandpiper House Inn, 94
San Francisco, 43–47
San Francisco 49ers, 317–18
San Francisco Giants, 316–17
San Francisco International
    Airport, 18
San Jose Sharks, 319–20
Santa Rosa
    history, 35–36
    restaurants, 133–34
Santa Rosa Chamber of Commerce, 10
Santa Rosa CityBus, 24
Santa Rosa Convention & Visitors
    Bureau, 10
Santa Rosa Junior College, 364, 374–75
Santa Rosa Junior College
    Planetarium, 332
Santa Rosa Junior College Summer
    Repertory Theatre, 265
Santa Rosa Memorial Hospital, 383–84
Santa Rosa Players, The, 265
Santa Rosa Senior Center, 358–59
Santa Rosa Symphony, 269
Santa's Arrival, 237
Sante at The Fairmont Sonoma
    Mission Inn, 130
Scandia Family Fun Center, 330
Scarlett's Country Inn, 79
School Bell Antiques, 256
Schoolhouse Canyon
    Campground, 113
schools. See also education and
    child care
    private, 368–74
    public, 366–68
Schooner Gulch, 285
Schramsberg Vineyards and
    Cellars, 173
Schug Carneros Estate Winery, 177
Scott Courtyard, 80–81
Seabird Lodge, 70
Sea Coast Hide-a-Ways, 71
Sea Cottage Real Estate, 353
Seafoam Lodge, 93

Seafood Brasserie, The, 134
Sea Gull Inn, 96
Sea Ranch Lodge, 66, 273
Sea Ranch Realty, 351
Sea Rock Inn, 96
Seasons of the Vineyard, 249
Sebastiani Theatre, 150
Sebastiani Vineyards, 178–79
Sebastopol Antique Mall, 256–57
Sebastopol Burbank Senior
    Center, 360
Sebastopol Chamber of Commerce, 11
Sebastopol Cinemas, 150
Sebastopol Golf Course, 291
Seguin Moreau Napa Cooperage, 196
senior centers, 357–61. See also
    retirement
Senior Citizens Center, 357
Senior Class, 355
senior services, 354–57. See also
    retirement
Service Corps of Retired Executives, 365
Sexually Transmitted Disease
    Hotline, 386
Shackford's, 240
Shady Oaks Country Inn, 77–78
Sharpsteen Museum, The, 198
Sheepshearing at the Adobe, 222
Sheraton Petaluma Hotel, 60–61
shopping, 240–61
    Mendocino County, 250–51, 253,
        257, 260–61
    Napa County, 240–45, 254, 257
    Sonoma County, 245–50, 254–57,
        259–60
shops, unique, 240–51, 253
Sign of the Bear, 245
Silverado Brewing Company, 151
Silverado Country Club & Resort, 99,
    145, 289
Silverado Museum, 197
Silverado Orchards, 362
Silverado Realty, 344
Silverado Vineyards, 164
Silver Oak Cellars, 165
Silver Rose Inn & Spa, 100–101
Simi Winery, 188–89
Simple Touch Spa, A, 108
Sinkyone Wilderness State Park, 288
Six Flags Marine World, 334
Skunk Train, 213, 333–4

Smalltown Christmas, A, 239
Smith Redwoods State Reserve, 284–85
Smith's Mount St. Helena Trout Farm
    and Hatchery, 328
Smothers Remick Ridge Vineyards, 180
Snoopy's Gallery and Gift Shop, 247
soccer, 320. *See also* sports, spectator
soil, 49
SolFest, 230
Sonoma
    historic sites, 201–2
    restaurants, 128–30
Sonoma Airporter, 21
Sonoma Bookends Bookstore, 257, 259
Sonoma Cattle Co. & Napa Valley Trail
    Rides, 293
Sonoma Cheese Factory, 246
Sonoma Cinemas, 150
Sonoma Coast
    history, 39
    restaurants, 137–38
    water activities, 307–8
Sonoma Coast State Beach, 281
Sonoma Coast Visitor
    Information/Bodega Bay Area
    Chamber of Commerce, 11
Sonoma County
    area overview, 5–8
    arts and culture, 263–65, 268–69,
        272–73
    bars and clubs, 146–49
    bed-and-breakfast inns, 83–91
    camping, 110–13
    day spas, 107–8
    education and child care, 367–68,
        371–73, 374–75, 376, 378, 380
    health care, 382, 383, 386, 387
    history, 33–39
    hotels, motels, and inns, 60–66
    kidstuff, 324–33
    limousine services, 26
    media, 388, 390–92, 394
    movie theaters, 150
    parks and recreation, 279–83,
        290–92, 293, 297, 298
    public transportation, 24
    real estate, 346–52
    resorts, 103–4
    restaurants, 128–40
    retirement, 355–57, 358–60, 363, 364
    shopping, 245–50, 254–57, 259–60

towns and cities, 1
vacation rentals, 71
water activities, 307–8, 309–10,
    312–14
wineries, 156, 157–58, 175–85,
    187–90
wine shops, 195
worship, 399–402
Sonoma County Airport Express, 21
Sonoma County Department of
    Health Services and Center for HIV
    Prevention and Care, 386
Sonoma County Fair and Twilight
    Parade (Healdsburg), 223
Sonoma County Fairgrounds, 323–24
Sonoma County Fair (Santa Rosa), 228
Sonoma County Folk Festival, 229
Sonoma County Harvest Fair, 236
Sonoma County Herald-Recorder, 391
Sonoma County Hilton, 63
Sonoma County Museum, 204
Sonoma County Repertory
    Theatre, 265
Sonoma County Tourism Program, 10
Sonoma County Transit, 24
Sonoma Fairgrounds Golf Center, 290
Sonoma Film Institute, 150
Sonoma Hotel, 60
Sonoma Index-Tribune, The, 390
Sonoma Management, 348
Sonoma-Marin Farm News, 391
Sonoma Mission Inn Golf Club, 290
Sonoma Museum of Visual Art, 273
Sonoma North Bay Biz, 393
Sonoma Outfitters, 247
Sonoma Rock & Mineral, 247
Sonoma Sky Park, 20
Sonoma Spa on the Plaza, 107
Sonoma State University, 264, 324, 376
Sonoma State University Art
    Gallery, 273
Sonoma State University Gerontology
    Program, 364
Sonoma Valley Airport, 20
Sonoma Valley Chamber of
    Commerce, 10
Sonoma Valley Chorale, 268
Sonoma Valley Cyclery, 292
Sonoma Valley Harvest Wine Auction,
    232–33, 234
Sonoma Valley Hospital, 383

Sonoma Valley Olive Festival, 218, 238
Sonoma Valley Regional Park, 279
Sonoma Valley Visitors Bureau, 10
Sonoma West Times & News, 392
Sonoma Wine Hardware, 195
Sons In Retirement, 357
Soo Yuan, 127
South Coast Senior Citizens, 361
Southwest Art in the Wine
    Country, 235
Spanish Flat Resort, 109
Sparks, 139
spas, day, 106–8. *See also* resorts
Spirits in Stone, 245, 272
Spoke Folk Cyclery, 292
sports, spectator, 316–25
    baseball, 316–17
    basketball, 319
    bicycle road races, 323
    college, 324–25
    football, 317–19
    golf, 320–21
    hockey, 319–20
    horse racing, 323–24
    marathons and running events,
        322–23
    motor sports, 321–22
    soccer, 320
Spreckels Performing Arts Center,
    264–65
Spring Lake Regional Park, 110–11, 280
St. Apollinaris Elementary School, 370
St. Clement Vineyards, 172
St. Francis Solano School, 371
St. Francis Winery and Vineyards, 181
St. Helena Catholic School, 370
St. Helena Chamber of Commerce, 10
St. Helena Community Pool, 297
St. Helena Cyclery, 292
St. Helena Hospital, 382–83
St. Helena Montessori School, 370
St. Helena Olive Oil Company,
    242, 259
St. Helena restaurants, 122–25
St. Helena St. Helena Antiques, 254
St. Helena Star, 389
St. Helena Wine Merchants, 194
St. John's Lutheran School, 370
St. Luke Lutheran School, 372
St. Mary's Mardi Gras, 219–20
St. Supéry Vineyards & Winery, 167–68

St. Vincent de Paul High School, 371
Stag's Leap Wine Cellars, 161, 164, 166
Standish-Hickey State Recreation
    Area, 284
Stanford Inn by the Sea, 69
Stanford University, 325
Starfish, 137–38
Steele Wines, 303
Stella's Cafe, 139–40
Steltzner Vineyards, 164
Sterling Vineyards, 173–74
Stevenson Manor Inn, 59
Stevenswood Lodge, 93
Stillwater Cove Regional Park,
    111–12, 281
Stuart School, 372
Studio Nouveau, 250
Stumptown Daze, 226
Sugarloaf Ridge State Park, 110, 279
Suicide Prevention, 386
Super 8, 70
Sutter Home Winery, 171
Sutter Medical Center of Santa
    Rosa, 384
Sutter Warrack Hospital, 384
Sweetriver Saloon, 148
Sweets River Grill and Bar, 140
Sweetwater Spa & Inn, 105–6
swimming, 297–98. *See also* parks and
    recreation
Swiss Hotel, The, 130
Symphony on the River, 230–31

Tanglewood House, 85
Tapioca Tiger, 243
Taste of Yountville, A, 220–21
taxi service, 27
Taylor & Norton Wine Merchants, 195
Taylor's Refresher, 124
Tayman Park Golf Course, 291
telephone numbers
    health care, 386
    for tourists, 10–11
television, 394. *See also* media
tennis, 298. *See also* parks and
    recreation
Terra, 124
Thanksgiving Festival, 237–38
theater, 263–66. *See also* arts and
    culture
theaters, movie, 150

Third Street Aleworks Restaurant and
    Brewery, 152
1351 Lounge, 146
Thistle Dew Inn, 83
Tides Wharf Restaurant, 138
Toobtown, 330
Topolos at Russian River Vineyards,
    Winery & Restaurant, 190
tours, 215–17
Toy Cellar, The, 328
Toyon Books, 260
Toyworks, The, 332
Tradewinds, 146–47
train service, 21
Train Town, 199, 201, 328–29
transportation, 14–27
    air, 17–21
    automobile, 14–17
    bus/train, 21
    limousines, 25–27
    public, 21, 23–25
    taxi, 27
Travelodge/Vineyard Valley Inn
    Motel, 64
Tra Vigne, 124
Tra Vigne's Cantinetta, 259
Trefethen Vineyards, 161
Trentadue Winery, 189
Triangle Tattoo Museum, 212–13, 334
Tributary Whitewater Tours, 315
Trojan Horse Inn, 83–84
Tucker Farm Center, 263
Turnbull Wine Cellars, 167
Tuscany, 119
Twisted Vines, 132

Ukiah Brewing Company, 153
Ukiah Chamber of Commerce, 11
Ukiah Daily Journal, 389
Ukiah Municipal Airport, 20
Ukiah Municipal Golf Course, 292
Ukiah Municipal Swimming Pool, 297
Ukiah Players Theatre, 265–66
Ukiah Senior Center, 360
Ukiah 6 Theatre, 150
Ukiah Valley Medical Center, 385
Union Hotel Restaurant, 140
University of California, 324–25
University of Northern California, 376
Upper Napa Valley Urgent Care,
    381–82

Up Valley Associates, 345
Ursuline High School, 372

V. Sattui Winery, 170
vacation rentals, 70–71, 348–49, 353
Valley Oaks Deli, 141
Valley of the Moon Vintage
    Festival, 234
Valley Orchards Retirement
    Community, 363
Van Damme State Park, 114, 286, 295
Vanderbilt and Company, 243
varietals, 186
Vella Cheese Company, 246
Velvet Rabbit, 251
Veterans Home of California, 197
Viansa Winery and Italian
    Marketplace, 177–78
Vichy Springs Resort, 105
Victorian Farmhouse, The, 93
Victorian Garden Inn, 83
Victoria's Fashion Stables, 330
Villa Ca'Toga, 199
Village Park Campground, 112
Villagio Inn & Spa, 99
Villa Missina, 89
Villa Mt. Eden Winery, 169
VINE, The, 23
Vineman Marathon, 322
vineyard calendar, 192
Vineyard Creek Hotel, Spa &
    Conference Center, 62
Vintage Aircraft Co., 201
Vintage Bank Antiques, 255
Vintage 1870 Father's Day Invitational
    Auto Show, 225
Vintage 1870 Wine Cellar, The, 194
Vintage House, 358
Vintage Inn, 56
Vintage Towers Inn, 90
Vintners Golf Club, 289
Vintners Inn, 63
Vista Manor Lodge, 70
visual arts, 269–74, 276. *See also* arts
    and culture
Viva Sonoma, 245
Volpi's Ristorante, 132–33
Volunteer Center of Napa County,
    The, 354
volunteer opportunities, 364–65. *See
    also* retirement

Volunteer Wheels of Sonoma County, 24

walk-in/prompt-care centers, 381–82.
 See also health care
Wally Johnson Realty, 353
Wappo Bar & Bistro, 127–28
water activities, 307–15
 Lake County, 301–2
 Mendocino County, 308–9, 310–11,
  312, 315
 Napa County, 309, 311–12
 Sonoma County, 307–8, 309–10,
  312–14
Wayside Inn, The, 82
W.C. "Bob" Trowbridge Canoe Trips,
 312
weather, 49–50
Weekly Calistogan, The, 389–90
Wellington Vineyards, 179
West County Museum, 206
West County Property
 Management, 348
Western Institute of Science and
 Health, 378
Westlake House Springs, 363
Westlake Wine Country House, 363
Westport-Union Landing State Beach,
 288
Wet Pleasure Jet Ski & Boat Rentals,
 A, 312
Wexford & Woods, 244–45
whale festivals, 221
Whale Watch Inn, 92
Wharf Master's Inn, 92
Wharf Restaurant, 144
Whistle Stop Antiques, 255
Whistlestop Antiques, 257
Whitegate Inn, 97
Whitehall Lane Winery, 170
White Sulphur Springs Resort &
 Spa, 100
Wikiup Golf Course, 291
Wildhurst Vineyards, 303
WilkesSport, 244
Willits Celtic Renaissance, 224
Willits Chamber of Commerce, 11
Willits Frontier Days, 228
Willits KOA, 113
Willits Municipal Swimming Pool,
 297–98
Willits Senior Center, 360–61

Windsor Bowl, 293
Windsor Chamber of Commerce, 10
Windsor Golf Club, 291
Windsorland RV Trailer Park, 111
Windsor Senior Center, 359
Windsor Times, 391
Windsor Vineyards Tasting Room, 184
Windsor Waterworks and Slides,
 206, 332
Windwalker Board Sports and School
 of Windsurfing, 314
wine
 appellations, 154–55
 California, 166
 varietals, 186
wine auctions, 232–33
wine caves, 162–63
Wine Country Cycling Classic, 323
Wine Country Inn, The, 58
Wine Country Kennel Club, 225
Wine Country Living, 393
*Wine Country Weekly Real Estate
 Reader,* 346
Wine & Dine Tours, 216
Wine Exchange of Sonoma, The, 195
Wine Plane, The, 214
wineries, 154–95
 Lake County, 156, 302–3
 Mendocino County, 156, 158–59,
  190–93
 Napa County, 155–57, 159–61,
  164–65, 167–75
 Sonoma County, 156, 157–58,
  175–85, 187–90
Wine Shop, The, 195
wine shops, 194–95
Winesong, 235
Wine Spectator Greystone Restaurant,
 124–25
wine tasting, 178
Wine Valley Lodge, 55
Wine Way Inn, 79
Wings Over Wine Country, 229
Wisteria Garden Bed & Breakfast, 81
Women's Weekend, 231
Woodbridge Village, 362
Wooden Duck Antique Shop, 256
Woods, The, 364
Working Gardener, 248
World Pillow Fighting Championships,
 227

worship, 396–403
  Mendocino County, 402–3
  Napa County, 396–99
  Sonoma County, 399–402

Yokayo Bowl, 293
Yorkville Vineyards & Cellars, 193
Yoshi-Shige, 119

Yountville Chamber of Commerce, 10
Yountville Inn, 56
Yountville restaurants, 119–21

Zazu, 134
ZD Wines, 168
Zin, 137

About the Author

Jean Saylor Doppenberg

A 15-year resident of Wine Country, Jean grew up on the outskirts of Des Moines, Iowa, surrounded by cornfields, not grapevines. She worked in the newsroom of the *Des Moines Register* for more than a decade, writing everything from obituaries to restaurant reviews. After visiting San Francisco and Wine Country in the early 1980s, Jean returned in 1988

and settled in Santa Rosa. She has completed courses in winery public relations and wine marketing, and has written for a publication that covers the business end of the wine industry. In addition, she has co-authored another guide to Wine Country and has written freelance articles for the local hospitality and wine industries.

Jean Saylor Doppenberg
PHOTO: WWW.STORYPHOTO.COM

(323) 268-
7241

X 306
308